OXFORD

UNIVERSITY PRESS

Oxford University Press, Inc., publishes works that further
Oxford University's objective of excellence
in research, scholarship, and education.

Oxford New York
Auckland Cape Town Dar es Salaam Hong Kong Karachi
Kuala Lumpur Madrid Melbourne Mexico City Nairobi
New Delhi Shanghai Taipei Toronto

With offices in
Argentina Austria Brazil Chile Czech Republic France Greece
Guatemala Hungary Italy Japan Poland Portugal Singapore
South Korea Switzerland Thailand Turkey Ukraine Vietnam

Published by Oxford University Press, Inc.
198 Madison Avenue, New York, New York 10016
www.oup.com

Oxford is a registered trademark of Oxford University Press

Library of Congress Cataloging-in-Publication Data
The story of sexual identity : narrative perspectives on the gay and lesbian life course /
edited by Phillip L. Hammack, Bertram J. Cohler.
   p. cm.
Includes bibliographical references and index.
ISBN 978-0-19-532678-9
1. Gender identity—History.   2. Gay and lesbian studies.   3. Homosexuality—History.
4. Lesbianism—History.   5. Sex role.   6. Sex differences.   I. Hammack, Phillip L.
II. Cohler, Bertram J.
HQ1075.S79   2008
306.76′609—dc22   2008023689

9 8 7 6 5 4 3 2 1
Printed in the United States of America
on acid-free paper

To our students

Foreword
On Narrative Pluralism

> World is crazier and more of it than we think,
> Incorrigibly plural...The drunkenness of
> things being various.
> > —Louis MacNeice, Snow

> We live in a pluralistic universe.
> > —William James

> A homosexual is not a homosexual
> is not a homosexual.
> > —John Gagnon and William Simon

I came out as a gay man between 1966 and 1970: between the swinging sixties of underground queer coffee bars in Soho and Carnaby Street of 1966 and the London School of Economics–based Gay Liberation Front of 1970. I moved from being an outlawed, criminalized, and sick little teenager to being an out proud gay man. In the same period, I got my first degree at Enfield College, started my Ph.D. on homosexuality, got a job as a sociology lecturer, and found my first serious boyfriend.

I had been born into a London working-class family—with no books but lots of loving aspirations. Before 1966, I cried and suffered the pangs of outlawed gay youth. I had had enough of this by 1966—when I was 20. I started going to gay bars in Soho (and by the way, I counted around 100 at that time!). I told close friends (and some turned out to be gay themselves). And finally I told my parents, who took me to the doctors! And all of this in the summer of 1966, a memorable period in the annals of my life. Homosexuality then was against the law, and it was also considered a mental illness. I had a short flirtation with psychiatrists and mental hospitals—well, that was the way of that time. It made me suspicious of much psychiatry, psychology, and even sociology. The social sciences were definitely not as neutral as they seemed, I learned. But by 1967 I had sorted all this out and had cheerfully started my gay career.

I decided to do a thesis on homosexual life in London, and as the law in England changed in 1967, I decided to give this a focus. In November 1970, I was amongst a very small group of people at the London School of Economics for the first meeting of the Gay Liberation Front—called by Aubrey Walter and Bob Mellors. I recall meeting Jeffrey Weeks there, and we became good friends.

The stories continue. Stories of my coming out then in the 1960s soon became embellished and changed. I have many versions of it. And indeed, I recall—20 years on—at a conference in Utrecht in 1988 (when I was speaking to a cluster of very keen neophyte lesbian and gay European students) announcing that I was postgay (Twenty years further on, it seems people are claiming this anew). Stories do not take a naturally linear form, nor do they develop in naturally linear ways. They bump you around and are contingent upon the events of everyday life. They change from place to place and from time to time. They offer you moments of choice and moments of utter fatalism. And stories themselves are never free-floating and random. They have historical roots, connect to wider patterns, cluster into structures and habits, and indeed become (often much loved) habits—part of what some sociologists now call our *habitus*.

Coming Out and Telling the Story of a Life

Here then is a highly truncated account of my coming out in the 1960s and a little glimpse of its aftermath. I could expand those years into a book or contract them into the opening line. Stories are like that. They are "incorrigibly plural." They can be long or short, focused or rambling, dense or thin, realistic or fictional, pedestrian or inspirational. And I find that I have been rewriting the stories of my life for all of my life.

We are, of course, meaning-creating animals, and we need to make sense of our lives. Stories and narratives are a major way we do this. As Joan Didion says, we need to tell our stories in order to live, hence the importance of stories and narratives for the human sciences. Making sense of our stories is one major key to understanding our humanities. More and more contemporary social thinkers, analysts, artists, and activists have come to identify with the importance of both the narrative and life-story telling traditions even as they seep back gently into history.

In some of my earliest writing I hover on the edge of all this. In *Sexual Stigma* (1975), I could sense the early stages of a coming-out story (clumsily called *sensitization, signification, subculturalization,* and *stabilization!*). But now we know this to be all far too simple, linear, and monolithic. In *Documents of Life* (initially 1983), which came out of research I was doing then on the life stories of a range of the sexually different—from pedophiles to sadomasochists—I sensed the power of life stories in social analysis. But now we can find—from Virginia Wolf to Marcel Proust—a much deeper sophistication in the linking of telling to lives, way beyond what I had imagined then. And in *The Making of the Modern Homosexual* (edited in 1981), we could certainly see that the modern homosexual was indeed a modern invention— though it was an argument that caused a lot of controversy at the time. But as we have documented and written about these experiences over the past 30 years, it has become manifest that the languages used and the experiences developed around same-sex experiences have so continuously managed to change and are so overwhelmingly connected to the structured historical moments that have emerged even since then that only the most historically ignorant and socially unaware could really deny it. Our sexualities are always deeply socially contingent. Of course, people come and people go, and nothing much changes. And yet, to be young and have sex with members of the same sex (whatever that might mean) in the early twenty-first century—the media society, the hi-tech society, the liquid society, the postmodern capitalist society—is, I suspect, ontologically very different from what it was even 30 years ago—just as my experiences as a young person were radically at odds with those of my grandparents 40 years before me, before the First World War!

Puzzling about it, I see that throughout my own life I have been many things and had many identities. Even the most coherent lives—and mine has actually and fortunately been quite coherent—are invariably multiple, plural. As a child, I kept thinking—amongst many other things—that I was a little sick queer boy. In my teen years—amongst many other things—I struggled with being a homosexual. After I came out (and for quite a while), I was unambiguously gay—through in a rather feminist, White, British, politicized, sociological, and male version! By my mid-40s, during the 1990s, I was often claiming more to be a "postmodern" gay, even truncating it to being "postgay." In the 2000s and approaching my old age, I have tried to give up calling myself anything in particular. Perhaps my central identity now is that of a partner (I have lived with the same partner for 30 years), and it is hard to imagine being without him. After childhood, I never wanted to call myself queer even as all around me did. To do that would have been to return to the pains of my childhood.

Gay Narrative Generations

One theme that comes across clearly within this book is the significance of narrative generations. The stories we tell of our lives, being richly bound up with our experiences and habits, always speak of lives lived at particular moments in history at particular points in the life cycle. Stories have very specific timings and generations, which should never be overlooked. The stories we tell at any time are also bound up with the historical moment and place. They are always tales about a time and a space. These are generational tales. Generations are not the same as age groups and have not been given adequate attention in the social sciences.

Throughout much of recent history, a generation could usefully be designated as a natural descent: a mother, daughter, and granddaughter would be three generations, and it meant approximately a third of a life (in turn, roughly 25 years). It was roughly the time between the birth of parents and the birth of their offspring. But these days, because change is so rapid, family organization is much less predictable, and birth patterns are much wider, cohorts cannot so easily be named. What seems to matter now are critical changing social experiences that demarcate groups from each other, though even in the same generation experiences are never that unified or held in common (think minimally class, ethnicity, and gender!). Generations are partially defined by a collective consciousness of shared experiences—usually a critical common life experience. It might help, then, to think about generations through shared critical life events—their crises and epiphanies—that are held in common and can generate what might be called *generational collective memories*. The war generation—living through World War II, for example—must be a critical shape for millions of the Western world. It could even be a key defining fact of identity. Past traumas and crises can help shape a collective memory life project.

Generations can be linked to many concerns—to objective world traumas (depressions, wars, terrorism), to the creation of social movements (the

Trade Union Movement, the Black Movement, the Women's Movement), to literature, film, music and other cultural events, and to shifts in intellectual fashions. They can also suggest the "fate" (or the structure of opportunities) of a group: sharing assumptions and ways of lives. Generations may also come to develop distinctive ways of seeing. Vito Russo's (1946–1990) wonderful book and film *The Celluloid Closet* implicitly shows a century's shifting world of gay imagery in film and imagines their multiple audiences. Films can provide memory books for different generations.

Such cohorts, then, need not be—indeed, often are not—linked to the mainstream orthodoxies. There are multiple subterranean worlds of generations, identifiable through their resistances to what is seen as the mainstream. Hence bohemian cultures, criminal cultures, political cultures of the left and right, hippy cultures, women's cultures, Black cultures, migrant cultures, and—of course—queer cultures come into being.

A number of the chapters in this book connect to these different gay generations. For example, Timothy McCajor Hall looks at the developing gay scenes in Prague through fieldwork since 1999. He suggests that the Velvet Revolution in 1989 marked a major generational transition for all Czechs and Slovaks, regardless of sexual orientation, and shows how, since then, gay life has been transformed with new organizations, cultures, and emerging identities. The legalization in 2006 of registered partnerships (as in so many countries of Europe) may well bring another turning point and generational moment for Czechs. Hall argues that "In some ways, gay men in the Czech Republic who came of age in the 1980s resemble gay men who came of age in the United States some 20 or 30 years earlier, while gay teenagers in the Czech Republic today have many attitudes and significant experiences comparable to those of their Western peers" (p. 58). This is a telling start to analyzing the ways in which different gay generations link up and connect across the gay disapora.

Plural and Cosmopolitan Sexualities

Whatever the different global generational gay histories may show, they bring us to a point toward the end of the first decade of the twenty-first century when any attempts to define gay and lesbian identities as fixed becomes futile. This book is full of examples of new categories and attempts to redefine the gay and lesbian experience—personally, socially, and politically. Alongside the massive informalization and consumerism of modern societies, we see also a bewildering fragmenting of same-sex identities across generations and across countries. As ever, there are always different and contested grounds both between and across generations that make for a portrait of gay and lesbian life (by whatever terms) as a vast patchwork of plurality of experience and ways of living. To grasp it is a bit like trying to reorder a kaleidoscope.

Over the years, there has been a rich blossoming of ideas around narrative and life story that now enable us to transcend many of the old debates and arguments. In lesbian and gay studies—or queer studies—the coming-out narrative has now become almost archetypal. But it should not be forgotten that this is indeed a very specific type of story that links to lives of people who connect to a specific generation. It is not universal in any way. At present, it hangs omnipresently and omnisciently over many gay lives, but there is no one way, and it is pointless now to remotely suggest that there is. We now know too much, and the chapters in this book amply testify to the growth of our knowledge.

This wonderful book shows a new maturity and confidence. It brings together a collection of elegant essays that provide the most up-to-date understanding of the ways in which stories of gay life are told, mainly in the United States but suggestive for other places too. It replaces older ideas of ages and stages with dynamic links to history and cultural moments. The power of place and history must be recognized in the analysis of stories and identities, and each chapter brings a sharp focus to some aspects that irrevocably fracture the idea that there is any one unitary or universal story to be told. There may be common themes; sameness—absolutely not. Here we have recognition of the many complex and shifting category terms used to describe gay desires and relationships, and detailed accounts of how they change over the same life, over lives through historical generational moments, and across cultures. More, in this book we have identity stories shaped by political conflict, urban change, Internet development, gender differences, ethnic situations. Here these are all explored with diverse forms of data and theory—making major advances in our way of thinking about social psychological realities. Our understandings of pluralistic sexual life and the historical social psychology of identity are richly advanced as a consequence.

Advancing Narrative Work: Narrative Engagement and Embodiment

We now know so much more about lesbian and gay life than the old psychological studies of personality types ever told us. Let us hope that this traditional line of reasoning and thinking amongst psychologists can now be laid to rest as the red herring it is. This book, by contrast, consolidates so much valuable recent work from history, sociology, psychology, anthropology, and queer theory and shows just how important the process of what Hammack and Cohler themselves call *narrative engagement* is. The authors make very clear their position on story, narrative, and identity. As they say:

> We view identity and culture as coconstitutive. It is for this reason that we speak of narrative *engagement* as a process of human development. The process of narrative engagement speaks to the ability of an individual or a group of individuals to contest the content of a master narrative from within, and in the process potentially repudiate and reformulate its story line. Hence narrative engagement represents a vitally *social* process and can, in fact, catalyze collective action for social change. (p. 455)

Narratives, then, are dynamic, political, and constantly contested. What I sense more and more in the reading and writing of stories is the way they work to undermine any sense of overarching, overriding consensus about narratives. When taken seriously, we find that many stories of lives are counterstories—they start to break down any claims for grand theories about lives. At their best, they challenge and redirect our thinking. At their worst, they tell us the same old story and utter it in cliché form. So many of the chapters in this book challenge us to think afresh our ideas about what we might now call the *pluralistic cosmopolitan sexual life*.

Stories, it seems to me, are also embodied. There is a complex linkage of story, identity, feeling, and body. I have become more and more convinced that the stories we tell of our lives are never simply narratives: they are heaving brutish encounters with our emotionally driven bodies. For instance, in the opening chapter of the book, the authors present a specific conflict between David and Paul—two gay men who disagree about the words to use to describe the story of their lives. One is *queer,* and the other is *gay.* But it is a disagreement that goes way beyond a simple conflict of stories, as Hammack and Cohler argue:

> Their conflict was not just abstract or intellectual; it was visceral, raw, and personal. The discourse between Paul and David was essentially *threatening* to a sense of enduring coherence and stability afforded by a life-story narrative (mostly to David). (p. 3)

What has to be realized in narrative theory is that stories are part of embodiment. The telling of stories is not just about the words we speak: it is about the ways in which we move through the world with hurting and joyful bodies—our feelings, our thoughts, our bodily sensations. Stories are embodied: they are told by tellers with body processes always at work. Narratives do not free-float in the world. Future work needs to bring these bodies to the forefront.

And why this is important rests in my concerns over the need for dialogues in many contested situations. When people disagree (and, indeed, when world cultures disagree), they need to communicate with each other, and part of this must be the telling of their stories. But their stories are never just the words they say: they come to their stories in full embodiment—pains and passions are often everywhere. Just watch the faces, the body language, the tones of voice, the hands. People embody stories. So we need to find ways of accessing the embodiment of narrative in our studies.

The study of lesbian and gay lives in all their global richness has, I believe, advanced enormously over the past half-century. History, anthropology, psychology, and sociology—alongside literature—have firmly killed off any idea of the universal or fixed homosexual "species." What we are left with are multiple worlds of ever-shifting and pluralistic sexual experiences, fleetingly grasped through a historically limited language that, in itself, and inevitably, continues to change. A homosexual is not a homosexual is not a homosexual.

—Ken Plummer
University of Essex

Preface

This book is the culmination of several years of conversation and collaboration between us. Our idea for the book emerged through our teaching and research on sexual identity and our strong conviction that a paradigm that integrates a narrative and life course approach transcends the boundaries of scholarly disciplines and, therefore, contributes to the evolution of sexual science. We both identify as interdisciplinary social scientists, and we have been frustrated over the years with the ways in which knowledge about sexual identity seems to have been so closely captivated by concerns more connected to ideology and the social control of desire. The obsession with issues such as a *gay gene* in the 1990s, framed within the unnecessarily dichotomized vision of sexuality as either *essential* or *constructed*, overlooked the lived experience of sexual desire because it reduced desire and identity to biological destiny. The approach we advocate, explicate, and explore throughout this volume seeks to move beyond such stifling paradigms by focusing directly on the lived experience of individuals with same-sex desire.

Biology is, of course, just as much a part of sexual desire and experience as it is of any aspect of human development. But we believe that the more interesting and relevant social science questions about human sexuality actually focus on the *meaning* individuals make of their desire in some social, cultural, and discursive context. In our view, a narrative approach restores a focus on the voices of sexual subjects and hence provides access to the meaning-making process as it is actively lived and embodied in word, thought, and action. This volume is intended to bring together a number of scholars who embrace just such an interdisciplinary approach to the study of sexual identity.

Though a narrative approach is necessarily skeptical of the transhistorical basis of social categories of identity, we do in fact speak of *gay, lesbian,* and *bisexual* lives. We recognize that desire does not necessarily map onto such social categories of identity, and we also recognize the historical basis of these categories. We want to acknowledge that the volume does not deal with transgender identity, but we hope that future volumes will do so. Since we view this volume as only the start of a longer and more substantive intellectual conversation, we trust that future conversations will include the voices of individuals whose desires do not map so comfortably onto labels like *gay, lesbian,* and *bisexual.*

We would like to acknowledge the support and guidance of Anthony R. D'Augelli and Ian Rivers throughout the development of this book. We would like to thank the editorial staff at the Press for their assistance throughout the course of our work on the book, including Lori Handelman, Jennifer Rappaport, Catherine Carlin, Jenna Hocut, and Stefano Imbert. We acknowledge the editorial assistance of Jessica Andrews during the final stages of editing and formatting. The students in our seminars on sexual identity at the University of California, Santa Cruz, and the University of Chicago have proven to be an important inspiration for the development of our thought on sexual identity, narrative, and the life course. Finally, as always, we thank our partners, Brendan M. Smith and Bill Hensley, for forming such an important part of our own personal narratives.

Contents

xvii

Contributors

BARRY D. ADAM, Department of Sociology and Anthropology, University of Windsor

MOLLIE V. BLACKBURN, School of Teaching and Learning, College of Education and Human Ecology, Ohio State University

DOUGLAS BRUCE, Department of Psychology, DePaul University

CHAD M. BURTON, Department of Psychological Sciences, University of Missouri, Columbia

BERTRAM J. COHLER, Department of Comparative Human Development, University of Chicago

DAVID DeBOER, Wellness Center, Loyola University Chicago

AARON C. GEISE, Department of Psychological Sciences, University of Missouri, Columbia

TIMOTHY McCAJOR HALL, Department of Psychiatry, UCLA Semel Institute for Neuroscience and Human Behavior

PHILLIP L. HAMMACK, Department of Psychology, University of California, Santa Cruz

GARY W. HARPER, Department of Psychology, DePaul University

ANDREW J. HOSTETLER, Department of Psychology, University of Massachusetts, Lowell

OMAR B. JAMIL, Department of Psychology, DePaul University

LAURA A. KING, Department of Psychological Sciences, University of Missouri, Columbia

STEVEN P. KURTZ, Center for Drug and Alcohol Studies, University of Delaware

ILAN H. MEYER, Mailman School of Public Health, Columbia University

SUZANNE C. OUELLETTE, Department of Psychology, The Graduate Center, City University of New York

JANETTE PERZ, School of Psychology, University of Western Sydney

MARY M. READ, Department of Counseling, California State University, Fullerton

DAMIEN RIDGE, School of Integrated Health, University of Westminster

PAULA C. RODRIGUEZ RUST, Spectrum Diversity, East Brunswick, New Jersey

DANA ROSENFELD, School of Criminology, Education, Sociology and Social Work, Keele University

PEDRO SERRANO, Department of Psychology, DePaul University

BENJAMIN SHEPARD, Human Services Department, City University of New York

JANE M. USSHER, School of Psychology, University of Western Sydney

JACQUELINE S. WEINSTOCK, Living and Learning Center, University of Vermont

REBECCA WRIGHT, School of Psychology, Deakin University

PART I

Time, Place, Story

Introductory Perspectives on Narrative and the Life Course

I

Narrative Engagement and Stories of Sexual Identity

An Interdisciplinary Approach to the Study of Sexual Lives

Phillip L. Hammack and Bertram J. Cohler

During a heated session of a seminar on sexual identity we were teaching at the University of Chicago in the spring of 2005, two young gay men suddenly began to scream at one another with a fervor neither of us had previously encountered in teaching. The tension between them had been building throughout the term. One of them, Paul, was a critical young scholar, and his desire to deconstruct the content of human consciousness extended to sexual identity, including his own. Based on his comments in the seminar, he might have fit nicely into what Savin-Williams (2005) calls a *postgay* identity. It was not that his same-sex attraction was not, in many ways, quite defining of his identity. It was, rather, that he assumed a critical stance toward the idea of an essentialized gay identity lurking inside him.

David, the other man in the seminar, was simply a young gay man, comfortable with his social identity and the social and sexual practice associated with it. He grew tired of Paul's constant deconstruction of gay identity and his views on "queerness." Their conflict was not just abstract or intellectual; it was visceral, raw, and personal. The discourse between Paul and David was essentially *threatening* to a sense of enduring coherence and stability afforded by a life-story narrative (mostly to David). David's evolving story as a gay man reflected a basic comfort with a *master narrative* of identity that was the product of a long struggle for recognition and rights over the twentieth century (see Plummer, 1995). Paul, on the other hand, was suspicious of this master story. He did not feel at home in the gay male community and thus came to question whether his personal narrative could, or should, integrate this master narrative of identity.

The tension between David and Paul that we encountered that spring in Chicago reveals two salient ideas about sexual identity that underscore the theoretical perspective developed in this book. First, social identity is by no means a stable, enduring index of categorization; it is, rather, always being contested from within. Because individuals engage with master narratives of social identity in diverse ways and at diverse times in both individual and social history, identity is better understood as a *process* of human development than a "task" to be "achieved" (cf. Erikson, 1968; Marcia, 1966; Vaillant & Milofsky, 1980).

Second, the role of *history* and *discourse* must be recognized in the process of identity development. Nowhere is this idea more evident than in the consideration of sexual identity. As Benjamin Shepard details in Chapter 2 of this volume, the discourse about sexual identity in the United States changed considerably over the course of the twentieth century, and it continues to evolve in the twenty-first century. Though Paul and David were born at around the same time and can clearly be counted in the same generation, the history of sexual identity now provides them with access to two distinct narratives that help them to make meaning of their same-sex desire (Cohler, 2007). What we have called the narrative of *struggle and success* is the classic gay youth narrative that evolved in the post-Stonewall era (Cohler & Hammack, 2007). It is a story of self-discovery, accompanied by struggle because of society's stigmas about homosexuality, but culminating in the resilient triumph of self-actualization realized by *coming out* and becoming a member of the gay community (Cohler & Hammack, 2007; Herdt & Boxer, 1993). David clearly identifies with this master narrative. Paul, on the other hand, questions its foundation. He questions whether there is a need for a unique narrative, segregated from that of his straight counterparts. He is suspicious of the homogenizing, exclusionary gay male community. He feels more of an affinity to what we have called a narrative of *emancipation* from society's social categorizations of sexual identity (Cohler & Hammack, 2007; see also Savin-Williams, 2005).

What is key in understanding the difference between Paul and David is, in our view, an appreciation of the historical factors that have produced them both as subjects inhabiting a particular *identity space* and influencing the discourse they appropriate to make meaning of their lives (Foucault, 1978). The life course perspective we have both used in our collaborative and independent research over the years helps us to stay committed to an analysis of history in understanding human development (e.g., Cohler, 2007; Cohler & Hammack, 2006; Hammack, 2006; Hammack, Thompson, & Pilecki, in press; see also Singer, 2004). This approach is also useful for its ability to transcend the insidious and intellectually inhibiting schism between *essentialist* and *constructionist* views of sexual identity development (Hammack, 2005b).

In the remainder of this introductory chapter, we further delineate a theoretical approach to the study of sexual lives that takes history, discourse, and culture seriously. Central to our perspective is the idea of *narrative engagement*. We argue that an approach that links the ideas of *life course* and *narrative* provides a paradigm for the study of sexual lives that maximizes our consideration of the contextual basis of human development. Following our theoretical exposition, we discuss the outline of the book and orient the reader to its content.

Stories and Selves

Central to the concept of narrative engagement is the idea of a *personal narrative*. A personal narrative portrays an account of lived experience that is organized as a story. It integrates experience into a coherent account that makes meaning of life events (Bruner, 1990) and provides unity and purpose to the individual life course (Cohler, 1982; McAdams, 1990, 1997, 2001). But the personal narrative cannot be analytically removed from the narratives of social identity available in a particular cultural and historical context (Hammack, 2008). In the West, the personal narrative is characterized by a concern with the linear organization of experience (Ricoeur, 1977).

The present significance attributed to narratives is founded in the work of Giambattista Vico (1725/1968), whose eighteenth—century proposal for a *new science* was based on his critique of the Enlightenment, with its focus on *rationality* rather than *reasonableness* (Toulmin, 2001). However, the importance of stories as guides to human actions is found in classical Greek drama as formulated by Aristotle in his essay on the *Poetics*. Aristotle recognized the significance of stories both for personal well-being and for the larger society.

Our present concern with the study of narratives is closely tied to a philosophy of inquiry developed by Wilhelm Dilthey (1833–1911), who distinguished between a concern for *interpretation* in the human sciences and *explanation* in the natural sciences (e.g., Dilthey, 1988). Dilthey questioned the value of a philosophy for the study of lives that was based on a rational-empirical foundation. He was particularly critical of mechanistic psychology that had little to say about the human condition (Betanzos, 1988).

Dilthey's critique of a strictly rational-empirical approach to the study of lives was rediscovered in the aftermath of the intellectual ferment of the late 1960s that questioned many aspects of contemporary life, including methods of study in psychology and other social sciences (Bruner, 1990; Gergen, 2001; Polkinghorne, 1983). Polkinghorne (1983, 1988) has documented this change in the way in which we understand the study of persons and cultures. He reviews the work of early twentieth century social philosophers such as Max Weber (1864–1920), who emphasized the study of intentions and purposes using an interpretative rather than an explanatory method (e.g., Weber, 1905/2001). Polkinghorne reviews much of the modernist debate in social philosophy across the nineteenth and early twentieth centuries that preceded the turn to what Gergen (2001) and Sarup (1996) have termed *postmodern* science. Polkinghorne (1988) and Toulmin (2001) have both independently argued for a study of lives founded on concern with the meanings that we make and that guide our actions using the systematic study of narratives of lived experience (Schutz & Luckmann, 1973, 1989). This approach to the study of human conduct has been termed by psychoanalyst Heinz Kohut (1959) an *experience-near* rather than an *experience-distant* mode of study.

Narrative approaches in the social sciences have contributed significantly to an integrated understanding of person, history, and culture. Bruner (1990) argues that the study of narrative is fundamental to cultural psychology, since it is through the symbolic system of language that we construct meaning (see also Mead, 1934; Vygotsky, 1934/2002). Thomas and Znaniecke's (1918–1920/1974) classic four-volume account of the experience of immigration to the United States in the early twentieth century, *The Polish Peasant in Europe and America*, relied largely on personal narratives for analysis. This study stirred such controversy that a special meeting of the Social Science Research Council was convened to evaluate the narrative approach. Blumer's (1939) critique of the study was followed by Allport's (1942) endorsement of the use of personal documents in psychology and a companion volume highlighting the importance of narrative approaches in history, anthropology, and sociology (Gottshalk, Kluckhohn, & Angell, 1942). In psychology, Henry Murray (1938), Robert White (1975), and Gordon Allport (1946/1965) all advocated strongly for the vitality of an approach that relied upon individual life stories.

With the encroaching *cognitive revolution* in psychology, the mechanistic approach of behaviorism was replaced with an equally mechanistic view of human cognition (Bruner, 1990). The application of the computer as a metaphor for the mind left little room for the individual's intentional construction of meaning through narrative. Jerome Bruner, one of the pioneers of the early cognitive revolution, gradually sought to counter this approach and revive a focus on the significance of narrative (e.g., Bruner, 1987, 1990).

In personality and social psychology, a significant intellectual movement in favor of narrative gained momentum with critiques of the historical enterprise of social psychology (Gergen, 1973) and the *situationist* critique within personality psychology (Mischel, 1977). These perspectives challenged the knowledge generated by an ahistorical, aggregate approach to psychological science. A renewed focus on narrative within both social (e.g., Gergen & Gergen, 1983, 1986; Sarbin, 1986) and personality (e.g., McAdams, Ruetzel, & Foley, 1986) psychology initiated a major intellectual movement within psychology beginning in the 1980s that sought to bring narrative approaches into the mainstream of the discipline.

By the 1990s, narrative perspectives had expanded well beyond psychology (e.g., Ewick & Silbey, 1995; Ochs & Capps, 2001; Plummer, 1995), and the narrative approach is now recognized as inherently interdisciplinary (e.g., Holland, Lachicotte, Skinner, & Cain, 1998). In psychology, a renewed focus on narrative has gained considerable ground, as evidenced by the publication of a number of major papers in journals considered to have a vast audience and a high impact in the field (e.g., Hammack, 2008; McAdams & Pals, 2006; McLean, 2005; McLean, Pasupathi, & Pals, 2007; Pasupathi, Mansour, & Brubaker, 2007). In addition, the publication of a series of books by the American Psychological Association Press on the narrative study of lives is indicative of the broad appeal of the narrative approach within psychology (e.g., McAdams, Josselson, & Lieblich, 2006).

Our approach to sexual identity relies heavily on the multidisciplinary perspectives on narrative that have been articulated in the late twentieth and early twenty-first century. An intellectual focus on the idea of narrative within the humanities and social sciences has interestingly paralleled radical narrative disruptions in the cultural construction of sexual identity, particularly in the West. By no means is this codevelopment a coincidence in our view, for the cultural transformations of the twentieth century sensitized us as social scientists to the historical relativity of lived experience. It is this emphasis on narrative and the life course, on the historical positioning of lives and the possibilities for story-making within a given discursive context, that distinguishes our approach to the study of sexual identity and that of the contributors to this volume.

History, Discourse, and Human Development: The Emergence
of the Life Course Paradigm

Our consideration of historical context in the study of sexual identity is grounded
in the life course paradigm of human development. Viewed through the lens
of this paradigm, the integration of personal and social identity through the
construction of a life story always occurs in a particular historical and cultural
moment. The life course perspective on human development ascribes primacy
to the historical positioning of individual lives (e.g., Elder, 1974, 2002; Elder &
Shanahan, 2006; Shanahan & Elder, 2002), with its focus on the significance of
generation-cohort. The German sociologist Karl Mannheim (1928/1993) long ago
observed that the common social location of a group of individuals in a particular
historical moment creates a shared context for thought and action. Sociologists
and developmental scientists throughout the twentieth century, recognizing
Mannheim's valuable insight, sought to increase our understanding of the significance of generational and social time for human development (e.g., Dannefer,
1984; Kertzer, 1982; Neugarten, 1979; Ryder, 1965; Sorokin & Merton, 1937).

One need only think of major historical markers, such as September
11, 2001, to realize the significance of generation. Individuals born after
September 11 inhabit a radically different social and cognitive space than individuals who, say, were adolescents or adults when the attacks occurred. In
the realm of sexual identity, there are equally important historical markers,
such as the Stonewall Inn riots of 1969 and the acquired immune deficiency
syndrome (AIDS) crisis of the 1980s. The course of many lives was radically
altered by these events—so much so that such events create distinct cohorts of
individuals with same-sex desire, whose narratives of identity, we will argue,
subsequently diverge in important ways (see Cohler & Hammack, 2006).

Construction of discourse regarding sexual identity takes place within a
cultural and historical frame, but it also occurs according to a particular conception of human development. That is, our narrative understanding of sexual
identity is inseparably linked to our cultural conception of human development itself. In contemporary society, sexual desire and same-sex attraction
are inevitably posed within a developmental scheme that assumes that earlier
events presage later ones and that narratives of sexual identity reflect the linear
order of lives (Conway & Holmes, 2004; Stewart, Franz, & Layton, 1988).

This developmental paradigm for understanding lives has long been characteristic of Western intellectual culture. The concept of a linear life course was
present in ancient Greece (Cole, 1992). Aristotle divided the course of human
life into three periods: growth, stability, and decline. Medieval Europeans

divided it into four periods: childhood, youth, maturity, and old age. However, many peasants were not aware of their actual age since they did not have access to new time-reckoning instruments (Le Goff, 1980).

The modern life course was first envisioned in Enlightenment Europe as a *career*, often represented in iconography as a staircase rising through the adult years and then descending into old age. With the emergence of the concept of distinct life stages in the seventeenth century, it was possible to determine one's own place within this linear progression at any point across the course of life. The beginnings of a stage-based account of human development can be traced to Freud's (1905) epigenetic conception of development in which early childhood figured prominently.

Freud's theory of development, heavily rooted in sexuality, can be considered an early *ontogenetic* account. An ontogenetic approach to human development tends to neglect or insufficiently consider the broader social context of development, viewing the individual as a self-contained entity passing through specific *stages* (Dannefer, 1984). The ontogenetic point of view was influenced by Darwin's (1859/1999) conception of evolution leading to more complex and differentiated structures. Freud's pioneering contribution fostered interest in development during early childhood, inspiring work on both cognitive and social development (e.g., Bühler, 1935; Isaacs, 1930, 1933; Piaget, 1967, 1970). Children at particular ages were presumed to have particular needs requiring the response of caregivers, and this relationship was recognized as fundamental to psychological development (e.g., Bowlby, 1969).

Much of the ontogenetic perspective in human development across the first half of the twentieth century was integrated in an innovative account by Erik Erikson (1963, 1982/1997). Erikson extended Freud's initial epigenetic concept beyond childhood to the life cycle as a whole, and he sought to reorient the focus from sexuality to *sociality*. As such, Erikson was intellectually committed to notions of historical and cultural relativity in human development (e.g., Erikson, 1963, 1968).

Particularly in his discussion of the adolescent's increasing awareness of futurity (Bluck & Habermas, 2001; Greene, 1986), Erikson maintained that adolescents struggle with the issue of creating a personal identity or coherent life story. Erikson can be credited with placing the idea of identity at the forefront of social science and popular concern in the mid-twentieth century. His emphasis on identity possessed resonance precisely because of its historical relevance at the time, with the massive cultural and political changes occurring across the globe.

Erikson's ontogenetic approach influenced much developmental study in the postwar era, but the study of human development quickly faced a significant paradigmatic challenge. Reports from a longitudinal study begun after World War I suggested that experiences of early childhood were less significant in determining the course of subsequent development than had been presumed (Kagan, 1998). The continuity and predictability of the life course were challenged by these studies, given the major social and political events that had transpired to influence individual lives. Evidence of the impact of politics and history on the life course called into question the ontogenetic approach to human development and suggested instead the need for a *sociogenic* paradigm (Dannefer, 1984; Riegel, 1979).

Another major challenge to the hegemony of ontogenetic approaches emerged from the translation of the writings of the Russian psychologist Lev Vygotsky. His pioneering work *Thought and Language* was first translated into English in 1962 (Vygotsky, 1934/2002), and a collection of his writings published in 1978 as *Mind in Society* (Vygotsky, 1978) proved very influential to the emerging cultural emphasis in developmental psychology (e.g., Cole, 1996; Rogoff, 1990; Wertsch, 1985, 1991). Vygotsky argued that mediated social practice, rather than fixed and sequentially negotiated stages in development, could best account for the child's social and cognitive development.

Vygotsky's emphasis on the significance of language connects his challenge to the ontogenetic view of development to that posed by the French social philosopher Michel Foucault. Foucault (1978) argued that any developmental scheme was embedded in a particular historical construction and that there was no "reality" to developmental accounts beyond the particular discourse of development deployed in a given power-infused cultural context.

Grounded in notions of the significance of generation-cohort (e.g., Mannheim, 1928/1993; Ryder, 1965), an increasing emphasis on the life course as historically positioned emerged in developmental science at the end of the twentieth century. The first clear shift away from the ontogenetic model was signaled by Baltes and his colleagues (e.g., Baltes, 1968; Baltes, Cornelius, & Nesselroade, 1979; Baltes & Nesselroade, 1984). The pioneering work of Glen Elder, beginning with his 1974 study *Children of the Great Depression*, represented the possibilities of this new paradigm for understanding human development.

According to Elder (1991), "historical influence takes the form of a cohort effect when social change differentiates the life patterns of successive cohorts" (p. 1126). His study of two distinct cohorts who experienced the social impact of the Great Depression at different developmental moments revealed this salient relationship between history and individual experience. Elder (1974) discovered that boys born in the early 1920s, who were already adolescents at the time of the Great Depression, fared better than boys in the cohort born a decade later. Members of the earlier cohort were old enough to serve in the Second World War. Returning to civilian life following the war, they were then able to move into adult life, completing their education, marrying, and having a family. These veterans enjoyed support from a grateful nation upon their return from military service and also benefited from federal government financial support to return to school.

Boys born at the end of the 1920s were preschoolers at the time of the Great Depression. By the end of the war, these boys were often in the midst of their education and may have married and become parents at the time when they were called to serve in the Korean conflict. This military service disrupted the life trajectory of these men who were in the midst of their education or beginning their work life. Returning from service, these veterans did not experience the relief of a grateful nation and were provided with few benefits. Military service had interrupted their transition from adolescence to adulthood, and their subsequent life course was more disrupted than that of the preceding generation.

The life course perspective on human development that emerged from studies such as Elder's offers a paradigm that recognizes lives as more than mere products of some biological or psychological sequence. Rather, the life course paradigm recognizes development as a socially situated process. The life course itself, then, becomes an experiential product of a given historical order. The connection between the possible trajectories of development *and the construction of those possibilities by a given social structure* is acknowledged and, indeed, rendered necessary for study.

Yet, the life course paradigm does not view social structure as inherently "driving" development, for it preserves a notion of individual agency (Elder, 1998; Elder & Shanahan, 2006; Hammack, 2005b; Shanahan & Elder, 2002). Hence, the focus on human development for which we advocate is characterized by a process of *engagement*. We do not privilege structure over agency, and in this way we argue that the relationship between culture and the individual is *reciprocal* and *coconstitutive*.

In sum, a life course paradigm emerged over the course of the twentieth century with the increased recognition of the significance of generation-cohort and the limits of an ontogenetic approach to development. The life course perspective embraces the reciprocity and coconstitutive nature of culture and identity. This intellectual stance makes it particularly suitable for the study of sexual identity development. When it is fused with a narrative paradigm, a perspective that recognizes the salience of history and discourse naturally emerges.

The Course of Sexual Lives

Our perspective on the development of sexual identity focuses precisely on the significance of cohort and context in the construction of identity. When applied to sexual identity development, the life course approach reconciles disparate accounts of essentialism and constructionism about sexual orientation (Hammack, 2005b). Because the idea of *human agency* is fundamental to life course theory—the notion that individuals actively engage with the possibilities of their social ecologies of development to chart their own developmental trajectories (Elder & Shanahan, 2006)—there is a general recognition that we "construct" our lives to the extent that the exercise of agency is possible. In other words, we make meaning of our lives using the tools that are available to us in a given cultural surround. Central to these tools are *language* and *discourse* (Foucault, 1978; Vygotsky, 1934/2002, 1978; cf. Mead, 1934).

Life course theory posits first and foremost that historical context matters deeply in human development. In our view, there is almost no other "index" of human development for which this point is more obvious than sexual identity. As all of the authors in this volume argue, we cannot understand sexual identity development apart from an understanding of history. In fact, as social scientists, we are perhaps foremost historians (Gergen, 1973). The data we produce are always historical data. They represent but a snapshot in time, never to be replicable, for the forces of history are always reconstructing the social ecologies in which our lives unfold.

This phenomenon is well explicated in this volume in Jacqueline Weinstock's chapter on lesbian friendship. Weinstock has been a key contributor to the literature on lesbian friendship for some time. But in her chapter, she argues that the changing historical context of lesbian identity has radically altered the character of relationships among lesbians. She questions whether the intimacy and intensity of the lesbian communities she once inhabited and studied were, in fact, emblematic of a certain time in gay and lesbian history—a time when the stigma of a sexual minority identity necessitated a more insulated community. Weinstock engages with the possibility that the normalization of gay and lesbian lives has perhaps radically altered the character of relationships.

Earlier work in the study of sexual identity development—particularly within psychology—failed to sufficiently recognize the inherently *historical* nature of data on sexual lives. Thus, early models of sexual identity development posited a series of stages presumed to characterize the typical identity formation process of sexual minorities (e.g., Cass, 1979; Troiden, 1979). The veritable explosion of research on gay youth that began in the late 1980s and continued throughout the 1990s constructed a particular narrative of the gay life course that was characterized by struggle and victimization (e.g., Hetrick & Martin, 1987; Martin & Hetrick, 1988) but culminated in resilience through coming out (Herdt & Boxer, 1993; Plummer, 1995). Because much of that work has recently been challenged as itself constructing a measure of grimness in the very life course it was seeking to illuminate (e.g., Savin-Williams, 2005), the utility of a life course approach again reveals itself.

Through the lens of life course theory, we can view the current contestation over the nature of gay youth identity development, exemplified by the encounter between Paul and David at the beginning of this chapter, through the lens of history. Fusing narrative and life course approaches, we can come to view the development of identity as a process of *narrative engagement*. As individuals navigate the discursive waters of a given social ecology, as they come to recognize the meaning of the social categories of identity available to them in a given cultural context, they must make decisions (conscious or otherwise) about the relationship between their own sexual desire and the discourse available to make sense of that desire (Hammack, 2005b). That is, individuals form their sexual identities through a dynamic engagement with the discourse of sexual desire that characterizes their sociohistorical location (Foucault, 1978).

Our approach to sexual identity development thus fuses a number of critical theoretical perspectives in the social sciences—perspectives that emphasize the significance of history and social time, language and symbol, power and discourse. Consistent with a number of scholars in narrative studies (e.g., Bruner, 1990; Josselson, 1996; McAdams, 1996, 2001; Mishler, 1999), we argue that it is through the construction of a coherent life story that individuals come to make meaning of their life experiences. But our focus on sexual identity makes us want to emphasize that it is not just *experience* that is integrated in the construction of a life story. Rather, we believe that the construction of a personal narrative serves the purpose of making sense of *desire* as individuals develop their sexual identities. For those whose sexual desire is largely heterosexual, this process is likely relatively unconscious and not particularly intentional. But for individuals with same-sex desire, living in the context of a heterosexist society, the process of personal narrative construction is extremely salient. It is through narrative that sexual desire becomes rendered sensible to us, given the social lexicon of our cultural surround.

An emphasis on personal narrative might initially seem to privilege the private world of individual consciousness—all too common among psychologists. Our view of sexual identity development as a *process* (not solely a *product*) of narrative engagement reveals our dynamic view of identity. Rooted in theories of human development that emphasize *practical activity* (e.g., Rogoff,

1990; Vygotsky, 1978; Wertsch, 1991), we view the construction of sexual identity as intimately linked to the *social practice* that mediates our understanding of sexual desire and of the social categories of identity (Holland et al., 1998). Thus, we emphasize identity not solely as *narrative*, but also as *narrative engagement*.

When we assume a comparative approach to sexual identity development, as most of the authors represented in this volume do, the variability in processes of narrative engagement becomes immediately apparent. Individuals born in the United States in the 1950s and coming of age in the late 1960s, with the historic event of the Stonewall Inn riots, engaged with narratives of "gay liberation" unavailable to same-sex attracted individuals born just 10 years prior. American youth in the twenty-first century engage with narratives of "queer" and "postlabel" identity that are antithetical to the recognition for which the Stonewall generation fought. But these narrative contrasts reveal the intimate connection to history and discourse that each individual life course assumes. We cannot make sense of a life without becoming "historians of the self" (Mishler, 2004). And we cannot make sense of sexual identity without careful attention to the discourse of sexual identity that characterizes a time and place, thereby constructing a master narrative to which individuals are exposed in the course of their development. Their personal narratives of identity are always constructed in reference to, or through engagement with, this master narrative.

Stories of Sexual Identity

The chapters in this book connect to the idea of sexual identity development as narrative engagement in a number of ways. For some contributors, the role of an historical discourse of sexuality is central to an analysis of life stories. Hall's chapter examining three generations of men in the Czech Republic offers a compelling account of the significance of changes in political discourse on the life stories of men with same-sex desire. Adam's chapter on the emergence of sexual practices and a "poz" sexual culture places an analysis of the historical context of sexual behavior at the forefront. Cohler's chapter on narratives of American boyhood reveals the way in which adult gay men integrate a certain discourse on gender retrospectively into their personal narratives as they seek to integrate their understanding of "difference" in childhood with a presently constructed life story. And a number of chapters detail the major transformations in narrative possibilities for many individuals with same-sex desire that have occurred with technological (e.g., Harper and colleagues' chapter on youth and the Internet) and social and political (e.g., deBoer's chapter on gay parenthood) change.

While many chapters emphasize the significance of history and discourse in life-story analysis, others focus more on the illumination of significant issues for same-sex attracted individuals through the use of narrative methods. Kurtz's chapter on the Miami "circuit" scene uses ethnographic and narrative methods to reveal the struggles young gay men face as they seek meaningful relationships and a sense of community. The Miami scene that Kurtz details represents, in our view, a site of cultural practice for gay men in creating meaningful social lives. Ridge and Wright's chapter uses narrative methods to highlight the navigation of sexual risk and relationship dissolution among contemporary gay men. The voices of their participants highlight the lived experience of a generation of gay men who inhabit a post-AIDS context for sexual behavior that requires the careful negotiation of risk.

The relationship between master narratives and personal narratives—and the tension of the contestation *within* a master narrative—is a focus of several chapters. Meyer and Ouellette argue in their chapter on the narratives of African American gay men and lesbians against the traditional narrative of conflict between racial and sexual identities. Their narrative data, rather, suggest that Black gay men and lesbians construct life stories characterized by unity, purpose, and coherence. Blackburn's fascinating case study of four tellings of the personal narrative of Dara reveals the process of narrative engagement in action. As a young Black lesbian from a working-class background, Dara experiments with the integration of her class- and race-based identities as she constructs a narrative of sexual identity. Across tellings of her life story, she actively engages with a master narrative of lesbian identity primarily scripted by white middle-class gay men and lesbians, gradually finding a voice of her own. Perz and Ussher's chapter on the experience of premenstrual syndrome (PMS) among lesbian couples challenges several narratives about gender, sexuality, and relationships. Most centrally, their narrative data argue against the view of lesbian relationships as characterized by an unhealthy level of fusion. By contrast, the way in which lesbian couples deal with the physical and psychological challenges of PMS reveals lesbian relationships as supportive and interdependent.

With a focus on history and generation, a number of chapters use narrative methods to highlight the unique experiences of the life course. Read's chapter reviews the published life stories of baby-boom lesbians, while the chapter by King and colleagues reviews their important work on ego development and the coming-out process. Hostetler's chapter on generativity among gay elders is exhaustive in its integration of a life course approach that fully contextualizes the stories of these men and their engagement within the larger process of historical change. Rosenfeld's chapter on a particular cohort of gay men and lesbians, over age 65 at the time of their interview, reveals the connection among social practice, politics, and sexual identity.

A Paradigm Shift

What unites all of the contributors in this volume is their epistemological faith in the idea of narrative and the responsible contextualization of sexual lives. In the science of sexual identity development—whether approached from sociology, psychology, or other social science disciplines—this commitment to contextualized knowledge has not always been explicit. Infused by the positivist-informed ontogenetic perspective, much work on the development of sexual identity has not typically recognized the historical boundaries of the knowledge it sought to produce (Gergen, 1973). We view this increasing desire to locate sexual identity development in its historical and cultural context as emblematic of a paradigm shift within sexual science itself.

The production of knowledge is always connected to the demands of a particular social order and is, in fact, a part of the social reproduction of that order (e.g., Foucault, 1972; Sampson, 1993). The discourse of sexual science has shifted from the ontogenetic, reifying view of the twentieth century to a more sociogenic paradigm (Dannefer, 1984) concerned foremost with social meaning and contextualized experience. This paradigm shift, which is itself part of a much larger turn toward *interpretation* as the fundamental epistemological approach of social science (Bruner, 1990), emerged because of the anomalies in sexual identity development that began to arise with the social and political change of the 1990s (see Hammack, 2005a). As Kuhn (1962) long ago argued, it is through the discovery of anomalies that science itself develops.

Our intention in this volume is to inspire a new generation of scholars of sexual science to embrace narrative and life course approaches, for these models of inquiry are ideal for their ability to fully contextualize the knowledge we produce. To that end, we hope to portray the voices of individuals with same-sex desire in such a way as to inform transformative social science (Sampson, 1993). The voices of sexual subjects, we believe, reveal possibilities for empowerment even as they illuminate the social injustice of subjugation in a heterosexist society. Transformations in the structural reality of sexual subjugation rely upon a new discourse on sexual selves—one that can only emerge from the lived experience of individuals themselves. The voices in this book, we hope, contribute to this transformative end.

REFERENCES

Allport, G. W. (1942). *The use of personal documents in psychological science*. New York: Social Science Research Council.

Allport, G. W. (1965). *Letters from Jenny*. New York: Harcourt, Brace. (Original work published 1946)

Baltes, P. H. (1968). Longitudinal and cross-sequential sequences in the study of age and generation effects. *Human Development, 11*, 145–171.

Baltes, P., Cornelius, S., & Nesselroade, J. (1979). Cohort effects in developmental psychology. In J. R. Nesselroade & P. B. Baltes (Eds.), *Longitudinal research in the study of behavior and development* (pp. 61–87). New York: Academic Press.

Baltes, P. B., & Nesselroade, J. R. (1984). Paradigm lost and paradigm regained: Critique of Dannefer's portrayal of life-span developmental psychology. *American Sociological Review, 49*, 841–847.

Betanzos, R. J. (1988). Wilhelm Dilthey: An introduction. In W. Dilthey, *Introduction to the human sciences* (R. J. Betanzos, Trans.) (pp. 9–64). Detroit: Wayne State University Press.

Bluck, S., & Habermas, T. (2001). Extending the study of autobiographical memory: Thinking back about life across the life span. *Review of General Psychology, 5*, 135–147.

Blumer, H. (1939). *Critiques of research in the social sciences: I. An appraisal of Thomas and Znaniecki's "The Polish peasant in Europe and America."* New York: Social Science Research Council.

Bowlby, J. (1969). *Attachment and loss* (Vol. 1). New York: Basic Books.

Bruner, J. (1987). Life as narrative. *Social Research, 54*, 11–32.

Bruner, J. (1990). *Acts of meaning*. Cambridge, MA: Harvard University Press.

Bühler, C. (1935). *From birth to maturity: An outline of the psychological development of the child*. London: K. Paul, Trench, & Trubner.

Cass, V. C. (1979). Homosexual identity formation: A theoretical model. *Journal of Homosexuality, 4*, 219–235.

Cohler, B. J. (1982). Personal narrative and the life course. In P. Baltes & O. G. Brim, Jr. (Eds.), *Life-span development and behavior* (Vol. 4, pp. 205–241). New York: Academic Press.

Cohler, B. J. (2007). *Writing desire: Sixty years of gay autobiography*. Madison: University of Wisconsin Press.

Cohler. B. J., & Hammack, P. L. (2006). Making a gay identity: Life story and the construction of a coherent self. In D. P McAdams, R. Josselson, & A. Lieblich (Eds.), *Identity and story: Crafting self in narrative* (pp. 151–172). Washington, DC: American Psychological Association Press.

Cohler, B. J., & Hammack, P. L. (2007) The psychological world of the gay teenager: Social change, narrative, and "normality." *Journal of Youth and Adolescence, 36*, 47–59.

Cole, M. (1996). *Cultural psychology: A once and future discipline*. Cambridge, MA: Harvard University Press.

Cole, T. R. (1992). *The journey of life: A cultural history of aging in America*. New York: Cambridge University Press.

Conway, M., & Holmes, A. (2004). Psychosocial stages and the accessibility of autobiographical memories across the life cycle. *Journal of Personality, 72,* 461–480.

Dannefer, D. (1984). Adult development and social theory: A paradigmatic reappraisal. *American Sociological Review, 49,* 100–116.

Darwin, C. (1999). *The origin of species.* New York: Bantam. (Original work published 1859)

Dilthey, W. (1988). *Introduction to the human sciences* (R. J. Betanzos, Trans.). Detroit: Wayne State University Press.

Elder, G. H., Jr. (1974). *Children of the Great Depression: Social change in life experience.* Chicago: University of Chicago Press.

Elder, G. H., Jr. (1991). Life course. In D. L. Sills (Ed.), *International encyclopedia of the social sciences* (Vol. L, pp. 1120–1130). New York: Macmillan.

Elder, G. H., Jr. (1998). The life course as developmental theory. *Child Development, 69,* 1–12.

Elder, G. H., Jr. (2002). Historical times and lives: A journey through time and space. In E. Phelps, F. F. Furstenberg, Jr., & A. Colby (Eds.), *Looking at lives: American longitudinal studies of the twentieth century* (pp. 194–218). New York: Russell Sage Foundation.

Elder, G.H., Jr., & Shanhan, M. (2006). The life course and human development. In R. Lerner (Ed.), *Handbook of child psychology: Vol. 1: Theoretical models of human development* (pp. 665–715). New York: Wiley.

Erikson, E. H. (1963). *Childhood and society* (Rev. ed.). New York: Norton.

Erikson, E. H. (1968). *Identity: Youth and crisis.* New York: Norton.

Erikson, E. H. (1997). *The life cycle completed* (Extended version). New York: Norton. (Original work published 1982)

Ewick, P., & Silbey, S. S. (1995). Subversive stories and hegemonic tales: Toward a sociology of narrative. *Law and Society Review, 29*(2), 197–226.

Foucault, M. (1972). *The archeology of knowledge and the discourse on language* (A. M. S. Smith, Trans.). New York: Pantheon.

Foucault, M. (1978). *The history of sexuality, Vol. 1: An introduction.* New York: Vintage.

Freud, S. (1905). Three essays on the theory of sexuality. In J. Strachey (Ed. and Trans.), *The standard edition of the complete psychological works of Sigmund Freud, Vol. 7* (pp. 130–243). London: Hogarth.

Gergen, K. (1973). Social psychology as history. *Journal of Personality and Social Psychology, 26,* 309–320.

Gergen, K. (2001). Psychological science in a postmodern context. *American Psychologist, 56,* 803–813.

Gergen, K. J., & Gergen, M. (1983). Narratives of the self. In T. Sarbin & K. Scheibe (Eds.), *Studies in social identity* (pp. 245–273). New York: Praeger.

Gergen, K. J., & Gergen, M. (1986). Narrative form and the construction of psychological science. In T. Sarbin (Ed.), *Narrative psychology: The storied nature of human conduct* (pp. 22–44). New York: Praeger.

Gottschalk, L., Kluckhohn, C., & Angell, R. (1942). *The use of personal documents in history, anthropology, and sociology.* New York: Social Science Research Council.

Greene, A. (1986). Future time perspective in adolescence: The present of things future revisited. *Journal of Youth and Adolescence, 15,* 99–113.

Hammack, P. L. (2005a). Advancing the revolution in the science of sexual identity development. *Human Development, 48,* 303–308.

Hammack, P. L. (2005b). The life course development of human sexual orientation: An integrative paradigm. *Human Development, 48,* 267–297.

Hammack, P. L. (2006). Identity, conflict, and coexistence: Life stories of Israeli and Palestinian adolescents. *Journal of Adolescent Research, 21*(4), 323–369.

Hammack, P. L. (2008). Narrative and the cultural psychology of identity. *Personality and Social Psychology Review, 12*(3), 222–247.

Hammack, P. L., Thompson, E. M., & Pilecki, A. (In press). Configurations of identity among sexual minority youth: Context, desire, and narrative. *Journal of Youth and Adolescence.*

Herdt, G., & Boxer, A. (1993). *Children of Horizons: How gay and lesbian teens are leading a new way out of the closet.* Boston: Beacon.

Hetrick, E., & Martin, A. (1987). Developmental issues and their resolution for gay and lesbian adolescents. *Journal of Homosexuality, 14,* 25–43.

Holland, D., Lachicotte, W., Skinner, D., & Cain, C. (1998). *Identity and agency in cultural worlds.* Cambridge, MA: Harvard University Press

Isaacs, S. F. (1930). *Intellectual growth in young children.* New York: Harcourt and Brace.

Isaacs, S. F. (1933). *Social development in young children.* London: Routledge.

Josselson, R. (1996). *Revising herself: The story of women's identity from college to midlife.* New York: Oxford University Press.

Kagan, J. (1998). *Three seductive ideas.* Cambridge, MA: Harvard University Press.

Kertzer, D. (1982). Generation and age in cross-cultural perspective. In M. W. Riley, R. P. Abeles, & M. S. Teitelbaum (Eds.), *Aging from birth to death, Vol. 2: Sociotemporal perspectives* (pp. 27–50). Boulder, CO: Westview Press.

Kohut, H. (1959). Introspection, empathy, and psychoanalysis: An examination of the relationship between mode of observation and theory. *Journal of the American Psychoanalytic Association, 7,* 459–483.

Kuhn, T. S. (1962). *The structure of scientific revolutions.* Chicago: University of Chicago Press.

Le Goff, J. (1980). *Time, work, and culture in the middle ages* (A. Goldhammer, Trans.). Chicago: University of Chicago Press.

Mannheim, K. (1993). The problem of generations. In K. H. Wolff (Ed.), *From Karl Mannheim* (2nd expanded ed., pp. 351–398). New Brunswick, NJ: Transaction Books. (Original work published 1928)

Marcia, J. (1966). Development and validation of ego identity status. *Journal of Personality and Social Psychology, 3,* 551–558.

Martin, A. D., & Hetrick, E. (1988). The stigmatization of the gay and lesbian adolescent. *Journal of Homosexuality, 15,* 163–183.

McAdams, D. P. (1990). Unity and purpose in human lives: The emergence of identity as a life story. In A. I. Rabin, R. A. Zucker, & R. A. Emmons (Eds.), *Studying persons and lives* (pp. 148–200). New York: Springer.

McAdams, D. P. (1996). Personality, modernity, and the storied self: A contemporary framework for studying persons. *Psychological Inquiry, 7,* 295–321.

McAdams, D. P. (1997). The case for unity in the (post)modern self: A modest proposal. In R. D. Ashmore & L. Jussim (Eds.), *Self and identity: Fundamental issues* (pp. 46–80). New York: Oxford University Press.

McAdams, D. P. (2001). The psychology of life stories. *Review of General Psychology, 5,* 100–122.

McAdams, D. P., Josselson, R., & Lieblich, A. (Eds.). (2006). *Identity and story: Crafting self in narrative.* Washington, DC: American Psychological Association Press.

McAdams, D. P., & Pals, J. (2006). A new big five: Fundamental principles for an integrative science of personality. *American Psychologist, 61,* 204–217.

McAdams, D. P., Ruetzel, K., & Foley, J. M. (1986). Complexity and generativity at mid-life: Relations among social motives, ego development, and adults' plans for the future. *Journal of Personality and Social Psychology, 50,* 800–807.

McLean, K. C. (2005). Late adolescent identity development: Narrative meaning making and memory telling. *Developmental Psychology, 41,* 683–691.

McLean, K. C., Pasupathi, M., & Pals, J. L. (2007). Selves creating stories creating selves: A process model of self development. *Personality and Social Psychology Review, 11,* 262–278.

Mead, G. H. (1934). *Mind, self, and society.* Chicago: University of Chicago Press.

Mischel, W. (1977). On the future of personality measurement. *American Psychologist, 32*(4), 246–254.

Mishler, E. (1999). *Storylines: Craftartists' narratives of identity.* Cambridge, MA: Harvard University Press.

Mishler, E. (2004). Historians of the self: Restorying lives, revising identities. *Research in Human Development, 1,* 101–121.

Murray, H. A. (1938). *Explorations in personality.* New York: Oxford University Press.

Neugarten, B. (1979). Time, age, and the life cycle. *American Journal of Psychiatry, 136,* 887–894.

Ochs, E., & Capps, L. (2001). *Living narrative: Creating lives in everyday storytelling.* Cambridge, MA: Harvard University Press.

Pasupathi, M., Mansour, E., & Brubaker, J. R. (2007). Developing a life story: Constructing relations between self and experiences in autobiographical narratives. *Human Development, 50,* 85–110.

Piaget, J. (1967). *Six psychological studies* (A. Tenzer & D. Elkind, Trans.). New York: Random House.

Piaget J. (1970). *Genetic epistemology* (E. Duckworth, Trans.). New York: Columbia University Press.

Plummer, K. (1995). *Telling sexual stories: Power, change, and social worlds.* New York: Routledge.

Polkinghorne, D. E. (1983). *Methodology for the human sciences: Systems of inquiry.* Albany: State University of New York Press.

Polkinghorne, D. E. (1988). *Narrative knowing and the human sciences.* Albany: State University of New York Press.

Ricoeur, P. (1977). The question of proof in Freud's psychoanalytic writings. *Journal of the American Psychoanalytic Association, 25*, 835–872.

Riegel, K. F. (1979). *Foundations of dialectical psychology.* New York: Academic Press.

Rogoff, B. (1990). *Apprenticeship in thinking: Cognitive development in social context.* New York: Oxford University Press.

Ryder, N. (1965). The cohort as a concept in the study of social change. *American Sociological Review, 30*, 843–861.

Sampson, E. E. (1993). Identity politics: Challenges to psychology's understanding. *American Psychologist, 48*(12), 1219–1230.

Sarbin, T. R. (1986). The narrative as a root metaphor for psychology. In T. R. Sarbin (Ed.), *Narrative psychology: The storied nature of human conduct* (pp. 3–21). New York: Praeger.

Sarup, M (1996). *Identity, culture and the postmodern world.* Athens: University of Georgia Press.

Savin-Williams, R. (2005). *The new gay teenager.* Cambridge, MA: Harvard University Press.

Schutz, A., & Luckmann, T. (1973). *The structures of the life-world.* Evanston, IL: Northwestern University Press.

Schutz, A., & Luckmann, T. (1989). *The structures of the life world* (Vol. 2). Evanston, IL: Northwestern University Press.

Shanahan, M., & Elder, G. (2002). History, agency, and the life course. In R. A. Dienstbier & L. J. Crockett (Eds.), *Agency, motivation and the life course* (pp. 145–186). Lincoln: University of Nebraska Press.

Singer, J. (2004). Narrative identity and meaning making across the adult life span: An introduction. *Journal of Personality, 72*, 437–459.

Sorokin, P., & Merton, R. (1937). Social time: A methodological and functional analysis. *American Journal of Sociology, 42*, 615–629.

Stewart, A., Franz, C., & Layton, L. (1988). The changing self: Using personal documents to study lives. *Journal of Personality, 56*, 41–74.

Thomas, W. I., & Znaniecki, F. (1974). *The Polish peasant in Europe and America.* New York: Octagon Books. (Original work published 1918–1920)

Toulmin, S. (2001). *Return to reason.* Cambridge, MA: Harvard University Press.

Troiden, R. (1979). Becoming homosexual: A model of gay identity acquisition. *Psychiatry, 42*, 362–373.

Vaillant, G., & Milofsky, E. (1980). Natural history of male mental health: IX. Empirical evidence for Erikson's model of the life cycle. *American Journal of Psychiatry, 137*, 1348–1359.

Vico, G. (1968). *The new science* (T. G. Bergin & M. H. Fisch, Eds. & Trans.) (3rd ed.). Ithaca, NY: Cornell University Press. (Original work published 1725)

Vygotsky, L. S. (1978). *Mind in society: The development of higher psychological processes.* (M. Cole, V. John-Steiner, S. Scribner, & E. Souberman, Trans.). Cambridge, MA: Harvard University Press.

Vygotsky, L. S. (2002). *Thought and language* (A. Kozulin, Trans.). Cambridge, MA: MIT Press. (Original work published 1934)

Weber, M. (2001). *The Protestant ethic and the spirit of capitalism.* (T. Parsons, Trans.). New York: Routledge. (Original work published 1905)

Wertsch, J. (1985). *Vygotsky and the social formation of mind.* Cambridge, MA: Harvard University Press.

Wertsch, J. (1991). *Voices of the mind: A sociocultural approach to mediated action.* Cambridge, MA: Harvard University Press.

White, R. W. (1975). *Lives in progress* (3rd ed.). New York: Holt, Rinehart & Winston.

2

History, Narrative, and Sexual Identity

Gay Liberation and Postwar Movements for Sexual Freedom in the United States

Benjamin Shepard

Throughout the post–World War II period in the United States, movements for social justice and sexual freedom battled over the management of queer sexuality. These struggles manifested themselves in a series of competing narratives of identity and meaning. During this historical moment, a narrative of queer sexuality as pathology proliferated in American society. Activists fought to shift the terms of discourse over queer sexuality toward liberatory understandings built on links with the era's other movements for personal freedom and social justice, including civil rights, women's liberation, and the antiwar movement. Yet, with every ensuing progressive discourse, a reductionist narrative followed which sought to relink queer sexuality with pathology.

This chapter reviews competing narratives of queer sexuality during the postwar years. It begins with the intermingling Cold War red and lavender scares over communism and sexual perversion, juxtaposed with calls for civil tolerance of homosexuals by the Mattachine Society and other early homophile groups in the 1950s. By the 1960s, narratives had shifted from treatment of homosexuals as second-class citizens—based on criminal and mental illness models—toward civil rights discourses centered on citizenship. By the 1970s, narratives had shifted toward a more assertive call for personal and sexual freedom. A backlash followed as liberationist

23

narratives competed with conservative story lines linking homosexuality with deviance, especially pedophilia. Throughout this era, panic narratives linking queerness with pathology seemed to follow each advance of progressive story lines for queer life.

With the dawn of the acquired immune deficiency syndrome (AIDS) pandemic in the 1980s, narratives of gay life shifted once again, as homosexuality was again linked with images of illness. Activists sought to turn this story line on its head. By the 1990s, panic narratives had become part of the ongoing debates about AIDS, sex, and pleasure as conservative and radical camps debated the contemporary meanings of queer sexuality. Within this debate, radicals accused assimilated gays of advancing a normative, commercialized form of citizenship that "whitewashed" any sense of difference out of their queerness.

Recognizing that the process of personal narrative construction relies upon larger discourses of identity, this chapter reviews the evolution of contested historical narratives of queer identity. The chapter explores a schism dating back to the earliest days of gay liberation. At its heart, this debate concerns questions about the very nature of queer identity and its social meaning. Do queers simply engage in same-sex sexual behavior or is queerness a fundamental critique of social, sexual, and political expectations and participation? The struggles of this period highlight core dilemmas about identity and historical change in a participatory democracy, illustrating the ways in which historically based narratives of sexuality influence the development of individual sexual identity.

While no one narrative or grouping of narratives speaks comprehensively to the shifting social and cultural context of same-sex desire, an analysis of competing narratives reveals the ways in which constituencies fought to define and redefine practices in queer community building. With the contestation of historical meta-narratives over the past 70 years, shifts in practices of the queer self have resulted in differing forms of same-sex social practices, expanding social networks, reduction of social isolation, and vitality within social movements for sexual freedom. The result is a shifting historical context for competing narratives of the queer self.

It Takes One to Know One

Throughout the 1930s, practices of queer life remained an uneasy, secretive part of American life in cities from San Francisco to Washington (Boyd, 2003). Shortly after Franklin D. Roosevelt became president, Prohibition came to an end. With its passing, a new era of social tolerance took hold in Washington. New Deal Washington would become a boomtown. Federal agencies created thousands of new jobs as the population doubled. Some 700,000 people— many young and single—descended on the nation's capital. Some stayed at the YMCA, and others met after work at Lafayette Park to enjoy the thriving queer culture that had become part of the New Deal openness (Johnson, 2004)—until the queer purges began in the late 1940s and 1950s.

Over the next two decades, competing narratives of queer life would shift between Cold War propaganda linking homosexuality to communism and Mattachine narratives calling for acceptance of same-sex desire. Discursive struggles between those who quietly expressed same-sex desire and those who viewed such practices as dangerous and worthy of investigation characterized much of the 1950s and 1960s. The political landscape shifted as the federal government began screening alleged "sex perverts" for employment (D'Emilio, 1983). The Cold War and the Kinsey Report (Kinsey, Pomeroy, & Martin, 1948) focused nationwide attention on the specter of "otherness" represented by both communism and homosexuality.

By 1950, the Republicans had been out of power for some 18 years. Unable to locate actual communists in the federal government, homosexuals served as the more accessible "security threat" that could be targeted in the Democrat-controlled government. The McCarthy era purges of "perverts" from the government based on morality charges were a way for Republicans to exact political revenge (Johnson, 2004). Historians such as George Chauncey (1993), Martin Duberman (1991), Estelle Freedman (1989), John D'Emilio (1983, 1992), and David Johnson (2004) have outlined the narrative links between the homosexual "sex crime panics" and the queer purges of the McCarthy years. Johnson, for example, notes that the 1950s fixation on sex perverts built upon the hysteria of the World War I–era Red Scare, in which large numbers of immigrants and anarchists were targeted and deported at will.

In the 1950s discourse, communism, homosexuality, and sexual perversion were linked into a single deviant story line. Within this narrative, outsider status signified criminality. Queers and communists were thought to recruit those who were weak, disturbed, or ill, as well as those who lived outside traditional norms. Many suspected that the two groups were actively collaborating to subvert the U.S. government.

Throughout the 1950s, communists were thought to be "infecting" the American body politic—and especially American youth. Their point of entry: homosexual desire. Yet, this line of thinking was anything but new. From the spring of 1919 through 1920, the U.S. Navy dispatched squadrons of enlisted men to investigate "immoral conditions" reported at the Naval Training Station in

Newport, Rhode Island. Volunteer decoys were sent to find the true "queers" operating at the station. Under oath, these decoys testified that they submitted to the
queers' sexual advances in order to rid the station of their presence. In fact, they
dedicated inordinate enthusiasm to the task, and many volunteered for multiple
assignments. During a trial, the defense cross-examined the one such volunteer:

Q.   You volunteered for this work?

A.   Yes, sir.

Q.   You knew what kind of work it was before you volunteered?

A.   Yes, sir.

Q.   You knew it involved sucking and that sort of thing, didn't you?

A.   Yes, sir.

Q.   And you were quite willing to get into that sort of work?

A.   I was willing to do it, yes, sir.

Q.   And so willing that you volunteered for it, is that right?

A.   Yes, sir. I volunteered for it, yes, sir.

(Chauncey, 1989, p. 306)

Many of the entrapped men testified that the decoys had initiated the sexual encounters. By 1920, the Navy gave up on the investigation (Duberman,
Vicinus, & Chauncey, 1989).

The problematic relationship between the investigator and his object of
scrutiny is a dominant feature within the hysteria of the lavender scare years.
This attraction/repulsion relationship has a distinguished history within U.S.
political thought. The sentiment finds expression in a fixation with things one
is taught to dislike. In Newport, right-thinking prosecutors fixed their gaze on
homosexuals in the Navy; during the 1950s lavender scare, the glare extended
to queers in government. Throughout these panics, moral guardians claimed
to be protecting the public from a predator, either communist or homosexual.
While feeding erotophobia, such Cold War scares brought out the propensity
in U.S. politics to define American citizenship in terms of what one is *not*, in
terms of "other" (Heale, 1990; Orr, 2006, Schrecker, 1998; Shepard, 2007).

This attempt to construct identity through "othering" is by no means
merely an American phenomenon. A brief review of German homophobic
discourses during the pre–World War II period is instructive. The specter of
guilt, questions about sexual performance, and accusation were key ingredients
of fascist propaganda. In his paper "National Socialism or Bolshevism," Adolf
Hitler's propaganda chief, Joseph Goebbels (1925/1995), used the association

of communism with homosexuality and lack of virility to rally Germans against the Soviets. Here, antiqueer narratives served a psychic economy that disavowed deviant forms of pleasure.

For the Nazis, the appropriate role of sexuality was in the service of power, control, and (re)production (D'Emilio, 1993). As with the U.S. lavender scare, communism and homosexuality—along with Jewishness—were identified as specters that could devour or dissolve the national will (Theweleit, 1989). The Nazis felt compelled to shut down most of Berlin's pulsating gay public sexual culture—including destroying the books and artifacts in Magnus Hirschfeld's Institute for Sexual Science—during their first days of power in 1933 (Gordon, 2000).

While many U.S. servicemen were able to experience same-sex contact throughout the Second World War, a similar backlash linked homosexuality with pathology. "There was a constant threat of being found out and cashiered out of the service," Stuart Loomis, a World War II veteran, recalled (quoted in Sadownick, 1996, p. 34). By the early 1940s, army psychiatrists began to establish elaborate screening processes for queer and deviant behavior among men in the armed forces. In 1942, the army began to differentiate between the "normal" and "persons habitually or occasionally engaged in homosexual or other perverse sexual practices" (Sadownick, 1996, p. 35). In the following years, narratives of queer life in the United States would become more and more reductive.

In the late 1940s and 1950s, Federal Bureau of Investigation (FBI) chief J. Edgar Hoover and Senator Joseph McCarthy saw desire through a lens of contagion. For those such as Hoover, queer desire was something that, if left unchecked, could overwhelm the nation's imagination. As D'Emilio (1983) notes, "Homosexuality became an epidemic infecting the nation, actively spread by communists to sap the strength of the next generation" (p. 44).

The process began with a chance revelation during hearings on the loyalty of government workers. On February 28, 1950, Undersecretary of State John Peurifoy testified to a government committee that 91 government officials who had been fired for moral turpitude were also homosexuals (D'Emilio, 1983). In so doing, the secretary tapped into a well of American sexphobia.

Senator McCarthy, who was just beginning his career as an anticommunist crusader, spent months railing about the dangers of "sexual perverts" in the government. He charged that the State Department had reinstated countless known queers, despite threats to national security. Others followed suit, accusing the executive branch of an inexcusable lack of resoluteness in weeding out spies and queers from the federal government. The District of Columbia issued a report stating that thousands of "sex deviants" had infiltrated the government. Word of a new "homosexual angle" at play swirled around capital. For many, "sex perverts" represented a threat as great as the communists themselves. In June 1950, the Senate authorized a full investigation of homo-sexuals and "sex perverts" in the U.S. government (D'Emilio, 1983).

What ensued was a grotesque example of the full Senate putting a premium on conformity, as tolerance for difference was lost for a generation (Duberman, 1991). The 81st Congress Senate Document, 2nd Session, No. 241, outlines the Senate subcommittee's position on "Employment of Homosexuals and Other Sex Perverts in Government." The subcommittee sought to establish how many perverts worked in the federal government and to examine useful ways to establish a solution to the "problem." The subcommittee defined sex per-verts as "those who engage in unnatural acts" and queers as "persons of either sex who as adults engage in sexual activities with persons of the same sex" (cited in Duberman, 1991, p. 182). They noted that "most authorities believe sex deviation results from psychological rather then physical causes" (p. 182). The subcommittee argued that "those who violate moral codes and laws and the accepted standards of conduct must be treated as transgressors and dealt with accordingly" (p. 182). Hence, official social and political discourse argued for the need to exclude queers from the government, and individuals with same-sex desire were framed as moral and political threats.

By this time, the American Psychiatric Association (APA) had defined homosexuality as a pathology. Freud's "Letter to a Young Mother," decrying condemnation of homosexuality, was withheld from the standard edition of his collected works. Indeed, Freud clearly noted that queer sexuality was nei-ther something to celebrate nor something to condemn (Freud, 1935/2001). Yet, the APA distanced itself from the more progressive elements of Freud's thinking (Danto, 2005).

From 1947 to April 1950, dismissals of suspected queers from government service averaged five per month. Eisenhower's addition of "sexual perverts" to the loyalty security program cost suspected queers their jobs at a rate of forty per month. More than 12,600,000 workers—a fifth of the U.S. labor force—faced loyalty investigations simply for subscribing to certain maga-zines or enjoying friendships with other suspects. And more people lost their jobs for being homosexual than for being communist during the Lavender Scare (D'Emilio, 1983; Johnson, 2004). As with so many panics, fear of difference was frozen into law. Yet, even then, counternarratives were beginning to emerge.

The Birth of the Gay Rights Movement

The Mattachine Society—the nation's first homophile group—formed in 1950 to fight the antihomosexual panic. At the time, most homosexuals in the United States were just trying to get by. Few conceived of the treatment of homosexuals in the State Department or in the culture at large as a social problem that needed to be addressed. Much of the vitality of this movement was incumbent on connecting isolated experiences or even yearnings for same-sex desire with broader, more liberatory narratives of the queer self.

Theorists of narrative have long suggested that communities need stories, just as narratives require an audience to find expression. The relationship between narrative and community is thus reciprocal (Plummer, 1995). These stories help social actors find meaning, coherence, and a way of connecting their story with larger social forces. Outside of community, the ambitions of such lives are pursued in isolation.

Consider the experience of lesbian activist Barbara Gittings, who mused about the feelings of isolation she experienced before joining the movement: "I had a lot of problems coming to terms with myself as a young lesbian. The stigma about homosexuality made me feel bad about it for a long time" (quoted in Tobin & Wicker, 1972, p. 205). Her story existed in a vacuum. "My main problem was that I suffered terribly as a young lesbian from a lack of intelligent information" (p. 206). At the time, medical narratives linked same-sex desire with sickness; so Gittings was treated by a psychiatrist.

> She took for granted that change was what I wanted and so did I. It was part of the culturally accepted outlook that if you had homosexual tendencies, this was a great misfortune and should be corrected. (p. 207)

It was only after reading stories of other lesbians that Gittings connected with the nascent movement, joining the Daughters of Bilitis in 1958 and editing a movement magazine, *The Ladder.* The aim of *The Ladder* was to spread a different story of queer experience—one that debunked narratives linking homosexuality with pathology.

Much of the power of the new movement involved the ways it built on the daily lives, practices, social ecologies, reading habits, networks, and friendships of early members. Sociologist Peter Nardi (1999) suggests that friendships often function as the nexus between personal membership and connection with broader macrocommunities and movements. There are few better examples of this than the early Gay Liberation organizing. When organizer Harry Hay moved to Los Angeles, he knew no one, except for a small list of contacts from friends. After making a few calls in his new town, Hay started to form a network, which became the foundation for the first U.S. gay rights organization, the Mattachine Society. Through informal contacts and practices rather than formal political networks, the U.S. gay rights movement was born (Foucault, 2005; Nardi, 1999).

Before Mattachine, Hay had been a member of the Communist Party. Thus, he was quite familiar with strategies for organizing. After a failed attempt at marriage in which his attraction to men never waned, Hay devoted himself to organizing a nascent movement of homosexuals. To begin, he wrote a manifesto with which to organize his new group. "We, the Androgynes of the world," the manifesto stated, "have formed this responsible corporate body to demonstrate by our efforts that our physiological and psychological handicaps need be no deterrent in integrating ten percent of the world's population towards the constructive social progress of man" (Hay, 1997, pp. 60–61). In his manifesto, he compared the mass arrests of queers in the State Department to the treatment of homosexuals in Nazi Germany only a few years earlier (Faderman & Timmons, 2006). And Hay started looking to connect with sympathizers.

On August 10, 1948, Hay organized a meeting near the University of Southern California, but no one attended. It was not until July 1950 that Hay found others to help start Mattachine. From April to October 1950, 382 homosexuals were dismissed from their jobs due to morals charges, up from 192 the previous two years (D'Emilio, 1983). The second Mattachine meeting was held on November 11, 1950, in a private residence in the Echo Park/Silverlake neighborhood of Los Angeles. Five men attended. The blinds were closed and the door was locked; one man served as a lookout for the police. Those who had come were worried that they could be arrested simply for attending such a meeting. "We didn't know," Hay recalled in Schiller and Rosenberg's 1985 film *Before Stonewall: The Making of a Gay and Lesbian Community*:

> None of us knew at that point that there had ever been a gay organization of any sort anywhere. We had no knowledge of that. So we felt that we had to be very careful with everything we did, very careful. Or we could make a mistake. Get in the papers for the wrong reasons. We could hurt the idea of a movement for years to come. We were terrified of that.

At the November meeting, the men detailed a plan for organizing homosexuals, which linked their cause with those of other progressive movements. It would take five months before the group gave itself the name "Mattachine," after a medieval French secret society of unmarried men. And it was just in time: By December, the federal government would formalize its policy on "The Employment of Homosexuals and Other Sex Perverts" (Faderman & Timmons, 2006; Hay, 1997; Kenney, 2001; Schiller & Rosenberg, 1985).

So, the group started to organize. Hay recognized that the group could be most effective if it followed basic organizing principles of reciprocity: votes for politicians in exchange for support. If the Progressive Party candidate Henry Wallace would support privacy protections for homosexuals, Mattachine would support his presidential bid. At the time, this was an outlandish proposition. After all, suspected homosexuals could be arrested simply for being accused of looking for sex, and homosexual gatherings were completely prohibited. Yet, Hay had the foresight to grasp the innovative idea that queers represented a distinct cultural minority. For Hay, homosexuality was a deeply spiritual disposition capable of unifying multiple aspects of an individual. In contrast to the *homophile* position of the era, which stipulated that homosexuals were just like heterosexuals, Hay suggested that homosexuality offered a distinct cultural perspective from which heterosexuals could learn a thing or two. Yet, Hay would clash with the more timid view of homosexuality that came to characterize the Mattachine approach, and his active participation in the group did not last (Bronski, 2002).

Other homophile groups also formed in the 1950s. The Daughters of Bilitis, founded by Del Martin and Phyllis Lyon in San Francisco in 1955, published the first-ever American magazine for lesbians, *The Ladder* (Gallo, 2006). ONE, Inc., a Mattachine offshoot founded in Los Angeles in 1952, also published a magazine, entitled *ONE* (Faderman & Timmons, 2006). All of these publications helped spread a more humanistic narrative of queer experience. They were part of a broad shifting story line.

Howling at the Panic

An early reader of *ONE* was the poet Allen Ginsberg. A leader in the Beat movement, Ginsberg was inspired by the literary quality and political perspective of the new publication. Such advocacy for free thought was exactly what he thought the movement—and the country—desperately needed. The publicity would continue when *ONE*, which sold some 5000 copies per month during the mid-1950s, successfully defended itself against obscenity charges by the U.S. Postal Service. The Supreme Court ultimately ruled that stories of queer life were not obscene and could legally be sent through the mail in 1958 (Faderman & Timmons, 2006).

For Ginsberg, the 1940s and 1950s were a time when homosexuals such as himself were just beginning to think that they did not need to be intimidated by the Nazis or the McCarthys of the world, "who did not know anything about life anyway," as he proclaimed in Schiller and Rosenberg's (1985) film. By the middle of the decade, he would create considerable notoriety with his own poetic narratives of cultural resistance.

Throughout the 1950s, San Francisco was becoming the center of a new literary and cultural explosion. The city had always been a place where social outsiders had come to reinvent themselves. Wave after wave of dreamers—from those panning for gold during the rush of 1849 to the Beats a century later—created new lives in "Baghdad by the Bay." World War II radically influenced urban queer politics, including those in San Francisco (D'Emilio, 1983). After the war, in which same-sex contact was common, many planted roots in the port city of San Francisco rather than return home (Sadownick, 1996). In between waves of outcasts, a different kind of story line of queer life found expression. Much of this vast civil society found expression within an underground bar culture, cross-dressing, performance, and conviviality. Over the decades to come this community became an enduring political constituency and a movement recognized around the world (Boyd, 2003; Shepard, 1997).

Among the waves of dreamers to find their way to San Francisco was a group of writers who came to inspire a new movement for freedom. According to Regina Marla (2004), editor of *Queer Beats*, the Beats were queer in the fullest sense of the word. Their fluid sexuality challenged both sexual and romantic conventions of the era. For most of those in the movement, sexuality was not a primary motivation or concern. Queerness was neither condemned nor a topic with which to be obsessed. Instead, the Beats celebrated the streets, jazz, and the road connecting ideas and possibilities within a "holy America." While Ginsberg was known to be homosexual and William Burroughs bisexual, others, such as Jack Kerouac, were known as heterosexual—although this did not stop some of the more heterosexual members of the movement from sharing their beds with Ginsberg, as he famously recounted in the poem "Many Loves."

Perched in a smoky coffee house deep in San Francisco's North Beach, Ginsberg would contribute to this burgeoning queer civil society of the era. He first read, performed, screamed "Howl" at the Six Gallery on October 7, 1955. The first lines are now familiar enough, yet from the vantage point of 1950s America, they are striking: "I saw the best minds of my generation destroyed by madness, starving hysterical naked, dragging themselves through the negro streets at dawn looking for an angry fix" (Ginsberg, 1956).

While "Howl" does not explicitly speak out about gay liberation, its striking imagery openly expresses a longing for another way of being in the world. The poem's heroes are those who struggle to live authentically, those who could feel, those who "broke down crying in white gymnasiums naked and trembling before the machinery of other skeletons," those who "shrieked with delight in police cars for committing no crime but their own wild cooking pederasty and intoxication" (Ginsberg, 1956). The poem refers to police enforcement of blue laws and harassment of homosexuals, those arrested for partaking in the public sexual culture of queer meeting spaces such as subways, parks, and streets—all historic cruising grounds for gay men (Munoz, 1996; Turner, 2003).

Throughout the poem, Ginsberg refers to the "heterosexual dollar." In so doing, he links capital with heterosexuality in a manner queer theorists of a generation later would describe as *heteronormativity*; herein, the opposition is to *normativity*, not necessarily heterosexuality itself (Warner, 1993). "Howl" reflects themes that would accompany many of the narratives of gay liberation: a call for an end to attacks on public sexuality, an appreciation for the spiritual potential of Eros, and a critique of consumer culture. For Ginsberg, the problem is "lacklove." Lack of love is a critique of capitalism and its own perversions.

The Beat movement and the San Francisco Renaissance that inspired it would provide a bridge between the "quiet" homophile movement represented by organizations like the Mattachine Society and the "loud" Gay Liberation era to come. The attacks on "Howl," the legal battles and ultimately unsuccessful attempts to ban the work—combined with the unsuccessful attempt to prohibit distribution of *ONE* magazine—contributed to publicity for the movement that helped spread its message and connect fellow travelers (Schiller & Rosenberg, 1985; Tobin & Wicker, 1972). The result was a proliferation of abundant narratives of queer experience.

Camp Arias and Police Batons

Within walking distance of the coffee shops, the jazz bars, and the Six Gallery where Ginsberg first read "Howl," a different, albeit no less significant, type of queer political performance was taking place at the Black Cat, a bohemian bar in San Francisco Ginsberg once dubbed "the greatest gay bar in America." José Sarria, a fixture in San Francisco's social and political scene for half a century, began working at the Black Cat after World War II. Dressed in heels, his accompaniment of the arias from Bizet's *Carmen*, mixed with camp and even a little politics, drew legions.

Sarria's performances included observations of the pulse of Baghdad by the Bay. "I started to preach that gay is good" (cited in Boyd, 2003, p. 23). In the face of arrests of homosexuals and raids on gay bars, Sarria defied the oppression with a high-octane dose of humor. "There is nothing wrong with being gay—the crime is getting caught," he argued while disseminating a far more affirmative narrative of queer life (Feinberg, 2005). "United we stand, divided they catch us one by one," Sarria exclaimed in an early expression of queer solidarity (Feinberg, 2005).

Sixteen years before Harvey Milk was elected to the San Francisco Board of Supervisors, Sarria's 1961 campaign for the Board of Supervisors marked the first such run for public office by an out gay individual. His run from the counterpublic of the Black Cat into the center of the city's public life garnered some 5600 votes. It was an impressive display of the burgeoning political power of the queer community, and it was the first time many noticed that homosexuals could wield political clout in the city. It is no stretch of the imagination to link Sarria's groundbreaking run with Milk's 1977 success (Shepard, 1997; Shilts, 1982).

In the years after his campaign Sarria stayed involved, turning his eyes outward to the ongoing harassment taking place at gay venues throughout the city (Boyd, 2003). The harassment continued, but now with greater public visibility. In June 1964, a coalition of progressive Christians, civil rights activists, and homophile advocates formed a new coalition called the Council on Religion and the Homosexual (CORH). On January 1, 1965, the group held a fund-raiser at California Hall in San Francisco. At the time, the police would arrest men who appeared in public dressed in women's clothing. And as was the case at many big events in San Francisco, this is exactly what happened. Police sought to shut down the event, arresting a few attendees, shining lights and photographing attendees, as the clergy watched in horror. While many had heard stories of such raids, the gap between hearing and witnessing the infringement of the most basic human rights was profound. The following day, CORH held a press conference at Glide Memorial Church and issued a press release chastising the San Francisco Police Department and the city itself for allowing such treatment to be part of official policy. The group served as a corroborating witness for complaints by queer activists, and their position as witnesses served as a vital source of support for the burgeoning movement (Shilts, 1982; Stryker & Van Buskirk, 1996).

Stories of queer resistance floated up and down the California coast. For example, "[I]n the Black Cat Bar in Los Angeles, at the stroke of New Year, plainclothesmen who had infiltrated the bar throughout the night started humiliating and beating the celebrants there," John Rechy (2006) recalls. "Subsequently 200 gay men and women gathered in the Silver Lake district to protest the raid before squadrons of armed police, stunned by the sudden resistance." A few months later, a similar event took place in the Bay Area after one too many insults from the police. In response, a group of queer patrons at Gene Compton's Cafeteria in San Francisco's Tenderloin district trashed the cafeteria and a police car before torching a nearby newsstand. The Compton riot signaled the emergence of a newly radicalized queer community (Lee & Ettinger, 2006; Stryker, 2005; Stryker & Van Buskirk, 1996).

Flash points lit up gay politics throughout these years, yet they were the exception rather than the norm. For much of the 1960s, the Mattachine Society maintained a politics of apology. Mattachine politics were disconnected from the affirmative tone of a new, liberating narrative. Yet, over time, the movement's narrative shifted tone from apologetic to transgressive. By the end of the decade, a mass of liberationist narratives coalesced to a crescendo.

Stonewall and a Different Story Line

In June 1969, a riot outside the Stonewall Inn in New York's Greenwich Village helped to transform Gay Liberation into a national movement. Marty Mumford, a member of New York's Gay Activist Alliance, was present at the riot. "It was beautiful," he recalled in an interview conducted shortly thereafter. He described the distinctly queer approach taken by those who fought back. "As the TPF [tactical police force] riot squad came down the street, about twenty-five gays broke into a chorus line. It was defiant camping" (quoted in Tobin & Wicker, 1972, p. 173).

The use of joy, play, and camp to organize queers would become a defining characteristic of the movement (Shepard, 2005). "It's sassy, arrogant, determined, headstrong, gonna win!" Mumford proclaimed (quoted in Tobin & Wicker, 1972, p. 167). With Stonewall, narratives of queer experience took a far more self-confident, assertive tone. The result was a dramatic shift in story lines of queer experiences of self and community. A good example of this shift is represented in Lige Clark and Jack Nichols' 1972 autobiography, *I Have More Fun with You Than Anybody*. The book—with a cover featuring affirming photos of the two men in Washington Square—was published by the mainstream St. Martin's Press. It offered a profound corrective to the narrative linking homosexuality with illness and tragedy typically witnessed in popular cultural representations of queers in films or other literature (Russo, 1987).

Gay Liberation fought the culture's persistent negative reaction to queers (Weeks, 1985). Among its goals, the movement aimed to free sexuality, to transform the family as an institution, to end antiqueer violence, and to develop a new vocabulary of the erotic (Altman, 1972). It was a social movement built on public visibility, exploration of personal growth, and an understanding that oppression based on sexual identity took place within a broad social context (Bronski, 1998).

Throughout the 1970s, gays helped build a public sphere for conversation, pleasure, and the free exchange of ideas. Titles such as *Orgasms of Light*, a gay poetry anthology from 1977, speak to the optimism and openness of "the new gay dawn" (Leyland, 1977, p. 7). New public spaces, including bathhouses, bars, movie houses, and tea rooms, for the practice of sexual liberation, and bookstores full of literature on the movement, functioned as profound cultural resources for the new movement,. According to Winston Leyland, the editor of *Gay Sunshine*, a San Francisco gay literary magazine, the Stonewall riot "was followed by the publication of newsletters and newspapers which acted as vehicles for the spread of movement ideas" (1977, p. 7). Notable examples include New York's *Come Out!*, Detroit's *The Gay Liberator*, Philadelphia's *Gay Dealer* and *Lavender Vision*, and Boston's *Fag Rag* (Leyland, 1977). These papers helped spread the liberationist story line of Gay Liberation across the nation.

This new narrative of Gay Liberation constructed a new reality for sexual consciousness. Eric Rofes, who worked at *Gay Community News* in Boston in the 1970s, said in a 2005 interview, "I think that came out of Gay Liberation. I feel like I got that from my years at *Gay Community News*, from being next door to *Fag Rag*, which was putting that out really boldly." Means and ends overlapped within the production of the stories of the new movements for sexual freedom.

> "What could it mean that after we did layout on Thursday night, the guys would be in Herbe's Ram Rod Room on their knees suckin' dick all night? Was that, an informal part of it, something to be ashamed of?" (Rofes, 2005).

As Rofes' personal narrative reveals, Gay Liberation helped advance a corrective to the sex-phobic narratives that had been so omnipresent: "Sexual pleasure had not been on anyone's agenda."

With Stonewall, the story line of the gay movement shifted from homophile calls for tolerance to a new defiant gay call for the total transformation of a society that harbored anti-sex attitudes, restricted sex roles, and institutionalized racial hierarchies. In the weeks after the June riots, gay activists adopted a new term for the movement—*Gay Liberation*—and sought to organize around a call for solidarity with movements for freedom taking place around the world. By mid-July, a flyer was plastered up around Greenwich Village: "DO YOU THINK HOMOSEXUALS ARE REVOLTING? YOU BET YOUR SWEET ASS WE ARE," the flyer declared.

With that flyer, the Gay Liberation Front (GLF) was born. "I'll never forget seeing that flyer," an early member of the group, Bob Kohler, recalled in an interview three decades later (Kohler, 2002). GLF would last for only a few months, but its call for a universalist discourse linking multiple forms of oppression was profoundly influential. The movement's call for struggle against injustice anywhere echoed similar sentiments of Martin Luther King, Jr., and Eugene Victor Debbs.

For others, however, this universalist attitude was not appealing (Tobin & Wicker, 1972). Many decided to take a different path within the burgeoning Gay Liberation movement, forming a new group to address strictly gay issues. GLF members condemned the new group as overly white and reformist, while the new Gay Activist Alliance (GAA) suggested that they had enough work to do just fighting homophobia. Harry Hay was initially inspired by the early Gay Liberation organizing, yet he worried that groups such as the GAA were overly fixated on assimilating into mainstream society rather than continuing the struggle to dismantle the oppressive forces that furthered homophobia (Bronski, 2002). The central tension would continue to involve a conflict between *assimilation* and *cultural transformation*. These competing story lines would follow the debates over the meaning of gay, lesbian, bisexual, and transgender liberation for decades to come (Shepard, 2001; see also Duberman, 1993; Warner, 1999).

The militancy of the early 1970s marked a stark contrast with the homophile calls for equality and tolerance that characterized groups such as the Mattachine Society and the early Daughters of Bilitis. A new ethos of direct action was part of the story line for Gay Liberation. This ethos of activism would contribute to the movement for the next two decades, providing continuity from GAA to the AIDS Coalition to Unleash Power (ACT UP).

Part of what these activists later brought to the AIDS struggle was an understanding of how to use direct action to shift social mores, create power, and alter political story lines (Gamson, 1991). It was a lesson they carried from one of the signature victories of Gay Liberation: the battle over psychiatric narratives of queer sexuality as illness. Throughout the early 1970s, Gay Liberationists borrowed from the lessons of antiwar groups such as Science for the People, which sought to disrupt the normal mechanisms of science (Moore, 2008). To do this, they pushed, prodded, disrupted meetings, zapped, and disrupted the daily mechanisms of psychiatric power until, in 1973, the APA rescinded their categorization of homosexuality as pathology.

The victory was a prime achievement of the burgeoning Gay Liberation movement. The rejection of narratives linking queer sexuality with pathology offered the marker of a new self-understanding. A vital element of this new consciousness was a rejection of the ruthless clinical logic of the pre-Stonewall world. For Gay Liberationists, it was that rationalized worldview that had consigned homosexual existence to the realm of mental illness and psychiatric wards (Foucault, 1978). After Stonewall, this worldview was largely rejected (although many conservatives continue to hold such a view). With this shift in the definition of same-sex desire, a proliferation of competing narratives found their way into public life.

Competing Narratives of Gay Life

With the successes of the Gay Liberation years, queers would start to draft different stories, cultivating differing experiences, practices, and meanings of queer life in the post-Stonewall era. While activists hoped to push the move-ment to continue fighting oppression wherever it manifested itself, others sought to build on the new visibility by marketing to a distinct gay community. Debate over the meaning of same-sex desire and community unfolded in gay papers across the country. At issue was the core question: Is queer sexuality normal, as the Mattachine society insisted, or did it represent a radical cri-tique of heterosexuality and patriarchy, as the GLF suggested (Bronski, 1998, D'Emilio, 1993)? What emerged was a series of competing narratives of gay life to be hashed out in the gay press, academic conferences, and street actions over the next four decades (Shepard, 2001).

In 1976, Lionel Biron published an essay in *Gay Sunshine* in which he attacked the *Advocate*, a national gay magazine, for its blatant consumerist approach. "During the past year the *Advocate* has been transformed into a show place of white, middle-class gay America," he wrote. "Features on travel, fashion and entertainment suggest an affluent, carefree lifestyle in which Gay means little more than fun and chic." Biron's (1976) primary critique was of the distance the *Advocate* was putting between itself and Gay Liberation politics. "Editorial statements, lashing out at the Gay Liberation Movement, have promoted a myopic gay politics whose sole end is the passage of gay civil rights legislation." Rather than achieve protections only for gays, the point was to fight to create a better world for all. After all, Biron suggested, few could argue that "all will be well with gay America once anti-gay discrimi-nation laws are enacted." Instead of a single-issue politics, Biron noted, Gay Liberation involved multiple overlapping narratives of queer experience. To think otherwise was "an affront" to gay communities of color and to "all other minority group gays who must struggle against oppression on *more than one front.*"

By the late 1970s, the movement had jettisoned much of its radical edge for a more limited gay civil rights agenda. In response, Harry Hay sought to create a different model of gay politics, forming the Radical Faeries in 1979. Rather than seek policy changes, the Fairies practiced community-building through rituals, environmentalism, and a view that queer sexuality offered spiritual possibilities unimaginable for those caught up in restricted gender norms or enforced social reproduction. "Harry was worried that gay life was too much about bars and drinking," New York Radical Faerie Donald Gallagher explained in a 2006 interview. Hay hoped that the Radical Faeries could contribute to a gay politics of difference. Over the next thirty years, the Faeries would be just that—a group of wild, often nude, outlandish queer men and women who embraced both male and female aspects of themselves, loved the earth, and participated in an egalitarian "genderfuck" in which social hierarchies were rejected in favor of a far more socialistic, utopian view of life (Bronski, 2002).

While radical queers struggled with assimilationist gays throughout the late 1970s, both camps were forced to contend with a larger social backlash to the advances of the gay rights movement. Here, dueling narratives of gay life confronted an ongoing debate over the meanings and appropriate policy responses to the issue of homosexuality. While San Francisco supervisor Harvey Milk called for gay people to come out and speak out as citizens and participate fully in public life (Shepard, 1997; Shilts 1982), antigay crusader Anita Bryant had other ideas: "Behind the high-sounding appeal against discrimination in jobs and housing"—which Bryant suggested was not a problem for closeted homosexuals—she proclaimed that queers hoped for a social blessing for "their abnormal lifestyle" (Romesburg, 2000).

Bryant sought to stymie the narrative of liberation—the coming-out stories that had become the core underpinning for the still-nascent gay rights movement (Plummer, 1995; Rofes, 1998). And Bryant was by no means alone in advancing this line of thinking. "Homosexuality is not a civil right," wrote conservative columnist Pat Buchanan. "Its rise almost always is accompanied, as in the Weimar Republic, with a decay of society and a collapse of its basic cinder block, the family" (Fairness & Accuracy in Reporting [FAIR], 1996). For her part, Bryant sought to relink discourses connecting queer sexuality with pathology and pedophilia. Since homosexuals cannot reproduce, "they can only recruit children," she proclaimed, "and this is what they want to do. Some of the stories I could tell you about child recruitment and child abuse by homosexuals would turn your stomach" (Romesburg, 2000).

Bryant deployed the most reductive antiqueer narratives to make a case that civil rights advances should be overturned across the country, antisodomy statutes should be retained or reinstated, and queers should be barred from teaching in the schools. When Boston sixth-grade teacher Eric Rofes heard Bryant's rant, he was so upset that he had to pull his car over as he trembled and fought tears (Rofes, 1998). Yet, instead of cowering or turning away, Rofes helped organize the first national Gay and Lesbian March on Washington. He would spend the next three decades struggling against Bryant's pathologizing narratives. It is hard to overemphasize the influence of such struggles on individual lives such as Rofes or Barbara Gittings, as well as on the movements in which those such as Rofes and Gittings found an outlet and a refuge.

While queers successfully contested many of these attacks during 1970s, the tenacity of narratives linking queer sexuality with pathology would gain momentum during the AIDS years to come. The 1970s would end with stories of political assassination, riots, and ongoing narratives of political redemption for gay people (Shepard, 1997).

Sexuality = Contagion

While "Gay Is Good" and sexual freedom represented central narratives of gay life in the 1970s, by the 1980s and 1990s such themes were challenged by narratives that relinked sexuality with pathology and contagion (Munoz, 1996). With the election of Ronald Reagan in 1980, prohibitive narratives from the 1950s, which linked nonprocreative sexuality with sexual deviance and criminality, found their way back into the center of public consciousness.

Many of these narratives took hold within the public spectacle of the Reagan-era Meese Commission on pornography and its chair's advocacy of "family values" at the expense of other, more diverse forms of sexual expression. Much of the commission's logic dates back to the 1940s and 1950s sex crime panics, as well as to attempts to ferret out homosexuals and "sex perverts" in the U.S. government and to censor different forms of sexual expression, such as ONE magazine. All the while, new antisex narratives gained momentum. In one example, a generation of antipornography feminists attempted to ban forms of sexual expression in the name of feminism (D'Emilio, 1992). In another case, North Carolina Senator Jesse Helms conflated homosexuality with obscenity (Hunter, 1995). A central stage for this cultural front was the Meese Commission hearings. The hearings began after Reagan decided that he was unsatisfied with the 1970 Johnson administration report on pornography, which concluded that pornography had no effect on behavior and called for the repeal of obscenity laws. In 1984, Reagan argued, "We have seen reports suggesting a link between child molesting and pornography. And academic studies have suggested a link between pornography and sexual violence against women" (Nobile & Nadler, 1986, p. 16). Therefore, he announced, he would call for a new commission to study the effects of pornography (Nobile & Nadler, 1986). And queers, who had witnessed multiple attempts to ban their literature by labeling it obscene, were particularly aware that censorship was bad for everyone.

Carole Vance witnessed the Meese Commission hearings firsthand, noting: "If these were the McCarthy hearings of sex, they were scripted by *Saturday Night Live*," she wrote. "The report and its two volumes, and 1960 pages, faithfully reflects the censor's fascination with the things they love to hate" (quoted in Watney, 1997, p. 69). The Commission brought together materials found in sixteen adult bookstores—725 books, 2325 magazines, and 2370 films—listing them in alphabetical order, beginning with *A Cock Between Friends* and ending with *69 Lesbians Munching* (Watney, 1997). Meese had put together perhaps the greatest porn database ever compiled.

The Meese Commission hearings linked 1950s Cold War fears of contagion with a new series of antisex narratives. Opponents argued that such anxieties of contagion were manufactured to uphold social roles and gender hierarchies (Kipnis, 1992). Noting that social control was a latent aim of the hearings, anticensorship feminists successfully outlined the ways the Meese Commission deployed fear to manipulate the populace (Hunter, 1995; Shepard, 2007).

AIDS Narratives

A primary ingredient in 1980s antisex narratives was the AIDS crisis. From its earliest days, stories of the AIDS epidemic would intersect with any number of competing narratives of queer experience (Treichler, 1988). The onset of the disease was heralded by a barrage of competing representations and high-contrast story lines: clean or dirty, hetero or homo, natural or immoral, pure or impure. Themes of morality and retribution, death and decay dominated stories cast with injection drug users, sex-crazed fags, whores, victims, disease carriers, and crack babies (Gamson, 1991). "The poor homosexuals they have declared war upon nature, and now nature is extracting an awful retribution," Pat Buchanan declared in 1983. Linking homosexuality with retribution; he declared in 1992 that "AIDS is nature's retribution for violating the laws of nature" (quoted in FAIR, 1996). These scripts privileged heteronormative cultural practices while utilizing the full administrative technology of the state to punish anything that deviated from them. All the while, legal and medical discourses utilized science to categorize people with AIDS in terms of deviance and stigma (Gamson, 1991).

ACT UP, and its offshoots such as Queer Nation, aimed to turn this story line on its head. The mantra "sexuality equals life" became a kernel of AIDS activism. Faced with court losses, bathhouse closures, and AIDS phobia, ACT

UP sought to reverse a cultural narrative that defined AIDS through a moralizing lens (Shepard, 1997).

Narratives of survival became an intimate part of queer life with the onset of the epidemic. In June 1990, an anonymous unsigned broadsheet bearing the words "Queers Read This" was distributed throughout the crowd during the New York City gay pride march. "How can I tell you. How can I convince you, brother, sister that your life is in danger," the broadsheet began: "That everyday you wake up alive, relatively happy, and a functioning human being, you are committing a rebellious act," it declared. "You as an alive and functioning queer are a revolutionary. There is nothing on this planet that validates, protects or encourages your existence. . . . You should by all rights be dead."

Echoing Frederick Douglass' old adage that power conceded nothing without a demand, the manifesto continued: "No one will give us what we deserve. Rights are not given; they are taken, by force if necessary." Within this call for self-determination, a narrative of a different sort of queer citizenship found its expression in the old Gay Liberation adage that an "army of lovers cannot lose." Such a brand of queer citizenship involved multiple overlapping layers of social and cultural experience: " . . . It is about the freedom to be public, to just be who we are. It means everyday fighting oppression; homophobia, racism, misogyny, the bigotry of religious hypocrites and our own self-hatred." From here, the broadsheet suggested queer life integrated any number of subversive cultural experiences. "Being queer means leading a different sort of life. . . . It's about being on the margins, defining ourselves; it's about gender-fuck and secrets, what's beneath the belt and deep inside the heart; it's about the night."

"Queers Read This" offered an outline of a queer life narrative that had far more to do with a 1970s brand of gay liberation than the antisex narratives that increasingly dominated the AIDS years. It also defiantly celebrated pleasure, even in the face of the epidemic, suggesting queers cultivate a brand of citizenship involving connections among bodies and polymorphous engagement with difference rather than interest-group politics.

Within narratives such as that of "Queers Read This," the stigma of the label "queer" waned (Berlant & Freeman, 1993). Along the way, a generation of sexual and social justice movement activists would seek to bring this voice to the fore. "Queers Read This" challenged homogenizing forms of gay experience, calling for resistance rather than assimilation. "So we've chosen to call ourselves queer," the broadsheet read. "Using 'queer' is a way of reminding us how we are perceived by the rest of the world. It's a way of telling ourselves we don't have to be witty and charming people who keep our lives discreet and marginalized."

The 1990s were characterized by conflicts between assimilationist gay politics and a radical queer approach to community-building (Shepard, 2001; Warner, 1999). The core of the debates involved narratives of the queer self. The implications of these shifting narratives continue to impact queer practices of self in the twenty-first century.

Normative Sexuality?

The competing narratives of queer sexuality explored in this chapter address the parameters of normal sexuality (see Warner, 1993). Within debate over the meanings and practices of same-sex desire, core questions about pluralistic democracy unfold. Can one choose a partner and enjoy intimacy without risking arrest, unemployment, or invasion of one's home (Rofes, 1998)? Should queerness be understood as a simple private act or as a fundamental critique of capitalist mores, as Harry Hay long suggested (Bronski, 2002; D'Emilio, 1993)? Are same-sex narratives part of a discourse linked with core notions of freedom of assembly and pursuit of happiness?

Harry Hay finally passed in 2002. He was 90 years old. The following year, in *Lawrence v. Texas*, the U.S. Supreme Court distanced queer sexuality from criminality by repealing state sodomy statutes. Hay would have appreciated the irony that Southern segregationist Strom Thurmond died the day of the ruling. While many cheered *Lawrence*, a bad taste was left for those whose lives failed to fit into the bourgeois mold of those who have sex only at home, as protected by the *Lawrence* decision. Once again, those on the margins—"kinky" queers and the economically marginalized, as well as those who make use of public sexual space for contact—were left to fend for themselves (Califia, 2004). Some suggested that the case only reminded them how close queer sexuality remained to criminality. After all, one of the judges who supported *Lawrence* stepped down shortly after the 5–4 decision, only to be replaced by a conservative who surely would have reversed the ruling (Rechy, 2006). Still, the decision amounted to a step forward for a progressive narrative of queer sexuality, one of countless intermingling stories and never-ending discourses of desire and regulation at the heart of a sixty-year debate over the meanings of queer sexuality in American life.

The interplay among narratives of the queer self, culture, and historical moment are contingent upon just such shifting discourses of queer experience. Few discursive terrains are more reflective of social flux than the narratives of the queer self over time. Diverse narratives of queer experience have resulted in the advance of a social movement for sexual freedom felt around the world. "[W]hat is being globalized about the international gay and lesbian movement," sociologist Peter Nardi (1998) writes, "is the creation of a political self based on sexuality and community" (p. 583).

Yet, the foundation on which stories of same-sex desire interact in the public arena remains precarious. Recall Barbara Gittings' personal narrative. While the story of Gittings' same-sex desire began with seclusion in the 1950s, she broke through this isolation, helping to disseminate narratives of queer experience that transformed understandings of same-sex desire for decades to come. By the time of her death, Gittings was viewed as a heroine, even if the *New York Times* took over a month to finally run her obituary (see Fox, 2007). And even that institutional recognition came only after prodding from Larry Kramer, who lamented the lack of an obituary during his March 13, 2007, ACT UP twentieth anniversary speech: "When the *New York Times* does not run an obituary on quite possibly the most famous lesbian in modern times, Barbara Gittings, then we are in trouble." Queer life stories continually reflect such struggles for recognition rather than social oblivion.

From Freud to Hoover, Newport to *Lawrence*, Mattachine to SexPanic!, the way these narratives have found expression became a primary story of life in the twentieth century, influencing countries the world over. These story lines are anything but settled. From the Cold War to Gay Liberation, competing narratives and definitional conflicts over the meaning of queer experience have intermingled, as contrasting struggles between social acceptance or criminality, health or pathology, liberation or retribution, connection or isolation, celebration or melancholia. They reflect ever shifting story lines of queer life experience, historical change, and a radically altered social ecology.

REFERENCES

Altman, D. (1972). *Homosexual oppression and liberation*. Sydney, Australia: Angus & Robertson.

Berlant, L., & Freeman, E. (1993). Queer nationality. In M. Warner (Ed.), *Fear of a queer planet* (pp. 193–229). Minneapolis: University of Minnesota Press.

Biron, L. (1976, Spring). The advocate: Capitalist manifesto. *Gay Sunshine*. Retrieved November 1, 2006, from http://www.photos-biron.com/advocate.htm

Boyd, N. A. (2003). *Wide open town: A history of queer San Francisco*. Berkeley: University of California Press.

Bronski, M. (1998). *The pleasure principle*. New York: St. Martin's Press.

Bronski, M. (2002). The real (radical) Harry Hay. *Z Magazine*. Retrieved October 16, 2006, from http://zmagsite.zmag.org/Dec2002/bronski1202.htm

Califia, P. (2004). Legalized sodomy is political foreplay. In Mattilda Bernstein Sycamore (Ed.), *That's revolting: Queer strategies for resisting assimilation* (pp. 69–72). Brooklyn, NY: Soft Skull Press.

Chauncey, G. (1989). Christian brotherhood or sexual perversion? Homosexual identities and the construction of sexual boundaries in the World War I era. In M. Duberman, M. Vicinus, & G. Chauncey (Eds.), *Hidden from history: Reclaiming the gay and lesbian past* (pp. 294–317). New York: New American Library.

Chauncey, G. (1993). The postwar sex crime panic. In W. Graebner (Ed.), *True stories from the American past* (pp. 160–178). New York: McGraw-Hill.

Clark, L., & Nichols, J. (1972). *I have more fun with you than anybody.* New York: St. Martin's Press.

Danto, E. (2005). *Freud's free clinics: Psychoanalysis and social justice.* New York: Columbia University Press.

D'Emilio, J. (1983). *Sexual politics, sexual communities: The making of a homosexual minority in the United States, 1940–1970.* Chicago: University of Chicago Press.

D'Emilio, J. (1992). *Making trouble: Essays on gay history, politics, and the university.* New York: Routledge.

D'Emilio, J. (1993). Capitalism and gay identity. In H. Abelove, M. A. Barale, & D. M. Halperin (Eds.), *The lesbian and gay studies reader* (pp. 467–478). New York: Routledge.

Duberman, M. (1991). *About time: Exploring the gay past.* New York: Meridian.

Duberman, M. (1993). *Stonewall.* New York: Plume.

Duberman, M., Vicinus, M., & Chauncey, G. (1989). *Hidden from history: Reclaiming the gay and lesbian past.* New York: New American Library.

Faderman, L., & Timmons, S. (2006). *Gay L.A.: A history of sexual outlaws, power politics and lipstick lesbians.* New York: Basic Books.

Fairness and Accuracy in Reporting (FAIR). (1996, February 2). Pat Buchanan in his own words. Press release. Retrieved October 10, 2006, from http://www.fair.org/index.php?page=2553

Feinberg, L. (2005). Pre-Stonewall gay organizing. *Workers World.* Retrieved April 18, 2008, from http://www.workers.org/2005/us/lavender-red-39/

Foucault, M. (1978). *The history of sexuality, Vol. 1: An introduction.* New York: Vintage.

Foucault, M. (2005). Sex and the politics of identity: An interview with Michel Foucault. In M. Thompson (Ed.), *Gay spirit: Myth and meaning* (pp. 33–35). Maple, NJ: Lethe Press.

Fox, M. (2007, March 15). Barbara Gittings, 74, prominent gay rights activist since '50s. *New York Times,* p. B8.

Freedman, E. (1989). Uncontrolled desires: The response to the sexual psychopath, 1920–60. In R. Padgug (Ed.), *Passion and power: Sexuality and history* (pp. 195–225). Philadelphia: Temple University Press.

Freud, S. (2001). Letter to an American mother. In C. Bull (Ed.), *Come out fighting: A century of essential writing on gay and lesbian liberation* (p. 18). New York: Thunder's Mouth Press/Nation Books. (Original work published 1935)

Gallagher, D. (2006). Interview with the author.

Gallo, M. (2006). *Different daughters: A history of the Daughters of Bilitis and the rise of the Lesbian Rights Movement.* New York: Carroll & Graff.

Gamson, J. (1991). Silence, death, and the invisible enemy: AIDS activism and social movement "newness." In M. Burawoy, A. Burton, A. A. Ferguson, K. J. Fox, J. Gamson, N. Gartrell, L. Hurst, C. Kurzman, L. Salzinger, J. Schiffman, S. Ui., *Ethnography unbound: Power and resistance in the modern metropolis* (pp. 35–57). Berkeley: University of California Press.

Ginsberg, A. (1956). *Howl and other poems.* San Francisco: City Lights Press. Retrieved November 1, 2006, from http://members.tripod.com/~Sprayberry/poems/howl.txt

Goebbels, J. (1995). National Socialism or Bolshevism. In A. Kaes, M. Jay, & E. Dimindberg (Eds.), *The Weimar Republic sourcebook* (pp. 127–129). Berkeley: University of California Press. (Original work published 1925)

Gordon, M. (2000). *Voluptuous panic: The erotic world of Weimar Berlin.* Los Angeles: Feral House.

Hay, H. (1997). *Radically gay: Gay liberation and the words of Harry Hay* (W. Roscoe, Ed.). Boston: Beacon Press.

Heale, M. J. (1990). *American anticommunism: Combating the enemy within, 1830–1970.* Baltimore: Johns Hopkins University Press.

Hunter, N. (1995). Contextualizing the sexuality debates: A chronology. In L. Duggan & N. Hunter (Eds.), *Sex wars: Sexual dissent and political culture* (pp. 16–29). New York: Routledge.

Johnson, D. K. (2004). *The Lavender Scare: The Cold War persecution of gays and lesbians in the federal government.* Chicago: University of Chicago Press.

Kenney, M. R. (2001). *Mapping gay L.A.: The intersection of place and politics.* Philadelphia: Temple University Press.

Kinsey, A., Pomeroy, W., & Martin, C. (1948). *Sexual behavior in the human male.* Philadelphia: W. B. Saunders.

Kipnis, L. (1992). (Male) desire and (female) disgust: Reading *Hustler.* In L. Grossberg, C. Nelson, & P. Treichler (Eds.), *Cultural studies* (pp. 373–391). New York: Routledge.

Kohler, B. (2002). From Stonewall to Diallo. An interview with Bob Kohler by Benjamin Shepard. In B. Shepard & R. Hayduck (Eds.), *From ACT UP to the WTO: Urban protest and community building in the era of globalization* (pp. 126–132). New York: Verso.

Kramer, L. (2007, March 13). ACT UP twentieth anniversary speech. Retrieved March 23, 2008, from http://www.actup.org/20th-year-anniversary/index.html

Lee, A., & Ettinger, M. (2006, May/June). Lessons for the Left from the radical transgender movement. *Left Turn.* Retrieved April 18, 2008, from http://leftturn.org/backissue&tid=206

Leyland, W. (1977). *Orgasms of light: Gay Sunshine anthology.* San Francisco: Gay Sunshine.

Marla, R. (Ed.). (2004). *Queer Beats: How the Beats turned America on to sex.* San Francisco: Cleis Press.

Moore, K. (2008). *Disruptive science.* Princeton, NJ: Princeton University Press.

Munoz, J. E. (1996). Ghosts of public sex: Utopian longings, queer memories. In Dangerous Bedfellows (E. G. Colter, W. Hoffman, E. Pendleton, A. Redick, &

D. Serlin, Eds.), *Policing public sex: Queer politics and the future of AIDS activism* (pp. 355–372). Boston: South End Press.

Nardi, P. (1998). The globalization of the gay and lesbian movement. *Sociological Perspectives, 41*(3), 567–786.

Nardi, P. (1999). *Gay men's friendships.* Chicago: University of Chicago Press.

Nobile, P., & Nadler, E. (1986). *United States of America vs. sex: How the Meese Commission lied about pornography.* New York: Minotaur Press.

Orr, J. (2006). *Panic diaries: A genealogy of panic disorder.* Durham, NC: Duke University Press.

Plummer, K. (1995). *Telling sexual stories: Power, change, and social worlds.* New York: Routledge.

Queers Read This (1990). Unsigned leaflet. June. Retrieved October 1, 2006, from http://www.qrd.org/qrd/misc/text/queers.read.this

Rechy, J. (2006). Address at the Adelante Gay Pride Gala in El Paso, Texas, on June 24, 2006. Retrieved December 13, 2006, from http://www.johnrechy.com/so_adel.htm

Rofes, E. (1998). *Dry bones breathe: Gay men creating post-AIDS identities and subcultures.* Binghamton, NY: Harrington Park Press.

Rofes, E. (2005). Interview with the author.

Romesburg, D. (2000, August 15). Straight from their mouths: Anti-gay attitudes of Anita Bryant and Dr. Laura Schlessinger. *The Advocate.* Retrieved November 1, 2006, from http://findarticles.com/p/articles/mi_m1589/is_/ai_63692908

Russo, V. (1987). *The celluloid closet: Homosexuality in the movies.* San Francisco: HarperCollins.

Sadownick, D. (1996). *Sex between men: An intimate history of the sex lives of gay men postwar to present.* San Francisco: Harper San Francisco.

Schiller, G., & Rosenberg, R. (1985). *Before Stonewall: The making of a gay and lesbian community.* First Run Features (www.firstrunfeatures.com).

Schrecker, E. (1998). *Many are the crimes: McCarthyism in America.* New York: Little, Brown.

Shepard, B. (1997). *White nights and ascending shadows: An oral history of the San Francisco AIDS epidemic.* London: Cassell.

Shepard, B. (2001). The suits vs. the sluts: The queer assimilationist split. *Monthly Review, 53*(1), 49–62.

Shepard, B. (2005). The use of joy as an organizing principle. *Peace and Change: A Journal of Peace Studies, 30*(4), 435–468.

Shepard, B. (2007). Moral panic in the welfare state. *Journal of Sociology and Social Welfare, 34*(1), 155–172.

Shilts, R. (1982). *The mayor of Castro Street: The life and times of Harvey Milk.* New York: St. Martin's Press.

Stryker, S. (2005). Roots of the transgender movement: The 1966 riot at Compton's Cafeteria. *Critical Moment.* Retrieved October 10, 2006, from http://criticalmoment.org/node/26/print

Stryker, S., & Van Buskirk, J. V. (1996). *Gay by the Bay.* San Francisco: Chronicle Books.

Theweleit, K. (1989). *Male fantasies, Vol. 2: Male bodies: Psychoanalyzing the white terror* (E. Carter & C. Turner, Trans.). Minneapolis: University of Minnesota Press.

Tobin, K., & Wicker, R. (1972). *The gay crusaders.* New York: Arno Press.

Treichler, P. (1988). AIDS, homophobia, and biomedical discourse: An epidemic of signification. In D. Crimp (Ed.), *AIDS: Cultural analysis/cultural activism* (pp. 31–70). Cambridge, MA: MIT Press.

Turner, M. W. (2003). *Backward glances: Cruising the queer streets of New York and London.* London: Reaktion Books.

Warner, M. (1993). Introduction. In M. Warner (Ed.), *Fear of a queer planet: Queer politics and social theory* (pp. vii–xxxi). Minneapolis: University of Minnesota Press.

Warner, M. (1999). *The trouble with normal: Sex, politics, and the ethics of queer life.* Cambridge, MA: Harvard University Press.

Watney, S. (1997). *Policing desire: Pornography, AIDS and the media* (3rd ed.). Minneapolis: University of Minnesota Press.

Weeks, J. (1985). *Sexuality and its discontents: Meanings, myths, and modern sexualities.* New York: Routledge.

PART II

Culture, Identity, Narrative

Context and Multiplicity in Sexual Lives

3

Stories from the Second World

Narratives of Sexual Identity in the Czech Republic Across Three Generations of Men Who Have Sex with Men

Timothy McCajor Hall

Different cultures in different eras emphasize different kinds of narratives and weight their components in different ways. Anthony Giddens argues that modern identities often orient themselves within a life project with a certain trajectory and following a particular kind of course (Giddens, 1991); one can easily imagine that not all forms of modernity encourage the same types of life narrative any more than they cultivate the same forms of literature or film. (Czechs, for instance, often feel that the happy endings of most Hollywood movies are contrived and emotionally unsatisfying, while Americans may express puzzlement at how French films stress characterization over plot.) Similarly, multiple genres may coexist within a culture. A detective story, for instance, may be cast as comedy, horror, or film noir, among other styles.

Empirically, we find that different individuals within a culture may piece together the elements of their life narratives in different ways, and that these narratives change over the life course, sometimes subtly and sometimes radically. On the one hand, these changes deeply complicate the study of sexual identities. As I will show in one of the case studies, individuals may present different narratives over time not merely because of deeper rapport with an interviewer, growing maturity, or the immediate effects of social context, but also because their self-concept changes, and in that process they organize and privilege or discount particular experiences differently. On the other hand, this awareness of flux and variation brings us to a better empiricism. We must be clear about our level of analysis: individual behavior, desires, goals, narrated identities, or (sub)culturally shared narrative genres and tropes. Each of these tells us something different and useful about how people in a given culture both live and make sense of their lives.

My own research examines processes of identity and community formation within the developing gay scenes in Prague, the Czech Republic, with nearly four years of fieldwork since 1999. Prague presents an unusual opportunity for the study of queer[1] identities in a cultural milieu that has been largely separated from Western European and Anglo-American culture for much of the twentieth century, but which is now both rapidly Westernizing (in some ways) and also serves as a major point of contact between Westerners[2] and postsocialist Central Europe.

Narratives of sexual identity among Czech men who have sex with men vary across generational cohorts in ways comparable to, though somewhat distinct from, those observed in Western countries. Taken as a whole, they also differ from some commonly observed patterns seen in Western gay men's self-narratives. Considering the historical Czech experience, it comes as small surprise that their narratives of sexual identity show much less political consciousness or that human immunodeficiency virus/acquired immune deficiency syndrome (HIV/AIDS) plays a far lesser role not only in terms of whether they know persons with HIV (mainly older gay men who lived abroad during the communist years[3]), but also in terms of their perceptions of the gay world. As in the United States, most Czech men who have sex with men have also had some sexual experiences with women, but most of them show less concern for demonstrating a dichotomous (homosexual vs. heterosexual) sexual orientation even when they do not represent themselves as bisexual.

More distinctively, the sexual narratives of Czech gay men do not foreground the adolescent conflicts with parents and alienation from peers described as standard elements of gay men's self-narratives in the U.S. (Cohler & Galatzer-Levy, 2000; Plummer, 1981; Troiden, 1989). To clarify, I do not claim that such conflicts never happen—for some of my informants do report them—but they are not represented with anywhere near the regularity or salience of U.S. and British gay men's narratives. I believe that this is because Czech men feel somewhat less need to monitor sexual feelings for same-sex attractions and because Czech society on the whole is both more secular (Froese, 2005; Goldsmith, 2000; Spousta, 2002) and less concerned with regulating private sexual behavior.[4]

This chapter examines how three cohorts of Czech men who have sex with men represent their experiences through narrative. One cohort, born in the 1930s and 1940s, lived through the show trials of the 1950s, and the liberalization and then repression following the Prague Spring in 1968. Another set, born in the 1950s, came of age during the period of socialist "normalization" in the 1970s. A third set, now young adults, were children or teens at the time of the Velvet Revolution in 1989 and have lived most of their lives in a relatively democratic capitalist society open to the exchange of goods and ideas with the West.[5] Some of these men identify as gay or homosexual, others as bisexual, and still others reject any sort of nonheterosexual identity. Their self-narratives also vary by age cohort, as they do in Western countries, but with a much shorter time span per cultural generation.

Czech men who have sex with men have developed their narratives of sexual identity and difference partly in dialogue with Western narratives, through film, literature, scholarly writings, health education, and direct experience with Western tourists or as tourists themselves in Western countries (Fanel, 2000; Hall, 2007; Prokopík, 2001). However, these dialogues have always been tempered by the distinctive Czech experience: a deep suspicion of identity politics stemming from the gross abuses of nationalist foreign occupiers (Austria-Hungary, Nazi Germany, and the USSR) and the cooptation of identities based on gender, class, religion, ethnicity, and occupation under state socialism (Čermáková et al., 2002; Sayer, 1998); the near-absence of a legitimate or effective local feminist movement (Nash, 2002; Šiklová, 1996); the high degree of ethnic and social homogeneity in the Czech Republic; escaping the ravages of HIV/AIDS in the 1980s in large part due to the closed borders; the more limited economic freedom of most Czech individuals until very recently (Hraba, Pechačová, & Lorenz, 1999; Večerník & Matějů, 1999); and a general feeling that Western models are ultimately merely options among many, and not the only possible way of organizing their lives.[6]

Analytic Considerations

Dan McAdams (1996) has argued that we should understand self-narratives of identity as an analytically separable level of personality: distinct from, though interacting with context-free traits and the more situation-specific motives, goals, and defense mechanisms. As he has suggested (McAdams, 2005), I would extend this insight to the lamentable cross-talk among sexuality scholars. The distinctions long recognized by sexologists among *sexual orientation, sexual behavior,* and *sexual identity* (Diamond, 2003; Kinsey, Pomeroy, & Martin, 1948;

Money, 1988; Zveřna, 2003) are clearly analogous to McAdams' distinctions among traits/temperament, mid-level constructs such as goals and defenses, and narratives of identity, respectively. While these aspects of human sexuality (and their constitutive components) tend to correlate, no level fully determines or is determined by any other level (Klein, 1990; Laumann, Gagnon, Michael, & Michaels, 1994; Pathela et al., 2006). Though it does not fully determine behavior, sexual orientation, defined as predominant attraction to female or male partners, appears to be fairly stable across the adult life course, at least in males (Mustanski, Chivers, & Bailey, 2002; Stokes, Damon, & McKirnan, 1997; Weinrich et al., 1993). Many heterosexually oriented males engage in occasional same-sex sexuality, particularly in adolescence (Sandfort, 1998), and most homo-sexually oriented males have had at least some sexual experience with women (Laumann et al., 1994). In fact, outside the late modern West, the expectation that homosexually oriented men would not engage in heterosexual relations has been the exception rather than the rule (Halperin, 1990; Murray, 2000).

As other contributors to this volume note, *sexual identity*, at least in part, belongs to an individual's project of self-narration. Specifically, it is that part of an individual's self-narration that selects, defines, organizes, and makes sense of one's sexual behaviors, desires, relationships, and experiences, relates them to (or segregates them from) the rest of one's life, and evaluates or dis-misses them in light of personal and cultural goals. What count as sexual acts and desires—whether they define certain types of persons and how, and how important or salient these questions are—all vary across cultures and eras. Of course, narratives of self and self-history do not comprise the totality of identity. Individuals can express many components of their identities propositionally, especially in regard to traits or statuses: "I am a conscientious person. I am a man. I belong to the Progressive Party." It is by incorporating (or excluding or minimizing) them in narrative, however, that individuals generally make meaning of their traits, statuses, and other propositionally expressible aspects of identity (Bruner, 1990).

Constructing Queer Identities

Cultures, subcultural groups, and individuals emphasize different elements of sexual experience, behaviors, and desires in constructing narratives of sexual and gender identity. However, many theorists of sexual identity (and particu-larly many scholars in queer studies) have extrapolated heavily from the more visible types found in Western, largely urban, late modern populations, and assumed (implicitly or explicitly) that particular features and developmental trajectories seen in these contexts should extend to other times and places. This leads to some perplexity and consternation when individuals or groups outside the urban, late modern, and often middle-class West construct their identities differently. In particular, members of these groups often *(1)* fail to demonstrate exclusively same-sex behavior (e.g., by marrying or intending to marry hetero-sexually); *(2)* do not embrace same-sex orientation or behavior as a primary or defining component of their social identity; and/or *(3)* do not form meaningful communities or political organizations above the level of sexual or friendship networks (Boellstorff, 2005; Essig, 1999; Muñoz-Laboy, 2004; Schluter, 2002; Woodcock, 2004). Queer scholars have often analyzed this phenomenon in one of two (nonexclusive) ways: as evidence for a strongly Foucauldian, cultur-ally determined sexual plasticity or as a primitive or incomplete precursor to a fully realized (i.e., Western, urban, 1990s-style) queer consciousness.

A comparable and usefully illuminating puzzle presents itself in the con-trast between the sexual identity narratives of men (both Czech and American) who identify as *gay* (or similar terms that indicate an identity based on same-sex orientation viewed as precluding heterosexual relations) and those who identify as *bisexual* or *straight* but who have had some period of engaging in sex with other men. I have not included case studies of men who identify as bisexual in this chapter, as they raise a different set of questions, but I shall consider them here briefly. The bisexual-identified men I have interviewed all acknowledge a qualitative difference in their sexual feelings for men compared with their sexual feelings for women, and they can identify one or the other as primary in terms of erotic attraction. However, they are able to enjoy sexual interactions with both, or feel a stronger attraction to one but are more compatible socially or emotionally with the other. On these bases, they often construct their identities either as bisexual or as heterosexual men who occasionally have sex with men. They typically tell stories of becoming aware of their same-sex attraction or their openness to it at later ages than do gay-identified men, and they less often tell of feeling gender-atypical as children. Gay-identified Western men, by contrast, often emphasize a dichotomous feeling, stating that their same-sex attractions are clearly primary and minimizing experiences with the opposite sex. This is confounded in younger generations, particularly those who came of age during the 1980s or later (in Western countries or following the fall of communism in Central Europe), by a tendency to self-monitor for same-sex attractions and to label such feelings as significant at younger ages, and a concomitant eschewing of opposite-sex relationships as incompatible with a gay identity.[7]

Queer scholars often become mired in debates over the status of bisexual versus gay identities in ways similar to the questions of essence and group consciousness (or the workings of hegemony) in relation to non-Western queer persons. Narrative analysis brings a welcome change of focus. Considered from the perspective advanced here, many of the distinctions between gay- and bisexual-identified men may be seen as engagement in different kinds of narrative projects based in part on a commitment to different subject positions and social relationships, rather than as differences in orientation or as conflicting forms of identity—where *identity* stands for orientation, behavior, and self-understanding all muddled together. In analyzing narratives, we expect not only that individual stories will vary within genres, but also that multiple styles and genres will coexist within a given (sub)cultural group, and we look for the possibility of variation in the forms and style of the genres themselves across cultures and cohorts (Bruner, 1990; Cohler & Hostetler, 2002).

Gay men's narratives in Britain and the United States, at least over the past few generations, have tended to follow certain general outlines, or *master narratives*—culturally shared expectations for particular elements and structures within a particular genre of narratives that shape both the expression and experience of life stories (Cohler & Galatzer-Levy, 2000; Plummer, 1995). Specifically, these men tend to present a story of at least some gender noncon- formity in childhood (e.g., preferring artistic or intellectual activities to sports), often strained relations with the father, a sense of alienation from heterosexual peers in adolescence, locating the source of one's difference in sexual orienta- tion, the emotional and social conflicts of coming out to friends and family, and the search for a romantic and sexual partner (cf. Troiden, 1989). It is not clear, however, that these narratives transparently represent a veridical past (Boxer & Cohler, 1989). Among British and American boys who later identify as heterosexual, not all like or excel at sports, many feel alienated from peers and parents during adolescence, and at least for those born since the 1960s, most will likely have multiple romantic relationships as adults. It remains an empirical question to what degree this Anglo-American master narrative of gay identity development will be found in other groups of gay-identified men. For example, many bisexual-identified men whom I have interviewed in both the Czech Republic and the United States tend not to emphasize early gender-atypical interests or a sense of adolescent alienation in their life histo- ries. Instead, they may draw on their more heterotypical experiences to explain their incomplete identification with the local gay community.

Comparing U.S. and Czech Narratives of Queer Identity

Scholars of Western queer identities have described a number of generation- defining moments for currently living gay men and lesbians in the United

States.[8] While forms of identity shaped around same-sex orientation were known at least in some urban settings from the nineteenth century and earlier (Chauncey, 1994; Newton, 1993; Norton, 1992), the mass population movements during World War II from farms and small towns to cities and then (for men) deployment in same-sex environments within the armed forces catalyzed the recognition and formation of homosexual identities among large numbers of men in the United States and other Western countries (D'Emilio, 1998).

In the United States, the early successes of the gay liberation movement represent another cultural watershed, enacted in legal and policy reform in many states during the 1960s and 1970s and epitomized in the Stonewall riots of 1969 (Duberman, 1993). Many same-sex oriented men who came of age in the United States after Stonewall made their way to a handful of well-publicized and relatively tolerant urban sites—particularly neighborhoods in New York City, Los Angeles, and San Francisco—where they created relatively openly gay communities and began sharing their narratives of self- and sexual discovery in both informal and formal venues (Cohler, 2007; Rechy, 1977; Reid, 1973). Men in this cohort who would identify as gay in adulthood rarely came out before their 20s. Most of them had some experience dating women, though fewer married and had children than in the pre-Stonewall cohort, and they often saw the expression of their sexuality as tied to the broader sexual liberation of the 1970s.

This period, often idealized in later American gay literature and film as a period of happy innocence, came to an end with the advent of the AIDS epidemic in the early 1980s. Large numbers of homosexually active men from the previous two generations died during the first years of AIDS, and the survivors reconceived their sexual identities in very different and highly politicized terms (Adam & Sears, 1996; Rofes, 1998). The public health crisis eventually forced public acknowledgment of homosexual persons and gay communities. The generation of men who developed their gay identities during the late 1980s came out at earlier ages, more often described themselves as politically aware, and also lived with a constant negotiation of sexual relations in the face of HIV. While their sense of identity is often less problematic, their sense of sexual intimacy is in some ways more so, as is the distinction between HIV-seronegative and seropositive men.

Yet another watershed moment was the introduction of highly active antiretroviral therapy (HAART) in 1996. This transformed HIV infection from a near-certain death sentence to a manageable (though complex, expensive, and potentially debilitating) chronic illness. While many regard this discovery as a decisive turning point in the fight against HIV/AIDS, few queer scholars have yet recognized its full social ramifications. Partly because of the decreased social stigma and the diminished urgency of collective political action, same-sex oriented men in many Western countries increasingly recognize multiple queer identities, differentiated by such factors as age, social class, ethnicity, and HIV-positive or HIV-negative status without necessarily embracing a broader gay identity either personally or publicly (Harris, 1997; Savin-Williams, 2001).

Cohort-defining events for homosexual men in the Czech Republic are less obvious and likely much closer together, with more recent cultural generations only a few years apart. Although consensual sexual acts between adults of the same sex were nominally decriminalized in 1961, homosexuals were still prosecuted under charges such as solicitation, disturbing the peace (a favorite catchall charge under communism), or "endangering the moral education of a minor" (Fanel, 2000, p. 434). The situation improved somewhat in the 1980s, but only since the early 1990s have homosexuality and heterosexuality generally been treated equally under the law.

Certainly the Velvet Revolution in 1989 marked a generational transition for all Czechs and Slovaks, regardless of sexual orientation. Since then, an increasingly differentiated set of gay institutions has emerged—student and sport associations, HIV/AIDS education and support organizations, and gay political associations, not to mention the spread of gay bars, clubs, and other venues (Hall, 2007; Prokopík, 2001). The legalization in 2006 of registered partnership (a form of same-sex marriage) that closely followed European Union (EU) accession in 2004 will likely constitute another watershed moment. In some ways, gay men in the Czech Republic who came of age in the 1980s resemble gay men who came of age in the United States some 20 or 30 years earlier, while gay teenagers in the Czech Republic today have many attitudes and significant experiences comparable to those of their Western peers.

Ethnographic Setting and Methods

My research examines processes of identity and community, life course, and mental health concerns among gay- and bisexual-identified men in the Czech Republic, particularly in Prague.[9] In accordance with standard participant-observation methods (DeWalt, DeWalt, & Wayland, 1998; Riemer, 1977), I became part of several gay social networks in Prague. I have established long-term working and friendly relationships with a core group of approximately 14 gay-identified Czech and Slovak men (born 1970–1982) who live or have lived in Prague, meeting their partners, roommates, and/or family members, spending significant time with them in diverse social settings over several years, and continuing to be in contact with most of them. I have also known a larger group of some 50 gay- or bisexual-identified men in Prague (born 1955–1982) over a period of years. With about half of them, I have conducted multiple open-ended life-history interviews (Plummer, 1983).[10] As part of a follow-up study in summer 2006 looking at generational differences, I recorded interviews with several older gay- and bisexual-identified men (born in the 1930s–1960s), two of which are presented here. The broader ethnographic project informs my interpretations of these more focused interviews.

In analyzing narratives of sexual identity presented here, I have drawn not only on standard approaches from the psychology of narrative (Bruner, 1990; Czarniawska, 2004) and cognitive anthropology (Quinn, 2005), but also on an approach sometimes called *person-centered* (Levy, 1973) or *clinical ethnography* (Herdt, 1999). Employing techniques from psychodynamic interviewing, clinical ethnographers build case studies so as to understand better their interlocutors' motives, experiences, and sense of self, particularly as these interact with local cultural forms (Briggs, 1970; DuBois, 1960; Levy & Hollan, 1998). The approach used here tacks between informants' own self-representations and my analysis of the cultural forms and social context in which they occur, as well as my interpretations of their motives and self-understandings over time.[11]

Son of the First Republic: Václav

Václav[12] was born in a small town in North Bohemia in the early 1930s. Except for a few years during university, he has lived in Prague since he was six. Asked about his early life, he recounts:

> Before the war, I cannot say, because when the war began I was seven and my erotic life, my sexual life, had not yet begun.... At the beginning of the 50s, when I finished high school [*gymnázium*] and got to university, not in Prague.... For political reasons I could not study in Prague: our family were not communists at all and there were problems because of that.... My first experience with this world, that is, with the gay world—was mostly academic, only vague awareness...and my first actual experience not until I was 20. Up till 1961 there was law 175, which prohibited homosexual intercourse.[13]

> I suspected, or maybe I read something, even though the literature was scant, but I remained in a phase of rather academic consciousness, nothing concrete.... My first contact—it was anonymous with a person...about 20 years older than I. I noticed along the way to

school, where I walked, as the way went through the park, through
Letná, which already in that time was a sort of center of potential
meetings.... The experience for my part was totally unpleasant...
even the act itself had for me, I would say, nothing sensational. It
was only a physical encounter...but the realization of that act left in
me afterwards a wish to repeat it somehow with someone.... In the
following period, I would say that I had—I don't know—two, three,
four contacts—anonymous again, because of consideration for my
situation in my family, among my friends...it was not appealing that
someone would know these things about me. So it remained hidden.
After about a year, I met someone of the same background—same
age, who studied here in Prague, and there began some brief friendly
contact, but I was not ready for a long-term relationship, so it ended.
But from that time we knew each other and some sporadic contact
remained—friendly, not sexual.

Afterwards he began a more serious relationship, though again the sexual
aspect did not last long:

We met in the theater, at the opera.... Gays [*Gayové*], I would say, are
to a notable degree lovers of theater and opera, because that inner
appearance of the opera is special, artistic, and I would say that it
suits many gays. In front of the theater, when I was buying the tick-
ets, I met another man, who was eight years older than I and whom
I met again during the performance and...from his side, I would say
that it had a serious character.... We knew each other a long time,
but only that first phase was really an attempt at long-term contact;
I was still not ready for something like that, so the fault was likely
on my side.... And today I regret that a bit, but what is there to do?
I could not go against my own situation in that moment.

Václav has never sustained a long-term romantic relationship, but this does
not bother him.

I am a person, I would say, who is sociable, easy to get to know, but
who is on the other hand solitary. To this day I have many acquaintances and many good friends, more and more of them younger....
But always from my side—sometimes unwanted, but it is my
nature—a certain distance. And that remains as a barrier to any
long-term relationship. I made several attempts, but it always foun-
dered on this.

One theme that shows up in Václav's narrative is that of being unable to change his "nature" (*povaha*), which relates both to Czech discourses of fatalism and to a broader Slavic ethnopsychology that posits emotions, or at least certain kinds of emotions (including those surrounding love and desire), as being intrinsically uncontrollable. Such references to one's nature, or implications that one has to follow one's feelings, recur throughout Czech gay men's narratives and inflect them in ways subtly different from corresponding North American discourses about "authenticity." Americans, I would argue, often construe being "true to oneself" as a morally good thing, possibly even a duty, but one that may conflict with other duties or moral goods (for example, some gay Christians in the United States try to negotiate between expression of their true selves, experienced as gay, and adherence to a code of sexual morality that condemns same-sex intercourse). In the Czech case, the matter is framed in a less volitional way; one cannot act against one's nature for very long, nor is it sensible to do so. I believe that this is one reason that many of my informants, particularly younger ones, have encountered primarily resignation from their families upon coming out to them, whereas U.S. informants (until very recently) have more often encountered admonitions to "try to change." The Czech construction of love and desire resonates with a view of sexual orientation as beyond individual control.

Speaking of his entrée to gay society, Václav recalls that public meetings were potentially dangerous in the 1950s, as homosexuality was still illegal. Some men would be blackmailed by their contacts, others threatened with violence by hustlers. When he was 23, Václav met an actor his own age. Though they did not sleep together, they became friends, and through him Václav became part of a circle of academics and artists, many of whom considered themselves homosexual or bisexual.

> That was a phase of my life which I remember fondly, because it was full of genuine friendship.... Public life in that time was somewhat risky, but what was wonderful for me then, what I liked quite a lot, was when I got close to that actor, and then my circle of acquaintances broadened...there existed then what we called the *salon*. There were people, obviously people with large flats—they were gay—and they invited some of their friends, who in turn brought their acquaintances...it wasn't possible to invite just anyone...a majority of the salon...had something—intellect, sociability, and so on...Sadly, as things developed later, with liberalization, democratization—such salons still exist, but they have a different character, more like gatherings of friends. And it lacks something....One pole

was elegance, and the other pole was a certain trusting camaraderie. Everyone was gay, so we were on the same footing and could speak about serious things, sometimes even intimate things.... It was an honor when a person was included in such a salon.

Partly through these connections, Václav later developed an international network of friends and colleagues and keeps in contact with many of them decades later. Though a majority were also gay, Václav says: "It was important that I never lost myself in the one-sidedness of gay society, because it is limiting.... It is far better and enriching to join with all levels of society."

Like many Czech men of his generation and since, Václav never came out publicly. Some of his colleagues knew or suspected his sexual orientation but said nothing. He came out to his sister early on but never spoke of it with their parents, and the wider family never commented on his failure to marry. He says of his parents, "I think that at the beginning they were worried, but when they saw that no tragedy came of it, they reconciled themselves to it." During the 1980s he was involved in an underground Catholic organization, and he saw no particular conflict between his sexuality and his participation in a religious group.

Václav finds many positive things in growing older. Regarding partners, he found that those he preferred grew older with him: "As I grow older, I like mature people.... I discovered that many people, at 50 or 55 ... have inside them some content, something to say—it's a wonderful thing. It also gladdens me, that process of development...that one doesn't remain the same...." He has not had a sexual partner for several years, but as he says at several points in his narrative, his intellectual and personal contacts were always more important to him than sex. He has taken on many gay younger colleagues and students as protégés over the years, introducing them to each other and to his wider network of friends in academia and the arts. Though many friends from his younger years have now passed on, he continues meeting new people, remains engaged in his academic work, and is generally quite happy with his life.

Child of the 1950s: Luboš

Luboš was born in South Bohemia in the mid-1950s and was in his early 50s when I interviewed him. His self-narrative is notably more pessimistic in tone than those of the other two interviewees. In part, this is a commonly observed difference between the generation who grew up in the 1950s and 1960s and those who grew up before or since. (It was in fact the flat, dysthymic affect of those who had their formative years during the so-called normalization after the Prague Spring that first inspired me to look at depression in the Czech Republic.) This pessimistic tone also reflects Luboš's more limited experiences and opportunities, as well as his choice of profession. As a high school teacher, Luboš has had to be circumspect throughout his adult life, and his gay friends are largely the same people he has known for decades.

Luboš recalls his feelings about girls and boys when he was in his teens as "not bounded [*neomezené*]."

> When I was growing up...I suspected, because boys interested me more than girls—but in that time, the 70s and 80s, it wasn't done.... I had a lot of girlfriends, I even lived with one girlfriend for a time, 8 years, but we never got married.... I grew up in a smaller town, and I came to Prague only for school during the week and then went back to my parents on weekends, and considering that I was studying pedagogy after I finished my military service—you couldn't just go out with someone anywhere, with some boyfriend or something. Those laws were still in effect...so many people hid it.... And if it somehow came out that one was gay or lesbian, everyone looked at them as if they had cholera or something, people were so prejudiced. That older generation, about 60 or older, are still like that now. They haven't changed.... And I know plenty of people from my own life who are gay, who got married. They have families and everything, and when it came to an end in the 90s and the laws changed, then they're already living their lives.

Luboš himself never married. He feels that he has worked much of his life to keep his orientation and his gay friendships and relationships hidden, both from the general prejudice of society and because as a teacher he has felt subject to heightened scrutiny. He has decidedly mixed feelings about the changes in gay life since the Velvet Revolution. He recalls the camaraderie of the few clandestine gay clubs of the 1980s with some fondness, despite the risk of exposure. "Everybody knew everybody then," he says. "We were all friends." These days, he sees drugs, prostitution, and materialism. He mentions in passing that he worries about AIDS among the younger gay men but says, "Here it's been minimal—knock on wood—and today it's still minimal, even though I've read some statistics that it's starting to increase."[14] His longest relationships have not lasted more than about 3 years, and the last was some time ago. He is still interested in sex but has relatively few opportunities.

Though he obtained a master's degree in pedagogy and teaches at a secondary school, Luboš comes from a working-class background, as do most of his friends, which distinguishes him from the other case studies here.

Czechoslovakia had some of the most effective class leveling of any social-ist country: the Jewish and German elites left the country or were expelled shortly after the end of the Second World War, true poverty was largely elim-inated by the communists, and income differentials were small even by com-munist standards (Večerník & Matějů, 1999). However, some class differences remained, and they are apparent in some of the differences between Luboš and the other two interviewees.

The Current Context for Sexual Identity in the Czech Republic

The group that I know best is the cohort born from the late 1960s to the mid-1980s. These men were still in school at the time of the Velvet Revolution and in university or beginning their adult careers during the 1990s. During their adolescence, homosexuality was technically legal in Czechoslovakia, though mostly clandestine. People learned of certain parks, met at public pools or saunas, occasionally had encounters with fellow students, and sometimes met through coded personal ads. Sex education in the schools did not men-tion homosexuality, and many who grew up in smaller towns say that they did not know what it was. For many of them whom I met in their 20s, coming-out stories formed a good part of our conversation, particularly for younger ones or for those just beginning to discover the gay community in Prague. This is characteristic of the United States as well, where coming-out stories serve simultaneously as means of introduction and as tokens of solidarity, as well as a way of working through one's own self-understanding (Gideonse & Williams, 2006; Plummer, 1981, 1995).

Coming out is the process of recognizing oneself as homosexual or bisex-ual and/or disclosing that information to others (Dank, 1971; Sedgwick, 1990). The term appears to have originated in the United States and has now, along with the word gay, been adopted by many other languages. According to older gay American informants, before the 1980s coming out more often referred to coming out to oneself—that is, one's own recognition and acceptance of one-self as having an exclusively or partially same-sex orientation. Plummer (1995) distinguishes among several levels or stages: coming out personally, to oneself; privately, to close friends and/or family; publicly, professionally, to coworkers, in ways that may become general knowledge; and politically, in ways that aim at broader social change or acceptance. Though Plummer does not assume that these occur in a fixed order, a number of scholars and activists do see such a progression as typical or desirable (Eichberg, 1990; Savin-Williams & Diamond, 2000; Troiden, 1989), and queer ethnographers often locate major differences in Anglophone and other conceptions of queer identities in non-Western queer persons' refusal or disinclination to come out other than to themselves or to other queer persons (Essig, 1999; Girman, 2004; Woodcock, 2004). Since the 1980s, however, at least in the North American communities I have known, coming out refers primarily to one's disclosure of one's sexual orientation to others. *Coming out to oneself* requires the additional qualifier, and it is usually assumed that most gay men recognize their orientation long before they disclose it to others.

Among gay men in the Czech Republic, on the other hand, the borrowed phrase *coming out* nearly always refers to one's own self-recognition and self-acceptance. This fits with the different Czech emphasis on the division between public and domestic (or individual) spheres and with a common sentiment that sexuality is a private matter, neither a subject for public airing nor a matter for social regulation. Czech queer activist literature (e.g., Procházka, 1995) and discussion within Czech gay associations such as student groups strongly emphasize self-recognition over disclosure, though many Czech gay activists do encourage same-sex oriented persons to come out to family and significant others in time. In a country where until recently homosexuals were prosecuted for their orientation, the formation of an identity is usually seen as a more realistic first step.

Adolescents and young men in the Czech Republic who have recognized themselves as having a same-sex orientation then face the question of whether and how to disclose their orientation to others—their families, friends, and colleagues—on the one hand, and of finding a romantic or sexual partner, on the other. Gay Czech adolescents and young adults often view coming out to their families with a great deal of trepidation. They are, after all, in a vulnerable position: often dependent on their families entirely for financial support and accommodation, not to mention the possibility of emotional rejection. Most gay Czechs therefore do not come out to their parents during adolescence. Instead, they try to have clandestine relationships while they are still living at home, if they can find a partner, or they postpone same-sex relationships entirely until they leave for university or find a job and a place of their own.

My impression from hearing the coming-out stories of dozens of gay Czech men is that most Czech parents are fairly accepting of their children's same-sex orientation, at least in comparison with the myriad coming-out stories I have heard from men in the United States and other Anglophone countries. Part of this acceptance might be due to a much lower concern among Czechs with traditional religion. It also reflects a general Czech fatalism. Parents may initially be disappointed or concerned about their child's happiness, believing that homosexuals are less able to find lasting relationships than heterosexuals, for instance, or worrying that their child will experience discrimination (two parental fears reported by several informants), but they generally seem to come to accept that sexual orientation cannot be changed and so reconcile themselves to it as a fact of life. A Czech and more broadly Slavic cultural model sees sexuality as a deeply authentic part of the person that cannot easily be controlled.[15]

Among my informants, a few revealed that their families did react badly, usually those from strongly Catholic or Evangelical backgrounds. Other informants had not come out to their parents and did not plan to do so, because their parents' behavior augured badly. One university student from a small town in Bohemia, for example, told me that his parents were pleased with his lack of apparent interest in girls because they thought it meant he was focusing on his studies and postponing sex until after university. He inferred from this disapproval even of heterosexual activity that they would be unlikely to approve of homosexual interests.

Another informant came from a family that had been strongly Catholic before the Revolution, even while religious activity was restricted, and converted to Pentecostalism in the early 1990s. When he came out, while still in high school and living at home, his family reacted very badly. His mother cried, his older brother refused to speak to him except occasionally to send him religious pamphlets,[16] and his father threatened to throw him out of the house and cut him off financially. He was eventually reconciled with his family, other than with the older brother, but his parents periodically made disapproving statements about his orientation. In general, it is more difficult to be openly gay in small towns and rural areas, and informants from small-town backgrounds were much more likely not to be out to their families.

Other families had more secular reactions and sought answers from the medical community. Sexology has a long history in the Czech Republic as an academic field of study and as a medical specialty (part psychiatry, part sociology, and part urology and reproductive medicine). Half a dozen informants related how their parents, upon hearing about or suspecting their son's same-sex orientation, took them to see a sexologist for diagnosis and treatment. In each case, the sexologist interviewed the putatively homosexual or bisexual adolescent, made a pronouncement on his sexual orientation, and then took the parents aside to reassure them. The sexologist explained that homosexuality is a normal variant of human sexual orientation that cannot be changed through therapy and assured the parents that their child could still grow up to have a normal and fulfilling life. While such a response seems enlightened in comparison with that of many psychiatrists and general physicians elsewhere in the world until very recently, this reliance on medical authority to pronounce on the validity of sexual orientation and particularly to make a diagnosis is striking—as though the sexologist, after a brief interview and assessment, could ascertain someone's sexual orientation better than the individual himself.[17]

Child of the 1970s: Radek

Radek belongs to my core group of interlocutors, and it has been interesting to see how his narratives have changed over time. In part this change has consisted of greater disclosure, but I can also see changes in emphasis and in how he incorporates particular incidents or facts into his overall narrative. During my fieldwork Radek was in his 30s (born in 1970), from a medium-sized town in Moravia. Now divorced, he has a daughter in grade school who lives with her mother and stepfather in a suburb of Plzeň. He initially identified himself more often as bisexual and now usually as gay, and has lived with his boyfriend in Prague for 7 years. Here is an excerpt from my field notes from 2001, when I asked how he came to get married:

> Well, it was the late 1980s and I was finishing high school and about
> to start my military service [*vojenská služba*]. I was dating women
> back then—I didn't know any better. There weren't any places back
> then where you could meet men. My friends and I would ride our
> bikes out to the villages on the weekends and drink beer in the pubs
> and try to meet girls. I started dating Radka, and after about a year
> she got pregnant, so we got married and moved in with her parents
> for a few months while we were waiting for a flat. You couldn't travel
> abroad then, and there was no point in studying. I was about to start
> my military training, and so Radka stayed home and took care of our
> daughter.

In her study of the changing Czech family structure, Rebecca Nash has noted how the tropes of "travel" and "study" recur in Czechs' accounts of life in the 1970s and 1980s (Nash, 2003). As the borders were closed to all but a few, travel outside the country was severely limited. With extreme wage leveling and the official encouragement to enter manufacturing jobs, there were few incentives to pursue higher education (Večerník, 1996; Večerník & Matějů, 1999). Many Czech women say that they got pregnant and married (usually in that order) because there was "no reason not to do so." Since the end of communism in 1989, however, the situation has changed. Age at first marriage has increased and birth rates have plummeted, so that many Czechs now complain of a demographic implosion (Maříková, 2000). The ideal family consisting of a mother, father, and two children (one boy and one girl) was never really abandoned during the pro-natalism of the 1970s and 1980s, though couples started that idealized family at younger ages and were more likely to add a third child. However, divorce rates have gone up and many women, as mentioned, are becoming anxious about the conflict between the previous pattern of early marriage and childbearing and the new opportunities for travel, education, and career advancement (Nash, 2003).

When I first knew him, Radek presented himself as something of a naive small-town boy and said that his initial same-sex experiences had come as something of a surprise. He even insisted on this stance when his boyfriend and I expressed incredulity that he could not have known that something was different about himself until his early 20s, as he then claimed. One evening in 2006, however, while talking with me about his life and his feelings about his current relationship, he told a somewhat different story. He now says that he felt an attraction to other boys from early adolescence and that he was clearly interested in other males, both in his fantasies and in daily life. However, he was living in a small town and did not even have a word to describe his orientation, and he certainly did not know that there was any possibility of doing anything about it. He had no sexual experiences with other males during adolescence. He hung out with a group of male friends from school, picked up girls with them, and eventually had sex with girls, though it did not interest him as much as the thought of having sex with other males. He got married and had a child.

A few years later, in the mid-1990s, he was posted to Brno for work-related training and got the first inkling that he might be able to act on his feelings. He began reading about homosexuality and homosexuals on the Internet and was torn between extreme sexual interest and fear—mainly of being caught. His first sexual encounter with a male was a man he met through the Internet. They only engaged in mutual masturbation, but Radek was intensely aroused, though terrified afterward. As time went on, he met other men for sex and took it further until he began dating someone. He also found his way to gay establishments in Brno. Eventually, he broke off the relationship with his wife, and they divorced. That first gay relationship ended, though the men are still friends, and about half a year after his divorce, he met and began dating the man with whom he has been living for the past 7 years.

Radek's narrative demonstrates a number of points aside from the specifically Czech features. I have known him very well for nearly 7 years, and I do not believe that his changing narrative represents a difference in our rapport. Rather, as he has spent more time socializing mainly in gay circles (other than at work-related events), his understanding of himself has changed. When I met him, he played up a certain small-town ingenuousness and a lack of concern with such things as particular singers or films with a gay following. Together with his occasional identification as bisexual, these traits emphasized a certain (potentially admired) masculinity in comparison to some of the gay-identified men around him. However, it also opened him to charges of ignorance, either of his own motives and history or of the gay subculture. Over time, he has come to see himself as more clearly gay and has foregrounded and connected elements from his personal history in new ways. Few scholars have looked explicitly at the effects of time within the gay community as a form of enculturation rather than as a more or less unproblematic process of revealing or developing one's gay identity. Many gay men, by contrast, recognize this as a significant dimension of the gay experience, shown here by Radek's changing self-perception and narrative presentation.

Making Sense of Sexual Narratives

What do these narratives tell us about the construction of sexual minority identities? Narratives must be interpreted within their ethnographic context. A narrative is not merely individual events strung together, but how those events and the stringing together make sense against a cultural background. Václav belongs to the minority of homosexually oriented Czech men who have not had any significant sexual or romantic experiences with women. As the narratives of gay Czech men born in the 1970s and 1980s reveal, many men still come to a sense of themselves as clearly gay only over time, and working out precisely what that means, in a culture where there are even fewer models of gay life than in the United States, takes time.

One expected theme—hardships or persecution under communism—rarely arises in these narratives of sexual identity, though certainly I heard many such stories over time in other contexts. Anthropologist Haldis Haukanes has found a lack of macrohistorical events in Czech life narratives generally and considers a number of possible explanations: big political events such as the Prague Spring in 1968 may not belong to the genre of life histories, at least not unless the individual in question is highly political or was directly affected. Another, nonexclusive possibility is that for most people, the social effects of grand events filtered down to their personal lives only gradually (Haukanes, 2006). Certainly some large-scale events do figure in personal narratives: both Václav and Luboš commented on the differences before and after the repeal of Paragraph 175 in 1961, legalizing at least some kinds of homosexual relations between adults. Likewise, the differences between conditions before and after 1989 are so stark, particularly from the vantage point of some 17 years later, that that year serves as a reference point for those who lived through it. Other events, however—Prague Spring, the separation from Slovakia in 1993, and EU accession in 2004—are notable for their absence. Also notable for their absence, for those of us who grew up on Cold War stories and stereotypes, are the hardships experienced under communism.

In contrast to middle-class U.S. gay narratives, gay Czechs' narratives display little concern for specifically queer politics. My interlocutors differed in the details of their opinions about the recent adoption of registered partnership, for instance. All of them also clearly had mixed feelings about the changes they saw in the gay community in Prague. Social tolerance and openness are increasing, but at the same time, many dislike what they see as the crass commercialism, materialism, and flamboyant behavior of gay men in their late teens and early 20s.

Consideration of HIV/AIDS is also notably absent from these narratives. It is hard to overstate the degree to which HIV/AIDS dominated gay public and private discourses in the United States during the 1980s and 1990s: whole subgenres of film and literature were devoted to HIV stories, HIV issues galvanized gay political activism, and the promotion of safer sex practices was embraced with an almost religious zeal. Like many other Central and Eastern Europeans, the Czechs experienced none of these events during the 1980s and 1990s, except for a handful of academics and medical professionals who know them largely secondhand or a few gay men who have lived abroad.

These case studies demonstrate some of the differences seen even in cultures drawing on a partially shared European heritage, Czech and Anglo-American, as well as within culturally defined generations across a period of rapid social and cultural change within a single relatively homogeneous society. Czech and Anglo-American men who identify as gay (or who acknowledge and endorse a same-sex orientation) are quite recognizable to each other. However, small but real differences cumulate in the structuring of their social lives and in the narration of their life stories, leading to our theoretical dilemma: how to address the part-strangeness, part-familiarity in thinking about sexual identities across cultures? By embracing the narrative turn in the study of selves and identities, we have the opportunity to transcend both this essentialist-constructivist binary and representations of ethnographic research that unduly imply homogeneity.

Narrative analysis provides one framework for understanding the production of culturally meaningful forms from idiosyncratic individual experience, and it reminds us to attend both to generic structures and to individual variation. The narrative approach also requires us to look for multiple genres and multiple styles or themes within a genre without discounting variation or needing to invoke such reifications as *hybridity* (cf. Brubaker & Cooper, 2000). Perhaps most important for the study of sexuality, through narratives we can see how individuals construct sexual identities by weaving together events (behavior), subjective desire (orientation), and cultural forms. We may also see that Western (urban, white, late twentieth-century) models carry no necessary privilege: the details of our own master narratives are particular to our time and place.

Acknowledgment

The research and writing of this chapter have been supported in part by the Jacob K. Javits Fellowship, U.S. Department of Education (PR# P170A70655); the Medical Scientist Training Program at the University of California, San Diego School of Medicine (NIH #5 T32 GM07198); and training grants from the Office of Behavioral Science Research, National Institute on Aging (#5 T32 AG000243), and the National Institute of Mental Health (#5 T32 MH019098-15). I am grateful to my friends and informants discussed herein for sharing their experiences with me. I also thank the editors of this volume and the participants in the Culture, Life Course, and Mental Health workshop at the University of Chicago for their helpful comments.

NOTES

1. I use *queer* here in a broad social science sense to refer collectively to various sorts of nonheterosexual or nonexclusively heterosexual forms of sexual behavior, orientation, and self-understanding and social forms (such as communities and organizations) based upon them. Many queer male identities in Central Europe are recognizably similar to and participate in some of the same historical discourses as Western gay and bisexual identities. However, I wish to avoid unreflexive assumptions of similarity across cultures that could be implied by using the word *gay* or the potentially clinical connotations of *homosexual*. As used herein, the word *queer* describes forms of same-sex sexuality cross-culturally without implying (or rejecting) strong similarity in local construal or experience.

2. *Western* as an analytic concept should always be qualified. In this chapter, *Western* describes the dominant cultures of a number of countries including but not limited to the United States, Britain, Ireland, Canada, Australia, and New Zealand (sometimes collectively termed the *Anglosphere*) and some countries of Western Europe. Among other things, these countries to a greater or lesser degree share a relatively long history of industrialization and urbanization, large population movements

during and after World Wars I and II, post-World War II prosperity, the sexual revolution and identity-based political and social movements of the 1960s and 1970s, an HIV/AIDS epidemic in the 1980s initially seen as confined to homosexual men, intravenous (IV) drug users, and sex workers (as well as recipients of blood products), and in recent years a particular framing of same-sex orientation and behavior as a civil rights concern. They also share many features of government and civil organization. Consequently, over much of the twentieth century, sexual identities in these countries developed in ways similar to each other and distinct from those in much of Latin America, Africa, Asia, and the Soviet Bloc.

3. In part because of closed borders (in contrast to Western Europe) and in part due to a lesser prevalence of IV drug use and better hospital hygiene (in contrast to Russia, Romania, and some other Eastern European countries), the Czech Republic had a low incidence and prevalence of HIV until about 2005, though both are now rising. Very few persons on the gay scene who are seropositive have chosen to disclose this fact publicly. There is no real local equivalent to the *Poz* identities now seen in Western countries among some HIV-seropositive men who have sex with men.

4. In addition to being one of the most secular countries in Europe on measures such as regular churchgoing, stated belief in God, and so on, the Czech Republic also differs from most Anglophone Western countries in that the dominant conception of morality is post-Catholic rather than currently Calvinist. One consequence is a far lesser concern with the social regulation of private sexual behavior.

5. Many in a still younger cohort, born in the late 1980s and 1990s, have entered the gay scene since the end of my main fieldwork. My impression and that of my Czech and expatriate informants is that they seem increasingly similar, though not identical, to their counterparts in Western European cities.

6. Moreover, the indigenous Czech models of sexual identity have developed much more in dialogue with German ideas than with Anglo-American ones.

7. However, some researchers have found that among the most recent cohorts in the urban United States, some homosexually oriented young men are having sexual relationships with women as well (Savin-Williams & Cohen, 1996; Savin-Williams & Diamond, 2000).

8. Scholarship in this area has largely focused on the experience of same-sex oriented men more than on women, and far more on the United States and Britain than elsewhere.

9. There is almost no ethnographic or historical research on sexual minorities in the Czech lands published in English and very little in Czech or other European languages. For a good overview of Czech nationalism and identity, see Derek Sayer (1998), *The coasts of Bohemia: A Czech history*. A more general history is Peter Demetz, (1997), *Prague in black and gold: The history of a city*. In Czech see Jiří Fanel (2000), *Gay historie*.

10. I also interviewed a number of local experts, community leaders, and entrepreneurs, as well as several gay foreigners living in Prague, for their perceptions of the local gay community. Unless interviewees were highly fluent in English, interviews were conducted in Czech. All interviewees were aware of my university affiliation and my status as an anthropologist, specifically that I was in the process of

writing about gay life in Prague for publication in English and in Czech. They were also aware that they could request that some or all of their statements not be used. Research protocols were reviewed for ethical and methodological considerations and approved by the social sciences institutional review boards (IRB) at the University of California, San Diego, and the University of Chicago.

11. This method also seems more appropriate for interpreting narratives that were largely collected in a language with both conceptual and grammatical categories about as different from English as one can find among Indo-European languages. Representing more than brief statements as direct discourse rather than paraphrase and summary would invite a microanalysis that the translation cannot bear or risk representing highly articulate and reflective interlocutors as far less so.

12. Individuals denoted only by given name have been given pseudonyms. Some biographical details have been changed to protect their identities.

13. All translations here are my own. Ellipses indicate deleted material.

14. HIV rates seem to have reached a tipping point around 2006, with a few dozen cases being noted monthly in 2006–2007 compared to a few dozen cases annually during 2000–2005. Future trends and their social impact are difficult to predict at this point.

15. Two informants, the children or grandchildren of Czechs who emigrated in the 1950s and 1960s, described a tacit assumption among their parents and grandparents that many men go through a phase of same-sex attraction and sex play during adolescence and young adulthood and that this may even be a good thing, as a mark of deep friendships that are good to have or that reduce the likelihood of an unplanned pregnancy before a young man is ready to marry. I have not heard such things volunteered by other informants, however, so this may be a view of an earlier generation of Czechs or of a particular group, or it could be entirely idiosyncratic to these two émigré families.

16. The older brother became heavily involved in a fundamentalist splinter group of their Pentecostalist church. His level and form of religiosity were atypical.

17. Melinda Reidinger (personal communication) notes that this also fits into a broader Czech reliance on authoritative statements from "experts" such as physicians or social scientists in regard to many issues of proper behavior or "normality," apparently a remnant of attitudes encouraged under state socialism.

REFERENCES

Adam, B. D., & Sears, A. (1996). *Experiencing HIV: Personal, family, and work relationships*. New York: Columbia University Press.

Boellstorff, T. (2005). *The gay archipelago: Sexuality and nation in Indonesia*. Princeton, NJ: Princeton University Press.

Boxer, A. M., & Cohler, B. J. (1989). The life course of gay and lesbian youth: An immodest proposal for the study of lives. *Journal of Homosexuality, 17*(3–4), 315–355.

Briggs, J. (1970). *Never in anger: Portrait of an Eskimo family*. Cambridge, MA: Harvard University Press.

Brubaker, R., & Cooper, F. (2000). Beyond "identity." *Theory and Society, 29*, 1–47.

Bruner, J. S. (1990). *Acts of meaning.* Cambridge, MA: Harvard University Press.

Čermáková, M., Hašková, H., Křížková, A., Linková, M., Maříková, H., & Musilová, M. (2002). *Relations and changes of gender differences in the Czech society in the 90s.* Praha: Czech Academy of Sciences, Sociology Institute. (In Czech)

Chauncey, G. (1994). *Gay New York: Gender, urban culture, and the making of the gay male world, 1890–1940.* New York: Basic Books.

Cohler, B. J. (2007). *Writing desire: Sixty years of gay autobiography.* Madison: University of Wisconsin Press.

Cohler, B. J., & Galatzer-Levy, R. M. (2000). *The course of gay and lesbian lives: Social and psychoanalytic perspectives.* Chicago: University of Chicago Press.

Cohler, B. J., & Hostetler, A. J. (2002). Aging, intimate relationships, and life story among gay men. In R. S. Weiss & S. A. Bass (Eds.), *Challenges of the third age: Meaning and purpose in later life* (pp. 137–160). New York: Oxford University Press.

Czarniawska, B. (2004). *Narratives in social science research.* Thousand Oaks, CA: Sage Publications.

Demetz, P. (1997). *Prague in black and gold: The history of a city.* London: Penguin Books.

Dank, B. M. (1971). Coming out in the gay world. *Psychiatry, 34*, 180–197.

D'Emilio, J. (1998). *Sexual politics, sexual communities: The making of a homosexual minority in the United States, 1940–1970* (2nd ed.). Chicago: University of Chicago Press.

DeWalt, K. M., DeWalt, B. R., & Wayland, C. B. (1998). Participant observation. In H. R. Bernard (Ed.), *Handbook of methods in cultural anthropology* (pp. 259–299). Walnut Creek, CA: AltaMira Press.

Diamond, L. M. (2003). What does sexual orientation orient? A biobehavioral model distinguishing romantic love and sexual desire. *Psychological Review, 110*(1), 173–192.

Duberman, M. B. (1993). *Stonewall.* New York: Dutton.

DuBois, C. A. (1960). *The people of Alor; A social-psychological study of an East Indian island. With analyses by Abram Kardiner and Emil Oberholzer.* New York: Harper.

Eichberg, R. (1990). *Coming out: An act of love.* New York: Plume.

Essig, L. (1999). *Queer in Russia: A story of sex, self, and the other.* Durham, NC: Duke University Press.

Fanel, J. (2000). *Gay historie.* Praha: Dauphin. (In Czech)

Froese, P. (2005). Secular Czechs and devout Slovaks: Explaining religious differences. *Review of Religious Research, 46*(3), 269–283.

Giddens, A. (1991). *Modernity and self-identity: Self and society in the late modern age.* Stanford, CA: Stanford University Press.

Gideonse, T., & Williams, R. (Eds.). (2006). *From boys to men: Gay men write about growing up.* New York: Carroll & Graf.

Girman, C. (2004). *Mucho macho: Seduction, desire, and the homoerotic lives of Latin men.* New York: Harrington Park Press.

Goldsmith, C. (2000). Czechs least religious of former Warsaw-Pact countries. Retrieved April 25, 2000, from http://www.radio.cz

Hall, T. M. (2007). Rent-boys, barflies, and kept men: The spectrum of men involved in sex with men for compensation in Prague, Czech Republic. *Sexualities, 10,* 457–472.

Halperin, D. M. (1990). *One hundred years of homosexuality, and other essays on Greek love.* New York: Routledge.

Harris, D. (1997). *The rise and fall of gay culture.* New York: Ballantine.

Haukanes, H. (2006). Telling lives: Autobiography and history after socialism. In T. M. Hall & R. Read (Eds.), *Changes in the heart of Europe: Recent ethnographies of Czechs, Slovaks, Roma, and Sorbs* (pp. 279–294). Stuttgart, Germany: ibidem-Verlag.

Herdt, G. (1999). Clinical ethnography and sexual culture. *Annual Review of Sex Research, 10,* 100–119.

Hraba, J., Pechačová, Z., & Lorenz, F. O. (1999). *Deset rodin po 10 letech, 1989–1999.* Praha: Academia. (In Czech)

Kinsey, A. C., Pomeroy, W. B., & Martin, C. E. (1948). *Sexual behavior in the human male.* Philadelphia: W. B. Saunders.

Klein, F. (1990). The need to view sexual orientation as a multivariate dynamic process: A theoretical perspective. In D. P. McWhirter, S. A. Saunders, & J. M. Reinisch (Eds.), *Homosexuality/Heterosexuality: Concepts of sexual orientation* (pp. 277–282). Oxford: Oxford University Press.

Laumann, E. O., Gagnon, J. H., Michael, R. T., & Michaels, S. (1994). *The social organization of sexuality: Sexual practices in the United States.* Chicago: University of Chicago Press.

Levy, R. I. (1973). *Tahitians: Mind and experience in the Society Islands.* Chicago: University of Chicago Press.

Levy, R. I., & Hollan, D. (1998). Person-centered interviewing and observation in anthropology. In H. R. Bernard (Ed.), *Handbook of methods in cultural anthropology* (pp. 333–364). Walnut Creek, CA: Altamira Press.

Maříková, H. (Ed.). (2000). *Proměny současné české rodiny.* Praha: Sociologické nakladatelství-Slon. (In Czech)

McAdams, D. P. (1996). Personality, modernity, and the storied self: A contemporary framework for studying persons. *Psychological Inquiry, 7*(4), 295–321.

McAdams, D. P. (2005). Sexual lives: The development of traits, adaptations, and stories. *Human Development, 48,* 298–302.

Money, J. E. (1988). *Gay, straight, and in-between: The sexology of erotic orientation.* New York: Oxford University Press.

Muñoz-Laboy, M. A. (2004). Beyond "MSM": Sexual desire among bisexually-active Latino men in New York city. *Sexualities, 7*(1), 55–80.

Murray, S. O. (2000). *Homosexualities.* Chicago: University of Chicago Press.

Mustanski, B. S., Chivers, M. L., & Bailey, J. M. (2002). A critical review of recent biological research on human sexual orientation. *Annual Review of Sex Research, 12,* 89–140.

Nash, R. J. (2002). Exhaustion from explanation: Reading Czech gender studies in the 1990s. *The European Journal of Women's Studies, 9*(3), 291–309.

Nash, R. J. (2003). *Re-stating the family: Reforming welfare and kinship in the Czech Republic.* Unpublished doctoral dissertation, Department of Anthropology, University of Virginia, Charlottesville.

Newton, E. (1993). *Cherry Grove, Fire Island: Sixty years in America's first gay and lesbian town.* Boston: Beacon Press.

Norton, R. (1992). *Mother Clap's molly house: The gay subculture in England, 1700–1830.* East Haven, CT: GMP.

Pathela, P., Hajat, A., Schillinger, J., Blank, S., Sell, R., & Mostashari, F. (2006). Discordance between sexual behavior and self-reported sexual identity: A population-based survey of New York City men. *Annnals of Internal Medicine, 145*(6), 416–425.

Plummer, K. (1981). Going gay: Identities, life cycles, and lifestyles in the male gay world. In J. Hart & D. Richardson (Eds.), *The theory and practice of homosexuality* (pp. 93–110). London: Routledge & Kegan Paul.

Plummer, K. (1983). *Documents of life: An introduction to the problems and literature of a humanistic method.* London: George Allen & Unwin.

Plummer, K. (1995). *Telling sexual stories: Power, change, and social worlds.* New York: Routledge.

Procházka, I. (Ed.). (1995). *Coming out.* Praha: Orbis. (In Czech)

Prokopík, P. (2001). *Hypermaskulinizace.* Unpublished MA thesis, Filosofická fakulta–Karlova univerzita, Praha. (In Czech)

Quinn, N. (2005). *Finding culture in talk: A collection of methods.* New York: Palgrave Macmillan.

Rechy, J. (1977). *The sexual outlaw: A documentary: A non-fiction account, with commentaries, of three days and nights in the sexual underground.* New York: Grove Press.

Reid, J. (1973). *The best little boy in the world.* New York: Putnam.

Riemer, J. W. (1977). Varieties of opportunistic research. *Urban Life and Culture, 5*(4), 467–478.

Rofes, E. E. (1998). *Dry bones breathe: Gay men creating post-AIDS identities and cultures.* New York: Haworth Press.

Sandfort, T. (1998). Homosexual and bisexual behaviour in European countries. In M. Hubert, N. Bajos, & T. Sandfort (Eds.), *Sexual behaviour and HIV/AIDS in Europe* (pp. 68–105). London: University College London Press.

Savin-Williams, R. C. (2001). A critique of research on sexual-minority youths. *Journal of Adolescence, 24*(1), 5–13.

Savin-Williams, R. C., & Cohen, K. M. (1996). Dating and romantic relationships among gay, lesbian, and bisexual youth. In R. C. Savin-Williams & K. M. Cohen (Eds.), *The lives of lesbians, gays, and bisexuals: Children to adults* (pp. 166–180). Fort Worth, TX: Harcourt Brace.

Savin-Williams, R. C., & Diamond, L. M. (2000). Sexual identity trajectories among sexual-minority youths: Gender comparisons. *Archives of Sexual Behavior, 29*(6), 607–627.

Sayer, D. (1998). *The coasts of Bohemia: A Czech history.* Princeton, NJ: Princeton University Press.

Schluter, D. P. (2002). *Gay life in the former USSR: Fraternity without community.* New York: Routledge.

Sedgwick, E. K. (1990). *Epistemology of the closet.* Berkeley: University of California Press.

Šiklová, J. (1996, February 25–31). Different region, different women: Why feminism isn't successful in the Czech Republic. *Replika, 1*(17). Retrieved April 23, 2008, from http://www.c3.hu/scripta/scriptao/replika/honlap/english/01/09fsik.htm

Spousta, J. (2002). Changes in religious values in the Czech Republic. *Czech Sociological Review, 38*(3), 345–364.

Stokes, J. P., Damon, W., & McKirnan, D. J. (1997). Predictors of movement toward homosexuality: A longitudinal study of bisexual men. *Journal of Sex Research, 34*(3), 304–312.

Troiden, R. R. (1989). The formation of homosexual identities. *Journal of Homosexuality, 17,* 43–73.

Večerník, J. (1996). Earnings disparities in the Czech Republic: The history of equalisation. *Czech Sociological Review, 4*(2), 211–222.

Večerník, J., & Matějů, P. (Eds.). (1999). *Ten years of rebuilding capitalism: Czech society after 1989.* Praha: Academia. (In Czech)

Weinrich, J. D., Snyder, P. J., Pillard, R. C., Grant, I., Jacobson, D. L., Robinson, S. R., et al. (1993). A factor analysis of the Klein sexual orientation grid in two disparate samples. *Archives of Sexual Behavior, 22*(2), 157–168.

Woodcock, S. (2004). Globalization of LGBT identities: Containment masquerading as salvation, or why lesbians have less fun. In M. Frunza & T. E. Vascarescu (Eds.), *Gender and the (post) 'East'/'West' divide* (pp. 171–188). Cluj-Napoca and Bucharest: Limes.

Zvěřina, J. (2003). *Sexuologie (nejen)pro lékaře.* Brno: Akademické Nakladatelství CERM. (In Czech)

4

Unity and Purpose at the Intersections of Racial/Ethnic and Sexual Identities

Ilan H. Meyer and Suzanne C. Ouellette

Something in Oz and me was amiss
But I tried not to notice
I was intent on the search for my reflection, love, affirmation in eyes of blue gray green.
Searching, I discovered something I didn't expect.
Something decades of determined assimilation cannot blind me to.
In this great gay Mecca I was an invisible man.
I had no shadow, no substance, no place, no history, no reflection.
I was an alien unseen and seen unwanted.... I was a nigger. Still.

I am angry because of the treatment I am afforded as a Black man.
That fiery anger is stoked additionally with the views of contempt and despisal shown me by my community because I am gay.
I cannot go home as who I am.
When I speak of home I mean not only the familial constellation from which I grew, but the entire black community: the black press, the black church, black academicians, the black literati, and the black left.
Where is *my* reflection?
I am most often rendered invisible,

Perceived as a threat to the family,
Or I am tolerated if I am silent and inconspicuous.
I cannot go home as who I am,
And that hurts me deeply.

—Riggs (1989)

Writers have described Black lesbians, gay men, and bisexuals (LGBs) as having conflicted and fractured identities. Black LGBs are said to experience their sexual identities as competing with their racial/ethnic identities, to suffer from a double burden (or "double jeopardy") of stressors related to their race/ethnicity and sexual orientation identities, and to have looser connections with the gay community than White LGBs. This view of Black gay identity is supported by identity theories that describe the postmodern self as a "protean self," which, rather than striving for coherence, thrives on dissonance (Gergen, 1991; Lifton, 1993). Our observations among a group of Black LGBs in New York City and our reading of more recent literature lead us to conclude otherwise. Where others have seen identity conflict and a double burden, we see a search for unity and purpose at the intersection of racial/ethnic and sexual identities. We hear in Black LGBs a recognition of the constraints of social forces but also a struggle—both internal and external—for coherence.

The theoretical question underpinning this chapter is: How do Black LGB individuals, who inhabit two socially significant identities, experience these identities? We address two dominant perspectives in identity theory. One perspective views multiple salient identities as competing; the other perspective argues that multiple identities coexist to form a coherent self. We supplement these perspectives with two notions: (1) that individuals recognize the social origin of constraints placed on their identities and (2) that identity is a dialectical process that occurs in distinctive interpersonal, sociocultural, and historical contexts. This conceptual framework enables us to appreciate how unity can exist alongside multiplicity and personal agency alongside social determination in Black LGB identities.

LGB and Racial/Ethnic Identities in Conflict

The view that identities are in conflict has been prominent in literature describing the lives of LGB individuals who are also members of racial/ethnic minority groups, especially the experiences of African Americans. Collins (2005) sees the source of this conflict in an affinity between racist and heterosexist ideology. Racist ideology views Blacks as primitive and as having abundant sexuality that is more connected to nature. Because homosexuality is seen as unnatural, it is seen as not inherently African. Following this reasoning, LGB Blacks are seen as less authentically Black.

We believe that the historical context of identity politics in the United States, where racial/ethnic and sexual identities have been foci of civil rights struggles, may help explain this casting of LGB and racial/ethnic identities as inevitably conflicted. During the civil rights struggles, it seems, identity conflict was experienced as a conflict in political allegiances. Acquiring two politically salient identities was not simply a personal matter; American politics required that only one identity be important: the one that guided one's political action and allegiance.

The depth of this conflict perspective is echoed in the identity labels used by some authors. *Black gay* and *gay Black* refer to the seemingly necessary primacy of one or other identity among Black LGBs (Wilson & Miller, 2002). In an article titled "Are You Black First or Are You Queer?," Conerly (2001) suggests not only a conflict but a competition between identities. He and others (Johnson, 1982) show that "black-identified gays" were equated with loyalty to Black culture and causes, whereas "gay-identified blacks" were associated with assimilation, abandonment, and, one gets the sense, *betrayal*, of Black roots.

In an examination of Black anthologies published primarily from the mid-1980s to the mid-1990s, Conerly (2001) finds that authors tended to employ the "black nationalist 'blacker-than-thou' rhetoric to discredit gay-identified black men" (p. 18). In the early anthologies of lesbian Black writers, gay-identified Blacks, or *interracialists*, were viewed as self-hating and their "blackness and their commitment to black politics" were questioned (p. 13). Conerly sees the source of identity conflict in the social circumstances of Black LGBs and the double oppression they experience in mainstream Black and gay communities. Black LGBs, he writes, "perceive racism among white lesbigays and heterosexism among straight blacks" (p. 11). Underlying this experience is not solely lack of acceptance and prejudice, but a complete lack of cultural relevance: a *"rift between two cultures"* (p. 12, italics added).

This perspective of identity conflict also underlies our understanding of stress and coping among Black LGBs. Authors have suggested that Black LGBs suffer from prejudice because of their race/ethnicity in their interactions in mostly White LGB communities and homophobia in their racial/ethnic communities (Loiacano, 1989). Writers have suggested that Black LGBs cope with the stressors suffered in each community by choosing to affiliate with one or the other. Battle and Crum (2007) explain:

> Black LGBs... often feel the pressure to "choose" between what are
> perceived as conflicting identities: their "Black self" or their "LGB
> self." Experiencing gay/lesbian culture as White and hegemonic,
> ethnic minority gay men and lesbians feel a strong need for contin-
> ued ties to their cultural communities.... They cannot "afford" the

rejection of the homophobic [Black] heterosexual world...because
the [mostly white] "homosexual world" does not deliver the same
social and psychological benefits for them as it does to the White gay
and lesbian community. (pp. 337–338)

Audre Lorde (1984) describes the influence of conflict on the self: because of
homophobia and racism, she says, Black lesbians are "constantly being encouraged to pluck out some one aspect of self and present this as the meaningful
whole, eclipsing or denying other parts of self" (cited in Loiacano, 1989, p. 21).

Identity Theory: Conflict versus Unity

The typical understanding of gay Black identities as torn and conflicted also
has roots in identity theory and identity development models that researchers have used to understand gay and (separately) Black identities (Cass, 1984;
Cross, 1995; Phinney, 1996; Sellers, Rowley, Chavous, Shelton, & Smith, 1997;
Troiden, 1989). Interestingly, although there has been little, if any, exchange
among writers discussing gay and Black identity development, both areas
suffer from a view of identity as singular and insular. In both areas, writers
describe identity development as a series of struggles to resolve identity crises
leading to a solid identity. In this view, there is competition between Black and
gay identities, which are seen as conflicting components in search of a resolution toward a unitary but singular identity. Such models have been criticized
as not fitting a multiplicity model of identity where several identities coexist
(Eliason & Schope, 2007).

Currently, most identity theorists recognize that individuals hold multiple
identities, but these theorists do not agree about how these identities coexist. The main theories highlight conflict versus unity. The conflict perspective
describes identity as comprising components that are at war with one another:
"...The life story is really more like a *conversation of narrators*, or perhaps a *war
of historians* in your head" (Raggatt, 2006, p. 16, italics in the source). Such
authors critique the notion that identity synthesis is required for healthy development. Instead, "the dialogical self" (Hermans, 2001), "the mutable self"
(Côté, 1996), and "the protean self" (Lifton, 1993) are presented as "models
[that] share the insight that the self need not be viewed as abhorring dissonance, requiring consistency and coherence as prerequisites for survival or
even psychic health" (Hartman Halbertal & Koren, 2006, p. 40).

Raggatt (2006) demonstrates the dialogical self using the case study of
Charles, a gay White man. Raggatt notes that Charles' narrative demonstrates

conflicts resulting from his social positioning between gay and straight—initially Charles tries to become heterosexual but then accepts a gay identity and becomes a gay rights activist. In Charles as an activist, Raggatt concedes, "we can see some evidence for integration, but this dynamic of change over the life course can also be interpreted dialogically. The voice of the activist is a dialogical response to the socially produced positioning of self as 'humiliated homosexual'" (p. 31). Thus, Raggatt's interpretation of Charles' life course retains the two conflicting parts (the prior heterosexual and the ultimate resolved gay activist).

Similarly, Hartman Halbertal and Koren (2006) take the conflict perspective in their analysis of the narratives of 18 Orthodox Jewish gay men and lesbians. These authors see in the life stories of their respondents so much identity dualism and conflict that, they say, "the very notion of identity synthesis [and] its usefulness as a model to account for [these respondents'] experience must be called into question" (p. 37). The life stories of the Orthodox Jewish lesbian and gay respondents represent, according to the authors, two identities that cannot be reconciled, each—religion and sexual orientation—seen as essential and even "divinely bestowed" (p. 37). Unlike other elements of identity, which could be incorporated into or unified with one's sexual identity, "religion represents a far more encompassing web of beliefs, values, ritual practices, and social and familial connections that cannot easily be uncoupled from the individuals' deepest sense of being" (p. 38).

The respondents in Hartman Halbertal and Koren's (2006) study all achieved acceptance of their sexual identities—they identify as both lesbian or gay and Orthodox Jews—but "nonetheless continue to experience these identities in stridently dualistic terms" (p. 39). The authors found in the life stories no concept of a singular self through which conflicting claims on their identities are mediated and processed, much less synthesized: "the notion of identity synthesis is far more than merely nonresonant: It is an oxymoron" (p. 57).

In contrast to this view, according to the unity perspective, the self strives for coherence by incorporating complex identities into an integrated and meaningful unity. Summarizing the unity perspective, Singer (2004) notes that an individual's life story provides "causal, temporal, and thematic coherence to an overall sense of identity" (p. 442). This coherence reflects progress through the "work of building a narrative identity" (p. 445)—work that progresses across the individual's life span. Referring to their data from a study of the life course of academics, McAdams and Logan (2006) find: "In neither case does the story suggest a simple unity and coherence in life. At the same time, neither story devolves into randomness and the kind of shifting, patternless mélange that postmodern theorists such as Gergen (1991) repeatedly invoke" (pp. 100–101).

Identity as a Dialectic of Persons in Context

The unity view of identity often found in narrative studies embeds identity processes and content in historical, social, and cultural, as well as personal, contexts. For Cohler and Hammack (2006), it is the interaction of the person and his or her sociohistorical context that determines identity constructions. When viewed this way, identity emerges as a result of individuals' active confrontation with several external forces. Applying the unity view, in a closer look at the narratives examined by Hartman Halbertal and Koren (2006), we disagree, in part, with the authors' interpretation of identity conflict: We see their respondents striving for and achieving consolidation of religious and sexual identities. For example, Amiram, one of the respondents in the study, talked about being "torn from the inside," but he clearly identified the *external* source of his seeming conflict when he said: "It hurts, it just hurts. I am not angry at God, I am angrier at society" (p. 54). A lesbian (Shlomit) reported that she stopped discussing her sexuality with rabbis, declaring, "I have studied [religious law] and I can explicitly say that I can be a religious person and I can be a lesbian and be *whole with it*" (p. 56, italics added). Such resolutions of identity conflict among religious LGBs, by reinterpretation of religious teachings, have also been described among Christian and Muslim LGBs (Minwalla, Rosser, Feldman, & Varga, 2005; Rodriguez & Ouellette, 2000).

Sociocultural Context

In terms of the broader sociocultural context of Black LGB lives, we recognize that the American cultural context has been changing significantly over the past 40 years. The context of Black LGBs described above, in which identity was described as conflicted and identity choice indicated loyalty, has changed to an extent. On the one hand, attitudes about gay men and lesbians have become more accepting. On the other, the urgent need of the Black civil rights movement for strict identity allegiance has subsided. In general, identity discourse has loosened, allowing more fluid identity constructions (Cohler & Hammack, 2007; Eliason & Schope, 2007; Glenn, 1999).

Perhaps reflecting these changes, in addition to the conflict view of Black LGB identities that we described above, a unity perspective has also emerged. For example, hooks (2001) maintains that homophobia and racism still characterize the experience of Black LGBs but rejects the notion that the lives of Black LGBs are lives of conflict and contradiction. hooks takes issue with the notion that Black communities are more homophobic than White communities. Rather than emphasizing competition between gay and Black identities, hooks highlights the synthesis of the struggles for Black civil rights and gay rights. She describes the experience of Black lesbians and gay men who have lived integrated lives in Black communities but warns that their stories are often missing from the public record. She notes (2001):

> This is a research project that must be carried out if we are to fully understand the experience of being Black and gay in this white-supremacist, patriarchal, capitalist society.... We [hear] hardly anything from black gay people who live contentedly in black communities. (pp. 68–69)

In this chapter, we directly aim to describe these voices.

Voices of Black LGBs

In this chapter we examine how Black lesbians, gay men, and bisexuals who are embedded in Black communities in New York City narrate their identities. In our view, the person, his or her contexts, and the transactions between person and context need to be seriously addressed when we consider identity conflict and unity among Black LGBs. In this chapter we consider the person's awareness of, feelings about, and movement toward action in response to the social and other external constraints upon his or her identities. We examine identity in multiple areas of participants' lives, particularly in the context of prejudice and discrimination—stressors related to both race/ethnicity and sexual orientation (Meyer, 2003). We include what is close at hand for identity construction in the form of close relationships and work commitments and less proximal connections such as those with religious institutions. We employ existential notions like Sartre's (1956) *look* and Greene's (1988) *situated freedom* in our interpretation of identity narratives.

To employ a multidimensional analytic approach, we rely on a dialectical view of identity processes. Borrowing from theorists like Ricoeur (1965), we seek to avoid simple dichotomies and recognize that identities at the intersections of race/ethnicity and sexual orientation are continuously being crafted in particular times and places in creative ways, with the potential for the production of radically new forms of personal and social identity.

Method

Sampling

This report relates to a small subsample of participants in a large epidemiological study. (Detailed information about the study's sampling and other

methodological issues is available online at http://www.columbia.edu/~im15/.)
We used a venue-based sampling method, with venues selected to ensure a
wide diversity of cultural, political, ethnic, and sexual representation within
the demographics of interest. Venues included business establishments (e.g.,
bookstores and cafes), social groups, outdoor areas (e.g., parks), and snowball
referrals (upon completing an interview, respondents were asked to nominate
up to four potential participants). Between February 2004 and January 2005,
25 outreach workers visited a total of 274 venues in 32 different New York City
zip codes.

In each venue, outreach workers approached potential study participants,
invited them to participate in the study, and completed a brief eligibility
screening form for each volunteer. Respondents were eligible if they were 18 to
59 years old, had resided in New York City for two years or more and self-
identified as *(1)* heterosexual or lesbian, gay, or bisexual; *(2)* male or female
(and their identity matched sex at birth); and *(3)* White, Black, or Latino; but
they could have used other labels referring to these identities. Eligible respondents were contacted by trained research interviewers and invited to participate in the study. Interviews lasting on average 3.8 hours were conducted in
English, in person, at the research office.

Of 524 respondents, 131 were Black LGBs. As Figure 4-1 reveals, most Black
participants resided in New York City neighborhoods that are predominantly
Black. This chapter reports on 22 Black respondents (11 men and 11 women)
who were selected at random from among the Black study participants to participate in a semistructured qualitative component of the study (see Table 4-1).
This portion of the interview lasted on average for 40 minutes.

Interview

We aimed to elicit brief self-referential narratives about identity but also
to improve quantitative gay and Black identity measures, which confine
respondents to singular identities. At the same time, we strove for precision
in obtaining answers to the research questions and efficiency in the data
analysis. We therefore opted for semistructured interviews so that respondents could describe their identities within sociocultural contexts and over
time, but also so that they were allowed complete freedom in choosing how
to relay these narratives. The interview aimed to *(1)* elicit descriptions of
and narratives about interrelations among identities, statuses, and roles;
(2) provide narratives about the enactment of identities and interactions
with institutional settings such as work, family, and community life; and
(3) describe social stressors associated with these identities and institutions.

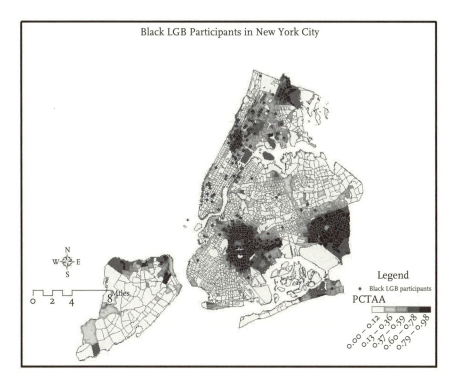

FIGURE 4-1 Participants' georgraphic residence. (Note: Black participants' (N = 131) residential location is indicated by a dot that is superimposed on New York City's neighborhoods grouped by proportion of Black residents. Darker areas indicate a greater concentration of Black residents.)

We used as a probe a sheet of paper with a drawing of a large circle with lines protruding from it. Four of the lines had preprinted labels for race/ethnicity, gender, age group, and sexual orientation, the focus of our investigation. Respondents were asked to list identities, statuses, and roles that described who they were near these labels and near the other blank lines. They were told that they could write as many or as few identities as they wished and that they did not have to fill in the prelabeled spaces if they did not wish to do so.

With this list at hand, the interview began by asking the respondent to describe what she or he had listed. Interviewers were allowed to alter both the order of questions and their specific content, depending on the flow of the interview. Interviewers probed narratives following standard guidelines for qualitative interviewing (Denzin & Lincoln, 2000). We devised specific instructions and probes to induce responses of interest to the main questions of the study and reduce possible biases related to social desirability.

TABLE 4-1 Select Sample Characteristics (N = 22)

Name*	Age	Education	Sexual Orientation Identity Label	Sexual Orientation Identity[†]	Race/Ethnic Identity Label[‡]
Women					
Monette	38	High school	Lesbian	Gay/love women	None listed
Corine	23	Some grad school	Bisexual	Bisexual	Mixed
Aretha	36	Some college	Lesbian	Lesbian	Black
Llysha	28	Some college	Lesbian	Futch (female butch)	Native American, Jamaican, Honduran
Belle	50	B.A. degree	Gay	Gay woman/ Black, aggressive gay woman	Black/Black aggressive gay woman only at times
Lela	37	Some college	Bisexual	Het/bi	None listed
Les	23	Some college	Gay	None listed	None listed
Tameca	23	B.A. degree	Lesbian	Queer/gay/ lesbian	Black
Candice	27	B.A. degree	Gay	None listed	None listed
Tiffany	32	High school	Bisexual	None listed	Black
Binta	27	Some college	Lesbian	None listed	None listed
Paulina	42	Some college	Lesbian	Lesbian	None listed
Men					
Aaron	28	High school	Bisexual	Bisexual	Black (African American)
John	34	High school	Homosexual	Gay	African American
Kahlil	45	High school	Gay	Gay/just being me	Black
Clifford	40	B.A. degree	Gay	Gay	Black
Perry	30	B.A. degree	Gay	None listed	None listed
William	41	High school	Gay	Ver.top	Black
Tyrone	23	Some college	Gay	Gay	Black
Adrian	46	B.A. degree	Gay	Homosexual	Black
Elijah	18	B.A. degree	Gay	Gay	Black
Duane	29	B.A. degree	Gay	Gay	None listed

* No real names are used to protect respondents' identity.

† Label was chosen by the respondent from multiple-choice categories given in the quantitative section of the interview.

‡ These labels were given by respondents in the qualitative section. We used as a probe a white 9 × 11 inch page with a preprinted illustration of a large circle centered in the upper half of the page with lines positioned around the perimeter protruding out of the circle. On four of the lines around the circle were written the words *sexual orientation, race/ethnicity, age group,* and *gender* as areas of identities and roles. At the beginning of the interview, respondents were asked to write any number of identities, statuses, roles, or other descriptors as they chose on this sheet. They were told that they could choose to write something under the prelabeled categories or not.

For example, if a respondent chose not to describe an identity related to his or her race/ethnicity, gender, or sexual orientation, he or she was asked to explain this choice (e.g., "I see that you did not write anything describing your race/ethnicity, I wonder why?"). If a respondent did not report identity conflict, he or she was asked about it; when a respondent reported general ideas or truisms, he or she was challenged to provide detailed and concrete examples. By probing, interviewers sought to elicit an honest discussion, not to influence the interviewee's response. To do so, they tried to put the respondent at ease, making it clear that all answers were acceptable, explaining that the researchers were interested in the respondent's own point of view, and expressing genuine interest in and curiosity about the respondent's identity narrative.

Data Analysis

Complete transcriptions of the interviews that included participants' and interviewers' words along with notation of pauses, overlapping speech, expressions of emotion, and unintelligible speech represented our data sources. Both authors conducted multiple readings of the transcripts alone and together, with conversations between readings.

We began our analysis with some ideas about relationships between the concepts that were based in several prior conceptualizations of identity as well as minority stress theory. This conceptual familiarity supported an initial coding analysis in which we looked for the appearance of concepts and themes. We then proceeded to a more intensive look at portions of identity narratives in light of the full narratives, that is, in light of the complete material on individual cases. In this thematic analysis, we relied on comparative examination across cases. We turned insights gained from single cases into questions that we posed to and across other individual cases. We moved between deductive and inductive forms of analysis. Although we approached the material with clear questions and prior conceptualizations, we allowed the interview material to confirm or disconfirm our preconceptions and to introduce new ideas. Guided by a specific research question, we present as results the themes that support an understanding of how it is that Black gay men and lesbian women of a variety of ages are able to maintain prominent and positive gay identities alongside equally prominent and positive Black identities. As our analysis evolved, we found ourselves relying more and more on existential and hermeneutical theories for interpretation. The conceptual formulation of identity at the end of our work is fuller and more complex than the one with which we began.

Results

ELIJAH (18-YEAR-OLD GAY MAN):   Well, it seems, well, all my identities seem to work together, no, nothing seem to conflict really, because most of my identities have to do with me expressing myself, so, you know, it's all like intertwined.

BELLE (50-YEAR-OLD GAY WOMAN):   I can't separate being a Black woman and a gay woman, there're still one and the same. So, a Black woman who's not afraid to go out there and meet challenges or face adversity, no matter what, because just being Black is gonna be an adversity. Being gay is gonna be adversity, but [I am] the type a person that I can face all'a that, you know what I mean? No matter what. I'm never gonna not be able to do it. I think that's why we treat that so much as important that is known, that this is the biggest part of me.

WILLIAM (41-YEAR-OLD GAY MAN):   ...A big dream, or not a dream, but a, I always think, if I go to my parents' church, and the preacher, you know we go as a family or whatever, and the preacher is saying antigay things from the pulpit, I would get up and leave. That would be my biggest moment, my biggest protest moment, in front of my parents, and in front of people that they know.

Each of these quotations represents one of the three key themes we identified in the interview data. The three themes interact with and complement one another. Instead of hearing conflict and competition, we were overwhelmed by voices that describe unity and coherence. We title this theme *unity and coherence*. But it is not an untroubled unity. We discuss a complex picture in which identity conflict is also present, yet acted upon in respondents' search for integration.

Our second theme, *struggle with social constraints*, helps to explain how this unity is achieved. Individuals engage in a long and ongoing process in which the self confronts and seeks to transcend limitations to coherence. As respondents contend with gay and Black identities, they are acutely aware of the external structures and processes that seek to limit their identity pursuits. In this theme, the narratives of respondents revealed the view that something is wrong with what *society* assumes about their identities—with what other people think about them and how they act toward them. Through their contemplation of social constraints (especially related to religion and family of origin), and by identifying these external forces as sources of struggle rather than internal doubt, our respondents built a foundation for a coherent view of themselves.

The third theme, *identity as a dialectical process,* is related to the first and second themes in that it helps to explain the process through which potentially conflicted identities become unified. With this theme, we describe the crafting of identities as a dialectical process that happens in context and over time. People contend with earlier undesired ways of being, seek resolution of these in the present, and project this work into the future when resolution can be imagined. Through their view of what might be, they choose life projects and commitments to new ways of expressing self in the future. Thereby, they experience an even more fundamental source of unity across identities and time.

Unity and Coherence

Our interviewers were trained to let participants frame identity issues as they subjectively experienced them. Given the interview guidelines and the tools used in the interview, however, there was plenty of opportunity for respondents to focus on identities in isolation and in conflict with each other. Nonetheless, respondents did not choose to cast their identities in these terms, struggling instead to present a unified self. Interviewers' efforts to encourage participants to talk about conflict were often and insistently redirected:

INTERVIEWER JT: I guess what we'd just like to know is, do you think that these different parts of yourself, how do you think that they fit together, or they don't fit together, are there ways that you see them similarly or different, or just, overall, like, how do you think that they fit together, or don't fit together?

CLIFFORD (40-YEAR-OLD GAY MAN):   I really don't see h-, what's the separation? I don't understand the separation. You, you're either, you're male or female, I', I'm male, I'm gay, I'm Black, I'm forty. It just,

INTERVIEWER JT: Okay, just so tell me what you mean by that in terms of the separation.

CLIFFORD: I don't see a separation at all…. Yes, that's who I am. I, I wake up every morning, I'm a Black, gay, male that's forty years old…. That's that.

INTERVIEWER ARG: In what ways do [your racial and sexual identities] compete with one another or are in harmony?

JOHN: Well, they don't compete against one another, for me. But, I guess it's society who looks at 'em.

Participants consistently refuted the notion of significant conflict between their racial/ethnic and sexual identities. Instead, participants' identity narratives were sites of construction for a coherent self. Elijah, an 18-year-old gay male poet, needs to inhabit all of his identities in order to be who he is: "...No, nothing seem to conflict really, because most of my identities have to do with me expressing myself, so, you know, it's all like intertwined."

A unified identity is what respondents find when they look in the mirror. For Perry, a 30-year-old gay man, being gay, a man, and a person of color are "inextricably bound.... They all come together." He and others talk about their necessarily multifaceted ways of being. Respondents were acutely aware that they have views about who they are and how they see themselves, and their self-reflections may produce images at odds with (and more positive than) images others would impose on them. Addressing the notion that you cannot be gay and Black, Duane, a 29-year-old man, says, mockingly: "Hello! [laugh] I'm here!"

In making this strong claim for unity narratives, we are not suggesting that participants never talk about conflict or the experience of clashes between identities, living more than one life, or having separate lives. For example, the majority of respondents talk about the relevance of religion and spirituality in their lives, and five of them explicitly depict conflict between being gay or lesbian and being a believer and member of a church or mosque. Most often, however, this experience does not represent as much an internal conflict as a conflict with clearly defined *external* oppressive forces.

Monette, a 38-year-old lesbian, describes the relationship between external oppression and the notion of clashing identities:

> Well, my spiritual and my gay. That, sometimes clashes, I mean, because I was brought up in church.... Sometimes it does cause a problem with my spiritual life because some of the spiritual people, they don't understand it, if you tell them, so now you got to live sort of like a double life, meaning that you don't want to tell too many people that are who go to the church, because they're going to judge you for who you are, so now you keep that on the back burner, keep that separate from your spiritual life, and sometimes it actually clashes because you never know when you're out in the streets and you're with your partner, or whatever, and you happen to see one of the church members, sometimes you find yourself, you say, "Oh this is just my friend," and you don't mean to be that way, but you see the spiritual, you see it clashing.

In this excerpt from Monette's narrative, she shifts from talking about the church to "church members." Her narrative echoes those of other respondents who describe this conflict not as abstract or distal, not only about ideology or institutions. Rather, it is a very *social* conflict in which respondents report feeling distance from and disagreement with important family members and friends who uphold the religious ideas and teachings that stigmatize gay identity.

Some respondents describe conflict as involving a split between gay identities and their membership in the Black community. But that experience is also not an internal conflict: Being gay or lesbian conflicts with expectations some perceive within the Black community about sexuality and gender. John, a 34-year-old man who identified as a "homosexual," perceives community norms as dictating that he cannot be both a "real man" and gay in the African American community. This perception questions his masculinity and prevents others from recognizing the paternal role he has assumed for his nephew. Aretha, a 36-year-old lesbian, reports that she has been ostracized by both men and women in the Black community because they perceive her as having too "aggressive" a look for a woman. Duane, a 29-year-old gay man, echoes other narratives in his articulation that the source of the conflict is not internal but in the community's attitudes. At the same time, he speaks of his rejection of these attitudes:

> In the Black community they see, and it's, you know, a crazy part,
> they see as being gay as sort of a White European thing for some
> reason. You know, "Black people are not gay," you know, we don't talk
> about those things.

The respondents acknowledge the negative consequences of such community attitudes for their lives. Along with the negative personal emotional responses captured by the terms *frustration* and *guilt,* respondents describe the negative effects this conflict has had on their relationships. Corine, a 23-year-old Catholic bisexual woman, misses being able to go to church with her parents the way her siblings do: "It's just confusing, it's frustrating, so it's just like a big thing." And Monette, sadly, says about her mother: "I love her to death, I love her, but I don't think she would ever be able to accept my lifestyle."

In essentially all of their expressions, respondents clearly present conflict as having to do with the role of social and cultural forces—forces that they typically dissociate from their internal voice. They typically depict conflict as outside the self, attributable to mistaken views held by others—specific others or society in general. Duane, a 29-year-old gay man, provides a typical instance of this attribution as he corrects the interviewer's perception of conflict:

> INTERVIEWER JXT: Um, tell me a little bit of where you feel like the
> conflict comes from. I mean, it sounds like there's a conflict somewhat
> between that, so if you could just say a little about...

DUANE: Um, conflict, I think it's a lot on society's views and how they
view people, you know.

Struggle with Social Constraints

When asked to talk about their identities in various spheres of life, many
respondents chose to talk about "freedom of expression" as a way of narrating their experience of what is limited in their lives. A theme common across
several identity narratives is the threat posed by others' "looks"—typically
encountered on the street, sometimes accompanied by threat—that strive to
negate their identity. Often such threats lead to an assertion of one's self. When
Duane is asked what impact such encounters had on him, he responds:

> Duane:... It keeps me going stronger... how am I gonna say this,
> if I... listen to what everyone else said, I'd be a crazy person
> [laughs]... so I try to do, you know, what I need to do for myself, um,
> to make myself a better person.

Duane does not only externalize the source of identity conflict but uses his
awareness of it as the impetus for coherent identity development.

Similarly, for Perry, the 30-year-old gay man who described his identities
as "inexorably bound," the struggles of being gay as a young person in his Black
community enabled him to escape negative influences in his environment,
provided him with pathways to better places like college, and enabled him to
set goals and to be courageous. Tameca, a 23-year-old lesbian of Caribbean heritage, appreciates the growth such struggles afforded her. She recounted how
she has become more politically and personally confident over time, noting:

> Tameca:... Maybe in opposition with those things [racism, homopho-
> bia, and sexism]... maybe that's a strange thing to say. But I think
> to a certain extent even the things that have been awful... but at the
> same time... you can also develop, personally.

Participants' stories about socially induced stress related to racism or
homophobia turn into discourses about the identity-unifying benefits of
being able to see oneself as someone who can rise to the challenge of stress.
Participants like Belle, whose narrative introduced the Results section, explicitly make a connection between facing multiple adversities and identity integration. Belle sees sexual orientation as a personal choice against homophobia
and racism, while she sees each of these forms of discrimination as a "societal
choice." She is resigned to the notion that these negative forces within society will always be there and contends with it through a view of herself as one

who will always respond to social pressures aggressively. Alongside her view of society as essentially stressful and debilitating is her view of herself as the person who is always there to step in when there is a problem.

Other respondents also often take an active role to counter social stressors, even in the most difficult area of religion. They take the position that church members, the church, and even God are wrong in their rejection of gay people. In this realization is also the promise (or hope) of self-assertion in front of God and people, a self-assertion that comes out of a struggle that has an almost rebellious connotation.

MONETTE: Yeah, and I think I keep [my gay and religious identities] separate because in one sense, I know the Bible says it's not right [to be gay], and then in one sense, I'm saying, "Well God, I can't help who I fall in love, I can't help what I feel," it's like a clashing, and the bad thing about our society is that it doesn't understand....

And it shouldn't clash, but, I think as you learn yourself and know who you are, eventually that won't clash, you'll just be free to say, well, "This is my girlfriend," whether the person, whether they judge or not, that takes a lot of experience and you've got to deal with your inner self with that....

John, a 34-year-old gay man, also describes a process that involves determination, choice, and action:

Being that from such a young age, at 5 years old up until I was 29, I was part of a religious organization, that had a very big impact in shaping and molding me into the person I am today. So if I do have one thing that's fighting, it's the fact that being gay does not agree with what I was taught as such a young child. So that's a constant conflict that I have going on even though I would like to have them resolve each other. I've gotten better with it, but it's still a sore spot, it's a very sentimental point for me cuz, if I could be openly gay in that organization, I would still be with it, but I had to, one of them had to be given up. And the one I gave up was the one that I had a, I had the ability to choose if I wanted to be in it or not. I didn't, I didn't choose to be gay, that's how it was.

Identity as a Dialectical Process

In the narratives we witness an identity dialogue, but it is not in Raggatt's (2006) sense of the warring internal voices or selves. Rather, the dialogue is between the self and what are perceived to be external forces seeking to limit the self. Duane nicely demonstrates the difference. He replaces Raggatt's metaphor of war with metaphors of fashion and dance. His identity, he says, is made up of many hats he carries with him in a "big suitcase." He presents himself as having become quite adept at knowing when and how to switch hats. He thus contends with the taboos surrounding race and gender in the Black and White communities. But, he says, he has to remain vigilant: remaining aware of context and staying "on my toes."

This dialectic goes on within intrapersonal, interpersonal, and larger social and cultural contexts. These contexts reveal something of the mechanisms and processes through which ongoing identity work happens. With regard to the intrapersonal, our participants' responses have taught us that although our focus is on racial/ethnic and gay identities, we need to broaden our view to include participants' many other identities and to understand the relationships among them. For example, for two artists within the group, the identity as an artist becomes a vehicle through which to experience a way of integrating Black and gay identities.

> ELIJAH: One of my identities is a [sic] artist. And the kind of way it fits together is because my poetry and also my song is based upon my, multi identities, like, you know, me being gay, I write a lot of poetry based on, you know, gay lives and the trouble that we go through. Also, also, I'm, I teach a lot of people about, information about, like Black culture, and one of the other things I write poetry about. So I kind of like intertwine my multi identities through my, my poetry or myself.

Binta, a 27-year-old lesbian poet, expresses similar identity possibilities in her art:

> BINTA: ...Do they work together? Yes, because without me being a poet, I couldn't be a friend, I couldn't be a counselor, I couldn't be a daughter, a good daughter at that. And, then I wouldn't be so much of a dreamer. I don't know.
>
> INTERVIEWER (YXN):   Can you tell me more specifically how they connect? Give me some examples of the way that you see yourself being a poet and a lesbian and these connecting for you.
>
> BINTA: Um. Oh, wow [laughs]. Because my views as a lesbian, what I can't do, such as getting married, it shows in my poetry.

With regard to interpersonal context, the narratives reveal that participants do not work on their identities in isolation. Identities happen *with* significant others. Clifford, the 40-year-old gay man who has had to live his gay life as separate from his life with his family, describes changes in his identity as critically connected with what his brother and other family members think and do regarding his sexuality. He reports that their attitudes have changed "drastically" over the past 10 years. His younger brother, with whom he typically only talks about sports, "just came out of the blue and said, 'I can deal with a gay man long as he doesn't wear a dress.'" Clifford's response to his brother was a simple "Okay," but he shares more with the interviewer. He sees his brother's statement as a sign that, despite their strong Baptist-based belief that homosexuality is wrong, he may at some point be able to share his sexual identity with his siblings.

Similarly, Duane's identity is interwoven with people in his life. For example, his attempts to help his White gay partner resolve identity issues are connected to his own identity reconciliations. An aunt is a kind of identity go-between—her conversations with a sister smooth the way for a resolution of the impasse he and his mother had reached concerning his sexual identity. He has always understood his mother as the source of his positive outlook on life, and casting her in that role has never sat well with her rejection of his homosexuality. But they are now beginning to talk about sexuality.

With regard to sociocultural context, religion is a prominent institution. But, interestingly, this context is not something to which people passively respond. Most participants who retain a connection with religion and spirituality can see the flaws, hypocrisy, and prejudices of those who see themselves out as representing the will of God. Monette, who worries that she will meet church members while walking down the street with her girlfriend, tells us that identity clashes stem from church members who do not understand what it means to be gay. The sources of the clashes our respondents experience are family members, neighbors, and society at large. Aretha, who has been rejected by members of her Black community, says that she is a "universal person" without conflict within herself; it is others who have a problem with the way she presents herself, and she does not want to internalize their problems.

Often, the respondents interact with religion and bring about changes in the context as they search for a more supportive environment. Most respondents who, like John, were troubled by their church's rejection, searched for and were able to find a new, more accepting church. Aaron, a 28-year-old bisexual man, describes how he moved from a conservative Pentecostal church to an openly gay church and now to a more inclusive—but not gay-identified—interdenominational fellowship. Others reject institutionalized religion altogether, keeping their spirituality separate from the church. Kahlil, a 45-year-old gay man for whom the mosque was once very important, now finds that he can no longer go to the formal institution because of its rejection of gay people and its hypocrisy (because he knew one or two other mosque members to be gay but closeted). "I don't have to go to a church or to a mosque to find God," he says. "So, I'm at peace with myself." Lela, a 37-year-old bisexual woman, also describes her journey from being born a Baptist to conversion to Islam and membership in a mosque to a more personal form of Islam:

> Oh, I was born um Baptist, um I converted to Islam in 1998 which
> I'm still Muslim and was practicing Muslim up until about a year
> ago, I'm still Muslim but I don't go to the mosque, I don't really
> practice, it's because now I have a different awareness of religion and
> I think that as long as I have a relationship with God personally, I
> don't need to be so disciplined and strict about, "oh I need to go to
> the church, oh I need to do this, oh I need to that, oh I'll be damned
> if I don't," and I really don't believe that anymore.

Tyrone, a 23-year-old gay man who had been raised in Islam, had felt very attracted to many aspects of the religion but found it too rigid, especially its ideas about sexual orientation. He is now considering Buddhism, where he is hoping to experience what he found positive about Islam while being free of its negative constraints. William expresses a commitment to a different way of being in a church. And Monette looks forward to a time when she can say to church members on the street: "This is my girlfriend."

For yet other respondents, college provided an important sociocultural context. Tameca tells us: "For me when I went away to college, that was a big shift for me, in terms of feeling like I can grow." It was in college that she came to see that the church and some of her other communities were homophobic. For Duane, an academic article he read in college provided the insight to contend with and resolve struggles over his multiple identities by arriving at a coherent, integrated gay and Black identity.

> ...And I'll never forget there was actually an article I read in college
> [laugh] by Peggy McKlintock or McKlintish, and I can't remember
> her last name, but it was on that same issue. It was identifying as a
> gay Black um, individual, or as a Black gay individual.

Work is another relevant identity context. When asked if there are specific circumstances in which identities are in harmony or in competition, Duane describes his current human immunodeficiency virus (HIV) prevention work as enabling him to express his multiple identities simultaneously and the New York City Gay Men's Chorus as a setting where he proudly sings as both a gay and a Black man. For Paulina, a 42-year-old lesbian, the lesbian, gay, bisexual, transgender (LGBT) youth group she runs is a safe place for her own identity work. Finally, 18-year-old Elijah, our youngest participant, sees new possibilities for a coherent gay and Black identity in the current historical sociocultural context.

> Well, you know, nowadays, like today, presently, it seems like people are more open-minded, so, but maybe like three four years ago, it was a little awkward. You know, people would look at, you know, have that look of disgust, you know, so, but now, you know, I see a gradual change in the whole, you know, way people perceive, you know, homosexuals, so.

Discussion

Although we approached the material with clear questions and prior conceptualizations, we allowed the interview material to inform us and were open to confirm or disconfirm our preconceptions. As we began to read through the interview materials, we were struck by the clarity of voice about two topics. First, while we expected, based on our reading of the literature, to find conflict between gay and Black identities, we found clear and consistent evidence for coherence and unity. Second, religion emerged quite clearly as a core locus of conflict and deliberation. Our analysis supports Hartman Halbertal and Koren's (2006) claim that religion represents a unique element of identity among religious LGB individuals because it creates challenges for unity and coherence. These authors noted that, among Orthodox Jewish lesbians and gay men, religious identity comprises a set of core values and beliefs that directly compete with LGB identity and are not malleable. However, unlike these authors, we found that our respondents—of Christian and Muslim denominations—actively engaged with religious identities, striving for identity unity and often finding ways to integrate religious and gay identities.

As we began to analyze respondents' identity stories, and as we discussed these in view of various contemporary readings on identity, we became dissatisfied with a simple dichotomy of identity integration versus identity conflict. Although concepts relevant to each pole of the binary were useful in our characterization of some of our respondents' stances concerning self, we found ourselves in need of a conceptual framework that allowed us to talk not about the "either-or," but about the movement between and beyond the two. The writings of hermeneutical philosopher Paul Ricoeur (1996) provide a more effective way of describing and understanding the narratives of our respondents.

Although identities are often discussed in the literature in static ways, we see in our respondents' stories identities on the move, with evidence of people working on identities to reshape them. Especially relevant are the observations of participants' reclaiming of religion and spirituality as aspects of their identity. Several of our respondents described how important religion had been to them in the past but also how damaging it had been to their developing gay identities, leading them to leave their church or mosque. Later, however, they found new ways to interpret religious teachings and be religious or spiritual. They reclaimed a religious identity and redefined it in ways that now are compatible with an LGB identity while engaging in an ongoing search regarding spirituality.

From Ricoeur's (1996) perspective, all of our narratives about self and identity reveal an attempt to maintain a sense of sameness while simultaneously facing the unknown and the incompleteness of the self. Ricoeur sees this process as a part of the human condition: We are constantly creating who we are. Ricoeur would have us recognize, in the interpretation of an identity narrative, the importance of what has happened in the person's past, but also how the person is contending with those influences and even healing their effects in the present. In addition, Ricoeur asks us to examine how a person's view of the future influences how he or she experiences the present. The person's movement toward both the past and the future provides some sense of unity—a different kind of unity than is present in much of the current psychological literature on identity, but a unity nonetheless. When they talk about their identities, respondents convey the "warmth and intimacy" that William James and later scholars of the self associate with the experience of the sameness of self (Barresi, 2002).

With the addition of participants' emphasis upon stress and struggle related to homophobia and racism, we can expand this interpretation. Participants bring to powerful life Jean-Paul Sartre's (1956) notion of the others' gaze as that through which the person comes to experience limitations on his or her own freedom and with which the person must come to terms if his or her exercise of freedom is to be authentic. In other words, from the existential perspective, freedom is freedom only if it is exercised in the midst of the limitations imposed by others, place, and time. Contemporary existential philosophers Charles Taylor and Maxine Greene call authentic freedom a *situated freedom*—that is, a freedom that must be exercised within the constraints that are inevitably part of lives lived with others (Greene, 1988).

Stress—external sources of demand and challenge in forms such as stigma, prejudice, and discrimination—forms the background against which participants construct, maintain, and change their identities (Meyer, 2003). Social stress represents the limitations and causes of suffering that Ricoeur

(1965) found essential to include as he wrote about men's and women's exercise of will and freedom through language and narrative. In their stories about social stress, respondents help us understand what they need to contend with as they seek to build any kind of identity. Further, it is through their awareness and recognition of these stressors that respondents move away from a debilitating sense of identity conflict toward identity coherence.

In these stressful challenges, respondents described identity as enacted on people—whether it be church members, family members, or members of the Black and gay communities in general. This finding is consistent with McAdams' (1997) "identity as a life story" approach, where, as Singer (2004) describes it,

> [The self] coheres around a narrative structure, which casts the individual as a protagonist in a lifelong journey, marked by the mutual challenges of intimacy and autonomy, and expressed through archetypical characters, turning points, and various outcomes of redemption or contamination. (p. 445)

There are many limitations to our study. First, we do not write here about everything that might be said about participants' identity narratives. We searched for answers to the specific questions we initially posed about the integration of Black and gay identities. Second, our respondents are a select group of Black LGB individuals, identified to a lesser or greater extent with both their gay and Black identities. We did not attempt here to discuss other forms of identification (or lack of identification) with same-sex behavior, such as men who have sex with men (MSM) and women who have sex with women (WSW) (Young & Meyer, 2005) or the much-discussed "down low" (Boykin, 2005). That being said, to the extent that we can talk about any representation from a small, mostly qualitative, study, it is important to note that our sample was not drawn from a traditional (White) gay community. As is demonstrated by the geographic residence of our participants, they are Black LGBs deeply embedded in New York City's Black communities.

We started this chapter with reference to the many writers who noted the difficulty that dual identities cause Black LGBs. But there have been other voices that are consistent with what we found from our respondents' identity narratives. For example, Hawkeswood (1996) documents the lives of gay men who reside in Harlem—a Black community in New York City—and are socially integrated into its community. He notes the rich history of Black men in Harlem who define themselves as Black and gay, the social networks available to them within the community, and the indigenous Black gay culture and society. Among the men he interviewed, he does not describe the kind of conflict and torn identities described by the writers we quote in the introduction to this chapter. Similarly, Wilson and Miller (2002) did not find evidence that Black gay and bisexual men experience a conflict among identities. Even though they confirm that some men experience the gay community as racist and the Black community as homophobic, this finding does not seem to lead to choosing an affiliation with one community against the other community. The authors discovered that some men changed their behavior, depending on the context, but they still sensed that they belonged to both communities. These men did not view their racial/ethnic and sexual identities as separate and certainly did not view one as subordinate to the other.

More recently, authors have taken biculturalism as a model for understanding the integration of racial/ethnic and sexual identities (e.g., LaFramboise, Coleman, & Gerton, 1993). Such authors explain that the challenges of Black LGBs are similar to the challenges of acculturation and underscore the possibility of engaging effectively in two cultures simultaneously. Indeed, Parks, Hughes, and Matthews (2004) note, "What is or has been a source of oppression may become a source of strength" (p. 251), so that experiences of racism may help Black LGBs cope with experiences of homophobia. Another study of Black gay and bisexual men suggests that a more cohesive identity is most psychologically beneficial. Crawford and colleagues found that men who had a positive identification as both African American and gay had higher levels of self esteem, better social support, more life satisfaction, better HIV-related coping strategies, and less distress than men who did not have a positive identification with both identities (Crawford, Allison, Zamboni, & Soto, 2002).

Changes in the situation of Black LGBs are presented in Marlon Riggs's film *Tongues Untied*. The quotation that opens this chapter illustrates Riggs's experience of identity conflict. By the end of the film, Riggs and his friends march for gay rights as an African American contingent and illustrate the unity of identities and, indeed, of political agendas. Unlike the attempts of Black heterosexuals to silence the sexual orientation of Bayard Rustin for the perceived benefit of the struggles for Black civil rights (D'Emilio, 2003), more recent discourse has explicitly allowed for the synthesis of the two identities. Hutchinson (2000), who describes himself as a heterosexual Black man, acknowledges that there is much homophobia among heterosexual Blacks and calls on Black leaders to confront it and see that "they should be the last ones in America to jettison other Blacks who may be in a position to make valuable contributions to the struggle for political and economic empowerment" (p. 6).

Similarly, hooks claims that there is no inherent conflict between Black and gay identities. Although hooks (2001) does not believe that homophobia and racism should be discussed as synonymous—she sees skin color as a stronger social indicator and a greater cause of harm to Black people than the more concealable sexual orientation—she believes that there is a "union between black liberation struggle and gay liberation struggle" (p. 73). Collins (2005) goes further. She sees an intersection between race and sexual identities and therefore a common political struggle: "Developing a progressive Black sexual politics requires examining how racism and heterosexism mutually construct one another" (p. 89). This work has been adopted by many current Black leaders, including such prominent figures as Coretta Scott King, Archbishop Desmond Tutu, Rev. Jesse Jackson, and Rev. Al Sharpton, indicating and leading to further significant changes in the Black community (Banerjee, 2006; "Tutu stops short of backing gay marriage," 2004).

Influenced by what we have read in the literature, we approached this research with the hypothesis that Black LGBs would experience great struggles in managing their sexual and racial/ethnic identities. We expected that these struggles would leave Black LGBs conflicted and fragmented. We thought that some would resolve this conflict by moving more toward the White LGB community, making their sexual identities primary, and others would resolve the conflict by making their racial identities primary. We consulted identity theorists and found Raggatt's (2006) and other postmodern theorists' description of the protean self (Lifton, 1993) to be a good theoretical orientation for our study. But the picture that emerged as we heard the voices of our respondents was quite different: We found a struggle, for sure, but a struggle that helps unite rather than separate identities, a struggle that, for most respondents, seems to have led to a unified sense of self, appreciation of their various identities, and a clear sense of the stressful impact of oppression. In understanding what we heard, we relied on Cohler and Hammack (2006) and Cohler (2007) to explain the social context of our respondents' identity stories and to recognize that the shifting social context over the past few decades has helped Black LGBs to construct a coherent identity. We also relied on McAdams (1997) and other identity theorists who describe not a warring self, but the strive for unity and purpose in identity construction.

Acknowledgment

The research reported in this chapter was supported by a grant from the National Institute of Mental Health to the first author (RO1-MH066058). The authors thank Michael Stirratt, Robert Kertzner, Rebecca Young, Rafael Narvaez, Michael Roguski, and Danielle Beatty for their contribution to the development and testing of the qualitative measure used to obtain the results reported in this chapter.

REFERENCES

Banerjee, N. (2006, January 21). Black churches' attitudes toward gay parishioners spur debate at conference. *The New York Times*. Retrieved May 2, 2008, from http://www.nytimes.com

Barresi, J. (2002). From "the thought is the thinker" to "the voice is the speaker": William James and the dialogical self. *Theory & Psychology, 12*, 237–250.

Battle, J., & Crum, M. (2007). Black LGB health and well-being. In I. H. Meyer & M. E. Northridge (Eds.), *The health of sexual minorities: Public health perspectives on lesbian, gay, bisexual and transgender populations* (pp. 320–352). New York: Springer.

Boykin, K. (2005). *Beyond the down low: Sex, lies, and denial in Black America.* New York: Carroll & Graf.

Cass, V. C. (1984). Homosexual identity formation: Testing a theoretical model. *Journal of Sex Research, 20*, 143–167.

Cohler, B. J. (2007). *Writing desire: Sixty years of gay autobiography.* Madison: University of Wisconsin Press.

Cohler, B. J., & Hammack, P. L. (2006). Making a gay identity: Life story and the construction of a coherent self. In D. P. McAdams, R. Josselson, & A. Lieblich. (Eds.), *Identity and story: Creating self in narrative* (pp. 151–172). Washington, DC: American Psychological Association Press.

Cohler, B. J., & Hammack, P. L. (2007). The psychological world of the gay teenager: Social change, narrative, and "normality." *Journal of Youth and Adolescence, 36*, 47–59.

Collins, P. H. (2005). *Black sexual politics: African Americans, gender, and the new racism.* New York: Routledge.

Conerly, G. (2001). Are you Black first or are you queer? In D. Constantine-Simms (Ed.), *The greatest taboo: Homosexuality in Black communities* (pp. 7–23). Los Angeles: Alyson Publications.

Côté, J. E. (1996). Identity: A multidimensional approach. In G. R. Adams, R. Montemayor, & T. P. Gullota (Eds.), *Psychosocial development during adolescence* (pp. 130–180). London: Sage.

Crawford, I., Allison, K. W., Zamboni, B. D., & Soto, T. (2002). The influence of dual-identity development on the psychosocial functioning of African-American gay and bisexual men. *Journal of Sex Research, 39*, 179–189.

Cross, W. (1995). The psychology of nigrescence: Revising the Cross model. In J. G. Ponterotto, J. M. Casa, L. A. Suzuki, & C. M. Alexander (Eds.), *Handbook of multicultural counseling* (pp. 93–122). Thousand Oaks, CA: Sage.

D'Emilio, J. (2003). *Lost prophet: The life and times of Bayard Rustin.* New York: Free Press.

Denzin, N., & Lincoln, Y. (Eds.). (2000). *Handbook of qualitative research.* Thousand Oaks, CA: Sage.

Eliason, M. J., & Schope, R. (2007). Shifting sands or solid foundation? Lesbian, gay, bisexual, and transgender identity formation. In I. H. Meyer & M. E. Northridge (Eds.), *The health of sexual minorities: Public health perspectives on lesbian, gay, bisexual and transgender populations* (pp. 3–26). New York: Springer.

Gergen, K. (1991). *The saturated self: Dilemmas of identity in contemporary life.*
New York: Basic Books.

Glenn, E. N. (1999). The social construction and institutionalization of gender
and race. In M. Marx Ferree, J. Lorber, & B. B. Hess (Eds.), *Revisioning gender*
(pp. 3–43). Walnut Creek, CA: AltaMira Press.

Greene, M. (1988). *The dialectic of freedom.* New York: Teachers College Press.

Hartman Halbertal, T., & Koren, I. (2006). Between "being" and "doing": Conflict
and coherence in the identity formation of gay and lesbian orthodox Jews. In
D. P. McAdams, R. Josselson, & A. Lieblich (Eds.), *Identity and story: Creating self
in narrative* (pp. 37–61). Washington, DC: American Psychological Association
Press.

Hawkeswood, W. G. (1996). *One of the children: Gay Black men in Harlem.* Berkeley:
University of California Press.

Hermans, H. J. M. (2001). The dialogical self: Toward a theory of personal and
cultural positioning. *Culture and Psychology, 7,* 243–281.

hooks, b. (2001). Homophobia in Black communities. In D. Constantine-Simms (Ed.),
The greatest taboo: Homosexuality in Black communities (pp. 67–73). Los Angeles:
Alyson Publications.

Hutchinson, E. O. (2000). My gay problem, your Black problem. In D. Constantine-
Simms (Ed.), *The greatest taboo: Homosexuality in Black communities* (pp. 2–6).
Los Angeles: Alyson Publications.

Johnson, M.L. (1982). *Influence of assimilation on the psychological adjustment of Black
homosexual men.* Ann Arbor: University of Michigan.

LaFramboise, T., Coleman, H. L. K., & Gerton, J. (1993). Psychological impact of
biculturalism: Evidence and theory. *Psychological Bulletin, 114,* 395–412.

Lifton, R. J. (1993). *The protean self: Human resilience in an age of fragmentation.*
Chicago: University of Chicago Press.

Loiacano, D. K. (1989). Gay identity issues among Black Americans: Racism,
homophobia, and the need for validation. *Journal of Counseling and Development,
68,* 21–25.

McAdams, D. P. (1997). The case for unity in the (post)modern self: A modest
proposal. In R. D. Ashmore & L. Jussim (Eds.), *Self and identity: Fundamental
issues* (pp. 46–80). New York: Oxford University Press.

McAdams, D. P., & Logan, R. L. (2006). Creative work, love and the dialectic in
selected life stories of academics. In D. P. McAdams, R. Josselson, & A. Lieblich
(Eds.), *Identity and story: Creating self in narrative* (pp. 89–108). Washington, DC:
American Psychological Association Press.

Meyer, I. H. (2003). Prejudice, social stress, and mental health in lesbian, gay, and
bisexual populations: Conceptual issues and research evidence. *Psychological
Bulletin, 129,* 674–697.

Minwalla, O., Rosser, B. R., Feldman, J., & Varga, C. (2005). Identity experience
among progressive gay Muslims in North America: A qualitative study within
Al-Fatiha. *Culture, Health & Sexuality, 7,* 113–128.

Parks, C. A., Hughes, T. L., & Matthews, A. K. (2004). Race/ethnicity and sexual orientation: Intersecting identities. *Cultural Diversity and Ethnic Minority Psychology, 10*, 241–254.

Phinney, J. S. (1996). When we talk about American ethnic groups, what do we mean? *American Psychologist, 51*, 918–927.

Raggatt, P. T. E. (2006). Multiplicity and conflict in the dialogical self: A life-narrative approach. In D. P. McAdams, R. Josselson, & A. Lieblich. (Eds.), *Identity and story: Creating self in narrative* (pp. 15–35). Washington, DC: American Psychological Association Press.

Ricoeur, P. (1965). *Fallible man* (C. Kelbley, Trans.). Chicago: University of Chicago Press.

Ricoeur, P. (1996). *Oneself as another* (K. Blamey, Trans.). Chicago: University of Chicago Press.

Riggs, M. T. (Producer/Director). (1989). *Tongues untied.* [Motion picture]. San Francisco: Frameline's Lesbian & Gay Cinema Collection.

Rodriguez, E., & Ouellette, S. C. (2000). Gay and lesbian Christians: Homosexual and religious identity integration in the members and participants of gay-positive church. *Journal for Scientific Study of Religion, 39*, 333–347.

Sartre, J. P. (1956). *Being and nothingness* (H. Barnes, Trans.). New York: Philosophical Library.

Sellers, R. M., Rowley, S. A. J., Chavous, T. M., Shelton, J. N., & Smith, M. A. (1997). Multidimensional inventory of Black identity: A preliminary investigation of reliability and construct validity. *Journal of Personality and Social Psychology, 73*, 805–815.

Singer, J. A. (2004). Narrative identity and meaning making across the adult lifespan: An introduction. *Journal of Personality, 72*, 437–459.

Troiden, R. R. (1989). The formation of homosexual identities. *Journal of Homosexuality, 17*, 45–73.

Tutu stops short of backing gay marriage. (2004, April 21). *Canadian Press*, p. B6.

Wilson, B. D. M., & Miller, R.L. (2002). Strategies for managing heterosexism used among African American gay and bisexual men. *Journal of Black Psychology, 28*, 371–391.

Young, R. M., & Meyer, I. H. (2005). The trouble with "MSM" and "WSW": Erasure of the sexual-minority person in public health discourse. *American Journal of Public Health, 95*, 1144–1149.

5

Bisexuality in a House of Mirrors

Multiple Reflections, Multiple Identities

Paula C. Rodríguez Rust

I tend to use lots of terms to describe my sexuality, because I think context is very important.

—Respondent "Lee-Anne,"[1] IBICIP study

The observation that sexual identity is mutable is common to both traditional and contemporary perspectives on sexual identity; what distinguishes different perspectives is the characterization of this mutability. According to traditional views of sexual identity as a reflection of inherent or essential sexuality, identity development is a goal-oriented process culminating in identity stability; as such, changes in sexual identity are cast as evidence of psychological immaturity. In contrast, social interactionist perspectives view identity as the result of interaction between individuals in a social context; in this view, an individual's identity is akin to an "agreement" made between the individual and others about who that individual is within a given social environment. Although identity change is therefore normative, implicit in this perspective is the assumption that psychological health will be achieved through a complete integration of personal and presented identities, after which further identity change would be unnecessary.

More contemporary social constructionist views of sexual identity posit that identity is a cultural product, produced by individuals within frameworks provided by culture; individual identities change over time as the cultural construction of sexuality changes historically. Finally, the idea of sexual identity as a narrative product combines social interactionist and social constructionist perspectives by examining the process by which identity is produced through a continuous narrative process that occurs at both the societal and individual levels.

Several distinct bodies of literature have grown out of the study of sexual identity as a social, cultural, and/or narrative product. One body of literature examines changes in sexual identity over the course of history. For example, in this volume, Shepard examines changes in the narratives of sexual identity possibilities in the post–World War II period in the United States. A second body of literature examines changes in sexual identity over the life course; whereas traditional views of identity have produced developmental models of the individual coming-out process, narrative analyses include Welle's examination of the development of *body narratives* among lesbian, gay, bisexual, transgender, and queer (LGBTQ) youth (Welle, Fuller, Mauk, & Clatts, 2006) and Hammack and Cohler's examination of the individual identity development process as a process of narrative engagement between an individual and a cultural environment (e.g., Cohler & Hammack, 2007; Hammack, 2005; Hammack & Cohler, this volume). A third body of literature, primarily anthropological, examines differences in the social construction of sexuality in different cultural contexts; these contexts might be entire societies or localized cultural venues. For example, in this volume Kurtz discusses gay men's construction of a public identity in relation to the sex-drug gay party cultural venue of Miami, and deBoer discusses the reconstruction of gay men's identities as gay fatherhood becomes a legal and then a personal reality.

These bodies of literature cover three quadrants of a two by two array (see Fig. 5-1). The two axes defining the array are the level of social analysis, which is classified as either Individual (I) or Social Group (G), and the dimension along which change occurs, which can be either Historical Time (T) or Cultural Space (S). The examination of life course processes, such as coming out, identity development, and individual processes of construction and reconstruction, inhabits the Individual/Historical Time (I x T) quadrant. The examination of historical changes in the social construction of sexual identity inhabits the Social Group/Historical Time quadrant (G x T). The examination of cross-cultural differences in the social construction of sexuality, including the examination of specific processes of construction in specific cultural venues, inhabits the Social Group/Cultural Space quadrant (G x S).

		Level of Analysis	
		Individual	Social Group
Dimension of Change	Time	• Coming out • Psychological identity development • Individual identity construction	• Historical changes in the social construction of sexual identity
	Space		• Cross-cultural differences in the social construction of sexuality • Identity construction within specific cultural venues • Ethnographic studies of sexual organization and identity

FIGURE 5-1 Bodies of literature on sexual identity classified by their perspective on identity change

Noticeably absent from the literature is an examination of identity construction in the realm of the individual as he or she moves through cultural space, that is, the fourth quadrant (I x S). Individuals do not live in a single cultural space throughout life or even throughout a single day. At minimum, most individuals experience home, work, and recreational contexts on a regular basis and might function in multiple layered contexts simultaneously. The construction of sexuality might differ in these different environments, providing different narrative vocabularies and opportunities for self-identification in each environment. Therefore, as an individual moves from one context to another— a movement that might itself occur over time, and simultaneous with both historical changes in culture and life course progression—different narratives come into play and different identities are produced. As a result, individuals might identify themselves differently in different contexts, change their identities over time, and maintain more than one identity simultaneously.

Some individuals experience greater variability in their personal narratives across context than others. Individuals whose personal biographies and experiences of self fit neatly into widely accepted cultural categories are likely to find that they can move from one context to another without having to alter their personal narratives. In contrast, individuals who do not fit neatly into widely accepted cultural categories are more likely to have to adjust their narratives as they move through cultural space. With regard to sexual orientation, because the predominant cultural construction is the gay/straight dichotomy, individuals whose sexual biographies include both same- and other-sex attractions or behaviors have more difficulty finding identities that accurately and consistently reflect their sexualities across different social contexts than individuals whose biographies are more consistently same- or other-sex oriented. Therefore, contextual identity variation should be more dramatic among bisexually attracted and bisexually behaving individuals. In this chapter, I use the concept of identity as a narrative product to explore the microconstructive processes that bisexual individuals go through as they move among the various social and cultural environments of their daily lives and life courses.

The data on which this chapter is based are taken from the International Bisexual Identities, Communities, Ideologies, and Politics study (IBICIP). The IBICIP is a self-administered survey of individuals who had ever identified themselves as bisexual and/or had ever been attracted to or had sexual contact with at least one man and at least one woman over the course of their lives. Previous publications based on the IBICIP data have explored the meanings of bisexual identity for individuals who identify as bisexual, perceptions of the existence of a bisexual community, and transitions to and from bisexual identity over the life course (e.g., Rust, 2001a, 2001b). This chapter focuses on individuals who reported more than one sexual identity and examines the ways in which these different identities allow them to function in the different cultural environments within which they live, work, and socialize.

Identity as a Narrative Product in Historical Context

Before turning to the data, it is necessary to clarify the relationship between narrative and identity and to locate the process of personal narration within larger historical constructive processes. A narrative is a story in the process of being told. A personal narrative is one's own story of one's self, told to one's self or to others; this narrative both reflects and constructs the self. One's identity is a representation of that narrative, functioning as the summary of the story. Identity is a sense of who one is, which may or may not be represented by labels symbolizing various aspects of the self, such as *African American, honest,* or *father.* Identity is, therefore, produced through personal narrative. An identity, especially an identity that is symbolized with a label, might vary in the degree to which it accurately represents the narrative story underlying it. Insofar as identity labels are imperfect representations of personal narratives, as one moves through cultural space it is possible for one's narrative to shift without causing observable changes in one's identity label. Like constantly shifting tectonic plates that might cause either a series of small tremors or a period of apparent quiet followed by a dramatic and apparently sudden adjustment, narratives and identities are in a state of constant production and re-production, whereas identity labels might display a more discrete pattern of apparently abrupt change whenever the fit between a label and its underlying narrative becomes too strained.

Narratives function at multiple social levels, including individual, social, and historical levels. At the individual level, in a particular social context, one's personal micronarrative explains who one is in that context—for example, defining one's relationships to others in the context and explaining one's reasons for being in the context. Despite the fact that the process of personal micronarration might vary as an individual moves from one context to another across time or space, most individuals feel a sense of narrative consistency that transcends context. In other words, individuals don't feel as if they are a "different person" in different situations, even though they might present themselves differently in different situations. Instead, they feel a sense of internal consistency that is maintained even as outward presentations change. This sense of internal consistency, or core self-identity, is the product of a personal metanarrative that encompasses situation-specific micronarratives. The metanarrative functions as the glue holding the micronarratives together by explaining differences between them to reconcile them with each other and with the metanarrative. The metanarrative is, in effect, a dialogue one has with oneself about the self. The product of this metanarrative is akin to the social interactionist concept of the *self-identity*, or the identity that one uses to describe the self to the self, as opposed to the *presented identities* one enacts for others as produced through context-dependent micronarratives.

Just as a whole is not the sum of its parts, but rather a system produced by its parts, social narratives are the product of individual narratives and historical narratives are the product of social narratives. Individual micronarratives and metanarratives form an individual's history, which in turn reflects and is part of larger social constructive processes of historical cultural change, that is, the process of historical narration. As individuals weave their micronarratives with each other in the context of a specific historical moment, the products they create alter that context, thereby creating historical change.

The Latitude and Longitude—and Temporality—of Cultural Space

Cultural difference is typically visualized in terms of geographic space. Children's textbooks about cultural differences often show a projection map, with national flags marking each country, and pointers extending from different regions of the world to photos showing the traditional clothing, foods, or activities of those regions. But cultural space is not two-dimensional, and movement through cultural space does not necessarily correlate with movement from one geographic location to another.

Cultural space is multidimensional. Along one dimension, cultural space is defined by social venue. Every social venue, no matter how small, constitutes a cultural space. Cultural differences between nations and states are usually clear and quite obvious; cultural differences between neighborhoods in a city or between classrooms or lunch tables in a public school might not be as evident to outsiders, but they are important to those who live or eat lunch in those environments. As an individual moves from one venue to another—for example, from one neighborhood to another, or one classroom to another—she or he moves from one cultural context to another. A single friendship or even a single conversation can also constitute a cultural space.

Along a second dimension, at any given moment, each individual exists and interacts simultaneously within multiple environmental layers. For example, a lesbian African American high school student sitting at the school lunch table in New Jersey is simultaneously enveloped by a predominantly heterosexual-cultured larger society, in a state with some of the most progressive civil rights laws in the country for LGBT students, at a table with other LGBT students who are probably predominantly white and might not understand racism, and sitting next to a table of students who are African American but might not be LGBT-friendly. At the moment she opens her mouth to speak, she is speaking simultaneously in all these contexts reflecting layers of different racial and sexual attitudes. As she leaves the lunchroom to go to class, the larger layers—nation, state, and school—remain the same, while the more local layers shift.

Along a third dimension, as individuals move from one cultural environment to another, they carry with them traces of each previous environment they have experienced and are influenced by their previous cultural experiences. Two bisexual Mexican American men might meet at a gay bar in Texas. Although they are inhabiting the same multiple environmental layers as they interact with each other, they might have come from families or segments of the Mexican community with different attitudes about gay sexuality. Perhaps one is an *activo* who recently immigrated from *La Ciudad de México* and identifies as heterosexual, whereas the other is an Americanized *hombre moderno* who identifies as bisexual; their previous cultural environments will affect how each can understand himself and interact with the other within their current cultural context.

The fourth dimension is time; cultures change over time, and individuals enter and leave social contexts as they progress through the life course. Consequently, individuals might find themselves changing identities over time in response to changes in cultural space that are related to the progression of either historical or personal time. Or, instead of changing identities, they might maintain identities adopted at earlier stages of their lives even as they, and the world around them, change. The result is an age-related cohort effect in which different generations of sexual minority individuals maintain different patterns of sexual identification. Like a core sample taken of the earth's layers or a slice of petrified wood showing the tree rings, the result is that a cross-sectional "snapshot" of age-related differences in self-identification, taken at any given moment, will show the reflections of historical change across multiple generations.

Bisexuality: A Look at the Scientific Literature

The current analysis of identity as a narrative product among IBICIP respondents is part of a growing body of literature that explores patterns of bisexual identification and sexuality. Although these patterns are of interest here because they shed light on narrative processes that individuals with a wide range of sexualities experience and not because they can be classified as bisexual per se, it is nevertheless helpful to locate the current analysis within the contemporary scientific discourse on bisexuality.

In contrast to persistent cultural notions that heterosexuality and homosexuality are mutually exclusive sexual orientations and that bisexuality does not exist, previous research and theory on bisexuality have provided ample evidence that many individuals are in fact attracted to both men and women, have had sexual contact with both men and women, and/or are able to enjoy sexual contact with and form romantic bonds with both men and women (Binson et al., 1995; Diamond, 2000; Fay, Turner, Klassen, & Gagnon, 1989; Klein, 1993; Laumann, Gagnon, Miachel, & Michaels, 1994; Rogers & Turner, 1991; Rust, 2001b; Smith, 1991; Weinberg, Williams, & Pryor, 1994). Whether or not such sexual patterns are called bisexual is a matter of social or scientific construction; what is clear, however, is that it is not scientifically practical to treat sexual orientation as a simple dichotomy consisting of an orientation toward one gender *or* the other.

Historically, the belief that sexual orientation must be directed toward one gender or the other, and the practice of defining individuals in terms of their attraction to gendered others, are recent developments. The concept of the *homosexual* person dates to the late nineteenth century. Most authors cite Kertbeny (1869) for coining the term *homosexual,* although the concept itself might be slightly older (Trumbach, 1977). Prior to that time, motivations for heterosexual coupling concerned economic viability and procreation; an individual's sexual desires were, if anything, antithetical to marriage because passion was short-lived and could not form the basis for an enduring partnership between man and woman (Katz, 1995; Seidman, 1991). Only with increasing economic prosperity and the rise of a cult of individualism did an individual's sexual desires acquire the legitimacy and importance needed for the shift toward personifying these desires in homosexual and heterosexual *types of persons* (Katz, 1990, 1997).

Prior to this time, evidence indicates that some individuals did feel attracted to and engage in sexual relationships with both men and women. For example, Smith-Rosenberg (1975) described married women of the nineteenth century who carried on extramarital sexual relationships with other women. I have argued that, ironically, individuals might have been freer to express bisexuality prior to the construction of the heterosexual and homosexual persons; once sexual desire became a basis for identity and that desire was classified as either heterosexual or homosexual, the cultural rug was, in fact, pulled out from under bisexuality (Rust, 2001a, 2001b).

In scientific circles, recognition of sexual orientation as a continuum including various degrees of combined attractions to men and women, rather than as distinct categories of attraction to men *or* women, is marked by the introduction of the Kinsey scales (Kinsey, Pomeroy, & Martin, 1948; Kinsey, Pomeroy, Martin, & Gebhard, 1953). Since then, other theorists have proposed modifications of the Kinsey scale that usually involve the use of multiple scales for the separate assessment of various dimensions of sexual orientation, including sexual behavior, sexual attractions, sexual fantasies, and sexual identity (e.g., Bell & Weinberg, 1978; Weinberg et al., 1994). Few of these modifications have been used by researchers other than their own authors, creating a lack of consistency in the measurement of sexual orientation. An exception is the Klein Sexual Orientation Grid, which is probably the most complex scalar model of sexual orientation to be used by researchers aside from its own authors (Klein, 1993; Klein, Sepekoff, & Wolf, 1985).

Some theorists have argued that the use of models in which orientation toward males and orientation toward females are placed at opposite ends of the same scale unnecessarily treats these orientations as contrary forces by implying that orientation toward one sex must decrease as orientation to the other increases. Authors such as Gonsiorek, Sell, and Weinrich (1995), Shively and DeCecco (1977), and Storms (1978) have argued that each dimension of sexual orientation (attraction, behavior, fantasy, identity, etc.) should be measured using a pair of scales, one assessing the strength of orientation toward males and the other assessing the strength of orientation toward females.

These advances in the scientific modeling of sexuality have had little impact on general public beliefs about bisexuality, which remain founded on the conceptualization of sexual orientation as categorically straight or gay. For example, many people still believe that bisexuality does not exist because heterosexuality and homosexuality are opposing drives that cannot coexist within a single person. In this view, the fact that some individuals identify as bisexual or behave bisexually is explained as psychopathology, inability to come out as gay or lesbian, psychological immaturity, hedonistic or youthful experimentation, lack of ability to commit to a single partner or lifestyle, an attempt to avoid prejudice by denying one's true homosexual nature, or an indiscriminate attempt to maximize one's chances for sexual contact. Insofar as the existence of bisexual individuals is acknowledged within this framework, bisexuals are stereotyped as nonmonogamous and promiscuous, because it is thought that the heterosexual and homosexual "halves" of the bisexual will vie against each other for sexual satisfaction.

Beliefs in the nonexistence and inauthenticity of bisexuality are also found within lesbian and gay minority subcultures. Among lesbians, for example, the rise of lesbian feminism was linked to the attitude that "if feminism is the theory, lesbianism is the practice." That is, a woman could not be a good feminist if she did not commit her life—politically and personally—to women. In this view, bisexual women were seen as traitors, as cowards who were afraid to come out, or as opportunists who wanted the pleasures of lesbian sexuality without shouldering their share of the burden of lesbian oppression.

Advances in theoretical modeling of sexual orientation have also been slow to inform scientific research. In research on sexuality, the nonexistence belief is reflected in the use of concepts that reconcile bisexual behavior with dichotomous sexual orientation, such as *secondary homosexuality, latent homosexuality, situational homosexuality,* and *pseudohomosexuality* (Rust, 2001b). Such characterizations were particularly common in scientific research conducted during the 1960s and 1970s. In the 1980s, the advent of human immunodeficiency virus (HIV) and public fears that bisexuals would be the gateway through which HIV would spread from the gay population to the straight population forced the recognition—although not the appreciation—of bisexual behavior.

During the 1980s, research on married gays and lesbians and the epidemiological consequences of bisexual behavior predominated. Researchers studying sexual minority populations began habitually referring to "gays, lesbians, and bisexuals" instead of "gays and lesbians," regardless of whether or not they had collected any information about the bisexuality of their respondents. Partly in response to biphobia intensified by the HIV epidemic, during the 1980s the bisexual community became increasingly politicized. This community coined the term *monosexual* to refer to heterosexuals and gays/lesbians, as distinct from *bisexuals,* thus creating a new dichotomy. Beginning in the mid-1980s and intensifying in the 1990s, researchers became aware of bisexual individuals as a distinct population available for study, and began to distinguish bisexuals from gays and lesbians in their study populations and to study bisexual men and women in their own right.

Although bisexuality remains understudied relative to monosexual forms of sexuality, there is a growing body of research literature. Since the publication of the Kinsey volumes, other large-scale nonprobabilistic studies with assessments of bisexual behavior, attraction, or identity include Hunt (1974), Cook (1983), and Janus and Janus (1993). Groundbreaking studies focused on bisexuality have been conducted by Fritz Klein and his colleagues (e.g., Klein, 1993), Martin Weinberg and his colleagues (e.g., Weinberg et al., 1994), Lisa Diamond (2000), and Ron Fox (2006). Other pioneering studies of bisexuality include the IBICIP study, which is the basis for this chapter. In recent years, several general population studies of probabilistic samples in various countries have used assessments of sexual orientation that acknowledge the existence of bisexual experience, including the General Social Survey (Binson et al., 1995; Smith, 1991) and the National Health and Social Life Survey (Laumann et al., 1994) in the United States, the Australian Study of Health and Relationships (Smith, Rissel, Richters, Grulich, & de Visser, 2003), and the Danish Quality of Life Population Survey (Ventegodt, 1998).

Method

The methods used in the IBICIP have been described elsewhere (Rust, 2001b). Over 900 individuals responded to a self-administered paper questionnaire that included questions about sexual identity, sexual behavior, attitudes and beliefs about sexuality, conceptions of sex and gender, and political views. No data were collected electronically, although the survey was publicized using both electronic (i.e., Internet) and nonelectronic methods. The questionnaire was distributed through multiple venues, and the target population was defined broadly as any individual who identified as bisexual at any time during his or her life and/or who had ever had sexual contact with or felt sexually attracted to at least one man and at least one woman. The data used in this chapter are from the 703 respondents who resided in the United States at the time they completed the survey.

Sexual identity was assessed with the question "When you think about your sexual orientation today, what term do you use most often to describe yourself? Do you think of yourself as bisexual, lesbian, gay, or heterosexual, or do you prefer another term?" The question was followed by the parenthesized instruction "If you use more than one term, you may circle all that apply, but indicate which one you use most often when you think about yourself" and by 26 response options including both traditional LGB identities and contemporary identities such as *queer, pansensual, polyfidelitous, ambisexual,* and *lesbian who has sex with men.* Respondents were also given the option of answering that they were "not sure" of their identity or that they "prefer not to label" themselves.

Respondents' supporting narratives were elicited with a question about the meanings of their sexual identities: "Sexual identity means different things to different people, and the same sexual identity might mean different things to different people. For example, two women might both call themselves 'bisexual,' but they might mean very different things and they might be two very different people sexually. What does your sexual identity mean to you? Explain why you call yourself _____. (fill in blank with answer to sexual identity question)." Respondents who had chosen more than one sexual identity were asked to explain the meaning of each of their identities.

Statistical Results

Sample Demographics

Demographically, the sample resembles most nonrandom samples of LGB individuals. White, college-educated young adults are overrepresented, although the large size of the sample ensured that members of a variety of racial and ethnic groups, high school dropouts and high school graduates without a college education, and the elderly were also represented. The majority of respondents were in their 20s (36%), 30s (34%), or 40s (19.6%) at the time they participated in the IBICIP, but ages ranged from 18 to 86. One quarter were students, one third of whom were also employed, 6% were unemployed, 6% were retired or not employed, and the remainder were employed full or part time. One third lived in large cities, one third lived in small or medium-sized cities, 17% lived in suburbs or large towns, and 13% lived in small towns or rural areas. Almost half of the sample had advanced education beyond college, and 88.8% identified themselves as White, Anglo, or of European descent. In order of representation, the remainder identified themselves as Latino/a (3.8%), of Black/African descent (3.0%), Native American (2.3%), and of Asian descent (2.3%). Almost 5% of the sample was transgendered; among nontransgendered respondents, women outnumbered men 2:1.

Self-Identities

One in seven respondents indicated that they preferred not to label themselves or were unsure of their identity, but because respondents were able to choose more than one response option to the question about self-identity, the majority of these individuals did also indicate a sexual identity. Two fifths of respondents (37% of women and 40% of men) chose only one self-identity; the remainder reported two or more sexual self-identities. Women chose an average of 2.6 identities and men chose an average of 2.3 identities, and the mean number of identities chosen decreased with age from 2.8 among those below age 25 to 1.8 among those over 50 years of age. Respondents employed full-time chose fewer identities (2.3) than respondents employed part-time and students (2.6–2.7).

Bisexual identity was the single most prevalent identity among IBICIP respondents, chosen by two thirds of both women (69%) and men (65%). The majority (76%) of bisexual-identified respondents indicated that their bisexual identity was their primary sexual identity, but most indicated that they also used other identities—lesbian, gay, heterosexual, queer, pansexual, polyfidelitious, and so on—to describe their sexual selves. Among women, for example, 27% of those who identified as bisexual also identified as lesbian or gay, and 33% also identified as queer.

The Stories Behind the Stories: The Narrative Production of Sexual Identities

> I like the word "Queer" because it is so all-encompassing and everyone who is living outside of a traditional heterosexual, monogamous lifestyle fits into this category. It's a friendly word that implies building alliances, not walls. Sometimes I'll call myself "Polyfidelitous" or "Bisexual" because they are more specific ways in which I'm considered "Queer" by societal standards.
>
> "Rosemarie," IBICIP study

When respondents in the IBICIP were asked about the meanings of their sexual identities, their answers clearly reflected the processes of narrative production that lay behind their choices to use particular identities. The idea that sexual identity is a "translation" of the self for others is a common thread in IBICIP respondents' explanations of their sexual identities, with the frequent implication that "something is lost in the translation." This was true even for the most commonly chosen sexual identity in this population, that is, bisexual identity. Many IBICIP respondents explained that they use *bisexual identity* because it is a commonly understood term that technically encompasses the range of their sexual experiences and feelings, but many said that in doing so, they were compromising. They did not feel that the term accurately conveyed the complete nature of their sexuality and therefore did not find the term adequate. For example, Elliot uses *Bisexual* "because, as with most labels, it saves time and is approximately correct," and Haley wrote, "I call myself Bisexual because it is the commonly used term in society for my sexual orientation."

The solution for many individuals in the IBICIP was to use multiple self-labels, treating these labels as a collection of identities whose combined meanings approached a reasonable representation of their sexual narratives. Almost 200 individuals explained why they used more than one sexual self-identity and provided narratives explaining the meanings that their identities held for them. Three broad themes emerge from their answers.

First, many individuals with both same-sex and other-sex histories or attractions find that there is no single identity term available to them that they feel completely and accurately reflects all aspects of their sexual self-narratives. They use multiple identities to create a more complete representation of themselves; each term fills in the gaps left by the other(s). Second, many individuals report that they use different identities in different situations, either because different narrative vocabularies are available or because the same labels have different meanings in different contexts. In one context, a particular label might function adequately to represent their sexual self-narratives, whereas the same label might mean something entirely different in another context. Third, some individuals distinguish between their private and public sexual identities; this parallels the interactionist distinction between self-identity and presented identity and reflects the distinction between context-specific micronarratives and personal metanarratives.

The Use of Multiple Identities to Reflect Different Aspects of the Self-Narrative

Sexual self-narratives encompass many different aspects of the sexual self, including sexual attraction, emotional or romantic attraction, sexual behavior, and fantasies, to name a few. Individuals whose sexual narratives are not consistently oriented toward either one gender or the other, or whose sexual narratives are not organized in terms of gender, often find the fit between their sexual experiences and the available vocabularies of sexual self-description less than perfect. For many of these individuals, there is no one label that can represent their entire sexual narrative. Therefore, these individuals often use different sexual identities to represent different aspects of their sexual narratives.

For example, Steven used different identities to reflect his present attractions as distinct from his present behaviors; he used Gay[2] identity "because my sexual preference is to males," but also identified as Bisexual because "I am married and have sex with my (female) spouse." Conversely, Gretchen is Bisexual, "by which I mean that I have the potential to be sexually attracted and sexually active with either gender," and Lesbian because "my partner is female." Irina distinguished between her emotional and sexual attractions, identifying as Lesbian because "I relate on a deep emotional level to women, and not to men" and as Bisexual because "I am physically attracted to both sexes."

Sexual narratives tell not only the story of an individual at the current moment, but also the story of who the individual has been in the past and how she or he came to be the person she or he is currently. This history is an important part of the story, adding meaning through explanation. However, each dimension of sexual orientation can vary over the life course, further complicating the individual's efforts to reflect her or his complete sexual narrative using available sexual self-labels. For this reason, many individuals use different identities to reflect their current sexual selves as compared to their past selves or to reflect the variety of their past behaviors. For example, in the IBICIP, Alex used Gay identity to reflect the fact that his "primary attraction at this time is to men," in contrast to his past behavior, which was reflected by his Bisexual identity: "Looking at my life holistically, I have had satisfying, loving, intimate, sexual relationships with women." Seth is Homosexual because "my present sexuality is strictly with male persons" and Ambisexual because "I've had relationships with men and women in the past." Geraldo uses multiple identities to reflect the variety of his past experiences; he identifies as Bisexual because he has had "seven long-lasting relationships with females" and Gay or Homosexual because "From 22 years old on I started having sex with males." These past experiences are still part of one's sexual narrative that explains who one is as a sexual person today, and as such, it is important to these individuals that these experiences be reflected in their sexual identities.

In slight contrast, some IBICIP respondents carried with them identities developed during previous stages of their lives, even though they did not feel that these identities truly reflected their current sexualities. In some cases, these were identities that reminded individuals of important stages in their lives, or of communities that played important roles in their lives, and that now linger as tributes to these past realities. Maggie calls herself a Dyke because the term "harkens back to a young active tomboy time in my life that is...a place of origin for my sexual feelings and attractions. No matter who, what, when, why—I will always be a Dyke." Francisco reported that he is Bisexual and not Gay, but still identifies as Gay as well as Bisexual because "I grew up in the gay male community; it was my last closet." Linda "began calling myself Gay on a women's college campus when it was a nongender-specific term."

Although the term Gay has changed in meaning, she still uses it—now in addition to her Lesbian identity.

As Klein (1993) has pointed out, the multidimensionality of sexual orientation is not exhausted by the recognition that past and current experiences might differ; Klein asserted that an individual's "ideal" or "future" experiences are also part of her or his sexual orientation. This can be seen clearly among IBICIP respondents, many of whom used their identities to describe differences between their current or past experiences, on the one hand, and their overall/lifetime, intended, or expected future sexual feelings or experiences, on the other hand. Amanda identified as Bisexual because she is "attracted to both men and women"—a current attraction—but also identified as Lesbian because "I'm not sure if I'll ever date a man again"—an expected future behavior. Marcus identified as Gay "because I have been in a relationship with another man for over 10 years"—a current behavior—but sometimes thinks of himself as Bisexual because "I occasionally have [relationships with] women"—an overall, or lifetime, behavior. Elizabeth distinguished between her current behavior, past behavior, and possible future behavior; she calls herself a Lesbian because "I am presently in a long-term, monogamous, committed relationship with a woman," but she is also a Lesbian-identified Bisexual because "I was once married to a man...I don't think it was a mistake, and I don't rule out a relationship with a man in the future." Mara distinguished between her current attractions and intended behavior; she is a Lesbian because lesbians are women who are "sexually, romantically, emotionally and spiritually attracted to other women and not men," and she is a Bisexual Lesbian "because I'm still attracted to men sexually but for the most part choose not to act on it."

Sexual identities can also reflect aspects of the self that are not directly sexual, such as social or political affiliations. Many IBICIP respondents used one identity to reflect their sexual interests or behaviors while using other identities to reflect the ways in which they relate to others, their relationships to certain social contexts, their social relationships including memberships in sexual minority communities, or their positions with regard to political or social change movements. Tammy-Lee explained that she is Bisexual because she "gets involved" with both men and women, but she is a Dyke because that is how "I relate to the world; how I relate to heterosexual women, how I relate to lesbians, how I see myself socially, how I sit in my med school class." Arnold is Bisexual because he is attracted to both men and women, but also calls himself Gay because "most of my current friends are gay." Similarly, Ingrid is Lesbian as well as Bisexual because, in part, "I engage in social activities related to lesbian community and culture." Larry is "Bisexual by sexual inclination and Gay by community affiliation." Chris is Bisexual "because I am attracted to men and women" and Queer "because I identify strongly with the queer community."

Queer identity is often used to reflect one's relationship to mainstream cultural institutions, that is, as an outsider; Sarah calls herself Queer because "I expect to remain outside many mainstream cultural institutions (e.g., marriage, nuclear family, competition-based lifestyle)," and Katrina uses Queer "to express my 'otherness'—from heterosexuality mostly, but also from gays and lesbians." Helen explained that "The reason I describe my identity [as a Bisexual Lesbian] is because it embraces both my sexual orientation and political perspective.... For me, my sexual orientation is bisexual, I am sexually and emotionally attracted to men and women. My personal politics are feminist, life-oriented and environmental.... [Lesbian] identity is politically important in a misogynist and patriarchal culture."

Narrative and Social Context: Telling Stories to Different Audiences

Sexuality is constructed differently in different social contexts, providing different languages and opportunity for self-description in different contexts. Whenever one tells one's story, one has to take one's audience into account and tell the story in a way that will be understood by a particular audience. One of the largest contextual differences pointed out by IBICIP respondents is the difference between mainstream cultural contexts and contexts within the LGBT community.

In general, there is a wider range of sexual identities, with subtler distinctions in meaning, available in sexual minority contexts than in mainstream cultural contexts. Sometimes identities that are available in sexual minority contexts are simply not available or understood in more general contexts, and many respondents said that they cannot use their preferred sexual identities in mainstream contexts because they would not be understood. For example, Minnie commented that she prefers to call herself a Bisexual Dyke because it is a true reflection of her sexual history, but it is "lost on the general population," so she reserves it for use within the queer community. Similarly, Giuseppe prefers the identity Multi-Queer, but it is understood only within certain cultural contexts, so he uses Bisexual identity for "occasions when I don't feel like explaining" the term "multi-queer." Mikayla prefers the Dyke identity but calls herself a Lesbian because "it is a common word that most people understand which describes a part of my life.... I do not feel any personal connection to 'Lesbian';...I use it as a translation for others."

Sometimes particular sexual identities might be available in different contexts but have different moral or political meanings that limit individuals' ability to use these identities across contexts. For example, Lee-Anne avoids the term Bi when she is at college, because she does not want to be "lumped in with" the " 'fakes'—bi women who really do embody lots of bad bi stereotypes." However, when she goes "somewhere more Bi-aware, such as Boston...I proudly use the term." Suzanne wrote, "I like 'Queer' as an identification with a political community, but I can't use it around, e.g., my mother," and Jonathan uses Queer to express his political identity but commented that "I generally use 'Bi' in straight circles, since 'Queer' is generally considered pejorative." Jinnie calls herself a Dyke "when I am with fellow bisexual women and lesbians. With them, I use it jokingly. Otherwise I would find it offensive."

Even within sexual minority communities, there are variations in the availability and meaning of different sexual identities. Each segment of the sexual minority community has a more developed vocabulary for identities that are relevant within that community. For example, identities such as *pansexual, pansensual*, and *polyfidelitous* have developed within bisexual communities to convey nuances in bisexual identities and concepts, and are not as well understood within lesbian or gay cultural contexts. Michael is Pansexual, but "ran across people that assumed it to mean having sex with people other than consensual adults, i.e., children, animals, objects. So for clarification I adopted the Bisexual moniker." Sandy uses her preferred identity Bi only "when I'm at a bisexual discussion group" because more general audiences might not recognize "bi" as an abbreviation for "bisexual." Sometimes, Etienne uses Bi identity anyway "because it's what I am," although he "dislike[s] it at the same time because there are few people around me who understand what it means. It takes explanation."

Within LGBT communities, there are also strong age-related generational and life course patterns in the meanings of some sexual identities. For example, the word *homosexual* is more acceptable among older generations of sexual minority individuals than among younger generations. For older individuals, the word is simply an accurate description of same-sex interest or orientation; it was a commonly accepted denotative term through the 1950s. For younger individuals, however, the term is associated with antiquated notions of same-sex interest as psychopathological. Newer terms like *lesbian* and *gay* carry much more positive connotations within this age group. Conversely, among younger generations, words such as *queer, fag*, and *dyke* are understood as "reclaimed" words with positive, proud meanings, whereas for older individuals these words remain extremely offensive and pejorative. The processes of narrative production within the sexual minority community reflect these age and cohort differences; for example, Karla identifies as a Dyke, but she uses Lesbian or Gay identity "when talking to older lesbians."

Private and Public Narratives: Private and Public Identities

Under traditional understandings of identity as a reflection of the essential self, any difference between privately held and publicly presented identities is taken as an indication that an individual has not yet finished the developmental process of sexual identity formation known as *coming out*. Such individuals are ostensibly at the stage of coming out in which they have personally realized their "true" sexual orientation—presumably a socially stigmatized orientation such as gay or lesbian—but are not yet prepared to acknowledge this true orientation to others. They are "in the closet," with the implication that their private identity is a true identity, whereas their public identity is dishonest and false.

Many individuals do experience their processes of narrative-building, which might include changes in identity as different identities are produced over time, as a process of coming out or of being in the closet. For example, Robert explained that he privately thinks of himself as Heterosexual, Bisexual, and Sexually Omnivorous, but he normally uses Heterosexual as an identity because "my bisexual nature is closeted." Similarly, Olga calls herself Queer because "It's a word I can use among gay men and lesbians without them knowing I'm bisexual."

However, some individuals who reported differences between their public and private identities did not characterize them as a reflection of the coming-out process or of coming out of the closet. Many respondents hold identities privately that they do not use when describing themselves to others because they simply would not be understood. For example, Ricky prefers a Polyfidelitous identity but doesn't "think many other people would understand what I [mean]," so he uses Bisexual "because I believe it translates well to most others."

These individuals' experiences show that the traditional interpretation of difference between private and public identities is incomplete. The concept of identity as a narrative product, which incorporates the distinction between personal micro- and metanarratives, offers a broader interpretation of difference between private and public identity. Public identities are constructed for audiences composed of others in particular social contexts; they are micronarratives designed for specific circumstances. Private identities, on the other hand, are the product of metanarratives that explain the self to the self. Metanarratives must reconcile one's multiple situation-specific micronarratives with each other, but they are not simply an amalgamation of these micronarratives because they must also account for any private experiences of the self that have not been revealed to others. In this view, differences between private and public identities are not—as traditional views of identity would characterize them—reflections of maturity or honesty, but reflections of the differences between the self as an audience and others as audiences.

The relationship between a narrative and an audience is mutually interactive. Whereas some individuals adapt their narratives to fit the constraints and possibilities of a given audience, other individuals purposefully construct their narratives—and their identities—with the intent of affecting an audience. For example, some individuals use identities for their political effects. Often the desired effect is visibility, either in heterosexual society or within the sexual minority community. For Justine, different identities function to increase visibility in different contexts; among lesbians and gay men, she uses Bisexual identity to enhance bisexual invisibility "because it is important to me that gay and lesbian folk see me as bisexual" and Queer identity to "resist the gay/lesbian stereotype that I am trying to pass as straight." However, among straights, where simply being a lesbian is a challenge to assumptions, she feels "less strongly about that...I let them assume when I say queer I mean lesbian." Similarly, Bonnie calls herself Bisexual "in political contexts like the gay liberation movement where I feel bi-visibility is necessary" and a Dyke "in political situations to combat homophobia, when I am angry about the patriarchy." Yolanda is Bisexual and Queer and calls herself a Bisexual Queer "to insist on recognition of bisexuals in the queer community." Ruth is attracted to both men and women and calls herself Bisexual "because I think it is important to assert that as a legitimate political/sexual identity."

When individuals consciously use sexual identity to affect their cultural environment, the processes by which individual narratives produce social narratives, which in turn produce historical narratives—that is, historical change—become particularly transparent. The individual process of self-narration, insofar as it is shared with others, always contains the potential to affect the social narrative. This is because, when shared, one person's personal narrative becomes part of the social context within which others are producing their own personal narratives. As these effects on the social context accumulate over time, the result is the cultural reconstruction of sexuality, that is, the production of a historical narrative.

Conclusion: The Self in Context

> I am Bisexual because I have fallen in love with both women and men. Politically I am Gay-identified, meaning I consider myself gay, not straight. My feminism has a very strong impact on this which is

why I am comfortable calling myself a Dyke (political meaning) but
not a Lesbian (a woman who is only with women).

—"Arlene," IBICIP study

Individuals whose sexualities do not fit into mainstream cultural categories of heterosexuality and gayness are the canaries of the sexual world. All
individuals live their lives moving between and among different social contexts within which sexuality is constructed in a multitude of different ways. For
individuals whose sexualities fit into widely accepted categories, the changes
in sexual meaning as one moves from one context to another do not often
require changes in the way they identify their sexualities; they inhabit a portion of the sexual landscape that remains relatively consistent from one context
to another. For example, a woman who identifies as a lesbian and has never
felt attracted to or had sex with a man can identify herself as a lesbian and
be understood as such in a variety of contexts. Although people in different
contexts—her family, her local gay bar, her conservative church—might have
different attitudes and beliefs with regard to her lesbian identity, the identity
itself has a currency of meaning that largely transcends these various contexts.
For such a person, whose identity is constant across context, it is easy to perceive the identity as a characteristic of the *self.* Traditional views of identity in
which identity is a static representation of an essential self reflect the experience of such individuals.

The canaries, however, are those who do not fit into these widely accepted
categories—individuals who have attractions to more than one gender or who
have histories of sexual contact with people of more than one sex—who live at
the fluid fringes of socially constructed meanings. Their sexualities are interpreted and classified differently in different contexts, which often causes them
to use more than one sexual identity either to describe their sexuality within a
cultural world that does not have a widely accepted label for their sexuality or to
meet the demands of the different social contexts within which they live their
lives. These individuals challenge traditional views of sexual identity—and the
sexual orientation that identity purports to reflect—as characteristics of the
self and experience firsthand their sexual identities as products of narrative
construction. As their daily life journeys take them through various contexts,
they must tell and retell their personal stories, differently in different contexts,
to make sense of themselves and to others in each context. For these individuals, an identity that makes sense and accurately reflects their sexuality in one
context might not be accurate, or might not even exist as an available identity,
in another context. They might have to use different identities in different contexts and tell their stories in different ways to support these different identities.

These individuals are aware that identity is a narrative product, produced for a given audience in a given social context. They exemplify the modern individual, who negotiates her or his sexual identity in multiple social contexts simultaneously, navigating a complex sexual landscape as she or he engages in the dynamic process of self-narration in a fluid, multidimensional social world.

NOTES

1. Names of respondents are pseudonyms.

2. Capitalization reflects usage of the term as an identity by the individual described. Respondents did not necessarily capitalize these terms themselves, even when they are capitalized within quotes.

REFERENCES

Bell, A. P., & Weinberg, M. S. (1978). *Homosexualities: A study of diversity among men and women.* New York: Simon & Schuster.

Binson, D., Michaels, S., Stall, R., Coates, T. J., Gagnon, J. H., & Catania, J. A. (1995). Prevalence and social distribution of men who have sex with men: United States and its urban centers. *Journal of Sex Research, 32,* 245–254.

Cohler, B. J., & Hammack, P.L. (2007). The psychological world of the gay teenager: Social change, narrative, and "normality." *Journal of Youth and Adolescence, 36,* 47–59.

Cook, K. (with Kretchmer, A., Nellis, B., Lever, J., & Hertz, R.). (1983, May). The *Playboy* readers' sex survey: Part three. *Playboy, 30,* 126–128, 136, 210–220.

Diamond, L. M. (2000). Sexual identity, attractions, and behavior among young sexual-minority women over a 2-year period. *Developmental Psychology, 36,* 241–250.

Fay, R. E., Turner, C. F., Klassen, A. D., & Gagnon, J. H. (1989, January 20). Prevalence and patterns of same-gender sexual contact among men. *Science, 243,* 338–347.

Fox, R. C. (2006). *Affirmative psychotherapy with bisexual women and bisexual men.* New York: Routledge.

Gonsiorek, J. C., Sell, R. L., & Weinrich, J. D. (1995). Definition and measurement of sexual orientation. *Suicide and Life-Threatening Behavior, 25,* 40–51.

Hammack, P. L. (2005). The life course development of human sexual orientation: An integrative paradigm. *Human Development, 48,* 267–290.

Hunt, M. (1974). *Sexual behavior in the 1970s.* Chicago: Playboy Press.

Janus, S. S., & Janus, C. L. (1993). *The Janus report on sexual behavior.* New York: Wiley.

Katz, J. N. (1990). The invention of heterosexuality. *Socialist Review, 20,* 7–34.

Katz, J. N. (1995). *The invention of heterosexuality.* New York: Dutton.

Katz, J. N. (1997). "Homosexual" and "heterosexual": Questioning the terms. In M. Duberman (Ed.), *A queer world: The center for lesbian and gay studies reader* (pp. 177–180). New York: New York University Press.

Kertbeny, K. M. (1869). Section 143 of the Prussian Penal Code of April 14, 1851, and its upholding of Paragraph 152 in the draft of a penal code for the North German Confederation. Open, expert letter to His Excellence Herr Dr. Leonhardt, Royal Prussian Minister of State and Justice, Berlin 1869. Reprinted in the *Jahrbuch für sexuelle Zwischenstufen* (Yearbook for sexual intermediate stages), 7(1).

Kinsey, A. C., Pomeroy, W. B., & Martin, C. E. (1948). *Sexual behavior in the human male*. Philadelphia: W. B. Saunders.

Kinsey, A. C., Pomeroy, W. B., Martin, C. E., & Gebhard, P. H. (1953). *Sexual behavior in the human female*. Philadelphia: W. B. Saunders.

Klein, F. (1993). *The bisexual option* (2nd ed.). New York: Harrington Park Press.

Klein, F., Sepekoff, B., & Wolf, T. J. (1985). Sexual orientation: A multi-variable dynamic process. *Journal of Homosexuality, 11*(1/2), 35–50.

Laumann, E. O., Gagnon, J. H., Michael, R. T., & Michaels, S. (1994). *The social organization of sexuality; Sexual practices in the United States*. Chicago: University of Chicago Press.

Rogers, S. M., & Turner, C. F. (1991). Male-male sexual contact in the U.S.A.: Findings from five sample surveys, 1970–1990. *Journal of Sex Research, 28*, 491–519.

Rust, P. C. (2001a). Make me a map: Bisexual men's images of bisexual community. *Journal of Bisexuality, 1*(2/3), 47–108.

Rust, P. C. (2001b). Two many and not enough: The meanings of bisexual identities. *Journal of Bisexuality, 1*(1), 31–68.

Seidman, S. (1991). *Romantic longings: Love in America*. New York: Routledge.

Shively, M. G., & De Cecco, J. P. (1977). Components of sexual identity. *Journal of Homosexuality, 3*, 41–48.

Smith, A. M. A., Rissel, C. E., Richters, J., Grulich, A. E., & de Visser, R. O. (2003). Sex in Australia: The rationale and methods of the Australian Study of Health and Relationships. *Australian and New Zealand Journal of Public Health, 27*(2), 106–117.

Smith, T. W. (1991). Adult sexual behavior in 1989: Number of partners, frequency of intercourse and risk of AIDS. *Family Planning Perspectives, 23*(3), 102–107.

Smith-Rosenberg, C. (1975). The female world of love and ritual: Relations between women in 19th century America. *Signs, 1*, 1–29.

Storms, M. D. (1978). Sexual orientation and self-perception. In P. Pilner, K. Blankstein, & I. Spiegel (Eds.), *Advances in the study of communication and affect: Perception of emotion in self and others* (pp. 165–180). New York: Plenum.

Trumbach, R. (1977). London's sodomites: Homosexual behavior and Western culture in the 18th century. *Journal of Social History, 2*, 1–33.

Ventegodt, S. (1998) Sex and the quality of life in Denmark. *Archives of Sexual Behavior 27*(3), 295–307.

Weinberg, M. S., Williams, C. J., & Pryor, D. W. (1994). *Dual attraction: Understanding bisexuality.* New York: Oxford University Press.

Welle, D. L., Fuller, S. S., Mauk, D., & Clatts, M.C. (2006). The invisible body of queer youth: Identity and health in the margins of lesbian and trans communities. *Journal of Lesbian Studies, 10,* 43–71.

6

Narrative Identity Construction of Black Youth for Social Change

Mollie V. Blackburn

So, my name is [Dara], and I'm 23 years old. I came out as a lesbian when I was 15. At the time I had just come out to my best friend, whom I had a crush on, and she had also had a crush on me so it wasn't a problem that I shared this information with her. Later on, maybe about a year later, I decided I wanted to come out to my immediate family, which consisted of my mother and my two younger sisters. Um, the reason why I wanted to come out to my mom, and my sisters, was because I didn't want to hide anything from them. And, I just didn't want to lie about who I was or whatever. So, my sisters were very supportive, and they continue to be. My mother, on the other hand wasn't very supportive. She just kind of, um, she thought that it was a phase, and, I think that I hurt her feelings, and it was just really hard for her to deal with. So, when I decided to come out to more people at school, I didn't have her support when things got really bad. So my eleventh grade year, I decided to tell more people, and my thought behind that was that I saw that most of my friends were developing close relationships with people, and, um, I wasn't doing that because I wasn't being honest, about who I am and all that. So, I felt kind of isolated, and, so, initially my isolation was because I wasn't sharing. Um, so I decided to come out to more people, and it just, it got out of hand, I was

harassed, and, um, I was called dyke and queer and all that stuff. I
cut classes a lot because I didn't want to deal with being called a dyke
and all that stuff. I didn't, some time I didn't go to school, uh, it was,
it was horrible.

(Dara, July 21, 1999)

Thus began the first working session between Dara and me. We had
known each other for over a year by this time because she was a youth at the
center where I worked, first as a volunteer, then as a staff member, and consistently as an ethnographer. The center is called the Attic, and it is a youth-run
center for lesbian, gay, bisexual, transgender and questioning (LGBTQ) youth
in Center City, Philadelphia. It serves diverse youth ranging in age from 12 to
23. At the time that I was there, the population consisted predominantly of
African American working-class young men. This was not, however, always
the case. Dara was a founding youth member and remembered when the Attic
served predominantly White youth.

Dara is an African American working-class lesbian; I am a White middle-class lesbian. Dara and I worked together in a variety of ways, one of
which was on the Attic's speakers' bureau. The speakers' bureau consists of a
group of youth who were hired and trained to conduct outreach to youth and
youth service providers to provide insights on how to work well with LGBTQ
youth. I served as an adult facilitator of this group. In this role, I worked
with speakers' bureau members, including Dara, to refine their coming-out
stories that were typically a part of their outreaches. In order to do this work,
I audiotaped the stories told by speakers' bureau members in our working
sessions and in our outreaches. I documented four versions of Dara's
coming-out story. These versions are the foundation of the study reported in
this chapter.

I begin by talking about how narratives, and counternarratives in particular, function in both emotive and ethico-political ways. Next, I consider the
narrative resources upon which a teller draws, such as coherence, multiplicity, and variability. I then examine scholarship on analyzing repeated tellings
before moving to Dara's repeated tellings of her narrative, which I analyze in
terms of functions, factors, and resources. I conclude by arguing that when
narratives that function both emotively and ethico-politically are repeated in
different contexts, for different audiences, and with different intents, the tellers have opportunities to draw on multiplicity and variability as they move
from incoherence to coherence, and thus they have great potential to work for
social change.

The Emotive and Ethico-Political Functions of Counternarratives

Most simply, personal narratives are "dramatized accounts of events as perceived by the speaker" (Labov, 2001, p. 89). Narratives, however, have tremendous effects. According to Carger (2005), personal narratives, or stories, represent the "most time-honored way in which cultures preserve the past and shape the future...the most fundamental way in which knowledge reveals itself" (p. 237). According to Mishler (1986), "narratives convey the ways that individuals attempt to arrive at a meaningful understanding of significant events in their lives" (p. 106). Thus, they preserve, present, and elucidate, but they also accomplish emotive and ethico-political work (Hogan, 2006).

The emotive accomplishments of narratives are evident by the ways in which respondents organize and make sense of their experiences and "find and speak in their own 'voices'" (Mishler, 1986, p. 118). Counternarratives, in particular, constitute and restore identities that are not always valued in society. Bacon (1998) argues that "In the case of coming out narratives,...the formulation of identity may serve a constitutive function, but it also serves to restore continuity and meaning to individual existence" (Bacon, 1998, p. 254). Similarly, Gilyard (1996) claims that counterstories have "healing qualities" (p. 99) for African Americans in particular. Narratives that function in such emotive ways, Hogan (2006) argues, are catalysts for action.

Mishler (1986) examines the relationship between narratives and action and asserts that one who is empowered through narrative will "not only...speak in one's own voice and tell one's own story, but...apply the understanding arrived at to action in accord with one's own interests" (p. 119). As such, narratives can effect "social change beginning with the individual and expanding into the greater community" (Phillion, He, & Connelly, 2005, p. 10). Moreover, counternarratives, by documenting the "feelings, beliefs, events, and practices of people who have been marginalized" (Chapman, 2006, p. 71), play a significant role in "counteract[ing] or challeng[ing] the dominant story" (Dixson & Rousseau, 2006, p. 35) and thus working for social change. For example, Wood (1999) argues that the life stories of queers "resist heterosexist boundaries" (p. 46). With respect to racism, Duncan (2006) shows how counterstories "provide potent counterpoints to challenge the existing narratives that shape how we understand" (p. 200) the experiences of people of color. Bloom (1998), in her application of feminism to narrative study, emphasizes that this political work is the point of counternarratives:

> One of the purposes of examining subjectivity in women's personal
> narratives is to redefine what it means for women to write, tell,

discuss, and analyze their life experiences against the backdrop of the prevailing discourses that seek to silence them. To change the master script is to change reality; to change reality is to participate in making a history different from the one the status quo would produce. (p. 64)

So, according to these scholars, the purpose of counternarratives is to accomplish ethico-political work.

I understand coming-out stories to be a kind of counternarrative. Instead of defying stereotypes of people of color (Chapman, 2006), or sometimes, as is the case with the narrative of focus in this chapter, *in addition to* defying race-based stereotypes, coming-out stories challenge heteronormativity. Such narratives accomplish, in Hogan's (2006) terms, both emotive and ethico-political work.

Coherence, Multiplicity, and Variability as Narrative Resources

There are serious obstacles, however, to the emotive and ethico-political work of narrative. All narratives are "'disciplined' by the diverse social circumstances and practices that produce them" (Holstein & Gubrium, 2000, p. 3). This discipline is particularly punishing (Foucault, 1975/1995) for those telling counternarratives because the tellers and their narratives, by definition, exist in a hostile context (Bacon, 1998; Orellana, 1999). With respect to African American tellers, Gilyard (1996) characterizes this dynamic as the "tension between expression and repression of the Black voice" (p. 102).

Bloom (1998) recognizes similar tensions in women's narratives as "tensions between conforming to and resisting hegemonic, feminist, heterosexist, and personal meanings of femaleness" (p. 102). Wood (1999) also sees analogous tensions in her study of narratives of deaf and hearing lesbians. She finds that "lesbian self-transformation stories are stories of resistance about women loving women" that are told "amid sexism and homophobia, facts that both constrain and provide resources for the realization of lesbian identities" (p. 48). That is to say, the stories are created, told, and heard in contexts that belittle both the stories and the tellers. One of the risks in telling such personal narratives is that "lesbians [for example] will be defined by those very forces that would deny their existence" (Bacon, 1998, p. 252). Tellers of counternarratives work within and against such tension, within and against that which oppresses them.

In order to make counternarratives possible, tellers draw on "culturally available resources in order to construct their stories" (Silverman, 2000,

p. 824). Wood (1999) claims that coherence, which she defines as "the logic invoked by [stories'] interactional and ideological context," is one available resource. She argues that coherence is "created by inferences, shared assumptions, and subsequent presuppositions that underlie the discourses of a community" (Wood, 1999, p. 47).

> Lesbians must therefore tell coming-out stories that index the pool of acceptable (that is, coherent) narrative selves, selves that are recognized as either conforming to or resisting heterosexist ideologies.
> (p. 48)

Notice that it is the *telling* that must be coherent rather than the *experience*. It is significant that Wood recognizes coherence not as a lived reality of the tellers but rather as a resource on which tellers draw in order to make " 'their actions explainable and understandable to those who otherwise may not understand' " (Miller & Glassner, 1997, p. 107; cited in Silverman, 2000, p. 824). In order for a teller to move a listener to social action, the listener must comprehend the teller's narrative in one way or another.

Another resource to consider is that of multiple and variable discourses, identities, and positions (Sawin, 1999). Barrett, for example, in his study of African American drag queens, found that the "polyphone of stylistic voices and identities they index serve to convey multiple meanings that may vary across contexts and speakers" (Barrett, 1999, p. 327). In other words, it was the multiplicity and variability of his respondents' discourses and identities that served them well.

Based on her study of coming-out narratives, Bacon (1998) advocates for narratives that allow for "multiple, perhaps even contradictory selves" (p. 258). In my own study of queer youth and schools, I found that youth who were able to claim multiple subject positions were better able "to understand power as circulating and to work against the oppressions in their lives" (Blackburn, 2007, p. 51). Stories told in ways that draw on the resources of multiplicity and variability of discourses, identities, and positions evade the dilemma of their stories being understood only relative to the normative and reflect more accurately the complicated nature of lived experience.

The two resources of coherence and multiplicity may seem mutually exclusive, as if the demand for coherence negates the possibilities of multiplicity and variability (Bloom, 1998; Kaufman, 2006; Roof, 1996). My analysis of four versions of Dara's narrative shows, however, that these resources are not contradictory. Rather, they are necessarily complementary, particularly in efforts at social change.

Analyzing Repeated Tellings

A variety of scholars call for the study of repeated tellings (Bloom, 1998; Chafe, 1998; Mishler, 2004; Schiffrin, 2003). In Chafe's (1998) study of repeated tellings, he illustrates how an investigator might move from four tellings to get at the underlying experience with a figure like Figure 6-1.

I am less interested, however, in what the tellings reveal of the underlying experiences and more interested in how "contexts, audiences, and intentions" (Mishler, 2004, p. 118) influence the tellings and thus the function of those tellings. In order to capture the focus of this study, I have modified Chafe's illustration of the relationship between the tellings and the underlying experience by adding the factors of context, audience, and intention (Mishler, 2004); the resources of coherence (Wood, 1999) and multiplicity and variability (Sawin, 1999) between the tellings and the experience; and the emotive and ethico-political functions (Hogan, 2006) beyond the tellings. I have also changed the direction of the arrows to indicate my particular interest as leading toward the kinds of work narratives accomplish and away from the underlying experience. The resulting figure looks like Figure 6-2.

In an effort to analyze Dara's narrative, I initially reviewed my field notes taken on the days of the recordings, listened to the four audiotapes, and indexed the content. Then I identified parts significant to the study at hand and transcribed those parts. The field notes allowed me to identify the context, audience, and intention of each of the tellings. From all four of the tapes, I sought a general overview of Dara's coming-out story. I used my indices and transcripts to chart the components of each version of Dara's narrative. By *components*, I mean parts of her story as lived experience rather than generic components

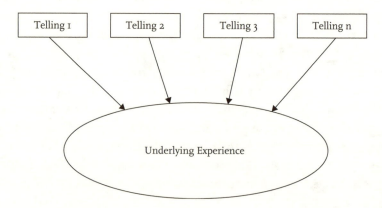

FIGURE 6-1

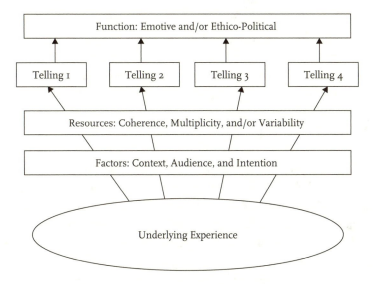

FIGURE 6-2

of a narrative. I then noted the parts that were similar across all four versions, the parts that were in some versions but not others, and the parts that were unique to particular versions (as recommended by Chafe, 1998). Next, I analyzed these patterns and discrepancy in patterns with the notions of resources (coherence, multiplicity, and variability) and functionality (emotive and ethico-political) in mind. Ultimately, my analysis considers how Dara negotiated various contexts, audiences, and intentions by using the resources of coherence, multiplicity, and variability in her narrative so that it functioned in both emotive and ethico-political ways and thus worked for social change.

Four Versions of Dara's Narrative

The four versions of Dara's narrative that comprise the data for this study were documented across approximately one year and nine months. During this time, she was mentored by a range of adults, including White gay men and lesbians and lesbians of color. She also worked with increasingly queer youth of color. Her status at the Attic shifted from youth employee (for the first three tellings) to adult employee (for the fourth telling). Her growth across this time was supported by regular counseling and a return to college. Much of her support developed as a result of her relationship with people at the Attic.

The first version, with which I began this chapter, was provided at a working session involving just the two of us at the Attic. The purpose of the session was to refine Dara's coming-out story for future outreaches. Dara expressed a desire to include more of her feelings in her story. Approximately a month later, I audiotaped an outreach in which she told another version of her story for local teachers of writing at a prestigious private university. The intention of this outreach was to demonstrate to teachers of writing ways in which they could better support their LGBTQ students.

A month after the working session, I audiotaped an outreach that included Dara telling her story to a class of preservice English teachers at the same university. As in the previous outreach, the intention was to teach English teachers ways in which they could better support their LGBTQ students. One of the instructors of the course, though, had asked that the members of the speakers' bureau include other aspects of their identities, such as race and class, in their stories. The fourth version was audiotaped approximately a year and a half later at another outreach, but this one was for a class of students preparing to be nurses at a local public university. For this outreach, the instructor of the course asked members of the speakers' bureau to talk about the impact of race and class on LGBTQ youth. All four of these versions included both a performance portion and a portion in which Dara responded to direct questions (Mishler, 2004).

There was remarkable consistency across all four versions of Dara's narrative. For example, in each of them, she began by introducing herself and stating her age. She talked about how she came out to her best friend when she was 15, when they realized that they had a mutual crush on each other, even though both of the girls had boyfriends. She described coming out to more people in her high school and being harassed for doing so. She also always mentioned the role of the Attic in her life.

There are some slight variations among the four tellings. In three of them, Dara talked about coming out to her sisters and mother, attending a high school for the creative and performing arts, the inadequacy of her high school counselor, being a vocal major there, and the significance of music in her life. In two of the four tellings, she talked about feeling different in middle school, not knowing the words to describe her difference but being teased as a result of it, and her efforts to conform to norms, particularly those defined by gender and sexuality.

For each telling, Dara modified her account for the context, the audience, and her intentions. For example, for the outreach to teachers of writing, she talked about using a male pseudonym when writing about her girlfriend in her journal that her teacher graded in an effort to conceal her attraction to other girls. In the outreach for preservice teachers of English, she talked about how her English curricula failed to represent her as a lesbian and how that impacted her performance in English classes. The focus of this chapter, though, is on the resources Dara used to incorporate the significance of race and class in her story and the emotive and ethico-political consequences for doing so, particularly how her story worked for social change.

Telling 1: Working Session

In the first documented version of her narrative, Dara and I met for approximately one hour in July 1999 at the Attic. I began by asking her whether there was anything she wanted me to help her work on with respect to her coming-out story, and she said:

> My feelings. I don't talk a lot about my feelings.... Because I think that that's important to say how I felt in these things. It's not that I'm consciously doing that. It's just what happens. I've told the story so many times.

Then she told me a clear and concise version of her coming-out story that she typically told on speakers' bureau outreaches. (This version serves as the introduction to this chapter.) She was well practiced at talking about her coming out as lesbian, and this was evident. I then asked her questions about various aspects of her story, particularly about her feelings related to the events she was sharing, and she discussed her story in greater detail with a focus on her feelings. Among many other details, she alluded to grappling with whether she self-identified, at the time of the telling, as either lesbian or bisexual:

D: I think it's really hard for me to say that I'm bisexual.

M: Yeah.

D: For a long time, I identified, I identified myself as gay and lesbian and...

M: To shift identity is hard. I think...

D: Well, were you here on Friday when we were doing the truth, truth

M: True, true, false thing? Yeah.

D: Yeah. Well, I was going to put in there bisexual, and that would have been a big deal.

M: Really? That would have been a good one. It would've stirred things up.

D: It would've. But I didn't. I don't know. It's weird. It's like coming out again almost.

Thus, Dara referenced her variable identities, particularly sexual identities, not in her story but in the discussion of it. She did not, however, refer to her racial and class-based identities. Because she told her narrative in a face-to-face interaction, I could make a reasonable interpretation of her racial identity as African American, and because I had known her for over a year by that time, such an interpretation was unnecessary. She claimed her African American identity freely and regularly. However, the words in this version of her narrative do not allude to her race or her class-based identity.

After we discussed her story, we talked about a plan for refining her story with her desired focus on feelings and turned off the tape recorder. The working session, however, was not complete. After the recorder was turned off, Dara wondered aloud whether to include her race and class identities in her story. I turned the recorder on again, and we got back to work.

In this portion of the working session, Dara began by saying, "So, I grew up in North Philadelphia," and I immediately asked her to characterize the neighborhood. She began again: "So, I grew up in North Philadelphia. North Philadelphia where I grew up was, there were a lot of, not, there were drugs." I then asked her to talk about race and class more explicitly in the neighborhood in which she was raised, and she named her neighborhood as predominantly African American, poor, and working class. She then characterized her family in class terms and relatively positively:

> My family, my mom's family is working class.... But I'm not sure
> though, in a way. I don't know what defines working class. My grand-
> father works a lot. He owns property. He's always made sure he had
> enough and then some.

As such, she described the maternal side of her family as working or middle class. In talking about her family and community, though, her identity as an African American seemed hardly worth mentioning, not because it was insignificant but because it was omnipresent. Instead, her sexual identity stood out in North Philadelphia, where she did not know any lesbians at the time that she came out. In contrast, once she came out and started attending gay functions, she found that there were few lesbians or people of color at the events. She said, "I would be the only African American lesbian or woman of color there."

I commented on the apparent isolation in both contexts, which she said was "really important" to her and triggered her statement that the local lesbian bar did not "cater to African American women, and they get a lot of people who are African American that come there, [but] they don't have African American staff." At the time, the bar regularly posted signs indicating that the managers were hiring staff. Dara applied twice but never received any response, even though, as she stated, "I know that I'm qualified." She told this to a girl whom she was dating and whom she did not name in racial terms. According to Dara, the girl responded by asking rhetorically and sarcastically, "Yeah, well, why don't you call the NAACP [National Association for the Advancement of Colored People]?" Dara acknowledged that she was infuriated by the comment because the girl was implicitly telling her to stop complaining about the fact that the local lesbian bar was racist, since the NAACP was as homophobic as the bar owner was racist. From Dara's perspective, this experience suggested that, as an African American lesbian, there was nowhere for her to be free of hatred.

In this second portion of our working session, Dara revealed that the significance of her multiple identities had varied over time. She said:

> For a while I thought that my gay identity was just as important as
> my African American identity, and I don't feel that way anymore.
> I thought everything was kind of equal, but it is really not like
> that.... As far as like basic needs and politically, I really feel like my
> African American identity and my identity as a working-class person
> is very important.

Much like Black feminists in the Combahee River Collective (1977/1982), Dara came to understand the power of her race and class identities in her life as a lesbian. Therefore, we agreed that her racial and class-based identities were important to include in her narrative, and I agreed to work on possible ways of incorporating them. I studied the audiotape of our discussion and suggested that she either revise her story entirely in ways that would allow her to foreground discussions of race and class or maintain her basic story and add more of her feelings to it. I drafted brief outlines for each of those possibilities based on what we had talked about in our working session. I put the revised story with a focus on race first, trying to encourage her to pursue it.

In this working session, she took the time to describe her various identities, first as having once worked hard to claim a straight identity, then identifying as lesbian, then as bisexual, and finally encompassing her multiple identities as an African American working-class lesbian. In doing so, her story was literally fragmented. She told her coming-out story; then we discussed it and her changing sexual identities; finally, we turned off the tape recorder, only to turn it back on to discuss her racial and class-based identities. Here, Dara drew on the resource of coherence during her brief coming-out story, but for the remainder of the telling (the majority of it) she drew on the resources of multiplicity and variability.

Tellings 2 and 3: Outreaches to Teachers

The first two outreaches took place in the next two months at the prestigious private university where I was a doctoral student at the time. The first of these outreaches was for a group of teachers who were becoming part of the Philadelphia chapter of the National Writing Project. I knew several of the teachers present as a result of our mutual affiliation with the university.

In this outreach, Dara's story was very similar to the one that begins this chapter and began our working session the previous month. As in the earlier version, she drew on the resource of coherence rather than multiplicity and variability. She talked about coming out as a lesbian and did not mention any contemplation of a bisexual identity. She did not talk about her sexual identity in relation to race and class identities. She did, however, make one change that I failed to notice at the time but can now interpret as the start of a version of her story that included race and class. After stating her name and age, she said, "I grew up in North Philadelphia." Insignificant as this sentence may seem, it was, for her, code for growing up in an African American poor working-class community. Because the audience consisted of local teachers, perhaps the explicit naming of her racial and class background was not imperative. Still, this telling, unlike the fourth one, lacked an insightful discussion of the tensions between her community of origin and local gay and lesbian communities.

The following outreach, two months after the working session and one month after the outreach for the Writing Project, was for a class of preservice secondary English teachers for which I was a teaching assistant. In this version of her story, Dara included the same general components of the earlier versions but with a significant addition. Dara referenced where she grew up at the beginning of her telling but then, unlike in the previous versions, she described her family. She depicted them primarily as a "very musical family." She said that she "lived in a house of about 12 people, which include my mom, my two sisters, my father, and his brothers and sisters, and some random people." Her parents divorced when she was in fifth grade, and her mother moved with her daughters "up the street" to live with Dara's maternal grandparents. She said:

> So my mom at the time was going to school and trying to get her GED and maybe get a job at some point. So, when I was in the fifth grade I went to a school outside of my neighborhood because my mom didn't want me to go to a neighborhood school. So, during that time, I was dealing with being in a new school and my parents' divorce.

Here she reveals her mother's shifting priorities in schooling, both for herself and for Dara.

This literal move "up the street" signals a move from a poor to a working-class household. The move from her neighborhood school to a magnet school was a move from a school with mostly African American students to a more racially diverse school. Thus, in this version of her narrative, Dara allocated a significant portion (25%) of her telling to an implicit discussion of her race and class background. Here, Dara relied on the resource of coherence and incorporated some details about her racial and class-based identities, albeit in coded ways.

It was in Dara's response to direct questions (Mishler, 2004), which followed the coming-out stories, that she explicitly discussed her race and class identities. Several people in the class had asked questions to which speakers' bureau members responded. Then, there was a distinct pause. At this point, Dara said:

> I also, I know, I know that Mollie brought up that we should, if we
> wanted, to talk about race and class issues, and I know that when I
> first came out, until maybe a few years ago, it was all about being
> gay, and nothing else. And, it wasn't that I wasn't aware that I was
> African American or anything like that, it was just like, well, okay,
> I'm African American and, I can deal with that when I go home,
> or I can deal with that when I go see my parents, or whatever. I
> don't have to deal with that here, at the Attic, or any other gay place.
> And then I started noticing that, I really do have to deal with that,
> especially in the gay community, and that has become like a really
> important part of my life, and, I remember when I was about 17
> and I went on this show...and they asked the question, "Is it more
> important, is your gay identity more important than your African
> American identity?" and I said, well, me being, I'm not even going
> to say about the age thing, but me just being the person that I was
> then, I was like, "Well, both of them are important." And, right
> now, I feel like, I don't feel that way. I feel like people see me as this
> African American woman/tomboy-looking person, but they don't see
> me as a lesbian first and foremost, and I would have to say that my
> African American identity is a lot more important to me, and, my
> social class. So.

This contribution to the discussion was longer than the segment of her coming-out story that was focused on her family; it was approximately one third of the total length of her coming-out story. The start of this piece, in which she said, "I know that Mollie brought up that we should, if we wanted, to talk about race and class issues," does not suggest that I brought race- and class-based identities to her attention. Race and class identities were likely salient to her long before they were to me, given what we know about the delayed conscious-ness of privileged identities by those embodying those identities. What the start of the story reveals, though, is apprehension about whether race and class were appropriate to discuss in the context of an outreach, particularly this out-reach, in which the audience was predominantly White and the setting was an expensive private school. This statement pointing to me provided Dara with a way to discuss race and class, a way that was sanctioned at least by me, who had a limited degree of authority in both the speakers' bureau and the class. What followed was similar to what she said in the second portion of our work-ing session about the shifting significance of her multiple identities, with the added benefit of some contextualization. After she finished, there was another notable pause followed by a question from a student on a very different topic.

Early in this outreach, then, Dara drew on the resource of coherence to tell her coming- out story in which she included a coded discussion of her race and class identities, but later in the outreach, she sacrificed coherence and instead drew on the resources of multiplicity to provide a more accurate sense of her lived experience as an African American working-class lesbian.

Telling 4: Outreach to Nursing Students

The fourth documented version of Dara's narrative took place approximately a year and a half later in an outreach for a class of nursing students at a public university near the community in which Dara was raised. At the request of the instructor, the outreach was designed to examine race and racism in LGBTQ communities. Therefore, Dara was responding to a direct question rather than performing more generally (Mishler, 2004). I was not present at the outreach, but Dara audiotaped it for me because of my interest in the focus.

This version included many of the details given in the earlier versions, but it was a complete revision that foregrounded discussions of race. In this version of her narrative, Dara said her name, her age, and where she was from, this time naming the specific intersection within North Philadelphia. She deleted the sections of her narrative about middle school and her high school coun-selor, but she talked about her high school, being a vocal major, and coming out to her best friend and to her family. She talked about coming out at school and the repercussions. This led her to an account I had never heard before:

> So, high school was a mess, and I remember one day coming home, and I decided to go to my aunt's house, and she was asking me what was going on with me and why were my grades so bad, and, and why

was I upset all the time, and she, she said, "Is it a problem with your boyfriend?" and I said, "No," and she said, "Is it a problem with your girlfriend?" like, but she was joking, and I said, "Yeah." And she laughed, and she was like, "Oh my god, this is crazy," and then she made this comment of "What White person introduced you to that?" and, and I was just like "Whoah." You know, that was kind of, not cool. And I didn't, I didn't know how to respond to that.

In this account, Dara provided a specific, coherent illustration of the isolation she experienced in her family and community as a result of being attracted to other women. Moreover, she included it in her story in a coherent way. She connected this account first to being harassed in school for being out as a lesbian and then to the way this experience, in which her "aunt made a comment about gay being a White thing," created an obstacle that prevented her from "dealing with my ethnicity, you know, I'm not dealing with being a person of color." As a result, Dara "tried to move away from [dealing with being a person of color] as much as possible" and instead just focused on being gay.

This focus, she said, was supported by "the gay community," in which people supported her acceptance of her sexual identity but allowed for her rejection of her African American identity. Her own racial stereotypes and the racism of the gay community, however, became visible to her in this context. Scholars of racial identity development argue that "African Americans can have negative stereotypes of Blacks (miseducation) that do not reflect self-hatred" (Vandiver, Fhagen-Smith, Cokley, Cross, & Worrell, 2001, p. 197). Rather, they reflect, as the parenthetical word suggests, the miseducation of African Americans that "results in individuals questioning their own worth as a Black person" (p. 177). With respect to Dara's stereotypes, she said:

I started to notice that some of the things I was rejecting about myself, like, when we started getting a lot of African American males started coming to the Attic, some of the things I rejected about myself, they exhibited, like my family were really loud and all this stuff, so I was dealing with that, and I saw that. You know, I saw that side, it made me face some of that, how I stereotype myself and my community.

Her reflection on this self-rejection showed that she had developed an awareness of this rejection and moved away from it. That is to say, in naming and discussing her own stereotypes in this version of her narrative, Dara worked to change them.

Concerning racism in the gay community, Dara said, "I started to notice, well, where is all the lesbians of color?... And then I noticed that we weren't talking about race and class issues in the gay community." The absence of people and conversation made her feel isolated again. She said:

> I didn't feel a part of that, because those are the things that I was
> dealing with. I was dealing with being poor. I was dealing with not
> seeing myself being represented. I was dealing with, with, well, like
> I said, not seeing myself represented as a person of color.

She provided three examples of the disjuncture she experienced as a result of being a person of color among LGBTQ people.

In the first example, she talked about her work at a cabaret, where the clients were predominantly gay White men. She said, "They wouldn't hand me their money, even though I was the person, you know, they had to like go through me. They would just kind of throw their money at me." In this context, gay White men treated her, as an African American lesbian, as if she either was not there or did not deserve to be treated with recognition and respect.

The second example related to local politics. Many gay people rejected a mayoral candidate, who was African American, because he did not support the recognition of domestic partnerships. The rival candidate, a White man, did but had made a collection of political decisions and moves that was not a "good thing for the African American people," according to Dara. She said:

> I felt that the reasons why the gay community didn't want [the
> African American mayoral candidate] was because he was against
> domestic partnership, when I felt like, as far as race and class issues,
> you know, if I don't have a job, why am I worried about domestic
> partnership? You know what I mean? People who don't have money
> aren't worried about those kind of things.

Here I understand her to say that people who do not have jobs or jobs with benefits do not have the luxury of voting for someone who is likely to offer domestic partnership benefits. They must, instead, vote for someone who is likely to improve their chances for employment or better employment. Therefore, she experienced a dramatic divide between herself and the gay community during this election year.

Her third example related to her work as a speakers' bureau member. She said that she did an outreach at a local teaching hospital with a gay White doctor. A student asked her "a question about how [she] saw people of color and people who were White and asked if people of color have a harder time coming out, as opposed to people who are White." She was unsure about how to respond, but the doctor gave the following answer: "The African American community is more homophobic, and so, it is hard for African American people to come out." Dara reflected on this experience in the context of this version of her narrative. She said:

> I was very upset with that because I don't feel like the African
> American community is more homophobic. I feel that, well, he said
> that it was because of the church, and I feel like it's about access and
> power and I feel like historically the African American community's
> access to power has been through the church and that the church
> is acting as, not a mouthpiece, but speaking for the community
> and that's what they're going to portray because it's a church. And,
> they're not really speaking for everyone in the African American
> community. And power looks very different in the African American
> community, as with different socioeconomic groups. If you're rich,
> then your access to power is very different than if you're poor. You're
> going to speak. Sometimes you're going to fight. For what you believe
> in in a very different way. You don't have access to government, like
> somebody who's rich or corporate or anything like that.

In this third example, she explicitly challenged a stereotype—that African American communities are more homophobic than, say, White communities.

Together, these three examples, as well as the account of Dara's conversation with her aunt, provided her listeners with insights regarding the tensions as she experienced between the communities in which she was raised and the one in which she was currently working in ways that the earlier versions of her narrative failed to do. In producing this counternarrative, Dara drew on the resources of coherence and multiplicity.

Functions, Factors, and Resources across the Tellings

Figure 6-3 takes the generic version of my modification of Chafe's (1998) figure and makes it specific to Dara's narrative. It delineates the factors and resources that influenced the telling and thus functioning of the four versions of Dara's narratives. Dara's coming out was the underlying experience for these four tellings. Across a variety of contexts, for distinct audiences and with a range of intentions, Dara drew on the resources of coherence, multiplicity, and even variability. My primary interest, though, is in how these four tellings functioned—that is, what sort of work they accomplished. More specifically, I am interested in whether the tellings accomplished emotive and/or ethico-political work.

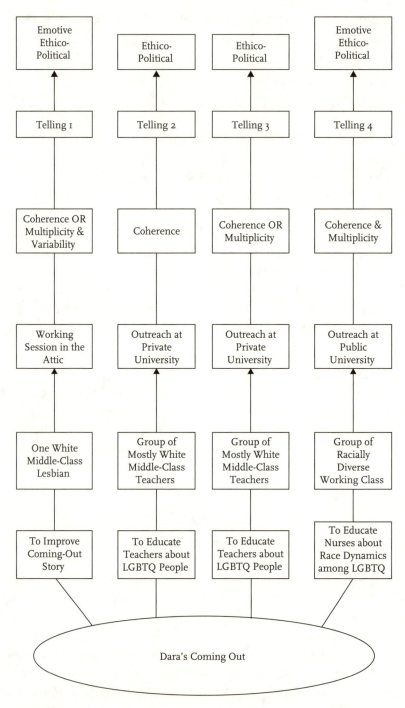

FIGURE 6-3

Functions

In the first version, Dara described how she felt about being the only lesbian in her community of origin and the only lesbian of color in her gay community. She also talked about her frustration with gay institutions that she perceived as racist, like the local lesbian bar, and with racially defined institutions that she perceived as homophobic, like the NAACP. This version allowed Dara to describe some of her feelings about being an African American lesbian; thus, it served an emotive purpose. The scope of its ethico-political work, however, was limited in two ways. Although this story revealed her feelings, she had not yet analyzed them enough to offer her insights on the tensions she was experiencing. Also, I was the only person privy to her exploration of feelings, so the number of people to be impacted by her discussion was limited.

In the second version Dara's audience was larger, but she did not discuss her multiple identities. In the third version, her audience was still larger, and she discussed the dynamics among sexual, racial, and class identities. As such, this telling functioned in an increasingly ethico-political way. However, the impact was both limited by its inaccessibility and problematic because of its potential to perpetuate stereotypes about poor and working-class African Americans. The portion of her telling that provided this disturbing potential accomplished some important emotive work regarding her feelings, thoughts, and beliefs about her race and class background. In this telling, she put into words her "internalization of negative stereotypes about Blacks" (Vandiver et al., 2001, p. 177), thus laying the foundation for the reflective work that appears in her fourth version. In her comment during the question-and answer-period of this outreach, Dara offered a more nuanced version of her experiences and understanding of the tensions of being an African American working-class lesbian, but it was still not as nuanced as the fourth version.

Dara's fourth version functioned in both emotive and ethico-political ways. As in the first version, Dara shared her feelings about being isolated in both her community of origin and her gay community. Also, as in her first version, she gave illustrative examples of how this isolation took shape in her life. Thus, this telling, like the first, functioned in emotive ways. However, unlike in previous versions, she closely examined these feelings and, based on her examination, she offered nuanced insights regarding the tensions of being an African American lesbian from a poor and working-class background, including a discussion of her negative stereotypes about Blacks that implies her efforts to combat them. She talked coherently and in front of a sizable audience. As such, this telling functioned in ethico-political ways. That this version functions in both emotive and ethico-political ways is its strength, as Hogan (2006) suggests.

Thus, the first and last tellings of Dara's narrative functioned most effectively in terms of their emotive work. The ethico-political work, however, increased across the four tellings. The difference between the emotive work and the progress of the ethico-political work was shaped by the variations of factors such as context, audience, and intention. Because of my interest in the emotive and ethico-political functioning of narratives, it is worthwhile to examine the factors and resources that surrounded the first and fourth versions as distinct from the second and third.

Factors

Mishler's (2004) factors—context, audience, and intent—distinguish the four versions. The first version was told in the queer-friendly context of the Attic and with a single person whom Dara had known for a year as the audience. Moreover, the purpose of the account was to help her improve her storytelling. These factors created an intimate telling in which Dara allowed herself to complicate the coherent version of her coming-out story by including her emotions and her race- and class-based identities. The intimacy, however, was likely limited by the fact that her one-person audience was a White middle-class educator.

The next three versions were told in invited outreaches at local universities. The invited nature of the outreaches suggested that at least the facilitators of the events were open to LGBTQ people. This did not necessarily indicate that all audience members shared that openness. Therefore, the outreaches did not necessarily offer a queer-friendly context. Thus, the versions told during the outreaches were not as intimate as the first version. This lack of intimacy was heightened in the second and third versions, which were presented at a local prestigious private university. The audiences were predominantly White, as well as middle class and upper middle class, particularly in the third telling. In both of these versions, the intent was to help teachers—a group of people who had not helped Dara very much when she was being harassed for not conforming to gender norms in middle school and self-identifying as lesbian in high school. As such, these two versions were likely the least intimate—the ones in which Dara was probably the most guarded.

The fourth version, however, was distinct from any of the previous three. It was presented at a local urban public university located near the neighborhood in which Dara was raised. As such, Dara was likely more comfortable in this context than in those of the previous two tellings. Furthermore, it is from this university that Dara ultimately graduated years later. Her comfort there was likely enhanced by the fact that the audience members were not White middle-class educators. Instead, this group was more diverse in terms of race and class and was preparing to become nurses. Moreover, the intent of the outreach was to help nurses better understand LGBTQ people and the racial diversity among them. So, Dara was invited to talk about a subject she had always known was important to her coming-out story but had not previously believed was appropriate to include in outreaches. In other words, when Dara was either in a queer-friendly setting or a setting with other working-class people of color, she was able to accomplish both emotive and ethico-political work through her tellings.

Resources

Across the four narratives, Dara drew most consistently on the resources of coherence and multiplicity and less on variability. In her first version, when she told the story she typically told on outreaches, her telling was clear, concise, and coherent, but when she tried to include her multiple identities, particularly those of race and class, her telling became literally fragmented, as highlighted by the break in our audiotaping. In the second version, she essentially sacrificed her discussion of multiple identities for coherence by focusing on her coming-out story. In her third version, though, she tried twice to include her multiple identities. Her first effort, in this version, was to incorporate her race and class identities into her coming-out story, but she did so in coded terms. As a result, it was difficult to understand. Her second effort came during the question-and- answer period when she waited for a pause and then talked about her race and class identities explicitly, but in ways that were not obviously connected to the discussion that preceded and followed her comments. The fourth version demonstrates how Dara effectively told a story of herself that was both coherent and representative of her multiple identities, thus illustrating that coherence and multiplicity are not mutually exclusive. As such, Dara became increasingly coherent in her efforts to reveal her multiple identities.

The question of variability, however, remains. In terms of race, her self-identification never revealed any variability across the four versions of her narrative, as well as across the years we worked together. The significance of her racial identity, though, did vary across time, as these four versions demonstrate. The variability of her sexual and class identities was evident in only one version of her narrative. She represented her sexual identities as variable when she grappled with whether she was lesbian or bisexual in the first documented version. Her variable class identities were also evident in this version when she vaguely alluded to her father's poverty, referred directly to her mother's working-class status, and hinted at her grandfather's middle-class status, as well as in the third version when she moved "up the street." In the fourth version of her narrative, though, none of this variability is named or even referenced. In Dara's narrative, as her coherence strengthened, her multiple identities stood strong but their variability did not.

Conclusion

Because the version of Dara's story that included her multiple identities became increasingly coherent and functioning, particularly in ethico-political terms, it seems to me that Dara needed opportunities to talk about her sexual, racial, and class-based identities in fragmented, incoherent, and even problematic ways in intimate spaces in order to be able to eventually craft a more coherent version that works against heterosexism, homophobia, racism, and classism. Based on these four versions of Dara's narrative, I argue that both emotive and ethico-political work requires factors that come together to create either an intimate or a comfortable space for tellers. Emotive work in narrative, however, often requires incoherence, particularly when incorporating multiple and perhaps variable identities. This emotive work is extremely significant to the teller, but it also lays the foundation for important ethico-political work (Hogan, 2006). Ethico-political work, however, often requires coherence because the listeners need to be able to access and make sense of stories in order to make changes in their lives and the lives of those around them. In other words, in shaping narratives that function in both emotive and ethico-political ways, coherence can be a resource, as Wood (1999) asserts. But incoherence can also serve as a resource, particularly when working to incorporate multiple and perhaps variable identities.

For narratives to work effectively for social change, their many versions must be told and heard. They must accomplish both emotive and ethico-political work. They can do so by being told and heard in intimate and comfortable spaces. Narratives must allow for incoherence but move toward coherence, even at the risk of being artificially linear. Such narratives, as Dara's illustrate, do not negate the possibility of drawing on multiplicity as a resource. In moving from incoherent tellings to coherent ones, tellers have opportunities to draw on the resources of multiplicity and variability while accomplishing both emotive and ethico-political work against not only heterosexism and homophobia but also racism and classism. Now, *this* is promising.

Acknowledgment

Many thanks to Adrienne D. Dixson and Trisha Niesz for reading an early draft of this chapter and offering invaluable insights for revision.

REFERENCES

Bacon, J. (1998). Getting the story straight: Coming out narratives and the possibility of a cultural rhetoric. *World Englishes, 17*(2), 249–258.

Barrett, R. (1999). Indexing polyphonous identity in the speech of African American drag queens. In M. Bucholtz, A. C. Liang, & L. A. Sutton (Eds.), *Reinventing identities: The gendered self in discourse* (pp. 313–331). New York: Oxford University Press.

Blackburn, M. V. *(2007)*. Gender rules and regulations as experienced and negotiated by queer youth. *Journal of Gay and Lesbian Issues in Education, 4*(2), 33–54.

Bloom, L. R. (1998). *Under the sign of hope: Feminist methodology and narrative interpretation.* Albany: State University of New York Press.

Carger, C. L. (2005). The art of narrative inquiry. In J. Phillion, M. F. He, & F. M. Connelly (Eds.), *Narrative and experience in multicultural education* (pp. 231–245). Thousand Oaks, CA: Sage.

Chafe, W. (1998). Things we can learn from repeated tellings of the same experience. *Narrative Inquiry, 8,* 269–285.

Chapman, T. K. (2006). Pedaling backward: Reflections of *Plessy* and *Brown* in Rockford public schools de jure desegregation efforts. In A. D. Dixson & C. K. Rousseau (Eds.), *Critical race theory in education: All God's children got a song* (pp. 67–88). New York: Routledge.

Combahee River Collective (1977/1982). The Combahee River Collective statement. In B. Smith (Ed.), *HOMEGIRLS: A Black feminist anthology* (pp. 272–282). New York: Kitchen Table: Women of Color Press.

Dixson, A. D., & Rousseau, C. K. (2006). And we are still not saved: Critical race theory in education ten years later. In A. D. Dixson & C. K. Rousseau (Eds.), *Critical race theory in education: All God's children got a song* (pp. 31–54). New York: Routledge.

Duncan, G. A. (2006). Critical race ethnography in education: Narrative, inequality, and the problem of epistemology. In A. D. Dixson & C. K. Rousseau (Eds.), *Critical race theory in education: All God's children got a song* (pp. 191–212). New York: Routledge.

Foucault, M. (1995). *Discipline and punish: The birth of the prison.* New York: Random House. (Original work published 1975)

Gilyard, K. (1996). *Let's flip the script: An African American discourse on language, literature, and learning.* Detroit: Wayne State University Press.

Hogan, P. C. (2006). Continuity and change in narrative study: Observations on componential and functional analysis. *Narrative Inquiry, 16*(1), 66–74.

Holstein, J. A., & Gubrium, J. F. (2000). *The self we live by: Narrative identity in a postmodern world.* New York: Oxford University Press.

Kaufman, J. (2006). Heteronarrative analysis: A narrative method for analyzing the formation of gender identity. *Qualitative Inquiry, 12*(6), 1139–1153.

Labov, W. (2001). The anatomy of style-shifting. In P. Eckert & J. R. Rickford (Eds.), *Style and sociolinguistic variation* (pp. 85–108). New York: Cambridge University Press.

Miller, J. & Glassner, B. (1997). The 'inside' and the 'outside': Finding realities in interviews. In D. Silverman (Ed.), *Qualitative Research* (pp. 99–112). London: Sage Publications.

Mishler, E. G. (1986). *Research interviewing: Context and narrative.* Cambridge, MA: Harvard University Press.

Mishler, E. G. (2004). Historians of the self: Restorying lives, revising identities. *Research in Human Development, 1*(1&2), 101–121.

Orellana, M. F. (1999). Good guys and "bad" girls: Identity construction by Latina and Latino student writers. In M. Bucholtz, A. C. Liang, & L. A. Sutton (Eds.), *Reinventing identities: The gendered self in discourse* (pp. 64–82). New York: Oxford University Press.

Phillion, J., He, M. F., & Connelly, F. M. (2005). The potential of narrative and experiential approaches in multicultural inquiries. In J. Phillion, M. F. He, & F. M. Connelly (Eds.), *Narrative and experience in multicultural education* (pp. 1–14). Thousand Oaks, CA: Sage.

Roof, J. (1996). *Come as you are: Sexuality and narrative.* New York: Columbia University Press.

Sawin, P. E. (1999). Gender, context and the narrative construction of identity: Rethinking models of "women's narrative." In M. Bucholtz, A. C. Liang, & L. A. Sutton (Eds.), *Reinventing identities: The gendered self in discourse* (pp. 241–258). New York: Oxford University Press.

Schiffrin, D. (2003). We knew that's it: Retelling the turning point of a narrative. *Discourse Studies, 5*(4), 535–561.

Silverman, D. (2000). Analyzing talk and text. In N. K. Denzin & Y. S. Lincoln (Eds.), *Handbook of qualitative research* (2nd ed., pp. 821–834). Thousand Oaks, CA: Sage.

Vandiver, B. J., Fhegen-Smith, P. E., Cokley, K. O., Cross, W. E., Jr., & Worrell, F. C. (2001). Cross's nigrescence model: From theory to scale to theory. *Journal of Multicultural Counseling and Development, 29,* 174–200.

Wood, K. M. (1999). Coherent identities amid heterosexist ideologies: Deaf and hearing lesbian coming out stories. In M. Bucholtz, A. C. Liang, & L. A. Sutton (Eds.), *Reinventing identities: The gendered self in discourse* (pp. 46–63). New York: Oxford University Press.

PART III

Identities in Process

Stories of Risk and Relationships

7

Between Kansas and Oz

Drugs, Sex, and the Search for Gay Identity in the Fast Lane

Steven P. Kurtz

The Scene

At midnight on a dark street in downtown Miami, small groups of men are beginning to congregate at the entrance to an old warehouse. Most are wearing tank tops or are already shirtless, and shaven chests with gym-built muscles are on display. The crowd grows quickly. By 1:30 A.M. it will take an hour or more to enter past the velvet rope. A Saturday night ritual has begun. Once inside, men head for either of two small barrooms that are open at that hour; only when these spaces are packed to their limit will the party begin. Most men order a $5 bottle of water and stand talking among friends while they "pre-heat," allowing the Ecstasy tablet they have ingested to bring on its warm, energetic glow. Others, already high on crystal methamphetamine or cocaine, are more animated. A television monitor above the bar entertains those who have come alone with videos of men having sex.

At 12:30 A.M., security guards remove the ropes from the entrances to the main room and the crowd pours out of the small bars and into the two-story dance club. The music is suddenly and thunderingly energetic; a drag queen opens with a lip-sync of a Madonna dance sensation. By 1 A.M., the party is in full swing. The energy of the music is reflected in the gyrations of the muscled go-go dancers perched on tiny platforms at the corners of the room. Some revelers carry multicolored laser-beam flashlights to shine on others who particularly catch their eye; others sport plastic liquid-filled tubes that glow in phosphorescent pastels. The mood is festive.

The dance floor is interrupted by a single central structural column where a handwritten sign uses arrows to direct "'muscle boys' to the left, 'losers' to the right." It is not possible to know whether the sign reflects someone's observed or desired reality, but the briefest inspection confirms that one side of the floor is packed with the "in" crowd: shirtless 25- to 45-year-old men who have worked hard to develop "six-pack abs" and big pecs. The other side of the floor, in front of the stage, is less densely inhabited by a more diverse group of men—men with shirts, skinnier and heavier men, older and younger men. On a platform next to the stage, a lone young blonde kid dances his heart out—he will still be there at 10 A.M., closing time.

As the Ecstasy "kicks in" across the floor of the packed house, the crowd is joyful. Men who have never met smile to each other; some share a dance, an embrace, or a sexual touch. The denseness of the crowd forces bodies against bodies; the inhibition-reducing properties of the drugs ensure that no one cares. The disc jockey spins the sound of a rhythmic whistle to signal that it is time for a "train," a simultaneous and sexually charged embrace of many men in a line, some facing forward, some backward, some friends, some strangers—a symbol of the universality of gay brotherly/loverly love.

At 3 A.M. the music shifts gears, slowing to announce the approach of a stage performance. The lights begin to brighten, the undercurrents of a gay disco classic are heard, and—suddenly—a fat bald man wearing a thong and bikini top makes his entrance. Her eyes are made up with glittering blue and green eyeliner, and the shaven eyebrows are replaced with multicolored streaks that are drawn up beyond his original hairline. The diva's only prop is a large toy headset, something that might be worn in a *Star Trek* movie. The song is "Love Will Save the Day." Muscle boys from the far side of the floor begin to congregate with the "losers" in front of the stage. Hoots and whistles fill the air. As the song moves toward its crescendo, the diva turns his back to the crowd, allowing the anticipation to build. The throng, hands in the air and eyes wide with drug-assisted awe, prepares for the finish. As the last refrain approaches, the fat man comes within inches of the edge of the stage, rips off the headset, opens her eyes wide, and, leaning down into the crowd, screams the message to them one last time: "LOVE WILL SAVE THE DAY." She closes quickly, and the crowd roars their approval.

The men drift back to their designated spaces and the music shifts to deep, heavy-bass mixes, seemingly signaling that it is time for "refreshment," as the drug high has become somewhat brittle for many. Small groups of friends gather to pass around glass vials from which to snort bumps of powdered ketamine or add a bit of gamma-hydroxybutyrate (GHB) to their drink. The lines for the bathroom stalls grow exponentially with those who want to ingest another dose of cocaine or crystal in privacy. The bartenders are confronted by a crush of customers, as some men switch to cocktails and others buy more water. As the night wears on, the search for someone to go home with appears more urgent. Single men cruise the balconies and hallways in search of a partner for the night. The action in the bathrooms increases: the seductive display of semierect penises at the urinals; several people having sex in the stalls; romantic liaisons in the lounges.

As some men begin to trickle out of the club, others are still arriving, and the space remains crowded for several more hours. By the time the disk jockey plays the opening lines of "The Party's Over," most of the men remaining on the dance floor seem oblivious to the impending close. Precisely at 10 A.M., bright lights fill the club as though it were midday. The music stops. The club is silent. Security guards probe every corner for the "crashed" bodies of those who got a little too high. Men gradually recover their bearings and head for the exit doors.

The Setting

Miami, Florida, is a very diverse community, having a large population of foreign-born (50.9%) residents (U.S. Census Bureau, 2000). Hispanics (60.0%) are the largest ethnic group, with the balance about equally split between "Anglos" (non-Hispanic Whites) and African Americans/Caribbeans. As a major gateway for international tourism and trade as well as a popular adult-oriented entertainment destination in its own right, metropolitan Miami lies amid a constant stream of vacationers, transients, temporary residents, immigrants, and political and economic refugees from across the globe.

Miami became a key migration point for gay men from the northeastern United States during the worst years of the acquired immune deficiency syndrome (AIDS) epidemic in the mid-1980s, before the availability of pharmaceutical treatments for the disease. Many of these men were "AIDS retirees" who came to south Florida expecting one grand but final party (Albin, 1995). Ecstasy, ketamine, GHB, and crystal methamphetamine became new sources of pleasure and escape in this traditionally cocaine-fueled city. Sex was as likely to be experienced on the stage, dance floor, or beach as in the bedroom. Together with fashion models, top designers, and avant-garde artists and architects, gay men were an integral force in the redevelopment of South Beach (part of the City of Miami Beach) as a chic tourist destination and as what Levine (1979) termed a "gay ghetto" (p. 384).

By the late 1990s, new treatments for human immunodeficiency virus (HIV) made it seem as though the party would go on forever. Modern gay culture in Miami—influenced by its circuit party–era origins, the city's perennial entertainment culture, and the tropical climate—is still epitomized by the nightclub scene, extensive drug and sex markets, and the glorification of the hypermasculine physique. Survey studies over the past 10 years have consistently revealed higher levels of regular drug use among gay men in Miami than among those living in other urban areas of the United States (Darrow et al., 1998; Kurtz & Inciardi, 2003). The sexual edge of the gay scene is also unique in this ethnic melting pot, where men of widely divergent sexual cultures share the space of a highly sexualized and sexually commodified geography (Kurtz, 1999).

In sum, Miami encompasses a host of social contradictions. The local population, with its politically and economically dominant foreign-born Hispanic majority, is in many ways characterized by a strong sexual conservatism. At the same time, the tourism industry has—since its beginnings in the early twentieth century—focused on adult entertainment and accommodated easy access to every variety of sexual experience and intoxicating substance. The city is also exemplified by sheer transience—of its cultural mix, of its sense of fashion and glamour, of its tourist hordes, and even of large numbers of residents who are also just "passing through." For many, metropolitan Miami is individualistic, hedonistic, spectacular and temporary, a truly postmodern place.

This chapter describes how gay men attempt to locate themselves in an environment in which change, spectacle, and the search for altered states of being are the main constants. As one respondent put it, "Living in Miami is like living in a hotel lobby. If you want a boyfriend, move to Chicago." I draw on extensive qualitative data collected over a decade to trace patterns in the narratives that gay men use to describe their experiences as they touch, confront, engage, embrace, absorb, and sometimes separate from the sex-drug pleasure dome that Miami often represents. In large part, this chapter presents the story of how men from diverse backgrounds integrate the sense of themselves as developed throughout childhood and adolescence ("Kansas") into this urban space that for most of them feels like "Oz."

The Stories

The research is theoretically and methodologically grounded in a social constructivist view of sexual cultures, masculinities, sexual behaviors, and drug use (e.g., Connell, 1995; Gagnon & Simon, 1973; Levine, 1992; Reback, 1997; Rubin, 1975). This perspective recognizes that social definitions of gender and sexuality categories, as well as the meanings associated with particular forms of entertainment, body shapes, sexual behaviors, and drug use, are relative to space, culture, and time. Although informed by quantitative survey studies conducted in Miami, the research presented here focuses on men's narratives of their experiences of the sex and drug party subculture, as well as their processes of reconciling the model it presents for gay male adulthood with their personal motivations and values.

Research was conducted in three stages from December 1996 through November 2006. Surveys and semistructured life history interviews conducted in the mid-1990s focused on men's integration of inherited masculinity norms with their gay identities and sexual practices. The second stage included 20 focus groups of gay and bisexual men conducted from 2003 to 2005 that examined the motivations for and consequences of living in the "fast lane" party subculture. Most recently, in late 2006, 11 young men were recruited for life history interviews that were designed to investigate how men's experiences of Miami had changed over the course of the prior decade.

All interview and focus group texts were analyzed following a constructivist-oriented grounded theory approach (Charmaz, 2000; Glaser and Strauss, 1967; Strauss & Corbin, 1990). Particular emphasis was placed on tracing patterns in the meanings men attributed to their engagement with local gay subcultures; their sexual identities, sexual behaviors, and drug use; and their relationships with family members, friends, and intimate partners. Excerpts from four of the recent life history interviews are described in some detail. These stories were chosen for their overall representativeness of the many narratives of men's experiences in Miami collected over the past decade, as well as to capture the diversity of narratives.

Edward

Edward, a 29-year-old European American, was raised a "hard-core Catholic" in southern California. His suburban middle-class childhood was turned upside down by the death of his mother when he was just 14. The next years were hard, as his father quickly remarried, and the family of three children was joined by his new stepmother and her three children. Edward's grades nose-dived even as his athletic performances soared. Family relationships deteriorated to the point where he was forced to move out of the house. During his junior year in high school, Edward moved into the home of his best friend. He was welcomed by his friend's parents, who were unaware that by that time Edward and his friend had been having sex together regularly for several years:

> Like at the end of the eighth grade, we finally experimented, and that was when it really clicked. He was a year younger than me, but he kind of pushed the envelope a little more. We actually ended up doing everything. We had this psychological game where we said we were just "practicing" on each other. We never admitted what it would mean...that a straight man would never receive. We just ignored that part until we got caught. His parents hated me after that.

Following high school, Edward put himself through college, where he continued to excel in sports. His athletic achievements made him quite popular, and he gradually took on a "jock" identity. He found his first real boyfriend on the team:

> We ended up falling in love. It was great, but I would still be saying, "This is great, but I still want to marry a woman and have kids." He was on a different level. I didn't think that it was possible to have a long-term relationship with a man, and a house and a dog and everything. Later, we moved in together, and, after him, I realized you could have those things.

The relationship did not last, and it was several years before Edward became comfortable having gay friends and dating other men. After a second relationship ended painfully, Edward decided to change his surroundings and move to Miami.

Having watched his best friend from high school and his brother both "go down the wrong path to hard drugs," Edward found the prevalent drug use in Miami's gay community to be a turn-off. But although he found new gay friends who did not do drugs, he said:

> We went through a weird phase for almost a year where we just party, party, partied. Like we were drunk three or four nights a week. Like we were losers, almost. After that, I experimented with all the drugs except the needle stuff. I had a great time. I don't beg to differ about why people do drugs. But it ruins your life. It's people who choose a healthy lifestyle versus people who do drugs. And it's financial, too—if you don't have money, how can you buy all this stuff, even drinking? How do you pay $400 or $500 a month drinking? That's rent.

So we stopped, but we didn't have fun anymore. Now we get together, but we really don't talk. You can see it in other gay groups, too; no one really talks to each other. Everyone just stares. If you don't go out all the time, then you don't know anyone. If you go out once in a while, you're stuck by yourself. The lifestyle sucks.

You know, I don't have sex with my friends, whereas it seems like in most groups everyone has sex together. And when I do meet someone, I can't seem to hold a relationship. I can't seem to find anyone I really like. I just feel like maybe there is something wrong with me. But how can you just date somebody when you don't have those feelings? And everybody who wants to be your friend wants to sleep with you. They want to be your boyfriend. If it doesn't work out that way, they don't want to be your friend.

Edward struggles to find a romantic partner in Miami. At the same time, he also continues to struggle with the conflicts between his jock identity and his perceptions of gay identity:

People in sports have great bodies, and they're competitive. It's a certain type of person, but they're all straight. I'm still fighting not wanting to be feminine, but knowing I do have feminine traits. I can never joke around, like doing a flaming voice, or acting like a girl, or whatever. It's too close to home to joke about that stuff. I find myself hating feminine guys. But I hate them because they're comfortable with themselves.

Having engaged in and rejected the local casual sex and drug scenes, Edward is still struggling with how to find close friends, financial stability, and self-acceptance as a gay man.

Felipe

Felipe, 29, grew up in New York City, the second oldest of six children, born to Colombian immigrants. His early life was unstable, as his father dealt cocaine, his parents fought constantly, and social service agencies made frequent visits to his home out of concern for the welfare of the children. When Felipe was 10, his father's involvement in the drug trade caused the entire family to be evicted in the middle of a blizzard, and they lived on the streets of New York until Felipe's mother was able to convince his grandmother to take them into her home in Miami. Although his parents still fought bitterly and his mother's psychiatric problems worsened, Felipe found structure there in church activities encouraged by his grandmother. His earliest memory of feeling "different" was

> when I had my first gay dream with Captain America when I was 5 years old. He was on top of me, just crushing me. It excited my danger zone. Later on, my friends would make fun of me when I would read a novel, like about the famous Latin group Menudo, the one Ricky Martin was in. And every time the Pentecostal pastor would say, "All gay guys go to hell," it was just like a stab in my heart.

Felipe began having sex with a male cousin when he was 11, and the sexual relationship continued until he was 16, when he became "more religious." He managed to avoid sex with men over the next couple of years, "except once, maybe twice actually." His next sexual experience was with a stranger in a park, and he felt so guilty afterward that he told his mother about it. She arranged for him to go to church and make a confession, but it made him feel worse and he stopped going to church altogether. Several months later, his brother told him in front of the rest of the family that he was unwelcome in the house if he was "going to be hanging out with faggots," and Felipe left home for good. He dropped out of school and found refuge among friends in the local gay "house" scene.

> I was mostly a club kid, that's mostly what my friends are. I was introduced to the club scene by doing shows; it gave us something to do, at least. I started experimenting, doing some sex here and there through online contacts. I started doing drugs when I ended a relationship. I guess I was feeling depressed, feeling bad, and didn't know what to do. I was 21. A friend at the time would say, "Oh, I took a pill and I had a threesome." So I was trying to be like my friend, but I was weak. First it was Ecstasy, then it was ketamine, and then it was Tina [crystal methamphetamine], and after Tina, GHB.

> First I would say to myself that I would never do what my parents did, you know, cocaine. You hear yourself: "You can do all the drugs besides coke." It was just stupid, but I was fascinated with the party scene, especially after the things I went through when I was a kid. The drugs would let me be a little more expressive, and little by little, just talk. Now I talk freely. But I don't know why I had to go through that route to become open, to be myself and to express myself. I also was doing sex scenes that I was regretting the next

day. The next day, I was like, "How could I do that, just because of the drugs?" Like putting myself at risk, doing things I didn't want to do. It started out because I was just wanting more. I was high and wanting more pleasure, and I wanted more pleasure, and more pleasure. I can't really regret anything. But it's like [hits his forehead with the palm of his hand], at the moment when an epiphany hits me.... "Why did I have to do it *that* way?" Now I'm doing the best I can. I just need to keep dusting myself off, and being more independent, and not so broken.

Felipe is now looking forward to going back to school, where he would like to get the training needed to become a nurse. He would most like to work for the American Red Cross in the Middle East. He continued:

I think my 20s were more like a learning experience, and getting to know myself. One of the things I got lately came from the Book of Solomon. Basically just to be happy. There's nothing in life that hasn't already been invented. There's a time for everything, like it says, a time to heal, a time to hurt, a time to love.... There's a time to die and a time to be happy, a time to weep. Don't be angry. There's a time for everything. Just be happy with what you have.

As the interview ended, I asked Felipe if there were anything that he does especially want in life. He said, "I want Captain America."

Carlos

Carlos, 24, is a performance artist who has lived in Miami for just 3 years. He grew up on the 28th floor of a "30-floor walkup," a housing project in a tough Bronx neighborhood so dangerous that his mother gave him a box cutter for self-defense to take to his first day of kindergarten. By the time he was 14, his father had moved away and his mother was rarely home. Carlos found social connections in New York's nightclub scene, gaining entry to adults-only environs by befriending the right people and attaining the right "look":

I already had about 20 piercings in my face, because in New York you could get into any club as long as you looked fabulous. You've got 5 pounds of makeup and 3-foot-tall platform shoes on, and you're wearing nothing but tighty-whities [briefs] and a little book bag. They'll let you in like that. You know, you look adorable. You're a cute little boy. They're going to let you in.

That's when I started falling into drugs, but I never paid for any of
them. That's one of the privileges that go along with being a night-
life celebrity. Being in that atmosphere, everything is so available.
You're just so fierce and so fabulous, people die to be around you.
They'll bump you for free. They'll buy you drinks all night. They'll
drive you home. You get paid to be at the club by the owners. At that
time, Ecstasy was out and ketamine was in, because it was the new-
est, most interesting drug. I loved it, and everyone loved it. It takes
you up and then it zones you out. Everything is so speedy, and then
the tranquilizer actually kicks in, so you're a zombie.

But in time, drug use and the nightclub scene led Carlos into sexual situations that he now regrets.

I performed at a lot of sex parties. Blackout parties. So I got involved
in scenes where I would make a show out of the sex. But there were
also many times I ended up at home with strange people after a
heavy night out. I mean, I would always be reluctant and say, "No,
I don't want to fool around," but they talked me into it. I woke up the
next day wanting to die. I felt dirty and felt like a whore. Of course,
I regret it now. I regret almost everyone I've ever slept with, actually.

It's the same here in Miami, or maybe worse. I'm very disappointed at
the gay community here. I mean everyone here sleeps with each other.
The tourists come; the locals sleep with the tourists. The tourists leave,
and, guess what, the guy you slept with last night slept with your best
friend. It was cute for a couple of months, which I guess is the point,
because it's for tourists. But people who live here are reduced to going
to clubs as a way to kill their spare time. And then you've put alcohol
and drugs together and you get the sex that you end up with that way.

Like some other men who have spent years in the club scene, Carlos believes
that he now sees his future in a different light.

Honestly, a good thing has come from moving here. I have been
forced into solitude. I have been stripped of my dignity, my life, and
even my social skills. But now I have more clarity. I notice the details
in things. I don't overlook things as easily as I used to. I'm more
in tune with how life works and how you really have to maintain a
positive flow. I've been trying to refine myself and love myself these

past two years. Trying to just focus on me right now, and not have a relationship, not going to school or working a 9-to-5 job. Just really trying to clarify me as a human being, what direction I want to take in my life, how to deal with issues and anger.

I have very low self-esteem. I'm very insecure with myself. I still feel ugly. I am so on top of my looks it drives me crazy half the time. I have spent thousands of dollars on resurfacing my face and microdermabrasion peels. I haven't gotten any surgery yet, but I am planning to. But I don't get anyone approaching me like I did in New York. I used to have to chase guys off with a baseball bat, but no one approaches me here whatsoever. And if they do, they're the wrong people, so it fucks up my self-esteem. Maybe I'm ugly after all. I just feel fat, old, and ugly. People don't even want to be my friend.

The kind of despair expressed in Carlos' narrative is a common refrain among men who have engaged in the fast-lane scene, especially those who are looking for strong social ties and those who feel that they do not fit the "muscle boy" ideal. Carlos was among many who say that they want to look for their futures elsewhere:

I'm stuck here, I'm stranded. I've got to go. I think San Francisco would be really good for me. I eventually see myself getting out of the country altogether.

Miles

Miles is a 22-year-old native Miamian, born to a Bahamian mother and a Haitian father. Because his mother was only 16 when he was born, Miles spent most of his childhood in the home of his paternal grandmother, together with several cousins who also stayed with her from time to time. He says that he always knew he was going to be gay. Although Miles began dating early and was having sex with girls by the time he was 12, he was soon fantasizing about having sex with boys. At age 14, he began a sexual relationship with a friend that lasted for several years. Although both boys continued to date and have sex with girls, the friendship ended when Miles had sex with another boy. His friend became so upset that a violent physical fight ensued in which both of them were wounded.

Miles gradually came to terms with his same-sex desire over the next several years, but not before going through a period of shame and overcompensating for what he perceived to be "feminine" behaviors. To find a path to self-acceptance, he has separated himself from his family and his church. At age 17, he began going to the local bars and nightclubs.

I couldn't believe that there were places for gay people. I used to think I was the only gay person in my neighborhood. When I first started to go to clubs, it was kind of scary, because one person just grabbed me and stuck their hands in my pants, and I'm like "What the fuck is wrong with you?" But then I started getting more into it. You know, it's hard to find a place where you can meet other people and actually hook up with people. In my neighborhood, I don't know who's gay. If I go to the club, everybody's gay.

Now I go out to a club every chance I get. I used to go by myself, but then I stopped. Because one time, I went to a club with somebody who came off as a cool person. The whole night was drinks, drinks, drinks. I got drunk and I said, "I want to go home," but they didn't want to take me. He drove me to a hotel and tried to have sex with me. He was really trying to force himself on me. Other times I would go out by myself and I would get high to the point that I felt I couldn't handle my drugs. Now I always go out with a group of friends, so I can feel safe around a bunch of people I trust.

One really bad drug I did was acid. That trip was so bad, I couldn't handle it. I was freaking out. I was looking crazy in the middle of the street. There are times when I look back on that time, and I still feel like I'll go back into that bad trip. And crystal meth, that drug I would never ever do again. When I first tried it, it was like "Oh my God, this is good! It's better than coke, it's better than everything else." But the day I tried crystal was like the day the world ended. I felt like I had no control that day, I had sex with people I would never have sex with. Just from getting high on that drug one time I had so many regrets. For three days I was still craving it. That was the first time I felt like I would do anything just to get more.

My drug of choice now is cocaine. Me and my friends get together on the weekends and we put money together and we get high together. It's something social. We stay up all night and talk about our problems, talk about good things and bad things. With cocaine, I can stop. If I run out of coke, that's it for the night, I don't need to go out and buy more.

Right now my life is not where I want it to be. I feel like my life is standing still. I'm not moving forward. I had a good job, but I quit, because one night I got high on coke and the next day I didn't feel like waking up. I guess the coke gave me the balls to quit, but it was a great job. I would like to see myself in school right now. I started thinking about beauty school. That's one thing I always wanted to do.

I would like to be in a relationship, but I think I'm good on my own, because there's so many things that I need to fix in my life. I don't even know how to say this. I think I am better off single, period, so that I can focus on myself. Even now, recently, I've gotten away from my friends. Like I still talk to them on the phone, but I don't hang out with them physically because, like last night, I got high, it was pure temptation. I want to quit coke so bad, so bad. Because whatever priority I have the day after I get high, I'm just not up to it.

Discussion

The men's stories have much in common and echo patterns found throughout the decade of research among gay men in Miami's party scene. Given the gradual but continuing change toward acceptance of gay and lesbian people in the United States, it is somewhat surprising that men's experiences of rejection by their families and struggles with heterosexual masculinity norms are as much in evidence in young men's life stories today as they were many years ago. Their decisions in early adulthood to engage in the gay fast-lane subculture, whether by moving across country or across town, reflect the need to escape rejection, victimization, and secrecy as much as the desire to find friends and sex partners.

The fast-lane subculture would appear to mirror this rejection in the homophobic and hypermasculine aspects of its structure of social stratification. The dominant theme of sexual competitiveness is built around a model of the male body that seems to be grounded in aspects of gay culture dating to earlier generations of men. While the muscled circuit party icon may have emerged in part as a subcultural response to the AIDS epidemic (Halkitis, 1999), Martin

Levine's (1998) posthumously published dissertation, *Gay Macho*, depicts a remarkably similar "gay clone" archetype in New York City during the pre-AIDS 1970s and early 1980s. Levine described the subculture of that era as epitomized by "the four D's: disco, drugs, 'dish' and 'dick.'" Similar to Levine's description, many respondents in this study found the masculinized Miami subculture to be both personally reassuring and visually attractive. For many men, the gym-honed body is an expression of masculinity, virility, health, and youth. At the same time, this form of social space seems to reinforce gay men's aversion to effeminacy. As a result, many continue to be self-conscious about their gendered self-presentations, and most continue to reject effeminate men as potential sex partners or boyfriends. For men who feel that they either do not fit or do not want to fit this model of attractiveness, frustration about the inability to find friends and intimate partners runs high. The difficulty in making connections seems to be especially acute for young men who grow up in Miami or move here to work or attend college. The predominance of the sex and drug party subculture means that younger men trying to negotiate intimidating straight and gay value systems find little room for self-discovery and intimate relationships. The code of this subculture reinforces men's secretiveness about their inner emotions and desires and buttresses the idea that emotion should be divorced from sex.

The sexual competitiveness of the scene and the difficulties in forging friendships often lead men to compensate by developing "attitude"—the construction of an attractive public identity that masks and protects their private needs for intimacy and friendship. This strategy often works initially, because at least for a time, the freedom, spectacle, and beauty of Miami's gay scene seem irresistible and priceless. The spectacle and excitement are enhanced by party drugs, which also serve as social lubricants that enable men to feel connected to each other, however momentarily.

In this regard, Miami's renowned party scene supports the predominance of the most extreme forms of gay entertainment: all-night dance and sex parties that frequently extend into three- and four-day nonstop, drug-assisted blowouts. Many men have observed that in these settings, the primary drugs of choice, Ecstasy and crystal methamphetamine in particular, serve to temporarily provide what the local gay subculture seemingly cannot: human connections, intimacy, and love. In some historical sense, it seems that different kinds of drugs became culturally intertwined to produce a rosier picture of life for gay men: steroids designed to improve the health of HIV-positive men in the AIDS era became mainstreamed for the production of the muscled physique; and this body, now embedded in a tourism-based culture that includes normalized recreational drug use, also became associated with a broad-based acceptance of mind-altering drugs, the most popular of which cause the user to feel connected and loved.

Many men emphasize that, at least initially, party drugs did help them feel more attractive, sexually desirable, and socially connected. To be sure, some men describe the sex and drug party subculture as empowering, welcoming, and providing an extraordinary sense of freedom (Westhaver, 2006). But this research suggests that those responses are largely temporary. The most popular drugs in the party scene, Ecstasy and crystal methamphetamine, are often used by gay men to escape feelings of loneliness, alienation, and stigmatization (Klitzman, 2006; Kurtz, 2005). The lack of other kinds of supportive gay community activities in Miami seems to make these problems especially difficult to manage.

As men engage the scene over a longer period of time, a theme emerges in their stories about the experience of the crossing of personal boundaries—sexual, physical, emotional, and spiritual—that risks the loss of self. These events may take the form of sexual activities under the influence of drugs that are regretted the next day, as a number of the men described. But the sense of violation may also come from the psychological effects of too much drug use, including depression and an inability to have sex or socialize without drugs. A third aspect of deepening problems for many men in the scene is an habituation to being "high" on sex, drugs, or sex and drugs together. Sexual sensation seeking has been shown in a number of studies to be associated with higher risks for sexually transmitted infections and HIV among gay men, as well as for other mental health problems such as depression (Dolezal, Meyer-Bahlburg, Remien, & Petkova, 1997; Ostrow, DiFranceisco, & Kalichman, 1997).

One aspect of sensation seeking that was not reflected in the men's stories related here is what some men describe as an inability to be satisfied with the kind of sex partners they attract. One respondent talked about the problems he developed after realizing that frequent casual sex was conditioning his life in ways he did not admire:

> It was a constant challenge to get a better person, which became excessive at the end. I was getting interesting people, but I was never satisfied. Then I woke up and realized that I was not going in the direction that I really wanted to go, that this would not fulfill me. Never, ever. It was destroying me psychologically, and it could be a big threat to my life.

Sexual sensation seeking and drug use often become intertwined in ways that are very difficult to resolve. The explosion of the Internet as a social and sexual connection point appears to increase the risks for sexual sensation seeking and simultaneously to reduce the social opportunities afforded by gay subcultures (McKirnan, Houston, & Tolou-Shams, 2006; Taylor et al., 2004).

Men who discover that they are rejected not only in their home environment but also in the gay subculture that they hoped would sustain them exit the party scene—and sometimes Miami itself—disillusioned and rudderless. Having left family behind, and living in a setting that many describe as devoid of community, they have few models or social supports to mediate new self-understandings or to guide the process of identity integration.

Nevertheless, the men's narratives share themes of hope and reconciliation that follow their disillusionment and rejection of the party scene. Though each man maps his own path to his dreams, their experiences of the scene seem to demand something more human, more intimate, and more meaningful from life. The men's stories suggest that the first step to the fulfillment of that demand is dedicated attention to the reflection on and achievement of acceptance and love for the self, which the spectacular Miami gay scene promises but ultimately fails to provide. Men who eventually succeed in constructing a meaningful life often express an appreciation for the freedom and empowerment that this subculture offered, however temporarily. Perhaps that is why it survives. Other men seem to get lost in the haze of the scene and do not fare as well later in adulthood.

Conclusions

In terms of late adolescent and early adult development, migration to an urban gay subculture (including migration within one's home city) appears to be a critical turning point. Although migration typically occurs in response to the real need to escape homophobia and secrecy, as well as to find safety and social support, it can come at a high price. The loss of close family relationships, established social and sexual mores, and years of social capital built up within the home community that occur upon migration are aspects of gay men's development that are seldom explored in the literature. This omission may relate to the perception that gay subcultures generally provide supportive environments for gay men and/or that to remain in an oppressive home community environment is untenable in any case.

The research described here indicates that these losses are very large in terms of economic prospects, drug use and sexual boundaries, and integration with the larger society and its breadth of social opportunities. Further, the fast-lane subculture appears to be somewhat limited in its capacity to be supportive because gay men bring their inherited masculinity norms, internalized homophobia, and emotional wounds (see Stall et al., 2003) to this new, less structured social realm. In this context, an underdeveloped area of research relates to understanding the factors men take into account in deciding where and how to engage gay-fast lane subcultures, as well as the factors that predict special risks or protections for them.

Implications for Men's Health

Drug use among gay men in Miami—and likely in other urban centers with similar fast-lane subcultural characteristics—is often perceived to be normative and is frequently initiated by men's needs for intimacy and friendship. Yet, men often find that connectedness remains elusive and that greater drug involvement actually leads to increasing social isolation. In addition, there is great risk that men's drug use will permanently harm their health. This research suggests that interventions to reduce drug use may be more successful among men in the fast-lane scene to the extent that they address men's needs for—and skills at attaining—social relationships with other individuals and stronger ties to the broader community. Community-level interventions that aim to reduce the social acceptance of drug use, and also those that target social expectations about physical attractiveness and sexual performance, are also needed.

Limitations of the Study

The main limitations of the research relate to the generalizability of findings. Certainly many gay men do find support within gay subcultures, and they are able to keep the fast-lane aspects of the scene at enough distance to lead highly productive and socially integrated lives (Cochran & Mays, 2006; Stall et al., 2003). Respondents in the various phases of the study described here may have been particularly motivated to participate because of social isolation, the monetary stipend, their relationships to other participants, or other factors. In addition, Miami's multiethnic, transient, and entertainment-focused gay subculture is unique to its space and time. In this regard, however, all large urban gay subcultures in the United States share some aspects of the fast-lane party scene, including drug use (Frye et al., 2006; Signorile, 1997).

REFERENCES

Albin, G. (1995, May). To live and die in South Beach. *Out*, 73–77, 125–128.
Charmaz, K. (2000). Grounded theory: Objectivist and constructivist methods. In N. K. Denzin & Y. S. Lincoln (Eds.), *Handbook of qualitative research* (2nd ed., pp. 509–535). Thousand Oaks, CA: Sage.

Cochran, S. D., & Mays, V. M. (2006). Estimating prevalence of mental and substance-using disorders among lesbians and gay men from existing national health data. In A. M. Omoto & H. S. Kurtzman (Eds.), *Sexual orientation and mental health* (pp. 143–166). Washington, DC: American Psychological Association Press.

Connell, R. W. (1995). *Masculinities*. Berkeley: University of California Press.

Darrow, W. W., Webster, R. D., Kurtz, S. P., Buckley, A. K., Patel, K. I., & Stempel, R. R. (1998). Impact of HIV counseling and testing on HIV-infected men who have sex with men: The South Beach Health Survey. *AIDS and Behavior, 2*(2), 115–126.

Dolezal, C., Meyer-Bahlburg, H. F. L., Remien, R. H., & Petkova, E. (1997). Substance use during sex and sensation seeking as predictors of sexual risk behavior among HIV+ and HIV- gay men. *AIDS and Behavior, 1*(1), 19–28.

Frye, V., Latka, M. H., Koblin, B., Halkitis, P. N., Putnam, S., Galea, S., et al. (2006). The urban environment and sexual risk behavior among men who have sex with men. *Journal of Urban Health, 83*(2), 308–324.

Gagnon, J. H., & Simon, W. (1973). *Sexual conduct: The social sources of human sexuality*. Chicago: Aldine.

Glaser, B. G., and Strauss, A. L. (1967). *The discovery of grounded theory: Strategies for qualitative research*. Chicago: Aldine.

Halkitis, P. N. (1999). Masculinity in the age of AIDS: Seropositive gay men and the "buff agenda." In P. Nardi (Ed.), *Gay masculinities* (pp. 130–151). Newbury Park, CA: Sage.

Klitzman, R. (2006). From "male bonding rituals" to "suicide Tuesday": A qualitative study of issues faced by gay male ecstasy (MDMA) users. *Journal of Homosexuality, 51*(3), 7–32.

Kurtz, S. P. (1999). Butterflies under cover: Cuban and Puerto Rican gay masculinities in Miami. *Journal of Men's Studies, 7*, 371–390.

Kurtz, S. P. (2005). Post-circuit blues: Motivations and consequences of crystal meth use among gay men in Miami. *AIDS and Behavior 9*(1), 63–72.

Kurtz, S. P., & Inciardi, J. A. (2003). Crystal meth, gay men, and circuit parties. *Law Enforcement Executive Forum, 3*, 97–114.

Levine, M. P. (1979). Gay ghetto. *Journal of Homosexuality 4*(4), 363–377.

Levine, M. P. (1992). The implications of social constructionist theory for social research on the AIDS epidemic among gay men. In G. Herdt & S. Lindenbaum, (Eds.), *The time of AIDS: Social analysis, theory and method* (pp. 185–198). Thousand Oaks, CA: Sage.

Levine, M. P. (1998). *Gay macho: The life and death of the homosexual clone*. New York: New York University Press.

McKirnan, D., Houston, E., & Tolou-Shams, M. (2006). Is the Web the culprit? Cognitive escape and Internet sexual risk among gay and bisexual men. *AIDS and Behavior, 11*(1), 151–160.

Ostrow, D. G., DiFranceisco, W., & Kalichman, S. C. (1997). Sexual adventurism, substance use and sexual behavior: A structural modeling analysis of the Chicago MACS/CCS cohort. *AIDS and Behavior, 1*(3), 191–202.

Reback, C. J. (1997). *The social construction of a gay drug: Methamphetamine use among gay and bisexual males in Los Angeles*. Executive Summary, City of Los Angeles, AIDS Coordinator.

Rubin, G. (1975). The traffic in women: Notes on the "political economy of sex." In R. Reiter (Ed.), *Toward an anthropology of women* (pp. 157–210). New York: Monthly Review Press.

Signorile, M. (1997). *Life outside: The Signorile report on gay men: Sex, drugs, muscles and the passages of life*. New York: HarperCollins.

Stall, R., Mills, T. C., Williamson, J., Hart, T., Greenwood, G., Paul, J., et al. (2003). Association of co-occurring psychosocial health problems and increased vulnerability to HIV/AIDS among urban men who have sex with men. *American Journal of Public Health, 93*(6), 939–942.

Strauss, A. L., & Corbin, J. (1990). *Basics of qualitative research: Grounded theory procedures and techniques*. Newbury Park, CA: Sage.

Taylor, M., Aynalem, G., Smith, L., Bemis, C., Kenney, K., & Kerndt, P. (2004). Correlates of Internet use to meet sex partners among men who have sex with men diagnosed with early syphilis in Los Angeles County. *Sexually Transmitted Diseases, 31*(9), 552–556.

U.S. Census Bureau. (2000). Census. *State and County Quickfacts: Miami-Dade County, FL*.

Westhaver, R. (2006). Flaunting and empowerment: Thinking about circuit parties, the body, and power. *Journal of Contemporary Ethnography, 35*(6), 611–644.

8

(My) Stories of Lesbian Friendship

Jacqueline S. Weinstock

If you want to know me, then you must know my story, for my story defines who I am. And if *I* want to know *myself*, to gain insight into the meaning of my own life, then I, too, must come to know my own story. I must come to see in all its particulars the narrative of the self—the personal myth—that I have tacitly, even unconsciously, composed over the course of my years. It is a story I continue to revise, and to tell to myself (and sometimes to others) as I go on living.

—McAdams (1997, p. 11)

Lesbian friendship has been at the center of the story I have told about myself for over 25 years, the whole of my adult life thus far. It has also been the main focus of my scholarly work for half of this time, the whole of my professional career. Indeed, my personal understandings of lesbian friendship have paralleled my scholarly writings and reflections. Yet, in recent years, the parallels have lessened, leading me to question the stories I have told thus far and to lose faith in their continuation.

In this chapter, I reflect upon my changing experiences and understandings of lesbian friendship in relation to the prevailing story lines evident in the literature on lesbians' friendships—including those in my own writings. I begin by placing myself in current and historical context and by examining select early childhood and adolescent experiences that informed my first views about the nature and power of friendship. From there, I examine select young adulthood experiences, through my college, graduate school, and postdoctoral years, with a focus on my coming out as a lesbian, connecting with lesbian and feminist communities, and making my initial decision to direct my scholarly attention to lesbian friendships. I then briefly review my published writings in this area, and the connections between these works and my own experiences, beliefs, and questions about friendship. Finally, I bring my story back to the present by identifying and exploring several emerging side plots, evident throughout my friendship experiences and writings, but now transforming the story and challenging the validity of the friendship narrative I have told to date.

Setting the Context: Identity Locations and Childhood Lessons of Friendship

My thoughts about friendship and my personal experiences with friendship cannot be examined without placing them in lived context. For me, this means acknowledging the privileges and forms of oppression I experience. I was born in 1961 in New York City to White, middle-class, heterosexual Jewish parents, and I was easily labeled female at birth and raised as a girl. Today I locate myself as a middle-aged, single, able-bodied, lesbian-identified trans ally and feminist living and working in the State of Vermont. With the exception of a few years in childhood, I have lived in, attended, and worked in predominantly White neighborhoods and institutions. With the exception of one year, I have been able to take care of myself financially as an adult; with the exception of this same year and a few of the years that followed, I have also been able to take care of myself physically.

I am a rather quiet, private person, shy until I get comfortable with the people and the settings I am in, and even then, I prefer not to be the center of attention. My mother, on the other hand, is very social and outgoing (she was voted "Class Clown" by her high school graduating class; I was voted "Most Likely to Succeed" by mine). One thing we do have in common is the value we place on and the commitments we make to our friendships.

I first became aware of my mother's investment in her network of friends when I was $5^1/_2$ years of age. A few months earlier, my twin sisters had been born, and our family of four (I have a sister 2 years older than me as well) became a family of six, living in a two-bedroom apartment in Queens, New York. It was a tight squeeze, but on the upside, our apartment was in a court-yard, and we were surrounded by many other families with young children. Many of the adults who lived here were my mother's good friends, and relatives were also near. More often than not, then, there were several women visiting together and watching us children as we played in the courtyard or on the swings in the back.

To accommodate our enlarged family, however, my parents moved us to a house in another area of Queens, in another neighborhood, away from both neighborhood friends and extended family. At the same time, my father began to work longer hours—into the evenings and on Saturdays—to support our family and the new house. My mother became isolated as a stay-at-home care-giver with four young children, a striking contrast to the courtyard experience. I remember this time period well, for my mother's stress level went up and her patience went down. I also remember the lesson I learned—that friendships may be viewed as a nice addition to life, but in reality they are essential, espe-cially in times of stress.

The second lesson about friendship that I learned from my mother came a few years later, after she did create a new friendship network and an especially close friendship with Bonnie.[1] This close friendship remains today, but there was a break in it for a time when our family planned to move again, one last time together, from Queens to Long Island and, as a result, away from Bonnie. I never knew exactly what occurred between them but I always envisioned that the break was about the move away from each other, something that was hard on both of them. They stopped being friends for a while not because of a lack of caring but because of the challenge of circumstances; from this I learned that while friendships may be essential, they may also be pretty precarious.

Adolescent Friendship Lessons

The lesson learned from my mother's friendship with Bonnie was further reinforced by my own experience of shifting from a local to a long distance friendship when my family moved from Queens to the South Shore of Long Island during the summer between my fifth and sixth grades. This move taught me a new lesson as well—that of the challenge of identity differences in friendships. I had been good friends with a girl named Denise, who was African American. Our interracial friendship was not common at the time (nor are these friendships common now), and we each suffered some teasing for it. But we managed to withstand the pressures and, through that, grew closer together. This changed, however, after I moved away. Not only did we lose access to a daily shared context, but we were now living in two very different communities. Mine was a suburban town comprised mostly of European American Jewish families, and hers was more city-like and racially mixed but composed predominantly of African American families. These location differences highlighted our identity differences. I remember Denise's first and only visit to my new home, when we went to the local pool. Denise stood out as the one Black person among a crowd of all White children and parents. Shortly thereafter, I attended Denise's birthday party; of the 10 or so girls there, I was the only who was White. We did not talk about either of these experiences; we did not know how to do so. Instead, we each in our own way avoided visiting the other again, and over time we simply lost contact.

Along with the shift in racial composition from Queens to our new Long Island suburb, I found myself entering a group of peers who were more embedded in adolescence than my group had been. I definitely had some learning and catching up to do. Eventually I became part of a mixed-sex peer group with shifting patterns of heterosexual dyads "going steady" for a few months at a time (making for a long-term relationship from our perspectives). Despite the emphasis on heterosexual dating, though, friendships were central; friendship pairs often determined the couples rather than the other way around.

Over the next several years, I learned that friends were the people I could talk to, trust, and depend upon; and also that they could betray, be competitive with each other, and sometimes just drift away or find other friends. I learned that while we espoused the belief that we could tell each other everything, there really were some topics of conversation, some thoughts, and some feelings that were better left unexpressed, especially if they did not fit within the norms of the friendship group. I knew, for example, not to complain about how much attention was paid to counting calories and related body-image issues or to articulate my plan never to get married and be a wife. I knew I walked a tight line by playing sports and dressing for comfort and movement rather than style, in contrast to the emphasis on self/body presentation among my female friends. I maintained my place in this group, my acceptance by this group, by being quiet about these differences and about the deeper differences I noticed emerging between us.

The most challenging silence during high school had to do with my friendship with Alana. From the start, I felt it was important to keep this friendship separate from my group and to talk about it only in broad superficial terms. Alana and I met through our part-time jobs, and we were immediately drawn to each other. She seemed to be much older than me in many ways, more comfortable with herself, and more herself with her parents than I was at that time. We started hanging out a lot together, just the two of us, having intense conversations that lasted for hours. But after about six months of this kind of intensity, there started to be fewer and fewer opportunities for just the two of us to hang out. Most of the time Mary joined us, and soon thereafter, I learned that the two of them began to get together without me. I was confused and pained by these changes, and I did not understand them or my feelings about them. I did not feel that I could talk with anyone in my life about this incident or my feelings about it, and it was a long while before I was able to raise the topic with Alana. Her response was positive—she missed me too, she said. She would make more time for us, she declared. And she did—at least for the few weeks that followed. But then things cycled back to the way they were before we talked until I raised my concerns again. We cycled through this pattern over and over for several months, despite my vowing to myself after each cycle to break free of it. By the time I left for college, we had established an uneasy truce: we would get together once in a while, just the two of us, with only occasional forays into discussions about how much things had changed between us. I was still confused and hurt, but I did my best to pretend otherwise. Meanwhile, Alana did her best to act as if nothing had changed and we were still the best of friends.

It was not until I returned home after my first semester of college that I learned that Mary and Alana had been involved with each other sexually. Mary, not Alana, told me, and, in fact, she did so not just to get my support as their relationship was ending but also to warn me about Alana. Alana was dangerous, she said. She lies, Mary said. She is controlling. Their relationship had been unhealthy; Mary was not really gay but Alana had played to her vulnerabilities, and Mary fell under her spell. Now that she was coming out of it, she wanted to warn me to protect myself.

I listened to Mary and offered what support I could, though I was emotionally confused and greatly shocked. When I was alone with my thoughts, I found myself not really focusing on Mary's warnings but instead wondering why Alana had lied to me about her and Mary. And then: Why hadn't Alana come on to me? Why hadn't she chosen me? Or had she come on to me and I missed her signals because I had no framework for seeing them? Did I want her to come on to me? Was I sexually attracted to her? Had I been in love with her? Was I still? I had no answers for these questions, and I did not ask Alana any of them. We did not talk about her relationship with Mary and I returned to college full of confusion, not just about this friendship but also about my feelings for this friend and about the line between friends and lovers. Had Alana and I been friends and sort of lovers without (my) knowing it?

Lesbian Friendship Stories in the College Years

A year later, at age 20, I began my (no "sort of" about it) first lesbian love relationship. Helen and I met early in our first year of college. We developed a
friendship over several months' time, with no inkling on my part (or Helen's,
I believe) of any sexual desire. Yet, such desire clearly developed for each of us,
and eventually, during our second year of college, we were ready to acknowledge
it to ourselves and to reveal it to each other. Even after expressing our shared
desire for each other, however, we decided—over and over again—not to act
on it. We did not want to harm our friendship, we said; we weren't lesbians;
we did not want to hurt our families or worry our other friends, we declared.
Other fears went unverbalized—fears about our emotional safety in our families and our physical safety in our communities and in society; and fears about
our future lives and our current identities. One night, however, despite these
fears, and while in Helen's dorm room studying together for an exam we had
the following day, we gave in to and acted upon our desire for each other.

Over the months that followed, it became clear to us both that we were
in love. But it was a secret love, both a wonderful and a horrible secret. At the
beginning, we mostly felt the wonder of it all. But eventually the context of
heterosexism filtered into our relationship, and we began to act out some of our
internalized hatred on ourselves and each other. It cut me deeply when Helen
asked me to leave her room early in the morning so that her residents would
not see me (she was a resident assistant); she felt my cut when I made her do
the same at my place. I felt it and brought it back to our relationship after I told
a friend of mine about being in love with Helen, and she responded by telling
me that she did not want to be my friend anymore. We both felt the cuts when,
in a memory that still sears, Helen and I were engaged in deep conversation
sitting in her car by my house, me with my hand on her thigh. A group of male
college students neared, heading most likely to their fraternity house farther
down the road. Without hesitation, without thought it seemed, I immediately
removed my hand. Helen later described this scene in a poem, emphasizing
the moment when the sureness of my hand became the feel of its absence. Fear
became pain, and love bled into shame, as we each strived to express our love
for the other and to feel this love in return, all the while separating ourselves
from questions of sexual identity. "It's just that I fell in love with you; this isn't
about my sexuality," one or the other of us would say. "If you were a man, you
would be the person I would want to make a life with," Helen said to me.

Despite our best efforts to hold our love for each other and our relationship with each other separate from our identities, we each began to

acknowledge that, just maybe, what we felt for each other might have meaning for our identities. We decided to try to explore this possibility together by
attending a meeting of the undergraduate gay student group. But the meeting was awkward and we did not stay long, nor did either of us go back for
another try. Instead, we returned to our cocoon, pushing aside questions
about the future and questions about identity, at least for a while longer. A
few months later, however, Helen decided that she needed to explore being
with men before she could consider whether she might be a lesbian or a
bisexual woman. We continued to see each other during these few months
of Helen's exploration, though it was a difficult time. Eventually, we came
back together more fully and began to tell our friends about our relationship.
We also connected with and became friends with another same-sex couple at
school and then with other lesbians. These connections became lifelines to
self-respect and self-pride, to acknowledgment and support for our relationship. These connections also brought us into the lesbian community, and
many members of this community became both friends and family to me.
Most of us were not out to family-of-origin members, so we turned to each
other for personal support, holiday celebrations, and a sense of belonging.
It was during these years that I also experienced a welcoming of intimate
conversations on all kinds of topics, including those that had been taboo in
friendships past, and I began to experience my own friendships as centrally
important to me. There was, as well, a growing awareness on my part that I
seemed to be drawn to and to follow a *friendship script*, common to many lesbian lover relationships (e.g., Rose, 1996; Rothblum & Brehony, 1993; Vetere,
1982; Weinstock & Rothblum, 2004).

Lesbian Politics, Lesbian Community, Lesbian Friendships

Helen and I remained together through college. She graduated before me and
left Ithaca; I took another year to finish and chose to stay in Ithaca thereafter.
We stayed together at long distance for some of this time but eventually agreed
that it would be better if we broke off our relationship and began to see other
people. Still, we continued in many ways to stay together. Meanwhile, in my
last year of college and in the few years that followed, I increasingly ventured
into lesbian community and lesbian politics, frequenting Smedley's Bookstore,
reading many of the books the owner recommended, and attending the various events advertised on the store's bulletin board. I was especially drawn
to the politics of lesbian separatism, Adrienne Rich's (1979) analysis of *com-
pulsory heterosexuality*, and the lesbian feminist critique of traditional family

structures and their conceptualization of alternative communities composed of multiple committed friendships. Yet, while I had my circle of friends, I was for the most part an observer, watching from the outside what I perceived to be Ithaca's lesbian feminist community.

Throughout this time, I continued to develop intimate friendships and, at times, to fall in love with these friends. Paula was one such friend. We worked together at a local retail store and got to know each other over time through this shared work experience and group gatherings after work for drinks. I was at first quite excited about this newly developing friendship because I saw it as an opportunity to work on separating friends and lovers. This friendship, it seemed to me, would be different from most of those I had recently been forming because Paula was (presumably) a heterosexual woman. She was living with her male partner, yet she seemed quite comfortable with my lesbian identity. So, it seemed a safe context, a safe friendship.

Over months of getting closer, however, I began to fall in love with her. I kept this quiet, since she was involved with someone. But when that relationship ended (at least temporarily), we got involved with each other. And we did so a few times over the years that followed. But we never seemed to last long as lovers, doing much better as friends. For a long while after our last breakup we were good friends, committed to visiting each other and staying connected. Today we remain connected as friends, though our contact is much more sporadic than in years past.

My next friendship-turned-lover relationship (and then back to friendship) was with a woman much older than myself. Toni was more connected to Ithaca's lesbian community, and she was closely connected to her ex-lover, Carol. Thus, as we became friends and eventually lovers, I became a little more connected to this community and especially to Carol, Toni's ex-lover, and Carol's current lover, Abby. I was still only peripherally connected, however, to the lesbian community Toni was a part of; I was much younger, I had been in Ithaca for school, and I was preparing to move in a few months to attend graduate school. All that changed one early summer afternoon, however. Toni and I were playing tennis, and I found myself unable to run after the balls that Toni was hitting back to me. At some point, I called out that I needed to stop and rest. I went to lie down on a bench and experienced such great pain in my lower back and down my leg that I couldn't get up. Thus began an immobilizing back injury that lasted a full year, followed by over 10 years of a very gradual recovery. I had been working full-time when this injury happened, and because I was unable to work, I received New York State Disability for six months. When that ran out, I was given welfare benefits and food stamps for the remaining six months of my incapacitation.

It was during this time that I was enveloped by a network of friends—my own friends, Toni's friends, and the few we had in common—with Toni as the central caregiver and coordinator of care. That role ended abruptly, however, about six months into my injury. Toni was lying down when the phone rang, and as she reached to answer it, she too "slipped a disc," as we came to describe it. For the next several months, we were both incapacitated. Fortunately, we were able to rely upon our friends and community to cook for us, shuttle us to doctors' appointments, keep us company, and in other ways offer us care and support. Eventually we ended up moving into Carol's home, which she shared with her new partner, Abby. Friends continued to care for us, but now it was Carol and Abby who were the main providers and coordinators of our care.

It is no exaggeration to say that we survived this time because of our friends, our ex-lovers, and our lesbian community. Linda Strega (1996) also came to rely on lesbians for care while she fought cancer; her circle of lesbian friends was broad, including those she knew well, those who were just acquaintances, and even those who did not know her at all but who came to her aid. She describes this friendship experience as creating "a sense of us belonging with each other as Lesbians and as Separatists in ways that go beyond personal conflicts or discomforts with each other" (p. 284). My circle of caring friends was not composed only of lesbians or only of women, yet lesbians predominated and, for me, it felt like lesbian community and lesbian politics being enacted and lived. It was these experiences, along with my observations of other circles of lesbian friendships and lesbian community, that led me to conceptualize friendships as "much more than simply individual, private affairs: they are building blocks of lesbian community and politics" (Kitzinger, 1996, p. 298).

Converging Stories

A year after my initial back injury, my mobility improved enough to enable me to move to Burlington, Vermont, and begin graduate school in developmental psychology. Toni and I broke up around this time, and soon thereafter she got involved with Liz, a mutual friend who had first been my friend. While we all struggled with these relationship shifts and the challenges they posed to our friendships, after some time and much effort, we worked through the challenges and came to build a friendship family together. I was fortunate enough to form other key friendships during my graduate school years, some with other graduate students, some with lesbian community members, some with faculty mentors, and some with new ex-lovers. Even Helen came back into my life at this time, though our friendship seemed always to work better when

I was single. Eventually, I got frustrated with Helen's unwillingness to support me in my love relationships, and she agreed that this was a challenge for her. We decided to get some help to learn how to be better friends to each other. I flew out to visit her, and she arranged for us to attend two therapy appointments together. While the first appointment went well, the second began to feel like an ambush. Our therapist articulated the traditional story line, telling us that our desire for continued connection had to mean either that one or both of us still wanted to be lovers or that one or both of us were holding on for some unhealthy reasons. We should either get back together or move on and stop trying to be friends. I was silent during this part of the session, but afterward, when we were alone, I shared my frustration with Helen about the therapist's traditional conceptualization of friends and lovers. Helen had a different reaction, however, and wanted us to talk about getting back together. When I said that this was not what I wanted, she got very angry. There was yelling, there was silence, there was a request for me to leave. Eventually Helen calmed down and let me stay; we went on with our plans for that night and the next day, and then she took me to the airport to catch my plane. I thought we were all right, back on track and committed to working at being friends. As I turned to board the plane, however, Helen said, "Have a nice life," and then turned and walked away. She did not respond to my phone calls or letters for years.

This experience shook me, but it did not deter me. I remained committed to maintaining friendships with other ex-lovers, even when one of us had romantic feelings and might have preferred a romantic relationship. There were also friendships that included sexual expression (what is referred to these days as *friends with benefits*). These were the ways my friends and I sought to prioritize friendship relationships and to create lesbian community centered on these friendships. We were aiming as well to challenge traditional partner and family forms.

As the years went by and many of us transitioned from our 20s to our 30s, maintaining close friendships and prioritizing them over partner relationships became more and more challenging. Some of us began to form primary romantic relationships and to make these into committed monogamous partnerships. As we did so, we maintained our friendships and continued to value them greatly, but these friendships were no longer placed at the center of the family. Still, they were not lost. There were frustrations, complications, struggles, and some pain, but in the end, we reconstructed our families to include a partner, ex-lovers, and other close friends. We committed to honoring the different dyadic relationships within these families and to making time for family gatherings as a whole. These patterns we were creating were also evident in other lesbian friendship groups with which we were peripherally connected.

Taken together, they gave me a strong, felt sense of lesbian community during my early to mid-30s. I was single, but I definitely did not feel alone.

It was around this time that I met Rebecca, and with the development of our friendship, new questions about and dilemmas of friendship arose. Rebecca moved to town with her partner, and through various lesbian community connections, we met and began to get to know each other. I was immediately taken by Rebecca; she was somehow both familiar and unfamiliar to me—familiar because of our similar identity locations and upbringings, unfamiliar because she seemed to be both direct and outgoing, neither of which could have been said about me at that time. We began to spend time together, sometimes as a threesome with Rebecca's partner but more often, over time, just the two of us. I was most drawn to this time together and came to insist on it, for it was with Rebecca that I came to feel most comfortable with myself and to learn how to open up about myself.

We kept a good balance for a while, sometimes all three of us hanging out together, sometimes just Rebecca and I, and once in a while just me with Rebecca's partner. Over time, we all developed a feeling of ease together, and I came to depend upon Rebecca as a close friend. But there were complications: (1) I began to question what I wanted from my relationship with Rebecca, for I knew that I was deeply drawn to her in a way that felt different from other friendships, and (2) I began to have concerns about Rebecca's relationship with her partner, for it seemed to me that Rebecca was less, rather than more, able to be herself when with her partner than apart from her. I am not sure which concern arose first, but together they confused me for a long while, and during that time, I lied with my silence (Rich, 1979). Indeed, that was just what Rebecca had struggled with when I finally did tell her how I felt. It was during a relationship break between Rebecca and her partner, one of several that I had witnessed by that time. This time, however, I chose to speak my truths—both of them. I did not think I could say one without the other and really be honest or a good friend.

Our friendship was deeply challenged by these truths, by my speaking them, and by my not having spoken them before. Rebecca did end up returning to her partner relationship, and she felt both great anger toward me and betrayal by me. Fortunately, we had built a strong enough friendship base to allow for the expression of these feelings and, over time, to begin, slowly but surely, to move through them. Together we committed to a process of exploring and working through not only this rift in our connection but also our differing feelings and what we each wanted from our friendship. Through these conversations, we came to a greater understanding of each other and our connection, and we recommitted to our friendship.

When I look back on this time, and on a few other close friendships from these years, I am profoundly aware of having learned to trust that I could speak my truths and that these would be respected and cared for, even if they did not match my friends' truths. I learned that talking things out—the good things, the hard things each of us was experiencing in her life, the hard things we were experiencing together—offered an opportunity to learn and grow, individually and in our friendship. I learned, in essence, how to love and be loved through these friendships. And I learned, through these experiences, that friendships were central relationships in my life, lifesavers and contexts for developmental growth.

With this deepened sense of the power of friendship for supporting adult development, I began to seriously consider exploring lesbians' conceptions of friendships, lover relationships, and community as part of my graduate work. Specifically, I began to consider focusing my dissertation on the role of lesbians' friendships in fostering positive identity development and building lesbian communities. I had already been reading all I could find—personal stories, research reports, works of fiction, and theoretical works—on friendships in general and on friendships among lesbian, gay, bisexual, and/or transgender (LGBT) individuals. (In reality, however, in 1990, this meant reading mostly about lesbians' and gay men's friendships.) But when I began to talk about my preliminary ideas for my dissertation, I was advised by some lesbian academics who had gone before me to hold off. They thought I should wait at least until I had an academic job, if not until tenure. The risks of being pigeonholed as a lesbian (and thus a nonserious scholar or, maybe worse, a potential troublemaker) were too great, they said; play it safe, they advised.

A Postdoc Education

I listened to those who had gone before me, and I played it safe through graduate school. I wrote my dissertation on friendships but not on lesbian friendships. After earning my Ph.D. in the summer of 1993 and moving to State College, Pennsylvania, to start postdoctoral training at Penn State, I was ready, though, to stop listening. In fact, I felt I had to stop listening if I was to survive for the next two years. I had to take the risk of coming and being more out, both personally and professionally. In part, this was a response to the shock of moving from Burlington to State College. During my first few weeks in town, I experienced the pervasive context of heterosexism and it reached deep into my core, triggering my own internalized heterosexism.

I watched the queer youth on campus and in the surrounding communities struggle with similar feelings, and I noticed the dearth of places where queers could see themselves reflected in any positive way. Some resources did exist on campus, but the only place I found off campus was a bar that "went gay" one night a week. This context did much to spur my own coming out. Not only did I feel less vulnerable than the undergraduate and graduate students around me, but I had become extremely uncomfortable with the depth of my internalized heterosexism. Finally, I was coming to the realization that I had to act as if I was ready to come out rather than wait until I felt ready, as that time might never come.

With this commitment, I contacted the out faculty connected with the queer student groups and learned of the need the undergraduate student group had for an advisor. Meanwhile, I was spending a lot of time with new female friends I had made, some heterosexual, some bisexual, and some lesbian, but all embedded in the women's community and focused on the problem of sexism. I did not realize the extent of this focus, however, until I shared with these friends my decision to serve as advisor to the queer student group. I learned then of the deep divide and distrust between the women's and queer communities. I was even warned by some that I would have a hard time remaining accepted by the women's community if I was viewed as part of the queer community.

I opted to stay on as advisor to the queer group, and I sought to maintain my friendships with and connection to the women's community. This attempt to stay connected to both communities enabled me to see firsthand the good reasons for the split between the two communities in this town. The sexism of many of the gay men was clearly evident and at times unbearable, while for the queers, the lack of understanding of and attention to heterosexism made the women's community seem irrelevant to their issues. But perhaps the greatest tension—and transformation—that I experienced at this time centered on the issues raised by members of the queer community who were beginning to self-identify as transgender. These members wanted the student group to add transgender to its name and to become a trans-inclusive and trans-positive group. But many queer community members were uncomfortable with this, and in this way aligned more with the prevailing views in the women's community. The tensions were palpable.

The response the student leaders came up with was education, both through public events and private lessons. One student in the group whom I had gotten to know as an activist lesbian-identified student came to my office one day to ask how I knew I was a woman when ze[2] had never felt that in per whole life even though ze had female anatomy and was raised as a girl. Over the next months I had trans-identified students in a course I taught, attended other trans-related events, and had many long, troubling conversations with some members of the women's community. We were all struggling to understand trans experiences and the meaning of trans inclusion in both queer and women's communities.

My incoming views about transgender people came from my undergraduate years when I was assigned Jan Raymond's (1979) *The Transsexual Empire* as a required text in a women's studies course. I remembered Raymond's argument that transgender women gave men the ultimate ability to invade women's spaces. But then in my role as advisor during my first year at Penn State, I attended the student-sponsored public talk by trans activist Leslie Feinberg and, in preparation, read Feinberg's *Stone Butch Blues* (1993). In my second year, I attended a talk and workshop by another trans activist, Kate Bornstein, and again prepared by reading Bornstein's *Gender Outlaw* (1994). My intent at first was simply to support the student group's ability to engage in conversations and education prior to putting the question of adding "T" to the group's name and focus to a vote. Through these learning opportunities, however, I experienced a great deal of personal unlearning, enough at least to be able to foster discussions among students with differing views and to create and conduct a few workshops in collaboration with some trans students for members of Penn State's Equity Committee. But I was still far from being a trans ally in some key respects, and I remained skeptical about bridging some of the divides I perceived between lesbian feminism, with its commitment to challenging gender roles, and some trans activism that seemed to reify those same gender roles. I managed to hold on to a middle ground that kept me from fully facing the question that was just beneath the surface—whether I could be a trans ally and a lesbian feminist. I could not risk posing the question to myself at that time, as I was not prepared to face the answer. I was still too embedded in and dependent upon the women's and lesbian feminist community, and on my friendships with other lesbian feminists, to put them at risk.

(Writing My) Three Stories of Lesbian Friendship

The personal narratives I have shared thus far center on three main themes: friends as uniquely significant in my life/friends as family; blurred lines between friends, lovers, and ex-lovers; and building lesbian community and challenging traditional (patriarchal) family forms. These are the themes most often identified in the scholarly discourse on lesbian friendships, including my own writings.

Friends as Uniquely Significant, Serving as Family

The strongest, most persistent theme in the literature on lesbians' friendships with other lesbians (and gay men's friendships with other gay men, and sometimes lesbians' and gay men's friendships with each other) has at its core the notion that these friendships are uniquely significant to us as critical sources of both social support and satisfaction (see, e.g., D'Augelli, 1989; D'Augelli & Hart, 1987; Kurdek, 1988; Kurdek & Schmitt, 1987; Nardi, 1982; Nardi & Sherrod, 1994; Stanley, 1996; Stanley & Weinstock, 2004; Weeks, Heaphy, & Donovan, 2001; Weinstock, 1998, 2000, 2004b; Weston, 1997). These friendships play key roles in fostering the development of positive sexual identities; in providing spaces where we are able to really be ourselves, without cover or explanation; and in validating our same-sex lover relationships.

Within this story line, there are two major subplots. In one, emphasis is placed on the importance of shared sexuality (and sometimes, as well, gender identity) in our friendships. When we are with others of the same sexual identity, we do not have to worry about acceptance, and we do not have to worry about explaining ourselves, our community, our inside jokes. As a consequence, the story goes, we are most likely to be closest to others like ourselves—lesbians with other lesbians, gay men with other gay men, and so forth.

Across available empirical studies on lesbians' and gay men's friendships, there is good evidence that we tend to form friendships with others like ourselves in terms of both sexual and gender identities (Nardi, 1999; Weinstock, 1998). Thus, gay men are most likely to form their closest friendships with other gay men and lesbians with other lesbians. This is quite similar to the patterns typically found among heterosexual friendship pairs. Yet, to date, little attention has been paid to other aspects of identity such as age, race, ethnicity, socioeconomic situation, physical ability and religion, as well as other aspects of experience such as partner context and parental role. It is likely that here too, as has been shown in the research on heterosexuals' friendships (for reviews, see Fehr, 1996; O'Connor, 1992), similarities are the norm.

The issue of similarities and differences has been central in my own work on lesbian friendships. My first published work on lesbian friendships (*Lesbian Friendships: For Ourselves and Each Other*) was an edited collection of personal stories, fiction, theoretical works, and empirical research reports (Weinstock & Rothblum, 1996a) in which we sought to examine "how being a lesbian affects our friendships" (Weinstock & Rothblum, 1996b, p. 13). Most of the included pieces centered on friendships among lesbians, but we also created a section entitled "Friendships Across Differences," which included pieces that examined the ways a nonshared lesbian identity or other differences between friends were negotiated (or not) in friendships.

The other subplot to this story about lesbians' (and gay men's) friendships as uniquely significant focuses attention on the functions that friends play in our lives. Specifically, the story goes, our friends serve more diverse functions and/or more often serve select functions than is typical in friendships—*typical* here referring to what is expected of and experienced among heterosexuals' friends. That is, our friendships are uniquely conducted in our communities. In many cases, in fact, our friends function as heterosexuals' family members do, such that our friends become our family.

While these two subplots and the overarching friendship story that frames them are often told by lesbian and gay male theorists, clinicians, personal storytellers, and fiction writers, only a few empirical studies have directly examined our friendships. Especially rare has been an examination of the meaning ascribed to friends as family. Yet, three different meanings have been identified (see, e.g., Weinstock, 2000, 2004b; Weston, 1997). The first—"friends as substitute family members"—appears to develop in response to rejection by and/or exclusion in other ways from families of origin. Unable to rely upon families of origin for typical support, we turn to our friends for these necessities. Through this reliance, we become family to each other. Similarly, for some lesbians and gay men faced with a cultural context that denies us access to and support for forming our own traditional families with a partner and children, it may have felt/still feel easier to form friends as family instead. Such friendship families need not be publicized or even visible to neighbors and coworkers, yet our needs for family may still be met.

As Weston (1997) initially noted, some lesbians and gay men sought to construct friendship families in order to offer a purposeful critique and alternatives to traditional notions of family. Meanwhile, a third meaning of friends as family identified by Weinstock (2000, 2004b) is "friends as in-laws," which may be a way for ex-lovers and/or friends, where there is some sexual attraction, to still be a part of one's family. These latter two conceptions of friends as family reflect aspects of the other two prevailing story lines about lesbians' friendships.

Blurred Lines Between Friends and Lovers, and Ex-Lovers as Friends

A second common story about lesbians' (and gay men's) friendships emphasizes both similarities and differences between friends and lovers, though particular emphasis is placed on the overlap between these two relational forms. One such overlap is recognized in the developmental pattern of moving from friends to lovers (a pattern particularly associated with lesbians) or from lovers to friends (a pattern particularly associated with gay men). A second overlap is recognized through the tendency for lesbians and gay men to maintain close connections with ex-lovers (often to the extent that ex-lovers become family).

In both forms of overlap, the underlying theme is the important and intimate nature of friends and lovers and a commitment to maintaining our connections with both even as they transform into other relational forms (see, e.g., Becker, 1988; Nardi, 1992; Rose, 1996; Rothblum, 1994, 2000; Rothblum & Brehony, 1993; Stanley, 1996; Vetere, 1982; Weinstock, 2004a; Weston, 1997). Evidence of the prevalence of this theme can be seen in the comment of social worker and author Suzanne Slater (1995) that "sustaining friendships with ex-lovers is normative in lesbian communities" (in Weinstock, 1998, p. 141). Meanwhile, evidence of the centrality of this theme in my own writings is clear: one section of our 1996 edited collection was devoted to "Exploring the Continuum: Friends, Lovers, and the Places in Between" (Weinstock & Rothblum, 1996a). Here we placed those works that focused on the many ways friends and lovers overlap as well as sexual tensions in friendships. More recently, Esther Rothblum and I named our edited collection focused on lesbian ex-lover relationships *Lesbian Ex-Lovers: The Really Long-Term Relationships* (Weinstock & Rothblum, 2004).

Despite the prevalence of this story line, few empirical studies examining sexual activity and sexual attraction in same-sex, same-sexuality friendships have been conducted. Those that have been conducted (see, e.g., Becker, 1988; Nardi. 1999; Nardi & Sherrod, 1994; Stanley, 1996), however, do support the presence of considerable overlap between sex/sexual attraction and friendship among lesbians and gay men. For example, Nardi and Sherrod (1994) found that most of the lesbians and gay men in their sample considered their partners to be their best friends. Related research has highlighted the tendency for lesbians to remain friends with ex-lovers (Becker, 1988; Stanley, 1996) and for lesbians to follow a path from friends to lovers, reflecting what has been named the *friendship script* (Rose, 1996; Rose, Zand & Cini, 1993; Vetere, 1982).

Challenging Family, Challenging Patriarchy, Building Lesbian Feminist Community

The third prevailing story line is a lesbian feminist narrative that emphasizes challenging traditional family forms and creating lesbian feminist communities composed of lesbian friendships. Lesbian friendships are viewed as the core of lesbian community building and political activism and as reflective of lesbians' commitment to prioritizing each other and working together to create shared feminist communities (see, e.g., Card, 1995; Jo, 1996; Kimmel, 1992; Kitzinger, 1996; Kitzinger & Perkins, 1993; Nardi, 1992; Raymond, 1986;

Strega, 1996; Weinstock, 2000, 2004b; Weston, 1997). One section of our 1996 book, titled "Fixed Points in a Changing World: Personal and Political Dimensions of Friendship," was also devoted to this story line. We placed selections here to "highlight, honor, and celebrate lesbian friendships and lesbian culture" and to "present powerful images of what we are—and what we can be—to each other through the building, sustaining, and honoring of our friendships" (Weinstock & Rothblum, 1996b, p. 21). In the Afterword to this collection, Kitzinger (1996, p. 295) writes that *Lesbian Friendships* as a whole "puts lesbian friendships firmly back on the agenda as a passionate, absorbing, and vital concern for lesbians today…[and] prioritizes friendship among lesbians." She goes on to note that this is a welcome contrast to the tendency to overemphasize lesbians' partner relationships and consider lesbians' friendships largely in terms of their impact on partner relationships.

Side Plots

Despite the many parallels between my personal narrative and the three prevailing story lines in the literature on lesbian friendships, several inconsistencies are also evident. In years past, I worked hard to ignore these inconsistencies, both personally and professionally. But avoidance is no longer an option; the side plots are taking over and becoming the story.

Friends on the Side?

As noted earlier, at least three meanings of "friends as family" have been identified in the discourse to date: "friends as substitute family members," "friends as a challenge to the core family structure," and "friends as in-laws" (Weinstock, 2000, 2004b; see also Nardi, 1982; Weston, 1997). Yet, all three constructions of friends as family may be on the wane and, along with this, a lessening of the unique role for friends in lesbians' lives. Heterosexism remains prevalent but there has been much progress, and with it, lesbians now have access to legal rights for their partner and parent-child relationships. Indeed, a brief examination of the major political goals of our national LGBT organizations reflects an emphasis on access to marriage rights and rights related to the raising of children. While there is great value in fighting for—and winning—equal rights to the institution of marriage, to foster parenting and adoption, and to insurance and retirement benefits for partners, I do think it important to consider the implications of this shift in discourse from challenging heterosexual practices and the underlying assumptions of normality that go with them to fighting for equal access to them. Is the radical potential of both lesbian identity and lesbian friendship erased in this discourse?

This shift in the discourse is evident in my own communities and friendship networks. Most of my closest friends who are lesbians have been in committed partner relationships for a long while now, and some are raising children. Only two of my closest friends from graduate school still live nearby, though it was this friendship/family group that prompted my move back to Vermont. The friends who moved away did not want to lose the ease of connecting within our friendship family, but there were other, more central considerations that ultimately determined the final decision to move—partner needs, closeness to families of origin, and work opportunities are just a few of the factors that were placed at the center. Our friendships have been sustained at long distance, but the distance has impacted our closeness and our ability to function as family to each other in day-to-day ways and even during holidays and personal celebrations. For those with partners and/or children, there is no doubt that these are now at the center of the family story. There remains great value placed on these friendships, to be sure, but friends are more on the side, supporting characters or extended family members, neither of whom is unique to lesbians' friendships.

Similarly, more and more of us are being welcomed into our families of origin even if we are not fully understood there, and more and more of us are finding it easier to create close friendships with people with whom we do not share a sexual and/or gender identity. This is not to say that friendships across sexual identity differences are easy, but the barriers appear to be lessening (see, e.g., Weinstock & Bond, 2002). It is becoming increasingly rare to read about or see lesbians working to form lesbian friendships as a challenge to the core family structure. All in all, these past several years have revealed for me more and more what Celia Kitzinger (1996) argued 10 years ago—that it is "surprisingly difficult, even in a lesbian context, to insist on the importance and centrality of friendship to our lives" (p. 296).

From Friends to Lovers or Passionate Friends?

What makes someone a lover versus a friend? This has been a central question in my own life to date, but Lisa Diamond's work (e.g., 2002, 2003, 2004, 2005) has come to pose a substantive challenge to my most comfortable way of answering this question for myself. Diamond describes some sexual-minority women who "recall intense but platonic adolescent friendships containing many of the feelings and behaviors typically associated with romantic relationships" (Diamond, 2000a, in 2002, pp. 6–7). For these young women, romantic passion is felt for friends but without a corresponding sexual desire. Diamond refers to this phenomenon as *passionate friendship*, and it defies the traditional view of friendships and romantic relationships as distinct interpersonal relationships, with "the sexual 'charge' of a romantic relationship giv[ing] rise to a heightened intensity that never emerges between platonic friends" (Diamond, 2002, p. 6). Diamond argues that, developmentally speaking, these passionate friendships "may be particularly likely and uniquely meaningful for *young* women owing to the normative developmental tasks of adolescence" (2002, p. 10).

Diamond's work has led me to revisit my own history of friendships and the stories I have typically told to make sense of this history. These stories have clearly emphasized my falling in love with my friends. First, there was Alana in high school, whom I came to view as probably my first same-sex love, though I was unable or unwilling to admit these feelings at the time. Then there was Helen, first a friend who then became a lover, and so too with Toni and Paula and others whom I have not named here. My friendship with Rebecca was different in some key ways but also the same; we did not become lovers, but I interpreted my loving feelings for Rebecca as attraction and an interest in a romantic relationship. Now I question this interpretation and wonder about a new possibility—passionate friendship—involving an intense feeling of love beyond that of ordinary friendship, but not akin to sexual desire or romantic love. This interpretation is supported by recent findings indicating that sexual desire and passion activate different parts of the brain than attachment and commitment (see, e.g., Aron et al., 2004; Diamond, 2004).

I am not sure which of these stories is more in line with my feelings at the time, my experience of these relationships, and at the same time reflective of any unconscious desires, early attachment issues or other developmental concerns, and personal protection or coping styles. I do know, however, that Rebecca recently recalled that I had tried to explain my feelings for her during graduate school in terms similar to these: as a "temporary state of heightened interest in and preoccupation with a specific individual, characterized by intense desires for proximity and physical contact, resistance to separation, and feelings of excitement and euphoria when receiving the partner's attention" (Tennov, 1979, in Diamond, 2004, p. 117). This way of feeling may also include, as Diamond acknowledges, unexpressed or unrequited sexual desire, but it may also simply, truly, and deeply reflect a kind of attached-at-the-heart-friendship (Brehony, 2003). Unfortunately, there has been and remains a tendency among researchers—and among the young women themselves (myself included)—to interpret these passionate friendships as unrequited romantic relationships and/or as indicative of young women's sexual identities. What new understandings of attachment relationships, of interconnections, might we construct free from these worn story lines?

Ex-Lovers as Friends or Ties That Bind Too Tight?

As the stories I have shared in this chapter indicate, I have both experienced and endorsed the maintenance of connections with ex-lovers as an important lesbian community value. I have long recognized that this may require great effort on the part of the ex-lovers, and also on the part of new lovers as they work to make room for and accept their lover's ex-lover connection. But it is only recently that I have begun to seriously question this full-fledged endorsement of ex-lover ties. I am not saying that my beliefs are in line with those of the therapist Helen and I went to, but I do see now that there is value in questioning any commitment to maintaining a close ex-lover connection. What if the lover relationship ended because of difficulties in being good friends? What if the commitment to an ex-lover relationship reflects an unhealthy attachment, one that might interfere with the building of a new lover relationship? Is there a point at which an ex-lover connection is too close? Perhaps so—if one desires a new lover relationship in the form of a committed partnership.

As I wrote a few years back:

> How do we know when (or which aspects of) our desire for close connection to an ex- is built upon positive and healthy factors and when (or which aspects of) it is more reflective of not being able or willing to let go, or evidence of unresolved feelings, a tendency towards self-torture or self-fooling? Conversely, when we are troubled by our new lover's close ties to her ex, how can we tell if we might have a legitimate concern—for example, perhaps the new lover and her ex- are not quite ready to let go of their lover relationship—or if the concern ought to be recognized as more with ourselves—for example, our own personal insecurities or jealousies?
>
> (Weinstock, 2004a, p. 195)

I remain an advocate for maintaining ties with ex-lovers and, when possible, being close friends and family to each other. But I am now more attentive to the possibility that some of these connections may reflect and reinforce unhealthy relational dynamics, either within the ex-lover relationship itself or for other or future lover relationships.

Becoming a Trans Ally and Questioning Lesbian Feminism
and Lesbian Identity

My development as a trans ally is the strongest side plot to my stories of friendship to date and poses the greatest challenge to a continued centralization of
lesbian friendships in my narrative. This side plot reaches back over 10 years
to my first introduction to trans identities and the questions these raised. It
reaches even further into my past by challenging core feminist beliefs and lesbian cultural values I first endorsed in the early 1980s. One particular feminist
tenet was that sex does not determine gender because anatomy is not destiny.
Gender, as I and others then understood it, was gender *role*—the behaviors,
personality characteristics, body movement and presentation styles, and other
characteristics associated with and expected only from one sex (male) or the
other (female). It was distinct from sex, a biological characteristic. I was particularly drawn to this feminist notion of separating sex and gender and the
related promotion of androgyny as a positive alternative to enacting one or
the other approved gender role. As I understood it then, an androgynous person was one who was skilled at and able to express the positive characteristics
traditionally associated with and expected only from each constructed gender
role. The concept of androgyny also offered a framework for critiquing both
traditional feminine passivity and masculine aggressiveness.

As I delved more fully into feminist politics and claimed a lesbian identity
for myself, I was drawn specifically to lesbian feminist community and politics, with its focus on challenging the oppressive systems of both heterosexism
and sexism and valuing women's relationships with other women. For over a
decade, I thrived within these lesbian feminist community and political contexts. My own experiences of lesbian friendships and my creation of a lesbian
family of friends were reinforced by these contexts, and my own writings about
lesbian friendships reflected these values.

Yet, for some time now, I have also been engaged in a personal and professional journey toward being a trans ally. The journey started slowly, during my
postdoc years at Penn State when, as I have already described, I experienced my
first direct confrontation between the feminism of the women's community and
the trans politics of the queer community. I chose, then and in the years that
followed, to stand somewhere in the middle of the two perspectives. In so doing,
I moved forward at times as a trans ally and at other times backward; the same
might be said about my feminist credentials. I found myself striving to remain
connected to both communities and making threatening missteps in each.

This pull of opposing allegiances reached its peak after I moved back
to Vermont to work as a faculty member at the University of Vermont.

I approached these opposing pulls as I had done before, and I again met resistance from all sides. I was challenged by some women's studies faculty, community activists, and students for my views about trans identities, and I was challenged by some genderqueer and trans community activists and students for my allegiance to certain feminist perspectives. More significantly, I was challenged internally to try to create coherence among my own beliefs and to find a place where I might belong, with all of my beliefs. Only in recent years have I found some success in this regard, and have discovered a sense of community with those who are committed to both trans and feminist politics. As a result, I have begun to find a trans ally voice that is also feminist and a feminist voice that is also trans positive.

Despite the recent easing of these tensions between my trans and feminist politics, other related tensions remain unresolved. These tensions center on my personal comfort with participating in and committing to political projects, personal gatherings, professional groups, and social issues explicitly centered on women or lesbians. It is not that I no longer believe there are such issues still to address. Nor is it that I think that gatherings of women or lesbians are unimportant. The question I ask myself, however, is this: If I am uncomfortable in such settings, why do I continue to be drawn to them? Why do I not just forgo women-only or lesbian-only gatherings, activities, issues, and groups that are or have this potential to be trans-exclusive?

It is, in fact, easy for me to opt out of things that are explicitly anti-trans. But I find it hard to opt out of all contexts simply because they gather women or lesbians together who were assigned female at birth, separate from those who are women or lesbians *not* so assigned at birth. Yet, when I am in such contexts, I experience discomfort, as I am on guard for negative comments about trans people or comments that reflect and reinforce essentialist notions of women and men, lesbians and heterosexual women. I am wary too of negative comments being made about trans and genderqueer people who used to identify with or participate in women's and lesbian communities. And at a personal level, I miss having some of these individuals as part of what is supposed to be my home community. It is all these things that have made it difficult for me to find/feel at home in spaces designated as lesbian or women's communities, the very spaces where I first found a home in my young adulthood years.

It is all these things too that have led me to wonder these days about the extent to which being lesbian-identified remains a core aspect of my sense of identity, community, and politics, and how a shift away from this core might influence my friendship experiences and stories. Most of my closest friendships continue to be with other lesbians, but this is not the case for many of these lesbian friends. In some cases, I am the only one or one of only a very few lesbians in their closest friendship circles, now composed mostly of heterosexual single women and couples. Furthermore, while my closest friends know each other and are connected in some way, these connections vary widely and are highly individualized. More to the point, only some of our friendships overlap, and they no longer combine for most of us to serve as a shared community. We are each a part of multiple communities now.

What I also have been struck by of late is that my friendships with other lesbians seem to have less and less to do these days with our shared lesbian identity. Our friendships may have formed more easily at first because of this connection, but it is no longer what keeps us together as friends. Our shared sexual identity is not at the center of our conversations, nor is it the central connecting point between us. My friendships with other lesbians have become too varied in texture, quality, and context for me to view them in some common lesbian friendship framework. At the same time as the centrality of a specific shared lesbian identity weakens for me in maintaining friendships, I find myself searching for other links, links centered more on political and personal values than on the specificity of our identities. Not surprisingly, one important link of late centers on an openness to exploring questions of gender identity and expression, critically examining trans-oppressive internalized beliefs, and working together against trans-based oppressions.

Concluding Reflections

Lessons from childhood and adolescence taught me the deep value of friendships and, at the same time, to beware the shifting ground underneath which friendships might at any moment disappear. My experiences through late adolescence and young adulthood continued to offer these lessons. But new friendship lessons occurred as well—this time gleaned from experiences that were embedded in a context of lesbian identity development, lesbian relationships, and lesbian community building and political organizing.

I came to understand the critical role that friends can play in supporting the development of a positive lesbian identity in a context of heterosexism and sexism and the impact their absence can have on the course of this development. I experienced the loss of some friendships because these friends could not accept my lesbian identity or my same-sex intimate relationships. I distanced myself from my family because I anticipated the same lack of acceptance and understanding. I fell into several of the traps posed by internalized oppression, especially during my first intimate relationship when I took in the negative messages from society, made them my own, and then enacted them within this relationship. But I also found ways—with my first lover and beyond—to challenge those messages and to come to recognize and appreciate the power of lesbian identity, same-sex lover relationships, and especially lesbian friendships and lesbian community.

One particular aspect of these experiences that I was most drawn to centered on relationship fluidity and on developing connections from friends to lovers and lovers to friends. At the same time, I struggled to distinguish between these two relational forms—friends and lovers—and to know when my feelings reflected more of one or the other of these relational desires. Needless to say, there was both great overlap and blurred distinctions between friends and lovers in my own experiences and understandings. Still, I was in good company, as many of my friends and other lesbians in the lesbian community worked to create our adult lives centered on friendships, rather than on traditional family forms that placed a partner and children at the core.

These themes reflect my central personal narrative, and they are at the center of much of the scholarly literature on lesbian friendships, including my own such writings. I have no doubt that the personal narratives "I have tacitly, even unconsciously, composed over the course of my years" (McAdams, 1997, p. 11) thus far have been intricately shaped by and have shaped these scholarly narratives. Yet, today I find myself at a point of disjunction, no longer so comfortable with the stories I have told about my friendships and no longer drawn as deeply to the telling of stories of lesbian friendship. In the past several years, it has been more the absence of lesbian friendship stories that has caught my attention.

Over these same years, I have moved from young to middle adulthood; from a lesbian feminist community context to one that is less woman and lesbian focused, indeed less identity category focused in general; and from a sense of family comprised largely of lesbian friendships to one that includes a greater diversity of individual identities and experiences. The textures of my friendships with other lesbians are deeply varied. At times, the shared lesbian identity seems simply irrelevant. I have observed similar shifts among many of the lesbians I know, though my lens is a narrow one, and there continue to be groups of lesbians working together to build lesbian community. I do continue to be drawn to these groups and even to participate in them. But it is an uneasy participation, an ambivalent participation, one that challenges my sense of identity, my commitment to my own central stories to date, and my faith in the future of the lesbian friendship narrative as a central narrative in my own life.

Part of the unease is tied to my reexamination of several central lesbian feminist beliefs claimed by me in my 20s—beliefs that included many negative views about gender identities and gender expressions. As I have shifted in my understandings and deepened my commitment to fighting transgender-based oppression, I have found myself in conflict with these lesbian feminist beliefs and with many lesbian feminists themselves. At the same time, I have struggled with the lessening of attention among many lesbians and gay men to the building of alternative family forms and communities centered on friends.

Ray Pahl (2000) credits the lesbian and gay community with originating the notion of *families of choice*. Yet, more and more, the focus in these communities has centered on forming more traditional families, a shift reflected in the focus on the strong push for marriage and other related family policies. Part of my continued yearning for and draw to lesbian community stems from the emphasis placed on building such alternative families and communities, in the past and, for some, still in the present. But I yearn for something broader too—a community based on shared political views and personal values, not simply on shared identities. This is the journey I am on today. I do not know where it will lead me, but I am pretty sure of where it will not.

I doubt I will continue to write about lesbian friendships, at least not through the same lens I have relied upon to date. That is, I doubt that I will focus on a shared lesbian identity and how it affects friendships. Like the queer voices of many of my students, and of some of the research scientists and theorists studying sexual orientation, I "have increasingly come to question the usefulness of [sexual identity] categories in light of the increasing evidence for nonexclusivity and plasticity in sexuality, especially among women" (Diamond, 2005, p. 119). I have also come to recognize that, as Diamond (2004) put it, "individuals are capable of developing intense, enduring, preoccupying affections for one another regardless of either partner's sexual attractiveness or arousal" (p. 116). It is this core of *affection* that I am most drawn to examining these days, regardless of the patterns of individual identities among the participants in a relationship. Thus, I suspect that any new midlife writings on—and I hope my personal narratives of—friendships will focus more explicitly on the felt depth of close friendship wherever it may occur, and on deepening insight into the ways friends support individual development, community activism, and social justice. The fact of shared or differing identities is likely to become just one of many side plots rather than the main story line.

NOTES

1. The names used in this chapter are pseudonyms.

2. *Ze* (in place of *she* or *he*) and *per* (in place of *her* or *him*) are used here intentionally as gender-neutral terms.

REFERENCES

Aron, A., Fisher, H., Mashek, D., Strong, G., Li, H., & Brown, L. L. (2004, July). *Passionate love as a research-oriented behavioral and neural system: An fMRI study.* Paper presented at the meetings of the International Association for Relationship Research, Madison, WI.

Becker, C. S. (1988). *Unbroken ties: Lesbian ex-lovers.* Boston: Alyson Publications.

Bornstein, K. (1994). *Gender outlaw: On men, women and the rest of us.* New York: Routledge.

Brehony, K. A. (2003). *Living a connected life: Creating and maintaining relationships that last.* New York: Henry Holt.

Card, C. (1995). *Lesbian choices.* New York: Columbia University Press.

D'Augelli, A. R. (1989). The development of a helping community for lesbians and gay men: A case study of community psychology. *Journal of Community Psychology, 8*(1), 12–22.

D'Augelli, A. R., & Hart, M. M. (1987). Gay women, men, and families in rural settings: Toward the development of helping communities. *American Journal of Community Psychology, 15,* 79–93.

Diamond, L. M. (2002). "Having a girlfriend without knowing it": Intimate friendships among adolescent sexual-minority women. In S. M. Rose (Ed.), *Lesbian love and relationships* (pp. 5–16). Binghamton, NY: Harrington Park Press.

Diamond, L. M. (2003). What does sexual orientation orient? A biobehavioral model distinguishing romantic love and sexual desire. *Psychological Review, 110,* 173–192.

Diamond, L. M. (2004). Emerging perspectives on distinctions between romantic love and sexual desire. *Current Directions in Psychological Science, 13*(3), 116–119.

Diamond, L. M. (2005). A new view of lesbian subtypes: Stable vs. fluid identity trajectories over an 8-year period. *Psychology of Women Quarterly, 29,* 119–128.

Fehr, B. (1996). *Friendship processes.* Thousand Oaks, CA: Sage.

Feinberg, L. (1993). *Stone butch blues.* Ithaca, NY: Firebrand Books.

Jo, B. (1996). Lesbian friendships create lesbian community. In J. S. Weinstock & E. D. Rothblum (Eds.), *Lesbian friendships: For ourselves and each other* (pp. 288–291). New York: New York University Press.

Kimmel, D. C. (1992). The families of older gay men and lesbians. *Generations, 17*(3), 37–38.

Kitzinger, C. (1996). Toward a politics of lesbian friendship. In J. S. Weinstock & E. D. Rothblum (Eds.), *Lesbian friendships: For ourselves and each other* (pp. 295–299). New York: New York University Press.

Kitzinger, C., & Perkins, R. (1993). *Changing our minds: Lesbian feminism and psychology.* New York: New York University Press.

Kurdek, L. A. (1988). Perceived social support in gays and lesbians in cohabiting relationships. *Journal of Personality and Social Psychology, 54,* 504–509.

Kurdek, L. A., & Schmitt, J. P. (1987). Perceived support from family and friends in members of homosexual, married, and heterosexual cohabiting couples. *Journal of Homosexuality, 14*, 57–68.

McAdams, D. P. (1997). *The stories we live by: Personal myths and the making of the self* (Rev. ed.). Boston: Guilford.

Nardi, P. M. (1982). Alcohol treatment and the non-traditional "family" structures of gays and lesbians. *Journal of Alcohol and Drug Education, 27*(2), 83–89.

Nardi, P. M. (1992). That's what friends are for: Friends as family in the gay and lesbian community. In K. Plummer (Ed.), *Modern homosexualities: Fragments of lesbian and gay experience* (pp. 108–120). New York: Routledge.

Nardi, P. M. (1999). *Gay men's friendships: Invincible communities.* Chicago: University of Chicago Press.

Nardi, P. M., & Sherrod, D. (1994). Friendships in the lives of gay men and lesbians. *Journal of Social and Personal Relationships, 11*, 185–199.

O'Connor, P. (1992). *Friendships between women: A critical review.* New York: Guilford.

Pahl, R. E. (2000). *On friendship.* Malden, MA: Polity Press.

Raymond, J. G. (1979). *The transsexual empire: The making of the she-male.* Boston: Beacon Press.

Raymond, J. G. (1986). *A passion for friends: Towards a philosophy of female affection.* Boston: Beacon Press.

Rich, A. (1979). *On lies, secrets, and silence.* New York: Norton.

Rose, S. (1996). Lesbian and gay love scripts. In E. D. Rothblum & L. A. Bond (Eds.), *Preventing heterosexism and homophobia* (pp. 151–173). Thousand Oaks, CA: Sage.

Rose, S., Zand, D., & Cini, M. A. (1993). Lesbian courtship scripts. In E. D. Rothblum & K. A. Brehony (Eds.), *Boston marriages: Romantic but asexual relationships among contemporary lesbians* (pp. 70–85). Amherst: University of Massachusetts Press.

Rothblum, E. D. (1994). Transforming lesbian sexuality. *Psychology of Women Quarterly, 18*, 627–641.

Rothblum, E. D. (2000). Sexual orientation and sex in women's lives: Conceptual and methodological Issues. *Journal of Social Issues, 56*, 193–204.

Rothblum, E. D., & Brehony, K. A. (Eds.) (1993). *Boston marriages: Romantic but asexual relationships among contemporary lesbians.* Amherst: University of Massachusetts Press.

Slater, S. (1995). *The lesbian family life cycle.* New York: Free Press.

Stanley, J. L. (1996). The lesbian's experience of friendship. In J. S. Weinstock & E. D. Rothblum (Eds.), *Lesbian friendships: For ourselves and each other* (pp. 39–59). New York: New York University Press.

Stanley, J. S., & Weinstock, J. S. (2004). Friendship. In M. Stein (Ed.), *Encyclopedia of lesbian, gay, bisexual, and transgender history in America* (pp. 412–420). New York: Scribner.

Strega, L. (1996). A lesbian love story. In J. S. Weinstock & E. D. Rothblum (Eds.), *Lesbian friendships: For ourselves and each other* (pp. 277–287). New York: New York University Press.

Vetere, V. A. (1982). The role of friendship in the development and maintenance of lesbian love relationships. *Journal of Homosexuality, 8(2)*, 51–65.

Weeks, J., Heaphy, B., & Donovan, C. (2001). *Same sex intimacies: Families of choice and other life experiments.* New York: Routledge.

Weinstock, J. S. (1998). Lesbian, gay, bisexual, and transgender friendships in adulthood: Review and analysis. In C. J. Patterson & A. R. D'Augelli (Eds.), *Lesbian, gay, and bisexual identities in families: Psychological perspectives* (pp. 122–153). New York: Oxford University Press.

Weinstock, J. S. (2000). Lesbian friendships at midlife: Patterns and possibilities for the 21st century. *Journal of Gay and Lesbian Social Services, 11*, 1–32.

Weinstock, J. S. (2004a). Lesbian FLEX-ibility: Friend and/or family connections among lesbian ex-lovers. In J. S. Weinstock & E. D. Rothblum (Eds.), *Lesbian ex-lovers: The really long-term relationships* (pp. 193–238). Binghamton, NY: Harrington Park Press.

Weinstock, J. S. (2004b). Lesbian friendships at and beyond midlife: Patterns and possibilities for the 21st century. In G. Herdt & B. de Vries (Eds.), *Gay and lesbian aging: A research agenda for the 21st century* (pp. 177–209). New York: Springer.

Weinstock, J. S., & Bond, L. A. (2002). Building bridges: Examining lesbians' and heterosexual women's close friendships with each other. In S. M. Rose (Ed.), *Lesbian love and relationships* (pp. 149–161). Binghamton, NY: Harrington Park Press.

Weinstock, J. S., & Rothblum, E. D. (Eds.). (1996a). *Lesbian friendships: For ourselves and each other.* New York: New York University Press.

Weinstock, J. S., & Rothblum, E. D. (1996b). What we can be together: Contemplating lesbians' friendships. In J. S. Weinstock & E. D. Rothblum (Eds.), *Lesbian friendships: For ourselves and each other* (pp. 3–30). New York: New York University Press.

Weinstock, J. S., & Rothblum, E. D. (Eds.). (2004). *Lesbian ex-lovers: The really long-term relationships.* Binghamton, NY: Harrington Park Press.

Weston, K. (1997). *Families we choose: Lesbians, gays, kinship* (Rev. ed.). New York: Columbia University Press.

9

Emergence of a Poz
Sexual Culture

Accounting for "Barebacking"
Among Gay Men

Barry D. Adam

Barebacking is a term that makes sense only in a particular social
and historical context. Sex without a barrier did not need a name
before the risks of Acquired Immune Deficiency Syndrome (AIDS)
and other sexually transmitted infections became increasingly
evident. Today it is an idea associated particularly with sex between
men, as communities of gay men have been heavily impacted by
Human Immunodeficiency Virus (HIV) and AIDS, but it has yet
to gain much currency among other populations despite the rising
prevalence of HIV disease around the world. *Barebacking* can be
used to refer to any kind of unprotected sex, but more often it refers
to *intentional* unprotected sex and not to various kinds of slips or
accidents where unprotected sex is a consequence. In the context
of elevated risk that characterizes communities of gay, bisexual,
and other men who have sex with men, barebacking has at times
been viewed as something of a scandal and its practitioners as
deviants, rebels, or irrational and irresponsible individuals. Yet,
closer examination reveals just how unsurprising and consistent it is
with widespread rules of conduct circulating in advanced industrial
countries.

This chapter delves into the history of the difficult relationship
that gay and bisexual men have had with HIV and its prevention as
they have sought pleasure and intimacy in an era marked by a

life-threatening disease. The chapter examines a converging set of social, psychological, and physiological factors that created the conditions for the beginnings of a bareback microculture and identity. In doing so, it is important to keep in mind that in the first decade of the twenty-first century, *barebacking* remains an emergent, inchoate, and contested term and identity. Some men whose sexual practices might appear to an outside observer to fit the category reject the term. Others employ bareback language and participate in bareback circuits and scenes but limit their unprotected sex to particular partners and situations and often express a willingness to accept protected sex with partners who initiate condom use.

AIDS and LGBT Communities

Since the first identification of AIDS in 1981, public conceptions of the significance and danger of HIV and AIDS have shifted substantially. Faced at first by an unprecedented deadly threat, lesbian, gay, bisexual, and transgendered (LGBT) communities mobilized to support those struck by the disease and to find ways to limit its transmission. By the 1990s, the sexual practices of men having sex with men had changed profoundly and rates of transmission, as well as deaths from AIDS, had fallen sharply as a consequence. But in the first decade of the twenty-first century, HIV has changed yet again. Now it seems that the transmission of HIV has begun to edge upward among gay, bisexual, and other men who have sex with men, especially in the major cities of the advanced industrial world. The question is: Why? How has the face of HIV been transformed, and what are its consequences for the health of thousands of gay men now and in the decades to come?

When the first reports of an acquired immune deficiency surfaced through the Centers for Disease Control in 1981, AIDS was an unknown and unimagined affliction. At first, it was hard to believe that such a syndrome could really exist. In the early years, scientists, journalists, religious leaders, and politicians stepped into a conceptual chaos, with a range of motivations and agendas, to make sense of this new medical peril. AIDS was, at first, a blank slate on which a range of conflicting narratives were inscribed (Epstein, 1996). What was all too clear to LGBT communities was that many gay and bisexual men, their friends, and their partners were falling gravely ill, that public authorities were quick to either cast blame or refuse to acknowledge the problem, and that few were willing to provide support, research, or practical measures to face the new health menace. As it turns out, at the time of its identification, HIV had already infected a substantial number of gay, bisexual, and other men who have sex with men, resulting in a rapidly rising death toll through the mid-1980s. In the early years, the causal agent for AIDS was unknown, nor was it clear how to avoid it. The fact that epidemiology pointed to sexual transmission led to the first steps taken to develop an AIDS avoidance strategy through condom use. The New York Gay Men's Health Crisis (Kramer, 1989) issued a first guide on how to have sex in an epidemic, and soon gay men, lesbians, their families, and frontline professionals were pulling together community-based AIDS organizations in virtually every city to assist people living with HIV and to get the word out about how to avoid contracting the disease (Altman, 1986; Levine, Nardi & Gagnon, 1997; Patton, 1985, 1990).

AIDS arrived in an historical era when LGBT communities were making their first gains in abolishing laws that criminalized their sexual and affective relationships, as well as winning basic protection from discrimination through human rights laws. But in the 1980s, many jurisdictions, especially in the United States, continued to marginalize gay men as outlaws. Full citizenship rights and participation in the many spheres of life, whether in employment, residence, religion, recreation, government, or corporate services, could not be taken for granted and required struggle with social institutions, the courts, and legislatures. Public authorities were typically slow to respond to a medical syndrome that affected gay men and other populations such as injection drug users, hemophiliacs, and immigrants from Africa and the Caribbean—none of whom commanded much power or status in Western societies. Some 16,000 died of AIDS in the United States—most of them gay men—by the time a test for HIV was developed and made available in 1985 and 1986. This number turned out to be just a fraction of a global epidemic. With inadequate treatments, the prospect of testing positive was often perceived as a death sentence. With an average 10-year period of disease progression from the time of infection to the development of AIDS, many people faced an apparently relentless and deadly disease that they had unknowingly contracted before anyone had heard of it.

By the 1990s, gay men responded with a massive reorientation of their sexual practices by using condoms most or all of the time, and with this reorientation came a major decline in new HIV infections. In the same decade, with the 1996 world AIDS conference in Vancouver, came the announcement of a new class of anti-HIV drugs, the protease inhibitors, and with them, new hope for effective treatment of AIDS. The combination of protease inhibitors with other classes of antiretroviral drugs succeeded in stabilizing the health of many people living with HIV, but at the cost of a rigorous and expensive drug regimen that risked failure if the drugs were not taken consistently and on time every day. By the late 1990s infection rates had fallen steadily, though gay communities remain impacted by HIV much more than other communities in advanced industrial societies. Public discourses of panic and siege began to give way to more medicalized narratives of disease, and some speculated about a turn toward a "post-AIDS" era (Rofes, 1998) in which HIV was to become an enduring but less dominant concern of gay communities.

The Contemporary Context of HIV

In the early 2000s, the HIV epidemic appeared to be changing yet again. Rates of infection began to increase in more and more cities after having fallen to a plateau in the mid-1990s. A series of speculative theories arose to account for the apparent resurgence of HIV transmission. As media attention turned increasingly to the massive worldwide heterosexual epidemic, infection among gay men became old news, though male-to-male sexual transmission continued to be the leading risk factor for HIV transmission in the advanced industrialized nations of northern Europe, North America, and Australia and New Zealand. Popular narratives arose describing "condom fatigue" among gay men, whose supposedly greater confidence in the effectiveness of medication to control HIV was resulting in complacency about condom use and reduced personal vigilance against HIV transmission. A meta-analysis of 25 studies on treatment-related beliefs found evidence of a persistent statistical relationship between decreased concern and fear of HIV (compared to the preprotease era) and unprotected anal intercourse (Crepaz, Hart, & Marks, 2004). However, relatively small numbers of gay and bisexual men overall showed a willingness to consider HIV a diminished threat. Indeed, the enduring proliferation of the condom fatigue or treatment optimism narrative raises this question: To what degree is it an account so readily available in the public sphere that it supplies ready-made recipe statements that take on a life of their own and circulate through the media in a grand feedback loop? The degree to which it is a leading or persistent narrative among men speaking of the occasions on which they have had unprotected sex is quite another question.

Perhaps the most noteworthy finding to emerge from the large amount of research done on gay and bisexual men facing the threat of AIDS is that most men, most or all of the time, continue to take protective measures to guard against the transmission of HIV. This change in sexual practice is the largest behavioral change in sexuality found in any population. The underlying conditions and narratives influencing sexual practices in everyday life turn out to be much more complex than mediatized public discourses. Gay and bisexual men remain at high risk of acquiring HIV if they have unprotected anal intercourse, and a good deal of investigation has mapped out a range of vulnerabilities, situations, practices, and discourses that contribute to the heightened risk. These fall into a few broad categories: condoms and erectile difficulties, momentary lapses and trade-offs, personal turmoil and depression, alcohol and drug use, disclosure and intuiting safety, and relationship formation. There are, then, a number of push and pull factors associated with unprotected sex. The convergence of a critical mass of these factors creates the conditions for the emergence of a set of men whose sexual practices become more and more consistently unprotected. With these conditions in place come social networks and mutual communication and subsequently narratives that reflect on, encode, and justify these practices.

Condoms, Erectile Difficulties, and Momentary Lapses

Large numbers of men employ condoms without difficulty and make them a routine part of their sexual lives. Some prefer the hygienic qualities of condoms; others simply accept them as a necessity. Using condoms every time, rather than making a decision about risk and safety at each encounter, remains the most reliable method for HIV avoidance (Hart et al., 2005). But for some men—especially those who have difficulty maintaining an erection—condoms may be experienced as an impediment to satisfactory sex. Condom-avoidance rationales tend to fall into two major categories: (1) physiological (they are desensitizing), and (2) symbolic (they signify a barrier to intimacy and to its sexual expression through insemination) (Díaz & Ayala, 1999; Mansergh et al., 2002; Zwart, Kerkhof, & Sandfort, 1998). The statement of this man, drawn from a Toronto sample of men having difficulty with safe sex, is typical:

> It will not stay hard if I put one on, come hell or high water. Believe me, I've tried. So, you know, since I've started having sex, I've basically always had unsafe sex.
>
> (Adam, Husbands, Murray, & Maxwell, 2005a, p. 240)

In addition to the men who report their own erectile difficulties are those who report them in their partners.

Recent research in Sydney and Toronto has identified the practice of delayed condom use among some gay men. The Polaris study in Toronto found a strong association between this practice and becoming HIV-positive (Calzavara et al., 2003). Delayed use or episodic use during a sexual experience is usually due to difficulties in resolving the tension between condoms and erections.

I find this more as I've gotten in my 30s. I find if I'm not into it, once I put the condom on, I can get soft.... We'd start with a condom and then if I got soft, I'd take the condom off and I'd put my dick inside and get hard again and then we'd put the condom back on. But sometimes the condom just never came back on.

(Adam et al., 2005a, p. 240)

In a number of instances, men report wrestling with a series of dilemmas about condom use: wanting to maintain an erection that refused to cooperate when sheathed, wanting to accommodate a partner experiencing similar difficulties, wanting to avoid exposure to the risk of infection, wanting to ensure that a partner does not become infected, attempting to keep up some degree of condom use even if inconsistent, and relying on a risk calculus that falls back on withdrawal, taking the top role, or avoiding tears to the rectal lining. For men who experience erectile difficulty with condom use, these are real dilemmas resolved through actions that may heighten the risk.

The urgency of passion and the opportunity to connect with a particularly desirable partner, sometimes facilitated by drugs or alcohol, account for some unsafe encounters. Heat-of-the-moment situations can be complicated by "trade-off" scenarios in which men who feel disadvantaged in some way— by age, ethnicity, or attractiveness—fear to offend a desirable partner and trade away safe sex lest it prove an obstacle to sexual interaction (Choi et al., 1999; Seal et al., 2000; Stokes & Peterson, 1998).

Personal Turmoil and Depression

A small but growing set of studies finds that men who report having experienced sexual abuse as children report higher rates of unprotected anal intercourse with casual partners when they become adults (Kalichman, Benotsch, & Rompa, 2001; Paul, Catania, Pollack, & Stall, 2001; Relf, 2001). Perhaps not surprisingly, then, men who are currently HIV-positive report having experienced childhood abuse at a higher rate than their HIV-negative counterparts (Greenwood et al., 2002; Kalichman, Gore-Felton, Benotsch, Cage, & Rompa, 2004; Paul et al., 2001). Childhood sex abuse also appears to be a predisposing condition to a number of additional factors associated with unsafe sex, including drug use, higher numbers of sex partners, sex work, and sexual adventurism (Díaz & Ayala, 1999; Kalichman et al., 2001, 2004; Klitzman, Greenberg, Pollack, & Dolezal, 2002; Paul et al., 2001). Dorais' (2004) interviews with gay and bisexual men in Québec who had experienced sexual abuse in childhood concludes that they frequently suffer "depression, confusion and uneasiness about sex, and even loss of control over their love lives, mak[ing] meaningful self-protection more difficult" (p. 119) as they become adults.

Broad-based surveys of risk factors frequently identify depression as more common among those who have unprotected anal intercourse (Kalichman, Cherry, Cain, Pope, & Kalichman, 2005; Semple, Patterson, & Grant, 2000b). Qualitative studies give some insight into the way this everyday depression works (Adam et al., 2005a; Adam, Sears, & Schellenberg, 2000; Odets, 1995; Schwartz & Bailey, 2005). Episodes of unprotected anal intercourse may follow major stressful events such as job loss, financial crisis, moving to another city, homophobic victimization, breakup with a partner, or death of a partner (Boulton, McLean, Fitzpatrick, & Hart, 1995; Vincke & Bolton, 1995). Personal disruption and depression can affect the sense of being in control of one's life and having the capacity to care for oneself. To be effective, then, the prevention message calls on an autobiographical narrative that life is worth living and that something done now makes sense because the future will be a desirable place. Yet, depression and personal turmoil can pull away the underpinnings of this belief. If life does not seem worth living now and the future appears bleak as well, then self-preserving actions no longer make much sense.

Alcohol and Drug Use

The relationship between drug and alcohol use with unprotected anal intercourse is one of the most developed areas of research. A plethora of studies reveal an association between rates of unprotected anal intercourse and the use of "club drugs" (Colfax et al., 2004; Klitzman et al., 2002; Parsons, Kutnick, Halkitis, Punzalan, & Carbonari, 2005) and the use of alcohol with or without other drugs (Hirshfield, Remien, Humberstone, Walavalkar, & Chiasson, 2004; Koblin et al., 2003; Vanable et al., 2004). Myers and colleagues (2004) conclude that

> the effects of substances varied not only by the type of substances used
> or the expectations of the participants who use them, but also by the
> context in which the same substance is used.... Risky sex does not
> result from the simple exposure to drugs or alcohol before or during
> sexual behaviours, but rather depends on mitigating factors such as
> the personal convictions of the individual, as well as the decision-
> making processes that occur well throughout the sexual act. (pp. 222, 225)

Observers of today's circuit parties and the "party and play" scene refer to the "tribalism," "esprit de corps," and sense of communion that attract a segment of the gay and bisexual population (Ghaziani & Cook, 2005; Green, 2001;

Kurtz, this volume; Slavin, 2004; Westhaver, 2005). Club drugs have found a function that is not easily displaced, as they facilitate a sense of connection so desired by participants.

Disclosure and Intuiting Safety

Some HIV-positive men inform their partners of their HIV status and may then have unprotected sex on the presumption that the partner, having been duly warned, will take appropriate precautions where necessary. Settings with a reputation for quick sex such as baths, parks, sex clubs, sex parties, public washrooms, and some Web sites tend not to make disclosure of serostatus easy and operate more by the rules of the marketplace, namely, *caveat emptor* or buyer beware. In these situations, knowledge about a partner's serostatus may be more an assumption than a fact based on reliable information, and unprotected sex may be riskier than is initially understood.

Relationships

Anticipating that a relationship will occur, or identifying a new partner as "boyfriend material," is enough to motivate some men to drop condom use as a sign of the seriousness of the relationship. As long as condom use implicitly communicates distrust of a partner, dropping it can function as a tacit sign of trust and of the increasing seriousness of a relationship. Gay and bisexual men are scarcely unique in this practice, and research confirms its pervasiveness (Adam et al., 2000; Carballo-Diéguez, Remien, Dolezal, & Wagner, 1997; Cusick & Rhodes, 2000; Díaz & Ayala, 1999; Flowers, Smith, Sheeran, & Beail, 1997; McLean et al., 1994). Even among serodiscordant couples (where one partner is HIV-negative and one is HIV-positive), these meanings can exert a strong influence (Adam & Sears, 1996; Odets, 1995; Remien, Carballo Diéguez, & Wagner, 1995). As Rhodes (1997) remarks:

> In the context of relationships where one partner is HIV positive, unprotected sex can be considered to communicate feelings of "love" and "commitment" in even more powerful ways than would be the case if both partners were negative. (p. 215)

Emergence of a Poz Sexual Culture

There is, then, a range of circumstances, assumptions, and vulnerabilities reported by men for whom unprotected sex is typically exceptional in a general pattern of consistent condom use. The uneven accumulation of these factors gives rise to conditions that increase the tendency for unprotected sex among particular individuals and microcultures. In recent years, a set of primarily HIV-positive men have given up on condom use most or all of the time, and their presence has now been well documented in major cities of the advanced industrialized countries. There are several conditions, incentives, and motivations that contribute to a bareback orientation, as well as an idea system to justify it. Yet, most gay men, especially HIV-negative men, and certainly nongay populations have little familiarity with the dynamics involved. This mutual misapprehension can result in sexual interactions where risk is indeed heightened, and these scenarios pose new challenges for effective HIV prevention messages in a context in which rates of HIV infection have begun to rise again among gay and bisexual men.

Certainly for most people who test HIV-positive the experience is disturbing—even devastating. But over time, as a sense of normalcy is restored and symptoms related to HIV disease may be resolved, some experience a sense of relief over not having to worry anymore about contracting HIV and indeed about sex with condoms. For many, the risk of infection with any other disease while being immunocompromised is incentive enough to maintain a policy of protection (Adam, Husbands, Murray, & Maxwell, 2005b). And for many other HIV-positive individuals, condom use remains the choice for sexual conduct with casual partners and any other partners who are not HIV-positive. For others, participation in support groups for HIV-positive people, getting used to seeing other positive people in the street, and developing friends and contacts among other positive people help contribute to a sense of living in a *poz* world where everyone "knows the score" and shares a number of assumptions about norms and expectations concerning sexual interaction. Combined with apprehension about having to explain their sero status to naive outsiders or the prospect of rejection by fearful or uncomprehending prospective partners, some people also actively seek to restrict their romantic and sexual connections to other positive people (Adam & Sears, 1996; Stirratt, 2005). In this context of poz-on-poz sex, leaving condom use behind can seem reasonable and become a habit over time.

The rationale for condomless sex is readily at hand. The AIDS service organizations have long sought to educate the public that everyone must take responsibility for HIV prevention and that simply presuming that prospective sex partners are HIV-negative, then blaming them later if it turns out that they are not, is scarcely a reliable method of HIV prevention. It is advice that relies on sex partners being well-informed adults who calculate risk rationally and appropriately and enter knowingly into an implicit contract with each other when sex occurs. Those who employ the language of barebacking typically presume that prospective partners will be "in the know"—that is, they will be fully knowledgeable about the HIV risk, they will be adult men capable of making informed choices and of consenting after having weighed all relevant risks, and often they will be HIV-positive themselves. Few, if any, actually insist on unprotected sex; they are nearly always willing to respect partners who prefer to use protection, but if a condom is not produced by a new partner, there is a ready-made explanation applied to the sexual inter-action that allows unsafe sex to occur. For the subset of men who have left safe sex behind, raw or bareback sex is justifiable by a rhetoric of individual-ism, personal responsibility, consenting adults, and contractual interaction. In other words, discourses of HIV prevention that postulate sexual actors as individuals acting defensively against potential threat converge with domi-nant narratives of consumption and competition in market societies in which they are to be responsible, contract-making individuals who must manage risk in a buyer-beware environment.

At a time when *serosorting* has become something of a buzz word in HIV prevention, many men who prefer barebacking consider that they are indeed serosorting—that is, selecting partners who share their HIV status. For those who go with a prospective partner for HIV testing and ascertain that they are in fact seroconcordant, reliable serosorting has been accomplished and, with a subsequent agreement about monogamy or shared risk prevention, they may not need to use condoms to avoid HIV infection (or reinfection). But few employ such a rigorous standard of verification. Some men rely on sometimes highly subtle clues to impute the seropositivity of a partner or to communicate to a partner that they are already seropositive (e.g., leaving pill bottles in view, men-tioning having volunteered for an AIDS organization) (Adam, 2005; Serovich, Oliver, Smith, & Mason, 2005; Stirratt, 2005). Indeed, many HIV-positive men read the willingness of their partners to engage in unprotected sex as evidence that the partners are already HIV-positive (Adam, 2005; Gorbach et al., 2004; Larkins, Reback, Shoptaw, & Veniegas, 2005; O'Leary, 2005; Rhodes & Cusick, 2002; Richters, Hendry, & Kippax, 2003; Semple, Patterson, & Grant, 2000a; Stirratt, 2005). By contrast, HIV-negative men rarely make this assumption or they assume the opposite—that partners willing to engage in unprotected sex must be negative (Van de Ven et al., 2005).

The development of a bareback current among poz men may account for a cascade of recent evidence showing elevated and rising rates of unprotected anal intercourse among HIV-positive men with casual partners of unknown or negative HIV status (Frankis & Flowers, 2006; Grulich, Prestage, Kippax, Crawford, & Van de Ven, 1998; Mansergh et al., 2002; Morin et al., 2005;

Rogers et al., 2003). Reback and associates (2004) typify the views of the men they interviewed as follows:

> Participants tacitly signed onto the social contract that states the primary responsibility to disclose HIV status is placed on the sexual partner. Many claimed to operate from the assumption that people are responsible for their own bodies, and that feelings of responsibility toward another are not obligatory. The participants referred to an "unspoken rule" that men in public sex environments who did not initiate a discussion on disclosure were either HIV-infected or did not care about their health. (p. 94)

In many ways, these accounts of unsafe sex participate in the moral reasoning widely propagated by government and business today that constructs everyone as a self-interested individual who must take responsibility for himself in a marketplace of risks (Adam, 2005). The problem is that this moral reasoning works no better in the sexual realm than it does in government or business. Rational calculation of risk is just one possibility among many when unprotected sex is associated with condoms and erectile difficulties, momentary lapses and trade-offs, personal turmoil and depression, alcohol and drug use, disclosure and intuiting safety, and relationship formation. When one person presumes that his partner's failure to introduce a condom indicates HIV-positive status and the partner does not use a condom for any of the many unintentional reasons, a high-risk encounter may ensue.

Conclusion

Networks of gay, bisexual, and other men who have sex with men have been among the populations most heavily impacted by HIV transmission, and gay communities have been leaders in developing responses to the AIDS epidemic, both in terms of supporting people living with HIV and promoting HIV prevention techniques. In the decades since the discovery of AIDS the losses have been great, and gay men in advanced industrialized societies are still contracting HIV at a rate comparable to that of the most heavily afflicted communities in Africa. The sizable research literature that has developed to account for HIV vulnerability points to myriad social and psychological factors that reduce condom use. In the absence of any other effective HIV prevention techniques short of abstinence, HIV transmission continues to present a daunting challenge to the health of gay and bisexual men. Despite advances in treatment and management, HIV remains an onerous and life-threatening syndrome.

Complicating this picture is the development of circuits or microcultures within gay communities acting on divergent norms and expectations concerning sexual conduct.

Narratives that call on individuals to act defensively and protect themselves against all others may collide with romantic scripts that prescribe how to show trust in relationships. The messages of AIDS service organizations intended to instill a sense of shared responsibility in sexual actors conflict with neoliberal discourses that posit citizens of contemporary societies as individual actors in a marketplace of risks. Disease-avoidance discourses rely on particularly middle-class autobiographical narratives that presume a life trajectory with a bright future. Without a personal narrative on preserving oneself now for a better future, avoiding a long-term infection that could compromise that future stops making sense. While criminal justice systems seek to enforce an obligation to disclose one's serostatus in advance of sexual engagement, disclosure may be inhibited in everyday social interaction by fear of being stigmatized or rejected. Ultimately, the routine use of condoms with every sexual encounter is a safety technique that works without disclosure, and those who make decisions to have safe sex, encounter to encounter, depending on the disclosure of serostatus, have considerably higher odds of acquiring HIV than those who simply use condoms consistently. Gay, bisexual, and other men who have sex with men continue to face a series of dilemmas in preserving and promoting their health and the health of their communities. To some degree, the clash of narratives of the marketplace, law, biography, and romance increase the vulnerability to HIV transmission. Barebacking comes about at one intersection of these circulating narratives, further complicating the question of how viral circulation might be disrupted.

REFERENCES

Adam, B. D. (2005). Constructing the neoliberal sexual actor. *Culture, Health & Sexuality, 7*(4), 333–346.

Adam, B. D., Husbands, W., Murray, J., & Maxwell, J. (2005a). AIDS optimism, condom fatigue, or self esteem? *Journal of Sex Research, 42*(3), 238–248.

Adam, B. D., Husbands, W., Murray, J., & Maxwell, J. (2005b). Risk construction in reinfection discourses of HIV-positive men. *Health, Risk and Society, 7*(1), 63–71.

Adam, B. D., & Sears, A. (1996). *Experiencing HIV*. New York: Columbia University Press.

Adam, B. D., Sears, A., & Schellenberg, E. G. (2000). Accounting for unsafe sex. *Journal of Sex Research, 37*(1), 259–271.

Altman, D. (1986). *AIDS in the mind of America*. Garden City, NY: Doubleday.

Boulton, M., McLean, J., Fitzpatrick, R., & Hart, G. (1995). Gay men's accounts of unsafe sex. *AIDS Care, 7*(5), 619–630.

Calzavara, L., Burchell, A., Remis, R., Major, C., Corey, P., Myers, T., et al. (2003). Delayed application of condoms is a risk factor for human immunodeficiency virus infection among homosexual and bisexual men. *American Journal of Epidemiology, 157*(3), 210–217.

Carballo-Diéguez, A., Remien, R., Dolezal, C., & Wagner, G. (1997). Unsafe sex in the primary relationships of Puerto Rican men who have sex with men. *AIDS and Behavior, 1*(1), 9–17.

Choi, K. H., Kumekawa, E., Dang, Q., Kegeles, S., Hays, R., & Stall, R. (1999). Risk and protective factors affecting sexual behavior among young Asian and Pacific Islander men who have sex with men. *Journal of Sex Education and Therapy, 24*(1&2), 47–55.

Colfax, G., Vittinghoff, E., Husnik, M., McKirnan, D., Buchbinder, S., Koblin, B., et al. (2004). Substance use and sexual risk. *American Journal of Epidemiology, 159*(10), 1002–1012.

Crepaz, N., Hart, T., & Marks, G. (2004). Highly active antiretroviral therapy and sexual risk behavior. *Journal of the American Medical Association, 292*(2), 224–236.

Cusick, L., & Rhodes, T. (2000). Sustaining sexual safety in relationships. *Culture, Health & Sexuality, 2*(4), 473–487.

Díaz, R., & Ayala, G. (1999). Love, passion and rebellion. *Culture, Health & Sexuality, 1*(3), 277–293.

Dorais, M. (2004). Hazardous journey in intimacy. *Journal of Homosexuality, 48*(2), 103–124.

Epstein, S. (1996). *Impure science.* Berkeley: University of California Press.

Flowers, P., Smith, J., Sheeran, P., & Beail, N. (1997). Health and romance. *British Journal of Health Psychology, 2,* 73–86.

Frankis, J., & Flowers, P. (2006). Cruising for sex. *AIDS Care, 18*(1), 54–59.

Ghaziani, A., & Cook, T. (2005). Reducing HIV infections at circuit parties. *Journal of the International Association of Physicians in AIDS Care, 4*(2), 32–46.

Gorbach, P., Galea, J., Amani, B., Shin, A., Celum, C., Kerndt, P., et al. (2004). Don't ask, don't tell. *Sexually Transmitted Infections, 80,* 512–517.

Green, A. (2001). "Chem friendly." *Deviant Behavior, 24,* 427–447.

Greenwood, G., Relf, M., Huang, B., Pollack, L., Canchola, J., & Catania, J. (2002). Battering victimization among a probability-based sample of men who have sex with men. *American Journal of Public Health, 92*(12), 1964–1969.

Grulich, A., Prestage, G., Kippax, S., Crawford, J., & Van de Ven, P. (1998). HIV serostatus of sexual partners of HIV-positive and HIV-negative homosexual men in Sydney. *AIDS, 12*(18), 2508.

Hart, T., Wolitski, R., Purcell, D., Parsons, J., Gómez, C., & the Seropositive Urban Men's Study Team. (2005). Partner awareness of the serostatus of HIV-seropositive men who have sex with men. *AIDS and Behavior, 9*(2), 155–166.

Hirshfield, S., Remien, R., Humberstone, M., Walavalkar, I., & Chiasson, M. (2004). Substance use and high-risk sex among men who have sex with men. *AIDS Care, 16*(8), 1036–1047.

Kalichman, S., Benotsch, E., & Rompa, D. (2001). Unwanted sexual experiences and sexual risks in gay and bisexual men. *Journal of Sex Research, 38*(1), 1–9.

Kalichman, S., Cherry, C., Cain, D., Pope, H., & Kalichman, M. (2005). Psychosocial and behavioral correlates of seeking sex partners on the Internet among HIV-positive men. *Annals of Behavioral Medicine, 30*(3), 243–250.

Kalichman, S., Gore-Felton, C., Benotsch, E., Cage, M., & Rompa, D. (2004). Correlates of childhood sexual abuse and HIV risks among men who have sex with men. *Journal of Child Abuse, 13*(1), 1–15.

Klitzman, R., Greenberg, J., Pollack, L., & Dolezal, C. (2002). MDMA ("ecstasy") use, and its association with high risk behaviors, mental health, and other factors among gay/bisexual men in New York City. *Drug and Alcohol Dependence, 66,* 115–125.

Koblin, B., Chesney, M., Husnik, M., Bozeman, S., Celum, C., Buchbinder, S., et al. (2003). High-risk behaviors among men who have sex with men in 6 U.S. cities. *American Journal of Public Health, 93*(6), 926–932.

Kramer, L. (1989). *Reports from the Holocaust.* New York: St Martin's.

Larkins, S., Reback, C., Shoptaw, S., & Veniegas, R. (2005). Methamphetamine-dependent gay men's disclosure of their HIV status to sexual partners. *AIDS Care, 17*(4), 521–532.

Levine, M., Nardi, P., & Gagnon, J. (1997). *In changing times.* Chicago: University of Chicago Press.

Mansergh, G., Marks, G., Colfax, G., Guzman, R., Rader, M., & Buchbinder, S. (2002). "Barebacking" in a diverse sample of men who have sex with men. *AIDS, 16,* 653–659.

McLean, J., Boulton, M., Brookes, M., Lakhani, D., Fitzpatrick, R., Dawson, J., et al. (1994). Regular partners and risky behaviour. *AIDS Care, 6*(3), 331–341.

Morin, S., Steward, W., Charlebois, E., Remien, R., Pinkerton, S., Johnson, M., et al. (2005). Predicting HIV transmission risk among HIV-infected men who have sex with men. *Journal of Acquired Immune Deficiency Syndromes, 40*(2), 226–235.

Myers, T., Aguinaldo, J., Dakers, D., Fischer, B., Bullock, S., Millson, P., et al. (2004). How drug using men who have sex with men account for substance use during sexual behaviours. *Addiction Research and Theory, 12*(3), 213–229.

Odets, W. (1995). *In the shadow of the epidemic.* Durham, NC: Duke University Press.

O'Leary, A. (2005). Guessing games. In P. Halkitis, C. Gómez, & R. Wolitski (Eds.), *HIV + sex: The psychosocial and interpersonal dynamics of HIV-seropositive gay and bisexual men's relationships* (pp. 121–132). Washington, DC: American Psychological Association Press.

Parsons, J., Kutnick, A., Halkitis, P., Punzalan, J., & Carbonari, J. (2005). Sexual risk behaviors and substance use among alcohol abusing HIV-positive men who have sex with men. *Journal of Psychoactive Drugs, 37*(1), 37–36.

Patton, C. (1985). *Sex and germs.* Boston: South End.

Patton, C. (1990). *Inventing AIDS.* New York: Routledge.

Paul, J., Catania, J., Pollack, L., & Stall, R. (2001). Understanding childhood sexual abuse as a predictor of sexual risk-taking among men who have sex with men. *Child Abuse & Neglect, 25,* 557–584.

Reback, C., Larkins, S., & Shoptaw, S. (2004). Changes in the meaning of sexual risk behaviors among gay and bisexual male methamphetamine abusers before and after drug treatment. *AIDS and Behavior, 8*(1), 87–98.

Relf, M. (2001). Childhood sexual abuse in men who have sex with men. *Journal of the Association of Nurses in AIDS Care, 12*(5), 20–29.

Remien, R. H., Carballo Diéguez, A., & Wagner, G. (1995). Intimacy and sexual risk behaviour in serodiscordant male couples. *AIDS Care, 7*(4), 429–438.

Rhodes, T. (1997). Risk theory in epidemic times. *Sociology of Health and Illness, 19*(2), 208–277.

Rhodes, T., & Cusick, L. (2002). Accounting for unprotected sex. *Social Science & Medicine, 55,* 211–226.

Richters, J., Hendry, O., & Kippax, S. (2003). When safe sex isn't safe. *Culture, Health & Sexuality, 5*(1), 37–52.

Rofes, E. (1998). *Dry bones breathe.* New York: Haworth.

Rogers, G., Curry, M., Oddy, J., Pratt, N., Beilby, J., & Wilkinson, D. (2003). Depressive disorders and unprotected casual anal sex among Australian homosexually active men in primary care. *HIV Medicine, 4,* 271–275.

Schwartz, D., & Bailey, C. (2005). Between the sheets and between the ears. In P. Halkitis, C. Gómez, & R. Wolitski (Eds.), *HIV + sex: The psychosocial and interpersonal dynamics of HIV-seropositive gay and bisexual men's relationships* (pp. 55–72). Washington, DC: American Psychological Association Press.

Seal, D., Kelly, J., Bloom, F., Stevenson, L., Coley, B., Broyles, L., et al. (2000). HIV prevention with young men who have sex with men. *AIDS Care, 12*(1), 5–26.

Semple, S., Patterson, T., & Grant, I. (2000a). Partner type and sexual risk behavior among HIV positive gay and bisexual men. *AIDS Education and Prevention, 12*(4), 340–356.

Semple, S., Patterson, T., & Grant, I. (2000b). Psychosocial predictors of unprotected anal intercourse in a sample of HIV positive gay men who volunteer for a sexual risk reduction intervention. *AIDS Education and Prevention, 12*(5), 416–430.

Serovich, J., Oliver, D., Smith, S., & Mason, T. (2005). Methods of HIV disclosure by men who have sex with men to casual sexual partners. *AIDS Patient Care and STDs, 19*(12), 823–832.

Slavin, S. (2004). Drugs, space, and sociality in a gay nightclub in Sydney. *Journal of Contemporary Ethnography, 33*(3), 265–295.

Stirratt, M. (2005). I have something to tell you. In P. Halkitis, C. Gómez, & R. Wolitski (Eds.), *HIV + sex: The psychosocial and interpersonal dynamics of HIV-seropositive gay and bisexual men's relationships* (pp. 101–119). Washington, DC: American Psychological Association Press.

Stokes, J., & Peterson, J. (1998). Homophobia, self-esteem, and risk for HIV among African American men who have sex with men. *AIDS Education and Prevention, 10*(3), 278–292.

Van de Ven, P., Mao, L., Fogarty, A., Rawstorne, P., Crawford, J., Prestage, G., et al. (2005). Undetectable viral load is associated with sexual risk taking in HIV serodiscordant gay couples in Sydney. *AIDS, 19,* 179–184.

Vanable, P., McKirnan, D., Buchbinder, S., Bartholow, B., Douglas, J., Judson, F., et al. (2004). Alcohol use and high-risk sexual behavior among men who have sex with men. *Health Psychology, 23*(5), 525–532.

Vincke, J., & Bolton, R. (1995). Social stress and risky sex among gay men. In H. ten Brummelhuis & G. Herdt (Eds.), *Culture and sexual risk* (pp. 183–203). Luxembourg: Gordon and Breach.

Westhaver, R. (2005). "Coming out of your skin." *Sexualities, 8*(3), 347–374.

Zwart, O. d., Kerkhof, M. v., & Sandfort, T. (1998). Anal sex and gay men. In B. S. R. Michael Wright & Onno de Zwart (Eds.), *New international directions in HIV prevention for gay and bisexual men* (pp. 89–102). New York: Harrington Park Press.

10

Connectedness, Communication, and Reciprocity in Lesbian Relationships

Implications for Women's Construction and Experience of PMS

Janette Perz and Jane M. Ussher

Lesbian Relationships: Fused and Dysfunctional or
Connected and Satisfying?

Lesbian relationships may have been so unimaginable to the
Victorian prelates who enshrined male homosexuality as a crime
within British law that their very existence was denied. However, over
the past two decades, researchers have more than compensated for
this neglect. There is now a substantial body of research examining
the nature of lesbian relationships, both in comparison to gay male
and heterosexual relationships and in their own right. This research
has been partly motivated by the desire to understand the unique
dynamics of lesbian relationships in order to be able to inform social
theory in relation to gender relationships (Metz, Rosser, & Strapko,
1994) or to inform clinicians working with lesbian clients and couples
(Ossana, 2000; Scrivner & Eldridge, 1995).

Early clinical literature positioned the lesbian relationship as
one of distress, manifested as fusion, enmeshment, and merger,
resulting in emotional distance, conflict, individual dysfunction,

223

and triangulation (Krestan & Bepko, 1980). While the authors of the work that became the classic family therapy statement on sexual relationships between women later recanted their initial positioning of fusion as pathological (Green, Bettinger, & Zacks, 1996), Krestan and Bepko's (1980) work has assumed the status of unquestioned truth in many clinical circles, spawning a body of similar writing (see Roth, 1989; Slater & Mencher, 1991). Lesbian relationship distress or dysfunction has been deemed to be caused by women's gender role socialization, which leads to merger (Krestan & Bepko, 1980); the oppressive forces of homophobia and heterosexism, which are assumed to be internalized (Brown, 1995); lack of legal validation and protection or support from family (Ossana, 2000); and overt discrimination (Fraser & Richman, 1999). Adding this list to the notion of "lesbian bed-death," lower rates of sex reported among some lesbian couples (Nichols, 2004), and the finding that lesbian relationships are more likely to dissolve than heterosexual marriages (Andersson, Noack, Seierstad, & Weedon-Fekjaer, 2004; Blumstein & Schwartz, 1983; Kurdek, 2004a), it would be easy to conclude that lesbian relationships are not good for women's mental or physical health.

Yet, it is not that simple. Questions have been raised about the generalizability of research based on lesbian couples attending therapy to the wider lesbian population (Green et al., 1996). Equally, there is now a significant body of research on nonclinical community samples demonstrating that, in the core aspects that define a successful relationship, lesbian couples have the same qualities as successful heterosexual couples. These include containment of relational conflict and psychologically intimate communication (Mackey, Diemer, & O'Brien, 2004) and a positive communication style (Julien, Chartrand, Simard, Bouthillier, & Begin, 2003), as well as humor and affection (Gottman et al., 2003). Equally, dissolution rates of lesbian relationships are similar to those of cohabiting heterosexual couples (Blumstein & Schwartz, 1983; Kurdek, 1995), leading one reviewer to conclude that the most notable thing about lesbian (and gay) relationships is not that they are unstable, "but rather that they manage to endure without the benefits of institutionalized supports" (Kurdek, 2005, p. 253).

These findings account for the conclusions that are regularly drawn in the research literature: that "lesbians and gay men are more like heterosexual women and men than they are different from them" (Scrivner & Eldridge, 1995, p. 328); that "the relationships of gay and lesbian partners appear to work in the same way as the relationships of heterosexual partners" (Kurdek, 2005, p. 253); and that "satisfaction and stability in gay and lesbian relationships are related to similar qualities as in heterosexual relationships" (Gottman et al., 2003, p. 24). This research has been used to demonstrate that gay and lesbian couples deserve equal status and recognition in society, leading the American Psychological Association (2004) to pass a resolution that it is unfair and discriminatory to deny same-sex couples legal access to marriage and all of its associated rights and privileges (Kurdek, 2005, p. 253).

As a political position, this desire for researchers to emphasize the similarities between same-sex and opposite-sex couples seems laudable. However, the emphasis on similarity detracts from the issue of difference, and the significance—as well as benefits—of being in a lesbian relationship, in terms of a woman's subjectivity and negotiation of life stresses. Lesbian couples report more cohesion or connectedness than gay male or heterosexual couples (Green et al., 1996), demonstrating a capacity for mutual empathy, empowerment, and relational authenticity (Mencher, 1990) associated with relational resiliency (Connolly, 2005). Greater egalitarianism, manifested as "highly flexible decision making and household arrangements" (Green et al., 1996, p. 197) and innovation and adaptability in dealing with both relational needs and domestic tasks (Connolly, 2005, p. 270), has also been observed in lesbian relationships. As a result, lesbian couples are more likely to share responsibilities (Matthews, Tartaro, & Hughes, 2003; Schneider, 1986) and to report an egalitarian power balance within the relationship (Eldridge & Gilbert, 1990) compared to heterosexual couples. Lesbian couples also tend to resolve conflict more effectively than heterosexual couples, even though they disagree over the same issues (Kurdek, 2004b). Discussions begin more positively, and a more positive tone is maintained throughout the discussion (Gottman et al., 2003). Lesbian couples tend to argue more effectively, being more likely to suggest solutions and compromises and less likely to use a style of conflict resolution in which one partner demands and the other withdraws (Kurdek, 2004a). There is also evidence that lesbian couples are more likely to report open exploration of feelings, empathic attunement to nonverbal signals, negotiation, and the conscious avoidance of contempt (Connolly & Sicola, 2006). Given all of the above, it is not surprising to find a growing body of research reporting that lesbian relationships are experienced as more satisfying than heterosexual relationships (Green et al., 1996; Kurdek, 2003; Metz et al., 1994), with predictors of this satisfaction being greater emotional companionship (Metz et al., 1994), greater liking, trust, and equality (Kurdek, 2003), cohesion and flexibility (Green et al., 1996), as well as intimacy, equity, and autonomy (Schreurs & Buunk, 1996).

This chapter considers this counternarrative to the positioning of lesbian relationships as either unhealthily fused or identical to heterosexual relationships and therefore "normal." Taking the issue of premenstrual syndrome (PMS) as a case example, this chapter will argue that the aspects of lesbian relationships that have been reported to differ from heterosexual relation-ships—connectedness, egalitarianism, and positive communication—are of key relevance in terms of the construction and experience of women's premen-strual distress and coping.

Premenstrual syndrome is an issue affecting 40%–60% of women (Steiner & Born, 2000), deemed to be of the same magnitude as major depres-sive disorder, yet often overlooked in epidemiological research (Halbreich, Borenstein, Pearlstein, & Kahn, 2003). While up to 150 different symptoms have been associated with PMS, it is primarily characterized by reports of pre-menstrual increases in irritation, anger, or depression. It has been argued that lesbians may feel doubly disabled by PMS (Poulin & Gouliquer, 2003), both their sexuality and their menstrual cycle variability marking them as "other" and leading to avoidance of professional intervention. However, we will argue in this chapter that lack of adherence to hegemonic discourses of (hetero) fem-ininity, as well as the mutuality, responsiveness, and responsibility-sharing that are much more likely to be found in lesbian relationships, lead to lesbians being more likely than heterosexual women to develop effective ways of deal-ing with premenstrual change and distress. We will argue that lesbians are also less likely to take up the position of *Monstrous Feminine* (Ussher, 2006) in relation to the reproductive body, with all the attendant guilt and self-blame associated with that position. This argument is embedded in recent feminist research demonstrating that PMS is a gendered illness and needs to be under-stood within a framework of intersubjectivity.

The Construction and Experience of Premenstrual Change as PMS within a Relational Context

Whilst PMS has historically been represented as a pathological entity caused by bio-medical or psychological factors (Ussher, 2003b), with women catego-rized dichotomously as PMS sufferers or nonsufferers (Bancroft, 1993), it has recently been recognized that premenstrual changes in emotion, behavior, or embodiment are not inevitably labeled as PMS, and equally, that these changes are not inevitably associated with distress (Cosgrove & Riddle, 2003; Ussher, 2006). Rather, the construction of premenstrual change as PMS is an ongo-ing process of negotiation, associated with the mode of appraisal and coping adopted by women (Ussher, 2002). In this view, PMS is not the underlying pathology that causes distress. Rather, it is the distress itself (Jones, Theodos, Canar, Sher, & Young, 2000; Ussher, 2004a), with the relational context within

which a woman experiences and expresses premenstrual change having a significant impact on its construction and impact.

Women report greater reactivity to family stresses and altered perception of
daily life stresses during the premenstrual period, reporting feelings of anger,
irritation, or a desire to withdraw in situations where there are overwhelming
demands from a partner or children (Ussher, 2002, 2003a). Women and their
families attribute these "symptoms" to an embodied disorder, PMS, even when
alternative explanations can be found, such as a woman's overresponsibility
(Ussher, 2006) or relationship difficulties (Steege, Stout, & Rupp, 1988). In an
attempt to explain the expression of premenstrual anger within relationships,
some argue that this is the only time that some women "allow" themselves
to be angry, as they can attribute anger to their hormones (McDaniel, 1988).
Elson (2002) describes this phenomenon as a "redeployment" of the reproductive body to meet women's emotional needs. This notion implicitly suggests a
calculated decision on the part of women to express anger and use PMS as an
excuse, a conclusion at odds with the extreme distress reported in relation to
premenstrual emotional expression (Ussher, 2003b, 2006).

The self-surveillance and repression of emotion that typify women's
accounts of the non-PMS self are akin to the pattern of "self-silencing" associated with women's depression (Jack, 1991), and women who report PMS score
significantly higher on levels of self-silencing than populations norms (Perz &
Ussher, 2006). But it is the premenstrual *break* in self-silencing that is associated with distress, being positioned as "out of control" and described by a "short
fuse" or "pressure cooker" metaphor (Ussher, 2003a). Differences between the
premenstrual and nonpremenstrual self are characterized by self-description
as "Jekyll and Hyde," reflecting the judgment imposed upon women who
transgress the ideals of (hetero) femininity, which dictate that "good" women
are eternally calm, in control, and self-sacrificing in relationships (O'Grady,
2005). The reproductive body is thus positioned as the site of the Monstrous
Feminine (Ussher, 2006; Ussher & Perz, 2006). Transgressions from gendered ideals are blamed on the body, and the interpersonal or political problems that are associated with women's premenstrual distress are disavowed
(Chrisler & Caplan, 2002).

Cultural expectations of appropriate gendered behavior are policed in the
privacy of intimate relationships, and the reactions of partners and family to a
woman's expression of her needs, or her discontent, play a significant role in
the construction and experience of PMS. Many heterosexual women express
the need to contain their emotions in relation to men so as not to be considered weak (Ussher & Perz, 2009). Men's constructions of PMS have also
been implicated in women's negative premenstrual experiences, with evidence

that many men treat premenstrual change or the notion of PMS in a belit-tling way (Sveinsdottir, Lundman, & Norberg, 2002). Conversely, support and understanding offered by partners appear to reduce feelings of guilt and self-castigation in women who experience premenstrual changes in affect, allow-ing them to engage in coping strategies premenstrually (Perz & Ussher, 2006; Ussher, 2008).

The majority, if not all, previous research on PMS has been (presumably) conducted with heterosexual women. The exclusion of lesbians is connected to lack of recognition of the relevance as well as lack of identification, as the majority of research studies do not indicate the sexual orientation of their par-ticipants. Thus, lesbians may have taken part in PMS research, but they have not been identified within the sample. We believe that this omission is signif-icant, as the gender of a woman's sexual partner, as well as the nature of their relationship, can play a significant role in the experience and construction of premenstrual distress. Drawing on interviews with lesbian-identified women who report that they experience moderate to severe PMS, as well as interviews with lesbian partners, we examine the experience of PMS among this impor-tant population.

Method

This analysis is part of a broader study on the experience of PMS in the context of relationships, involving interviews with 60 Australian women aged 22 to 46 (average age 34) who presented as experiencing PMS and 23 of their partners. These women were purposefully selected for interview from a larger group of women who were taking part in a mixed-methods study examining the experience and positioning of PMS. This chapter will focus on the accounts of PMS in the interviews with 18 lesbian women and 10 of the interviewees' partners. The average age of this subsample was 36. Relationship duration ranged from 2 to 20 years, with a median of 5 years. Four interviewees had dependent children.

One-on-one semistructured interviews were conducted to examine women's subjective experience of PMS and the negotiation of PMS in the context of relationships. The interviewer began by asking women to describe how a woman, or her partner, was when she had PMS, then to describe a typical experience of PMS, and finally to explore how this experience var-ied across relational contexts. The interviews ranged in duration from 45 to 90 minutes. After transcription, the interviews were read and reread in order to identify themes relating to the construction and experience of PMS.

Themes were then grouped, checked for emerging patterns, variability and consistency, commonality across women, and uniqueness within cases. Thematic coding of the interviews was conducted, line by line. This process follows what Stenner (1993) terms a *thematic decomposition*, a close reading that attempts to separate a given text into coherent themes that reflect subject positions allocated to or taken up by a person (Davies & Harré, 1990). A number of consistent themes emerged in the interviews, which will be discussed under three categories: *(1)* connectedness and mutuality; *(2)* communication and conflict resolution; and *(3)* reciprocity and responsibility-sharing.

The Experience of PMS in the Context of a Lesbian Relationship

Accounts of premenstrual change and of experiences positioned as symptoms of PMS were identical to those reported by heterosexual women, both in the present study and in previous research (Cosgrove & Riddle, 2003; Perz & Ussher, 2006; Ussher, 2006). Common symptoms of PMS were described as anxiety, anger, irritability, moodiness, paranoia, vulnerability in the face of life stresses, dislike of the body, desire for time alone, and need for support and reassurance. The relational context within which premenstrual distress was experienced and expressed (particularly the reactions of partners) played a significant role in women's negotiation of premenstrual change and their construction of PMS (see also Ussher & Perz, 2008).

Mutuality and Connectedness

Jordan's (1991) definition of mutuality as "openness to influence, emotional availability, a constantly changing pattern of responding to and affecting the other's state" (p. 82) has been used in previous research examining connectedness in lesbian relationships (Connolly, 2005). In the interviews with lesbians and their partners, this mutuality was manifested by awareness and recognition of PMS and by responsiveness and reciprocity.

AWARENESS AND RECOGNITION OF PMS. In heterosexual women's accounts, male partners are often described as having little awareness or understanding of PMS, resulting in the women's experience being denied, ignored, or pathologized (Ussher, Perz, & Mooney-Somers, 2007). In contrast, lesbian interviewees consistently reported a high level of awareness and understanding on the part of their partners, even though premenstrual changes in behavior "may be weird." This was experienced as nonjudgmental acceptance, as Shea (age 23) commented:

> In terms of the response, like, yeah, it's just really understand-
> ing and I guess supportive.... Like, it's not that big an issue that it
> becomes an issue... it's just like, "This is how I'm feeling." "That's
> okay."

Awareness of the importance of taking a nonjudgmental position was present in the accounts of many of the lesbian partners. As Denise (age 51) told us about her partner, Stephanie:

> I don't ever feel like it's okay to say to that person, you know, "You're
> premenstrual. You're just out of control. Things are unrealistic, and
> next week you'll see things differently." I never feel good about say-
> ing that, because it just devalues what they're feeling.

Indeed, the majority of the lesbian interviewees reported being taken seriously by their partners, with their premenstrual distress being positioned as "real."

> (I know) how important it is to have someone kind of go, "Yep, you
> really do... " and it's not being silly and it's not, um, dismissed as
> being, you know, um.... Like, it's actually real. "I get that. I believe
> you." That sort of stuff. It's not just an excuse for having an off day,
> sort of thing.
>
> (Casey, age 40)

This awareness was sometimes precipitated by a woman naming herself as having PMS, with her partner accepting this positioning, without further explanation (Mooney-Somers, Perz, & Ussher, in press). As Jacinta (age 31) commented:

> I generally just admit that I'm premenstrual. And she goes, "Oh.
> Yeah." So I don't necessarily talk about the feelings that I have—that
> I'm feeling... you know, not as worthy, or less worthy, or whatever.

Self-awareness and self-positioning as "having PMS" were often used to provide an explanation for premenstrual reactivity or irritability, with communication of this awareness often acting as an apology. As Linda (age 36) describes:

> She certainly understands and so if I was to turn around, you know
> after a couple of times, you know I might be snappy for half a day
> and then I finally sort of realize that I'm like that, um I will say to

her, "Look, I'm really sorry" and it's actually better then. And then she'll, she'll just take it in her stride. Not a problem.

A number of lesbian interviewees described their partner as being aware of PMS before they were. This awareness precipitated an empathic discussion about premenstrual changes in behavior or mood, as well as the provision of practical support.

> She knows that it's coming and we talk about the fact that I'm proba-
> bly premenstrual, so she'll say something like "Um, you know you've
> probably got PMS," and I'll say, "Yep, I think that's what it is." So
> what normally would have, I guess in past relationships, become an
> argument, um, these days would probably just mean that she would
> make me a cup of tea and a hot water bottle and I'd lie down and,
> um, get a bit pampered.
>
> (Sheridan, age 35)

Jacinta reported that she had previously thought PMS was "a crock of shit" but that her partner's recognition of her premenstrual change had allowed her to recognize it in herself, which was beneficial to her coping:

> She said, "This happens all the time. This happens around your
> period, you know," and you go, "Oh, okay. Oh. Okay." Yeah, and so,
> then recognizing that that's what it is.

For Jacinta and other women, this kind of recognition functioned to protect the relationship, because irritability and moodiness could be positioned as "just my bad day" rather than "something personal," or something that would have a major impact upon the relationship. Jocelyn (age 47) described it thus:

> If anyone's a little bit short-tempered or acting very frustrated, then
> we just understand that that's what it is and so the behavior's sort
> of not valid in our relationship. It's just a time of our relationship
> that needs a little bit more understanding, care, and concern, I sup-
> pose...or my partner knows that it's purely a behavior thing, it's not
> personal, and to just let it go by.

In apparent contrast to Casey, who wanted her partner to acknowledge that her premenstrual distress was real, Jocelyn described her partner, Deborah (age 40), as letting "me have a little spit or whatever I need to do.... She under-stands, and she knows it's not real." Equally, Deborah described the premen-strual changes Jocelyn experienced as "not usually affect[ing] me because I'm aware that it is, um, not real, that it's just blown out of proportion. So,

I don't usually take much notice of it, unless, of course, it is a genuine issue that's the basis of it. But if it is something trivial I think, 'Oh, she'll be over it tomorrow.'"

Deborah's account is not about dismissing premenstrual distress as "not real." Rather, it is about understanding that a woman's irritability or desire to be alone is associated with premenstrual changes in state or emotion, rather than reflecting an underlying problem in the relationship. However, if there was a genuine issue underlying the irritation, the majority of interviewees reported that this issue was addressed, sometimes when emotions were less heightened. This flexibility and responsiveness in dealing with changing emotions and needs, central to descriptions of mutuality (Connolly, 2005; Jordon, 1991), were common in lesbian accounts of PMS in this study.

RESPONSIVENESS AND EMPATHY. In heterosexual women's accounts of PMS, it is commonly reported that male partners are not responsive to women's changed moods or needs premenstrually, which results in the woman being pathologized or rejected (Perz & Ussher, 2006; Ussher et al., 2007). A number of the lesbian interviewees contrasted the responsiveness of their current partners to the reaction of a previous male partner who could not, or would not, empathize with their experience of premenstrual change. For example, in contrast to her ex-husband, who "tried to understand it, and I think he just gave up," June (48) described her current partner as acting to alleviate her distress and to smooth tensions with her children, a common focus of her premenstrual irritation.

> I'll just say, "I'm about to get my period, so I'm ... tired, or ... I've been cranky with the kids.... She's supportive about it.... I suppose she can actually make me feel happier. She can bring me out of it, a little bit.... And she has talked to my children.... "Mummy's a bit angry at the moment." You know. "Try and behave." Or "Try and do what Mummy asks you to do." And stuff like that. She's much more supportive than my ex-husband was.

Equally, in response to the premenstrual woman's feeling of insecurity, many lesbian partners described themselves as offering reassurance. Christy (age 29), the partner of Janna (age 24), told us that she offered emotional support by "actually commenting that she looks nice, without being prompted, without being asked, 'Do I look all right?' So to say, 'Oh, that looks nice.'" Elspeth (age 39) said of her partner, Sheridan:

> I just have to adapt the way I interact with her ... I will often be more affectionate with her. Because I think that's ... I don't know, just feels

appropriate...lots of looking in to each other's eyes.... In psychological terms I make sure that I'm not withholding. Like, I make sure that I validate and don't avoid her and that seems to help.

At the same time, there was conscious awareness of the avoidance of conflict or of situations that might trigger a negative reaction or emotion premenstrually. Hayley (age 30) said, "Around period time I will usually be extremely flexible and don't do things that I know are going to annoy her." Denise said, "I can be extra—what's the word?—extra thoughtful and extra making sure we don't do anything that will trigger some of those responses."

Many of the partners interviewed described their acceptance and support of the partner with PMS as resulting from empathy. As Elspeth commented, "Well, I guess being a woman as well, I can kind of empathize with her." Ashley (age 31) said, "Having a female partner, I think, just makes all the difference...because I think they understand." Ashley went on to describe the implications of empathy in relation to the experience of premenstrual change in her relationship:

> Well, for instance, if I'm having a bad time with my period, or
> Coral's having a bad time with her period, we are just able to empathize, and just go "Okay." Not actually make it mean anything, but more like "Oh, okay, it's her period." Rather than, um, "Oh well, she doesn't like me."

Emotional availability was a key aspect of this responsiveness. For example, Pip (age 29) described her partner thus: "She's generally very supportive and she talks through things with me as well, I think. She won't avoid the issue, she'll talk it through."

In sum, mutuality and connectedness facilitated awareness and recognition of premenstrual change and distress on the part of women and their partners, which acted to protect relationships from possible escalation of tension or conflict premenstrually, as a PMS attribution for irritation could be made. The empathy and lack of judgment women obtained from their female partners premenstrually were experienced as supportive and contributed to the low level of "pathologization" among the lesbian participants.

Communication and Conflict Resolution

Communication is a key aspect of the construction and negotiation of premenstrual change, associated with recognition and naming of distress, resolution of relational conflict, and the responses of partners to premenstrual needs and vulnerability. Two subthemes were identified in the narratives: *(1)* explicit discussion of premenstrual feelings and concerns and *(2)* the partner's emotion work in relation to PMS.

EXPLICIT DISCUSSION OF PREMENSTRUAL FEELINGS AND CONCERNS. Heterosexual women commonly report that issues or feelings that are raised premenstrually are ignored by their partner or dismissed as "just PMS" (Perz & Ussher, 2006; Ussher, 2003a). In contrast, the majority of lesbian interviewees in this study provided accounts of open discussion of premenstrual feelings leading to open communication about concerns and needs within the relationship. As a consequence, women reported that conflicts were resolved more effectively. For example, Casey (age 40) told us that she and her partner had very different sexual needs premenstrually, with her own libido disappearing, while her partner's "went through the roof when she's got PMS." However, because they could "talk about it, there's a respect." Casey's sexual rejection of her partner was not meant as "a personal thing":

> So it's a really hard kind of negotiation, because I'm just like, (groan),
> you know, so.... But we've got there. I mean, it was.... It was a bit
> tricky there for a while, because it's a hard.... You know, it's really
> one of those hard things to talk about initially, but then it was like,
> well, you know, we have to. And just that understanding of it's not
> about personal rejection or, you know, whatever. It's bigger than that.
> So...we kind of worked it out. Worked the zones out. Almost like
> there's a map on the wall.

For Casey and her partner, the management of PMS reflected a pattern of communication developed within the relationship. There were similarities for Jocelyn and her partner. As Jocelyn commented, "We've been together for over 20 years, and we sort of talked a lot when we first got into a relationship about how a relationship would run, and it's always run on being very up front with each other, ah, discussing any issues we have and just keeping each other informed of how we are, and who we are, and just being caring for each other."

A number of interviewees drew contrasts with previous relationships with both men and women in which issues could not be discussed. In these relational contexts, self-silencing had increased their premenstrual irritability. As Vicki (age 26) commented:

> In other relationships, and particularly the latter parts of those rela-
> tionships that were bad, I would have more severe PMS experiences
> and also kind of more PMS that was characterized by anger, or just

like really small things making me really angry and getting really
irritable, and a lot of [them] were the kind of things that were unspo-
ken at other times or maybe frustrations.

As Sheridan remarked, "It [PMS] had been named in past relationships, I think,
as well, but I don't at all feel attacked now." Many of the lesbian interviewees
gave accounts of the delicate balance between describing feelings as related to
PMS, and thereby risking their dismissal as not real, and the need to express
their premenstrual emotions or concerns about other issues within the relationship. Discussing the same issues after the premenstrual phase had passed
was one solution. As Sophia (age 28) said:

> I generally preface any conversation with, "Look, oh no, I'm feeling
> really premenstrual but, look, I'm thinking about this," and usually
> Tina will frame everything with that understanding that there's pre-
> menstrual behavior going on, and it might make sense or it might
> not. And in a week from now, you know, I might come back and
> go, "Hey, that was a bit unrealistic," or...yeah. So she's pretty good
> around that stuff.

At the same time, Sophia described how her partner, Tina, would let her know
that she had been "really fully on" premenstrually after it had passed:

> A couple of days later, or something, I say, "Oh, f..., I'm bleeding,"
> and she goes, "Woo-hoo! Everything's good!" and she really actively
> goes, "Guess what you just did! Oh my God, you were so full-on!"

Yet, this did not mean that premenstrual anger or annoyance was disregarded.
Sophia continued, talking about Tina's PMS:

> You don't challenge them on it, or anything, because something's
> going on for them, and they're working through it in their own
> time and space. I think if Tina gets really mad, sometimes that can
> happen, and we'll be having an argument of some proportion and
> something...in my brain, I'll go, "Oh, man...she's premenstrual.
> Okay.... Right." And then I start saying phrases like, "Oh, you know
> what? Maybe I could be wrong. Maybe you've got a point and I'd like
> to listen to it a bit more." And it's...in a way, you just allow them
> space to be who they are at that time.

Sophia's narrative account of the management of PMS within the relationship suggests that many lesbian couples negotiate the timing of raising major
issues, with an acknowledgment that the premenstrual distress impacts emotional dynamics and interpretations.

Maintaining a positive tone in communications and avoiding confrontation and aggression were important features of partners' responses to premenstrual emotion. Pip gave an account of being out with her partner, Helen (age
41), and suddenly wanting to go home because she felt anxious and insecure
premenstrually. Pip described Helen's response as "level-headed," and said
that even though Helen is a "very social person, she will say, 'Well, okay, let's
go home' or 'Do you want to go home?'" Many partners recognized that this
positive tone was needed to avoid or diffuse conflict. As Denise noted, when
her partner, Stephanie, was distressed or angry premenstrually, she would "go
up and say gently, 'Okay, look, I know that's how you feel, I understand the
point, that's enough.'" Or as Elspeth said, "If you pick it early enough...that's
when you, sort of, quickly, say, deflect the situation, diffuse the situation or say,
'All right, why don't you have a bath?'"

At the same time, a number of partners also gave accounts of maintaining
boundaries around what was acceptable premenstrually. As Sophia commented:

> People are accountable for what they do, and, um, if I felt like Tina
> was really out of control and saying and behaving in a way that
> I really felt strongly was not okay under any circumstance, pre-
> menstrual or otherwise, I would certainly say it at that time.... So
> I might say, "Your behaviour right now is really shit and makes me
> feel like you don't care about me right now. And if you did care about
> me, you wouldn't be raising your voice."

Sophia described herself as not having become a "passive person," concluding, "I think you still engage, and you still, you know, respond. But you have
a framework for it." The need for boundaries reflects the "emotion work"
(Duncombe & Marsden, 1998) being conducted by lesbian couples in which
one partner experiences premenstrual distress.

PARTNER'S EMOTION WORK IN RELATION TO PMS. The position of responsive
partner, who is understanding, supportive, and able to communicate positively
about a woman's premenstrual change or distress, is not a position without
cost or consequence. As Helen acknowledged when talking of her partner, Pip,
"If she gets cranky about something and at me, it's not pleasant." Or as Casey
said about her partner, "I find it very hard to be around her when she's in that
zone. And I have to work very hard at not reacting to it. So, actually having a bit
of separateness is actually a healthy thing for both of us." Having to figure out
how to support their premenstrual partner each month could also be exhausting. As Denise said, "I think part of my problem is...I don't want to have to
find the solution every month."

Awareness of how the situation could escalate into an argument if it was not handled sensitively was evident in a number of accounts. Elspeth described the situation as "a bit like stumbling in to a trap." She went on to say:

> Like it takes you a couple of minutes to realize that you have stumbled into a trap, that it wouldn't really matter what you said. It's not about that, it's about, there's a "making trouble" thing going on. . . . I just have to adapt the way I interact with her.

For Elspeth, this adaptation was sometimes difficult and could result in irritation or resentment on the part of her partner:

> You feel pissed off, well, you know, you feel like throwing something, not caring and empathic but like. . . . It's almost like the . . . (a) is something you would say, (b) is the reaction you got and (c) is an opportunity for you to escalate the situation. But if you don't do (c), then you don't get the argument. It doesn't escalate into something much more heated and severe that might cause us not to speak for half a day or so.

So, while Elspeth was aware that she could say, " 'Well, stuff you,' and I could walk away," she acknowledged, "But that's not usually what I do." However, she had clearly considered such a response. Similarly, while Lorna (age 36) reported that she offered her partner, Linda, "lots of love" premenstrually and made sure "not [to] react to bad moods, to aggravate the situation more," she said that this response could be difficult, depending "on my mood at the time."

A number of partners described this kind of emotion work as invisible within the relationship.

> So I guess another impact from that is then that, you know, I'm actually doing all this bending over backwards. This is how I feel it is. Um, but it's actually not seen that way. Sometimes I don't tell her that I'm doing it either, so she doesn't even know that I'm doing that.

(Hayley, age 30)

But Hayley's account stands in contrast to accounts of interviewees who realize that premenstrual mood or behavior change can exact consequences on the relationship or on their partners. As Linda told us:

> First and foremost it's a horrible feeling because I know that I'm irritable and I might be a little bit snappy. That's what I'm aware of mostly, is that you know like my partner might say something to me and I'll just say, "Oh don't talk to me like that," just for an example,

and then I, as soon as I say it, as soon as it's come out of my mouth I just go, I take a step back and I go "Oh, I wish I wasn't like this."

Thus, while many of the interviewees reflected positively on the difference between previous relationships with men and their current relationship with a woman, there was also acknowledgment that two women with PMS could be difficult. As Ellen (age 29) said, "Being with a woman during the time just makes it entirely exhausting and difficult, um, and far more complex than I ever thought it would be."

In sum, effective communication and conflict resolution thus served to facilitate discussion of issues that were raised premenstrually. Constructive discussion could take place rather than escalation of conflict, even if this did require significant emotion work on the part of both parties, with partners sometimes experiencing exhaustion as a result.

Reciprocity and Responsibility Sharing

The burden of overresponsibility, in relation to household tasks and the emotional needs of one's partner and family, is a consistent theme in heterosexual women's accounts of PMS (Ussher, 2003a, 2004b; Ussher, Hunter, & Browne, 2000). Many women report that it is difficult to engage in self-care, which serves to increase premenstrual distress. In contrast, all of the lesbian interviewees in this study gave accounts of an egalitarian relationship context in which they could reduce their responsibilities premenstrually, receive rather than provide care, and not feel guilty as a result.

> It's about...someone just...recognizing that you're actually feeling really out of sorts, um, and, um, I guess taking...taking some of the responsibility off you to actually manage it. It's more about, well, now you're feeling crap. And I know there's nothing that much that can fix that, except if...you don't have to worry about...where the food's coming from, or, you know, I mightn't even think about a bath, and then she'll say, "How about you go and have a bath? And I'll run it for you," and I'll be like "Oh, that would be really nice!" That not having to think about how to fix it. Yeah. Just kind of being able to just be. And have someone else like just take control of...of that.
>
> (Casey)

This feeling was described as serving to "just protect you a bit from the rest of the world, um, just for the moment," allowing Casey to "be able to just go home and just go, fall apart."

Sharing responsibilities also allows women who experience premenstrual distress to engage in self-care or take time for themselves. As Jocelyn says:

> I've got a really big garden that I maintain and I like to take myself out there.... I do like to be a little more alone around that time.... She's very understanding, maybe does a little bit of housework on those days, ah, doesn't expect too much from me at those times.

Jocelyn describes a reciprocal caring, adding that "we just sort of care for each other around those times. Deborah has a lot of pain during her periods, so it's kind of like I give back a lot too."

The importance of accommodating a woman's need for time alone premenstrually was recognized to be important by many of the lesbian partners we interviewed. Denise described her partner Stephanie as saying:

> "Oh, look, you know, I just want to be on my own." So she'll go to her own room, and that's fine. You know. Or she'll potter in the garden. And I go, "Well that's fine," you know. It doesn't...you know, I'm...it doesn't actually bother me; I don't need to be, you know, around. In fact, I'd rather that she found whatever it is that...that helps her resolve it, that's my preference.

In a similar vein, Sophia said of her partner, Tina, "You've got to give the person space to be themselves in that, and experience that."

A number of the lesbian couples described experiencing premenstrual change simultaneously and thus needing to be aware of their mutual needs for space or support. As Casey reported:

> There's a couple of days where we're exactly in the same place, which isn't a great place to be, but on either side of that, we can both recognize what the other needs are...and we're very clear.... We have a very clear understanding of what makes the difference, and what helps.

There is thus a reciprocal caring during the premenstrual and menstrual phases of the cycle rather than a situation in which one woman is pathologized or positioned as needy.

> She'll come home from work, and...she'll be really cranky. Like, really, really cranky. And um, almost simmering on explosion. And I'll be like, "Ooooh. Okay." And her thing is to go and play video games. So she'll go and play video games. And I'll go in and try and talk to her, and she'll just be like one-word responses, and I'm like,

"All right." And there would be things like...um..."Dinner's going to be ready soon. Do you want me to bring it in here?" "Yes, please." (whispering) "Okay." And so, it's just things like, she just needs to be on her own, doing her thing in her zone. And you know, normally for me, that wouldn't be acceptable, to have meals in different rooms and not talk and stuff. But she needs...that's what she needs. And so that's what we do.

(Casey)

For Casey and her partner, there is a mutual, reciprocal recognition of emotional needs and space that accompanies the premenstrual and menstrual periods.

Responsibilities are not just in the home. Indeed, many of the lesbian interviewees talked of wanting to let go of "big girl responsibilities" at work when they were premenstrual. Women reported that they could express this desire within the relationship. As Elspeth said:

When I'm getting PMS, I feel very fragile, and I don't want to go to work. I feel scared to go to work, because it's hard what I do, and it takes a lot and I guess you kind of need to be properly resourced to do what I do.... I often say I feel like I want to be small, I want to be a little girl, not have sort of big girl responsibilities. And so they are the sort of things that I will say, and it's almost very straightforward. Sheridan will say, "You must be getting your period."

Work tensions and pressures were described as a major cause of distress premenstrually. However, the need to maintain the persona of a calm professional worker meant that frustrations built up during the day and often needed to be expressed at home. A supportive context for the release of these frustrations allowed for a cathartic release among the women in this study.

I can come home and say, "I've had a shit day, and this is what's gone on," and a lot of debriefing around that time too, about you know, "And they did this and this and they are really pissing me off because they did this," and then there's just that exactly... "Yep. I understand." So...yeah. It's really, you know, thank the Lord for it.

(Casey)

Casey's experience stands in contrast to accounts of many heterosexual women, who report coming home from a stressful day at work when they are premenstrual to find that they then have to provide emotional and practical care, which

makes it more likely that they will respond with irritation and anger, resulting in relationship tension and a cycle of self-blame and guilt (Ussher et al.,
2000). Thus, reciprocity and responsibility sharing act to alleviate the burden
premenstrually and to facilitate self-care, reducing women's premenstrual distress and increasing their ability to cope with premenstrual change.

Discussion

Previous research on the nature of lesbian relationships has presented us
with a picture of dysfunction and distress, manifested as fusion, enmeshment, and merger, resulting in emotional distance and conflict (Krestan &
Bepko, 1980). Alternatively, research has suggested that there is no difference between lesbian and heterosexual relationships at all: a good (or bad)
relationship includes the same features, regardless of the gender of either
partner (Kurdek, 2005). This chapter provides a counternarrative to both of
these positions, arguing that lesbian relationships are distinct, positive, and
beneficial for women.

Using the example of the construction and experience of PMS in lesbian
relationships, we have argued that while experiences of premenstrual change
and distress were similar to those previously reported by heterosexual women,
the lesbian relationship context and positioning of PMS was markedly different. In contrast to the lack of understanding or responsiveness, rejection,
pathologization, and overresponsibility reported by many heterosexual women
(Perz & Ussher, 2006; Ussher, 2003a, 2004b), the lesbians interviewed in this
study reported awareness and recognition of their premenstrual change and
distress, responsiveness to their needs, open communication, and reciprocity
and responsibility sharing on the part of their partners. These dynamics had
significant consequences for the construction and experience of premenstrual
change, facilitating open expression of needs, self-care, and avoidance of guilt
and self-blame. Indeed, the accounts of PMS in this study were most notable
for what was absent in the accounts of PMS commonly reported by heterosexual women.

All of the women in this study used *PMS* as a term to describe their premenstrual change, as would be expected in a study that specifically targeted
women who experience PMS. However, PMS was not positioned as a medical
illness or an unspeakable dysfunction, as is common in heterosexual wom-
en's accounts (Ussher, 2003a; Ussher et al., 2007). Rather, it was used as a
term to make sense of changes women experienced premenstrually, acting to
communicate these changes to their partners. Confirming previous research

on premenstrual change in women with positive attitudes toward menstrua-tion (Lee, 2002), none of the women in the present study adopted a stance of self-pathologization or used derogatory terms to describe themselves premen-strually, such as *mad, loony-tune, bitch, monstrous-mummy,* or *Jekyll and Hyde*—terms commonly found in heterosexual women's accounts of PMS (Cosgrove & Riddle, 2003; Ussher, 2002). The position of Monstrous Feminine, wherein the reproductive body is deemed abject and the woman deviant or dysfunctional as a result (Ussher, 2006), was thus resisted by these lesbian interviewees and their partners. The direct implication of this resistance was the almost com-plete absence of accounts of guilt and self-blame—a major focus of distress in heterosexual women's accounts of PMS (Ussher, 2003b).

Equally, there were very few accounts of feeling "out of control" premen-strually, as premenstrual change was accepted as part of a woman's expe-rience, even if it was not necessarily a pleasant experience for a woman or her partner. Women were thus able to avoid the concomitant distress associ-ated with feeling out of control in Western culture (Chrisler & Caplan, 2002). Acceptance and nonpathologization of premenstrual change is a plausible explanation for the finding that PMS is not reported in non-Western coun-tries such as China (Chang, Holroyd, & Chau, 1995), a finding that has led to the conclusion that PMS is a "culture bound" syndrome (Chrisler & Caplan, 2002). However, the results of the present study suggest that acceptance and nonpathologization can also operate in a Western cultural context, strongly influenced by the construction of PMS adhered to by a woman and her part-ner, as well as the relationship dynamics associated with negotiation of pre-menstrual experiences.

In the present study, there were no accounts of relationship conflict or tension escalating premenstrually as a result of a woman's partner rejecting or dismissing her, a common theme in heterosexual women's accounts of PMS (Ussher, 2003a; Ussher et al., 2007). These results do not suggest that lesbian partners are passive in the face of premenstrual irritation or intemperance. Rather, the women in our study adopted a positive and conciliatory mode of communication that served to diffuse conflict and offer support. The narra-tives of women and their partners suggested that dealing with premenstrual distress is the subject of a complex negotiation between two women, requir-ing emotion work from both parties to manage the feelings of both of them. Among the women we interviewed, this emotion work was not described as a burden but rather as part of being in a committed relationship. This narrative framing stands in contrast to many heterosexual women's accounts, in which premenstrual emotions are positioned as "too much" work by their male part-ners (Ussher et al., 2007).

Evidence of open discussion of feelings and needs, in the context of partner understanding and support, refutes the notion that PMS serves as a redeployment of the reproductive body, which allows the expression of otherwise repressed feelings and needs (Elson, 2002; McDaniel, 1988). Equally, there was little evidence of women attempting to live up to unrealistic ideals of (hetero) femininity, resulting in the positioning of the PMS self as "not me" (Cosgrove & Riddle, 2003; Ussher et al., 2000). At the same time, there were no accounts of women feeling overburdened by emotional or practical responsibilities in the home premenstrually, described in heterosexual women's accounts through a "short fuse" or "pressure cooker" metaphor (Ussher, 2003a, 2004b). The absence of such accounts in the narratives of women suggests that it is not simply resistance of hegemonic discourses of femininity that leads to lower rates of self-silencing among lesbians. Rather, it is the egalitarian, empathic, and mutually supportive relationship context described by all of our interviewees that repositions PMS as a normative process for women.

The relationship context described in the current study is consistent with previous research on positive aspects of lesbian relationships. There was strong evidence of cohesion and connectedness in the narratives of women, supporting the findings of Green et al. (1996) and Connolly (2005). Narratives also revealed evidence of closeness and caregiving, consistent with the findings of O'Brien (2003). These findings suggest that Jordan's (1991) notion of *mutuality* as "openness to influence, emotional availability, a constantly changing pattern of responding to and affecting the other's state" (p.82) is a more applicable term for lesbian relationships than *fusion,* the oft-critiqued term that refers to lesbian couples' supposed pathological enmeshment and merger (Krestan & Bepko, 1980). The accounts of positive and effective communication strategies, and the absence of aggression and contempt associated with relationship distress and dysfunction (Gottman et al., 2003), are consistent with previous findings that lesbians are more likely than heterosexual couples to use a positive tone in resolving conflict (Gottman et al., 2003), are more likely to argue effectively (Kurdek, 2004a; Metz et al., 1994), and make more effort to resolve conflict (Metz et al., 1994). The open exploration of feelings and explicit discussion of issues also support Connolly and Sicola's (2006) study of communication in long-term lesbian relationships. In the current study, these patterns were evident regardless of relationship length, but many interviewees did talk of learning to communicate and deal with emotions over the course of their relationship. Finally, the finding of responsibility sharing and flexibility in relation to household arrangements supports previous reports that lesbian relationships are more egalitarian than heterosexual relationships (Connolly, 2005; Green et al., 1996; Matthews et al., 2003; Schneider, 1986).

There are a number of explanations for these differences between lesbian and heterosexual relationships. Gender is the key to each of them, following the assumption that gender, and the gendering of power, both constructs and affects relationships (Laird, 2000). It has been argued that similarity in gender role may benefit women by allowing them to empathize with each other (Metz et al., 1994), a view that is supported by the accounts of empathy in the narratives of our interviewees. Expectations of empathy from a partner are also gendered. Metz and colleagues (1994) have argued that "if women are generally more likely to be cautious, scrutinize themselves, or worry more about a male partner's reactions, or if they have concerns about being substantially understood by a man, then women may be more self-assured when addressing conflict with another woman" (p. 304). This phenomenon may be of particular relevance in coping with distress associated with the reproductive body, where women expect a female partner to be better able to understand their premenstrual experience than a male partner.

The finding that lesbians are less likely to conform to the traditional feminine gender role (see Bailey & Zucker, 1995) is also of relevance and was evidenced by the absence of accounts of ideals of (hetero) femininity among the narratives of women. This gendered nonadherence has been linked to greater instrumentality, masculinity, and expressiveness among lesbians (Kurdek, 1987). Green and colleagues (1996) emphasize that lesbians are not like heterosexual men. Rather, they are more androgynous than heterosexual women. According to Green and colleagues (1996), lesbians might be less likely to be susceptible to fusion in relationships because the greater instrumentality of lesbians leads to assertiveness of their own needs. While there were accounts of increased vulnerability premenstrually in the narratives of lesbians in this study, there was no evidence of "clinging" and certainly no evidence of distancing on the part of partners. These findings stand in contrast to many heterosexual women's accounts of PMS (Perz & Ussher, 2006; Ussher et al., 2007). Indeed, the narratives of women supported the notion of lesbian relationships as "extremely close and highly differentiated" (Green et al., 1996, p.197).

The absence of children in the majority of lesbian relationships has also been proposed as an explanation for differences between heterosexual and lesbian couples, as the burden of family responsibility falls disproportionately on heterosexual women after having children (Metz et al., 1994). However, accounts of unsupportive relationships, overresponsibility, and self-silencing associated with PMS have been reported by heterosexual women with and without children (Ussher, 2004b). Equally, lesbian couples are less likely to adopt gendered divisions of labor even if they do have children and have been reported to rate relationship satisfaction very highly compared to child-free lesbian couples (Koepke, Hare, & Moran, 1992). In the present study, there was no evidence of a difference between lesbian couples with and without children. Future research on PMS could usefully explore this issue further, systematically examining the difference between couples with and without children among women in both same-sex and opposite-sex relationships.

In conclusion, the findings of the present study appear to belie the suggestion that "the relationships of gay and lesbian partners appear to work in the same way as the relationships of heterosexual partners" (Kurdek, 2005, p. 253). In relation to PMS, the experiences of lesbians and heterosexual women appear to be markedly different, with significant implications for women's negotiation and experience of premenstrual change. However, we do not intend to suggest that heterosexual couples cannot experience awareness, recognition, understanding, communication, and responsibility sharing in relation to PMS. Many heterosexual women do have partners who provide a supportive context for their experience of premenstrual change, which acts to facilitate self-care and reduce distress (Ussher et al., 2007). Unfortunately, these women rarely appear in the research literature, as they cope with PMS and avoid the spirals of guilt, self-blame, and pathologization that often motivate participation in a research study on PMS. Further study of these women who experience premenstrual change but do not position it as problematic is warranted.

Supportive heterosexual relationships share the qualities of the lesbian relationships discussed in the present study. Thus, we might conclude that a good relationship is a good relationship, regardless of gender or sexuality (see Gottman et al., 2003). However, the suggestion that there is nothing distinct about lesbian relationships in particular underestimates the positive aspects of lesbian relationships. When compared with previous research on lesbian relationships, the narratives of women in this study suggest that same-sex relationships are far more likely to be egalitarian, empathic, and supportive than opposite-sex relationships. As a consequence, there are significant implications for psychological well-being, such as coping with the emotional experience of PMS. But this phenomenon is not unique to the experience of PMS. In other areas of women's reproductive health, such as perinatal depression (Ross, 2005) and menopause (Winterich, 2003), the gender of a woman's partner appears to have an impact on her experience of distress.

The implications of this research are far broader than the positioning and experience of the reproductive body. We argue that these findings provide insight into the high levels of satisfaction reported in many lesbian relationships and have broader implications for understanding and facilitating women's mental health and well-being. Difference does not necessarily mean disadvantage: being in a lesbian relationship can undoubtedly be beneficial for many women. The narratives of women collected in this study, demonstrating the psychological advantage of having a same-sex partner for coping with PMS, reveal that the larger narrative of lesbian relationships as fusion is worthy of substantial revision. The positive distinctiveness of lesbian relationships is illuminated in the narratives of women and highlights new prospects for research.

Acknowledgment

This research was funded by a Discovery Grant from the Australian Research Council. Thanks are offered to Julie Mooney-Somers, Lee Shepard, Beverley Johnson, Caroline Joyce, and Helen Vidler for research support and assistance. Sections of the analysis presented in this chapter also appear in Ussher, J. M., & Perz, J. (2008). Empathy, egalitarianism and emotion work in the relational negotiation of PMS: The experience of lesbian couples. *Feminism and Psychology, 18*(1), 87–111.

REFERENCES

American Psychological Association (2004). Resolution on sexual orientation and marriage. Retrieved November 14, 2004, from http://www.apa.org/pi/lgbe/policy/marriage.pdf

Andersson, G., Noack, T., Seierstad, A., & Weedon-Fekjaer, H. (2004). The demographics of same-sex "marriages" in Norway and Sweden. Rostock, Germany: Max-Planck Institute for Demographic Research. Retrieved November 14, 2004, from http://www.demogr.mpg.de/papers/working/wp-2004-018.pdf

Bailey, J. M., & Zucker, K. J. (1995). Childhood sex-typed behavior and sexual orientation: A conceptual analysis and quantitative review. *Developmental Psychology, 31*, 43–55.

Bancroft, J. (1993). The premenstrual syndrome: A reappraisal of the concept and the evidence. *Psychological Medicine, suppl 241*, 1–47.

Blumstein, P., & Schwartz, P. (1983). *American couples: Money, work, sex.* New York: William Morrow.

Brown, L. S. (1995). Therapy with same-sex couples: An introduction. In N. S. Jacobson & A. S. Gurman (Eds.), *Clinical handbook of couple therapy* (pp. 274–291). New York: Guilford.

Chang, A. M., Holroyd, E., & Chau, J. P. (1995). Premenstrual syndrome in employed Chinese women in Hong Kong. *Health Care for Women International, 16*(6), 551–561.

Chrisler, J. C., & Caplan, P. (2002). The strange case of Dr. Jekyll and Ms. Hyde: How PMS became a cultural phenomenon and a psychiatric disorder. *Annual Review of Sex Research, 13*, 274–306.

Connolly, C. M. (2005). A qualitative exploration of resilience in long-term lesbian couples. *The Family Journal: Counseling and Therapy for Couples and Families, 13*(3), 266–280.

Connolly, C. M., & Sicola, M. K. (2006). Listening to lesbian couples: Communication competence in long term relationships. In J. J. Bigner (Ed.), *An introduction to GLBT family studies* (pp. 271–296). New York: Haworth Press.

Cosgrove, L., & Riddle, B. (2003). Constructions of femininity and experiences of menstrual distress. *Women & Health, 38*(3), 37–58.

Davies, B., & Harré, R. (1990). Positioning: The discursive production of selves. *Journal for the Theory of Social Behaviour, 20,* 43–65.

Duncombe, J., & Marsden, D. (1998). Stepford wives and hollow men? Doing emotion work, doing gender and authenticity in heterosexual relationships. In G. Bendelow & S. Williams (Eds.), *Emotions in social life: Critical themes and contemporary issues* (pp. 211–227). London: Routledge.

Eldridge, N. S., & Gilbert, L. A. (1990). Correlates of relationship satisfaction in lesbian couples. *Psychology of Women Quarterly, 14,* 43–62.

Elson, J. (2002). Menarche, menstruation, and gender identity: Retrospective accounts from women who have undergone premenopausal hysterectomy. *Sex Roles, 46,* 37–48.

Fraser, M. W., & Richman, J. M. (1999). Risk, protection, and resilience: Toward a conceptual framework for social work practice. *Social Work Research, 23*(3), 318–342.

Gottman, J. M., Levenson, R. W., Gross, J., Frederickson, B. L., McCoy, K., Rosenthal, L., et al. (2003). Correlates of gay and lesbian couples' relationship satisfaction and relationship dissolution. *Journal of Homosexuality, 45*(1), 23–43.

Green, R. J., Bettinger, M., & Zacks, E. (1996). Are lesbian couples fused and gay male couples disengaged? Questioning gender straightjackets. In J. Laird & R. J. Green (Eds.), *Lesbians and gays in couples and families: A handbook for therapists* (pp. 185–230). San Francisco: Jossey-Bass.

Halbreich, U., Borenstein, J., Pearlstein, T., & Kahn, L. S. (2003). The prevalence, impairment, impact, and burden of premenstrual dysphoric disorder (PMS/PMDD). *Psychoneuroendocrinology, 28*(Suppl 3), 1–23.

Jack, D. C. (1991). *Silencing the self: Women and depression.* Cambridge MA: Harvard University Press.

Jones, A., Theodos, V., Canar, W. J., Sher, T. G., & Young, M. (2000). Couples and premenstrual syndrome: Partners as moderators of symptoms? In K. B. Schmaling (Ed.), *The psychology of couples and illness: Theory, research, & practice.* (pp. 217–239). Washington, DC: American Psychological Association Press.

Jordan, J. V. (1991). The meaning of mutuality. In A. G. Kaplan, J. B. Miller, I. P. Stiver, & J. L. Surrey (Eds.), *Women's growth in connection: Writings from the Stone Center* (pp. 81–96). New York: Guilford.

Julien, D., Chartrand, E., Simard, M. C., Bouthillier, D., & Begin, J. (2003). Conflict, social support, and relationship quality: An observational study of heterosexual, gay male, and lesbian couples' communication. *Journal of Family Psychology, 17*(3), 419–428.

Koepke, L., Hare, J., & Moran, P. (1992). Relationship quality in a sample of lesbian couples with children and child-free couples. *Family Relations, 41*, 224–229.

Krestan, J., & Bepko, C. S. (1980). The problem of fusion in lesbian relationships. *Family Process, 19*, 277–289.

Kurdek, L. A. (1987). Sex-role self schema and psychological adjustment in coupled homosexual and heterosexual men and women. *Sex Roles, 17*, 549–562.

Kurdek, L. A. (1995). Assessing multiple determinants of relationship commitment in cohabiting gay, cohabiting lesbian, dating heterosexual, and married heterosexual couples. *Family Relations, 44*, 261–266.

Kurdek, L. A. (2003). Differences between gay and lesbian cohabiting couples. *Journal of Social and Personal Relationships, 20*, 411–436.

Kurdek, L. A. (2004a). Are gay and lesbian cohabiting couples really different from heterosexual married couples? *Journal of Marriage and Family, 66*, 880–900.

Kurdek, L. A. (2004b). Gay men and lesbians: The family context. In M. Coleman & L. H. Ganong (Eds.), *Handbook of contemporary families: Considering the past, contemplating the future* (pp. 96–105). Thousand Oaks, CA: Sage.

Kurdek, L. A. (2005). What do we know about gay and lesbian couples? *Current Directions in Psychological Science, 14*, 251–254.

Laird, J. (2000). Gender in lesbian relationships: Cultural, feminist, and constructionist reflections. *Journal of Marital and Family Therapy, 26*(4), 455–467.

Lee, S. (2002). Health and sickness: The meaning of menstruation and premenstrual syndrome in women's lives. *Sex Roles, 46*(1–2), 25–35.

Mackey, R. A., Diemer, M. A., & O'Brien, B. A. (2004). Relational factors in understanding satisfaction in the lasting relationships of same-sex and heterosexual couples. *Journal of Homosexuality, 47*(1), 111–136.

Matthews, A. K., Tartaro, J., & Hughes, T. L. (2003). A comparative study of lesbian and heterosexual women in committed relationships. *Journal of Lesbian Studies, 7*(1), 101–114.

McDaniel, S. H. (1988). The interpersonal politics of premenstrual syndrome. *Family Systems Medicine, 6*(2), 134–149.

Mencher, J. (1990). *Intimacy in lesbian relationships: A critical re-examination of fusion.* Work in Progress No 42. Wellesley, MA: Wellesley College, Stone Center for Women's Development.

Metz, M. E., Rosser, B. R. R., & Strapko, N. (1994). Differences in conflict-resolution styles among heterosexual, gay, and lesbian couples. *Journal of Sex Research, 31*(4), 293–308.

Mooney-Somers, J., Perz, J., & Ussher, J. M. (In press). A complex negotiation: Women's experiences of naming and not naming premenstrual distress in couple relationships. *Women and Health.*

Nichols, M. (2004). Lesbian sexuality/female sexuality: Rethinking "lesbian bed death." *Sexual and Relationship Therapy, 19*(4), 363–371.

O'Brien, S. M. (2003). Intrusiveness, closeness-caregiving, and relationship adjustment in lesbian cohabiting couples. *Dissertation Abstracts International,* Section B: The sciences and engineering (64[6-B]), 2933.

O'Grady, H. (2005). *Women's relationship with herself: Gender, Foucault, therapy.* London: Routledge.

Ossana, S. M. (2000). Relationship and couples counseling. In R. M. Perez, K. A. DeBord, & K. J. Bieschke (Eds.), *Handbook of counseling and psychotherapy with lesbian, gay, and bisexual clients* (pp. 275–302). Washington, DC: American Psychological Association Press.

Perz, J., & Ussher, J. M. (2006). Women's experience of premenstrual change: A case of silencing the self. *Journal of Reproductive and Infant Psychology, 24*(4), 289–303.

Poulin, C., & Gouliquer, L. (2003). Part-time disabled lesbian passing on roller blades, or PMS, Prozac and essentializing women's ailments. *Women and Therapy, 26*(1–2), 95–110.

Ross, L. E. (2005). Perinatal mental health in lesbian mothers: A review of potential risk and protective factors. *Women and Health, 41*(3), 113–128.

Roth, S. (1989). Psychotherapy with lesbian couples: Individual issues, female socialization and the social context. In M. McGoldrick, C. M. Anderson, & E. Walsh (Eds.), *Women in families: A framework for family therapy* (pp. 286–307). New York: Norton.

Schneider, M. S. (1986). The relationships of cohabiting lesbian and heterosexual couples: A comparison. *Psychology of Women Quarterly, 10,* 234–239.

Schreurs, K. M. G., & Buunk, B. P. (1996). Closeness, autonomy, equity, and relationship satisfaction in lesbian couples. *Psychology of Women Quarterly, 20,* 577–592.

Scrivner, R., & Eldridge, N. S. (1995). Lesbian and gay family psychology. In R. H. Mikesell, D. Lusterman, & S. H. McDaniel (Eds.), *Integrating family therapy: Handbook of family psychology and systems theory* (pp. 327–345). Washington, DC: American Psychological Association Press.

Slater, S., & Mencher, J. (1991). The lesbian family life cycle. *American Journal of Orthopsychiatry, 61,* 372–382.

Steege, J. F., Stout, A. L., & Rupp, S. L. (1988). Clinical features. In W. R. Keye (Ed.), *The premenstrual syndrome* (pp. 88–96). Philadelphia: W.B. Saunders.

Steiner, M., & Born, L. (2000). Advances in the diagnosis and treatment of premenstrual dysphoria. *CNS Drugs, 13*(4), 287–304.

Stenner, P. (1993). Discoursing jealousy. In E. Burman & I. Parker (Eds.), *Discourse analytic research* (pp. 114–134). London: Routledge.

Sveinsdottir, H., Lundman, B., & Norberg, A. (2002). Whose voice? Whose experiences? Women's qualitative accounts of general and private discussion of premenstrual syndrome. *Scandinavian Journal of Caring Sciences, 16*(4), 414–423.

Ussher, J. M. (2002). Processes of appraisal and coping in the development and maintenance of premenstrual dysphoric disorder. *Journal of Community and Applied Social Psychology, 12,* 1–14.

Ussher, J. M. (2003a). The ongoing silencing of women in families: An analysis and rethinking of premenstrual syndrome and therapy. *Journal of Family Therapy, 25,* 388–405.

Ussher, J. M. (2003b). The role of premenstrual dysphoric disorder in the subjectification of women. *Journal of Medical Humanities, 24*(1/2), 131–146.

Ussher, J. M. (2004a). Blaming the body for distress: Premenstrual dysphoric disorder and the subjectification of women. In A. Potts, N. Gavey, & A. Wetherall (Eds.), *Sex and the body* (pp. 183–202). Palmerstone North, New Zealand: Dunmore Press.

Ussher, J. M. (2004b). Premenstrual syndrome and self-policing: Ruptures in self-silencing leading to increased self-surveillance and blaming of the body. *Social Theory & Health, 2*(3), 254–272.

Ussher, J. M. (2006). *Managing the monstrous feminine: Regulating the reproductive body.* London: Routledge.

Ussher, J. M. (2008). Challenging the positioning of premenstrual change as PMS: The impact of a psychological intervention on women's self-policing. *Qualitative Research in Psychology, 5*(1), 33–44.

Ussher, J. M., Hunter, M., & Browne, S. J. (2000). Good, bad or dangerous to know: Representations of femininity in narrative accounts of PMS. In C. Squire (Ed.), *Culture in psychology* (pp. 87–99). New York: Routledge.

Ussher, J. M., & Perz, J. (2006). Evaluating the relative efficacy of a self-help and minimal psycho-educational intervention for moderate premenstrual distress conducted from a critical realist standpoint. *Journal of Reproductive and Infant Psychology, 24*(2), 347–362.

Ussher, J. M., & Perz, J. (2008). Empathy, egalitarianism and emotion work in the relational negotiation of PMS: The experience of lesbian couples. *Feminism and Psychology, 18*(1), 87–111.

Ussher, J. M., & Perz, J. (in press). Disruption of the silenced-self: The case of pre-menstrual syndrome. In D. C. J ack (Ed.), *The depression epidemic: International perspectives on women's self-silencing and psychological distress.* Oxford: Oxford University Press.

Ussher, J. M., Perz, J., & Mooney-Somers, J. (2007). The experience and positioning of affect in the context of intersubjectivity: The case of premenstrual syndrome. *International Journal of Critical Psychology, 21*, 145–165.

Winterich, J. A. (2003). Sex, menopause and culture: Sexual orientation and the meaning of menopause for women's lives. *Gender & Society, 17*(4), 627–642.

11

Postcards from the Edge

Narratives of Sex and Relationship Breakdown Among Gay Men

Damien Ridge and Rebecca Wright

Gay men are no different from others when they narrate their lives as stories with characters, motivations, reasons, and even heroes and villains (Gold & Ridge, 2001). Like others, gay men grasp their senses of self through the meaningful way the story of their lives unfolds and is told and retold (Plummer, 1995). People tell stories to themselves and to others in order to understand the world and their place in it (Elwyn & Gwyn, 1999). Skillful and life-invigorating stories can support better health, while stories of despair may be detrimental to well-being (Bochner, 1997; Holmes, 1992; Jackson, 1998; Pennebaker & Seagal, 1999; Smith, 1999). Stories are thought to be valuable for their ability to engage people, aid reflection, transmit ideas, invigorate lives, tackle stigma, and aid recovery from ill health (Panford, Nyaney, Amoah, & Aidoo, 2001; Ridge & Ziebland, 2006).

When viewed across a few short decades, remarkably powerful narratives of homosexuality have emerged in the West (see Shepard, this volume). These narratives have included struggle against social oppression through gay liberation, accompanied by a shift from homosexuality as a criminal activity or diagnosable mental illness to an acceptable social identity. Yet, societies continue to be characterized by homophobia (Plummer, 1999), which is ultimately detrimental to all citizens, including heterosexual men (Plummer, 2001).

In this chapter, we explore some of the complex challenges that are part of the lives of gay men in the early twenty-first century. To examine these challenges, we consider two potential experiences in the gay male life course that remain poorly understood. First, we examine challenges facing human immunodeficiency virus (HIV)-positive gay men in preventing the forward transmission of HIV and establishing positive sex lives. Second, we look at the experience of relationship dissolution for gay men. We seek to gain a deeper and more nuanced understanding of these potential experiences of the gay male life course through the use of narrative methods. In concluding our exploration, we will present inferences about gay narratives, identity, and the life course in the new century.

Sex, Risk, and Pleasure for HIV-Positive Men

Over the decades, HIV prevention campaigns for gay men have moved away from a universal "condoms always" message for anal sex toward more complicated constructions of "risk" and "risk reduction" (Bartos, McLeod, & Nott, 1993; Parsons et al., 2005). Current approaches recognize the complex ways in which gay men actually negotiate sex to minimize risk, understanding that not all risk is unhealthy and that risk cannot be eradicated entirely. The multiple complex sexual risk-reduction strategies that gay men have adopted in the real world include withdrawal before ejaculation in unprotected oral and anal sex, always using condoms for anal sex, *strategic positioning* (in which the HIV-positive partner is receptive in unprotected anal sex and the HIV-negative partner is insertive), and *serosorting* for partners of the same HIV status for unprotected anal sex (Elford, 2006; Parsons et al., 2005). Strategies like serosorting are greatly aided by new Internet technologies that allow sophisticated database searches for like-minded sex partners of the same HIV status (Davis, Hart, Bolding, Sherr, & Elford, 2006).

Along with the diversification of actual sexual risk-reduction strategies and critiques of rational models of sexual risk, narrative research highlights the need to move beyond simplistic health behavior models of gay men (Martin, 2006; Rhodes & Cusick, 2002). In contrast to a rational model of human behavior, narrative research has suggested that the meanings of sexual risk are fluid, multiple, emotionally based, contradictory, layered, not necessarily available to conscious awareness, and context dependent (Davis et al., 2002; Gold, 2000; International Collaboration on HIV Optimism, 2003; Martin, 2006; Ridge, 2004).

In the first part of this chapter, we examine online narratives (collected by DR) of the sexual lives of 24 HIV-positive gay men in the United Kingdom. These narratives are available to the public via a research and public-information Web site we created (http://www.healthtalkonline.org/hiv). We explore these online narratives as a way to identify the primary concerns of HIV-positive gay men as they negotiate safe and rewarding sex.

Negotiating Sex

Negotiating sex with serodiscordant partners was a key struggle identified in the narratives of positive men. For instance, positive men were at times confronted with the need to respond to a negative partner's desire to engage in unsafe sex (Ridge, Ziebland, Williams, Anderson, & Elford, 2007). Desires to engage in unsafe sex are difficult to explain using rational models of health behavior. As such, urges for unsafe sex could take men or their partners by surprise.

> And over a period of time with one of them [ongoing partner] it was
> the urge to then have unsafe sex.... He would push towards that....
> Until it would freak him out completely. (H03)

Some men speculated about the reasons underpinning their partner's sexual risk, including recklessness, the desire to express closeness, and the perceived inevitability of infection anyway.

Interestingly, while some negative sexual partners seemed comfortable with their partner's positive status, others appeared particularly frightened of HIV. Even if it was difficult for fearful partners to fully communicate their anxieties, their fears could emerge during sex.

> And they [ongoing sexual partners] all had issues around it [HIV],
> and you know they all said no, no, it is fine, it is not a problem you're
> HIV positive.... [With] one it was a case of them just drawing away
> from having safe anal sex, and then [me] suddenly thinking, I don't
> know if I am comfortable with [only having] oral sex.... And it is like
> why? What is different now? I am healthy, things are great. (H03)

As this narrative suggests, positive men were sometimes forced to confront their partners' anxieties about various sex acts, and a kind of "fatigue" in having to manage such anxieties can develop among men.

It was clear from the narratives that the addition of HIV to a relationship could create significant challenges. Sometimes there were long-term implications for the enjoyment of sex within relationships. A number of men reported that their relationships were no longer sexual, and some linked HIV to their celibacy within their relationship.

> We have given up sex, com, completely. I think mostly because of the risk involved. Which in a way it was quite...it's quite ironic because we were in a way, our relationship, our relationship was maturing in[to] something more honest, closer. And perhaps was getting to a stage where we probably would have been able to have a...a bit of a revival in this respect. But it's...it's...certainly in the first few months after my diagnosis there was too much going on to kind of think about that. Too much going...too much going on...too much risk to think about, too many things to adjust to...in our own, in our relationship, to kind of...add this additional layer of, of complication in a way. (H17)

The need to consider discordance in status can create anxieties for men and introduces a degree of complexity that can work against the more spontaneous aspects of sex.

While positive men wondered about the motivations of some partners who were prepared to have unsafe sex, others admitted that their own interpretations could also present problems for HIV risk reduction. A number of men noted that before their own HIV infection, they had made assumptions about their HIV status that influenced their behavior. Although he was practicing unprotected anal sex, Jorge, an immigrant from South America who did not consistently use condoms for anal sex, was so convinced that he was HIV-negative that he tried to persuade his reluctant partner to dispense with condoms.

> I really do like to do sex without the condom and he said no. Because his last boyfriend for 10 years their relationship, have died of HIV. And he said, "No, I don't want to." I said, "But why, because you are positive?" He said, "No, I'm not positive. But I have been with someone that is positive for 5, for 6 years. And I said to myself, never do sex without condom, and I don't want this to happen again." Then he asked me, it's very funny because he asked, "What happened if you are, if you discovered that I was positive?"...So we didn't have sex without a condom, I stayed very upset about that. Then I go back to London I said, "I will do some tests, to prove for you that I don't have nothing, and I want to have sex without condom." And he said, "Whatever you do, I will not do sex without condom." I said,

"Okay, but I will do this test anyway." After 2 weeks I went to take
the result.... And I never remember, I never forget...they said,
"Unfortunately, you are positive."...The whole world stopped. I just
remember that I just was start to cry, cry, cry....

On the other hand, Robert, a retired general practicioner, was so sure that he
was HIV-positive from a previous partnership that he was prepared to have
unprotected sex with a partner he knew to be HIV-positive. Robert assumed he
had already been infected with HIV from his long-term partner (who had died
from acquired immune deficiency syndrome [AIDS]) and so felt that unprotected anal sex with an HIV-positive man would not pose a health problem.

The two of us went out for dinner nearby here. And we had more to
drink and sort of came home between the two of us on three legs
here and.... And [I] remember...I assumed that I had HIV at the
time. And I knew he had, and we were sort of comforting each other
really, it was a sort of.... Very affectionate, very intimate session of
comforting after the funeral of his partner. And actually we had
a lovely night! But I was certainly exposed to infection and...and
in...proper time afterwards I had my seroconversion illness. I never
told him that I'd got HIV, he died not all that long afterwards.
I felt very much that it was certainly nothing that I could blame
him for. That it was a joint misadventure and it had actually been
lovely, being together that night. The HIV was a most unfortunate
consequence.

As the narratives of Jorge and Robert reveal, gay men take calculated risks
including information on their perceived HIV status.

Participants had differing views about telling sexual partners about their
HIV status. Some felt that they did not have to disclose to new or casual partners, provided that they had safe sex. Others, though, felt that risk could never
be completely eliminated, even with the use of condoms, or they were worried
about the perceptions of partners should they discover their status later on.
These individuals tended to feel an obligation to try to inform new partners of
their HIV status.

First of all, I think you have to have safe sex. Secondly, I think it's
not one person's responsibility. And I would never, I mean if anybody asked me [about my HIV status], I'd say immediately, yes. So
people are free to ask and everybody should have safe sex if they're
concerned, either...[about] getting it or giving it. Even so it worries

me a bit, and I'm beginning to move towards the idea that you
should at least provide, I should at least provide people with the
opportunity to find out [about my HIV status]. I'm just concerned
about people being appalled if they find out subsequently.... (H25)

Telling new and casual partners about HIV was an ongoing concern for many
HIV-positive men. Most positive men who told partners about their status
faced rejection at one time or another.

The narratives of HIV-positive men reveal the complexities of negotiating
sex with partners. Decisions about the use of protection raise issues for men of
responsibility for the health of partners, but the narratives of men reveal sexual decision making as a complex, fluid process of both internal and external
negotiation.

Emotional Complications

In the age of effective HIV treatments, what the narratives of the men mostly
revealed was that living with HIV—including anxieties about health, sexual
risks, and disclosure of status—continues to be difficult to manage at an emotional level. As one young man said, "God, what a mess. I fucking hate it. It's
awful, that's the truth. You know it's a minefield, and that's why I say there's
nothing manageable about living with HIV."

In terms of sex, some men admitted to avoiding opportunities for sex
because of the added emotional difficulties involved, while a few chose to have
sex with other positive partners only.

If, if I go out to a gay bar or ... I mean [pause] it won't particularly
bother me if someone makes an advance and I reject it. It doesn't
bother me. Because I always said to myself in the back of my mind
that I would not want to pass this thing on to anyone [pause] under
any circumstances. And that was going back to when I got it.
Because putting two and two together, you know, didn't have to be a
Sherlock Holmes, it's someone that I went with who knew that they
had it, but, you know, could have told me. But maybe didn't because
they, they felt as if they'd be rejected if they did. You know. Now I am
experiencing the same thing. The only, the case is ... The only difference here is that if I, if I do ever go with anyone, it will probably more
likely be someone who is also HIV-positive. Because I wouldn't want
to run the risk. My, my conscience wouldn't allow me to do anything
like that. You know. (H02)

Many men choose to partner only with other positive men in order to avoid the challenges of negotiation and disclosure that accompany sex with serodiscordant men. They serosort not only out of a desire to reduce the anxieties of sex with a negative partner, but also out of a sense of responsibility not to infect other men.

The emotional aftermath of an HIV diagnosis can run deep for men. While it could be easier for men to initially try to cope with an HIV diagnosis rationally, it is more difficult to escape the emotional work that needs to be done in the long run. For instance, David talks about how he first focused on the advantages that came with his identity as an HIV-positive White middle-class gay man. It took him a full year to connect with his true feelings about an HIV diagnosis.

> The first response wasn't to go, "Oh my God! Argh!" It was to say, "Well, at least I'm a, a White gay middle-class man in a developed country." You know, that really was ... I think the second year of my diagnosis was really then thinking about feelings. And I think a pattern in life had been to overrationalize.... As a, as a sort of coping mechanism, maybe. And also just because that's the way I am. But the second year was much more about connecting with my feelings about me, anyway generally. And my feelings about life. But also about HIV diagnosis. And sort of actually ... Rather than just saying, "Oh well, shit happens. And it's ... You know, it is shit, but I'll get this, this, this, and this out of it." And I've rationalized, rationalized, rationalized. Just thinking.... Actually, for the first time since telling a couple of very close friends, sort of getting, yes, a bit upset about it. And a bit angry about it.

In the process of coping with an HIV diagnosis, men are confronted with a barrage of emotions, some of which are deliberately avoided and worked through slowly. David's narrative reveals this process.

In many narratives, an HIV infection tended to bring deeper emotional issues to the surface. For instance, men sometimes wanted to shield their parents from the diagnosis. While this desire for secrecy could be about protecting parents from unpleasant news, even men who were out also grappled with the possibility that residual shame about their sexuality played a role in their decision.

> But I never told [my parents] ... and so they were wonderful about me, they love and accept [my current partner], but I never told them about my HIV status. And the reason for that I tell myself is because

I didn't want to hurt them, and that is true because I didn't want
to worry them.... And I thought I'll wait until I really absolutely do
have to tell the...And then treatment came along and I just, you
know.... I'm offered advice from various friends that you should
tell them.... But my instinct is not to tell them, why impose this
worry onto them? That no matter what I told them about therapy,
treatments, they'd just see HIV, AIDS, death. Then another side of
me thinks, am I really doing this because I am actually deep down
quite ashamed of myself?...I think if I had been diagnosed with and
treated for a cancer, which would probably...would now probably
lie in remission with good treatment for a lifetime, I wouldn't worry
about them finding out or telling them. I think that is definitely
something to do with it. No matter how un-PC this might sound
and things like that, and no matter how much work I've done on this
or how much I've lived through it, there is still part of me which is
ashamed of having HIV. (H12)

An HIV diagnosis raises issues about both self-acceptance and acceptance of
significant others in one's life, including one's family.

Finally, many men in the study had lived with HIV for decades and were
now moving into middle or older age. These men were coping with multiple
issues, and it was difficult for them to disentangle the challenges they faced as
their bodies and feelings changed. For instance, Edward talked about a time
when he was simultaneously struggling with relationship dissolution, depression, grief, the approach of middle age, unemployment, and improved health
because of the new HIV treatments.

So it was difficult adjusting. I went through a very bad time. I got
very depressed, because a second relationship of 10 years...the first
one died, the second one I decided...yeah, that was enough. And
you know it was the right decision. We shouldn't be together, but we
are best friends now. It was just at the time it was very difficult. I was
you know 44 or something, 43, 44. I am thinking, oh no, I just don't
want to go through this whole scene of going to the bars and trying
to meet people and all of this...a bit of a mid-life crisis. It was a very
strange time for me. And you know healthwise I am thinking, well
what have I got to do? Here I am.... I'm you know, I am not working.
I'm you know feeling better now with the medication. I don't know,
you know, it has its benefits in one way, but I couldn't go back and do
the [type of work I was doing before HIV].

A confluence of factors related to HIV status, relationship status, and the life course can converge to create unique emotional challenges for positive men, as Edward's narrative reveals.

Simon, who had been on medication for many years and was taking 19 tablets a day, described the situation in which he found himself concisely: "I don't know what it feels to feel normal." He described not knowing what in his subjective experience was due to moving into middle age, lack of testosterone, viral infection, or medication:

> I mean one, one of the things that I was talking about with...to somebody recently, and this is very pertinent. You get to a stage.... Certainly I've got to the...this stage. And my friend has got to this stage. And my friend is a, a consultant psychiatrist. Where you don't know what is normal. You don't know how you should be feeling. I, I have no idea what I should feel like at 40 years old, without hepatitis, without HIV. I have no idea. I've forgotten what normal nerve function feels like.... I, I will know if it gets worse, or if it, if it changes. But I don't know what it feels to feel normal.... Either physically or psychologically.... Sort of I'm nearly 40. And I, I basically know that I, I am menopausal. Because I'm not producing testosterone. Even though I've got testosterone and I've got a bit of sex drive. And then to be told I've got osteoporosis. It makes me feel like a little old lady. [laughs]

Simon's narrative suggests that coping with the normative biological and social changes of the life course can be unique for HIV-positive men, whose treatments impact on their physiology.

Relationship Dissolution and Coping

Despite some vigorous opposition (often articulated on religious grounds), there is increasing official recognition of gay relationships, especially in Europe. Legal recognition of same-sex committed relationships is supported by research showing the substantial psychosocial benefits of marriage (Herek, 2006), as well as the similarities of committed relationships irrespective of sexual orientation. Gay and lesbian couples develop and sustain loving and committed relationships with levels of satisfaction, commitment, duration, and quality similar to those of heterosexual couples (Kurdek, 1997, 2004; Peplau, Veniegas, & Campbell, 1996; Sarantakos, 1996). Further, if there are any differences, it appears that same-sex relationships demonstrate greater levels of functionality than heterosexual partnerships (Kurdek, 2004).

But what is the story when same-sex relationships dissolve? The psychosocial implications of the ending of same-sex relationships are currently unclear (Oswald & Clausell, 2006). Negotiating the end of an intimate relationship can be a traumatic life experience for anyone (Frazier & Cook, 1993). The reasons attributed to—and level of distress following—the dissolution of same-sex relationships are comparable to those of heterosexual separations (Kurdek, 1997).

In this section of the chapter, we examine narratives from a study of 10 gay men conducted by RW in Melbourne, Australia. The men interviewed for this study discussed their personal experiences of the dissolution of an intimate relationship that had lasted for more than 2 years. They provided detailed accounts of their feelings and coping strategies during the separation. Nearly all of the men were cohabiting with their partners at the time of separation. All of them, with one exception, reported a high level of distress following the separation. Most of the men did not initiate the separation.

The range and severity of the impact resulting from the loss of an intimate partner will ultimately depend on issues such as the degree to which the separation was anticipated, the level of communication in the relationship, and available coping mechanisms (Kurdek, 1997). The unique circumstances of individual couples also play an important role (James & Cody Murphy, 1997; Oswald & Clausell, 2006). For instance, characteristics of the relationship (e.g., degree of visibility, length of the relationship, living status, meanings of the partnership), the separation (e.g., reasons for the separation, how the separation was instigated, and whether it was anticipated), and the availability of support following the breakup are all thought to influence the way that gay men experience and cope with relationship dissolution.

Newly separated individuals report high levels of distress during and immediately following a relationship breakup (Hetherington, Cox, & Cox, 1982). This often highly emotional experience was well captured in the current study. Regardless of whether the men had actually initiated the separation, they reported experiencing feelings of emotional distress and grief, which could include deep sadness, devastation, loneliness, abandonment, disillusionment, and anger. One man articulated his profound reaction to a breakup in the following way:

> It was terrible. I felt like getting out of the city. I just felt like
> I couldn't live in the same city as him. I felt so abandoned and

really depressed and really disillusioned with the whole idea of gay relationships.

(Jim)

For the majority of men who had cohabited with their ex-partner, the breakup of a household was also a consideration and a complication following relationship dissolution. As in the study by Kurdek (1991), the men in our study noted the additional burdens of finalizing housing commitments, leaving the shared home, and seeking alternative living arrangements. These issues further compounded feelings of emotional distress and contributed to the feeling of being "transient" and less "grounded" during this time. As the narratives of Douglas and John illustrate:

> I went to visit my brother for a week and I was actually there for 10 days and when I came back the house was totally empty.... Here's this house and I owe a month's rent or something.... I was in no fit mental condition to cope with the fact that I had to get out of this house where I couldn't pay the rent.
>
> (Douglas)

> I felt really displaced because I came back with nowhere to live. I stayed with a friend and then I got in with a colleague.... I stayed with another colleague for a week. Then I stayed in a hotel for 2 weeks, so it was quite disruptive. I didn't have a base, I was groundless.... Being groundless is not a good place to try and work through any issues.
>
> (John)

Significant challenges exist for gay men when their meaningful relationships dissolve, particularly during the early stages of dissolution. The self-reported mental health consequences for gay men were overwhelmingly negative in the short term and could manifest in a reduced sense of self-worth, depression (ranging from depressed mood to a formal diagnosis of major depression), and, of particular concern, suicidal ideation and attempts. Elevated rates of suicidal thoughts and suicide attempts among gay men compared with nongay men are evident in the literature; however, concerns about suicide are typically associated with the coming-out process (Cochran & Mays, 2000; Remafedi, French, Story, Resnick, & Blum, 1998; Skegg, Nada-Raja, Dickson, Paul, & Williams, 2003). The results of the current study suggest that the first stages of relationship dissolution represent an additional "transitional" period when gay men may seriously consider suicide. While all of the men who participated in the study were ultimately able to move beyond the initial trauma of separation, their narratives revealed that getting on with living felt impossible at the time. The narratives of Chris, Jim, and Robert illustrate:

> I attempted suicide again in May this year and a lot of the feelings
> were the same, the sense of powerlessness, a sense of inability, a
> sense of hopelessness and ultimately a real sense of loneliness....
> And that sense of desperation, the pain is so bad that you don't want
> to go on anymore.
>
> (Chris)

> Immediately following, I felt terrible about myself. I just didn't
> want to be alive, I just felt that bad that you couldn't even put it into
> words.
>
> (Jim)

> I was practically picking it (antidepressant medication) up daily, for
> his (doctor's) sake as much as mine, so that I didn't overdose. At the
> time, I suppose if I had the chance just to take a bunch of sleeping
> tablets and just lay down and go to sleep, I probably would have taken
> the opportunity.
>
> (Robert)

The intensity of difficult emotions associated with relationship dissolution gradually dissipated as men worked through their separation issues. At the same time, the longer-term process of healing included many positive outcomes that were not anticipated by the men. A regaining of independence and an increased awareness of oneself, as well as personal growth in terms of being more assertive, feeling more compassionate for others, and having a greater sense of empowerment may well enhance the mental well-being of gay men in the long term. The narratives of John and Jim suggest such a longer-term outcome:

> I feel confirmed in knowing what I feel comfortable with and what
> I don't feel comfortable with, so I've decided that if I do have another
> relationship...I've decided that there are certain matters that I will
> not be going near, like the monogamy thing. It's going to be really
> important for me to protect my emotional security.
>
> (John)

There definitely have been some positives. It was a very interesting experience in that something that made you so depressed could end up being such a positive learning experience. It was like a double-edged sword.... You go through something negative but you can learn something positive.

(Jim)

Self-Help Strategies

What is currently less well understood in the literature is how men's partic-ular ways of coping with difficult events can be adaptive in terms of mental health. Understanding men's ways of coping with emotional problems requires an understanding of how coping is connected to valued ways of being male (Emslie, Ridge, Ziebland, & Hunt, 2006; Ridge, Plummer, & Peasley, 2006). In the current study, the narratives revealed that a combination of self-help and help-seeking coping strategies were used in the healing process. Interestingly, even though seeking the assistance of a professional counselor was a criterion for inclusion in the current study for ethical reasons, there was a tendency to prefer more autonomous coping strategies over help-seeking. The men reported using many different types of self-help strategies, including cutting ties, writ-ten and spiritual forms of self-discovery, and instrumental approaches.

CUTTING TIES. Some men made a conscious effort to increase the social dis-tance between themselves and their ex-partners, such as by removing personal effects, avoiding contact, and distancing themselves through geographic relo-cation. A few men had difficulty letting go, and they linked this problem with obsessional thoughts. They discussed behaviors such as phoning their partner several times a day, going to places where their partner was going to be, walk-ing past their home, and waiting outside their home.

The first thing I did to help myself was go overseas and to be inde-pendent, that was really important. I had some difficult times with alcohol on that trip, but generally I didn't drink a huge amount, and I really appreciated not working because I'm a slave to time, and to be able to do things in my own time was fantastic.

(John)

Robert found himself engaging in obsessive behaviors and only later under-stood the effects of his behaviors on his ex-partner. However, at the time, he felt that his actions were a way of displaying his love.

I suppose I would have been scary.... But that wasn't my point of being there. I was there to show him that I still loved him and I couldn't live without him.

WRITTEN AND SPIRITUAL SELF-DISCOVERY. Some men used bibliotherapy (reading literature, particularly self-help books) as a way of understanding themselves and working through their feelings. Additionally, self-discovery through their own writing (e.g., keeping a journal or writing letters to an ex-partner without necessarily sending them) was popular with some men. Participants reported that writing helped them find a way to express and explore their feelings and experiences.

> I kept that [a journal] through the relationship and certainly when the relationship finished I wrote avidly.... I was still looking for some kind of structure or reason to it.... I've got lots of different approaches to it because I'm an Aquarian so I come at things from lots of different angles. I'd write lists of stuff, then I'd write things in blocks of dates, then I'd just do scrambled writing, or other times I'd be really structured and try and really think it through. Other times I try and concentrate on my emotions, but trying to do it [understand the relationship breakup] with words that were about emotions... It's really hard. One thing my partner said which was complimentary was, I love the way your record your madness.
>
> (John)

While one participant claimed that he did not find writing useful, his narrative suggested that writing might have actually helped him identify how he was feeling and reacting to his separation.

> I started writing a lot but there was a lot of pent-up anger because I was always looking for someone else... to blame.
>
> (Rod)

Some men interpreted their experiences through a spiritual narrative. John's understanding of being on a spiritual journey contributed to a feeling of hope and a sense of well-being, and he framed his life events as occurring within an ultimately compassionate universe:

> I've done a lot of letting go, that's why the AA [Alcoholics Anonymous] process is very closely aligned with my spiritual path, well it's part of it, actually. Because it's about letting go and handing

over rather than grasping and clinging at your problems and creating more anger and resentment.

(John)

I was displaced, I was thrown out basically but it fixed itself up and I
kind of knew I was being looking after, so that's part of the spiritual
journey to know that it will be okay. But it was really scary and that
goes back to being really scared about coming out of a relationship,
to being by myself for the first time.

(John)

INSTRUMENTAL APPROACHES. Men also used instrumental approaches such
as engaging in activities (e.g., new hobbies, work) as a way of finding distraction from difficult thoughts and feelings. Finding a balance seemed to be the
key in instrumental activities. For instance, work could provide some relief from
emotional pain. Half of the men reported immersing themselves in work following the relationship dissolution. Some men used work effectively as a distraction to avoid thinking about the separation or as a means of gaining a sense of
achievement.

I started to feel a bit better about myself because I was keeping busy
and I wasn't thinking about [my ex-partner] 24 hours a day because
I had a job to do.

(Robert)

I needed to achieve beyond what I had to begin with.

(Ben)

Men such as Robert and Ben channeled their energy into work and identify
this coping strategy as beneficial. However, for some men, work could be an
additional source of strain in an already emotionally draining period.

[My ex-partner] left in September like I said, and from then through
till the end of September I stayed on still working. I was working
three jobs at the time, working up to about 50 hours a week. I was
getting home, like I'd work a day job then a night job, and I'd get
home at midnight and I was drinking heavily and then going back
in to work the next day.... The impact of this really heavy period of
work and stress that was going on...I was drinking more and more.

(John)

For John, immersion in work did not necessarily prove to be a beneficial coping strategy and even seemed to increase his level of stress.

Men reported using other instrumental strategies such as engaging in sex as a distraction and using drugs and alcohol to dull the emotional pain. While the men perceived that some of these strategies were less helpful, they tended to be reported primarily in the short term.

> I'd end up being with other people that I didn't want to be with just for the sake of company.... And started getting into some really strange situations so I wasn't alone.
>
> (Rod)

> I started drinking heavily.... I started drinking so heavily that I was going to work blind drunk.... I started taking drugs as well to cope with it [dissolution of the relationship]. My idea at the time was that if I block out that memory I also block out the pain.
>
> (Robert)

Help-Seeking Strategies

In addition to self-help strategies, men sought external resources to cope with the relationship dissolution. Although they were important, social, familial, and professional networks were less emphasized in coping with the separation than self-help approaches. There was also great variability among the men regarding the availability and appropriateness of social network supports.

The men's experiences with professional counseling were mostly positive, though this depended on the characteristics of the counselor. Most counselors who provided positive support to the men were gay themselves. Participants believed that gay counselors could better understand their experiences. Helpful counselors not only assisted by providing a safe and understanding space for talking, but also helped the men work through a range of specific issues including self-perception and intimacy needs.

> My counselor helped me to isolate what it was I was still missing about him by making me write down a list of all the things I missed about him. We narrowed these down through the sessions until I could isolate exactly what I missed about him. I was missing someone in my life that loved me, I was missing companionship and intimacy, I wasn't necessarily missing [my partner] per se.
>
> (Ben)

This man's experience with counseling provided him with the self-awareness and knowledge to cope effectively with the loss of his partner.

Support from friends after relationship dissolution was reported as quite mixed. Several men felt that friends dropped off after the separation because of the perceived need to choose sides. Some men admitted that their relationship had been so all-encompassing that it tended to marginalize friendships before the breakup. Alternatively, some men chose to stop socializing because of their own distress, and this decision contributed to further feelings of isolation.

> We were so firmly established as a couple that a lot of people sort of shied away. I suppose it happens when people get divorced as well, they don't want to be in that position where they are taking sides. The fact that some people wanted to keep [my partner] as a friend, so they avoided me, and some people wanted to keep me as a friend, so they avoided [my partner]. A lot of people avoided both of us because, as I said, we did everything together.
>
> (Douglas)

> I was extremely isolated. I'd just go to work, I'd come home and I'd drink. Then I'd go back to work again. I'd pretend to be sociable but in fact I wasn't interested in other people. All I wanted to do was drink.
>
> (John)

The narratives of Douglas and John illustrate the role that friendship can play following relationship dissolution. Because Douglas and his partner had been inseparable, it was difficult for him to reconfigure a social network after they split up. John maintained a social life after his relationship ended, but internally he continued to be highly focused on the loss of his partner.

Relationship dissolution created significant social and emotional challenges for the men in this study. Many of them reported that their ex-partner was the single most valuable source of support, offering emotional, social, financial, and practical assistance. Therefore, the consequences of the separation were particularly significant, involving multiple levels of loss.

Conclusion

In this chapter, we have traced some "narratives on the edge" of our understanding of the gay male life course in the twenty-first century. Using narrative methods, we illuminated the experiences of HIV-positive gay men in the United Kingdom as they negotiated sex and gay men in Melbourne, Australia, as they negotiated the end of their relationships.

In terms of HIV-positive gay men negotiating sex, we began by arguing that, in practice, sexual risk reduction approaches have diversified over the years. The narratives of the men in our study revealed a high level of complexity in preventing the transmission of HIV and negotiating rewarding sex lives. In particular, we highlighted the emotional complexities involved for HIV-positive men—the "mess" and the "minefield," as one man put it.

There is increasing recognition that the sexual and well-being needs of men with HIV can be quite different from those of men who do not have HIV. "Positive prevention" involves primary prevention (reducing the risk of spreading HIV and sexually transmitted infections) as well as secondary prevention (helping to promote the mental and physical health of people living with HIV) (International HIV/AIDS Alliance, 2003). While historically there has been a reluctance to focus on the specific prevention needs of HIV-positive gay men, the mood is now changing (Kalichman, 2005). As is evident in the research presented here, we are still in the early stages of understanding the various complex elements that make up positive prevention. Narrative research will play a key role in better understanding the needs of HIV-positive men to reduce sexual risk and increase sexual fulfillment.

Of particular interest is the finding that an HIV diagnosis can bring deeper emotional issues to the surface. Try as some men might to approach an HIV diagnosis rationally, complex feelings and narratives arise nonetheless. For instance, men discussed their underlying shame about gay sex, midlife crisis, anxiety and depression, fear of death, coming-out issues, and past family dysfunction after their diagnosis. The finding of residual shame about sexuality even in very out men reminds us that coming out does not necessarily resolve deeper problems that emerge from the deeply antigay messages that gay men receive from early boyhood (Plummer, 2001; Ridge, Hulme, & Peasley, 2003).

In terms of the life course, it is interesting that 15 of the 24 gay men in the study had been diagnosed with HIV before 1996. With or without the aid of treatment, these men considered themselves to be long-term survivors. Many of the men diagnosed before 1996 were now moving into middle age and beyond. The conflation of aging, the effects of the virus and medication on the body, and psychological issues (e.g., the midlife crisis) were central to their narratives. Long-term survivors commented on their longevity and its social meaning. One man who was infected in the 1980s described it this way: "It's like watching these films about people that live forever. Because I've basically just kept going while I've watched everyone else die." Another man said, "I'm going to live for considerably longer, which is incredibly scary." The stories of these men represent the cutting edge of future narrative research: positive gay men are surviving longer because of effective treatments, and they are getting older. "What the hell do I do with my life now?" one man asked?

The results of our Melbourne-based study on relationship dissolution identified the early stages of the breakup as a time of heightened vulnerability for some gay men. The results suggest that in addition to coming out, breaking up is another transition point where mental health and suicide risks can be elevated. However, the results also suggest that, following the initial trauma and grief, gay men do find ways to recover. Indeed, in the long term, some men feel that their lives are somehow improved by the narrative journey from breakup to recovery and establishing life again.

Given current research on masculinities, it is not surprising that the men in this study reported some preference for autonomous self-help coping strategies when their intimate relationships dissolved. Socially, men are encouraged to idealize dominant (hegemonic) forms of masculinity. These forms of masculinity are not set in stone but tend to be based on notions of physical dominance, strength and control, competition, and emotional invulnerability (Connell, 1995; Golombok & Fivush, 1994). Our research with heterosexual and gay men who experienced depression in the United Kingdom showed that recovery frequently involved reworking their personal narratives to (re)establish a valued sense of identity, including their own masculinity (Emslie et al., 2006). Men frequently aspire to hegemonic forms of masculinity, but some men can also negotiate different expressions of masculinity, such as those who value emotional sensitivity or intelligence.

In summary, the narratives in this chapter highlight the discovery of knowledge about the gay male life course as it is uniquely configured. The narratives of HIV-positive men reveal the strategies of sense-making that accompany life's challenging decisions about sex and relationships. The narratives of gay men coping with relationship dissolution reveal the diverse strategies men employ to deal with what can prove to be a major rite of passage in the gay life course. The methodological emphasis on narrative that we employ helps to raise awareness about uncharted territory in social inquiry of sexual lives by providing direct access to the voices that construct lived sexual experience.

REFERENCES

Bartos, M., McLeod, J., & Nott, P. (1993). *Meanings of sex between men*. Canberra: Australian Government Publishing Service.

Bochner, A. P. (1997). It's about time: Narrative and the divided self. *Qualitative Inquiry, 3*(4), 418–438.

Cochran, S., & Mays, V. (2000). Lifetime prevalence of suicide symptoms and affective disorders among men reporting same-sex sexual partners: Results from NHANES III. *American Journal of Public Health, 90*(4), 573–578.

Connell, R. W. (1995). *Masculinities.* St. Leonards, Australia: Allen & Unwin.

Davis, M. D. M., Hart, G., Bolding, G., Sherr, L., & Elford, J. (2006). E-dating, identity and HIV prevention: Theorising sexualities, risk and network society. *Sociology of Health & Illness, 28*(4), 457–478.

Davis, M. D. M., Hart, G., Imrie, J., Davidson, O., Williams, I., & Stephenson, J. (2002). HIV is HIV to me: The meanings of treatment, viral load and reinfection for gay men living with HIV. *Health, Risk & Society, 4*(1), 31–43.

Elford, J. (2006). Changing patterns of sexual behaviour in the era of highly active antiretroviral therapy. *Current Opinion in Infectious Diseases, 19*(1), 26–32.

Elwyn, G., & Gwyn, R. (1999). Narrative based medicine: Stories we hear and stories we tell: Analysing talk in clinical practice. *British Medical Journal, 318*, 186–188.

Emslie, C., Ridge, D., Ziebland, S., & Hunt, K. (2006). Men's accounts of depression: Reconstructing or resisting hegemonic masculinity? *Social Science & Medicine, 62*, 2246–2257.

Frazier, P. A. & Cook, S. W. (1993). Correlates of distress following heterosexual relationship dissolution. *Journal of Social and Personal Relationships, 10*(1), 55–67.

Gold, R. S. (2000). AIDS education for gay men: Towards a more cognitive approach. *AIDS Care, 12*(3), 267–272.

Gold, R. S., & Ridge, D. T. (2001). I will start treatment when I think the time is right: HIV positive gay men talk about their decision not to access antiretroviral therapy. *AIDS Care, 13*(6), 693–708.

Golombok, S., & Fivush, R. (1994). *Gender development.* New York: Cambridge University Press.

Herek, G. M. (2006). Legal recognition of same-sex relationships in the United States: A social science perspective. *American Psychologist, 61*(6), 607–621.

Hetherington, E. M., Cox, M., & Cox, R. (1982) Effects of divorce on parents and children. In M. Lamb (Ed.), *Nontraditional families* (pp. 233–288). Hillsdale, NJ: Erlbaum.

Holmes, J. (1992). *Between art and science.* London: Routledge.

International Collaboration on HIV Optimism. (2003). HIV treatments optimism among gay men: An international perspective. *Journal of Acquired Immune Deficiency Syndromes, 32*(5), 545–550.

International HIV/AIDS Alliance. (2003). *Positive prevention: Prevention strategies for people with HIV/AIDS.* Draft background paper. Brighton, U.K.: International AIDS Alliance.

Jackson, P. S. (1998). Bright star—black sky: A phenomenological study of depression as a window into the psyche of the gifted adolescent. *Roeper Review, 20*(3), 215–221.

James, S., & Cody Murphy, B. (1997). Gay and lesbian relationships in a changing social context. In R. Mackey, B. O'Brien, & E. Mackey (Eds.), *Gay and lesbian couples: Voices from lasting relationships* (pp. 99–121). Westport, CT: Praeger.

Kalichman, S. C. (2005). *Positive prevention: Reducing HIV transmission among people living with HIV/AIDS.* New York: Springer.

Kurdek, L. A. (1991). The dissolution of gay and lesbian couples. *Journal of Social and Personal Relationships, 8*(2), 265–278.

Kurdek, L. A. (1997). Adjustment to relationship dissolution in gay, lesbian, and heterosexual partners. *Personal Relationships, 4*(2), 145–161.

Kurdek, L. A. (2004). Are gay and lesbian cohabiting couples really different from heterosexual married couples? *Journal of Marriage and Family, 66*(4), 880–900.

Martin, J. (2006). Transcendence among gay men: Implications for HIV prevention. *Sexualities, 9*(2), 214–235.

Oswald, R., & Clausell, E. (2006). Same-sex relationships and their dissolution. In M. Fine & J. Harvey (Eds.), *Handbook of divorce and relationship dissolution* (pp. 499–513). Mahwah, NJ: Erlbaum.

Panford, S., Nyaney, M. O., Amoah, S. O., & Aidoo, N. G. (2001). Using folk media in HIV/AIDS prevention in rural Ghana. *American Journal of Public Health, 91*(10) 1559–1562.

Parsons, J. T., Schrimshaw, E. W., Wolitski, R. J., Halkitis, P. N., Purcell, D. W., Hoff, C. C., & Gomez, C. (2005). Sexual harm reduction practices of HIV-seropositive gay and bisexual men: Serosorting, strategic positioning, and withdrawal before ejaculation. *AIDS, 19*(Suppl. 1), S13–S25.

Pennebaker, J. W. & Seagal, J. D. (1999). Forming a story: The health benefits of narrative. *Journal of Clinical Psychology, 55*(10), 1243–1254.

Peplau, L. A., Veniegas, R. C., & Campbell, S. M. (1996). Gay and lesbian relationships. In R. C. Savin-Williams & K. M. Cohen (Eds.), *The lives of lesbians, gays, and bisexuals: Children to adults* (pp. 250–273). Orlando, FL: Harcourt Brace.

Plummer, D. C. (1999). *One of the boys.* New York: Haworth.

Plummer, D. C. (2001). The quest for modern manhood: Masculine stereotypes, peer culture and the social significance of homophobia. *Journal of Adolescence, 24*(1), 15–23.

Plummer, K. (1995). *Telling sexual stories: Power, change and social worlds.* London: Routledge.

Remafedi, G., French, S., Story, M., Resnick, M., & Blum, R. (1998). The relationship between suicide risk and sexual orientation: Results of a population-based study. *American Journal of Public Health, 88*(1), 57–60.

Rhodes, T., & Cusick, L. (2002). Accounting for unprotected sex: Stories of agency and acceptability. *Social Science & Medicine, 55*(2), 211–226.

Ridge, D. (2004). It was an incredible thrill: The social meanings and dynamics of younger gay men's experiences of barebacking in Melbourne. *Sexualities, 7*(3), 259–279.

Ridge, D., Hulme, A., & Peasley, D. (2003). Queering health: The health of young same-sex-attracted men and women. In H. Gardner & P. Liamputtong Rice (Eds.), *Health, social change and communities* (pp. 282–305). Oxford: Oxford University Press.

Ridge, D., Plummer, D., & Peasley, D. (2006). Remaking the masculine self and coping in the liminal world of the gay "scene." *Culture, Health and Sexuality, 8*(6), 501–514.

Ridge, D., & Ziebland, S. (2006). The old me could never have done that: How people give meaning to recovery following depression. *Qualitative Health Research, 16*(8), 1038–1053.

Ridge, D., Ziebland, S., Williams, I., Anderson, J., & Elford, J. (2007) Positive prevention: Contemporary issues facing HIV positive people negotiating sex in the UK. *Social Science & Medicine, 65,* 755–770.

Sarantakos, S. (1996). Same-sex couples: Problems and prospects. *Journal of Family Studies, 2*(2), 147–163.

Skegg, K., Nada-Raja, S., Dickson, N., Paul, C., & Williams, S. (2003). Sexual orientation and self-harm in men and women. *American Journal of Psychiatry, 160*(3), 541–546.

Smith, B. (1999). The abyss: Exploring depression through the narrative of the self. *Qualitative Inquiry, 5*(2), 264–279.

PART IV

Making Gay and Lesbian Identities

Development, Generativity, and the Life Course

12

In the Beginning

American Boyhood and the Life Stories of Gay Men

Bertram J. Cohler

The essence of homosexual boys has until now either been silenced or stigmatized. Bullies identify sissies. Psychiatrists identify sissy-boy syndromes. There has been virtually no effort to speak of the boyhood experience of homosexuals other than to characterize their youth as a disordered and/or nonconforming realm from which it is hoped they will break free. The fate of these boys is contemplated with the kind of hushed charity that obscures antipathy.

—Corbett (1999, p. 108)

Personal accounts of self-identified gay men writing or telling about their lives during the post–World War II period have emphasized rejection of such gender-stereotyped boyhood interests as "rough-and-tumble" play (Friedman & Downey, 2002) and "tough-guy" denial of feelings (Pollack, 1998). These accounts often emphasize awareness of oneself as different from other boys and early childhood recognition of unusual interest in other boys and men (Green, 2003; Jennings, 2006; Miller, 1997; Sedgwick, 1991). The significance of boyhood experiences presaging adult same-sex desire has been emphasized in psychoanalytic accounts ranging from Freud's (1905/1953) account of the formative role of childhood in the development of sexuality through the reductionist accounts of Rado (1949), Socarides (1968), the Biebers and their colleagues (Bieber et al., 1962; Friedman, 1998; Green, 1987).

This chapter discusses the impact of the American "boy code" from the boy books of the nineteenth century to our own time upon present representations of boyhood in the accounts of men self-identifying as gay. These men represent four postwar generation-cohorts: *(1)* men who came of age in the 1960s, a time of nascent activism; *(2)* men who came of age in the 1970s with the emergence of the gay rights movement; *(3)* men who came of age in the 1980s with the appearance of the AIDS pandemic; and *(4)* men who came of age in the 1990s, when same-sex desire had become a recognized lifeway among urban men (Hostetler & Herdt, 1998).

Boyhood in the American Life Story: Gender Stereotypes and Narratives of Gay Men

Lives and stories in bourgeois Western culture are presumed to be linear, with a beginning, middle, and end (Ricoeur, 1977). Personal accounts such as memoirs and autobiographies have placed particular emphasis on beginnings and on the significance of childhood experiences for the course of adult life (Coe, 1984; Freud, 1905). In his account of childhood and education, Rousseau (1762) emphasized the importance of childhood well-being for adult outcomes. Rousseau stressed the emotionally fragile character of childhood, which was a dramatic shift from the earlier presumption that children were either "little adults" (Aries, 1962), replete with adult desire, or uncivil beings in need of "taming" (Plumb, 1975). This view of childhood as a time of particular vulnerability for subsequent experience has been reflected in autobiographies and memoirs from Rousseau's statement about education and his personal account to those of the present time.

Coe (1984) has observed that while it is possible to verify accounts of events taking place in the adult years, verification is more difficult when portraying childhood experiences. While some critics maintain that all life-writing is inevitably fiction (Eakin, 1985; Spengemann, 1980), Lejune (1989) has observed that readers of autobiography and memoir presume an "autobiographical pact" between writer and reader in which the account is assumed to be "a retrospective prose narrative written by a real person concerning his own existence, where the focus is his individual life, in particular the story of his personality" (p. 120). The reader of a memoir or an autobiography believes that this personal account refers to actual persons, places, and events (Popkin, 2005). The autobiographical pact requires only that the life-writer provide a presently remembered rather than a deliberately fictional account of childhood, but it does not assume that this account needs to be factually accurate since we presume that we remember anew our past as we successively revise our life stories (Freeman, 1993; Schafer, 1981). Regardless of whether or not the memory is "accurate," it is a part of the writer's presently recalled life story and is "true" to the extent that the writer believes that the event recalled in this memory took place in a particular manner at a particular time (Eakin, 1999; Freeman, 1993).

The "Boy Code" and the American Boy Book

The boy code of a tough, self-reliant youth, unable to talk about feelings, portrayed by Pollack (1998, 2000) and supported by the observations of Kindlon and Thompson (1999) and a *Newsweek* cover story (Tyre, 2006), extends a view of American boyhood that had emerged in the "boy books" of the late nineteenth and early twentieth centuries. Evans (1999) has observed that lifewriting by men since the nineteenth century has been dominated by this view of boyhood featuring toughness and denial of feelings.

The concept of a tough boyhood characterized by rough-and-tumble play, the defining concept for gender-stereotyped activity of boys across middle childhood (Friedman & Downey, 2002; Pollack, 1998), began in the second half of the nineteenth century with the emergence of urban culture. This culture provided the luxury of free time apart from the inevitable round of chores expected of boys growing up in farm families. Mintz (2004) notes that genderspecific norms governed boys' activities: boys were expected to be physical, not sentimental or emotional, but daring and aggressive, adventurous, fun-loving, and self-reliant, although noble in spirit. Tom Sawyer and Huck Finn became the icons of late-nineteenth-century boyhood and fostered a tradition of "boyology" (Kidd, 2004). This idyll of late-nineteenth-century unsupervised boyhood in the neighborhood and community has been supplanted over the past century by increased parental supervision and involvement in leisure activities such as scouting that provided regularized, disciplined activities. Influenced by an emerging technology of education and child rearing, school and home conspired in this new control.

This concept of boyology is reflected in the American boy book and begins with Aldrich's (1869/1990) account of an impudent boy (Kidd, 2004). The genre is best reflected in Mark Twain's (aka Samuel Clemens') paired autobiographical novels of two boys growing up in a still-rural Midwest, *Tom Sawyer* (1876/1981) and *Huckleberry Finn* (1884/2003). *Tom Sawyer* is the quintessential American boy book. Tom is mischievous yet well-meaning. He is clever and charismatic, impudent and tough (Kidd, 2004). He is the "good" bad boy (Fiedler, 1966), the inspiration for the boy code later portrayed by Pollack

(1998). Tom's innocent boyish tricks are preparation for the heteronormative gender role expected of the American man. However, there is a darker reality implicit in these American boy books—that of desire that conflicts with the portrayal of childish innocence, including the complex same-sex relationship between Huck Finn and his companion, the runaway slave Jim. Written in the first person, *Huckleberry Finn* is the expression of true rebellion against middle-class values (Kazan, 1981).

Mintz (2004) argues that across the twentieth century, there was increased focus on gender differences, including emphasis on gender asymmetry in such activities as dating, and particular concern about the appropriate expression of masculine interests among boys. Boys with other than gender-stereotyped interests were contrasted with those "little Rascals" portrayed in movie matinees, lacking in adult supervision, daring and defiant, and constantly in trouble (Horrigan, 1999). These defiant boys were the heirs of the boyology that originated with Mark Twain's stories of Huck Finn and Tom Sawyer. Parents of boys who did not live up to these gender-stereotyped expectations sought expert advice and reassurance when they believed that their son was not showing sufficient expected masculine interests and was acting like a sissy (Corbett, 1999; Sedgwick, 1991; Shyer & Shyer, 1996). In the conservative era following the Second World War, it was assumed that boys became sissies as a consequence of having overindulgent mothers and emotionally distant fathers (Bieber et al., 1962).

Remembered Boyhood in the Life Stories of Gay Men

The emergence of life-course perspectives in the study of lives has emphasized the interplay of social and historical change and change in our understanding of such aspects of identity as sexual desire. This life-course perspective focuses on the meaning of life changes for particular generation-cohorts. While these events may be experienced by all generations—a so-called period effect—different cohorts construe significant events in quite different ways, depending upon the sequence of other events influencing a particular generation (Elder, Johnson, & Crosnoe, 2003). The life stories that are told or written by members of a particular generation reflect these distinctive life experiences (Cohler & Hostetler, 2003).

Among men seeking sexual contact with other men, boyhood awareness of being different from other boys or of the experience of same-sex desire takes on quite different significance across generation-cohorts. For example, the experience of acceptance of same-sex desire reported by many young people born in the generation of the 1980s is markedly different from that reported by earlier postwar generations (Jennings, 2006; Miller, 1997; Savin-Williams, 2005, Savin-Williams & Ream, 2003; Shyer & Shyer, 1996). According to the observations of Green (2003), Sedgwick (1991), and Stockton (2004), the experience of growing up for men in these generations was more like growing "sideways," since it was presumed that men with same-sex desire were psychologically "stuck" at some point in preadult personality development and were psychologically still "little boys" in adult guise.

Time and Place in Writing About a Gay Boyhood

American men seeking sexual and social ties with other men and coming to adulthood during the postwar years inevitably read *Tom Sawyer* and *Huckleberry Finn* in school. Twain's accounts of the experiences of boys growing up in nineteenth-century rural America have become the ideal type of the American boy book (Gribben, 1985; Jacobson, 1994). Boys aware of their same-sex desire often felt estranged from typical gender-stereotyped interests in competitive team sports and roughhouse play (Miller, 1997). They grew up at a time when the mental health professions regarded nongender-stereotyped interests in boys as evidence of a disturbance in psychological development (Corbett, 1999; Green, 1987; Shyer & Shyer, 1996). Being forced by anxious parents to seek counseling by psychotherapists educated in this tradition, and reading popular accounts that labeled them as sissies, further damaged their self-esteem and fostered an enduring sense of shame (Lassell, 1999; Meyer, 2003). Their sense of shame and stigma may have led many of these boys to compensate by becoming high achievers in such areas of their lives as school, scouting, and individual athletic and outdoor activities. Consistent with Bem's (1996) argument in his essay "Exotic Becomes Erotic," these boys might even have found themselves attracted to Tom and Huck, the ideal type of the boy code and so different from their own experiences.

The very concept of nonstereotyped gender interests told or written about by gay men might be understood as a subversive account. As a representative of the dark side of boyhood, Huck Finn's story is more congenial than that of Tom Sawyer among men seeking same-sex contact who may have also experienced a dark boyhood in which their sexual desire was as unaccepted as Huck Finn's delinquency. A contemporary gay reading of *Huckleberry Finn* might see in Huck's relationship with Jim the elusive homoerotic tie of boyhood (Kidd, 2004; Tierney, 2000). The significance of homoerotic elements in accounts of boyhood among men self-identifying as gay has been considered by Kincaid (1992), by Moon (1998), and in edited collections by Rottnek

(1999) and Bruhm and Hurley (2004). As both Bruhm and Hurley (2004) and Kincaid (1992) note, within our own culture there is a conflict between portrayal of the purportedly innocent boy and the reality of desire as an intrinsic element of the human condition (see Foucault, 1978).

Freud's (1905/1953) signal contribution was an emphasis upon a diffuse erotic tie to others beginning in earliest infancy and responsible for later variation in the capacity for intimacy. This subversive view of childhood emphasizing the child as erotic is consistent with contemporary "counterhegemonic" writings on sexuality (e.g., Sedgwick, 1991). The boy code and the labeling of same-sex desire as evidence of psychological disturbance during the postwar era provided the basis for a new postwar master narrative (Plummer, 1995) in which same-sex desire was at odds with the boy code and was the reason for an enduring sense of shame and personal deficit. This master narrative shaped the manner in which these life-writers coming of age in the postwar era portrayed their own boyhood, following in the tradition of the Western canon of adult lives that can only be understood in the context of boyhood experiences (Coe, 1984).

The portrayal of boyhood in the memoirs of men seeking sex with other men reflects a presently remembered past shaped by both professional and popular accounts of same-sex desire in a particular sociohistorical context (Elder et al., 2003; Mannheim, 1928/1993; Settersten, 1999). Sears (1991) has portrayed the dilemma of men and women growing up in the American South in the postwar years, while Fellows (1996) has provided multigenerational personal accounts gathered through interviews with men growing up on farms and self-identifying as gay. The narratives gathered by Fellows provide a useful contrast to the memoirs of urban-living counterparts, albeit recognizing that these accounts are brief and are told rather than written.

Since World War II, three major social changes have impacted the manner in which men who have sex with other men have viewed their lives. The first event, the emergence of the gay rights movement in the 1970s, may be traced to patron resistance to a raid on New York City's Stonewall Inn, a bar in which men and women could meet others with same-sex desire (Carter, 2004; Duberman, 1994). It is important to realize that this defining event of the gay rights movement, and the annual gay pride parades in a number of cities celebrating the anniversary of this event, was itself presaged by political organization of the incipient gay community across the preceding decades (Clendinen & Nagourney, 1999; D'Emilio, 1998; Quimby & Williams, 2000).

The second major event that impacted men's self-understandings was the emergence of the acquired immune deficiency syndrome (AIDS) pandemic. Ironically, the enhanced visibility of the community of gay men gathering at bars and bathhouses in the decade following the Stonewall riots made it possible for men seeking sex with other men to recognize each other more easily than in past times of "tea rooms" and furtive sexual encounters (Humphreys, 1970). Economic journalist Andrew Tobias (1998) recalls a sunny morning over the long July 4th holiday in 1981, sitting with his housemates on the veranda of their Fire Island home overlooking the tranquil Long Island Sound and reading the *New York Times* over breakfast. One of them reported on a brief item, buried on page 20 of the *Times*, about a rare illness striking homosexual men. He recalls that a chill went through him as he immediately grasped the significance of the account of the Centers for Disease Control bulletin in the *Times*. Tobias reports that AIDS would eventually claim four of these housemates and about half of the men on his Sunday brunch list. Soon the newspapers were full of obituaries of men dead from the consequences of AIDS. Shilts' (1987) passionate portrayal of the AIDS pandemic in the 1980s captures the desperation of this era, as do the portraits of caring for a lover dying of AIDS by Doty (1997), Johnson (1996), and Monette (1988).

A third, more recent cohort-defining event may be the discovery of the antivirus medication in 1995 that has successfully controlled the course of HIV infection for many men experiencing serocoversion. While a diagnosis of human immunodeficiency virus (HIV) and the progress of infection to AIDS destroyed several hundred thousand infected men over the preceding decade and a half, the antivirus medication has changed an almost certain death sentence into a chronic disease. Taking place alongside increasing social acceptance of same-sex intimacy and even support for diversity, particularly in more liberal and affluent communities, for many boys coming to adulthood in this generation born in the 1980s and early in the 1990s, "hooking up" with others of the same sex is merely a matter of choice and is not regarded as deviant or subversive. These new gay teens and young adults do not define themselves as gay and resist any categories or labels that define their life in terms of a particular identity (Cohler & Hammack, 2007; Savin-Williams, 2005).

Postwar Narratives of the Boyhood of Men
Self-Identifying as Gay

The interplay of history and social change on the construction of boyhood among men seeking sex with other men can be observed from the memoirs of men born in the postwar period and explicitly discussing boyhood in their personal accounts. The life stories I have selected for discussion were told or written by men seeking other men for social and sexual intimacy. I have followed the suggestion of sociologist Ken Plummer (2001) by selecting life stories of men telling or writing about self and sexual desire within a particular generation that are "information rich." That is, these life stories provide particular insight into the period of boyhood in shaping the important life experiences of men with same-sex desire. Clearly, no claim can be made that these accounts are representative in any statistical sense. They are, rather, intended as descriptive accounts of the relationship between personal narrative construction and the larger social ecology of boyhood in the context of development.

Something's Different: Men Born in the 1940s Coming to Adulthood in the 1960s

Recollections by men born in the 1940s and telling or writing as middle-aged adults about their boyhood portray vague awareness of being different from other boys (Helms, 1995; Poole, 2000). The conservative society of this postwar period was particularly intolerant of homosexuals. Postwar personal accounts often begin with a story of a childhood experienced as different from what was to be expected for a boy, including early awareness of same-sex desire and more or less obvious preference for nongender-stereotyped activities.

Fellows' (1996) accounts of boys born in the postwar period and growing up on Midwestern farms are particularly relevant sources of information since these boys who grew up in Midwestern communities like those of Tom Sawyer and Huck Finn were supposed to share the same traditions of enjoying adventure, eschewing expression of feelings, and feeling a shy attraction to girls depicted in the nineteenth-century boy books. Farm life demanded much of their time apart from school and chores. Attracted to other boys whom they met at 4-H and church events, many of these boys did not connect this attraction to sexual desire. Some of these men reported gender-atypical interests such as collecting flowers or cooking. This led to conflict with older brothers who derided their interests.

While there are some important differences in personal accounts that are told to another or written, these narratives of farm youth coming of age in the postwar era can be contrasted with the experience of urban and suburban youth born in the same decade, such as the memoir of Arnie Kantrowitz (1977/1996, 1999), who grew up in a lower- to middle-class New York suburb. Born in 1940, Kantrowitz traces his awareness of same-sex desire to attending Saturday movie matinees where handsome leading men stirred the hearts of desirable women (Horrigan, 1999). The title of Kantrowitz's narrative is taken from the hit song "Somewhere Over the Rainbow" from the movie *The Wizard of Oz*. The film, first released in 1939, begins with a monochrome narrative of Dorothy, played by a young Judy Garland, living in Kansas, where she is not understood by her aunt and uncle. A cyclone transports her to the land of Oz, where the movie is transformed into Technicolor. Kantrowitz's gay "reading" of *The Wizard of Oz* portrays a new home over the rainbow complete with an empathic Wizard who would understand his personal pain and grant him permission to realize his gay desire (Tierney, 2000).

Kantrowitz's account features what Plummer (1995, 1996) and Corbett (1999) have portrayed as the master narrative for becoming gay: knowledge of same-sex desire from boyhood, including distaste for competitive athletics, accomplishment in studies, and desire for the beautiful boys of the locker room during the school years coupled with an obsessive fear of being discovered to have such desire. Kantrowitz's account is the ideal type of memoir portraying a nongender-stereotyped boyhood that presages adult same-sex desire. Kantrowitz recounts a childhood in which he liked to skip rope and play house with the neighborhood girls but lied in the evening when his mother interrogated him about what he had done during the day (a hint that she already suspected something amiss with his sexual orientation). Apparently aware of this same-sex desire, he reports that at the age of 6 he managed to encourage a 14-year-old boy to satisfy his desire to be tied up and embraced while playing a game of "pirates"—an event that presaged his later interest in gay S & M.

In a world in which both Arnie and his mother felt bereft of beauty, like Dorothy in the depressing black-and-white opening scenes of Kansas in *The Wizard of Oz*, Kantrowitz spent much of his early life searching for the technicolor world of Oz. His mother, anxious about her son's apparent lack of masculinity, made feeble efforts to induct young Kantrowitz into the "man's world" with hormone shots to help him grow taller and boxing lessons and summer camp in order that he could learn "manly" ways. Kantrowitz was much more interested in the locker room than in the ring, although he was terrified that he might be caught looking at his naked locker-room schoolmates. He was much more interested in enticing a camp counselor to wrestle with him and to be physically close than in the baseball game the counselor was supposed to be coaching.

Similar to Kantrowitz's narrative, Andrew Tobias (1973/1993, 1998), growing up in the socially conservative decade of the 1950s, writes that he devoted much effort to hiding his secret same-sex desire. The title of his memoir—*The Best Little Boy in the World* (BLBITW)—reveals the significance of his childhood sense of difference, which motivated a desire to achieve. Tobias' life story recounts the struggle of a well-socialized boy to please his family and community. It is this same desire to please—or not to *displease*—that leads Tobias to originally write under a pseudonym (John Reid) in order not to upset his parents. As he observes:

> How could I write a book that might cause my parents so much
> pain? I am writing it because I want to, because like everyone I want
> to try to do something meaningful with my life, because I *do* want to
> be the BLBITW, and because I think they will understand.
>
> (Tobias, 1973/1993, p. 174)

The internalized sense of shame and struggle over same-sex desire is revealed in the manner in which Tobias chooses to narrate his life story—anonymously so as not to upset his parents. (It is noteworthy that the memoir was republished under Tobias' actual name in 1998 to coincide with the publication of his follow-up, *The Best Little Boy in the World Grows Up.*)

Tobias' account begins prophetically at age 5, with a memory of playing hide-and-seek and hiding in the hall closet. This metaphor of hiding in the closet, so common to men of Tobias' generation, represents the major theme of Tobias' life story through his college years. He introduces himself in his first memoir, saying, "I am five years old. I am the best little boy in the world, told so day after day" (Tobias, 1973/1993, p. 5).

Socialized within an upper-middle-class family in the 1950s, Tobias was expected to achieve. He learned to please others while desperately trying to cover up the secret of the closet—his same-sex desire. He did not even allow himself to masturbate until he was in college, even though he shared a room with his older brother, who regularly masturbated. Sex was not a topic of discussion in the Tobias household.

Tobias traces his first boyhood awareness of his same-sex desire to age 11. By the time he was 13, Tobias reports feeling very guilty about his desire and working ever harder to please his parents. He sought refuge in his schoolwork, where he excelled in highly competitive New York private schools. He reports not being well accepted at summer camp. Once again, as in Kantrowitz's account, awareness of same-sex desire was accompanied by pervasive guilt and an effort to hide this desire.

Accepting Difference: Boyhood and Same-Sex Desire Among Life-Writers Born in the 1950s

Kinsey, Pomeroy, and Martin's (1948) report on homosexuality received wide press coverage and brought same-sex desire to public awareness. Published at a time when postwar conservatism was emerging in response to the unsettled

war years, and with the fear of difference symbolized by a national preoccupation with communism, the work of the Kinsey Institute raised troubling issues
that remained in the background as the Army-McCarthy hearings played out
on the new technology of televison (see Shepard, this volume).

Boys growing up in the 1950s learned early that same-sex desire was
viewed as a threat to the social order and would be suppressed at whatever cost
to personal liberty (Poole, 2000). For the boys of this generation, growing up
in a time of stereotyped social conventionality, the pressure to conform to the
heterosexual norm of a tough, self-reliant boyhood was particularly powerful—
and the sanctions for deviance were equally powerful and visible. Boys born in
this decade came of age with the gay rights revolution of the 1970s. Enjoying
newfound freedom of assembly, these men found opportunities to meet other
men with same-sex desire in the newly visible gay bars and bathhouses, where
they were not aware of the emergence of HIV as they enjoyed sexual freedom.
The generation of men born in the 1950s was particularly devastated by the
AIDS pandemic three decades later.

Fellows' (1996) accounts of nine men growing up on farms in the 1950s
reflect a more evident struggle with their sexual desire than was present in the
accounts of boys growing up in the 1940s. Several of the participants recalled
their boyhood attraction to shirtless boys and men working on nearby farms.
Although several of the boys reported an erotic tinge to childhood friendships,
there was no physical intimacy. The story of Everett is particularly clear in
talking about the place of boyhood experiences and of not becoming like the
stereotyped tough farm boy. Everett's father had little use for him because he
was not macho enough. In elementary school his teachers praised his academic abilities and his musical gifts. He was mesmerized by the Tarzan films
shown in Saturday matinees (Horrigan, 1999). Everett was 3 years older than
his brother. The two of them slept in the same bed and frequently engaged in
sex play; by day the two brothers were rivals for their father's attention, but at
night they were lovers.

With greater public attention on homosexuality in this era, the parents of
these boys were open in their distaste for sex between men, and the boys early
learned that their same-sex desire was shameful and must be hidden. Several
of the men born in the 1950s, in contrast with those born in earlier eras, felt
pressure to get married and pretend to be "normal" men. In time, with the
social changes taking place in the 1970s, "backward socialized" by a vibrant,
visible gay youth movement, these men divorced their wives and adopted a gay
"lifeway" (Hostetler & Herdt, 1998).

Memoirs by men growing up in cities and suburbs, born in the 1950s,
frame their accounts in terms of the influence of early boyhood awareness of

their same-sex desire upon the subsequent course of their life. Two particularly dramatic accounts by men born in the 1950s and coming of age in the 1970s illustrate the emergence of this master narrative of "always having been different" or aware in boyhood of same-sex desire: poet Mark Doty (1999) (born in 1953) and performance artist Tim Miller (1997, 2002) (born in 1958).

Doty's memoir was written following the 1996 publication of a moving account of his relationship with his lover, who had died in 1994 of complications related to AIDS. When I asked Doty about the order of his life-writing, first the account of Wally's death and then his story of his own boyhood, he suggested that the work of mourning had freed energy to complete his memoir. Doty grew up in the South and West in a bizarre and troubled family where his father worked for a defense contractor. It is almost trite to say that his memoir is of a boy growing up with nonstereotyped gender interests. His parents had hoped for a girl. Doty learned in childhood that his mother had had a miscarriage prior to her last pregnancy, and he comments that he could have had an older brother who could have guided him through the mysteries of being a boy. From boyhood, Doty was attentive to beauty and to colors. The title of his memoir, *Firebird* (Doty, 1999), refers to a fourth-grade experience at a dancing school when his teacher played Stravinsky's "Firebird." Transfixed by the music, Doty danced in front of the class, imagining the vivid colors of the firebird dancing into the destruction of its own flames.

Like so many boys sensitized to the feeling of difference because of their same-sex desire, Doty excelled in school in order to make up for his feelings of deficiency and gender atypicality. His first reference to his same-sex desire was as a young boy going to the beach with his sister and her handsome boyfriend and seeing so many boys in their revealing bathing trunks tanning themselves. He recalls riding on his sister's boyfriend's motorcycle, his arms around the waist of the shirtless boy. For Doty, this experience was accompanied by a "strange" sensation, a desire that needed to be controlled. Doty was puzzled by this stirring: no one could know about this private, perhaps shameful, appreciation of beauty that marked him as different from other boys. Doty was particularly attracted to bare-chested men in the Saturday matinees he attended with his older sister (Horrigan, 1999).

Doty views his own boyhood as different from that of American boys growing up in the postwar period. Fellow life-writer Tim Miller (1997), also born in the 1950s, expresses similar awareness of being different from other boys who were fascinated with sports. Indeed, Miller sees himself as different from the moment of conception, although he could not name the desire he felt until he was 14. Miller grew up in southern California. The title of his memoir refers to the practice in school gym class of one team taking off their shirts in order to identify the two teams. Drawn to body contact with the shirtless boys on the other team in school football games, he reports feeling "weird" looking at those boys and feeling desire for them.

The New Gay America: Men Born in the 1960s and Coming to Adulthood in the 1980s

Beginning with a sense that the promise of postwar prosperity had apparently been fulfilled, the 1960s ended with a society at war with itself and enmeshed in a war half a world away, a society exhausted by social conflict at home and three inexplicable murders of a president, his brother, and a national spiritual leader (Gitlin, 1987; Tipton, 1982). A sexual minority that had been invisible at the beginning of the decade had burst into national awareness by the end of it, along with the rebellion and the accompanying riot at the Stonewall Inn in New York City. Across the decade social activism had been stirring within the homophile community, and reports of something called a *gay identity* had appeared in national news magazines (Clendinen & Nagourney, 1999). Rural, suburban, and sophisticated urban cultures alike were affected by this stirring of social activism. As the reality of same-sex desire became a recognized life-way for men and women, there was an accompanying increased media focus and increased psychological study.

The boy story of life on the farm and participation in the "manly" activity of farming largely disappears from the 10 accounts of men born in the 1960s and coming of age in the midst of the AIDS pandemic. Sexuality entered into self-awareness in a more explicit form than in earlier generations, perhaps influenced by increased coverage of same-sex desire in the media and increased access to publications explicitly for the gay community (see Shepard, this volume). Accounts from both rural and urban men born in the 1960s focus less on understanding a "strange desire" than of being aware from an early age of the meaning of same-sex desire.

Rural and suburban boys alike felt unable to act in accordance with the boy code, and perhaps because of increased media coverage, their parents were aware of the extent to which they boys were different from early childhood. As Marlene Shyer writes in a memoir that she coauthored with her son Christopher, born in 1961:

> People are always incredulous when I say I foresaw Chris's destiny as early as kindergarten.... The differences between my two boys were conspicuous and marked, if not to Dr. Greene, at least to me. Here we have Exhibit A, Kirby, resisting the entire process of

civilization. It was a monumental struggle to get past his Tarzan
tendencies...his friends in constant motion...pushing each other,
spilling things.... Chris, Exhibit B, was genteel and polished...he
liked dressing up for Sunday school. He liked museums and was
interested in interior design, sculpture and painting.

(Shyer & Shyer, 1996, pp. 126–127)

Older brother Kirby is the ideal type of the boy code, in contrast with Chris'
behavior, which his mother portrays as "ladylike." Dr. Greene is a pseudonym
for Richard Green (1987), a psychiatrist specializing in the identification of
homosexuality in boyhood on the basis of nongender-stereotyped interests.
Apparently, he did not see Chris as demonstrating the pattern expected of a
boy destined to become homosexual. Based on the prevailing view that homosexuality in boys was due to an overprotective mother (Bieber et al., 1962),
a psychologist consulted by Chris' parents warned Mrs. Shyer against being
overprotective. Another doctor they consulted encouraged Chris' father to
spend more time with him playing sports. In this memoir, both mother and
son express their awareness of Chris' difference from other boys; both are
aware of the meaning of this difference. Yet, Chris' mother does not acknowledge his homosexuality until he finally comes out to her, his father, and his
older brother in adulthood.

This account of Chris' childhood, as noted above, is coauthored by Chris
Shyer and his mother. Chris grew up in a typical upper-middle-class suburban
neighborhood in which boys were expected to enjoy athletics and to be tough
and self-reliant. The account begins with the report by Mrs. Shyer that Chris'
kindergarten teacher had informed her at a parent-teacher conference that her
son was probably going to grow up to be a homosexual. Chris' difference from
other boys was evident in his concern with his clothes and with being neat,
clean, and obedient. Mrs. Shyer immediately understood and compared Chris
with his older brother, who was indifferent to cleanliness and etiquette. Chris
was not rough, like his mischievous older brother. Chris reports that at age 5
he was already playing games with a friend in which they would crawl under
a blanket, pulling up their shirts and touching their bodies together, all the
while feeling a sense of shame. In stark contrast to his older brother, Chris
reports hating the round of athletic activities at summer camp. In short, Chris
failed to conform to the boy code that had come to construct childhood gender
roles and stereotypes.

Boyhood for Chris was a confusing time. With parental preoccupation
regarding his sexual orientation, repeated visits to specialists, and warnings from teachers and camp directors that Chris was destined to become

a homosexual, his difference from the expected American boy code was a continuing source of concern for his parents. Later in boyhood, Chris reports trying to clown around like the other boys while at the same time being concerned with his academic performance. At camp he refused the rough play of his fellow campers; the camp director warned Chris' parents that he had some sort of "problem." A sixth-grade gym teacher insulted Chris in front of the class, noting his inability to play sports as evidence that he was not a "real boy." He tried to look the part of a real boy but was regularly ridiculed by his classmates.

An even more complex response to the American boy code has been provided in a memoir by performance artist Martin Moran (2005). First in a one-man performance and then in a book describing his central memory of childhood sexual intimacy with an older man, Moran describes growing up in Denver in a lower-middle-class neighborhood where a boy code of hiking and camping in the mountains was emphasized. Moran, one of four children, was aware from an early age of his attraction to neighborhood boys who were tough and physical. His best friend was a boy whose father was a wrestling coach; the boys in this family tussled with each other. Moran recalls his attraction to the lifeguard at the swimming pool and also to other boys and men, all the time feeling guilty about his desire, which he perceived as unlike that of his playmates.

The story Moran tells is of his seduction by Robert, a sometime seminarian who had worked in the Catholic camp that both Moran and his father had attended during childhood. Having met the seminarian at camp, and with his parents' ready assent, Moran accepted Robert's invitation to come along with some other boys on a weekend expedition to build Robert's cabin in the mountains. Robert succeeded in seducing Moran the very first evening as they shared sleeping bags zipped together. These sexual intimacies lasted for several years as he worked on the cabin with Robert, sometimes alone and sometimes together with other boys whom his friend had also seduced. Moran observes that he did learn valuable outdoor skills working with Robert in this rugged terrain.

Moran is ambivalent about his times with Robert in the mountains. There is a photograph that captures this ambivalent experience that Moran uses both in his performance art and also on the cover of his memoir, of a grinning, pudgy 12-year-old boy sitting in a canoe, wearing a life preserver, proudly holding his canoe paddle above his head, expressing his pleasure at having learned this outdoor skill. However, particularly relevant is the picture that Moran provides of the boy code, growing up in a social world in which toughness and survival skills in the mountains were essential parts of boyhood. Moran was permitted to attend public high school, where he excelled in his studies and became part of a group enjoying the "alternative lifestyle" of the late 1970s, which offered a way to escape the boy code. During his high school years he was admired for both his acting and his musical talent.

Moran's memoir does not implicate Robert as the source of his same-sex desire. As Moran (2005) muses to himself during his student years, walking about the still Stanford campus one evening, "a clear and tender thought came up to surprise me. Came up from the deep and fell out of my mouth. He didn't make you this way, you know. Bob didn't do it. This is who you are" (p. 195). However, participating in sexual experiences with Robert added to his sense of shame. Moran suggests that his continued search for anonymous sex during his adult years, which his loving partner understands as a problem he is struggling to overcome, represents both an effort to master his feelings regarding this earlier sexual seduction and a means of dealing with the feeling of personal depletion in the aftermath of his childhood experiences.

Growing Up Gay in the Aftermath of the Gay Rights Revolution

Boys born in the 1970s and 1980s had opportunities that had been less available to previous generations for escaping the boy code. The social ferment of the 1960s led over time to increased tolerance for minorities and for diverse sexual lifeways. The experiences of the prior two decades led to awareness of same-sex desire and to assumption of a gay identity, no longer presumed to be criminal or psychopathological. While parents worried at first that a gay son might die of AIDS, or at least have a more difficult time in society than a boy less aware of this same-sex desire, in many suburban and urban high schools, gay-straight alliances (GSAs) developed. Parents and Friends of Lesbians and Gays (PFLAG) provided support for families learning of their offspring's same-sex desire. Herdt (1989) and Herdt and Boxer (1996) have documented the emergence of this sexual minority lifeway for urban youth born in the 1980s. Support systems provided a refuge for boys aware of same-sex desire and able to avoid the tyranny of the boy code.

The "parent-blaming" perspective to which boys growing up in the 1970s and their families were exposed was called into question in the 1980s. New studies suggested that it was difficult to know the determination of sexual orientation. Some suggested that many gay boys developed an erotic tie to their fathers. Uncomfortable with this tie, the father of the prospectively gay boy attempted to develop increased emotional distance and greater personal comfort in an effort to avoid this intensity (Isay, 1986, 1987, 1996). Phillips (2001, 2003) has suggested that it is less that the father withdraws from his relationship with his prospectively gay son than that the son experiences such withdrawal in an effort to deal with conflicting feelings about his father.

There are few published memoirs authored by men growing up gay in the 1970s and 1980s. In part, the emergence of the Internet has provided an alternative means for writing about the experiences of boyhood among boys with same-sex desire (Cohler, 2007). From online magazines managed by gay and lesbian youth, providing opportunities for other youth to tell their story of growing up gay, to the more recent creation of the blog and the e-book, the Internet may replace more formal means of publication for gay life-writers to tell their life stories (Hamilton, 2004; Phillips, 2004). These online accounts provide valuable resources for boys with same-sex desire who live in rural communities and small towns.

One of the few published memoirs of the boyhood of men born following the social upheavals of the 1960s is Kirk Read's *How I Learned to Snap* (2001). Read, born in 1973 in the South, describes a boyhood in which his career military father and his mother paid little attention to his interests or to his difference from other boys. Hoping that his youngest son might follow him in a military career, Kirk's father sent him to a rugged camp at age 10. Kirk's main problem there was his attraction to his two counselors. He got into fights with other boys where he held his own, and although he avoided most athletic events, he learned to play soccer and later starred in his community's soccer team even as he was producing a play about being a gay boy. When classmates called Read a "faggot," he silenced them with withering comments. In his last year of high school, he was applauded by his class for being proud of what he was and standing up for his rights.

Conclusion

Kirk Read rejected the boy code and saw little problem both in being an accomplished actor and playwright and serving as the soccer coach of the town's Little League team, even though parents in the community knew that Kirk self-identified as gay. He could fight to protect his rights and excel in athletics without seeing a contradiction with his same-sex desire. Savin-Williams (2005) and Cohler and Hammack (2007) have documented this changing master narrative of sexual identity in American culture. It is a shift from an identity script of "struggle and success" to "emancipation" from the confines of rigid categorizations of sexual identity (Cohler & Hammack, 2007; see also Savin-Williams, 2005). Many boys aware of having same-sex desire no longer see themselves as different in any way from their heterosexual counterparts. They report fewer of the problems confronted by Arnie Kantrowitz (1977/1996), growing up in the 1950s, or Chris Shyer (Shyer and Shyer, 1996), growing up in the 1960s.

Savin-Williams (2005) argues that today's same-sex attracted youth do not view their sense of difference as traumatic and in fact display remarkable resilience. While they prefer to have sex with other men, they do not see this preference as marking them as necessarily different from other men. They shun the term *gay* as one belonging to a past generation that "carries too much baggage" (Cohler & Hammack, 2007). While aware of AIDS and the social activism its devastation inspired, these young men have never known anyone with AIDS. The new antiviral medication virtually ensures that HIV-positive people look as healthy as anyone else. These youth, aware of their same-sex attraction from childhood, may be forging a new concept of the life course in which sexual attraction is only one of the many things important about them. That is, as narratives of sexual identity in American society shift toward increasing acceptance, the centrality of sexual desire to the personal narratives of youth might diminish. As these boys forge a new conception of boyhood apart from the traditional American boy code that encourages a nongender-stereotyped boyhood, they are having an impact on the manner in which boys more generally understand their emotions and interpersonal relations. Supported by other cultural changes focusing on the importance of relatedness in realizing a more satisfying life, these boys eschew a definition of normal boyhood as presuming rough-and-tumble play and denial of feelings. They are helping to foster a "sideways socialization" (Stockton, 2004), calling into question the value of the boy code for morale and relations with others.

REFERENCES

Aldrich, T. B. (1990). *The story of a bad boy*. Hanover, NH: University Press of New England. (Original work published 1869)

Aries, P. (1962). *Centuries of childhood: A social history of family life*. New York: Random House.

Bem, D. (1996). Exotic becomes erotic: A developmental theory of sexual orientation, *Psychological Review, 103*, 320–335.

Bieber, I.,Dain, H., Dince, P.,Drellich M., Grand, H., et al. (1962). *Homosexuality: A psychodynamic study of male homosexuals*. New York: Basic Books.

Bruhm, S., & Hurley, N. (2004). (Eds.). *Curiouser: On the queerness of children*. Minneapolis: University of Minnesota Press.

Carter, D. (2004). *Stonewall: The riots that sparked the gay revolution*. New York: St. Martin's Press.

Clendinen, D., & Nagourney, A. (1999). *Out for good: The struggle to build a gay rights movement in America*. New York: Simon & Schuster.

Coe, R. (1984). *When the grass was taller: Autobiography and the experience of childhood*. New Haven, CT: Yale University Press.

Cohler, B. J. (2007). *Writing desire: Sixty years of gay autobiography* Madison: University of Wisconsin Press.

Cohler, B. J., & Hammack, P. L. (2007). The psychological world of the gay teenager: Social change, narrative, and "normality." *Journal of Youth and Adolescence, 36,* 47–59.

Cohler, B. J., & Hostetler, A. (2003). Linking life course and life story: Social change and the narrative study of lives over time. In J. T. Mortimer & M. J. Shanahan (Eds.), *Handbook of the life course* (pp. 555–578). New York: Kluwer Academic/Plenum Publishers.

Corbett, K. (1999). Homosexual boyhood: Notes on girlyboys. In M. Rottnek (Ed.), *Sissies and tomboys: Gender nonconformity and homosexual childhood* (pp. 107–139). New York: New York University Press.

D'Emilio, J. (1998). *Sexual politics, sexual communities: The making of a homosexual minority in the United States, 1940–1970* (2nd ed.). Chicago: University of Chicago Press.

Doty, M. (1997). *Heaven's coast.* New York: HarperCollins.

Doty, M. (1999). *Firebird: A memoir.* New York: HarperCollins.

Duberman, M. (1994). *Stonewall.* New York: Plume.

Eakin, P. J. (1985). *Fictions in autobiography: Studies in the art of self-invention.* Princeton, NJ: Princeton University Press.

Eakin, P. J. (1999). *How our lives become stories: Making selves.* Ithaca, NY: Cornell University Press.

Elder, G. H., Jr., Johnson, M. K., & Crosnoe, R. (2003). The emergence and development of life course theory. In J. T. Mortimer & M. J. Shanhan (Eds.), *Handbook of the life course* (pp. 3–19). New York: Kluwer Academic/Plenum Publishers.

Evans, M. (1999). *Missing persons: The impossibility of autobiography.* New York: Routledge.

Fellows, W. (1996). *Farm boys: Lives of gay men from the rural Midwest.* Madison: University of Wisconsin Press.

Fiedler, L. (1966). *Love and death in the American novel* (Rev. ed.). New York: Stein & Day.

Foucault, M. (1978). *The history of sexuality, Vol. 1: An introduction.* New York: Vintage.

Freeman, M. (1993). *Rewriting the self: History, memory, narrative.* New York: Routledge.

Freud, S. (1953). Three essays on the theory of sexuality. In J. Strachey (Ed. and Trans.), *The standard edition of the complete psychological works of Sigmund Freud* (Vol. 7, pp. 130–243). (Original work published 1905)

Friedman, R. C. (1998). *Male homosexuality: A contemporary psychoanalytic perspective.* New Haven, CT: Yale University Press.

Friedman, R. C., & Downey, J. I. (2002). *Sexual orientation and psychoanalysis: Sexual science and clinical practice.* New York: Columbia University Press.

Gitlin, T. (1987). *The sixties: Years of hope, days of rage.* New York: Bantam Books.

Green, J. (2003). Growing up hidden: Notes on understanding male homosexuality. *American Journal of Psychoanalysis, 63,* 177–191.

Green, R. (1987). *The "sissy boy syndrome" and the development of homosexuality.* New Haven, CT: Yale University Press.

Gribben, A. (1985). "I wish Tom Sawyer was there": Boy-book elements in *Tom Sawyer* and *Huckleberry Finn.* In R. Sattelmeyer & J. D. Crowley (Eds.), *One hundred years of* Huckleberry Finn: *The boy, his book, and American culture* (pp. 149–170). Columbia: University of Missouri Press.

Hamilton, L. D. (2004). *A gathering of angels.* Bay City, TX: Sigma Σ Books.

Helms, A. (1995). *Young man from the provinces: A gay life before Stonewall.* New York: Avon Books.

Herdt, G. (1989). Introduction: Gay and lesbian youth, emergent identities, and cultural scenes at home and abroad. In G. Herdt (Ed.), *Gay and lesbian youth* (pp. 1–42). New York: Harrington Park Press.

Herdt, G., & Boxer, A. (1996). *Children of horizons.* (Rev. ed.). Boston: Beacon Press.

Horrigan, P. E. (1999). *Widescreen dreams: Growing up gay at the movies.* Madison: University of Wisconsin Press.

Hostetler, A., & Herdt, G. (1998). Culture, sexual lifeways, and developmental subjectivities: Rethinking sexual taxonomies. *Social Research, 65,* 249–290.

Humphreys, L. (1970). *Tearoom trade: Impersonal sex in public places.* Chicago: Aldine.

Isay, R. (1986). The development of sexual identity in homosexual men. *Psychoanalytic Study of the Child, 41,* 467–489.

Isay, R. (1987). Fathers and their homosexually inclined sons in childhood. *Psychoanalytic Study of the Child, 42,* 274–294.

Isay, R. (1996). *Becoming gay: The journey to self-acceptance.* New York: Pantheon.

Jacobson, M. (1994). *Being a boy again: Autobiography and the American boy book.* Tuscaloosa: University of Alabama Press.

Jennings, K. (2006). *Mama's boy, preacher's son.* Boston: Beacon Press.

Johnson, F. (1996). *Geography of the heart: A memoir.* New York: Washington Square Press.

Kantrowitz, A. (1996). *Under the rainbow: Growing up gay.* New York: St. Martin's Press. (Original work published 1977)

Kantrowitz, A. (1999). Such a polite little boy. In M. Rottnek (Ed.), *Sissies and tomboys: Gender nonconformity and homosexual childhood* (pp. 226–235). New York: New York University Press.

Kazan, A. (1981). Afterword. In M. Twain (1884/1981). *The adventures of Huckeberry Finn* (pp. 294–305). New York: Bantam Books.

Kidd, K. B. (2004). *Making American boys: Boyology and the feral tale.* Minneapolis: University of Minnesota Press.

Kincaid, J. R. (1992). *Child-loving: The erotic child and Victorian culture.* New York: Routledge.

Kindlon, D., & Thompson, M. (1999). *Raising Cain: Protecting the emotional life of boys.* New York: Ballantine.

Kinsey, A., Pomeroy, W., & Martin, C. (1948). *Sexual behavior in the human male.* Philadelphia: W. B. Saunders.

Lassell, M. (1999). Boys don't do that. In M. Rottnek (Ed.), *Sissies and tomboys: Gender nonconformity and homosexual childhood* (pp. 245–262). New York: New York University Press.

Lejune, P. (1989). *On autobiography.* Minneapolis: University of Minnesota Press.

Mannheim, K. (1993). The problem of generations. In K. H. Wolff (Ed.), *From Karl Mannheim* (2nd expanded ed., pp. 351–398). New Brunswick, NJ: Transaction. (Original work published 1928)

Meyer, I. H. (2003). Prejudice, social stress, and mental health in lesbian, gay, and bisexual populations: Conceptual issues and research evidence. *Psychological Bulletin, 129*(5), 674–697.

Miller, T. (1997). *Shirts and skins.* Los Angeles: Alyson Books.

Miller T. (2002). *Body blows: Six performances.* Madison: University of Wisconsin Press.

Mintz, S. (2004). *Huck's raft: A history of American childhood.* Cambridge, MA: Belknap–Harvard University Press.

Monette, P. (1988). *Borrowed time: An AIDS memoir.* New York: Harvest Books/ Harcourt Brace.

Moon, M. (1998). *A small boy and others: Imitation and initiation in American culture from Henry James to Andy Warhol.* Durham, NC: Duke University Press.

Moran, M. (2005). *The tricky part: One boy's fall from trespass into grace.* Boston: Beacon Press.

Phillips, B. (2004). www.amongthepopulace.com

Phillips, S. H. (2001). The overstimulation of everyday life: I. New aspects of male homosexuality. *Journal of the American Psychoanalytic Association, 49,* 1235–1267.

Phillips, S. H. (2003). Homosexuality: Coming out of the confusion. *International Journal of Psychoanalysis, 84,* 1431–1450

Plumb, J. H. (1975). The new world of children in eighteenth-century England. *Past and Present, 67,* 64–95

Plummer, K. (1995). *Telling sexual stories: Power, change, and social worlds.* New York: Routledge.

Plummer, K. (1996). Intimate citizenship and the culture of sexual story telling. In J. Weeks & J. Holland (Eds.), *Sexual cultures: Communities, values and intimacy* (pp. 34–52). New York: St. Martin's Press.

Plummer, K. (2001). *Documents of life 2: An invitation to a critical humanism.* London: Sage.

Pollack, W. S. (1998). *Real boys.* New York: Henry Holt.

Pollack, W. S (with T. Shuster). (2000). *Real boys' voices.* New York: Penguin.

Poole, W. (2000). *Dirty Poole: The autobiography of a gay porn pioneer.* Los Angeles: Alyson Books.

Popkin, J. D. (2005). *History, historians and autobiography.* Chicago: University of Chicago Press.

Quimby, K., & Williams, W. L. (2000) Unmasking the homophile in 1950s Los Angeles: An archival record. In J. A. Boone, S. Silberman, C. Sarver, K. Quimby, M. Meeker, et al. (Eds.), *Queer frontiers: Millennial geographies, genders, and generations* (pp. 166–195). Madison: University of Wisconsin Press.

Rado, S. (1949). An adaptational view of sexual behavior. In P. H. Hoch & J. Zubin (Eds.), *Psychosexual development in health and disease* (pp. 159–189). New York: Grune & Stratton.

Read, K. (2001). *How I learned to snap: A small-town coming-of-age coming-out story.* Athens, GA: Hill Street Press.

Ricoeur, P. (1977). The question of proof in Freud's psychoanalytic writings. *Journal of the American Psychoanalytic Association, 25,* 835–872.

Rottnek, M. (Ed.). (1999). *Sissies and tomboys: Gender nonconformity and homosexual childhood*. New York: New York University Press.

Rousseau, J. J. (1979). *Emile, or on education* (A. Bloom, Trans.). New York: Basic Books. (Original work published 1762)

Savin-Williams, R. C. (2005). *The new gay teenager*. Cambridge, MA: Harvard University Press.

Savin-Williams, R. C., & Ream, G. L. (2003). Suicide attempts among sexual-minority male youth. *Journal of Clinical Child and Adolescent Psychology, 32*(4), 509–522.

Schafer, R. (1981). *Narrative actions in psychoanalysis*. Worcester, MA: Clark University Press.

Sears, J. (1991). *Growing up gay in the South: Race, gender, and journeys of the spirit*. New York: Harrington Park Press.

Sedgwick, E. K. (1991). How to bring your kids up gay: The war on effeminate boys. *Social Text, 29,* 18–27.

Settersten, R. A., Jr. (1999). *Lives in time and place: The problems and promises of developmental science*. Amityville, NY: Baywood.

Shilts, R. (1987). *And the band played on: Politics, people, and the AIDS epidemic*. New York: St. Martin's Press.

Shyer, M., & Shyer, C. (1996). *Not like other boys*. Los Angeles: Alyson Books.

Socarides, R. (1968). *The overt homosexual*. New York: Grune & Stratton.

Spengemann, W. C. (1980). *The forms of autobiography*. New Haven, CT: Yale University Press.

Stockton, K. B. (2004). Growing sideways, or versions of the queer child: The ghost, the homosexual, the Freudian, the innocent, and the interval of animal. In S. Bruhm & N. H. Hurley (Eds.), *Curiouser: On the queerness of children* (pp. 277–316). Minneapolis: University of Minnesota Press.

Tierney, W. G. (2000). Undaunted courage: Life history and the postmodern challenge. In N. K. Denzin & Y. S. Lincoln (Eds.), *Handbook of qualitative research* (2nd ed., pp. 537–554). Thousand Oaks, CA: Sage.

Tipton, S. (1982). *Getting saved from the sixties: Moral meaning in conversion and social change*. Berkeley: University of California Press.

Tobias, A. (1993). *The best little boy in the world* (Rev. ed.). New York: Ballantine. (Original work published as J. Reid in 1973)

Tobias, A. (1998). *The best little boy in the world grows up*. New York: Random House.

Tyre, P. (2006, January 30). The trouble with boys. *Newsweek, 147*(5), 44–52.

Twain, M. (1981). *The adventures of Tom Sawyer*. New York: Bantam. (Original work published 1876)

Twain, M. (2003). *The adventures of Huckeberry Finn*. New York: Bantam. (Original work published 1884)

13

The Role of the Internet in the Sexual Identity Development of Gay and Bisexual Male Adolescents

Gary W. Harper, Douglas Bruce, Pedro Serrano, and Omar B. Jamil

Identity Development Among Adolescents

Adolescence is marked by increased exploration of sexual, occupational, ideological, and cultural roles as the adolescent attempts to form a unique and mature personal identity. The formation of identity has been considered by many theorists to be the primary developmental goal of the adolescent years (Erikson, 1968; Gullotta, Adams, & Montemayor, 1992). More recent theorists have suggested that the developmental period between childhood and adulthood is expanding for young people in industrialized societies, and they consider the life period between the late teens and the mid-20s to be a distinct developmental period called *emerging adulthood* (Arnett, 1997, 2000). Identity development is viewed by these theorists as a critical developmental milestone addressed during emerging adulthood (Arnett, 2000). Regardless of when identity development occurs, it is important to understand that the construct of adult identity is not unidimensional. It is actually composed of a mosaic of multiple identities within various realms of the adolescent's life, and each of these identities may form at varying rates and be influenced by both similar and unique factors.

For lesbian, gay, and bisexual (LGB) adolescents the identity formation process can be complicated by experiences of heterosexism, stigma, and prejudice, as their exploration of sexual identity involves same-gender sexual thoughts, feelings, and behaviors that are not generally accepted by the larger society (Harper & Schneider, 2003; Ryan & Futterman, 1998). In addition to the traditional developmental difficulties that adolescents must face, LGB adolescents must manage what Ryan and Futterman (1998) define as a *stigmatized identity* since these youth often contend with the negative impact of living in a heterosexist society. Stigma related to being LGB and the concomitant isolation, rejection, and discrimination that many of these youth face have been shown to be related to a range of negative behavioral, social, and health outcomes (Blake et al., 2001; Rosario, Hunter, Maguen, Gwadz, & Smith, 2001; Rotheram-Borus, Reid, Rosario & Kasen, 1995; Waldo, Hesson-McInnis, & D'Augelli, 1998).

Ethnic minority LGB adolescents experience unique challenges to their identity formation due to experiences of both individual-level and institutionalized racism (Harper, Jernewall, & Zea, 2004). Often LGB youth of color must contend not only with the negative societal reactions to their sexual orientation, but also with racial prejudice, limited economic opportunities and resources, and limited acceptance within their own cultural community (Diaz, 1998; Martinez & Sullivan, 1998).

One critical aspect of identity formation for LGB adolescents is their sexual identity development. This process helps youth to explore and understand their sexuality and to define their individual sexual self. Since LGB youth often develop their sense of sexuality and sexual orientation within the context of many societal systems that do not support same-gender sexual attraction and activity, they may need to find creative ways to explore and understand their sexuality. One emerging avenue for this sexual exploration is the Internet, which offers young people the ability to investigate their sexuality in a manner that allows for varying degrees of anonymity. The purpose of this chapter is to examine the role of the Internet in the sexual identity development process of gay and bisexual male adolescents. Since the sexual identity development processes of lesbians and bisexual young women have been proposed to differ from those of gay and bisexual young men (Diamond, 2003; Schneider, 2001), this chapter examines only gay and bisexual male youth.

Gay/Bisexual Identity Development among Adolescents

There is evidence that adolescents are self-identifying as gay or bisexual earlier now than in previous generations, and they are doing so at a time when they are still living with parents and attending school (D'Augelli, 2006). Gay and bisexual adolescents are active participants in multiple ecological social systems, especially family, school, and peer networks (Bronfenbrenner, 1979; D'Augelli, 2005). Although these social institutions often provide support and guidance for heterosexually identified youth, gay and bisexual adolescents may find that their family, peers, and teachers do not accept, support, and/or nurture them as they develop their gay/bisexual identity and may actually perpetrate harmful verbal and physical acts of violence against them (D'Augelli & Hershberger, 1993; Pilkington & D'Augelli, 1995; Savin-Williams, 1995; Telljohan & Price, 1993). Thus, the decision to disclose their sexual identity to others can be complicated for gay and bisexual adolescent males, who may fear expulsion from their home if parents become aware of their sexual orientation and who may lack a supportive network of peers and/or mentors to buffer the difficulties of juggling adolescent development and gay victimization (D'Augelli, 2005; Travers & Schneider, 1997).

When youth are able to feel comfortable with their sexual identity and disclose it to selected others, there is evidence that acceptance of a sexual identity and acculturation into a larger gay community can serve to buffer some of the negative effects of heterosexism and concomitant stigmatization. This is especially true with regard to sexual risk behaviors. Rosario et al. (2001) found that more positive attitudes toward same-gender sexual expression (including attitudes related to their own sexual orientation) were linked to decreased unprotected sexual activity for youth between the ages of 14 and 21, and limited involvement in gay/lesbian activities was associated with more unprotected sex. Waldo, McFarland, Katz, MacKellar, and Valleroy (2000) found that among younger gay and bisexual male adolescents (ages 15–17), self-acceptance of a gay or bisexual identity was associated with lower rates of sexual risk behaviors; and Ridge, Plummer, and Minichiello (1994) found that young gay men (under age 25) who did not belong to gay organizations reported higher rates of recent unprotected anal intercourse. Given the steadily increasing rates of human immunodeficiency virus (HIV) infection among gay and bisexual male adolescents and the substantial toll that HIV takes on their healthy growth and development (Garofalo & Harper, 2003; Harper, 2007), decreases in sexual risk behaviors associated with gay/bisexual identity acceptance are notable.

Gay Identity Development Theories

Research and theoretical literature on the development of a sexual identity have conceptualized it primarily as a process of progression through stages.

Common to the most predominant theories is an initial stage in which an individual experiences same-gender sexual attractions, with subsequent feelings of confusion since these attractions are different from those of her or his heterosexual peers (Cass, 1979; Coleman, 1982; Troiden, 1989). Following this stage, both Cass (1979) and Troiden (1989) identify a period during which an individual becomes aware of the heterosexism present in the larger society and withdraws from the heterosexual community. Exploration of the gay and lesbian community then follows, involving personal contacts with publicly identified (or *out*) gay or lesbian individuals (Cass, 1979; Troiden, 1989). Participation in dating and romantic/sexual relationships with openly identified gay or lesbian individuals also occurs during this time (Coleman, 1982). Once the individual has had positive contact with members of the gay and lesbian community and is able to accept and integrate the sexual orientation into his or her identity, the individual has reached the final stage of sexual identity development (Cass, 1979; Coleman, 1982; Troiden, 1989).

Some theorists caution that these traditional models are somewhat limited since they typically do not consider the sociopolitical, historical, and environmental contexts within which the adolescent is developing his or her sexual identity. Critics of these original theories encourage the acceptance of more comprehensive and fluid interdisciplinary models that address sociopolitical and historical issues related to heterosexism, homophobia, and oppression (D'Augelli, 1994; Eliason, 1996). From a critical constructivist theoretical perspective, the unique multiplicity of identities for gay and bisexual youth requires a reinterpretation of how identity development is socially constructed and defined, thus further challenging predominant developmental models of sexual identity. Additionally, critical constructivist theory urges researchers to examine the contexts within which identity development occurs, as well as the socially constructed nature of the labels used to define various identities.

Many existing theories of sexual identity development also were based on retrospective reports of identity development solicited from samples of primarily White adult gay men. These reports may have been impacted by the passage of time and by current life factors as adult gay men at the time of the interviews, and they failed to include the voices of youth of color. In order to better understand some of the unique factors that impact the sexual identity development processes of contemporary gay and bisexual male adolescents, it is necessary to listen to the voices of diverse youth as they currently engage in the identity development process. This narrative approach also allows youth to discuss their identity development within both cultural and historical contexts.

Learning Gay Culture

As adolescents develop their sense of adult identity, they learn new information and ways of being from individuals in their immediate surroundings, which often involves informal mentoring by significant adults in their lives, as well as through peers (Erikson, 1959; Marcia, 1966). This form of mentorship and learning has become an integral part of multiple identity development processes, and as a result, most individuals eventually develop a positive and healthy adult identity. This presents a challenge for gay and bisexual youth, who are often developing their sexual identity without supportive individuals, institutions, and communities to assist them. In addition, while many youth learn about aspects of their other identities, such as ethnic identity, through parents and family members who teach them cultural history, traditions, and practices, they typically do not receive similar types of information about gay culture. Therefore, these youth often learn about gay culture and its accompanying language, rituals, symbols, and normative behaviors and practices from nonfamilial adults, peers, mass media, and the Internet (Harper, 2007).

In Herdt's (1997) analysis of same-gender sexual relations across multiple cultures, he stresses the importance of understanding varying "sexual cultures" that exist in societies, which he views as generally accepted models of cultural ideals regarding sexual behavior within a specific group. Sexual cultures include sexual and gender norms, emotions, beliefs, rules, and symbolic meanings attached to the nature and meaning of sexualized social interactions. Thus, a sexual culture creates a system for categorizing certain sexual acts and behaviors as desirable and appropriate. As young people explore their sexuality and learn about sexual cultures, they develop an individualized sense of sexuality within the context of a larger cultural social system.

For many gay and bisexual male adolescents, the sexual culture that they must learn is the larger gay culture. The existence of a distinct gay culture has been supported by anthropologists, sociologists, and psychologists and involves language, rituals, symbols, and other culturally normative images and practices (Flowers, Smith, Sheeran, & Beail, 1998; Herdt, 1992, 1997; Hersker, & Leap, 1996; Leap, 1998, 2007; Pope, 1995). Pope (1995) argues that the existence of a gay culture is supported when the standards often used to define ethnic/racial groups as cultural groups or cultural minorities within the psychological literature are applied to the lives of lesbians and gay men (i.e., geographic living areas, economic and social organizations, cultural traditions and rituals). Therefore, adolescents who begin to develop an identity as gay or bisexual must learn the larger gay culture's norms and expectations concerning ways of being, acting, and knowing (Gee, 1990).

Various forms of mass media, including books, television, movies, and music, have been identified as sources for gay youth to become acculturated to gay culture, including gay-related styles of speaking (Leap, 1994; Linné, 2003). The Internet also has been recognized as an important socializing force for youth seeking to learn about gay culture (Driver, 2006; Linné, 2003). Russell (2002) states that the Internet provides gay youth with a way to form their own communities, explore their identities, and create social change as they connect with one another. Given the increased use of the Internet in all of its various forms (e.g., Web sites, blogs, chat rooms, instant messaging [IM]) by adolescents and its potential for assisting youth to learn about gay culture, it is imperative to explore the role of the Internet in the sexual identity development processes of gay and bisexual adolescent males. In order to understand the complex ways in which gay and bisexual adolescents are using the Internet to explore their sexuality, we examined the narratives of gay and bisexual adolescents who participated in a larger qualitative study focused on multiple identity development processes for gay and bisexual male adolescents.

Before we present the findings from our qualitative inquiry regarding the Internet's role in identity development, it is important to examine the role of the Internet in the lives of adolescents in general. Research is beginning to emerge on the ways in which adolescents may use the Internet as a means of acquiring information, communicating with peers, and developing new social networks. Little research, however, has been done on how gay and bisexual adolescents may utilize the Internet in their sexual identity development.

Adolescents' Use of the Internet

Early research on adolescent use of the Internet revealed trends that pointed to increased parental perceptions of social isolation (Turow, 1999) and decreases in well-being and local social network size among first-time Internet users (Kraut et al., 1998). Much of this early research focused on early Internet applications such as message boards and multiuser dungeons (MUDs). Subsquently, far from being an isolating influence on adolescent users, as predicted by early Internet research, the Internet has been shown to afford opportunities for lonely adolescents to improve their social competence through experiments with online identities (Valkenburg & Peter, 2008). The rapid expansion in the breadth of online communication applications, including IM, personal

Web pages, and chat rooms, challenges these earlier findings (Gross, 2004; Schmitt, Dayanim, & Matthias, 2008; Valkenburg & Peter, 2008).

Adolescents' adoption of new Internet applications, such as IM and personal Web sites, may even precede their use by adults in some cases. The creation of personal homepages has been shown to be associated with adolescents' perceptions of mastery and expressions of identity (Schmitt, et al., 2008). Theorists have suggested that the reduced importance of physical appearance on the Internet may facilitate social interaction in this medium (McKenna & Bargh, 2000). However, the popularity of personal Web sites such as MySpace and Facebook, as well as the increased accessibility of webcams, may suggest that the invisibility promised by previous Internet-based innovations (email, message boards, chat rooms) may now be superseded in some ways by new youth-created, image-laden, and identity-driven communication forums. Significantly, it has been proposed that personal homepages may function as forums for expressions of identity rather than explorations of identity (Schmitt et al., 2008).

Adolescents appear to use online communications in a range of personal and social contexts. For some, online communication serves as an extension of face-to-face offline communication within established peer networks, and friendships begun online tend not to last as long as those begun offline (Mesch & Talmud, 2006). Adolescents who experiment with various online identities have been found to do so more with persons of different ages and cultural backgrounds (Valkenburg & Peter, 2008). Further, early adolescents and preadolescents tend to experiment with identities more frequently, while later adolescents tend to report less experimenting (Gross, 2004; Huffaker & Calver, 2005; Valkenburg & Peter, 2008).

Gender differences were remarked upon in early adolescent Internet utilization research, with male adolescents reporting more game playing and Web surfing than female adolescents, but these differences appear to have become less distinct as the Internet has diffused across the adolescent population and as diverse Internet applications emerged (Gross, 2004). Male adolescents have been found to use more explicitly sexual themes in teen chat rooms, while female adolescents use more implicitly sexual themes, as well as sexualized and gendered nicknames and user names (Subrahmanyan, Smahel, & Greenfield, 2006). Research in Australia has discovered that Internet use, especially chat room use, is associated with less developed identity status and higher social anxiety among young men but not among young women (Mazalin & Moore, 2004). A survey of Canadian college students found that young men reported going online for sexual entertainment at earlier ages than young women, although young women reported equal utilization rates of sex chat rooms (Boies, 2002). In the same study, 21% of respondents reported getting their first sexual education material from the Internet, and 40% spent an average of 20 minutes a week meeting new people online.

Most of what little research that has been conducted on Internet usage and gay and bisexual adolescents has focused on the degree to which young men seek out sexual partners on the Internet and engage in sexual risk behavior. Research from the United Kingdom has documented an increase in the percentage of gay and bisexual young men who met their first male sexual partner through the Internet from 1993 (2.6%) to 2002 (61%) (Bolding, Davis, Hart, Sherr, & Elford, 2007). A majority of young gay/bisexual men (68%) surveyed in Chicago reported using the Internet to find a romantic or sexual partner, while 48% reported having had sex with a partner found on the Internet, and 23% reported inconsistent condom use with Internet partners. In this study, White young men were more likely (65%) to have met sexual partners through the Internet compared to African American (20%) or Latino (51%) young men (Garofalo, Herrick, Mustanski, & Donenberg, 2007). Among a study of two chat rooms used by young gay/bisexual men of color, 84% of participants stated they were online primarily to look for some kind of sexual encounter (Fields et al., 2006).

The ways in which gay and bisexual male adolescents utilize the Internet in the development of their sexual identity is largely unknown. One exception is the work of McKenna and Bargh (1998), which has suggested that "demarginalization" may be one positive outcome associated with Internet use for gay/bisexual adolescents who feel socially isolated within their offline communities. In a series of studies conducted in the 1990s, McKenna and Bargh (1998) found participation in Internet newsgroups associated with marginalized sexual identities to be significantly associated with improvements in self-acceptance and coming-out processes, as well as decreased social isolation. In these studies, the more participants in the newsgroup found the newsgroup to be important to their identity, the more they perceived their marginalized sexual identity to be more acceptable.

In summary, emerging research on Internet use by adolescents is somewhat contradictory, with differing effects associated with the use of various applications (e.g., newsgroups, weblogs, IM, chat rooms, personal Web pages). Also, varying motivations of identity expression and experimentation exist regarding online interactions with peer group members and with persons of different backgrounds.

The development of online relationships and online identities may in some cases parallel the development of offline relationships and identities. For some adolescents, online relationships may present unique opportunities for identity development not afforded by offline interactions. As such, the Internet may provide a range of social interactions that pose significant opportunities for stages of development and personal trajectories of gay and bisexual male youth.

Exploring Gay/Bisexual/Questioning Male Adolescents' Sexual Identity Narratives

Sample and Methods

In order to examine the role of the Internet in the sexual identity development processes of gay and bisexual male adolescents, data from a qualitative exploration of the specific processes by which youth developed their sexual identities were examined. Qualitative interviews were conducted with African American, Latino, and White male youth between the ages of 15 and 23 years who identified as gay, bisexual, or questioning (GBQ) and who lived in either the Miami/Dade County or Chicago metropolitan areas. These data were part of a larger study focused on issues of identity, sexuality, substance use, and sexual behaviors among GBQ youth.

A total of 200 GBQ male youth were recruited through a diverse array of LGBT (lesbian/gay/bisexual/transgender)-focused support organizations, community agencies, and social venues where GBQ young men congregate. After being screened for eligibility, all participants were administered a survey assessing demographic factors, sexual identity, ethnic identity, sexual behaviors, and substance use. From the initial 200 participants (Chicago $N = 97$; Miami $N = 103$), 63 were selected to participate in qualitative interviews based on various identity-related characteristics in order to create a stratified purposive sample of individuals representing different backgrounds and life experiences. This sample included youth who identified ethnically as African American ($N = 19$), Latino/Hispanic ($N = 22$), or White ($N = 22$).

The in-depth qualitative interview explored four aspects of GBQ male youths' identities: masculine identity, ethnic identity, sexual identity, and an integrated identity. The data reported here were derived primarily from sections of the interview that focused on sexual identity. Phenomenological and constructivist frameworks were used in the creation of the semistructured interview guide. Thus, for each identity, participants were asked to first define and describe their identity using their own words and conceptualizations, and then were guided through an in-depth exploration of factors that have influenced each specific identity development. Participants were encouraged to expand on details of individual stories and collective cultural narratives when discussing their identities. Since predetermined heteronormative sexuality labels were not imposed on the participants, they provided less restrictive responses.

Phenomenological and Narrative Analyses

Since we were seeking to learn about the lived experiences of GBQ male adolescents with regard to their sexual identity, our analysis was conducted using both phenomenological and narrative frameworks (Creswell, 1998; Mankowski & Rappaport, 1995, 2000; Patton, 1990). This approach allowed us to learn about the sociocultural behaviors, language, roles, and interactions within a culture-sharing group and to focus on individual (i.e., stories) and shared (i.e., narratives) experiences and meanings given to those experiences. The stories were viewed as individual personal accounts of lived experiences, and the narratives were common stories or experiences shared across individuals (Mankowski & Rappaport, 1995, 2000). By understanding each individual's experiences, the researcher can determine the larger framework to describe the structure (or "essence") of the phenomenon (Schutz, 1970). Given our phenomenological/narrative approach, we offer segments of the individual stories from the youth in this chapter and present them clustered together into categories of common narratives or shared experiences.

After the participants were interviewed, their transcripts were analyzed and additional codes were created and/or clarified based on our phenomenological framework. For the purposes of this inquiry, the Internet was defined as any one of the multiple computer-based applications included in the worldwide network of electronic communication modalities that carry information from one computer to another. This included applications such as Web sites (including social networking Web sites), IM, email, chat rooms, newsgroups/ discussion forums, and blogs. Initial a priori codes were created to capture the primary concepts being explored regarding the Internet's potential role in sexual identity development. Pattern codes were created to connect subsequent concepts under larger headings within each transcript; then consistent patterns in meaning, concepts, and themes across all interviews were identified (Creswell, 1998; Miles & Huberman, 1994). Given the phenomenological and narrative frameworks that guided our data collection and analysis, we ensured that different voices were represented and that conceptual "outliers" were not silenced by the average or dominant perspective by presenting all voiced themes instead of only those that were endorsed by a majority of participants.

In order to ensure the quality and credibility of the overall emergent themes from the qualitative interviews, several credibility checks were performed. The first involved "member-checking" interviews (Guba & Lincoln, 1981) of three GBQ male youths that occurred after approximately half of the qualitative interviews had been conducted, with these youths responding to initial interview themes and identifying additional areas for inquiry. The second check was "peer-debriefing" interviews (Lincoln & Guba, 1985) with three adult experts that occurred at the same time as the initial member-checking youth interviews. These experts had extensive experience working with GBQ youth and were asked to verify independently the initial emergent themes from the qualitative analyses. The third validation check consisted of two focus groups, where interview participants returned after all interviews were completed to verify general patterns and themes revealed in the initial analyses.

GBQ Male Adolescents' Internet Narratives

The interviews concerning GBQ male adolescents' sexual identity development processes were explored for stories and narratives regarding the role of the Internet in sexual identity development. Participants reported the use of a variety of Internet resources, including Web sites, chat rooms, IM, blogs, and email. The youth used these applications in a variety of ways, representing four increasing levels of connecting with other people via the Internet: (1) anonymous exploration, (2) casual posting, (3) online conversations, and (4) offline meetings.

The Internet served a range of functions related to their sexual identity development, including (1) developing increasing self-awareness of sexual identity, (2) learning about sexual identity and gay culture, (3) connecting with other gay/bisexual youth, (4) finding support for and acceptance of sexual identity, (5) developing increasing comfort with sexual identity, and (6) facilitating the coming-out process.

Varying Levels of Connection through the Internet

Narratives of GBQ male youth indicated that they used the Internet and its applications in a variety of ways. Given the relative anonymity of the Internet, young men could control the degree to which they revealed either a real or fabricated identity to others. Four levels of connection with others on the Internet regarding their sexual identity, representing progressive levels of communication and decreasing levels of anonymity, were revealed. These included (1) anonymous exploration, (2) casual posting, (3) online conversations, and (4) offline meetings.

ANONYMOUS EXPLORATION. The anonymous exploration level is the most anonymous form of communication regarding sexual identity. It involves no direct attempts to interact physically or virtually with other Internet users. At this first level, participants reported primarily searching and reading Web sites in order to obtain information about their same-gender sexual feelings, attractions, and desires. This typically did not involve exploration of interactive modalities such as chat rooms, IM, or email. As the following excerpt from a participant's narrative illustrates, most youth used this level to research various sexual identity-related topics.

> Um, well, when I first identified, when I first realized, again I was in fifth grade, that's what, 10 or 11 years old, that's young. So um, I had all these messages already, like these preconceived notions of what a gay guy was, what a gay person was. And most of them were negative because that's just how like at school, for example, that's how they're portrayed, and the Church doesn't necessarily have the nicest stances. My parents had never had any problem with gay people, but again, it was just something that never came up in my family. I never knew how my parents thought, so being good Irish Catholics, I assumed they would have had a problem with it and think that it was wrong. But um, so I did, for instance, like I kind of researched on my own. I did some research on the Internet, but again I didn't go into chat rooms. I mean, I looked up homosexuality in the encyclopedia just to see what they said. I read articles about it when I could find them. Um, and so like I kind of educated myself and I kind of came to terms with myself. By the time that I came out, I was already like very proud of the fact that I was gay, and wouldn't have changed it had I been given the opportunity.

CASUAL POSTING. The next level of Internet use to explore sexual identity, which involved increased communication with other users, was the casual posting stage. This involved posting comments, information, and/or pictures on Internet applications such as Web sites, blogs, or message boards. There were varying levels of anonymity, with some youth using pseudonyms, fake pictures, or ambiguous email addresses when posting and others using all or part of their real names and pictures. The purpose of the postings varied as well; most were either focused on obtaining new information related to sexual identity or attempting to judge how others felt about a sexual identity–related topic or about the youth. As the following narrative illustrates, some youth used these postings as a way to "test the waters" before progressing to more direct contact with others on the Internet (R = respondent; I = interviewer).

> R: Just kind of, initially it [posting on a Web site] was just kind of to test the waters and like see how people felt.
>
> I: About you?
>
> R: Yeah. And just a lot of people's experience and advice and stuff like coming out. Like they had helped me to come out, kind of, and like it was

kind of, they would kind of hold my hand about it and tell me how things would be. But um, some of it's just like having to, like I got close to, also this Broadway thing like now. Like it's kind of the only thing posted now. And like, like I just posted um, because last night I met AD [Broadway actress] like I posted a picture of like, hey, like I look like AD and like, like some replies were like, oh, really cool, but then like there's also like along with that there are those guys are like, oh, like you're looking cute.

ONLINE CONVERSATIONS. The next level of communication took the form of online conversations—interactive and reciprocal conversations with other Internet users, typically through chat rooms or IM. The length of the connection with the other Internet user varied from a one-time contact, to intermittent contact, to regular and successive contacts. The level of anonymity also varied during these interactions. Some individuals reported that they used pseudonyms, did not offer any personal information, and refused to share photographs. Other users did reveal their real name, used accurate sociodemographic information, and posted actual photos. Although some youth used these conversations primarily to gain more information about topics related to their sexual identity, others used them as a way to build some type of social connection with another gay or bisexual youth. For those youth who were apprehensive about meeting another gay or bisexual individual in person, these virtual online conversations provided the safety and anonymity they needed until they were ready to meet such individuals face to face. The following narrative illustrates how one youth was able to get close to other gay and bisexual youth and still maintain his anonymity through online conversations. Such conversations served as a "stepping stone" on the way to conversations in person with other gay and bisexual individuals.

I: How are you connected to the gay community now?

R: Um, solely, not solely, I'd say in person. I'd say the Internet was just a way of getting close without really meeting anyone. It was like I was scared, but not scared enough, and then now it's like I'm not, I'm not afraid to actually like talk to someone. So I'd say in person.

I: Okay. So it sounds like the Internet community made it, was kind of like a bridge?

R: Yeah, like a stepping stone.

OFFLINE MEETINGS. The last level of communication involved the most direct physical contact with users in the form of offline meetings. These were real-time physical meetings that were arranged through various interactive Internet applications, such as chat rooms, email, or IM. The role that these meetings played in the sexual identity development processes varied across gay and bisexual youth. For some, they represented their first meeting with a gay or bisexually identified person. For others, they were a way to initiate friendships with gay or bisexual peers, and for still others, they were a way to find sexual or romantic partners. As the two narratives below demonstrate, for some individuals these offline meetings occurred after prolonged online conversations with the other user, while for others, the Internet contact let to a meeting that same day.

> R: Um, there was this guy [LC]. I'd known him for kind of a while again, like I'd known him, we met on the Internet. But we hadn't actually met, we, just someone to talk to. And he lives in the City. And I was in the city with some friends and they just kind of ditched me so I called [LC], we hung out a couple times, and then there was, like hang out for a while and then it um...
>
> I: How long ago was this?
>
> R: Um, well, the first time we met up was about 6, 8 months ago. And then um, we met up and then we just kind of hung out with his friends.
>
> It's, I mean, I feel that um, like even in chat rooms, like I go into chat rooms and chat with people and it's like oh, you want to meet up and mess around, or like, I just want to have fun. Enjoy myself.

Functions of the Internet with Regard to Sexual Identity

In exploring the narratives of GBQ youths' sexual identity developmental processes, it was clear that the Internet played a variety of roles in facilitating aspects of sexual identity development. The young men reported using a range of Internet applications when engaged in the various components of exploration and acceptance of their sexual identity, depending on the specific function and the relative need for anonymity. The following functions will be discussed and relevant sections of these youths' narratives will be offered to further illustrate them: (1) increasing self-awareness of sexual identity, (2) learning about gay/bisexual community life, (3) communicating with other gay/bisexual people, (4) meeting other gay/bisexual people, (5) finding comfort with and acceptance of sexual identity, and (6) facilitating the coming-out process.

INCREASING SELF-AWARENESS OF SEXUAL IDENTITY. Some youth found the Internet useful in helping them to understand and acknowledge their sexual attraction to other males. Two subthemes emerged in this area, with the Internet either (1) providing sexually explicit images of men that prompted arousal and subsequent exploration of same-gender attraction or *(2)* providing images of gay and bisexual men that affirmed that gay/bisexual men do exist. The former typically involved Internet-based pornographic or erotic Web sites, whereas the latter involved these Web sites plus others that showed images of gay/bisexual men displaying various forms of attraction to other men. For participants who had experienced sexual attraction to other men but had never seen two men showing any displays of affection or sexuality toward each other, viewing these images was very validating. In several of these instances, viewing these images set the stage for further exploration of their sexual identity.

> Okay. Um, first off, like porn. (chuckles) Yeah. Like you don't like straight porn or whatever, like I used to always find myself like always watching the guy and not the girl.

> During eighth grade I got Internet. And I started talking online and I started making friends. At first, at first what I would do is I would go online and start meeting girls. But then I'm like, hey, I saw these pictures that I kind of like when I would watch straight porn, then be like, oh, that guy's hot. Then I'd be like, hey, wait. Maybe I could find some other things I like. So I start getting curious and I started searching. That's how I discovered there's some like areas for gay people. And like you're chatting there. And all that stuff... that's kind of when I started to be more into the community.

* * *

R: In high school, like I'd see other boys, and I'd think about it but then I'd be like, whatever. Like of course they were straight, and then like on the Web sites, it was like, it was, they were really gay and doing gay things.

I: So was it seeing another man with another man that helped you kind of put those pieces together?

R: Yeah.

I: And what did you think of it before?

R: I had never really seen it before.... It was seeing these images that I was really attracted to.

I: That you were aroused by?

R: Yeah. And that I had never seen before.

* * *

I: So was there something particular, specific that kind of like got you to the point where you're, you said I'm gay?

R: I don't think there was, but I think it was um, like the gay Web sites
and things like that. And that's when I was like, wow, yeah. Um, I just
saw everything and I think I knew that it was like for real.

I: What did you see?

R: Like a guy with another guy. A naked guy!

LEARNING ABOUT GAY/BISEXUAL COMMUNITY LIFE.   The Internet served as a
resource for youth to learn more about the gay/bisexual community and what
it meant to identify as gay or bisexual. These youth used a variety of resources
that included varying degrees of anonymity representing a range of levels of
connection through the Internet. At the most anonymous level, some youth
searched for gay-related Web sites that included articles on a range of gay/
bisexual issues to help inform them of the concerns that gay/bisexual men
face. Others learned about the realities of living as a gay/bisexual man by reading the life narratives and stories of other gay/bisexual individuals posted on
Web sites, blogs, chat rooms, and discussion boards. Those youth who felt comfortable seeking stronger connections engaged in discussions with more experienced gay/bisexual men and youth in order to get advice on a range of topics
related to dating, sexuality, sexual health, and safety. Some youth with specific concerns regarding sexually transmitted infections and HIV expressed by
friends and confidants found on the Internet explored these issues further via
the Internet as well.

And um, I look at gay Web sites that have articles about gays, like gay
issues.

Yeah. And just a lot of people's experience and advice and stuff like coming out. Like they had helped me to come out, kind of, and like it was
kind of, they would kind of hold my hand about it and tell me how things
would be.

* * *

I: How did they help you?

R: Just like seeing their stories and like giving me advice and stuff.
What to do and safety tips and stuff like that.

I: Safety tips for?

R: Um, just for the rest of the world. Like um.

I: But for bisexuals specifically?

R: Bisexual or gay or whatever. For guys that sleep with guys.

I: Okay. And so these were safety tips for sexual behavior or just for living your life as a "fill- in-the-blank" male?

R: Both.

* * *

I: Any specific sites on the Internet that have been helpful to you [in learning about sexually transmitted infections]?

R: I usually Google them.

I: Google them? Like what do you type in?

R: Yeah. STD's and, I usually go from like sexually transmitted diseases or infections, etc. I have a Merck manual, too, so I like read through that and go eew. Yeah. I usually like, I can't think of, I can't think of any specific Web sites, but I know there's a lot of really good like medical Web sites that have like detailed graphic pictures and whatnot. Which is perfect for scaring the crap out of somebody, just let them view some things…. I think that's the best way to do things. Show them a picture. Because you can describe gonorrhea to somebody all you want, but show them a picture of what it might look like, something like that, and they'll think twice, because everyone says, oh, I can't get that, that sounds too weird. You look at it and you're like, oh, God. I don't know. I can't think of any Web sites.

COMMUNICATING WITH OTHER GAY/BISEXUAL PEOPLE. For the vast majority of the youth we interviewed, the Internet served as a way to communicate with other gay and bisexual people, especially other youth. These connections were first established through a variety of Internet-related venues, and continued communication occurred through email, IM, and chat rooms. For some, these connections with other gay/bisexual people represented the first time they realized that there were other gay people in the world. One young man remarked that the day he first found a gay chat room was "when I first started discovering there were people like me." Due to the relative anonymity of the Internet, those young men who were not ready to meet others in person were still able to converse with other gay/bisexual individuals in a setting that provided them with the comfort of communicating freely without the fear of revealing their identity. For others who did not live in communities where they could easily access a physical gay/bisexual community, these Internet connections also served a positive connective role.

I'd say the Internet was just a way of getting close without really meeting anyone. It was like I was scared, but not scared enough, and then now it's like I'm not, I'm not afraid to actually like talk to someone.

> Yeah, there's gay communities I feel on the Internet. It's, it's a way
> for people who don't have that um, who don't have that external con-
> nection in their town, in their, wherever they live that being on the
> Internet it's easy to find people that are similar to yourself and, and
> bond through, through similarities.

Many of the youth reported that being able to communicate with other individuals who were experiencing similar same-gender attraction, desires, and
sexual behaviors was very beneficial to their sexual identity development and
to their overall well-being. Some reported decreased feelings of loneliness
since they had found out that they were not alone with regard to their sexual
identity. Others discussed enjoying the ability to bond and find connections
with other young men who shared their life experiences and feelings. They
felt that these young men were able to understand them in a way that nobody
else could.

> Well, it's one of the main social lines, because you talk to people
> there, you share your thoughts, it's like oh, this happened to me or
> people share information with you and you just know what's going
> on. And you don't feel alone. Because that's what's nice.

> Yeah, I actually go on gay chat lines, but I'm more in the bisexual
> community because everyone there, I think I get along with more of
> them, because like they're in my place. They feel what I'm feeling.
> They're going through what I'm going, and I can, we can share the
> same connections.

MEETING OTHER GAY/BISEXUAL PEOPLE. The young men who wanted to go
beyond online communications with other gay/bisexual people found that the
Internet was a reliable way of meeting other gay and bisexual people offline.
Three primary types of meetings occurred: (1) meeting friends, (2) meeting
boyfriends/romantic partners, and (3) meeting sexual partners. Although previous literature on gay/bisexual youth's use of the Internet has focused on the
last of these three, this type of meeting was not the most predominant type.
While some youth did report using the Internet for all three purposes, several
stated that they never use the Internet to find sexual partners. These youth
typically said that the Internet provided them with a safe venue for identifying
other gay/bisexual young men through chat rooms and Web sites for potential
friendships. Thus, they did not have to guess who in their social environment
might or might not be a potential gay/bisexual friend.

For many of the youth who developed offline friendships, these began as online communications such as those described in the previous section. Some of these friendships involved individuals who lived close by, and the young men were able to interact on a regular basis. Other friends lived farther away, and the two visited each other from time to time. Still other youth discussed how the Internet helped to facilitate friendships with other gay/bisexual youth in their schools by providing a safe forum for first assessing whether or not the other person was gay/bisexual.

> Um, I met one of my best friends, but I would say that I met a lot of people, I met a whole lot of people, but from those like maybe 15, 20 guys, I met like my best friend and we still best friends to this day.

* * *

> R: But then um, like D, like the guy I met in Utah, like we still talk and he's just somebody who's become a good friend that we've just been able to talk about gay issues and stuff. But it's not even, like it's not even like specifically, like you talk about whatever.
>
> I: So how would you describe your connection to that gay Internet community?
>
> R: I guess I'm kind of a part of it.
>
> I: A part of it? Would you say that it is, it doesn't sound like you access that community for sex.
>
> R: No
>
> I: What made it easy for someone to approach you in high school to ask you if you were gay?
>
> R: He approached me on the Instant Messenger first, though (chuckles). I think it's a lot easier to do something, again which is why I think chat rooms are so popular, to do something online rather than in person where no one can see your face.
>
> I: So the um, the Internet and all the computer advances that we've had have really made high school or connecting in high school easier?
>
> R: Um hum

Finding boyfriends and romantic partners was discussed by several of the participants, and this occurred through various modalities including Web site chat rooms, Weblogs, and social networking Web sites. While some of the youth were actively pursuing a romantic relationship through the Internet, others reported that young men who began as online friends later become offline boyfriends.

I've met a lot of people off the Internet, too, like my first boyfriend I met through just a friend, but then I met um, another one off of [young gay men's magazine Web site] and we had just talked for a long time, and then he ended up doing a play with one of my friends and I went to see it and that's how we first met in person. And then there's um, this thing called [general Weblog site] which is like um, online journal kind of thing. And my next boyfriend found me off of [gay Web site] and then I found my next boyfriend off of that, and then my current boyfriend I found off [general social networking Web site] which kind of sounds bad, but it wasn't, it was more like, I don't think that, D's really the only, the only one that I found specifically off of that, but I think it's easier to talk to gay guys when like you know them through other people. Like the first way to like start talking to them is like to like IM them or talk to them or whatnot.

Other participants did discuss using the Internet as a way to meet other men for sexual encounters. They typically reported that they entered chat rooms or posted messages on forums/message boards for the specific purpose of obtaining a sexual partner. The majority of these encounters occurred only once, but some youth did report having multiple contacts over time with a sexual partner they met through the Internet.

Um, the only person that I've really um, had full anal sex with since my boyfriend, um, was some, was the person I met off the Internet, who's going to school at [local university] and um, we met a couple of times and then I think I was just at that point where I was like, I wanted to have sex and nothing was really gonna stop me. And so I used protection and had an amazing time with this person, and we knew that it wasn't really going anywhere other than just like a sexual encounter. Um, but it was a mutual respect for that, that it was, that's all it was going to be and it was having fun and it was being safe. And, and um, it was a nice time.

It's, I mean, I feel that um, like even in chat rooms, like I go into chat rooms and chat with people and it's like oh, you want to meet up and mess around, or like, I just want to have fun. Enjoy myself.

FINDING COMFORT AND ACCEPTANCE WITH SEXUAL IDENTITY. Finding both online and offline connections with other gay and bisexual people helped many youth feel more connected to a larger gay/bisexual community. This sense of connection and community helped many of the youth to accept their sexual identity and feel comfortable with their sexuality. For some, this comfort and acceptance came about after connecting with others online; for others, it occurred after meeting in person someone else who was gay/bisexual. Regardless of the level of connection with others that was established through the Internet, these affirmations served a positive role in helping youth to come to terms with their sexual identity.

> Um, well, at 14, when I came out, um, I would say Internet discussion boards, like forums and chat rooms, just hearing other people's experiences and stuff like that. And reading what they had to say um, really helped me. Um, to I don't know, come into acceptance.

* * *

I: So it was kind of the, being able to, having that online computer community, if you will, was, what?

R: Beneficial.

I: Beneficial and sort of got the ball rolling in that regard?

R: Yeah.

I: Okay. Do you think had you not had that connection, that Internet connection, that it would have taken you longer to solidify your gay identity?

R: Um, I don't know if it would have taken me longer to realize that I was gay, but I think it might have taken longer to decide to come out and like be okay with it.

R: Even um, there's this kid D [whom he met online], who's my age and he lives in Utah and we go out to Utah every year and like um, I wasn't like gonna meet him or anything, but then our flight got delayed actually from snow in Chicago and the hotel we were in ended up being like really close to him. And so like I ended up meeting him and he was the first person that I really talked to like in person, like that knew I was gay. And like I thought that was kind of an important point.

I: Why?

R: Just because it was the first time like being comfortable like in person with someone who like knew I was gay.

I: Are you more comfortable now meeting people who know you're gay?

R: Yeah.

FACILITATING THE COMING-OUT PROCESS. The Internet was the medium used by many of the participants to reveal their sexual identity to others. They used a variety of Internet-based applications and also revealed their sexual identity to many different people on the Internet, including strangers, friends, and family members. The methods used and the people to whom they revealed their sexual identity represented varying levels of intimacy and connection. At the least intimate level, some youth reported coming out to strangers in discussion forums or chat rooms, usually as a way to gauge their reaction when this information was revealed. The information was then used by some to make decisions about coming out to others with whom they had personal relationships.

> Like, like our generation, or my generation is so like computer savvy and whatever, like I think I had come out um, no, I'd gone on this one message board that was, it, it's actually a [female pop star] like fan message board and there was like a gay section on it, because that's like some of her friends are gay and whatnot. And like I just started talking to people there, but that was like, it wasn't really a coming out, because it's just kind of like, and they're gay. But then there's actually this other message board that was just a general talk line and I remember I came out on that. And then like I got like a good response from that just from like, but from people I don't really know. But after that, like I became like confident enough that I was planning on telling my first friend.

Several participants discussed how they came out to their friends over the Internet. This was sometimes seen as an easier way to tell friends with whom they had been connected for a longer period of time or who they considered to be their best friend, since they felt that those individuals would require more explanation and the Internet allowed them to take time to carefully craft and articulate their message.

> I knew it [coming out] wouldn't be an issue. I mean, my friends are all liberal, so it was, it was kind of, it was very difficult for me actually like verbalize and it just took me a while to, I think, I told him [close friend] in person, but other people I told like over the Internet and stuff like that. Because it was a really difficult thing for me to kind of verbalize to them because how long I've known them.

> Like for example, my best friend, he's straight. He's straight, plus when we were like young, when we were like 12, 13, he was mean to me. He was, and now we were talking on the Internet, I told him I'm gay. And he's like, wow, I didn't know. I'm sorry for everything that I made you go through when we were young, make you feel like shit

or gay or now, now I see you as a guy, as a person. Because you're gay doesn't mean that I have to treat you like an asshole. We have more, we have very connection right now, like we used to have. So it's good.

Still other participants reported using Internet-based communication applications to come out to family members. These were typically used when family members were not living in the same geographic region as the participant.

> R: I think, during my junior, senior year, like my sister and I both came out to each other at the exact same time. So that was helpful. To see it. Yeah. Because we were always like really close, like best friends, so that just like brought us closer together.

> I: Tell me about that. How did that happen?

> R: Um, she came out to me first like initially she's like, J, I have to tell you something. She's being like really dramatic. And um, she's like, I'm gay. And then, I'm like, I just like said LOL, and then um, it was over instant messenger, because she was at college already. So then I'm just like, I am, too. And she's like, oh, okay. (chuckles)

Conclusions

Sexual identity development is a critical aspect of the overall identity formation process of gay and bisexual adolescents. These youth must develop their sexual identities against a backdrop of heterosexism and homophobia and must explore their sexuality within multiple social ecological systems that often do not support and encourage same-gender sexual desires—especially the family, school, and peer networks (Bronfenbrenner, 1979; D'Augelli, 2005). Given the increased access and relative anonymity of the Internet, gay and bisexual male adolescents are using resources such as Web sites, chat rooms, IM, blogs, and email to facilitate their sexual identity development. These venues offer gay and bisexual adolescents the ability to explore their sexuality in virtual environments where they can control when, how, and how much disclosure about their personal identities and emerging sexuality they want to provide to others. Internet modalities also give gay and bisexual youth the option to go beyond virtual connections by facilitating face-to-face connections with other gay and bisexual people.

The sense of control and independence offered by the Internet is developmentally important for all adolescents, as gaining autonomy from parents and other adult caretakers is an important milestone of adolescent development

(Havighurst, 1972; Noom, Dekovic, & Meeus, 2001). The Internet and its various applications also have become a pervasive part of youth culture. Recent empirical data demonstrate that the vast majority of adolescents (93.9% of boys and 94.7% of girls) use the Internet throughout their high school years and use it, on average, 1–2 hours per day (Willoughby, 2008). The varying levels of anonymity offered by the Internet may be especially beneficial for gay and bisexual adolescents who may experience multiple levels of violence and victimization from adults and peers who do not accept their same-gender sexual attractions and behaviors (Pilkington & D'Augelli, 1995; Rivers & D'Augelli, 2001). Thus, the Internet often provides these youth with a relatively safe and supportive environment where they can develop their sexual identities.

The narratives of the gay and bisexual male adolescents we interviewed revealed a great deal about the ways in which they use the Internet and the roles and functions that the Internet plays in their sexual identity development process. These adolescents reported using a range of Internet applications (Web sites, discussion boards, IM, email, etc.) that provided them with varying degrees of anonymity and connection to others. A youth's comfort with and acceptance of his sexual identity often influenced both his use of the various Internet modalities and the degree to which he revealed personal information during these interactions. The participants' narratives revealed that their use of the Internet and its applications could be categorized into four increasing levels of connection with other people: (1) anonymous exploration, (2) casual posting, (3) online conversations, and (4) offline meetings.

The varying ways in which they used the Internet often served a range of potentially health-promoting functions for gay and bisexual male adolescents and played an integral role in their psychosocial and sexual identity development. The primary functions of the Internet included (1) increasing awareness of their sexual identity, (2) learning about sexual identity and gay culture, (3) connecting with other gay/bisexual youth, (4) finding support for and acceptance of their sexual identity, (5) increasing their comfort with their sexual identity, and (6) facilitating their coming-out process. These six functions could be collapsed into three primary content areas, indicating that the Internet provides gay and bisexual male adolescents with a forum where they can (1) learn about and explore their sexuality and the gay community, (2) connect and socialize with other gay and bisexual peers, and (3) gain self-acceptance and share their sexual identity with others. Although the focus of the current inquiry was on sexual identity development, an examination of these three content areas reveals that the Internet could also be helpful in addressing other critical developmental issues that involve independent learning, connecting/socializing with similar others, and accepting oneself and sharing one's identity with others.

Future Focus on the Internet

In order to better understand the unique factors that impact the sexual identity development processes of contemporary gay and bisexual male adolescents, it will be important for future researchers, theorists, and practitioners
to explore the role of the Internet in these critical processes. Although lesbian
and bisexual female adolescent narratives were not included in the empirical
investigation reported in this chapter, it will be important to explore the role
of the Internet in the lives of young women, since recent evidence suggests
that female adolescents are using the Internet at levels comparable to those of
their male counterparts (Willoughby, 2008). Part of developing an LGB sexual
identity also involves learning about the larger gay culture and its traditions,
rituals, symbols, norms, and ways of being, acting, and knowing (Gee, 1990;
Pope, 1995). The Internet is a relatively safe and convenient way for gay and
bisexual adolescents to do this, and it has been recognized as an important
socializing force for youth seeking to learn about gay culture (Driver, 2006;
Linné, 2003). As suggested by Russell (2002) and supported by the data presented in this chapter, the Internet also serves as a way for gay and bisexual
youth to create their own communities and connect with one another.

Although this virtual environment has many benefits in facilitating the
sexual identity development of gay and bisexual adolescents, there are real dangers to the Internet that should not be overlooked. Inexperienced adolescents
who are exploring their sexuality via the Internet may be vulnerable to adults
who prey on their naiveté. Thus, it is critical for parents/caretakers, teachers,
community workers, and others who have contact with gay and bisexual adolescents to educate them about the potential dangers of adults who use the
Internet to exploit and victimize youth.

Interventionists who wish to use the Internet to promote the healthy
growth and development of gay and bisexual male adolescents should realize that such programs will need to be tailored to the specific needs of their
population. The following factors may be considered in the development of
Internet-based interventions: *(1)* participants' relative desire for anonymity,
(2) the level of sensitivity of intervention messages, *(3)* the complexity of intervention messages, *(4)* participants' level of desired interaction, *(5)* immediacy
of desired interaction with participants, *(6)* participants' accessibility of technology, *(7)* comfort with technology, and *(8)* desired reach of intervention.

The Internet, and its many applications, has become a mainstay of daily
life for adolescents and young adults. This technology provides exciting novel
opportunities, as well as challenges, for youth and those who work with and
care about them. The ever-expanding array of Internet-based applications that

are continually introduced into youth culture is creating new virtual spaces and communities that provide gay and bisexual male adolescents with affirming environments where they can learn, explore, connect, and grow.

REFERENCES

Arnett, J. J. (1997). Young people's conceptions of the transition to adulthood. *Youth & Society, 29,* 1–23.

Arnett, J. J. (2000). Emerging adulthood: A theory of development from the late teens through the twenties. *American Psychologist, 55*(5), 469–480.

Blake, S. M., Ledsky, R., Lehman, T., Goodenow, C., Sawyer, R., & Hack, T. (2001). Preventing sexual risk behaviors among gay, lesbian and bisexual adolescents: The benefits of gay-sensitive HIV instruction in schools. *American Journal of Public Health, 91*(6), 940–946.

Boies, S. C. (2002). University students' uses of and reactions to online sexual information and entertainment: Links to online and offline sexual behavior. *Canadian Journal of Human Sexuality, 11*(2), 77–89.

Bolding, G., Davis, M., Hart, G., Sherr, L., & Elford, J. (2007). Where young MSM meet their first sexual partner: The role of the Internet. *AIDS and Behavior, 11,* 522–526.

Bronfenbrenner, U. (1979). Contexts of child rearing: Problems and prospects. *American Psychologist, 34*(10), 844–850.

Cass, V. C. (1979). Homosexual identity formation: A theoretical model. *Journal of Homosexuality, 4,* 219–235.

Coleman, E. (1982). Developmental stages of the coming out process. *Journal of Homosexuality, 9,* 105–126.

Creswell, J. W. (1998). *Qualitative inquiry and research design: Choosing among five traditions.* Thousand Oaks, CA: Sage.

D'Augelli, A. R. (1994). Identity development and sexual orientation: Toward a model of lesbian, gay, and bisexual development. In E. J. Trickett, R. J. Watts, & D. Birman (Eds.), *Human diversity: Perspectives on people in context* (pp. 312–333). San Francisco: Jossey-Bass.

D'Augelli, A. R. (2005). Stress and adaptation among families of lesbian, gay, and bisexual youth: Research challenges. *Journal of Gay, Lesbian, Bisexual, and Transgender Family Studies, 1*(2), 115–135.

D'Augelli, A. R. (2006). Developmental and contextual factors and mental health among lesbian, gay, and bisexual youths. In A. M. Omoto & H. S. Kurtzman (Eds.), *Sexual orientation and mental health: Examining identity and development in lesbian, gay, and bisexual people* (pp. 37–53). Washington, DC: American Psychological Association Press.

D'Augelli, A. R., & Hershberger, S. L. (1993). Lesbian, gay, and bisexual youth in community settings: Personal challenges and mental health problems. *American Journal of Community Psychology. 21*(4), 421–448.

Diamond, L. M. (2003). Love matters. In P. Florsheim (Ed.), *Adolescent romantic relations and sexual behavior* (pp. 85–107). Mahwah, NJ: Erlbaum.

Díaz, R. M. (1998). *Latino gay men and HIV: Culture, sexuality and risk behavior.* New York: Routledge.

Driver, S. (2006). Virtually queer youth communities of girls and birls: Dialogical spaces of identity work and desiring exchanges. In D. Buckingham & R. Willett (Eds.), *Digital generations: Children, young people, and new media* (pp. 229–245). Mahwah, NJ: Erlbaum.

Eliason, M. J. (1996). Identity formation for lesbian, bisexual and gay persons: Beyond a "minoritizing" view. *Journal of Homosexuality, 30*(3), 31–58.

Erikson, E. H. (1959). *Identity and the life cycle.* New York: Norton.

Erikson, E. H. (1968). *Identity: Youth and crisis.* New York: Norton.

Fields, S., Wharton, M., Marrero, A., Little, A., Pannell, K., & Morgan, J. (2006). Internet chat rooms: Connecting with a new generation of young men of color at risk for HIV infection who have sex with other men. *Journal of the Association of Nurses in AIDS Care, 17*(6), 53–60.

Flowers, P., Smith, J. A., Sheeran, P., & Beail, N. (1998). Coming out and sexual debut: Understanding the social context of HIV risk-related behaviour. *Journal of Community and Applied Social Psychology, 8*(6), 409–421.

Garofalo, R., & Harper G. (2003). Not all adolescents are the same: Addressing the unique needs of gay and bisexual male youth. *Adolescent Medicine: State of the Art Reviews, 14*(3), 595–612.

Garofalo, R., Herrick, A., Mustanski, B. S., & Donenberg, G. R. (2007). Tip of the iceberg: Young men who have sex with men, the Internet, and HIV risk. *American Journal of Public Health, 97*(6), 1113–1117.

Gee, J. (1990). *Psycholinguistics and literacies: Ideology in discourse.* London: Falmer Press.

Gross, E. F. (2004). Adolescent Internet use: What we expect, what teens report. *Journal of Applied Developmental Psychology, 25*(6), 633–649.

Guba, E. G., & Lincoln, Y. (1981) *Effective evaluation.* San Francisco: Jossey-Bass.

Gullotta, T. P., Adams, G. R., & Montemayor, R. (Eds.). (1992). *Adolescent sexuality.* Newbury Park, CA: Sage.

Harper, G. W. (2007). Sex isn't that simple: Culture and context in HIV prevention interventions for gay and bisexual male adolescents. *American Psychologist, 62*(8), 803–819.

Harper, G. W., Jernewall, N., & Zea, M. C. (2004). Giving voice to emerging science and theory for lesbian, gay, and bisexual people of color. *Cultural Diversity and Ethnic Minority Psychology, 10*(3), 187–199.

Harper, G.W., & Schneider, M. (2003). Oppression and discrimination among lesbian, gay, bisexual, and transgendered people and communities: A challenge for community psychology. *American Journal of Community Psychology, 31,* 243–252.

Havighurst, R. J. (1972). *Developmental tasks and education* (3rd ed.). New York: McKay.

Herdt, G. (1992). *Gay culture in America: Essays from the field.* Boston: Beacon Press.

Herdt, G. (1997). *Same sex, different cultures: Gays and lesbians across cultures.* Boulder, CO: Westview Press.

Hersker, A. L., & Leap, W. (1996). Representation, subjectivity and ethics in urban gay ethnography. *City & Society, 8*(1), 142–147.

Huffaker, D. A., & Calvert, S. L. (2005). Gender, identity, and language use in teenage blogs. *Journal of Computer-Mediated Communication, 10*(2). Retrieved April 16, 2008, from http://jcmc.indiana.edu/vol10/issue2/huffaker.html

Kraut, R., Patterson, M., Lundmark, V., Kiesler, S., Mukophadhyay, T., & Scherlis, W. (1998). Internet paradox: A social technology that reduces social involvement and psychological well-being? *American Psychologist, 53,* 1017–1031.

Leap, W. L. (1994). Learning gay culture in "a desert of nothing": Language as a resource in gender socialization. *High School Journal, 77*(1–2), 122–132.

Leap, W. L. (1998). Staking a claim on history and culture: Recent studies in the anthropology of homosexuality. *Anthropological Quarterly, 71*(3), 150–154.

Leap, W. L. (2007). Language, socialization, and silence in gay adolescence. In K. E. Lovaas & M. M. Jenkins (Eds.), *Sexualities and communication in everyday life* (pp. 95–104). Newbury Park, CA: Sage.

Lincoln, Y., & Guba, E. (1985). *Naturalistic inquiry.* Newbury Park, CA: Sage.

Linné, R. (2003). Alternative textualities: Media culture and the proto-queer. *Qualitative Studies in Education, 16*(5), 669–689.

Mankowski, E. S., & Rappaport, J. (1995). Stories, identity and the psychological sense of community. In R. S. Wyer, Jr. (Ed.), *Advances in social cognition* (Vol. 7, pp. 211–226). Hillsdale, NJ: Erlbaum.

Mankowski, E. S., & Rappaport, J. (2000). Narrative concepts and analysis in spiritually-based communities. *Journal of Community Psychology, 28,* 479–493.

Marcia, J. (1966). Development and validation of ego-identity status. *Journal of Personality and Social Psychology, 3,* 551–558.

Martinez, D .G., & Sullivan, S. C. (1998). African American gay men and lesbians: Examining the complexity of gay identity development. In L. A. See (Ed.), *Human behavior in the social environment from an African American perspective* (pp. 243–264). Binghamton, NY: Haworth Press.

Mazalin, D., & Moore, S. (2004). Internet use, identity development and social anxiety among young adults. *Behaviour Change, 21*(2), 90–102.

McKenna, K. Y. A., & Bargh, J. A. (1998). Coming out in the age of the Internet: Identity "demarginalization" through virtual group participation. *Journal of Personality and Social Psychology, 75*(3), 681–694.

McKenna, K. Y. A., & Bargh, J. A. (2000). Plan 9 from cyberspace: The implications of the Internet for personality and social psychology. *Personality and Social Psychology Review, 4*(1), 57–75.

Mesch, G., & Talmud, I. (2006). The quality of online and offline relationships: The role of multiplexity and duration of social relationships. *The Information Society, 22,* 137–148.

Miles, M. B., & Huberman, A. M. (1994). *Qualitative data analysis: An expanded sourcebook.* Thousand Oaks, CA: Sage.

Noom, M. J., Dekovic, M., & Meeus, W. (2001). Conceptual analysis and measurement of adolescent autonomy. *Journal of Youth and Adolescence, 30*(5), 577–595.

Patton, M. Q. (1990). *Qualitative evaluation and research methods*. Thousand Oaks, CA: Sage.

Pilkington, N. W., & D'Augelli, A. R. (1995). Victimization of lesbian, gay, and bisexual youth in community settings. *Journal of Community Psychology, 23,* 33–55.

Pope, M. (1995). The "salad bowl" is big enough for us all: An argument for the inclusion of lesbians and gay men in any definition of multiculturalism. *Journal of Counseling & Development, 73,* 301–304.

Ridge, D. T., Plummer, D. C., & Minichiello, V. (1994). Young gay men and HIV: Running the risk? *AIDS Care, 6*(4), 371–378.

Rivers, I., & D'Augelli, A. R. (2001). The victimization of lesbian, gay, and bisexual youths. In A. R. D'Augelli & C. J. Patterson (Eds.), *Lesbian, gay and bisexual identities and youth: Psychological perspectives*. New York: Oxford University Press.

Rosario, M., Hunter, J., Maguen, S., Gwadz, M., & Smith, R. (2001). The coming-out process and its adaptational and health-related associations among gay, lesbian, and bisexual youths: Stipulation and exploration of a model. *American Journal of Community Psychology. 29*(1), 113–160.

Rotheram-Borus, M. J., Reid, H., Rosario, M., & Kasen, S. (1995). Determinants of safer sex patterns among gay/bisexual male adolescents. *Journal of Adolescence, 18*(1), 3–15.

Russell, S. T. (2002). Queer in America: Citizenship for sexual minority youth. *Applied Developmental Science, 6*(4), 258–263.

Ryan, C., & Futterman, D. (1998). *Gay and lesbian youth: Care and counseling.* New York: Columbia University Press.

Savin-Williams, R. C. (1995). Lesbian, gay male, and bisexual adolescents. In A. R. D'Augelli & C. J. Patterson (Eds.), *Lesbian, gay, and bisexual identities over the lifespan: Psychological perspectives* (pp. 165–189). New York: Oxford University Press.

Schmitt, K. L., Dayanim, S., & Matthias, S. (2008). Personal homepage construction as an expression of social development. *Developmental Psychology, 44*(2), 496–506.

Schneider, M. (2001). Toward a reconceptualization of the coming-out process for adolescent females. In A. R. D'Augelli & C. J. Patterson (Eds.), *Lesbian, gay and bisexual identities and youth* (pp. 71–96). New York: Oxford University Press.

Schutz, A. (1970). *On phenomenology and social relations*. Evanston, IL: Northwestern University Press.

Subrahmanyan, K., Smahel, D., & Greenfield, P. (2006). Connecting developmental constructions to the Internet: Identity presentation and sexual exploration in online teen chat rooms. *Developmental Psychology, 42*(3), 395–406.

Telljohann, S. K., & Price, J. H. (1993). A qualitative examination of adolescent homosexuals' life experiences: Ramifications for secondary school personnel. *Journal of Homosexuality, 26*(1), 41–56.

Travers, R., & Schneider, M. (1997). A multi-faceted approach to reduce risk factors for lesbian, gay and bisexual youth. In M. Schneider (Ed.), *Pride and prejudice:*

Working with lesbian, gay and bisexual youth (pp. 49–67). Toronto: Central Toronto Youth Services.

Troiden, R. R. (1989). The formation of homosexual identities. *Journal of Homosexuality, 17,* 43–73.

Turow, J. (1999) *The Internet and the family: The view from the parents – the view from the press* (Report Series No. 27). Philadelphia: Annenberg Public Policy Center of the University of Pennsylvania.

Valkenburg, P. M., & Peter, J. (2008). Adolescents' identity experiments on the Internet: Consequences for social competence and self-concept unity. *Communication Research, 35*(2), 208–231.

Waldo, C. R., Hesson-McInnis, M. S., & D'Augelli, A. R. (1998). Antecedents and consequences of victimization of lesbian, gay, and bisexual young people: A structural model comparing rural university and urban samples. *American Journal of Community Psychology. 26*(2), 307–334.

Waldo, C. R., McFarland, W., Katz, M. H., MacKellar, D., & Valleroy, L. A. (2000). Very young gay and bisexual men are at risk for HIV infection: The San Francisco Bay Area Young Men's Survey II. *Journal of AIDS, 24*(2), 168–174.

Willoughby, T. (2008). A short-term longitudinal study of Internet and computer game use by adolescent boys and girls: Prevalence, frequency of use, and psychosocial predictors. *Developmental Psychology, 44*(1), 195–204.

14

Focus on the Family

The Psychosocial Context of Gay Men Choosing Fatherhood

David deBoer

A woman must have money and a room of her own if she is to write fiction.

—Woolf (1929, p. 4)

In *A Room of One's Own*, Virginia Woolf articulated the totalizing forces of male privilege that had conspired against creative literary production by women. Unable to inherit wealth or to keep earned money, compelled to perform domestic labor, denied access to equal education, and socialized to a sense of inferior intellect, women were unable to produce literature on a level playing field. The shifts in gender roles and opportunities in the United States over the past decades have resulted in more equal opportunities for women; yet, ongoing complaints of working women who come home to work the "second shift" reflect the fact that such social changes have not in a structurally significant way affected the daily lives or roles of men as husbands and fathers. Extremely common now is the mother who has a full-time professional career. The father who chooses to work as a primary caregiver or stay-at-home dad remains a rare phenomenon, if not an oddity.

Lacking a female spouse to literally and psychologically carry their reproductive desires, gay men choosing fatherhood outside of a coparenting role with a woman are akin to Woolf's psychologically androgynous writer, both in challenging the totalizing forces of heterosexual privilege and in needing to draw on inner resources not ordinarily cultivated by or valued for one's own gender. And like Woolf's female Victorian writer, gay fathers face a host of obstacles from a perplexed public.

If what a woman needed to participate in a man's domain as a writer was "money and a room of her own," what then does a gay man need, and what does he experience, when he wishes to tread on a woman's traditional domain, when social roles, religious and cultural beliefs, institutional practices and laws, and the reproductive realities of the body all combine to militate against such desires? This chapter seeks to address these questions.

Previous and ongoing work on gay and lesbian parenting has been necessarily focused on outcome studies on the children of gay men or lesbians. Such studies were and remain driven by the need to provide courts with evidence to use in resolving child-custody disputes involving the divorce of a married couple after one of the parents identifies as gay or lesbian (see Patterson, 2005, for a comprehensive review). Empirical evidence supports the conclusion that the children of same-sex parents do not differ significantly in their psychosocial and developmental outcomes compared to the children of opposite-sex parents (Patterson, 2005). Also, research has found no evidence of unsuitability for parenthood among lesbian mothers and gay fathers, but has instead suggested an ability to provide a good home environment for children equivalent to that of heterosexual parents (Patterson, 2005).

In reading the mainstream literature, one is struck by the pervasive, if unavoidable, defensiveness of much of the work done on this topic, which has sought to demonstrate the "normality" of same-sex relationships and to highlight the lack of difference or negative influence of same-sex parents. The human sciences are beginning to extend the reach of essential outcome studies to make a more holistic analysis of the *processes* of these newer family forms. This chapter draws on existing narrative accounts and family research, together with my own experience (socially located as a White, upper-middle-class gay man) of adopting an infant girl with my partner in 2004, to continue to frame the outlines of this nascent research program. In providing and reviewing such first-person narrative experience and observations, this chapter seeks to return to a focus on the family life experiences of gay men who choose to become fathers. In the first section, I review internal and external obstacles that gay men may face as they make the decision to become parents. In the second section, I describe the vicissitudes of adjustment to parenthood under the hegemonic shadow of American culture's master narrative that equates parenthood with heterosexuality. In the third section, I address changes in gay fathers' relationship to their gay male social context and their own evolving gay identity. The concluding section offers suggestions for further family-focused research.

Making the Decision to Become a Parent

Overcoming Internal Obstacles

My own inner process leading to adoption was catalyzed when my partner urged me to read Dan Savage's (2000) adoption story, a counternarrative that contests American culture's master narrative that equates parenthood with heterosexuality. Such counternarratives may thus come to play a crucial role in the social practice of sexual identity. In the absence of any actual gay parents in our social circle at the time, reading about the step-by-step process of an admired figure made the adoption process seem more possible and practical than I had imagined, and it directly led my partner to investigate local agencies, which in turn led us to informational seminars. I knew very early in this process that we would proceed further when, at each seminar, I experienced an overwhelming sense of tearfulness that felt like a reunion with a missing part of my self. On reflection, I felt that part of this experience was the ability to reclaim what I thought I had lost by coming out: my wish to be a father, to have a child of my own. This wish had long been a major presumptive part of my imagined future life course and of my identity, and I know it assumed a significant role in the delay of the initiation of my coming-out process. For in my North American suburban childhood and 1980s and 1990s urban adulthood experience, assuming a gay identity seemed to automatically entail losing this prospective parent identity. My tears were also tears of mourning, with the more profound realization of the pain that had been inflicted by society's dehumanization of me by treating me like an unsuitable candidate for parenthood simply by virtue of my sexual orientation. Just participating in these seminars that affirmed our capacity to parent restored a part of my personhood that had been taken from me.

Whereas biological reproduction can be achieved without a significant encounter with personal identity beyond that of role transitions, gay fathers typically face issues of role transition after first encountering deeper existential concerns and issues related to identity. For example, as part of the adoption process, prospective parents complete a checklist to identify a host of characteristics of babies that they would or would not feel comfortable taking on. (Families choosing surrogacy face similar choices and dilemmas when choosing egg donors and surrogate mothers.) These characteristics include an array of heritable medical and mental health risk factors, together with ethnic and racial characteristics. Thus, from the outset of our adoption process, we had to engage in a heightened encounter and dialogue with our identities across a range of features. This very difficult process challenged my abstract ideals and beliefs.

I devote my professional life to promoting mental health, but in my personal life, was I willing to risk parenting a child vulnerable to psychosis, fetal alcohol syndrome, or attention deficit disorder? I like to consider myself committed to civil rights and multiculturalism, but did I want to make my conspicuous gay family more conspicuous still by becoming an interracial family as well? Would adding that additional factor compound a child's difficulties with identity formation or would it simply strengthen a capacity for understanding and appreciating difference? Such an inner dialogue unfolds in the social context of family and associates directly and indirectly conveying their often conflicting opinions and beliefs on these matters. For example, an African American colleague said to me, with a familiar kind-heartedness but in utter seriousness, "Dave, you can't adopt an African American baby, and I'll tell you why: you don't know *anything* about taking care of Black hair." It seemed clear that the hair, although a very real issue, also represented an entire cultural experience that my colleague feared a White couple would be unable to help a Black child disentangle.

Gay fathers may thus benefit if they develop their capacity for nonconformity (Mallon, 2004), including an ability to overcome all manner of community skepticism or even hostility, possible family disapproval, and an entire parenting culture that equates primary caregiving with motherhood. Toward this end, a degree of psychological-mindedness is helpful. A psychotherapy client of mine—a gay man who, with his partner of 13 years, had considered but rejected the possibility of adoption—stated that a significant motive against moving forward with adoption was that he felt his conservative Catholic parents would not approve of them as same-sex parents, even though his parents have remained extremely affirming of them as a couple. It was clear that even if this client were reading his parents accurately, which seemed doubtful, a major task for him was to work on a sense of internalized homophobia, to allow himself at least to question his own assumptions about what constituted a suitable environment for children.

Early in our own adoption process, our awareness of our second-class citizenship status was heightened as we heard expectations, from both straight and gay contacts, that we would have a long wait and that we would likely receive a "difficult-to-place" child. There has been a longstanding and widespread assumption, both popularly and in the research literature, that a heterosexual couple would be first chosen by most birth mothers. Bozett (1987) stated as a given that agencies give first preference to heterosexual parents and that gay parents receive more "challenging" children. In Bozett's narrative and era, single-parent adoptions were the only ones allowed. Gay men have historically been ranked as the least desirable prospective parents. In fact, in Florida, much of the early debate about the legal rights of gay parents involved the matching of some of America's untouchables; that process seemed to say, "Okay, we'll allow gay parents to foster babies with acquired immune deficiency syndrome (AIDS)—but only those babies, and not without a fight that reminds you of your stigmatized status."

As it happened, our own experience (in 2004) and those of other gay fathers at our agency proved happily to be the opposite of the messages we had been given: to expect to be "last in line." We were chosen as parents before our profile was ever placed in the profile book by a birth mother who explicitly requested placement with a gay family. Our daughter's birth mother, a college student with tricolored hair who met Grace's birth father as fellow performers in a punk rock festival, was very open about her (conscious) reasons. In essence, our daughter's birth mother was playing a kind of identity politics of her own, counting on the reliability of assumptions she made based on our social identities as gay men. First, knowing she had an "artsy" persona outside of the mainstream, she felt better about the story that she imagined that an urban gay couple might tell her child about her birth mother compared with the suburban couples populating the waiting list, whom she had stereotyped as pious and conservative. Our professional identities as clinical psychologists may have further enhanced her greater trust in our capacity to truly empathize with her over time. Second, she cited an altruistic motive. Having confirmed her pregnancy too late for an abortion and angry that she had to carry the baby to term, she said that at least she could try to make someone else's life better by giving her child to a couple who otherwise might not be able to become parents. We felt there may have been another reason that she may not have articulated even to herself: that with this arrangement, she would not be replaced by another mother, so that eventually, when she was more ready for involvement, her daughter might be more amenable to that relationship. Perhaps feeling stigmatized or marginalized herself, she may have felt a sense of identification with another stigmatized group. In any event, it was a corrective experience to have our sexual identities work in our favor for a change, especially in the domain of parenting.

Overcoming External Obstacles

Returning to the question of what gay men choosing parenthood require, part of the answer is the same as it was for Virginia Woolf: money. In the 2003

Chicago domestic adoption market—it *is* a market—our 3-week-old daughter, Grace, cost $25,000 in agency fees. Attorney fees for the legal proceedings were an additional $1,500. Estate planning to provide legal stipulations that are a given in a legal marriage cost us an additional $500. Parents choosing international adoption usually incur significant additional expenses. Individuals and couples choosing surrogacy can usually spend more than $100,000 over the course of the process.

Legal barriers represent another significant obstacle to overcome, and they also shape the nature of gay families at least as tangibly as does economic opportunity. As of this writing, the Human Rights Campaign Fund (2007) reports that 46 states and the District of Columbia allow adoption by *single* gay men or lesbians. The law is either unclear or adoption is only allowed in some jurisdictions in three states. One state—Florida—explicitly bans adoption by gay men and lesbians. Adoption by same-sex *couples* is affirmatively allowed in only 10 states and the District of Columbia and explicitly prohibited in 5 states; the law is unclear in some jurisdictions in 35 states. Second-parent adoption of a partner's child is affirmatively allowed in 8 states and the District of Columbia and disallowed in 5; it is allowed in some jurisdictions or the law is unclear in 37 states.

Would-be fathers in states with significant restrictions continue to face choices among conflicting loyalties and obligations. Many will likely choose not to become parents as a result. Some may disconnect from local ties and relocate to areas where family law is more inclusive, while those who do choose parenthood may be forced to form families in which only one parent is legitimated and protected by law. We attended a 2006 summer camp for gay and lesbian families in a Midwestern state that forbids second-parent adoption by partners. In this experience, we encountered a group of gay fathers who had used an agency with a relationship with Central American countries seeking North American placement. In their locale, this agency happened to be one of the few available to gay men seeking to adopt. While the adoption agency's social workers colluded with a knowing wink, these fathers mostly needed to present to the Central American officials as heterosexual men who were becoming single parents, in spite of the fact that most were planning to parent within an established couple relationship. This secrecy raises the question of the psychological effects of a coerced return to the closet for an out gay man. Given that adoption under any circumstance presents challenges to a sense of legitimacy as parents, what is the effect on power relationships within these families of different legal statuses? Will separation rates in these states and families become higher, given that each partner does not have an equal amount to lose in the event of a split? Will laws whose rhetorical aim is to protect the conceptual family from imagined harm result in real harm to actual children in these actual families?

Even when the law is not a barrier to becoming a parent, legal issues often have other consequences, as do cultural, social, and bureaucratic factors that present further obstacles for families. In many areas of the country, prospective parents undeterred by legal barriers continue to face the last-in-line social bias. Issues such as access to health-care and domestic partnership benefits may have highly significant effects that influence family formation and functioning.

Adjusting to Parenthood in Developmental and Social Context

In this section, I consider the issue of adjustment to parenting within the unique developmental context of gay couples living under the hegemonic shadow of the heterosexual parent paradigm. It is well documented that heterosexual couples experience some short-term decline in marital satisfaction during the transition to parenthood due to role strain related to caregiving (Cohler & Galatzer-Levy, 2000; Cowan & Cowan, 1987; Feldman, 1987). Parenthood strain appears to be greater for (heterosexual) spouses who have to perform an inordinate number of "cross-sex" tasks, suggesting "that cultural stereotypes condition the expectation of couples even among those who generally regarded themselves as modern and egalitarian" (Feldman, 1987, p. 32) For gay male couples, all domestic tasks become cross-sex, which has implications for the adjustment to parenthood.

Previous research suggests that the division of labor among gay male couples tends to be egalitarian and that partner satisfaction is highest when tasks are seen to be equitably negotiated and shared according to skill and preference (Johnson & O'Connor, 2002; McPherson, 1993). In the process of coming out, gay men typically have to challenge all manner of gender norms, so one might expect that this experience would prepare them well for also doing so in the realm of parenting tasks. There seems a greater likelihood for reduced role resentment, since the roles will be negotiated and chosen rather than assigned by existing social convention. Savage's (2005) narrative engages this issue aptly:

> Embrace and inhabit sex roles while mocking them at the same
> time? We've had some experience with that. Ever since we became
> parents and Terry quit his job, we've joked about being "husband"
> and "wife." While the roles we play in our family have traditional
> outlines, we don't feel oppressed by them.... It helps that these are

roles we play willingly, not roles we're obligated or expected to play because of our gender.... Terry doesn't spend a lot of time wondering if being the stay-at-home "mom" is something he freely chose. (p. 147)

Research on marital satisfaction among heterosexuals suggests that the management and negotiation of problems is key to adjusting to parenthood (e.g., Ball, 1984, cited in Cowan & Cowan, 1987). There is little reason to believe that the dynamics would be different for gay male couples.

There are additional reasons why it is a reasonable hypothesis that postparenting morale and relationship satisfaction may differ for gay male couples. It is a truism of popular psychology and folk wisdom that a new father may feel excluded from the intense infant–mother bond and feel a sense of resentment for being neglected. For gay fathers, it may be that the absence of breast-feeding, together with the absence of the presumptive primary role of mother, may facilitate more equal caregiving and therefore reduced feelings of either being overburdened (with caregiving) or neglected (by the overburdened caregiver). In fact, perhaps one of the best aspects of parenthood for us is that my partner and I do not have to encounter the greater sense of ownership and entitlement that inevitably comes with having carried and birthed a baby. As fellow fathers, we each enjoy a more level playing field, a chance to establish a bond with our daughter not colored by that feeling of being the second-string comforter, of cutting in on the intimate mother–baby dance. For gay dads, this experience may not be without a darker side, however. Heterosexual dads, during times when their child prefers to be comforted by mother, might console themselves with a depersonalizing emotional defense by telling themselves that this preference is about gender or the mother role—about wanting mommy, not about their unique personal characteristics. Our daughter's preferences, on the other hand, may carry a more potent and personal sting and require an even greater capacity to manage these feelings and vicissitudes without withdrawing from or retaliating against either our daughter or each other.

As I noted, coming out as a gay man has historically been presumed to entail a renunciation of one's striving for or expectation of becoming a parent. The joyful experience of reclaiming a mourned loss and a highly valued aspect of self may play a significant role in mitigating the stressors of infant caregiving that normally contribute to a decline in satisfaction during adjustment to parenthood. As parenthood in the future becomes a more normative developmental possibility in the anticipated life course of gay men, this aspect of enhanced morale may prove to have been a short-term, cohort-specific phenomenon. A related mitigating factor may have to do with the buffering effect of community support and celebration of the couple's relationship. With the initiation of the parent role, there is typically a shift in adult children's relationship with their aging parents, who not only take pride in their new role as grandparents but who now identify in a different way with their adult children. They may become better able to adapt their parental stance with a fuller recognition of their children's adult responsibilities and separateness. Although this dynamic is perhaps shared by most parents, there is an added dimension for gay fathers. Notwithstanding the Massachusetts marriage law and the increasing popularity of commitment ceremonies for many gay couples, it is a nearly universal phenomenon for gay couples to feel that their relationship has not received a sense of affirmation, validation, and celebration equivalent to that of their heterosexual peers. The extended family rituals surrounding the birth of a baby, and the subsequent attention to the prized grandchild, nephew or niece, may therefore take on a very different meaning for gay couples than for heterosexual fathers.

Cohler and Galatzer-Levy (2000) note the issue of "social timing" as a factor in adjustment to parenthood. The current cohort of gay fathers appears anecdotally to be "off-time late" in comparison to their heterosexual counterparts, a fact that may ease adjustment to parenthood given that previous identity issues are more likely to have been largely resolved (Cohler & Galatzer-Levy, 2000). That the current cohort arrived at parenthood developmentally "late" was inevitable given the sociopolitical realities of their lives. However, there is every reason to believe that the average age of parenthood transition in future cohorts of gay fathers is likely to trend downward and to approach the average age of their heterosexual counterparts. However, developmentalists must remain sensitive to the coming-out process as a task that, for many, may continue to delay the formation of intimate partnerships and the transition to parenthood for gay fathers versus their heterosexual peers.

Developing Credibility while Managing Conspicuousness

Gay parents who adopt face the challenges both of feeling a sense of credibility as "real" parents and of countering an internalization of the norms of the traditional nuclear family. While this struggle for credibility is also an issue for heterosexual parents who adopt, gay fathers face unique challenges. Although "da-da" was in fact one of our daughter's first vocalizations, as with most children worldwide, Grace also vocalized "ma-ma" very early. Later, when Grace had become very verbal, from time to seemingly random time she might say something like "I want my Ma-Ma." While we were confident that she was parroting something she heard her playmates say, such moments can at the time undoubtedly play on one's worst fears: Does she have an innate, essential sense of "Mommy," and could it be possible that she really misses the woman who carried and gave birth to her? Does she wish she had a mommy?

As time goes on, such challenges to one's sense of legitimacy may take different forms. Grace is a high-spirited, feisty child, eager to explore, and never more so than when she was $2^{1}/_{2}$. When in a camping store, Grace was particularly overexuberant and heedless of repeated efforts to calm and contain her until she had run completely away and out of sight of each daddy. That was the last straw for my partner, Drew ("Da-Da"), who whisked her away for an impromptu time-out in our car in the crowded parking lot of a shopping mall. Furious at being contained, Grace pulled the classic toddler gambit of screaming for the nondisciplining parent—"I WANT MY DADDY!"—all the while writhing to free herself from Da-Da's arms. Much attention was drawn to this scene, and a couple in a coffee shop, obviously childless, would not avert their critical stares. Just as I came out to check on their delay, a police cruiser slowly drove by and surveyed the scene; it even caused us to wonder whether someone had suspected a child abduction and called the police! Our awareness of our conspicuousness was a maddening distraction from the parenting task at hand.

A heterosexual dad in the same situation would only have had to deal with the embarrassment of his toddler's tantrum in public. Gay fathers must contend with such experiences because our language and our culture have not caught up with the possibility that there may be two dads or two moms. This sociological reality may create tension not only internally but also within the couple as partners decide what last name to give the child and how the child will address each dad. A gay fathers must be able to retain his sense of legitimacy, for example, even as his child may not have his own surname or even as the child may address him with a term other than the traditional "Daddy." Gay men who choose parenthood, of course, cannot escape the cultural narrative and scripts given by the dominant heterosexual paradigm of parenthood and family. Further research may show that it is the particular quality and process in which that engagement is made by individuals and couples that will determine the choice to parent as well as the nature and quality of parenting and family life.

Encountering the Primacy of Motherhood

A gay male couple, the adoptive parents of a 3-year-old son, adopted their second child, a daughter. When their extended family came to meet the new baby, the newborn began to cry in what turned out to be demands for feeding. Perhaps overeager for time with the new baby, a sister-in-law immediately and instinctively reached to pick up the baby and said she would take care of it. The child's father and primary caregiver reported feeling displaced, feeling that she behaved as if making a reflexive assumption that even his own baby would want a woman first. Whatever she intended, gay fathers in this manner get a double dose of what every father encounters when venturing out without mother: a persisting cultural presumption of male ineptitude or uninvolvement with babies.

Strah's (2003) and Mallon's (2004) informants echoed our own experience of what in the race literature are referred to as *microaggressions* (Sue et al., 2007). One form such microaggressions take is that women may approach fathers and say things they most likely would not say to a mother. For example, a woman intruded into a private cubicle during our consultation with a banker to lecture us about the suffocation risks posed by the bank's promotional balloon, whose baby-distracting capacities were helping us to plan financially for her future education. There have also been significant smiles and raised eyebrows in restaurants and airports that seem to say, "Well, that was a valiant effort; not how *I* would do it, but *nice* try!" Gay fathers may at times feel such unchecked impulses of the maternal instinct as an undermining intrusion, even as we gratefully benefit from the examples and wisdom of the mothers and other women in our lives.

On the other hand, we also get a lot of smiles from women in public, and one sometimes senses a wistfulness, a wish that their husbands were as involved in caregiving as we are. Straight men might be forgiven for opposing adoption by gay dads, because the assumption of all caregiving roles by gay fathers exposes the feigned helplessness of heterosexual fathers to their wives. Gay fathers in Mallon's (2004) study elaborated on this dynamic and on their social relationships with heterosexual parents. These informants reported a common experience of feeling more of a bond with the straight moms than with the dads, primarily on account of a shared role as a more primary caregiver or parent. However, as much as commonalities with heterosexual parents may lead to enhanced social ties, these, of course, have their limits. Even the most supportive heterosexual allies may fail to grasp fully the extent of their heterosexual privilege. The current sex-and-gender system provides a built-in structure for heterosexual parents to share crucial information about the quality of neighborhood schools, tips for toilet training, and a great deal of parenting wisdom. These are highly gendered, mother-dominated networks that exclude fathers, who must work harder to tap into such support lifelines.

Parenting Arrangements

Further research might examine the diversity of gay male parenting arrangements. Some arrange family life according to traditional forms of a primary breadwinner and a stay-at-home primary caregiver. Others remain committed to some form of dual careers with an assortment of child-care arrangements. Couples who choose the latter course may do so against considerable pressure from both gay and straight sources who may assume the former. It was not an uncommon experience for us to hear from acquaintances—but usually gay ones—the assumption-laden question "So, which one of you is going to stay at home?" At such times, there has seemed to be on the part of some gay peers an overidentification with a traditional model of the nuclear family, and we sometimes even feel a kind of urgency to "get this right" for the gay community at large.

It was not without some trepidation that we each decided to continue working, although not completely full-time. Savage (2000, 2005), for example, frequently alludes to his partner as "the stay-at-home parent" in a locution that seems to presume that there should be one—that this arrangement is optimal for children and families. He is quick to clarify that his son's preschool is *pre-school*, not *day care*, as if anticipating criticism that his parenting choices are irresponsible. The current cohort of gay fathers thus establishes our sense of identity as fathers in a social context inevitably dominated by the master script of traditional heterosexual parenthood.

Changes in Relationships within the Gay Male Social Context

Shortly after we brought Grace home, a gay couple with whom we are very close, who were the hub of a wide circle of gay friends, generously hosted an elaborate baby shower. We were the first in the group to become parents, and for most of those in attendance—ourselves included—this was their first gay-father baby shower. Complete with silly shower games, it was a memorable spectacle to see a circle of men sniffing diaper after diaper to guess which candy bar had been melted in the microwave. Already overwhelmed by the joy of Grace, we experienced this gathering and generous outpouring of gifts and encouragement as profoundly supportive. And then a funny thing happened. As guests began to leave, our host passed each guest his party favor: a brown manila envelope with an old issue of a soft-core porn magazine! Our good friends were packing up 17 years worth of living to move across country, and this was one way to clean their basement. So, they were ending what was in many ways a very traditional baby shower with a campy gay twist.

Upon later reflection, this rather unexpected and vivid reminder of a shared attraction took on a certain kind of logic. Over time we came to sense and comprehend more deeply in the gay community at large a highly understandable ambivalence about children—perhaps an anxiety that a hard-won sense of community, defined in solidarity against an often misunderstanding and hostile straight world, might feel threatened or impinged on by the reproductive priorities of that straight world.

An ambivalence within the gay community toward parenting is even reflected in its social services system. Chicago's principal social service agency for the gay and lesbian community has a long history of programming for youth and coming out, for managing human immunodeficiency virus (HIV), for antigay violence, for mental health counseling, and for needs of the aging, yet only now is the agency identifying the needs for programming services for gay parents. In part because of the relative rarity of gay male parenthood, social life in the gay community is organized around *not* having children. In heterosexual social circles, many gatherings, such as summer barbecues or outings to the beach, may be assumed to be family events that include children. Within the gay community, children are typically not expected at such events, and they may even be experienced as an intrusion or a nuisance.

It is over the longer term, then, that such social realities, along with the demands of parenting, may threaten to loosen or alter previous ties to the gay community, which may in turn come to significantly impact one's earlier incarnation and sense of gay identity. As with heterosexual fathers, then, the rite of passage of parenthood for gay men may begin a process in which friendship relationships may undergo significant transitions. While some social ties may recede in intensity due to role demands, important and enduring connections adapt to a new reality, and the search for role partners (Cohler & Galatzer-Levy, 2000) often leads to the development of new social ties.

Our experience of this tension within our own social context has its analog in the queer theory academic literature. In *The Trouble with Normal*, Warner (1999) stakes a position that seems to suggest that gay men who choose to become fathers are ipso facto assimilationists who have been coopted into a heterocentric system and who thus have developed a false consciousness and betrayed the queer community and movement. Warner's critique includes a concept of "the good gays"—those who are willing to conform their intimate lives to the monogamous, heterosexual marriage model. It is these gays that heterosexuals may be willing to welcome into mainstream society through an institution like gay marriage or civil unions. Warner rightly fears that this might serve to further marginalize those who fall outside of marriage, and becoming a father certainly validated some of Warner's fears for me. As we walked down the street, with Grace in her baby pack, during a popular street festival in Chicago's gay neighborhood, an acquaintance who ran into us said, "Wow, you guys are like the poster boys for a gay relationship." His comment seemed to reflect the dynamic Warner warns about, and remarks like this make me uneasy in that our status and identity as parents can at such times seem to distance us from other gay men. We do not want to play the sociopolitical role of the good gays or be used by heterosexuals as an evidentiary counterpoint to a condemned "other" kind of gay man. But we do want to be parents.

Warner's critiques of the hypocrisies and inequities contained within the current legal and social organization of intimate ties are a valuable contribution to the ongoing debate on issues of gay marriage and the political priorities of gay men and lesbians (see also McRuer, 1997, 2006). These critiques rightly question the fundamental assumptions of the current social, legal, and bureaucratic organization of sexuality and family and of the governmental privileging of resource allocation based on particular relationship and ontological statuses. They find significant resonance in me as a gay man who continues to endure the effects of second-class citizenship. Yet, Warner's vision seems limited when it comes to parenthood. He is highly critical of work like Bawer's (1993) A Place at the Table for being too assimilationist, but he makes little room at his own table for gay fathers and their children. For adherents to this brand of orthodoxy in the queer community, a crowning achievement and an ongoing ideal of the gay liberation movement was sexual liberation and freedom unfettered by any legal or social strictures or pressures, while becoming mainstream or assimilated was a cardinal sin. That some gay men may also wish to realize the joys of vital nonsexual desires that may impact their sexual autonomy and relationships, such as the sublime pleasures of parenting, seems a threat to the fight against ongoing oppression, and so may be dismissed, devalued, or ignored.

While I am not alone in feeling that becoming a parent has been my most radical action as a gay man, in that it challenges our sex and gender system in its heterocentric reproductive core, there is no doubt that becoming a parent also does have a conservative influence. For example, parent couples in previously nonmonogamous relationships may find that the presence of children changes or limits that arrangement. Further, as a father, I feel the protective instincts to provide for my daughter in every way possible, and so it is a powerful impulse to agitate for the tangible here-and-now benefits that legal marriage would confer on our family and on Grace, however flawed that institution is. Though the odds are long, legal marriage seems a more likely and attainable goal in our lifetime than does the wholesale reorganization of our social structure implied by Warner's admirable, yet utopian, vision. In dividing my loyalty to my family with my loyalty to the wider gay community, the dilemma I experience exemplifies a conflict I regularly feel in my dual identities as gay man and parent. I am certain this will remain a tension lived rather than resolved.

It is interesting to note that in his role as a sex-advice columnist, Savage's rhetoric relies on a kind of "in your face" shock value and taboo-busting candor in all matters, both sexual and otherwise. While certainly this appears to have been his writing voice prior to parenthood, it seems apt that its continuation might demonstrate a kind of "street cred" within the gay community that he has not allowed parenthood to tame or domesticate his sexual persona. If nothing else, his ongoing public narrative exemplifies the dual identity conflicts faced by gay fathers. At times he seems to reassure the straight world of his parenting credentials, in a parallel way to the research literature, while at other times he more strongly emphasizes aspects of his sexual identity. In presenting counternarratives in dialogue with the master narratives of both parenthood and of gay male sexual identity, he ultimately refuses to adhere fully to the orthodoxies of either. But through engagement and dialogue with each, he seeks instead to articulate and so find his own truth and voice. Such is the prototypically postmodern task of all gay fathers in the contemporary environment. Alarmists on the right threaten to ban gay marriage and the legal right to parent, while agitators on the left seem to declare gay marriage or parenthood as unworthy of a self-respecting gay identity. Gay fathers are caught in the middle of these polarities as they strive to narrate and navigate their own way.

Beyond "Playing Defense" in Future Research on Gay Fathers

Much can be gained by progressing beyond the previous century's overly dichotomized gender roles and its romanticizing of the nuclear family. Just as the feminist movement created major shifts in (heterosexual) marriage and family roles, in the workplace, and in expanding career and personal possibilities in individual lives, so also can same-sex parenting. When marriage and family rights are ultimately more secured, there may be a greater willingness to move beyond the defensive position in research and writing, beyond trying to prove reassuringly through outcome research that the world will be safe with gay parents. A likely outcome is that there may come to be a greater emphasis for all families on parenting *processes and practices* not reified by gender or overly gendered roles.

It is hoped that one will not have to wait for the current sociopolitical controversies to settle to reorient research on children of gay and lesbian parents by keeping a focus on these children and families themselves, outside of judicial and political demands. This chapter has focused on the ways in which gay fathers negotiate the transition to parenthood while integrating multiple aspects of private self and social identity. The emphasis has been on the manner in which this dialogue is taken up against the powerful forces of the wider society's master narrative of normative parenting, together with gay culture's own expectations for normative gay male identity, relationships, and life course. Researchers and social service providers interested in understanding and assisting gay fathers and their families would do well to further develop our understanding of these identity processes. As further research is performed, narrative methods will offer an essential contribution by providing inductive data and testimony not filtered by the preconceived theories or hypotheses brought to bear by any sides on the controversial debates about the family lives of gay men and lesbians.

There are many avenues for research exploration. For example, a developmentalist interested in scaffolding (Vygotsky, 1978) might examine how children of gay men and lesbians come to an understanding over time of their family's differences and how they develop skills in stigma management. A friend who is a heterosexual mother has a daughter by a man who, in their child's first year, comes out as a gay man. Playing with a peer at the age of 3, she mentions to her friend that her dad is gay. "What does gay mean?" the friend asks. "Gay means that he has a rainbow bumper sticker on his car." A year later, in response to a similar question, she says, "Gay means that if he gets married they will both wear tuxedoes." As their daughter grows older, her parents continue to explain to her within her current developmental frame of reference, language, and understanding what it means that her father is gay. As a young teenager, she now divides her time between living with her father and his partner and with her mother, her mother's new husband, and her half-sister, and she has grown to understand and love her unique family very much.

While there are 2000 census data estimating that 163,879 households were headed by gay or lesbian parents, that number is estimated to be both low and outdated (Dingfelder, 2005; Smith & Gates, 2001). A starting point might be the undertaking of a rigorous descriptive national survey. Collecting enough data to associate local and regional legal, public policy, and cultural factors with the choice to parent and family compositions would be ideal. Besides economic and legal factors, what other variables contribute to the choice of the pathway to parenthood? Beyond choice of pathway, legal and economic obstacles also seem likely to determine such matters as family size or preferred caregiving arrangements. Moving forward, acquisition of national data on these matters would facilitate comparison with data from those nations with public policy and cultural norms and attitudes more affirmative of gay and lesbian parenting.

Further research should investigate gay fatherhood with a sensitivity to diversity of family forms. It might explore in more systemic detail the role of money as a determinant of the choice of method of parenting—domestic or international adoption, surrogacy, kinship adoption, or formation of shared parenting with a woman. Those with the fewest financial resources are perhaps the more likely to seek the latter two forms. Surrogacy will almost certainly remain the choice of the very affluent, while adoption is likely to displace parenthood from previous heterosexual unions as the most common family form for gay fathers. Do same-sex fathers tend to have more egalitarian parenting roles or do they mimic the (formerly) traditional heterosexual model of primary breadwinner and stay-at-home parent? What factors may influence variations in such choices of family arrangements? In short, what is needed is research that *describes* the experience of gay parenting.

In families created through donor insemination and surrogacy, what impact does the primary biological tie have over time on each parent's sense of parental credibility and on the quality of the child's relationship with each parent? Does the presence or absence of second-parent legal adoption change this dynamic or act as a protective factor in the relationship with the nonbiological parent? What level of curiosity will the children of donor eggs have concerning the identity of the biological and/or surrogate mothers? What issues of special concern apply to gay men who adopt as a single parent?

Psychoanalytic explorations may find a fertile ground for study in our newer family forms. Is there a common pattern of psychodynamic configurations that emerge in families with same-sex parents? What are the effects—on parents and on children—of having same-sex versus opposite-sex children? Does a child tend to form a more intense primary attachment in the early preoedipal years, and does this tend to depend upon the primary caregiver or on personality or other factors? Do these dynamics shift at all during what has historically been called the oedipal phase?

Psychoanalytic formulations themselves may be strengthened by a close consideration of the psychodynamics within gay families. One anticipates that some writers might take a simple accommodationist approach, as Isay (1989) did in reformulating the oedipal theory for gay men. He suggested that the dynamics were essentially the same but that mother and father simply changed positions within the triangular drama, as if the gendered nature of primary caregiving and bonding and work roles had a minimal impact. Ideally, theories will instead evolve that account for a multiplicity of factors, that do not over-value the creation of a reified, overarching deductive theory at the expense of lived experience and inductive data. It will further be interesting for observers to note what the effect may be on such matters of identity formation and sep-aration-individuation of children of the same and opposite genders as parents across developmental periods. Some evidence from lesbian parents (Patterson, 2005) suggests that one likely outcome may be greater fluidity and openness with respect to gender roles.

While heterosexual families may initially experience some anxiety about threats to their status quo, they may ultimately benefit from these new fam-ily forms. One important way is that gay fathers may reclaim some aspects of mothering (i.e., nurturing) as a possibility for all dads. In settings where they are exposed to gay fathers, straight fathers might then actually use these fathers as role models, might feel a greater sense of permission to adopt more nurturing aspects of the parent role. It seems likely that an important influ-ence of gay parents might in such ways reinforce and accelerate the shift in some aspects of U.S. culture toward more egalitarian parenting and partner roles begun by the feminist movement decades ago.

Finally, gay men of future cohorts may one day come of age in an era in which gay fathers have been part of their frame of reference all along. Parenthood may be experienced as an option open to them regardless of their sexual orientation, easing one barrier in the coming-out process. That gay par-ents were once seen as a feared anomaly may in that day seem as strange as it seems today that her contemporaries would begrudge Virginia Woolf her humble desire for a room of her own.

Acknowledgment

For their very thoughtful comments on previous drafts of this chapter, I am grateful to this volume's editors and to Drew McLeod, Jon Barrett, and Grayson Holmbeck.

REFERENCES

Ball, F. (1984). *Understanding and satisfaction in marital problem solving: A hermeneutic inquiry.* Unpublished doctoral dissertation, University of California, Berkeley.

Bawer, B. (1993). *A place at the table: The gay individual in American society*. New York: Simon & Schuster.

Bozett, F. (1987). Gay fathers. In F. W. Bozett (Ed.), *Gay and lesbian parents* (pp. 3–22). New York: Praeger.

Cohler, B. J., & Galatzer-Levy, R. M. (2000). *The course of gay and lesbian lives: Social and psychoanalytic perspectives*. Chicago: University of Chicago Press.

Cowan, C. P., & Cowan, P. A. (1987). Men's involvement in parenthood: Identifying the antecedents and understanding the barriers. In P. W. Berman & F. A. Pedersen (Eds.), *Men's transitions to parenthood: Longitudinal studies of early family experiences* (pp. 145–174). Hillsdale, NJ: Erlbaum.

Dingfelder, S. (2005, December). The kids are all right. *Monitor on Psychology, 11,* 66.

Feldman, S. (1987). Predicting strain in mothers and fathers of 6-month-old infants: A short term longitudinal study. In P. W. Berman & F. A. Pedersen (Eds.), *Men's transitions to parenthood: Longitudinal studies of early family experiences* (pp. 13–36). Hillsdale, NJ: Erlbaum.

Human Rights Campaign Fund (2007). Adoption laws: State by state. Retrieved January 8, 2007, from http://www.hrc.org

Isay, R. (1989). *Being homosexual: Gay men and their development*. New York: Farrar, Straus & Giroux.

Johnson, S. M., & O'Connor, E. (2002). *The gay baby boom: The psychology of gay parenthood*. New York: New York University Press.

Mallon, G. P. (2004). *Gay men choosing parenthood*. New York: Columbia University Press.

McPherson, D. (1993). *Gay parenting couples: Parenting arrangements, arrangement satisfaction and relationship satisfaction*. Unpublished doctoral dissertation, Pacific Graduate School of Psychology, Palo Alto, CA.

McRuer, R. (1997). *The queer renaissance: Contemporary American literature and the reinvention of lesbian and gay identities*. New York: New York University Press.

McRuer, R. (2006). *Crip theory: Cultural signs of queerness and disability*. New York: New York University Press.

Patterson, C. J. (2005). Lesbian and gay parents and their children: Summary of research findings. American Psychological Association, *Lesbian and gay parenting* (pp. 5–22). Retrieved May 14, 2008, from http://www.apa.org/pi/lgbc/publications/lgparenting.pdf

Savage, D. (2000). *The kid: What happened after my boyfriend and I decided to go get pregnant*. New York: Penguin Putnam.

Savage, D. (2005). *The commitment: Love, sex, marriage and my family*. New York: Penguin.

Smith, D., & Gates, G. (2001). *Gay and lesbian families in the United States: Same-sex unmarried partner households, a preliminary analysis of 2000 United States census data—A human rights campaign report*. Retrieved January 8, 2007, from http://www.hrc.org

Strah, D. (2003). *Gay dads*. New York: Penguin Putnam.

Sue, D. W., Capodilupo, C., Torino, G., Bucceri, J., Holder, A., Nadal, K., et al. (2007). Racial microaggressions in everyday life: Implications for clinical practice. *American Psychologist, 62*(4), 271–286.

Vygotsky, L. S. (1978). *Mind in society: The development of higher psychological processes.* Cambridge, MA: Harvard University Press.

Warner, M. (1999). *The trouble with normal: Sex, politics, and the ethics of queer life.* Cambridge, MA: Harvard University Press.

Woolf, V. (1929). *A room of one's own.* New York: Harcourt, Brace.

15

Midlife Lesbian Lifeworlds

Narrative Theory and Sexual Identity

Mary M. Read

To (re)create lesbian presence, it is necessary to reclaim lesbian existence and identity by rewriting what has been erased.

—Imbra (1998, p. 42)

The goal of this chapter is to use narrative identity theory to describe and facilitate an understanding of issues regarding the formation of a positive lesbian identity among a particular cohort of women: midlife North American lesbian women who were born between approximately 1940 and 1965. The life experiences and recollections of North American lesbians of the baby boom cohort (Stewart, 1994) reflect the integration of multiple aspects of the self, continually emerging and re-forming across diverse settings. My aim here is to display the narrative identity processes midlife lesbians, who experience at least three forms of diminished privilege in North American society (being women, older, and of stigmatized sexual orientation), have used to create lives of meaning and fulfillment. These issues are explored through the lens of a conceptual model (Read, 2004) created by analyzing narrative data gathered from life story portions that were available in existing literature.

Narrative Identity

Narrative identity theory posits that we "story" ourselves into a sense of self and identity and that we are innately structured to do so (Polkinghorne, 1996). Identity narratives serve to communicate a coherent, stable sense of self (McAdams, 1996) while recognizing multiple layers of self and identities. Life stories represent not only the expression of narrative identity but also its content (Lieblich, Tuval-Mashiach, & Zilber, 1998). Like a text, lived experience has no fixed, intrinsic meaning, only that which unfolds through interpretation. Events become meaningful episodes though narrative emplotment, relating them to the developing story. This process imbues the experience of time with meaning (Ricoeur, 1983). The complexity of identity as it develops requires conceptual models that can reflect shifting tides of self-response. Since recollections of identity issues expressed in life story form involve the flow of time, and since narrative is a form that specifically deals with temporality, narrative identity represents an integrative option for understanding the flow of the developing sense of self over the life course. This view provides the launching point for my exploration of identity issues among midlife lesbians.

Narrative Data

The central role of self-narration in identity formation may be seen through the lenses of multiple life stories, which serve as *field texts* (Clandinin & Connelly, 2000). For this chapter, those field texts consisted of life story portions drawn from different sources and representing a variety of identity aspects of older lesbians' lives. The literature I drew from in order to build my conceptual model is located primarily in psychotherapy-related fields, including psychology, counseling, women's studies, sociology, gerontology, social work, lesbian studies, and philosophy. Studies that have included the voices of lesbians over age 40, 50, or 60 have provided rich narrative details about how the women interviewed have come to see their lives as lesbians. To gain a rich narrative perspective, I chose to examine life story portions gathered by previous researchers (see Table 15-1) from approximately 524 self-identified midlife lesbians interviewed for various projects from the late 1980s through 2004. These sources fall into five categories: *(1)* topical books about lesbian lives and issues, providing the author's perspective and retaining midlife lesbians' worldview through brief quotations in the text; *(2)* autobiographies of self-identified lesbians; *(3)* collections of brief self-reflections made by midlife lesbians about their

TABLE 15-1 Sources of Narrative Data on Midlife Lesbians

Source Category	Author(s), Year	N Participants over Age 40
1. Topical books with life-story excerpts		
	Johnson, 1991	14
	Kehoe, 1988	100
	Kennedy & Davis, 1993	45
2. Autobiographies		
	Berzon, 2002	1
	Faderman, 2003	1
	Nestle, 1987	1
3. Brief life-story collections		
	Adelman, 1986	22
	Gershick, 1998	9
4. Issue-related collections		
	Abbott & Farmer, 1995	46
	Cassingham & O'Neil, 1993	28
	Curb & Manahan, 1985	50
	Holmes, 1988	23
	Penelope, 1994	34
	Penelope & Wolfe, 1989	46
	Sang, Warshow & Smith, 1991	41
5. Unpublished doctoral dissertations		
	Anderson, 2001	15
	Bennett, 1992	4
	Bourne, 1990	6
	Imbra, 1998	4
	Jackson, 1995	11
	Pedersen, 2000	19
	Read, 2004	1
	Silberkraus, 1995	3
Total participants		524

lives; (4) works focusing on a particular aspect of midlife lesbians' lives (such as having been married or in a religious order) related through life story portions; and (5) unpublished dissertations containing significant self-reflections from midlife North American lesbian lives about one or more dimensions of lesbian identity. The demographics and backgrounds of the contributors of narrative data included in these sources roughly correspond with the diversity of the North American populace in terms of race (with both being about 25% non-White), socioeconomic status, and religious practices.

I chose to analyze narrative data gathered from women who were (by self-report, author's description, or contextual clues) considered to be at midlife, that is, from 40 to 65 years of age (Sheehy, 2006) when interviewed. These

TABLE 15-2 Outline of Conceptual Model

I. Historical Context and Generational Cohort

II. Personal World: Where Difference Is Noticed and Integrated
    A. Life Cycle Effects on Identity
    B. Progression of Identity
    C. Self-Concept and Related Identity Plots About Lesbianism
        1. Lack of Lesbian Role Models: Denial – "I'm not lesbian"
        2. Dealing with Shame, Stigma and Self-Doubt: Non-acceptance – "I'm lesbian and therefore defective, sick or sinful"
        3. Coming Out to Oneself: Acceptance – "I'm lesbian, so what, I'm okay and will live with it"
        4. Honoring a "Tangential Perspective": Celebration – "Yes! I am lesbian, and proud, glad to be one"

III. Social World: Where Difference Is Processed and Expressed
    A. Sexuality
        1. Exploration and Development of Lesbian Sexuality
        2. Lesbian Sexuality Absent in Cultural View
    B. Family Life
        1. Family of Origin
        2. Family of Choice
    C. Work Life
        1. Closeted at Work
        2. Out at Work

IV. Political World: Where Difference Is Enacted and Celebrated
    A. Building Lesbian Community
        1. Enjoyment of "Like" Others
        2. Alliances Across Differences
        3. Reducing Heterosexism and Homophobia
    B. Celebrating Diversity
        1. Addressing Issues of Race and Class
        2. Making a Contribution

---

women belong primarily to the baby boom cohort, having been born between approximately 1940 and 1965. Information from these life story portions was examined iteratively to explore their varied *lifeworlds* (Husserl, 1925). This integrated information was examined for commonalities, which were then coordinated to form a conceptual kaleidoscope (see Table 15-2) through which to view the experiences and self-reflections of these women regarding their lesbian identity. The use of a collage of life story portions helps to represent a variety of pathways through which the common destination of positive identification as a lesbian was reached. From this narrative data emerged a complex, recursive, fluid process of dealing with multiple dimensions of identity, across common issues and in a variety of contexts, which is reflected in my conceptual model.

Women who did not experience their lesbian identities as possible or positive would have been unlikely to volunteer for the kind of interview research that produced the sources of life story data analyzed for this project. Voices representing the worldviews of women who did not develop a positive sense of lesbian identity are therefore missing from this data collage, except as represented by women who moved through a time of negativity and conflict in their identity journeys. However, it was not my goal to produce a monolithic model for understanding all midlife North American lesbian lives, suitable for inclusion in the mythical "big book of everything that ever happened to all gay women" (Van Gelder & Brandt, 1996, p. 13). Rather, this conceptual model is similar to a kaleidoscope, with many separate yet integrated elements contributing to a complex, shifting view of this cohort's lifeworlds and identity processes, gathered from the narrative collage of life story portions.

My position in this project was that of a feminist researcher and member of the cohort under study (Reinharz, 1994). Even though I did not collect the life story portions used as data from the participants myself (except for excerpts of my own story), the vehicle of narrative identity theory allowed me to experience an involved stance as I conducted my research. While my focus was particularly on the issues involved in having, at midlife, a positive sense of lesbian identity, I did not impose this constraint on the data. I sought, through reading and rereading life story portions, and by immersing myself in the lesbian studies literature for contextual richness, to hear what each woman had to say about her own lived experience and to reflect the commonalities and differences accurately.

All of the life story portions used for this study reflected first-person retrospective recollections of a personal historical past produced in a sociocultural historical context. The voices of these women storying their lives can help enrich our understanding and appreciation for lesbian identity at midlife. The fact that these 524 women were able to forge a positive lesbian identity (and willingly discuss that aspect of their lives with researchers) is remarkable, given the level of societal oppression and repression they faced, especially as they traversed adolescence with their fellow baby boomers. Browning, Reynolds, and Dworkin (1991) said that "we must be sensitive to the needs of the older lesbian[s] by recognizing the impact on their identity of coming out in an era when lesbians were viewed as sick or sinful" (p. 183). Since the construction of personal identity is always interdependent with the historical context within which the life being storied is lived (Cohler & Hammack, 2006), examining the cultural forces active as this cohort evolved is important. Fortunately, more members of the baby boom generation of lesbians (currently at midlife) are "out" than ever before (Adelman, 2000), giving rise to greater access for lesbian scholarship.

Generational Cohort

As with all narratives, the ever-changing historical context impacted both the lives as lived and the stories produced by the women whose narrative data fueled my research. Barker (2004) comments on the pivotal role that one's generational cohort plays in the developmental process. The historical period in which an individual grows and develops has a shaping effect on his or her identity processes (D'Augelli & Patterson, 1995), influencing access to and membership in cultural subgroups (such as lesbian and gay communities) in the future. Being born during and after World War II, the baby boom generation entered a society that had suffered a massive loss of innocence. Homophobia was firmly entrenched in the social milieu that first welcomed the new cohort, evidenced by a presidential ban in 1950 on the employment of homosexuals in government (Williams & Retter, 2003) and a media proscription from the 1930s to the late 1960s against images portraying any "sexual perversion" (including, by definition, homosexuality) enforced by the Motion Picture Production Code (Nardi, 1997). Unfortunately, when portrayals of lesbians and gays reentered the media, their characterizations had become "lonely, predatory, and pathological" (p. 428). However, in the late 1940s and 1950s, the Kinsey studies (Kinsey, Pomeroy, & Martin, 1948; Kinsey, Pomeroy, Martin, & Gebhard, 1953) greatly expanded dominant cultural views of sexuality, including an increased perception of same-sex attraction.

Tremendous social change was evident in the 1960s and 1970s as the baby boomers came of age. The civil rights movement was influential in helping American minority groups believe they could achieve more equality, a legacy that continues to positively affect lesbian lives. The shrinkage of the globe that worldwide war efforts had touched off was continued through both technological advances (including instant global communications) and greater exposure to Eastern philosophies and cultures. Changes in postwar North American social roles—encouraged in part by the Women's Liberation movement (Sheehy, 2006)—recursively affected the identity processes of this unique generation. Through activism by pioneering gays and lesbians, the psychological community removed homosexuality from its published list of mental disorders in 1973 (Berzon, 2002), a move that continues to have positive cultural ramifications for lesbians.

Lesbian Identity

Although historical references to women loving women extend in Western culture back to Sappho on the Isle of Lesbos (circa 580 B.C.E.), the concept of lesbianism is argued to be a fairly recent development (Faderman, 1991). In North America, Western Eurocentric ideas about sexuality condition and constrain the definitions of lesbianism through which lesbian identity is viewed (Brown, 1995). With the influence of postmodernism and especially feminism, as the baby boom cohort of lesbians approached midlife, the definitions of lesbianism moved beyond the pathologized, male-dominated, phallocentric, heterosexist, patriarchal models to more inclusive, multilayered conceptions of *women-identified women* (Brown, 1995). Brown's working definition of lesbian identity is "primarily a self-ascribed definition held by a woman over time and across situations as having primary sexual, affectional, and relational ties to other women" (p. 4). Brown makes it clear that this inner perception of being lesbian may not be congruent with outer behavior, and that both (the inner and outer) may fluctuate from the background to the foreground of the woman's life over time.

Speaking from my own experience, although I had known for many years that I loved women deeply (and had already been viciously persecuted for being "queer" during my adolescence), I did not know I was lesbian until I was 24. I fell in love with a woman at college and kissed her. I remember the exact date because we later chose it as our anniversary, since lesbian couples did not have the usual markers of engagements and weddings available to them in 1978 in the United States. The first time we made love—a conscious act, not reframable as simply the affection of friendship between women—I realized that I had translated "being sexual" into the realm of two women's bodies and felt I had come *home* to myself. In my interior world, I could finally know I was lesbian, even though it would take many more years for this identification to become something I shared comfortably. Now, at midlife, I embrace my lesbian identity with both joy and pride. The intention to ease that journey for others was a major motivation for this research.

Lifeworlds

Since *lesbian* is not a unidimensional identity descriptor, conceptualizing narratives of lesbian identity needed to embrace flexibility and fluidity across the life span. Therefore, to explore the identity processes of this cohort of midlife women and what it means to them to self-identify as lesbian, I use the construct of lifeworld developed by Husserl (1925) in his discussion of the phenomenology of psychology. As Husserl argues, entering the perspective of another is never completely possible. Yet, sharing one's perspective of what life feels like in the experiencing can offer an authentic view of one's lifeworld, by which mutual understanding and empathy are increased (Bugental, 1965). Habermas (1981) later used the term *lifeworld* to indicate shared common understandings developed through contacts taking place over time within a variety of social groupings (e.g., families, communities). The lifeworld construct is particularly useful in speaking of identity because inherent in it is a sense of mutual participation and community action, the recursive coconstitution of a sense of who "we" are.

I created my own conceptualization of the overlapping lesbian lifeworlds sketched in the life story portions that were analyzed, aiming to reflect shared issues encountered by unique means. Within the model, the contextual nature of identity is highlighted by the recursive incorporation of the historical epoch that the baby boom cohort of lesbians experienced, interwoven with the imagery of lifeworlds (personal, social, and political) and a unifying theme of *feeling different*. The boundaries between the lifeworld domains are somewhat arbitrary, an organizational pattern imposed on complex data to facilitate the creation of a recognizable picture of midlife lesbian identity. The model focuses on reflecting the varied experiences of these women, portrayed in their own voices, leaving room for the variety and irregularity that the narrative voice preserves. A discussion of each section of the model follows, including supporting examples drawn from the narrative data categorized in that section.

Personal World: Where Difference Is Noticed and Integrated

In this model, the personal world is first viewed through a *life cycle* lens, showing how the progression of the life cycle influences the formation of lesbian identity, visible retrospectively from midlife through narrative data. Pedersen (2000) and Bennett (1992) both explored a life cycle framework to describe lesbian lives, drawing from (and critiquing) the work of Erik Erikson (e.g., 1959), whose views of women's identity are flawed in the fashion of the 1950s—oppression, marginalization, and androcentrism are ignored as influences that might account for the developmental patterns observed in women's lives. Generically, the expected life course that women in the baby boom cohort faced included the necessity for an intimate partner, especially as the time to leave the family of origin approached.

Another important aspect of the life cycle is finding appropriate role models to assist in the development of the self-concept. The lack of lesbian role models left many baby boom lesbians unaware of their identities as they developed, which led to a feeling of isolation, as evidenced by one of Silberkraus' (1995) contributors:

> I always knew I had a special place for women. But I didn't know what it was.... I had a special feeling. I wouldn't even know if it *was* special, maybe a different feeling for women.... I couldn't put a word to it. I felt really alone. (p. 220)

In the second aspect of the personal world, a *progression of identity* represented in the narrative data is presented, with the caveat that it is not universally experienced and does not imply linearity. For example, Anderson (2001) refers to this theme as "a growing awareness" (p. 105), noting that while most of the women she interviewed did not have a name for what they were experiencing as "difference," they all described a strong pull in the direction of being attracted to other women. An inner realization of same-sex attraction, sometimes preceding actual sexual contact with other women, most often initiated the identity-questioning process (Silberkraus, 1995). An alternate pattern of being dissatisfied with heterosexual attraction or activity was cited as a precipitating factor in exploring a lesbian identity for some women in the narrative data. This pattern might or might not include a sense of gender incongruence, as some women stayed in their "tomboy" roles, developing more masculinized or "butch" personae (Bourne, 1990).

Sometimes the "knowing" of difference is seen, upon reflection from a midlife standpoint, to have always been present and felt rather definitely. Anderson (2001) gathered statements from her interviewees to this effect: "I was born this way," "I knew from day one," "I knew it as soon as the hormones kicked in—I was about 8 years old" (p. 106). At times, the realization of difference came from family members, not from the lesbian herself. Imbra (1998) collected this quote from an interview with a Chicana over 50 years old:

> My grandmother would...look at me and tell me that I was different and that I was special, and outside of her husband, men weren't worth very much. It was very interesting because she was widowed at the age of 46, and she didn't die until she was 94, but she never remarried. (p. 65)

Conflict with culturally approved religious practices also set in motion the questioning that began a progression of identity for some lesbians in this cohort. Speaking of her Catholic upbringing, one of Bourne's (1990) participants wondered—after making love to a woman for the first time—"What do I do? What does this mean? Does this mean I'm a lesbian now? Does this mean I'm weird?" (p. 142), struggling to reconcile her religious beliefs with her personal experience.

Some women do not seem to go through a period of feeling generally attracted to other women (or girls, while they are still girls themselves). However, these same women may, in a specific instance or with a particular partner, notice the attraction and take action. A wonderful statement about the possibilities for lesbian identity and experience comes from Suzanne Judith, interviewed by Zsa Zsa Gershick in 1987:

> So, in terms of being born that way, what I really think now is that some women are born that way for reasons that we don't know and that other women figure it out as they go. And that other women fall into it accidentally, and discover they love it. And that some women never do get around to it. Maybe most women. But I do think that it's a natural impulse....

> (Gershick, 1998, pp. 127–128)

The potential for lesbian identity without lesbian (sexual) activity was also expressed in other narrative data. One of Imbra's (1998) participants recalled her high school teacher and wondered if, despite living alone and remaining unmarried throughout her life, "Perhaps she was lesbian. I would say yes, because I don't believe that whether you're lesbian or not has anything to do with intimate genital knowledge of another woman" (p. 171).

In the third component of the personal world reflected in the data, the *self-concept* of midlife baby boom lesbians is explored in four domains: *(1)* the effects of not having lesbian role models available in the culture (particularly as this cohort was passing through adolescence and experimenting with social roles); *(2)* dealing with shame, stigma, and self-doubt; *(3)* the process of coming out to oneself; and *(4)* honoring a "tangential perspective" (see Bourne, 1990; Silberkraus, 1995). Each of these domains is associated with a narrative plotline (available from the sociocultural context; cf. Faderman, 1991) with which any woman attempting to identify as lesbian would have to deal at some point. Johnston (1973) describes the prescriptive force of such sociocultural plots, noting that identity is "what you say you are according to what they say you can be" (p. 58).

Through an iterative analysis process, four distinct plotlines arose from the life story data, as recalled from midlife: *(1)* denial ("I'm not lesbian"), *(2)* nonacceptance ("I'm lesbian, and therefore defective, sick, or sinful"), *(3)* acceptance ("I'm lesbian, so what, I'm okay and will live with it"), and *(4)* celebration ("Yes! I am lesbian and proud, glad to be one"). Each plot was found in the narrative data to describe and/or affect some woman's life accurately, at least for a particular time in her life. These self-concept domains are not freestanding but interdependent and contextualized, interacting recursively with the historical milieu and the other "worlds" in which the midlife lesbian lives and moves.

In the decades when baby boom lesbians were being imprinted by their cultural surroundings, several plotlines were available for women. The use of these plots here does not imply that they were the only ones available at the time or that there is always a progression from one plot to another during the life course. Some early stage theorists (e.g., Cass, 1979; Sophie, 1987) posited that a woman's pathway to lesbian identity consistently traveled developmentally through one plotline to the next in sequential order. However, few of the women whose life story portions were analyzed for this study identified such a clear, progressive sequence in their lives.

LACK OF LESBIAN ROLE MODELS: DENIAL. Bourne (1990, p. 144) described this first cultural plotline derived from the narrative data by stating that the events and/or feelings associated with being a lesbian may be experienced by the individual, and may even be acknowledged as having occurred while the personal, sexual components of those events/feelings are denied. One example of this denial involved limiting the type of sexual contact engaged in to avoid identifying inwardly as lesbian.

> I had a girlfriend through high school. When we would spend the night, we would make out but we never did anything below the navel because we thought that would make us lesbians. We would sit there kissing each other and say "We are not lesbians." (p. 151)

This plotline may have been associated by many lesbians in the baby boom cohort with a lack of lesbian role models. Browning et al. (1991) noted that during the time period in the United States when these women were developing their sense of sexuality, most young lesbians did not have adult lesbian role models to follow. Cultural visibility for lesbian lives might have helped ease their transition from the ubiquitous expectation of heterosexuality (heteronormativity) to a positive lesbian identity through modeling and/or mentoring. Many of the women's stories (in both the participant and author categories) used as data in this project include information reflecting this lack of cultural support and visibility. For example, one author from this cohort, Mary Hayden, wrote in *Sexualities* (1996):

> Like many lesbians who are now middle-aged and beyond, I had no experience dating with women, having become life partners with my first lover. For our generation there was no popular culture to aid us in our socialization as lesbians. In effect, we lacked an adolescence. (p. 8)

For women developing their self-concepts without undergoing an adolescent sexual discovery process (complete with culturally relevant lesbian "markers"), identifying as lesbian may have been denied almost as a technicality—"I love a woman but I'm not a lesbian." This form of denial may be seen less as an inward negation of feelings eventually identified as lesbian attraction for another woman than as a lack of accurate interior language, owing to both the lack of attractive cultural images of lesbian lives and the pervasive societal hostility attached to the term *lesbian*. Van Gelder and Brandt (1996) noted that many of their interviewees had passed through a time of such quasi-identification on the way to facing the next, larger step of affirming lesbian attraction, activity, or identity. Additionally, women's freedom to be emotionally close to and even physically affectionate with friends further blurred the boundaries between heterosexual and homosexual women's lives, adding to adolescent confusion (and potential denial) in the face of adopting a persecuted sexual identity.

DEALING WITH SHAME, STIGMA, AND SELF-DOUBT: NONACCEPTANCE. The second sociocultural plotline involves recognition of one's lesbianism while staying grounded in a heterosexist, homonegative, androcentric paradigm. Many voices from the literature reflecting older lesbians' voices include a reference to the confusion and loss engendered by the stigmatization of sexual relationships between women (e.g., Berzon, 2002). At times, these losses occurred in adolescence because other observers began to question the orientation of the developing young woman. Sometimes no sexual contact had yet transpired, but the power of the felt connection and the intense desire for the addition of a sexual component to the relationship made those losses resonant even many decades later. A poignant passage from Joan Nestle's (1987) autobiography illustrates this dynamic:

> I showed you the best way I could that it was your touch I
> sought...because I was a girl-woman it was a dangerous thing to
> touch me...your touch would have healed me. But we had been
> judged unclean, and you would not harm me with the power of what
> they called our sin. (p. 20)

One of Anderson's (2001) interviewees commented on the difficulty of acknowledging an attraction to other women, given the cultural myths and stereotypes about lesbians prevalent as she came of age.

> I think that when you hear about gay/lesbian people or homosexuality as a young kid, you are told that it is bad, wrong, evil, or sick.

I heard all of that, and I guess I believed it. I didn't want to, but there
was no one to tell me otherwise. (p. 129)

The plotline of nonacceptance can be seen as a natural reaction to feedback from the sociocultural environment that implies that lesbianism equates
with deviance. Pathologized, stigmatized, censured identities cannot be fully
embraced without some cost to self-esteem. Shame, secrecy, stress, and self-
censure are all linked to this plotline by life story portions dealing with nonacceptance of the self.

COMING OUT TO ONESELF: ACCEPTANCE. Acceptance is the third cultural plotline explored in the narrative data collage. Falling short of celebrating diversity,
this plot recognizes a neutral space, often hard won, where a woman can dare
to be herself at least *to* herself. She may not speak up loudly or often, but if
questioned, she is less likely to deny her lesbian orientation and may *come out.*
The issue of coming out is one that many midlife lesbians struggled with at
some point in their lives.

Due to the invisibility of lesbianism under the assumptions of heterosexism, Blumenfeld (1992) noted that this is a lifelong process, reenacted as each
out lesbian encounters new social situations. Coming out may also take place
at different times in various areas of life, as this quote from a contributor to
Curb and Manahan's (1985) collection on the lives of lesbian nuns demonstrates: "I identified as a political lesbian about three or four years before I
came out to my sexuality" (p. 64). The choice of whether to come out publicly is
a significant, even at times traumatic, issue. The National Lesbian Healthcare
Survey (Bradford, Ryan, & Rothblum, 1994) found a considerable level of suicidal thoughts and attempts associated with the contemplation of coming out,
both to oneself and to others.

To reach the point of self-acceptance, the difficulty of coming out to oneself
must be neutralized. Midlife can make this neutral acceptance more available
by contextualizing the brevity of life. One of Adelman's (1986) participants
noted, "The realization that my life was half over finally helped me accept my
lesbianism" (p. 94). For others, the developmental path to self-knowledge as a
lesbian was more gradual and varied by context. Robin Teresa Santos described
her process of coming out to herself in this way:

My coming out wasn't a single act of cathartic honesty; it happened
a bit at a time over a period of years. First, I had to be truthful with
myself, then I was able to come out to a few, select others, which did
not include...my parents, who I still feared would shame me....

> Coming out was scary, but being congruent with who I was, was
> such a joy.
>
> (Abbott & Farmer, 1995, pp. 38–39)

For some women, finding their experiences echoed in print eased their passage to lesbian identity. Other women found conversations with gay male friends or other lesbians enlightening, drawing on similarities of experience to begin to reach new conclusions, paving the way to enhanced self-acceptance.

HONORING A "TANGENTIAL PERSPECTIVE": CELEBRATION. This fourth cultural plotline represents a joy in being a "woman-loving-woman" that transcends mere acceptance and moves to active, open celebration. The fact that the cultural context "otherizes" lesbians is not accepted as the final word. Rather, strength and resilience (required to transform the negativity aimed at lesbians through heterosexism and homonegativism; Sears & Williams, 1997) are used to bolster the self-esteem and lesbian identification of women developing this *tangential perspective* (Bourne, 1990; Silberkraus, 1995). Bourne (1990) defines this perspective as

> [a]ffirming rather than denigrating one's culturally-incongruent
> characteristics ... or developing self-supportive beliefs and attitudes
> which are tangential to those espoused by the majority culture....
> Tangential perspective refers to the ability to question cultural
> norms and then to either accept, reject, or adapt them for personal
> use. (p. 127)

Bourne argues that a tangential perspective, which operates both inwardly (toward oneself) and outwardly (toward the world), "is achieved by creating an internal value system which evaluates the relevance of social norms to one's own life" (p. 127). The inward focus thus reinforces one's own self-perceptions and experiences as authentic rather than privileging contrary cultural views. Simply put, if a woman perceives her lesbian desires and actions as positive, then for her, they are. Similarly, the external focus critiques and challenges the societal view of lesbianism as negative, allowing only concepts that mirror one's internal perceptions (e.g., that living as a lesbian is constructive and growth-producing) to affect one's self-concept.

Those embracing a tangential perspective know that they do not represent society's norms. This sense of difference was significant for one of Bennett's (1992) contributors: "I liked being part of this underground sub-culture of deviance.... The root of the identity was in my otherness" (pp. 109–110). Another of Bennett's participants focused more on the positive sense of being lesbian versus the feeling of difference: "It's affirming of me as a woman to have women central in my life" (p. 107).

Yolanda Retter (1999), speaking of her own life experience, outlines another variation of the acceptance scenario—resistance:

> I argue that lesbian behavior has always existed and that women who consistently felt a primary affectional (sometimes sexual) inclination toward females, thought of themselves as "different" and marginalized.... I say this as a lifelong lesbian who when young felt "different" but who did not have a theoretical or political framework from which to analyze what I felt.... My unwillingness to give up my feelings gave rise to a resistant, incipient identity. (p. 365)

The personal world is an arena where many of the joys and struggles, pains and pleasures of being a lesbian are noticed for the first time, then integrated into personal identity through multiple recursions with the other lifeworld domains and the historical context.

Social World: Where Difference Is Processed and Expressed

The interconnectedness some women find as central for their identity processes (Gilligan, 1982) is a key element of the social world. Indeed, Bennett (1992) found that connection with others was "[t]he most significant component of identity development" (p. viii) for all the contributors in her study. Several realms of the social world, all emerging from a relational base, are examined by the themes associated with this category, including sexuality, family life, and work environments.

SEXUALITY. Dealing with (recognizing, celebrating) sexuality is an intimate part of the personal world, yet one that also takes place in a social context. For example, in Betty Berzon's (2002) autobiography, the integration of sexuality into identity plays a central role. She establishes at the outset that her triumphs included allowing her emerging self to experience desire, passion, and change, thus forging her identity, noting "the power that love and sex, experienced as one, can have on redefining identity" (p. 3). Questions about sexuality also represent an area where lesbian identity is often challenged by one's family or the larger culture, both of which may be hostile. One of Van Gelder and Brandt's (1996) interviewees reported that her mother asked how she knew she was gay if she'd never yet had sex with a woman. Her reply was to ask the reverse—whether her mom knew before engaging in sex with men that heterosexual activity was what *she* wanted for herself.

As stressed throughout this volume, there is a sociodevelopmen-
tal aspect to sexuality across the life span, reflected in individual's self-
stories. Women of the baby boom cohort related some gaps in terms of
their life experience and knowledge of sexual development as a lesbian,
attributing this partly to a lack of supportive models for women's sexual
identity in general, and lesbian identity in particular, as they grew up.
Barker (2004) notes that women from different generational cohorts vary
in the degree of comfort they feel discussing their sexuality—including
their sexual orientation—with others, even their health-care providers.
Midlife baby boom lesbians reported the effects of avoidance, erasure, and
editing regarding their own developing sexuality. Relative to developing
a social sense of sexual identity, Berzon (2002) describes a lack of direct
sexual content in her nascent thoughts of attraction toward other women,
combined with a subtle awareness of the transgressive nature of her not-
quite-sexual desire:

> My daydreams were not sexual per se, though I did think about hold-
> ing these women, and I knew that was not what I was supposed to be
> thinking about.... I was embarrassed by what was happening to me,
> hoping that no one could read my mind. (p. 12)

Nancy Manahan, reflecting on her own experience in a convent, wrote: "I
didn't know I was in love with her. I only knew that the chapel vibrated when
she walked in, and my stomach lurched when she knelt soundlessly behind
me. I longed for her touch" (Curb & Manahan, 1985, p. xxxvi).

A quote from one of Imbra's (1998) interviewees also reflects the developmental nature of identifying as a lesbian:

> When I was 26 I finally figured out that I really was attracted to
> women. I think with many of us it's like, "I'm very unique and we're
> the only two people in the world and this is really close friends stuff."
> I did not start out using the "l" word.... "L" was not used in any of
> the social interactions that my partner and I had at the time.... It
> probably took a year and a half to two years after I recognized that I
> was a lesbian to use the "l" word. (pp. 124–125)

This "not knowing" place regarding a sense of one's sexual self is echoed repeatedly across narratives of midlife lesbians. Speaking of her own as well as her
participants' development, Bourne (1990) observed: "Due to an absence within
the majority culture of visible alternatives to heterosexuality, almost all young
women begin the process of defining a personal sexual identity by assuming
they are heterosexual" (p. 133). One of Silberkraus' (1995) participants clearly

struggled with her identity in the absence of cultural markers for nonhetero/ sexualities, given the prurience of systemic homophobia:

> From the little that I read, and the psych [sic] books, it was a mental illness and I could get electroshock therapy...when I first identified my feelings I didn't think, "Gee, I'm a lesbian or gee I'm gay or gee I'm a homosexual." I thought, "oh, my God, I'm a pervert." 'Cause I didn't know what those feelings were about or that they were normal and other people had them. I had no basis [on which] to couch them or where to fit them. (p. 219)

The navigation of sexual identity cannot be dissociated from the social worlds of lesbians, regardless of how personal a process identity development might be. Because a lesbian identity is a socially stigmatized identity and was viewed very negatively during the life course of these women, sexual identity development is a socially salient process depicted in women's narratives.

FAMILY LIFE. Any study of identity must take into account the first social laboratory in which the exploration of self and other begins—the family unit. At the turn of the twenty-first century, the definition of family in North America has become considerably different from that of the 1940s and 1950s—when the majority of the baby boom generation entered the social world. The life stories of midlife lesbians examined in this chapter reveal that family is universally important for social development and a feeling of life satisfaction. They also reveal that, for many midlife lesbians, the conflicts presented by their identification as lesbian made ongoing contact with their families of origin impractical, if not impossible. At times, making the choice to follow one's own heart meant forsaking the plans one's family had mapped out based on heterosexist assumptions. For example, one of Bourne's (1990) interviewees had to choose between her family's view of spirituality and her own budding awareness at age 14 that she loved women:

> My grandmother brought me to the church so they could pray over me and get this demon out of me. This had to be a demon that had taken over my otherwise good nature, and they were going to try to save me from burning in hell for it. In the middle of all this...I got up and walked out. My grandmother never recovered from that. It hurt her real deep. It also meant that I was walking out on plans to follow in her footsteps and be a minister. (p. 130)

For many women in this cohort, embracing and celebrating their lesbian identity resulted in alienation from their families of origin.

A salient aspect of family life for many baby boom lesbians, particularly those whose original families proved less than accepting of their lesbian identity, is what Kath Weston (1991) calls a "family of choice." The importance (and often primacy) of this allegiance in a lesbian's life is attested to by many women's experience. This can be especially true for single lesbians (Pedersen, 2000), who may be more vulnerable to the effects of heterosexism without the buffering effect of a primary intimate attachment.

Decisions about child rearing also fall under the domain of family life in the social world. Until recently, the decision to live openly as a lesbian often meant giving up bearing and/or raising children (de Vries & Blando, 2004). Fortunately, the so-called gayby boom and concurrent advances in lesbian civil rights may mean that fewer women have to choose today between making a life with a lesbian partner and raising children.

WORK LIFE. Work life is a significant feature of the social landscape for most adults. The social milieu of the workplace therefore has a tremendous impact on the life satisfaction and self-image of those who share it. Whether or not a lesbian at midlife is comfortable being out at her place of employment is a significant social concern to be negotiated. Harry (1993) noted: "As a result of highly selective comings out to different audiences, the large majority of gays and lesbians are only partly out of the closet. In some settings they are self-disclosing while in others they are not" (p. 27). Even in the academy, where critical thinking is valued, coming out at work can be problematic. Cruikshank (1996) found that "most professors who are lesbian are still in the closet" (p. 161).

Jackson (1995) underscored the risks in identifying as lesbian at the workplace while noting as well the costs of passing for straight. "Lesbians who pass in order to make it to the top do so by paying a price.... In the end it's a tradeoff—job advancement or validation—an unfair decision" (p. 188). Jackson described several ways lesbians can weave their lesbian identity into their work life, including *censoring* and *passing*. One of Jackson's participants framed her lack of disclosure at work as a privacy issue, not related to shame or the risk of losing privilege: "[W]hy does someone not talk about who they are? In part, it's how you were raised and...how much you are invested in other people's views of you and what you think the appropriate thing is to do" (p. 195).

Arguably, the lack of out lesbian role models at work can make the process of self-identification more difficult. For example, one of Imbra's (1998) participants stated:

> The primary obstacle and barrier in those early years—when I'm just figuring it out—was being...surrounded by closeted dykes. They all

knew. I didn't know, so there was this code language going on that I
was not getting. (p. 125)

The same woman went on to say that "you can't be as effective (closeted) because
you can always be blackmailed, and that blackmail is self-blackmail...just like
self-homophobia" (p. 129).

In Jackson's (1995) study about the interaction of occupation and lesbian
identity, she found that workplaces could be places for positive expressions
of lesbian identity and that many lesbians long to be authentic in their workplace identities. The narratives of women throughout the literature suggest
that having one or more out role models at work provides encouragement and
support:

> One role model I do remember, sometime in the [19]70s, involves
> the first out person on this campus who I ever knew...she was
> wearing a pin on her lapel that had the woman sign (two women).
> It was the first visible symbol that she was a lesbian and in a lesbian
> relationship. I think having someone like her here—we all need to
> have those pioneers who step up and let us know it's ok.... If I have
> any model here of "being a lesbian" it would be her, and I think she
> has given so many of us courage. I think she has given voice to those
> of us who have struggled within the academy.
>
> (Imbra, 1998, p. 137)

Now, later in her own career, this woman makes sure to wear an identifying
symbol (such as a rainbow flag, the Greek letter lambda, or an inverted pink tri-
angle—used by the Nazis to identify homosexuals in concentration camps) on
campus during new student orientation week and during interviews for hiring
new personnel. Such identification may give a sense of safety to those who feel
alone or unsupported in a new environment and helps ensure that the topic of
being lesbian can arise openly (and hopefully, safely) in the workplace.

The social world, as a lifeworld domain, includes the arenas of sexual,
family, and work life—vital to the lived experience of identity for all persons.
The varied expressions of lesbian identity found in the narrative data flowing
from this central arena paint a unique, complex view of a social phenomenon
for this cohort of women.

Political World: Where Difference Is Enacted and Celebrated

The third lifeworld domain through which to understand the narratives of
midlife lesbians is the political world. Recursively interdependent with both of

the prior worlds (personal and social) and contextually dependent on a sense of history for the baby boom cohort, this identity dimension embraces the world of action. For the generation that energized the second wave of feminism (Brown, 1995), the phrase "the personal is political" illuminates the overlapping, interlocking nature of the domains in which the self is created and expressed, experienced in the form of identity. Many lesbians from the baby boom cohort have been politically active in multiple realms, addressing issues from civil rights to acquired immune deficiency syndrome (AIDS) activism, from global ecology to reproductive rights.

A political education and a sense of solidarity with women and other oppressed groups were two of the benefits of lesbian identification noted by one of Bennett's (1992) interviewees.

> One really positive thing about coming out...is I feel politically and spiritually, it really opened my eyes about other people and other things in the world.... I felt that I learned a lot about the world and about the structures of the world and political and spiritual repression...and I think it's stuff that I needed to know.... I identified as an oppressed person with other oppressed people. (p. 108)

Fundamental to the political lifeworld of baby boom lesbians was the explicit construction of a lesbian *community*. It was in community that the women could practice a lesbian identity in the service of social action and change.

BUILDING LESBIAN COMMUNITY. The term *lesbian community* is used in various ways, including referring "to a group of lesbians living in one geographical area, or...to a larger political sense of solidarity" (Darty & Potter, 1984, p. 305). Weston (1991) construes lesbian community as implied by "collective identities, organized urban space, and...significant relationships" (p. 124). As the baby boom lesbians came of age, the beginnings of lesbian community and culture were becoming more visible in America. Music festivals, bookstores, coffee shops, and a range of cultural gathering places for lesbians began to gain popularity (Van Gelder & Brandt, 1996). This activity, in turn, generated the capital and/or collaboration necessary to support women-oriented printing establishments, recording labels, catalog supply businesses, and the like.

Sharing common experiences also creates the feeling of community, whether those experiences are pleasant or not. A woman interviewed by Imbra (1998) stated, "I think being lesbian plays a very significant role in my life.... I'm an 'other' and because I'm an 'other' I understand the pain of otherness, and I understand the pain of not being included, or the pain of confusion" (p. 129). Another of Imbra's interviewees saw feminism, more than lesbianism, as central to the supportive community in which she functioned: "Some of the strongest women in the feminist community are lesbian. Perhaps that's coincidental. I would give feminism the credit that some people give to lesbianism alone" (p. 175).

One of the functions of any minority community is the sense of appreciation and safety that accompanies being with "People Like Us" (PLUs). In lesbian communities, the experience of being an oppressed minority can, for a time, be laid aside, at least ideally (Eliason, 1996). This can be a powerful experience, especially for a minority as invisible as lesbians (Deevey, 1990). So many women reported feeling that they were "the only one" that the realization of the possibility of fellowship, social events, and political action with other lesbians was simultaneously a shock and a relief (Weinstock, 2000). The power of community can also aid in the identification process, as one of Adelman's (1986) participants noted:

> It wasn't until I was 50, and still with Susan, that I first began to
> identify as a lesbian. I met these two lesbian women and they were
> my introduction to the women's community. They also helped me to
> self-identify. (p. 62)

Becoming a part of an active community, for many midlife lesbians, was associated with their own identification process. Exposure to similar others helped them to construct narratives imbued with social meaning.

In addition to experiencing PLUs in lesbian community, lesbian women reported reaching across a variety of differences to establish working alliances. These alliances might be personal, incorporating small-scale interactions, or more expansive, encompassing broader domains of social action. A White, middle-aged lesbian educational administrator put it this way:

> I think it has helped my relationship with [an African American
> male staff person] that I'm lesbian.... There are ways in which he
> and I are such strong allies on issues.... Being a lesbian can really
> serve as a bridge when you are trying to work with other people
> around other inequities or other issues of civil rights or social justice
> or inequality—because of the common factor of "otherness" and
> oppression, having shared oppression.
>
> (Imbra, 1998, p. 130)

Lesbians of this generation created political and personal alliances across forms of oppression to construct a sense of solidarity with other minorities in the culture.

CELEBRATING DIVERSITY. The goal of lesbian scholarship, and of all education at its best, is to foster the celebration—not mere tolerance—of diversity. This aspect of lesbian life was important to many of the midlife lesbians whose narratives were examined in this study. Two crucial elements of diversity—race and class—have historically been used to divide the less powerful from full participation in society. By reclaiming equality and working to redress social injustice, midlife lesbians are involved in the creation and maintenance of true social change.

Issues of race and class become especially salient when focusing on the positive embrace of diversity. Like other aspects of identity, the categories defined as racial are not essential and immutable (although certain aspects of racial categories may be genetically identifiable), yet they are often used as "justifiable" grounds for oppression (Fukuyama & Ferguson, 2000). For some narratives examined in this study, racial issues outweighed sexual orientation in terms of their impact on the quality of life and affected lesbian identification:

> No one walks around with a sign on them that says, "I'm gay." But
> there's a sign on me that says, "I'm black," and I can't come home,
> put on a dress, change my walk and nobody know it. What I have
> done with the blackness is that I have become me.
>
> (Adelman, 1986, p. 79)

The visibility of racial identity, in contrast to sexual orientation, increases the salience and significance of race for lesbians of color.

Penelope's (1994) work on lesbians and class offers several levels of critique important to an understanding of lesbian identity for midlife women. A quote from Christian McEwen appears in Penelope's introductory chapter: "I wanted to make sense of things, to tell the truth of what I knew. Talking about class was part of that: an attempt to face the tangles, to draw the pain and awkwardness into the open" (p. 32). McEwen viewed the opportunity to discuss her class background as a way of coming to know herself more fully as a midlife lesbian.

While the majority of the women whose voices are reflected in the narrative data analyzed in this chapter were both White and able-bodied, they remain vulnerable to losses of class and status not only through heterosexism but also through ageism. Rothblum, Mintz, Cowan, and Haller (1995) note that "for able-bodied, middle-class, white women...ageism may be the first recognized experience of oppression" (p. 62). Ageism minoritizes both men and women, but women's lesser earning power over their life span makes them even more vulnerable to the reduction of power and choice that accompanies the aging process in American society (Friend, 1990).

MAKING A CONTRIBUTION. For women experiencing the difference of les-bianism, an important part of integrating that difference can be using it to accomplish good in the world. A quote from one of Imbra's (1998) participants highlights this aspect of making a contribution to the larger social good:

> I work at the college level with students, and part of what they strug-gle with is their own identity. I think it gives me incredible empathy into their struggles.... So I interact with people of color, or people of different religions, who are seeking social justice, or are seeking equality, I understand that. It makes me a stronger advocate around issues of social justice...it makes me more empathic in dealing with people. It's who I am. (p. 129)

A participant in Bennett's (1992) study commented:

> We're obviously in the forefront of so many movements, political movements, who care so much about oppression—ending oppres-sion, work around racism and stuff.... I love the fact that, like I said before, we're important to all these movements for social change...leading the way, that we're committed, that we understand that all oppressions are linked together and that people have to work together. (p. 109)

Enacting and celebrating the difference that is lesbian identity can be a potent force for social justice, springing from the political lifeworld of women at midlife and beyond. The narratives of baby boom lesbians suggest that, for this cohort in particular, the political lifeworld represented a vital and insepara-ble piece of the personal narrative. The social change these women witnessed and the movements for social and political change with which they necessarily came into contact created the context for a narrative understanding of identity that was as much *political* as *personal*.

Summary

To explore the issues and challenges faced by women from the baby boom cohort in North America on their pathway toward a positive sense of narra-tive identity as a midlife lesbian, I reviewed portions of life story recollec-tions from 524 self-identified midlife North American lesbians gathered by previous researchers. Set against the historical context in which the baby boom generation witnessed tumultuous social change, the multiple identity dimensions of this cohort of lesbians were framed as lifeworlds, depicted by a collage-like, multilayered representation of the data. The overlapping, recursive nature of the personal, social, and political worlds as processing points in the ongoing development of narrative identity was demonstrated. The unifying construct of difference was explored through each lifeworld domain and viewed in light of the historical context of this unique cohort of women. A sense of the variety and unity of midlife lesbian identity was presented by viewing the narrative data collage through a kaleidoscopic lens that recognized the variability in women's narratives even as their common historical location created a common narrative to make meaning of the course of their lives.

REFERENCES

Abbott, D., & Farmer, E. (1995). *From wedded wife to lesbian life: Stories of transformation*. Freedom, CA: Crossing Press.

Adelman, M. (1986). *Long time passing: Lives of older lesbians*. Boston: Alyson.

Adelman, M. R. (Ed.). (2000). *Midlife lesbian relationships: Friends, lovers, children, and parents*. Binghamton, NY: Harrington Park Press.

Anderson, C. A. (2001). *The voices of older lesbians: An oral history*. Unpublished doctoral dissertation, University of Calgary, Canada.

Barker, J. C. (2004). Lesbian aging: An agenda for social research. In G. Herdt & B. de Vries (Eds.), *Gay and lesbian aging: Research and future directions* (pp. 29–72). New York: Springer.

Bennett, E. L. (1992). *The psychological and developmental process of maintaining a positive lesbian identity*. Unpublished doctoral dissertation, Boston University, Boston.

Berzon, B. (2002). *Surviving madness: A therapist's own story*. Madison: University of Wisconsin Press.

Blumenfeld, W. J. (Ed.). (1992). *Homophobia: How we all pay the price*. Boston: Beacon Press.

Bourne, K. (1990). *By the self defined: Creating a lesbian identity*. Unpublished doctoral dissertation, University of Southern California, Los Angeles.

Bradford, J., Ryan, C., & Rothblum, E. D. (1994). National Lesbian Health Care Survey: Implications for mental health care. *Journal of Consulting and Clinical Psychology, 62*(2), 228–242.

Brown, L. S. (1995). Lesbian identities: Concepts and issues. In A. R. D'Augelli & C. J. Patterson (Eds.), *Lesbian, gay, and bisexual identities over the lifespan* (pp. 3–23). New York: Oxford University Press.

Browning, C., Reynolds, A. L., & Dworkin, S. H. (1991). Affirmative psychotherapy for lesbian women. *Counseling Psychologist, 19*, 177–196.

Bugental, J. (1965). *The search for authenticity: An existential-analytic approach to psychotherapy*. New York: Holt, Rinehart, & Winston.

Cass, V. C. (1979). Homosexual identity formation: A theoretical model. *Journal of Homosexuality, 4*, 219–235.

Cassingham, B. J., & O'Neil, S. M. (1993). *And then I met this woman: Previously married women's journeys into lesbian relationships*. Racine, WI: Mother Courage Press.

Clandinin, D. J., & Connelly, F. M. (2000). *Narrative inquiry: Experience and story in qualitative research.* San Francisco: Jossey-Bass.

Cohler, B. J., & Hammack, P. L. (2006). Making a gay identity: Life story and the construction of a coherent self. In D. P. McAdams, R. Josselson, & A. Lieblich (Eds.), *Identity and story: Creating self in narrative* (pp. 151–172). Washington, DC: American Psychological Association Press.

Cruikshank, M. (1996). Lesbians in the academic world. In G. Vida (Ed.), *Our right to love* (pp. 160–163). New York: Simon & Schuster.

Curb, R., & Manahan, N. (Eds.). (1985). *Lesbian nuns: Breaking the silence.* Tallahassee, FL: Naiad Press.

Darty, T., & Potter, S. (Eds.). (1984). *Women-identified women.* Palo Alto, CA: Mayfield.

D'Augelli, A. R., & Patterson, C. J. (Eds.). (1995). *Lesbian, gay, and bisexual identities over the lifespan: Psychological perspectives.* New York: Oxford University Press.

Deevey, S. (1990). Older lesbian women: An invisible minority. *Journal of Gerontological Nursing, 16*(5), 35–39.

de Vries, B., & Blando, J. A. (2004). The study of gay and lesbian aging: Lessons for social gerontology. In G. Herdt & B. de Vries (Eds.), *Gay and lesbian aging: Research and future directions* (pp. 3–28). New York: Springer.

Eliason, M. J. (1996). Identity formation in lesbian, bisexual, and gay persons: Beyond a "minoritizing" view. *Journal of Homosexuality, 30,* 35–62.

Erikson, E. H. (1959). Identity and the life cycle: Growth and crises of the healthy personality. *Psychological Issues, 1*(1), 100–171.

Faderman, L. (1991). *Odd girls and twilight lovers: A history of lesbian life in twentieth-century America.* New York: Columbia University Press.

Faderman, L. (2003). *Naked in the promised land: A memoir.* Boston: Houghton Mifflin.

Friend, R. A. (1990). Older lesbian and gay people: A theory of successful aging. *Journal of Homosexuality, 20*(3–4), 99–118.

Fukuyama, M. A., & Ferguson, A. D. (2000). Lesbian, gay and bisexual people of color: Understanding cultural complexity and managing multiple oppressions. In R. M. Perez, K. A. DeBord, & K. J. Bieschke (Eds.), *Handbook of counseling and psychotherapy with lesbian, gay, and bisexual clients* (pp. 81–105). Washington, DC: American Psychological Association Press.

Gershick, Z. Z. (1998). *Gay old girls.* Los Angeles: Alyson.

Gilligan, C. (1982). *In a different voice: Psychological theory and women's psychological development.* Cambridge, MA: Harvard University Press.

Habermas, J. (1981). *The theory of communicative action: Lifeworld and system* (T. McCarthy, Trans., Vol. 2). Boston: Beacon Press.

Harry, J. (1993). Being out: A general model. *Journal of Homosexuality, 26*(1), 25–39.

Hayden, M. (1996). When a lesbian client is attracted to her therapist: A lesbian therapist responds. In M. Hall (Ed.), *Sexualities* (pp. 7–13). Binghamton, NY: Harrington Park Press.

Holmes, S. (1988). *Testimonies: A collection of lesbian coming out stories.* Boston: Alyson.

Husserl, E. (1925). *Phenomenological psychology* (J. Scanlon, Trans.). The Hague, the Netherlands: Martinus Nijhoff.

Imbra, C. M. (1998). *Lesbian leaders in higher education.* Unpublished doctoral dissertation, University of Minnesota, Minneapolis.

Jackson, J. M. (1995). *Lesbian identities, daily occupations, and health care experiences.* Unpublished doctoral dissertation, University of Southern California, Los Angeles.

Johnson, S. E. (1991). *Staying power: Long-term lesbian couples.* Tallahassee, FL: Naiad.

Johnston, J. (1973). *Lesbian nation.* New York: Simon & Schuster.

Kehoe, M. (1988). Lesbians over 60 speak for themselves. *Journal of Homosexuality,* 16(3/4), 1–111.

Kennedy, E. L., & Davis, M. D. (1993). *Boots of leather, slippers of gold: The history of a lesbian community.* New York: Routledge.

Kinsey, A. C., Pomeroy, W. B., & Martin, C. E. (1948). *Sexual behavior in the human male.* Philadelphia: W. B. Saunders.

Kinsey, A. C., Pomeroy, W. B., Martin, C. E., & Gebhard, P. (1953). *Sexual behavior in the human female.* Philadelphia: W. B. Saunders.

Lieblich, A., Tuval-Mashiach, R., & Zilber, T. (1998). *Narrative research: Reading, analysis, and interpretation.* Thousand Oaks, CA: Sage.

McAdams, D. P. (1996). Narrating the self in adulthood. In J. E. Birren, G. M. Kenyon, J. E. Ruth, J. J. F. Schroots, & T. Svensson (Eds.), *Aging and biography: Explorations in adult development* (pp. 131–148). New York: Springer.

Nardi, P. (1997). Changing gay and lesbian images in the media. In J. T. Sears & W. L. Williams (Eds.), *Overcoming heterosexism and homophobia: Strategies that work* (pp. 427–442). New York: Columbia University Press.

Nestle, J. (1987). *A restricted country.* Ithaca, NY: Firebrand.

Pedersen, H. L. (2000). *Singled out: Exploring lesbians' experiences being single.* Unpublished doctoral dissertation, University of Southern California, Los Angeles.

Penelope, J. (1994). Class and consciousness. In J. Penelope (Ed.), *Out of the class closet: Lesbians speak* (pp. 13–98). Freedom, CA: Crossing Press.

Penelope, J., & Wolfe, S. (Eds.). (1989). *The original coming out stories: Expanded edition.* Freedom, CA: Crossing Press.

Polkinghorne, D. E. (1996). Explorations of narrative identity. *Psychological Inquiry, 7,* 363–367.

Read, M. M. (2004). *Identity in midlife lesbians: A kaleidoscopic view.* Unpublished doctoral dissertation, University of Southern California, Los Angeles.

Reinharz, S. (1994). Feminist biography: The pains, the joys, the dilemmas. In A. Lieblich & R. Josselson (Eds.), *Exploring identity and gender: The narrative study of lives* (Vol. 2, pp. 37–82). Thousand Oaks, CA: Sage.

Retter, Y. G. (1999). *On the side of angels: Lesbian activism in Los Angeles, 1970–1990.* Unpublished doctoral dissertation, University of New Mexico, Albuquerque.

Ricoeur, P. (1983). *Time and narrative* (K. McLaughlin & D. Pellauer, Trans., Vol. 1). Chicago: University of Chicago Press.

Rothblum, E. D., Mintz, B., Cowan, D. B., & Haller, C. (1995). Lesbian baby boomers at midlife. In K. Jay (Ed.), *Dyke life: From growing up to growing old; a celebration of the lesbian experience* (pp. 61–76). New York: Basic Books.

Sang, B. E., Warshow, J., & Smith, A. J. (Eds.). (1991). *Lesbians at midlife: The creative transition*. San Francisco: Spinsters Book Company.

Sears, J. T., & Williams, W. L. (Eds.). (1997). *Overcoming heterosexism and homophobia: Strategies that work*. New York: Columbia University Press.

Sheehy, G. (2006). *Sex and the seasoned woman*. New York: Random House.

Silberkraus, S. L. (1995). *A Sapphic sojourn: Evolution of a lesbian identity*. Unpublished doctoral dissertation, University of Southern California, Los Angeles.

Sophie, J. (1987). Internalized homophobia and lesbian identity. *Journal of Homosexuality, 14*(1–2), 53–65.

Stewart, A. J. (1994). The women's movement and women's lives: Linking individual development and social events. In A. Lieblich & R. Josselson (Eds.), *Exploring identity and gender: The narrative study of lives* (Vol. 2, pp. 230–250). Thousand Oaks, CA: Sage.

Van Gelder, L., & Brandt, P. R. (1996). *The girls next door: Into the heart of lesbian America*. New York: Simon & Schuster.

Weinstock, J. S. (2000). Lesbian friendships at midlife: Patterns and possibilities for the 21st century. *Journal of Gay and Lesbian Social Services, 11*(2/3), 1–32.

Weston, K. (1991). *Families we choose*. New York: Columbia University Press.

Williams, W. L., & Retter, Y. (Eds.). (2003). *Gay and lesbian rights in the United States: A documentary history*. Westwood, CT: Greenwood Press.

16

The Good (Gay) Life

The Search for Signs of Maturity in the Narratives of Gay Adults

Laura A. King, Chad M. Burton,
and Aaron C. Geise

What makes a life good has been a topic of concern for human beings throughout the ages (e.g., Aristotle, 350 B.C.E/1962 C.E; Becker, 1992; Cottingham, 1998; Russell, 1930/1960; Ryff & Singer, 1998). Good lives may be thought of as truly exemplary in some way in terms of fulfillment, moral character, health, success, or excellence. In contemporary political discourse some have asserted, in no uncertain terms, that the phrase "good *gay* life" is somehow an oxymoron. Life experience and empirical evidence suggest otherwise, of course. Indeed, good lives—lives well worth living—occur even in the face of the harshest oppression. For our purposes, a good life is one that reflects a sense of well-being coupled with insight. In this chapter, we trace the narrative reflections of these virtues in the coming-out stories shared by a sample of 107 gay men and lesbians. We first consider the place of the coming-out story in narrative approaches to identity.

The Life Story and Coming Out

The life story has been described as an internalized narrative that links the past, present, and future (McAdams, 1993; McAdams, Josselson, & Lieblich, 2006)—an integrative frame for life experiences. The stories that people construct out of life experiences can be viewed as the creation of meaningful units out of potentially chaotic experience. From the perspective of identity as life story (McAdams, 1993), the coming-out story can be seen as an instantiation of meaning-making and self-construction, with particular relevance to integrating sexual identity into the larger life narrative (Cohler & Hammack, 2006).

From a narrative perspective, the stories that create meaning out of important life transitions may be thought of as particularly important chapters in the life story. It is in these narrative constructions that individuals are compelled to confront those moments when life is at variance with expectation. Loevinger (1976) stated that only when the environment fails to meet the person's expectations can development occur. Such potentially troubling moments provide the engine for moving the life story forward (Labov & Waletzky, 1997). Indeed, Bruner (1999) argued that stories can function as a source of identity and meaning only when there is some disturbance or imbalance. The moment of discovery of the imbalance between "who I thought I was" and "who I really am" or "who I might be" is a moment of self-discovery that might well color the rest of the life story.

The coming-out narrative, then, might represent a vital turning point (McLean & Pratt, 2006) for gay people. As such, we assume that these stories are particularly relevant to the question of what makes a good gay life. Research has shown that during such turning points, the individual is challenged to identify what makes life meaningful and the ultimate moral values of one's existence (McLean & Pratt, 2006)—essentially the defining features of a good life. We assumed that these important constructions of meaning would make explicit the themes that set the foundation for such a life.

These ideas have special resonance for a group of adults who may have engaged in self-conscious self-construction—who have been forced by circumstance to think about issues that may remain implicit in many lives (e.g., D'Augelli, 1994). Surely, the story that is the self may be incidentally constructed in some lives. Individuals who are afforded the opportunity to simply "go with the flow" of societal expectations may never engage in self-conscious construction of the life story. As one respondent in our research asserted about coming out as a gay man,

> It forced me to do some very difficult work...accepting myself as
> a person who faces prejudice. As a straight person, my life would
> be much more contented, peaceful, and happy. I don't know that I
> would ever have felt the need to do all the work I have done.

Examining significant autobiographical memories for correlates of maturity illuminates the ways that meaning-making within an important life transition reflects and/or contributes to these important outcomes. In examining the relations of the content of coming-out stories, we examine how these stories reflect the capacities of the mature person to make meaning out of life circumstance.

The construction of the life story is necessarily contextualized in the personal and social time in which the events take place and in which the story itself is told (Baddeley & Singer, 2007). Because societies, cultures, and historical time periods inform the very meaning of sexual identity, the construction of gay identity is especially sensitive to the particular social context in which it occurs (Cohler & Hammack, 2006). As such, the coming-out stories examined in the present research are necessarily contextualized in a particular place and time, a geographic and social/historical context.

Dallas, Texas, though located in the Bible Belt of the United States, is a large metropolitan area. Dallas boasts a large and vibrant gay community, including the largest predominantly gay church in the world. It is safe to say that the city of Dallas represents the libertarian "maverick" Texas sensibility, a "live and let live" mentality, alongside a general Southern conservatism.

The data for this study were collected in the mid-1990s at a time when homosexuality might have seemed to be an explicit topic in the political landscape. All of the respondents in this study had lived through the reality of acquired immune deficiency syndrome (AIDS), but the fevered hysteria of the 1980s had perhaps dampened. President Bill Clinton had approved the "Don't Ask, Don't Tell" policy in 1993. Although this policy has come to be viewed in a more negative light, it is notable that at the time, it was the first acknowledgment that gay and lesbian individuals could serve (though not openly) in the military. That same-sex marriage had taken on more than just a glimmer of reality is evidenced by the fact that the Defense of Marriage Act was passed by Congress and signed by President Clinton in 1996, ensuring that states would not have to recognize legal marriages between same-sex partners. These data were collected before Ellen Degeneres came out in 1997 and prior to the appearance of *Will and Grace* on American television in 1998. Americans' attitudes about homosexuality have shown a steady trend toward heightened acceptance since such attitudes have been measured (e.g., Pew Research Center, 2007). As such, at this point in time, gay Americans were living in a context in which attitudes about gays were more positive than at any other point in history but, as is still the case today, there was much progress to be made.

From the vantage point of the mid-1990s, these individuals looked back on their lives to yet another time and in a variety of places. The coming-out experiences described in the narratives had taken place years or even decades earlier. Many of these individuals came out in the 1970s and 1980s. As such, they were generally looking back to times when homosexuality enjoyed less acceptance than it did in their current lives. Whether these narratives represent accurate portrayals of experience is not as important as the notion that the stories themselves reflect the frame of reference of the person in the present moment constructing or reconstructing an important life experience from the past. As narratives authored by adults looking back on an earlier time in their lives, these stories provide a glimpse of the "meta-perspective" of the self taken by these authors looking back on a particular event in the evolving life story.

The particular historical context of these stories is important for at least two reasons: its relevance to the meaning of coming-out stories and to the meaning of gay identity itself. For our participants, coming out meant acknowledging and, at times, announcing their identity in a presumably unsupportive social environment largely lacking role models. For these individuals as a whole, coming out included risking rejection from family and friends and taking on a maligned minority identity. Thus, the social and historical context rendered the dramatic stakes of the stories quite high. These stakes—the very meaning of the coming-out story and its place in gay culture—may change particularly as societal attitudes about homosexuality themselves change.

Researchers have increasingly come to recognize the potentially fluid nature of human sexuality (e.g., Diamond, 2003), and individuals more generally have come to embrace less reified constructs in labeling their own sexual identities (e.g., queer). None of our participants balked at labeling themselves as gay or lesbian. For them, being gay or lesbian was viewed as largely a matter of fact, not a negotiable or ever-changing phenomenon, regardless of how outsiders or future individuals might conceive of sexuality. Within their particular place and time, these coming-out stories represent milestones in the life stories of our sample. As such, they are stories of life transition in which an individual describes the powerful process by which identity itself changed, presumably forever.

The Good Life and the Good Gay Life

Scholars interested in studying the good life often draw upon Aristotle's (350 B.C.E/1962 C.E.) classic distinction between hedonism and eudaimonia. For Aristotle, hedonism (the pursuit of pleasure) was distinct from eudaimonia (the experience of happiness that emerges from the expression of virtue). Perhaps any consideration of the good life must include an obligatory nod to

Aristotle. But his distinction is particularly apt in a discussion of the good *gay* life. The very meaning of homosexuality, as hedonistic or eudaimonic happiness, is clearly at stake in the question of what it means to live a good gay life.

In the realm of political propaganda, homosexuality is often equated with hedonism, with seeking pleasure for its own sake. Recall the words of evangelical minister Ted Haggard after it became known that he had engaged in sex with a male prostitute: "There is a part of my life that is so repulsive and dark that I've been warring against it all of my adult life." For Haggard, hedonic impulses and eudaimonic living were clearly experienced as explicitly in conflict. This conflict is surely represented in religious and societal notions of controlling one's "baser" impulses in the service of religiously defined greater goods or higher principles. The partitioning of hedonics from eudaimonia is reflected in the separation of one's "natural impulses" from behavior.

In considering the good gay life, the ethical characterization of these natural impulses would appear to be a central concern. The position of the Catholic Church on homosexuality is a case in point. While acknowledging that being gay may be part of an individuals' constitution (and represent a vulnerability to evil), acting on this impulse is considered morally wrong. As such, the individual presumably must forsake sexuality in his or her life, subjugating hedonic impulses to religiously defined eudaimonia. Yet, in examining the psychology of well-being, there are reasons to think that hedonic pursuits might themselves play a role in the achievement of a good life, gay or otherwise. Furthermore, this research indicates that the definition of eudaimonia proffered by psychologists interested in the good life may differ in central ways from the definition derived from religious sources.

Psychological Approaches to Happiness

In contrast to religious or societal notions of the good life, the psychological approach to this concern is based on the notion of optimal human functioning, including such constructs as psychological and physical thriving, the experience of fulfillment from meaningful pursuits, and well-being. Aristotole's distinction between hedonism and eudaimonia has often been applied to research in the area of well-being. Researchers interested in hedonic well-being (e.g., Diener, Suh, Lucas, & Smith, 1999) focus primarily on the individual's assessment of how he or she feels about his or her life. Eudaimonia, in contrast, has typically been defined as fulfillment that comes from engagement in meaningful activity and the actualization of one's potential (e.g., Ryan & Deci, 2001). Eudaimonia has also been characterized as authenticity, living in accord with and expressing one's true self or enacting one's deeply held values (Waterman, 1993).

The contrast between hedonism and eudaimonia in psychology might appear to be a distinction between happiness and, essentially, something better than happiness (King, 2008). That is, hedonism would seem to be the potentially meaningless pursuit of pleasure, while eudaimonic happiness is more authentic or virtuous. Alternatively, the distinction may be seen as primarily about the "why" of happiness. Eudaimonic happiness emerges out of the pursuit of meaningful attributes such as kindness or integrity, while hedonic pleasure might be found in buying a new car. Thus, hedonic and eudaimonic impulses may lead an individual down very different roads to the experience of happiness, but they might also converge.

Indeed, the research literature has demonstrated that the boundary between hedonic well-being and eudaimonia is fuzzy (King & Hicks, 2007, in press). For example, research has shown that individuals who are dedicated to intrinsic values (such as relatedness, autonomy, and competence) are better off psychologically than those who espouse extrinsic values (such as money, prestige, or social status; Kasser, 2002). Thus, the pursuit of eudaimonic values might enhance hedonic well-being. In general, eudaimonic living is related to heightened hedonic well-being, and simply being in a good mood can enhance the individual's experience of and sensitivity to meaning in life (King, Hicks, Krull, & Del Gaiso, 2006; Sheldon, 2004), lending credence to the humanistic ideal that following one's heart (i.e., following one's values or doing what "feels right"; Rogers, 1961) is the surest pathway to authentic fulfillment.

The very definition of eudaimonia as the expression of one's true self, or in the words of Carol Ryff (1995), "a striving for perfection that represents the realization of one's true potential" (p. 100), would seem to indicate that this highest form of happiness is likely to be found in a life that is an expression of one's true nature. In the words of a participant in our research, "The choice is not whether to be gay or not, but whether to live true to yourself or live a lie." The experience of eudaimonia would seem to require insight into the reality of the truths and lies that might characterize one's life and the courage to live in accord with the truths. Indeed, Aristotle recognized insight as a defining feature of the good life.

The distinction between intrinsic and extrinsic values may also be applied to gay and lesbian identity. Inasmuch as the struggle against one's same-sex desire is inspired by the potential extrinsic losses of coming out (e.g., loss of status, disapproval from others), one might draw a parallel to previous research demonstrating the role of extrinsic values in decreased well-being and heightened distress. In fact, research has demonstrated that acceptance of one's same-sex desire and being out is associated with enhanced hedonic well-being (e.g., King & Smith, 2004). For a variety of reasons, sexuality is often implicated in discussions of the "baser" impulses of human beings. But other impulses, such as the dire need to conform or to gain social approval, and to subjugate genuine impulses in pursuit of extrinsic goods, might also be viewed as natural impulses with moral and ethical consequences.

For adults, what makes a life good is likely some compromise between personal desires, abilities, dispositions, and environmental constraints. One way to think about eudaimonia in adulthood is to consider the concept of maturity (King & Hicks, 2007). In terms of development, we might say that adults exist in varying degrees of the fruition (and continuation) of a variety of developmental tendencies. They are, at least to some degree, *mature*—representing the ripened fruits of earlier development. In the research reported here, we relied on two aspects of the admittedly multifaceted construct of maturity: well-being (or happiness) and ego development (or complexity and insight). We consider the convergence of these two characteristics to represent a kind of mindful happiness that might well represent eudaimonia (King & Hicks, 2007). We describe each of these potential aspects of the good life in turn.

Well-Being: The Place of Happiness in Maturity

Theories of psychological development often include an implicit sense that development culminates in positive feelings. Of course, Erikson (1968) did not include "happy versus unhappy" as a psychosocial conflict, but it is not hard to imagine that some modicum of happiness comes along with the resolution of Erikson's conflicts: trust, autonomy, initiative, industry, identity, intimacy, generativity, and integrity. Moreover, well-being increases with age (Mroczek & Spiro, 2005; Vaillant & Mukamal, 2001). Contemporary models of adult development often include the notion that with development comes enhanced emotion regulation and, as such, higher levels of hedonic well-being (Carstensen, 1995; Labouvie-Vief, 2003).

There is, then, good reason to consider happiness as one facet of the good life in adulthood. In our research, we have included a range of self-report questionnaires of well-being, including life satisfaction, self-esteem, and meaning in life. A sample item from one of these demonstrates the transparency of these measures. The measure of life satisfaction includes "The conditions of my life are excellent" (Satisfaction with Life Scale; Diener, Emmons, Larsen, & Griffith, 1985). For those unfamiliar with these measures, it may be rather surprising that something as seemingly ineffable as happiness ought to be measured via these straightforward self-report questionnaires. In fact, such subjective measures have been used routinely to measure happiness in a variety of samples. It is a general assumption in the well-being literature that the best judge of the happiness in a life is the person living it (Larsen & Fredrickson, 1999).

Happiness alone would not appear to do justice to maturity, however. First, as anyone who can read a t-shirt message knows, "Denial is not just a river in Egypt." It is fairly easy to imagine (and to find corroborating YouTube clips for one's imaginings) Reverend Ted Haggard smiling broadly and expounding on his amazingly happy heterosexual life prior to the public scandal in which he was outed. Similarly, when Senator Larry Craig was arrested for soliciting sex in an airport men's room, a common theme among some prognosticators was that he simply was incapable of acknowledging his own sexual proclivities. Apparent happiness may belie deep defensiveness, lack of insight, or at the very least profound lack of understanding about one's life.

Second, even if an individual's avowed level of happiness reflects a realistic appraisal, some aspects of maturity are not well captured by happiness (e.g., compassion, insight). Many important activities of adulthood do not relate in simple ways to happiness (King & Hicks, 2007). Being true to oneself may not always be a way to maximize momentary happiness. Thus, while acknowledging the importance of happiness to maturity, in considering the full range of the good life, we must consider other potentially valuable developmental outcomes, such as wisdom, insight, character, or a broad, complex sensibility.

Finally, in considering individuals such as gay and lesbian adults, who by definition must forego some social norms, it is important that we consider some goods in life that are not linked to conformity with social expectations. If heeding the call of eudaimonia implies that one must also defy convention and sacrifice (even temporarily) (hedonic) happiness, then a measure of personality development that is independent of well-being is required (Helson & Wink, 1987). Essentially, we faced the challenge in this research of finding a measure of personality development on which a person who is (justifiably) unhappy might still qualify as mature on some other level. We found a suitable solution in Jane Loevinger's construct of ego development.

Ego Development

Ego development refers to the level of complexity with which one experiences oneself and the world (Loevinger, 1976). Loevinger's ego is a buffer between the self and the world. It is the lens through which the individual engages in life (King & Hicks, 2006). Importantly, Loevinger (1976) emphasized the ego as process, as the making of sense. This function of the ego is not simply something it *does*. It is, rather, what the ego *is*: the active striving to master experience is its very essence. Speaking from the perspective of story, McAdams

(1998) has referred to Loevinger's ego as the *selfing* of experience (p. 29) and the author of the life story.

At the earliest stages of ego development, individuals are dominated by impulses and engage in simplistic thinking. As ego level increases, the individual's organismic frame of reference becomes more complex. With development comes the abilities to control and channel impulses. In the middle stages of ego development, individuals rely on convention and societal norms to evaluate and dictate behavior. People at the higher stages of ego development recognize that life's lessons are contextualized and that life's big questions may have a variety of valid answers. Ego development involves an increasing capacity to recognize conflict and experience ambivalence. Identity and mutuality become concerns at the highest stages, leading to a more expansive view of the self and the world.

Ego development has been described, quite aptly, as the development of character (Westen, 1998). Ego development relates to openness to experience (i.e., a sophisticated sensibility that values art, poetry, etc.), increased compassion, intellectuality, and tolerance (Helson & Roberts, 1994; Helson & Wink, 1987), articulateness, intuition, and sublimation (Vaillant & McCullough, 1987), empathy, and the capacity for interpersonal connectedness (Carlozzi, Gaa, & Liberman, 1983; Pals & John, 1998). Ego development provides the individual with a framework in which to experience life in vivid and complex ways, to appreciate nuance, and to author a life story that represents the concerns of identity, integration, and intersubjectivity. For the developed ego, concerns about convention and norms may be less pressing than the recognition that what makes a life good may be personalized, contextualized, and dynamic.

In order to measure ego development, participants in this research completed the Sentence Completion Test (SCT; Hy & Loevinger, 1996). This measure asks individuals to complete a variety of sentence stems (e.g., "Education...," "A man's job...," "A woman has a right to..."). Responses are then coded according to the scoring manual (Hy & Loevinger, 1996), and the scores provide a measure of the level of complexity and insight with which individuals conceive of themselves and the social world. Although time-consuming, this measure has been shown to track changes in personality and complexity over time (e.g., Gilmore & Durkin, 2001; Helson & Roberts, 1994). In contrast to measures of well-being, the SCT does not rely on the respondent's intuitive sense of the construct or the conscious experience of his or her own level of ego development.

Importantly, ego development is independent of indicators of happiness and psychological adjustment (Helson & Wink, 1987; Noam, 1998; Vallaint & McCullough, 1987). An individual may be quite content but maintain a relatively simple orientation to the self and the world. The independence of these variables suggests that wiser is not always sadder. The sophisticated and complex orientation of one high on ego development can be found in the happy and unhappy alike (King & Hicks, 2007).

Research suggests that, generally speaking, well-being and ego development relate to quite different narrative characteristics. Well-being is associated with closure, resolution, coherence, and intrinsic and communal themes (Bauer & McAdams, 2004; King & Raspin, 2004, King, Scollon, Ramsey, & Williams, 2000). In contrast, ego development relates to imagery suggesting an active struggle to make sense out of difficult experiences (Bauer & McAdams, 2004; King & Raspin, 2004; King et al., 2000). Indeed, it has been suggested that such results represent two independent pathways to the good life: one that leads to happiness and one to heightened insight (King, 2001).

In sum, to capture two sides of the good life in adulthood, participants completed measures of well-being and ego development. In addition, they shared narratives of their coming-out experiences that were coded for imagery relevant to power and intimacy. Before describing the relations of these themes to maturity, we offer a detailed description of our sample. We hope this description will give the reader a full appreciation of the "everydayness" of these individuals. Participants in our study were generally individuals whose lives are spent going to work, paying taxes, mowing the lawn, buying groceries, walking the dog—exceptional only in the way that all human beings are exceptional.

The Sample

Participants were recruited in Dallas through advertisements in local and gay and nongay publications, through flyers posted in a gay bookstore and a women's bar, and at meetings of the Dallas Gay and Lesbian Alliance Against Defamation. They were told that they were being recruited because gay people would represent an interesting, even expert, sample in which to examine the issues of life change and well-being. Most participants (60%) reported learning about the study from the print ads. Others heard through friends (15%), responded to the flyers (15%), or attended a meeting where the study was described (10%). The packet of questionnaires was mailed to interested participants, along with a postage-paid return envelope. Participants were encouraged to complete the questionnaires at their own pace, not necessarily in one sitting. When the packet was returned, participants were sent a check for $20.

Vital Statistics

The final sample of 107 included 65 men and 39 women (with 3 not reporting). Though their age ranged from 18 to 66 years, the sample is best characterized as "30-somethings." Mean age was 36.65 (mode = 34, median = 35). The sample was largely White/Anglo-American (87.90%). Although a small proportion of participants had completed only grade school (3.8%) or high school (11%), the modal education level (25.5%) was a bachelor's degree, and a substantial proportion of participants had completed some postbaccalaureate training (25.5%). Nearly 40% reported earning more than $40,000 per year, and the majority (66%) were in a committed long-term relationship (with a mean length of 4 years, ranging from 10 months to 23 years). Thirty-seven percent reported attending church services at least three times per month, and participants rated religion/spirituality as a rather important aspect of their lives ($M = 6.87$ on a 10-point scale).

Gay "Credentials"

Participants completed a variety of measures about their lives as gay people. The mean age of first same-sex desire was 12.38 ($SD = 6.10$), and the mean age of first homosexual relationship was 18.05 ($SD = 13.43$). The mean age of committing to a gay identity was 22.7 ($SD = 7.4$), with a range of 5 to 53. Compared to previous research on lesbians and gay men, these descriptive statistics are fairly typical (e.g., Cohen & Savin-Williams, 1996; D'Augelli, 1991, 1994).

How gay were these individuals? Participants were asked to rate their perceptions of their sexuality on two scales ranging from 1 (not at all) to 6 (exclusively). For the homosexuality rating, 89% gave themselves a rating of 5 or 6 ($M = 5.6$). For heterosexuality, 87% gave themselves a rating of 1 or 2 ($M = 1.3$). In sum, these individuals were decidedly gay.

Another question asked participants to rate the provocative statement "If I could take a pill that would make me straight, I would take it" on a scale from 1 (strongly disagree) to 5 (strongly agree). Mean endorsement was quite low (1.57, $SD = 1.10$). In fact, 74% of the sample gave this item a rating of 1 (82% responded with a 1 or 2). This level of response would seem to indicate that members of our sample were not struggling with "repulsive and dark" tendencies but rather were living lives comfortably true to themselves.

Participants estimated the percentage of people with whom they interact regularly who know they are gay. Responses ranged from 0 to 100% ($M = 71.95\%$, $SD = 27.76$). Just 30% of the participants estimated themselves to be out to less than 50% of the people with whom they interact regularly. Generally speaking, these individuals appear to be out to even their most casual acquaintances.

Participants also rated the degree to which they were out to a variety of individuals in their closer social circles, including their best friends (gay or straight), their closest straight friends, other straight friends, their closest coworkers, other coworkers, mother, father, and siblings. Ratings were made on a scale from 1 (does not know at all, to my knowledge) to 5 (knows and we've talked about it). The mean level of outness across participants ($\alpha = .80$) was high ($M = 4.22$, $SD = .83$), indicating that most participants in the study were indeed living openly gay lives with regard to their closest social contacts. Fully 71% of the sample gave a rating of 5 for their mothers, while 56% gave this rating for their fathers.

Overall, then, the research we review in this chapter included a wholly nonexotic sample of people: (generally) White, educated, middle class, "married" professionals who happen to be exclusively, comfortably, and openly gay or lesbian. What might such a seemingly typical group of presumably atypical individuals tell us about the good gay life? This is the topic to which we now turn.

The Stories

All participants were asked to write their coming-out story. The instructions were left intentionally open, relying on the participant's intuitive sense of the meaning of this story label. The stories included a broad range of topics—from intense self-examination, to developing romantic relationships, to negotiating the announcement of one's identity to another. Some stories focused primarily on coming out to oneself, that is, the intrapersonal discovery of one's sexual orientation:

> It was a slow process that took a lot of spiritual and self-exploration to come to self-acceptance.

> (It)...caused me to look even more deeply into my own soul.

Other stories focused on the act of publicizing identity:

> I ended up setting aside a special day when I had a list of a lot of my friends and phone numbers. I called them all in order and came out to them....

Some of the stories bore an intensely positive emotional tone:

> When I first went to a gay bar I felt comfortable and knew this was where I should be....

> But I still remember that first kiss. It was the most wonderful sensation I have ever felt. It opened up doors that I never knew existed.

Other stories were imbued with the sober admission of the difficult lesson of conditional love:

> Part of accepting that you are gay means accepting that you will probably lose your friends and possibly your family. You can come out to your loved ones and they'll say it's okay, but it's not. You can tell.

And finally, others included abject despair and self-hatred:

> My "coming out" experience was perhaps the most difficult period in my life.... I had what I consider a "nervous breakdown."

> Coming out...was a terrible experience.... Anything I ever heard about gay people was bad. I did a lot of drugs—pot, cocaine, LSD, speed, heroin, etc.—to try to be "happy" even though I didn't know I was doing it to try not to think about being gay. I even tried to commit suicide.

As a rule, the 107 stories were quite varied. The settings, for example, ranged from the aisles of a library, where a young man surreptitiously looked up information on the dreaded topic of homosexuality to verify his suspicions; to a boy's bedroom, where a group of 9-year olds ogled erotic pictures of women and the young hero realized he was dangerously uninterested; to a car parked in the driveway of a house, where a married woman recognized that she had some important news for her husband; to a little boy awaking from a dream in which a knight in shining armor came to rescue him from his life.

At this point, some discussion of our treatment of this bounty of rich data may be warranted. Our approach to these stories is generally in keeping with that of mainstream personality and social psychology. Thus, the tradition represented by this work is primarily quantitative. While acknowledging the value of more purely qualitative studies of individual lives (e.g., Cohler & Hammack,

2006), here we focus on identifying general principles that might apply to the prediction of happiness and ego development in this sample and beyond. Such an approach certainly represents a compromise: we sacrificed what might be learned about the uniqueness of each person in the pursuit of replication and generalizability (King, 2004). One might well spend a lifetime analyzing each of these stories in order to come to an understanding of the coherence and incongruity that characterize each of these lives. For our purposes, we rely on group-level analyses to examine whether there are general trends suggesting that coming-out narratives in general do indeed reveal themes relevant to the intermingling of hedonism and eudaimonia.

Power and Intimacy in Coming-Out Stories: The Good Gay Life

Coming out arguably includes many of the essential dilemmas of adulthood—potential social rejection versus acceptance, surrendering one's majority identity for that of a maligned minority (e.g., Crocker & Quinn, 2000), standing up for one's rights versus risking the loss of social power. To capture this tension between standing out/standing up for oneself and being connected, we analyzed the content of coming-out stories for the motive themes of power and intimacy. *Power motive* refers to an enduring concern about having impact on the social world (Winter, 1989, 1992). *Intimacy motive* refers to an enduring concern about warm interpersonal encounters for their own sake (McAdams, 1985).

Power and intimacy represent two basic and orthogonal dimensions of human life—communion and agency (e.g., Bakan, 1963; McAdams, 1985). McAdams (1993) has described these two themes as the "prime determinants and reflections of the central thematic lines in a person's self-defining life story" (p. 228). It is notable that both power and intimacy motives are by definition social motives; they concern interpersonal life. Even if coming out refers to coming out to oneself, it remains a social process—for the intrapersonal process of coming out to oneself means discovering how one engages in what are often considered the most important relationships of adulthood. Coming out to oneself means recognizing how one experiences sexual fulfillment, intimacy, and commitment—ultimately, how one loves.

Power is scored for having influence, persuading or convincing others, for positive affect associated with exerting social influence, negative emotion associated with lack of power, and concern for status symbols and prestige (Winter, 1989). Excerpts of stories high in power motive include the following:

> I would not have had any problems pursuing my sexuality if it had
> not been for the pressures (negative influence) of family teachers,

neighbors and peers.... I soon realized that I would NEVER let myself be sexually repressed. The process took a while but it has been rewarding. I insist on being respected for the person I am.

A friend's mother gave me the "Stay away from my family" religious speech. One friend still tries regularly to "save me" through her religion....

It is noteworthy that in the coming-out stories, power tended to be exerted on the person in the form of family and friends trying to "change" the person into a heterosexual.

Intimacy imagery is coded when individuals mention a relationship producing positive affect or reciprocal dialogue. Intimacy images include psychological growth via relationship, commitment to and concern for another, transcending time or space, interpersonal union, harmony, surrender, escape to intimacy, and connection with the outside world. Excerpts from stories that were high in intimacy imagery follow (from King & Smith, 2005).

...I realized at a very young age that women are beautiful and soft and loving.... So I guess you could say that it was not really a conscious decision, I just felt that women were what made me feel love and to be loved. And I still feel that women are the most sensitive, loving, giving creatures God ever made.

...Honestly, I never knew what it felt like to love and want someone before.

I was late to a college course that I was taking with my lover.... As she spoke I watched her and felt the most intense love you could have for someone—her intelligence, her looks, the tone in her voice. I finally knew what it meant to be in love.

These excerpts demonstrate the definitive features of intimacy as warm, interpersonal encounters, dialogue, and transformation via relationships

We examined the relations of the themes of power and intimacy to the outcomes of well-being and ego development. Essentially, power motive imagery was negatively related to well-being, particularly for men (King & Smith, 2005). This result is not entirely surprising in that the power motive here tended to reflect not the individual's heroic influence on others, but rather the social world's unwelcome attempts to change the gay person. Power imagery was unrelated to ego development. Results with regard to intimacy imagery were more promising and provocative.

Strikingly, intimacy imagery in the coming-out stories was significantly related to *both* well-being and ego development (King & Smith, 2005). Recall that, in past research, well-being and ego development have been not only unrelated but predicted by differing narrative variables. In the case of coming-out stories, however, happiness and insight shared independent positive relationships with the occurrence of rich, warm, interpersonal imagery. Essentially, the coming-out stories of those who were happy and complex tended to be stories of receiving loving support or stories of the experience of first love. Indeed, for many of these individuals, coming out implied the discovery of one's capacity to love and to receive love.

Examining the stories told by individuals who scored high on both well-being and ego development reveals the remarkable way in which these accounts of coming out, as told by adults looking back on that moment in their lives, set forth explicit scripts for eudaimonic living. Coming-out stories represent a context in which happy, complex individuals describe the eudaimonic framework provided by that experience. Again and again, in these stories, the hedonic experience of joy is linked inextricably with a sense that the good life has been defined for the individual as a commitment to love, integrity, and honesty.

Rather than partitioning the experience of hedonics from eudaimonia, these individuals tell of moments in their lives when self-discovery occurred in the dramatic convergence of these two sides of the good life. These happy, insightful gay adults frankly refused to compartmentalize hedonic and eudaimonic happiness, to separate their inner nature from their outer lives. Coming out (even to oneself) was not only a private discovery but also an event with implications for public identity and future behavior.

Often in these stories, hedonics is represented in the experience of attraction and the excitement of first love. For instance, one man, faced with his experience of love for another man along with societal condemnations of these feelings, concluded, "I realized I must follow my heart and be true to myself." Here we see subjective hedonic experience translated explicitly into the principle of authenticity. Following one's heart provides the backdrop for the courageous commitment to eudaimonic principles. Hedonic experience justifies a personalized definition of the good life, an approach to eudaimonia that is not only principled and guided by virtue but also livable.

Similarly, a happy and insightful lesbian wrote, "I loved her so much—I realized there was a righteousness about it that made the transition from heterosexual to homosexual very natural for me." This experience of "righteousness" again highlights the coming-out experience not as a surrender to a life of hedo-nism but as a commitment to higher principles—the heroic assumption of the mantle of what is right in the name of love.

These short excerpts might appear to reveal a sentimental romanticism that seems to fall short of insight. It is first notable that these individuals were not simply happy; they also scored high on ego development. As such, we know that these are not happy dullards, incapable of acknowledging the negatives in life. The lens through which they experience life is one that is sensitive to detecting conflict, difficulties, and the richness of that experience.

Furthermore, an interesting characteristic of these stories is the gentle, even fond self-deprecation that characterizes the perspective taken by these individuals on the previous version of the self whose story they were sharing (King & Hicks, 2007). It was not uncommon, for instance, for these partici-pants to note that, although this first love was quite profound at the time, it did not necessarily last. Some admitted that the object of their first love eventually turned out to lie, cheat, or steal. However, these narrators afforded the expe-rience of love an incandescence, a momentary elevation out of the context of all that happened next. One lesbian commented about her first love, "I didn't know at the time that she was lying to me. And in retrospect, I'm kind of glad that she did. It made the experience seem magical for us both." Here, the frame of reference of the author looking back through the lens of happy matu-rity is clear.

The Good Gay Life: Eudaimonia Revisited

These analyses have direct relevance to our understanding of the reality of the good gay life and of good lives more generally. These lives are characterized by personalized definitions of eudaimonia based on intuitive and self-defined principles. Within the stories of those who report high levels of well-being and ego development, the implicit questions answered by the stories are clearly "How did I know that this identity was mine?" and "How did I know that this life might be a good one?" The answers are found explicitly in both the hedonic pleasure of the experience and the recognition that this moment was calling to a better way of life, an imperative to do the right thing.

If we think of eudaimonia as the actualization of one's potential, these stories convey coming out as the actualization of the individual's capacity to love. If eudaimonia involves the recognition of conflicting impulses and the conscious decision to pursue the difficult path of virtue, these stories dem-onstrate that these gay adults pursued the virtuous path. Coming out was not the easy thing to do, but for these participants it was the right thing to do. If eudaimonia is a well-earned happiness founded on a life of principle, these stories demonstrate that, for these individuals, two such principles are love and authenticity. These adults, within their own beliefs, contexts, and expectations, made a heroic choice to live their lives in accord with these principles.

Regardless of whether their gayness is an expression of some true nature or is a fluid quality that might change overtime, these individuals accepted a stigmatized label and all of its presumably "spoiling" consequences in the service of eudaimonia. They allowed themselves to be marked (and marked themselves) in the name of the higher principles of love and a dedication to honesty. These adults, who might have done otherwise, found in these moments of difficult and costly joy an inspiration for eudaimonic living.

There are a multitude of lessons here for scholars interested in the narrative construction of identity and the good life more generally. Within narratives of life transition, adults make explicit their own definitions of the good life. For these gay adults, these definitions are clearly interpersonal ones, informed by assumptions about the nature of human intimacy and the importance of love to human thriving. Happy and insightful gay adults make clear the wisdom that has emerged from their personal experiences of coming out in a particular social context. As adults they looked back and noted the naive assumptions of their youth, as well as the outdated social mores of those days. Clearly, these individuals had not only negotiated coming out, they had emerged as generally successful midlife adults.

As gay and lesbian identities become less of a mark of stigma, the heroism that characterizes these stories may itself be lost on future generations. The terror that marked the lives of these individuals in those moments may be viewed as a historical curiosity. Until that time, we can perhaps only marvel at the human capacity to recognize and follow the call of eudaimonia and write its lessons large in the story of how one's life changed forever.

REFERENCES

Aristotle. (1962 c.e.). *Nichomachean ethics* (M. Oswald, Trans.). Indianapolis, IN: Bobbs-Merrill. (Originally published 350 b.c.e.)

Baddeley, J., & Singer, J. A. (2007). Charting the life story path: Narrative identity across the life span. In D. J. Clandinin (Ed.), *Handbook of narrative inquiry: Mapping a methodology* (pp. 177–202.). Thousand Oaks, CA: Sage.

Bakan, D. (1963). *The duality of human existence: An essay on psychology and religion.* New York: Rand McNally.

Bauer, J. J., & McAdams, D. P. (2004). Growth goals, maturity and well-being. *Developmental Psychology, 40,* 114–127.

Becker, L. (1992). Good lives: Prolegomena. *Social Philosophy and Policy, 9*, 15–37.

Bruner, J. (1999). Narratives of aging. *Journal of Aging Studies, 13*, 7–9.

Carlozzi, A. F, Gaa, J. P., & Liberman, D. B. (1983). Empathy and ego development. *Journal of Counseling Psychology, 30*, 113–116.

Carstensen, L. L. (1995). Evidence for a life-span theory of socioemotional selectivity. *Current Directions in Psychological Science, 4*, 151–156.

Cohler, B. J., & Hammack, P. L. (2006). Making a gay identity: Life story and the construction of a coherent self. In D. P. McAdams, R. Josselson, & A. Leiblich (Eds.), *Identity and story: Creating self in narrative* (pp. 151–172). Washington, DC: America Psychological Association Press.

Cottingham, J. (1998). *Philosophy and the good life.* Cambridge: Cambridge University Press.

Crocker, J., & Quinn, D. M. (2000). Social stigma and the self: Meanings, situations, and self-esteem. In T. F. Heatherton, R. E. Kleck, M. Heble, & J. G. Hull (Eds.), *The social psychology of stigma* (pp. 153–183). New York: Guilford.

D'Augelli, A. R. (1994). Identity development and sexual orientation: Toward a model of lesbian, gay, and bisexual development. In E. J. Trickett & D. Birman (Eds.), *Human diversity: Perspectives on people in context* (pp. 312–333). San Francisco: Jossey-Bass.

Diamond, L. M. (2003). What does sexual orientation orient? A biobehavioral model distinguishing romantic love and sexual desire. *Psychological Review, 110*, 173–192.

Diener, E., Emmons, R. A., Larsen, R. J., & Griffin, S. (1985). The satisfaction with life scale. *Journal of Personality Assessment, 49*, 71–75.

Diener, E., Suh, E. M., Lucas, R. E., & Smith, H. L. (1999). Subjective well-being: Three decades of progress. *Psychological Bulletin, 125*, 276–302.

Erikson, E. H. (1968). *Identity, youth, and crisis.* New York: Norton.

Gilmore, J. M., & Durkin, K. (2001). A critical review of the validity of ego development theory and its measurement. *Journal of Personality Assessment, 77*, 541–567.

Helson, R., & Roberts, B. W. (1994). Ego development and personality change in adulthood. *Journal of Personality and Social Psychology, 66*, 911–920.

Helson, R., & Wink, P. (1987). Two conceptions of maturity examined in the findings of a longitudinal study. *Journal of Personality and Social Psychology, 53*, 531–541.

Hy, L. X., & Loevinger, J. (1996). *Measuring ego development* (2nd ed.). Mahwah, NJ: Erlbaum.

Kasser, T. (2002). *The high price of materialism.* Cambridge, MA: MIT Press.

King, L. A. (2001). The hard road to the good life: The happy, mature person. *Journal of Humanistic Psychology, 41*, 51–72.

King, L. A. (2004). Measures and meanings: The use of qualitative data in social and personality psychology. In C. Sansone, C. C. Morf, & A. T. Panter (Eds.), *The Sage handbook of methods in social psychology* (pp. 173–194). Thousand Oaks, CA: Sage.

King, L. A. (2008). Interventions for enhancing SWB: The pursuit of happiness. In R. J. Larsen & M. Eid (Eds.), *The science of subjective well-being* (pp. 431–448). New York: Guilford.

King, L. A., & Hicks, J. A. (2006). Narrating the self in the past and the future: Implications for maturity. *Research in Human Development, 3,* 121–138.

King, L. A., & Hicks, J. A. (2007). Whatever happened to "what might have been"? Regret, happiness, and maturity. *American Psychologist, 62,* 625–636.

King, L. A., & Hicks, J. A. (In press). Positive affect and meaning in life: The intersection of hedonism and eudaimonia. In P. T. Wong & S. P. Fry (Eds.), *The human quest for meaning.* New York: Oxford University Press.

King, L. A., Hicks, J. A., Krull, J., & Del Gaiso, A. (2006). Positive affect and the experience of meaning in life. *Journal of Personality and Social Psychology, 90,* 179–196.

King, L. A., & Patterson, C. (2000). Reconstructing life goals after the birth of a child with Down syndrome: Finding happiness and growing. *International Journal of Rehabilitation and Health, 5,* 17–30.

King, L. A., & Raspin, C. (2004). Lost and found possible selves, subjective well-being, and ego development in divorced women. *Journal of Personality, 72,* 603–632.

King, L. A., Scollon, C. K., Ramsey, C. M., & Williams, T. (2000). Stories of life transition: Happy endings, subjective well-being, and ego development in parents of children with Down syndrome. *Journal of Research in Personality, 34,* 509–536.

King, L. A., & Smith, N. G. (2004). Gay and straight possible selves: Goals, identity, subjective well-being, and personality development. *Journal of Personality, 72,* 967–994.

King, L. A., & Smith, S. N. (2005). Happy, mature, and gay: Intimacy, power, and difficult times in coming out stories. *Journal of Research in Personality, 39,* 278–298.

Labouvie-Vief, G. (2003). Dynamic integration: Affect, cognition, and the self in adulthood. *Current Directions in Psychological Science, 12,* 201–206.

Labov, W., & Waletzky, J. (1997). Narrative analysis: Oral versions of personal experience. *Journal of Narrative & Life History, 7,* 3–38.

Larsen, R. J., & Fredrickson, B. L. (1999). Measurement issues in emotion research. In D. Kahneman, E. Diener, & N. Schwarz (Eds.). *Well-being: The foundations of hedonic psychology* (pp. 40–60). New York: Russell Sage Foundation.

Loevinger, J. (1976). *Ego development: Conceptions and theories.* San Francisco: Jossey-Bass.

McAdams, D. P. (1985). *Power, intimacy and the life story: Personological inquiries into identity.* New York: Guilford.

McAdams, D. P. (1993). *The stories we live by: Personal myths and the making of the self.* New York: Morrow.

McAdams, D. P. (1998). Ego, trait, identity. In P. M. Westenberg, A. Blasi, & L. D. Cohn (Eds.), *Personality development: Theoretical, empirical, and clinical investigations of Loevinger's conception of ego development*. (pp. 27–38). Mahwah, NJ: Erlbaum.

McAdams, D. P., Josselson, R., & Leiblich, A. (Eds.). (2006). *Identity and story: Creating self in narrative*. Washington, DC: American Psychological Association Press.

McLean, K. C., & Pratt, M. W. (2006). Life's little (and big) lessons: Identity statuses and meaning-making in the turning point narratives of emerging adults. *Developmental Psychology, 42,* 714–722.

Mroczek, D. K., & Spiro, A. (2005). Change in life satisfaction during adulthood: Findings from the Veterans Affairs Normative Aging Study. *Journal of Personality and Social Psychology, 88,* 189–202.

Noam, G. I. (1998). Solving the ego development-mental health riddle. In A. Blasi & P. Westenberg (Eds.), *Personality development: Theoretical, empirical, and clinical investigations of Loevinger's conception of ego development* (pp. 271–295). Mahwah, NJ: Erlbaum.

Pals, J. L., & John, O. P. (1998). How are dimensions of adult personality related to ego development? An application of the typological approach. In P. M. Westenberg, A. Blasi, & L. D. Cohn (Eds.), *Personality development: Theoretical, empirical, and clinical investigations of Loevinger's conception of ego development* (pp. 113–131). Mahwah, NJ: Erlbaum.

Pew Research Center (2007, January 9). *A portrait of "Generation Next": How young people view their lives, futures, and politics*. Washington, DC: Author.

Rogers, C. R. (1961). *On becoming a person*. Boston: Houghton Mifflin.

Russell, B. (1960). *The conquest of happiness*. London: George Allen & Unwin. (Original work published 1930)

Ryan, R. M., & Deci, E. L. (2001). On happiness and human potentials: A review of research on hedonic and eudaimonic well-being. *Annual Review of Psychology, 52,* 141–166.

Ryff, C. D. (1995). Psychological well-being in adult life. *Current Directions in Psychological Science, 4,* 99–104.

Ryff, C. D., & Singer, B. (1998). The contours of positive human health. *Psychological Inquiry, 9,* 1–28.

Sheldon, K. M. (2004). *Optimal human being: An integrated multi-level perspective*. Mahwah, NJ: Erlbaum.

Vaillant, G. E., & McCullough, L. (1987). The Washington University Sentence Completion Test compared with other measures of adult ego development. *American Journal of Psychiatry. 144,* 1189–1194.

Vaillant, G. E., & Mukamal, K. (2001). Successful aging. *American Journal of Psychiatry, 158,* 839–847.

Waterman, A. S. (1993). Two conceptions of happiness: Contrasts of personal expressiveness (eudaimonia) and hedonic enjoyment. *Journal of Personality and Social Psychology, 64,* 678–691.

Westen, D. (1998). Loevinger's theory of ego development in the context of contemporary psychoanalytical theory. In P. M. Westenberg, A. Blasi, &

L. D. Cohn (Eds.), *Personality development: Theoretical, empirical and clinical investigations of Loevinger's conception of ego development* (pp. 59–70). Mahwah, NJ: Erlbaum.

Winter, D. (1989). *Manual for scoring motive imagery in running text*. Unpublished manuscript. University of Michigan, Ann Arbor.

Winter, D. G. (1992). A revised scoring system for the power motive. In C. P. Smith (Ed.), *Motivation and personality: Handbook of thematic content analysis* (pp. 311–324). New York: Cambridge University Press.

17

Generativity and Time in Gay Men's Life Stories

Andrew J. Hostetler

The developmental task of generativity is fundamentally about relationships of and to time. First popularized by the work of Erik Erikson (1963), generativity has been defined in terms of "establishing and guiding the next generation" (p. 247) and/or investing in projects that will "outlive the self" (Kotre, 1984). At the most obvious level, then, generativity concerns an individual's relationship to the future. But given that *narration*, or the incorporation of generative accomplishments into one's life story and identity, is a key aspect of the developmental process (McAdams & de St. Aubin, 1992; McAdams, Hart, & Maruna, 1998), generativity is also about the construction of the personal past. And from the perspective of its individual and collective recipients, generativity not only provides a connection to the past, but also an obligation to return the favor by "paying it forward" to the next generation. In short, generativity anchors the individual life course in the flow of sociohistorical time in a way that is true of no other developmental task in adulthood.

Although concerns related to sexual identity and same-sex intimacy have received more attention in political discourse and in scholarship on gay life, generativity is arguably more closely linked—for better or worse—to the prospects for the cultural integration of lesbian, gay, bisexual, and transgender (LGBT) persons.

Undoubtedly, questions about intimacy (i.e., will same-sex relationships be institutionalized?) and generativity (i.e., what will a lasting gay contribution to society look like?) are both at the heart of debates about the meaning of the gay good life and the desirability of a normalized gay life course (e.g., Chauncey 2004; Vaid, 1995; Warner, 1999). And given that the concepts of same-sex intimacy and gay generativity both continue to strike many nongay observers as oxymoronic, neither issue is necessarily more relevant to questions of social acceptance. Nevertheless, more seems to be at stake in the problem of gay generativity, for to deny LGBT people opportunities for culturally valued generative expression is to shackle them to an eternal present, locked out of both developmental and historical time.

Drawing on life-story interviews with 42 gay men representing roughly four different historical cohorts, this chapter explores the meaning and experience of gay generativity through intersecting narratives of personal-developmental and collective-historical time. These narratives reveal both cohort-specific shifts in gay men's time orientation and a more continuous pattern of historical change, with corresponding transformations in opportunities for making a generative contribution. But more than just identifying sociohistorical context as an important antecedent or independent variable, the narratives suggest a more dynamic intertwining of developmental and historical processes in the construction of the generative self. Specifically, I argue that the men are engaged in an intergenerational "multilogue"—with members of our research team and, by proxy, with each other—that is rewriting the individual experience and collective meaning of generativity. I conclude with a discussion of the future prospects for building a generative society and the potential contributions of LGBT people to such a project.

Theoretical and Methodological Framework

This chapter draws on life course, ecological, and narrative perspectives. According to both life course (e.g., Elder, 1998) and ecological (Bronfenbrenner, 1979, 1986) theories, developmental processes must be understood in the context of distal influences in addition to the proximal influences typically studied by developmental psychologists. For example, Bronfenbrenner (1979) identified institutional/structural (or *exosystemic*) and cultural (or *macrosystemic*) factors relevant to individual development, and Bronfenbrenner (1979, 1986) and Elder (1998) both addressed the important roles of historical change, developmental timing, and the interplay between personal and historical time.

Both approaches also recognize the important role of human agency, or active, conscious self-engagement in developmental processes. According to Giddens (1991), agency in late modern societies often takes the form of a "reflexive project of the self, which consists in the sustaining of coherent, yet continuously revised biographical narratives" (p. 5). In turn, the life course becomes coherent only through this reflexive and socially situated biography. Thus, the life story or narrative approach becomes an indispensable tool for understanding life-course development (Bertaux, 1981; Bruner, 1987, 1990; Cohler, 1982; Denzin, 1989; Edwards & Potter, 1992; Gagnon, 1992; Gergen, 1991, 1994: Gergen & Davis, 1985; Giddens, 1991; McAdams, 1993; Plummer, 1995a; Sarbin, 1986; Sarbin & Kitsuse, 1994).

Given the central place of generativity in the meaning-making efforts of adults, the general approach outlined above is particularly well suited to an examination of this developmental task. Erikson (1963) clearly privileged the biological/procreative route to generativity and also defined the previous task, *intimacy versus isolation*, in primarily heterosexual and procreative terms. However, he also appreciated the meaning-centered nature of generativity and the important role of dynamic sociocultural contexts in shaping human development—topics further explored in subsequent scholarship on generativity (e.g., Cohler, Hostetler, & Boxer, 1998; Kotre, 1984, 2004; McAdams et al., 1998; Stewart & Vandewater, 1998). For example, Kotre (1984) has elaborated on nonparental forms of generativity, including technical forms (the direct transmission of knowledge, skills, and/or traditions) and broader cultural forms. Similarly, McAdams and colleagues (1998) have explored the important role of cultural demands and opportunities in the experience of generativity, and they have highlighted the essential function of narration—understood as a collaboration between person and context—in this developmental process.

A few studies have explored the experience of generativity in the lives of gay men and/or women from a sociocultural, life-course and/or narrative perspective (Cohler et al., 1998; Cornett & Hudson, 1987; deVries & Blando, 2004; Kertzner & Sved, 1996; Vaillant, 1977), though general patterns have not yet been identified and important aspects of gay generative experience remain unexplored. This chapter begins with the assumption that although parenting is an important avenue for generative expression that should be open to gay men and lesbians, it is not and should not be the only way for LGBT individuals to make a lasting cultural contribution. At the same time, I acknowledge that the future prospects for nonparental forms of gay generativity are somewhat unclear. Building on earlier collaborative work (Cohler et al., 1998; Cohler, Galatzer-Levy, & Hostetler, 2000), this chapter is also grounded in the conviction that generativity narratives are *psychosocial constructions* "coauthored" by persons and cultures (McAdams, 1996) and by teller and listener as a part of a shared activity (Fontana & Frey, 2000; Plummer, 1995a). In addition, I highlight the ongoing intergenerational nature of this collaborative process, which is part of a larger multigenerational dialogue about questions of meaning and what matters.

The necessity of expanding generativity's temporal dimension in this way is well illustrated by Csikszentmihalyi's (1996) somewhat controversial contribution to the study of creativity. According to Csikszentmihalyi, true creativity is a product of the interaction between the person, the domain of his or her (would-be) creative contribution, and the field of experts who will evaluate the contribution. To be considered creative, the individual must either have his or her contribution validated by experts in an existing field or establish a new field.

But what if the creative contribution is disregarded and devalued, irrespective of any inherent value, simply because of the identity of the producer? What if there is no appropriate audience for evaluation? In other words, does creativity—or generativity—exist apart from its (timely) social reception and the individual internalization of this reception? The approach proposed here acknowledges the important role of social reception and evaluation but also draws attention to both the individual-developmental and historical revision that become possible when an appropriate audience is finally ready to listen— ideally, but not always, during the lifetime of the generative individual. This process of revision takes the form of a temporal dialectic characterized by ongoing processes of intergenerational negotiation—a position informed by recent research on the bidirectional socialization often involved in generative relationships (e.g., Vaillant, 2002).

I explore this intergenerational multilogue through the life stories of 42 predominantly White, middle-class gay men ranging in age from 36 to 77 and representing roughly four historical cohorts (see below). The racial and class composition of the sample is not surprising given the profile of the typical volunteer in research on sexual orientation (e.g., Meyer & Colten, 1999), but it is also reflective of a demographically homogeneous research team.[1] Likewise, the focus on men is attributable to their disproportionate representation in our sample but also to my specific interest in single gay men, who are purposely overrepresented. Given the common association of generativity with parenting and the more specific association of caring relationships with women, the mature gay men in our sample provide particularly informative examples of adaptive responses to the crisis of generativity. Finally, the age range was selected because, although certain dimensions of generativity may remain relatively constant throughout adulthood, this developmental task takes prominence and is fully realized starting only with the years of settled and middle adulthood (Cohler & Boxer, 1984; McAdams et al., 1998).

Given our sample, generalizability was not a goal. However, the concept of *narrative saturation* (Bertaux, 1981), or the idea that even relatively small interview samples can exhaust the range of narrative themes on a given topic, informed the analysis of life stories. Analysis was also guided by Strauss and Corbin's (1990) open coding methodology and followed an inquiry-guided perspective (Mishler, 1990). This perspective highlights the meaning-making efforts of individuals as they construct identities, build relationships, cope with life events, and maintain a sense of continuity over time (for more information about the study, see Hostetler, 2004). As the concept of *cohort* figures prominently in the following analysis, a few words about cohort classification are in order before we turn to an exploration of the narratives.

Cohort Classification among American Gay Men

The notion of cohort is integral to the life-course perspective (e.g., Clausen, 1993; Elder, 1998), and its usage is informed by Mannheim's (1928) classic work on generations. Cohorts are technically defined by birth year(s) but derive their developmental meaningfulness in reference to significant historical events that shape the experience and ethos of a generation during a formative period, typically adolescence or early adulthood (Clausen, 1991, 1993; Elder, 1974, 1992; Elder & Caspi, 1988, 1990). Accordingly, developmental and historical scholarship has identified at least five historical cohorts of currently living American gay men (Boxer & Cohler, 1989; Chauncey, 1994; Cohler & Galatzer-Levy, 2000; Cohler et al., 1998; Herdt & Boxer, 1996; Savin-Williams, 2005).

According to Herdt and Boxer (1996), four distinct cohorts of homosexual men and women men came of age in the twentieth century during or in the wake of different formative historical events: World War I, World War II, the Stonewall Riots and the beginning of the modern gay rights movements, and the acquired immune deficiency syndrome (AIDS) pandemic. More recently, Savin-Williams (2005) and others have documented another generational shift. They note that LGBT youth are coming out at earlier ages in a context shaped by the long-term impact of human immunodeficiency virus (HIV)/AIDS on gay politics and community life, its eventual transformation into a largely manageable chronic illness, and the increasing cultural integration of gays and lesbians. Young men and women of this generation are less preoccupied with sexual labels or with being different, and they expect to live openly and to have the same opportunities as their heterosexual peers.

Despite these important distinctions, the assignment of individuals to a particular cohort is far from an exact science, considering the idiosyncratic timing of "coming of age" (particularly for LGBT persons) and given gender, race, class, regional, and other within-cohort differences. The coexistence of multiple age strata ensures a diversity of generational worldviews at any given time. Moreover, even the most significant and far-reaching historical events rarely remake the cultural zeitgeist overnight. Finally, to overemphasize the importance of cohort membership would suggest a static view of the relationship between the sociohistorical context and individual development and obscure the important role of individual agency. For all these reasons, I try to avoid rigid classification by cohort.

Nevertheless, and in keeping with other historical and developmental scholarship, our data indicate clear historical shifts and a gradual transformation in the possibilities for constructing affirmative gay identities and happy, healthy gay lives. Specifically, the narratives of our older participants bear the marks of a particularly hostile ecological context that continues to take an existential toll. The lives of these men, born between 1919 and 1943, span the period from the end of Herdt and Boxer's (1996) first historical cohort to the end of the second. The younger participants were born between 1946 and 1962, with the youngest men straddling the third and fourth historical cohorts. Although these men undeniably benefited from the modern gay rights movement, they also faced their own cohort-specific challenges, most notably in the form of HIV/AIDS. These and other generational differences are reflected in the men's efforts to narrate the generative self—efforts characterized by shifting relationships to developmental and historical time.

Generativity and Time in Gay Men's Life Stories

Although Erikson (1963) believed it to be a universal experience, generativity—like identity (Giddens, 1991; Plummer, 1995a, 1995b)—seems to take on particular developmental and cultural significance in contemporary Western societies, given their marked future-time orientation and strong emphasis on individual expression (Markus, 2003; Markus & Kitayama, 1991, 1998). But while the freedom to express a sexual minority identity has dramatically expanded, homosexuality and generativity remain, in the popular imagination, somewhat mutually exclusive, defined in opposing terms that have much to do with the temporal dimensions of selfhood. Specifically, enduring homophobic stereotypes, uncontrollable historical circumstances, and other factors have worked in concert to reinforce the cultural construction of homosexuality as a "dead-end" lifestyle. Fortunately, gay people have actively resisted these definitions, working to redefine generativity and rewrite the meanings of gay experience—an ongoing dialectical process of individual and collective revision that is reflected in our data.

Narratives of Personal-Developmental Time

Traditional connotations of generativity and homosexuality could not be more at odds. Whereas generativity denotes healthy development, the flowering of maturity, and the creation of a positive, prosocial legacy, homosexuality was long believed to preclude these accomplishments. Whereas generativity invokes a utopian vision of progressive movement toward a better future for humankind, a collective endeavor that binds generations together, homosexuality was seen as destructive to the social fabric. And whereas generativity is fundamentally about the future, homosexuality has been portrayed as a hedonistic, present-oriented "lifestyle" that is at the same time firmly rooted in a primitive phylogenetic (i.e., animalistic) and/or ontogenetic past.

Unfortunately, many of our oldest participants, who straddled the first and second historical cohorts (Herdt & Boxer, 1996), internalized these and other homophobic ideas, and their narratives indeed reflect a preoccupation with the distant past. This preoccupation does not appear to be just a methodological artifact of participating in a life-story interview; nor is it merely a matter of ego integrity (Erikson, 1963). Rather, the developmental past seems to serve as a general interpretive anchor. Specifically, several of the oldest men we interviewed continued to grapple with the question of why they were gay, and this central focus functioned as both the lens through which they interpreted their experience and an obstacle to the articulation of more generative concerns. Some even adopted a psychoanalytic story line of developmental fixation. For example, James, a gay White man who was 77 at the time he was interviewed (b. 1922), reported a history of quasi-romantic, quasi-platonic relationships with much younger men. Although it would have been reasonable for him to interpret some degree of mentorship in these relationships, he instead situated them within a narrative of oedipal pathology (with the encouragement of a therapist):

> [My therapist] said the problem with my relationship with Monty,
> and the pattern I had established that I didn't know if I would ever
> break, was that I acted toward Monty like I was my mother and

treated Monty as though he were me.... I began to see, subconsciously, that this bonding was something more important than the sex. Once the sex was done the bonding was the important thing. As the psychiatrist pointed out later, it was this mother–son relationship that we were reenacting over and over and over.

Interestingly, our data suggest an important symbolic shift starting with representatives of the second historical cohort, whose narratives show the first signs of the emergence of coming-out narratives. Identified by Plummer (1995b) as paradigmatic modernist narratives of "suffering, surviving, and surpassing," coming-out stories provide gay men and women with the possibility, if not the guarantee, of moving beyond the internal struggles of a troubled past or a conflicted present. Although coming out provided new opportunities for the realization of gay generativity, the men and women of the second cohort still faced a difficult path. Participant narratives suggest that a preoccupation with causation and the developmental past remained a common theme (and it would eventually become a familiar American motif for understanding a wide range of atypical experiences [e.g., Rieff, 1966]). Indeed, several of the men we interviewed recounted difficult childhood and adolescent experiences, a common narrative theme among men who came of age in the middle decades of the twentieth century (see Cohler, this volume).

But gay developmental time starts to be reckoned somewhat differently in this period, and a narrative of *developmental delay* (Siegel & Lowe, 1994) emerges. Specifically, socialization into a heterosexual lifeway and the relatively late formation of a gay identity lead many gay individuals to experience a life course out of synch with normative developmental timetables (Cohler et al., 1998; Herdt & Boxer, 1996; Hostetler & Herdt, 1998), and this was particularly true for our participants from the second cohort. These men were likely to have grappled with identity and intimacy issues long after their straight counterparts had turned their attention to other concerns, diverting and delimiting time and energy that could have been dedicated to the achievement of generativity.

The life story of Tom (White, 65, b. 1934) bears the imprint of both early developmental struggles and a protracted coming-out process. A self-described "outsider," he retreated back into social isolation in his 40s after a relatively short period of more active social and community involvement:

I had a sense of being different from early on, 4 or 5, although I don't know that I could have pinpointed it as potential [sic] gay.... I remained pretty much isolated for the remainder of my childhood years because boys didn't play with girls and I wouldn't play with

boy.... [D]uring my 20s, which would have been a really good time
to have been identified as gay, and to have been living a gay life, I was
in knots and depressed. I wasn't living a heterosexual life, I wasn't
living a homosexual life.... [A]s I got to be in my 40s, I stopped having a sex life in terms of looking for men.... I think it would be nice
to expand my social horizons but, as I said, there's a bit of a problem
there...the opportunities seem few....

While the experience of being perpetually "off-time" (Neugarten, 1964) seems
to have channeled Tom and other men away from generative investments, the
implications of developmental delay depend on the timing of coming out and
the experiences that precede the assumption of a gay identity. For example,
Daniel (White, 71, b. 1923) was a father of two who came out relatively late in
life (and he was the only representative of the second cohort with children from
a previous heterosexual marriage). He would agree that he went through a
"second adolescence" once he came out, and he reported a near-exclusive preference for relationships with significantly younger men. However, he did not
experience an uncomfortable sense of being developmentally off-time when
he came out, in large part because his generativity needs had previously been
met. Rather, Daniel felt a marked sense of freedom to explore his sexual identity and to focus on self-realization in ways that had not been possible earlier.
He listed the birth of his children as high points in his life, but he nevertheless
felt liberated by his divorce:

A lot of my life has been the tension between other people's expectations and the cultural expectations that are around me and my own
possibilities and my own choices, and that's the reason I think I got
married.... I was 50, and that was a watershed event, when I really
decided, yes, I'm gay...I'm tired of conforming, trying to fit not only
my expectations but other expectations from other people. I'm gonna
do it [i.e, come out]!

In short, Daniel—like many men of his generation—adaptively deployed a
narrative of developmental delay in a way not incompatible with other developmental tasks.

While the experience of coming out well into adulthood led to a general
developmental delay for many gay men from the second cohort (and beyond),
the emergence of the AIDS epidemic was even more disruptive to the developmental timing of gay lives, particularly for men of the third cohort. At the most
obvious level, the disease robbed many gay men of a full life span in which to
achieve generativity and other developmental tasks, disrupted intergenerational

continuity, and denied future generations of any number of intellectual, artistic, social, and political contributions. For long-term survivors and the uninfected, AIDS decimated friendship networks, leaving many men isolated and without a supportive context in which to realize generative concerns. Many of our participants from the third cohort were personally impacted by HIV/AIDS, including at least four men who were living with the illness and many others who had lost, in some cases, dozens of friends over the years. In the following excerpts from life-story interviews, two participants from the third cohort and one from the second cohort (with a mostly younger social circle) discuss their many losses:

> There was a group of us. I think at one time we had a large group, something like 16 or 17 and now it's down to 5 and we lost 2 last year.
>
> (Wally, White, 69, b. 1927)

> It's getting smaller, HIV losses basically. About 20 people. I have friends in San Francisco who have lost hundreds of people....
>
> (Les, White, 54, b. 1942)

> I had a decent-sized circle of friends and that circle has been decimated a bit by AIDS. And now one in the circle now has AIDS. So there's five of us left and, like I said, one has AIDS. Who knows how long he'll be around. So that will be down to four, then.
>
> (Bill, White, 46, b. 1949)

For some of the men, such multiple losses led to increasing social detachment. Randy (White, 45, b. 1950) told us that "[a]fter my friends started dying of AIDS, I just thought, well, why bother meeting more people."

More than just producing a widespread experience of being developmentally off-time, the loss of so many significant others and the anticipation of death so early in life removed an entire generation of gay men from the expectable flow of life-course events. For men living with HIV and AIDS, the disease led to a dramatic "developmental telescoping," at least in the years before the development of life-prolonging antiviral drugs. Specifically, HIV-positive gay men were forced to resolve a variety of developmental concerns, typically spread out over the course of adult life, within a relatively short span of time prior to their premature deaths (Bennett & Thompson, 1991; Borden, 1989; Cohler et al., 1998). Such pressures can result in a sense of being completely outside of time (Hagestad, 1996) or in a defensive (and sometimes destructive) retreat into an eternal present. For men like Bill, AIDS imposed a twofold blow to gay generative expression, rupturing the continuity of gay history while also shifting the time orientation of an entire generation of gay men away from the future:

> Well, I think one of the main things is that almost all our main political national gay leadership have all died of AIDS. I mean, I think that's just devastating to the movement and to our continuity of history. That has been devastating. I think it's perpetuated the gay community's kind of myth of live for today and not for tomorrow. I think it's perpetuated that because it's like, well, people die, so why save?

Martin (White, 46, b. 1953), who has remained HIV-negative, characterized the attitude among his friends in the 1980s as resigned: "Pass the donuts, we're all going to die." This present-time orientation was reinforced by the necessity of caring for a sick and dying generation of mostly middle-aged men, draining resources that might have been invested in, among other things, the care and development of youth.

But for many men from the third cohort—both HIV-positive and -negative—the epidemic channeled generative energies into new and surprising directions, providing further examples of developmental agency. Several of our participants became even more dedicated to activism, volunteerism, and community-building, and at least two of the men viewed HIV as a potential resource, attributing positive changes in their social and community lives to the epidemic. Robert (White, 67, b. 1932), despite being older than most of his fellow HIV-positive peers, was profoundly influenced by the spirit and activism of the AIDS generation. He came out publicly in the context of AIDS activism following his long-term partner's death and his own seroconversion:

> [M]y HIV status has everything to do with where I'm at now.... I'm thankful HIV is here, not here but that I had it. Because it brought me to meet people, it brought me to accept people I never would've accepted.

And Terrence (African American, 36, b. 1959) recently started volunteering in the community and described his own fears of HIV as a "blessing" that helped to get his life back "on the right track" through community service, spirituality, and a more open and accepting attitude.

It could even be argued that the community service and activism inspired by the epidemic perfectly reflect the combination of "agency and communion" that, according to McAdams and colleagues (McAdams et al., 1998; McAdams, Hoffman, Mansfield, & Day, 1996; see also Bakan, 1966), characterizes generativity. Although it is certainly unfortunate that the present-time orientation of many gay men of this cohort interfered with direct, explicit efforts to address the needs of younger generations, the necessary attention paid to a dying generation was in the interest of all generations and therefore an essential expression of generativity. The communion dimension of this generative contribution is obvious in the heroic work of gay men, lesbians, family members, and allies to nurture those living with and dying from AIDS and is reflected in the words of David (White, 48, b. 1947):

> Right now, I feel like I'm in midlife because things are more important to me. Sitting holding hands with a friend who is dying is vitally important to me.

The experience of caring for the sick and watching friends die also inspired agentic efforts to transform the political and cultural landscape through political activism, philanthropy, and artistic expression—vital community-building efforts that paved the way for subsequent political and cultural achievements and created a lasting legacy for future generations (Chauncey, 2004). Although the caretakers and activists were often one and the same, many dedicated their energies primarily to one area or combined the two diachronically rather than synchronically. Moreover, an explicit motivation to help the next generation was not always present, as was also the case for the community-building activities of the two earlier cohorts. But focusing on the future is a luxury reserved for those not locked in a struggle to reconcile the past or forced to live in the moment by the specter of impending death (in the same way that self-actualization is an unrealistic goal in conditions of war or poverty). For this reason, generativity must be understood as more than an individual psychological and developmental issue; it must also be understood as a collective and historical process, a set of creative and adaptive responses that, whether by design or not, benefit future generations.

Narratives of Collective-Historical Time

Taken individually, the life stories speak—among many other things—to the generative concerns, accomplishments, and (in many cases) struggles of each man. Taken together, they tell a broader story of gay American life in the twentieth century—a story in which issues related to generativity play an important role. However, whether the plotline is one of sociopolitical progress, cultural loss, or something in between is a matter of continuing debate.

Narratives of inevitable progress have a long history in the American and broader Western traditions (e.g., Benjamin, 1986; Lyotard, 1984; White, 1973), and undeniably, the possibilities for leading an open, integrated lesbian and gay life expanded dramatically over the course of the twentieth century. However, progress narratives have been criticized because of their linear reading of history and because the meaning of *progress* is far from transparent and highly subjective. With respect to the interpretation of gay lives, these concerns are reflected in a shift away from *presentist* accounts of gay history (e.g., Chauncey, 1994) and in continuing debates about the implications and desirability of gay cultural integration (e.g., Chauncey, 2004; Vaid, 1995; Warner, 1999). Nevertheless, our younger participants have clearly been able to be generative *as* gay men in ways unimaginable to their older counterparts, whether through relatively traditional or more innovative routes.

For those members of the first cohort (and beyond), who led heterosexual public lives and never came out, their generative accomplishments were primarily in the traditional areas of work and family. These individuals remain largely invisible to gay and lesbian history, and they were not represented in our data. The creative and expressive arts offered a generative alternative, and gay men and lesbians have made lasting contributions in these areas. The most visible gay men worked in artistic and creative occupations, which had acquired a reputation of tolerance for sexual difference. But even these men were typically forced to hide their sexuality from family members and heterosexual society more generally. Many other individuals more thoroughly compartmentalized their homosexuality, participating in gay social and/or sexual life on the side while leading otherwise conventional lives.

One of our oldest participants, Bennett (White, 77, b. 1922), chose an arguably more difficult middle path, not unlike many men of his cohort, neither marrying nor ever fully accepting his same-sex desires and attractions. He compartmentalized his personal and professional lives and never achieved lasting intimacy. He told us that he never married or had a family because "I loathe children. I never wanted children." Bennett had relatively short-lived relationships with several married men, never came out, and avoided contact with the gay community and its "creepy people." He recalled his response to a written greeting from a new neighbor, a young mother: "Welcome, but I think I should tell you right off that I loathe children." Though once involved in different mainstream community organizations, he became a virtual recluse as his relatively few close friends died. From an Eriksonian perspective, Bennett failed to progress beyond identity concerns and consequently never formed truly intimate or generative relationships.

Although Bennett was particularly isolated, he was not alone in his decision not to marry; very few of our older participants ever did so. Less surprisingly, few had considered parenting as an openly gay man. Indeed, the idea of gay parenting was inconceivable when many of the older men in the study came of age. In the words of Peter (White, 64, b. 1931), "It kinds of robs a kid.... I think a kid that did have gay parents would take some abuse from other kids." And Robert (White, 67, b. 1932) articulated a sense of loss over the eventual abandonment of his desire to have children:

[I] absolutely thought of a family. That is the only thing I miss in having a gay relationship. I think it was something that [my part- ner] missed, too, because we used to talk about it to the point that it would be nice to have a kid.... I would've loved to, I think [my part- ner] would've loved to. I think he wouldn't have for his family's sake.

Despite the barriers to parenthood, the older men found other ways to fulfill their desires to mentor young people. Several were actively involved in the lives of their siblings' children, and all the uncles reported that their rela- tionships with nieces and nephews were at least somewhat important, even if physical distance from and/or lack of emotional closeness to siblings prevented more frequent contact. For example, although Daniel never wanted children of his own, he viewed the uncle role as a very significant facet of his life. He bought a home for his sister's family, is recognized as "Uncle Dan" by his part- ner's nieces and nephews, and reports that his own nieces and nephews "come to me for help lots and lots of times, and money." Similarly, Tony (White, 72, b. 1922), whose life centered primarily on career and a quiet domestic life with his partner of 31 years, noted that he was "trying to be the head of the family" following the loss of his parents and a brother. A disproportionate number of men had been teachers, including Jack (White, 62, b. 1933), who was also an activist for gay veterans' issues and was very involved in intercultural and interracial community-building efforts throughout his career. He said of his work, "I don't understand the word 'burnout.'"

In comparison, the men of the third historical cohort—the Stonewall generation—confronted fewer barriers to, and more opportunities for, gen- erative expression. The expansion of opportunities to parent as an openly gay person, in particular, has had profound implications (Patterson, 2006; Stacey, 2006). Not surprisingly, more participants from the third cohort (about half) than from the first and second cohorts (one or two) had considered the pos- sibility of parenting as gay men. However, men on the leading edge of the third cohort were likely to see their desire to have children unfulfilled, whereas younger counterparts were much more likely to view gay parenting as a via- ble option. The following three men reflected on their abandoned hopes to become fathers:

Now that I'm in my 40s and set in my ways, I mean, I wouldn't want to deal with kids in my life. But I think there was a real regret earlier on because I liked kids. I think I would have made a great dad in a way.... It was something I had crossed early on. I wasn't going to get married anyway.

(Martin, White, 46, b. 1953)

I know I wanted to have kids.... That urge to have children lasted way beyond when I knew I was gay.... I didn't go on forever, I think by the time I was in my late 20s. I had this longing to have my own children.

(Marc, White, 53, b. 1946)

God, would I have made a good father.... It would have been just wonderful. Could I have ever done it? I doubt it, because of the problem involved. I don't know whether I could. Maybe 25 years further on I could do it. But right now...the children that I would be raising would be constantly a victim of... "Oh, your father's a faggot...." Would I put a child through that? No, absolutely not.

(David, White, 48, b. 1947)

In contrast, four of the younger participants—two of whom straddle the third and fourth cohorts—have parented as openly gay men or are planning to do so. Interestingly, three of these fathers/prospective fathers were men of color, suggesting the possibility of racial differences. Mark, a 45-year-old African American man (b. 1949), adopted his sister's two sons when she became unable to take care of them. Being a father has made him feel "anchored in time and space," his "generativity needs hav[ing] been met" (see also Cohler et al., 1998). Keith (African American and Latino, 40, b. 1960) had an adult son from a previous heterosexual marriage. Coming to terms with his sexuality and coming out seem to have had a positive impact on his son, who eventually came out himself and with whom he enjoys a close relationship. Here Mark discusses his choice to stay married for many years and expresses his hopes for his son:

When you divorce, you divorce your children, too, and for me that was not an option. My father and my mother divorced very early, when I was about 8 years old...I felt like he divorced me.... And I hope my child did not feel the same, that's what I was working hard not to [have happen].... And I always tell my son, I think the important thing that I wanted to be for me son is a father, and to be that firs.... The best I can hope for him is that he's happy, I think that's probably the greatest gift he can ever give me....

Although gay men in particular continue to face significant obstacles in their efforts to become fathers, including antigay adoption restrictions or outright bans in five states (National Gay and Lesbian Task Force, 2006), more and more are able to enjoy the rewards and challenges of parenthood.

More generally, and in addition to its more tangible outcomes, the modern gay rights movement has led to the gradual normalization of lesbian and gay life-course pathways (Cohler & Galatzer-Levy, 2000; Hostetler & Herdt, 1998), and this development is both celebrated and lamented within LGBT communities. Indeed, the outline of a counternarrative of gay cultural loss is evident even in the words of our relatively conservative Midwestern participants. Many gay men and women of the Stonewall generation were strongly influenced by the counternormative and experimental ethos of the late 1960s and early 1970s, and many explored alternative modes of relating to, living with, and having sex with others—forms of intimate expression they hoped would replace traditional, patriarchal, nuclear family structures.

Although few of our participants could be described as radical or strongly counternormative, several had been actively involved in the gay rights movement and community-building efforts. For example, Edward (White, 43, b. 1952) helped organize gay bartenders and played an important role in the founding of the city's first gay community center. Les started the first local chapter of a national organization dedicated to serving the needs of friends and family members of gay men and women. He describes this as an important growth experience:

> It's probably the closest experience that I'll ever get to raising a kid. It was like helping it along when it couldn't walk.

Even before the gay rights era, there are examples of gay-specific forms of generative expression, forms that were lost somewhere en route to cultural assimilation. For example, two of the older men (one from cohort 1 and one from cohort 2) spoke about the mostly vanished tradition of being a gay "auntie" or giving "Fred Astaire dance lessons" to newly out young gay men to help them navigate same-sex intimacy and gay community life. A younger man, Bill, reflected on what it meant to him to have such a mentor:

> When I came out it was really good...because an older guy took me under his wing and so I had a real gay mother.... It was a sexual relationships with him in the sense that he didn't bring me up sexually, per se, but he was the type that that we would get out and say, "Okay,

we haven't done this sexual activity yet. You need to know what it's like, how to do it, and how to perform it well so that you'll be good in bed." So we literally, you know, did all the ABC's of sexual activity.

Admittedly, the sexual component of many of these "mentorship" relationships would disqualify them, in the eyes of many, from being generative.

Other gay contributions to the art of living are less controversial, most notably in the area of *families of choice* (Nardi, 1999; Weeks, Heaphy, & Donovan, 2001; Weston, 1991), a concept that resonated with many of our participants. Although there are many examples of "fictive kin" relationships in the cross-cultural record (many of which involve same-sex intimate relations) (Blackwood & Wieringa, 1999; Herdt, 1997; Hostetler, in press-a), gay and lesbian families of choice—which can include various combinations of partners, biological and/or adopted children, ex-lovers, friends, and biological kin—seem to have played a particularly important role in recent transformations of the American family. Above and beyond their significant cultural contribution, gay and lesbian families have provided a warm, supportive context for intimate and generative relationships.

As marriage and family rights have come to dominate the LGBT political agenda, many worry that the radically transformative potential of early gay liberation is being completely diffused, and that queer cultural innovation is becoming a thing of the past. As Gould (2000) has noted, the oscillation between assimilation and accommodation in gay politics and other progressive movements is nothing new and is perhaps an inevitable part of the political process. Moreover, given the "bricolage" quality of new cultural forms (Hebdige, 1981), a sharp distinction between assimilation and accommodation, tradition and innovation, is not justified. Even among those gay men pursuing a more conventional path to generativity through parenthood, many are putting their own spin on the experience, creating nontraditional family structures and often caring for those children with the greatest needs, children who might otherwise be abandoned.

Trevor, a 42-year-old African American man (b. 1958), describes his plans to become a foster parent, preferably to an adolescent struggling with sexual identity issues:

I think I have a pretty good life and I think there are a lot of kids out there, particularly gay youth, that either, for whatever reason, don't have a home, are estranged from their parents, and need an adult in their life, and, so, okay, there's an opportunity to really contribute and really support someone in doing what they have to do in life.

Trevor's commitment to generativity is related to the desire for family, but it reveals an innovative approach to creating a nontraditional family structure.

Although this kind of gradual renovation and creative tweaking of social institutions is the norm (even when disguised as something more radical), generational blind spots often interfere with the recognition of historical continuity. This is somewhat ironic given that the idea of cultural loss through gradual assimilation is a linear narrative that purportedly pays tribute to the past. On the other hand, endorsement of a progressive narrative runs the risk of casting older generations in the role of victim, deprived of opportunities for generative expression by a hostile ecological context. Fortunately, our data reveal a more active, constructive, and dynamic process of intergenerational negotiation regarding the meanings of gay contributions to society and to the art of living, an ongoing multilogue that is rewriting the past and hopefully laying the groundwork for a more generative future.

Between Generations: Generativity as Sociohistorical Process

The nature of the conversation in which our participants were engaged—with members of the research team and with a multigenerational imagined audience—indicates that generativity (like identity) remains a work in progress throughout the life course, a perspective in keeping with that of Erikson. And although the inability to achieve generative accomplishments during the course of one's life undoubtedly has significant psychological implications, our data also suggest that a lack of success in resolving generative concerns prior to death is not the same as generative failure. Indeed, the matter of ultimate success or failure may have to be decided by survivors and future generations. Ecological, life span, and other contextual approaches recognize not only the structural and symbolic constraints on development, but also the contributions of individuals—particularly in the face of such constraints—in the ongoing dialectic between person and environment. From this perspective, generativity must also be understood as a collective, intergenerational endeavor that plays out in historical time as well as developmental time, not necessarily in the sense of inevitable, linear progress but rather in the form of a running intergenerational dialogue about what matters and the meaning of experience.

By simply coming out and living their lives with integrity, the men from cohorts 1 and 2 paved the way for future generations of gay men and lesbians to do the same. Even participation in the present study can be interpreted as a generative act—sharing their stories not just for their own benefit but also for the benefit of others. At least one man, Saul (White, 71, b. 1923), was very much aware of this motivation:

> That's the reason you're here. That's the reasons I made the [documentary about older gay men]. I feel we have a legacy to leave. I feel that I was an architect that helped with this.

The narration of generativity is as much about convincing others as it is about convincing oneself and, in this passage, Saul engages me—a representative of a younger generation—in a conversation that he hoped I would continue and advance long after the completion of our interview. And while their opportunities for generative expression were relatively greater, several of our participants from cohort 3 were engaged in the same dialogue, reflecting on the contributions of the previous generations as well as those of their own:

> The generation before me, I think, were much more circumspect, much more careful about what they chose as gay people. And if they were gay in a career that they felt was somehow precarious, they were extremely, extremely closeted.
>
> (Bill, White, 46, b. 1949)

> Things are different now in the '90s and how it came about. That had to be somebody's hard work, lots of people had to get beat up, lots of people had to show themselves and be chastised, whatever, forced to get to this point, and they were the martyrs that make our world better.... The 1970s, early '70s, you had no good future. I mean, you could not look toward the future and say the remaining years are going to be fun. We had our own little segment of the world, where you go to [gay religious organization] or go to private parities or bars or something, but it wasn't going to give us well-rounded comfort that we have now.
>
> (David, White, 48, b. 1947)

> Yes, it's changed in a positive fashion. Because of the exposure, because of all the work that the people of my generation have done to make it know that we're not awful, ugly, sick.... We fought for that for a long time. And there are a lot of us that did it out there, in the headlines all the time, and a lot that just kind of did it in our community.... And then, as a result, people just accepted us for who we are.... Gay life in the '90s is very much everyday life.... When you

were a lawyer in the '70s and you were gay, you were a lawyer first
and gay later. Now you can be gay and still be a lawyer.

(Edward, White, 43, b. 1952)

To acknowledge the important contributions of earlier cohorts of gay men
and women—to validate their generative efforts—is not to fix their meaning
or to pin down their continuing implications, as the aforementioned debates
attest. Nevertheless, LGBT communities have unquestionably joined a broader
conversation, in which issues of generativity are of paramount importance,
about the future of the American (and global) way of life. In the final section
of this chapter, I address the potential contributions of LGBT people to a more
generative future.

Discussion: The Future of Gay Generativity

For better or worse, and despite the current conservative political climate,
some degree of cultural assimilation for LGBT people seems inevitable. Gay
parenting will likely become even more common and will provide the primary
generative outlet for a significant proportion of gay men and lesbians. Among
our seven youngest participants, who were on the trailing edge of cohort 3
or the leading edge of cohort 4, a greater sense of ease about being gay and
optimism about the future seemed to prevail. All but one of these men were
single and somewhat preoccupied with intimacy concerns, yet most of them
expressed some degree of hope and confidence that the coming years would
bring love, companionship, and a continuing sense of place and purpose. For
these men, parenting was in no way incompatible with being openly gay. Three
were actively engaged in parenting and mentoring, including Trevor and Keith.
Another man, Hector (Latino, 38, b. 1962), was heavily involved in the lives of
friends' children, serving as the godfather to the son of a lesbian couple. He
says of this relationship, "[It's] probably the most important thing in my life
right now."

At the same time, alternate generative outlets may no longer be as readily available. Increasing cultural integration, the emergence of the Internet,
and the widespread availability of life-extending drug "cocktails" to treat HIV/
AIDS—though in many ways positive developments—have eliminated much
of the impetus and energy behind gay organizing and community-building
efforts. And many of the urban "gay ghettoes" have been depopulated as
LGBT folks feel more and more at home in a variety of locations (Brown,
2007; Sullivan, 2007). Nevertheless, for other men, activism and volunteer

opportunities in the LGBT community continue to provide an avenue for creative and generative expression. For example, Terrence (African American, 36, b. 1959) reported recently being "in soul search" that led him to community service at the local LGBT community center to "give something back."

Increasingly, as gay culture is woven into the fabric of American life, gay and straight individuals confront similar obstacles to the realization of generativity. Consumerism and hyperindividualism are obviously widespread and, unfortunately, not especially compatible with building generative relationships and communities. The trends described more than 20 years ago by Bellah and colleagues (Bellah, Madsen, Sullivan, Swidler, & Tipton, 1985) seem only to have intensified, as middle-class Americans have continued to flock to suburbs and exurbs, isolating themselves from community life in mammoth SUVs and "McMansions." In a recent study, the average American reported having two or fewer close friends, and a full 25% claimed no close friendships—a marked decrease since the 1970s (McPherson, Smith-Lovin, & Brashears, 2006). In addition, ageism is pervasive in the United States and few opportunities exist for young and old Americans to interact with each other; even relationships between grandparents and grandchildren have been strained by distance in an increasingly mobile society (AARP, 2002; Bellah et al., 1985).

But visions of a more generative future are also emerging and, as has long been the case, gays and lesbians are at the forefront of cultural innovation. For example, Hector and Terrence frame recent changes in their lives and their renewed commitment to community in contradistinction to the more superficial aspects of gay and American culture:

> You had to have the latest in the fashion, the names, a lot of the attitudes. And it's just, that's the crowd I came out in and then stayed in for about 8 or 9 years.
>
> (Terrence)

> The whole gay community is buying into the whole Madison Ave. crap. We've become a marketing destination.
>
> (Hector)

Within the LGBT community at large, many men and women are refusing to internalize ageist attitudes and perceptions and are providing a model for nonfamilial forms of generativity as they create and sustain vibrant LGBT community centers that provide not only age- and developmentally appropriate services, but also mentorship opportunities, including in New York City, Los Angeles, and Chicago. Openhouse in San Francisco, a nonprofit residential community for gay and lesbian retirees, provides a wonderful model of senior living that is immersed in, rather than walled off from, community life. And gay men and women have played an integral role in the creation and maintenance of innovative, intergenerational, "green," and self-sustaining communities like EcoVillage in Ithaca, New York (Stephanie Greenwood, personal communication). At the same time, senior centers across the country still face an image problem (i.e., as bingo and knitting warehouses for the old and inactive) and could learn a lot about successful marketing and programming, including intergenerational programming, from LGBT centers.

Whether or not yesterday's senior centers become the vibrant intergenerational community centers that they could be, images and profiles of the "average senior" will undoubtedly change as baby boomers enter late adulthood, poised to take advantage of a longer, healthier, and more active "third age" (Laslett, 1991; Rubinstein, 2002; Weiss & Bass, 2002). These emerging seniors, many of whom have a history of collective political activism, could embrace volunteerism on an unprecedented scale, transforming late adulthood into the most generative of developmental periods and laying the groundwork for the creation of a truly caring society. Given that Americans are volunteering more than ever (Corporation for National and Community Service, 2006), the prospects for such a future are good, though far from guaranteed.

The single biggest impediment to the realization of such a transformation may be the lack of a compelling cultural narrative of collective generative commitment. "Family values" rhetoric and, more recently, post-9/11 nationalistic discourses, with their intolerance of difference and dissent, have proven unable to unite an increasingly pluralistic society through a positive and forward-looking vision of the common good. On the other hand, one of the most important, if not yet widely recognized, cultural contributions of gay and lesbian people is a narrative of and model for mutual acceptance, friendship, and community that is neither defined by traditional bonds of kin or clan nor, ideally, delimited by gender, race, class, age group, or even sexual orientation. The innovative efforts of lesbians and gay men to build families and communities of choice (Nardi, 1999; Weeks et al., 2001; Weston, 1991), though not an unqualified success (Hostetler, 2004, in press-b), should nevertheless prove inspirational. The words of Terrence capture the spirit of this important gay contribution to the art of living:

> If I [weren't gay] I'd be so restricted. I would be less accepting of
> other's people's values and other people's disciplines. You know, it's
> almost like a blessing. It's opened up a lot of doors that I would never
> have been open to understanding.

To the extent that there is a distinctly LGBT vision for a more inclusive, respectful, and caring future, its temporal grounding is somewhat unique. To begin with, it is not anchored in the kind of natalist or nationalist ideology that so often places history and the imagined future in service of parochial and exclusionary interests. Sexual minority identities and communities have brought people together across divisions of age, class, race, ethnicity, ability, and—given the increasingly global reach of the Internet—space. Moreover, the lived experience of LGBT people, perhaps more than that of any other minority group, has helped to demonstrate the fluid and multidimensional nature of identity (Butler, 1990, 2004; Warner, 1999). At its best, a queer vision is not beholden to specific narratives of the past, nor is it synonymous with the nihilism and hedonism of an eternal present; rather, it gestures toward an inclusive, equitable, and always provisional imagined future informed by the multiplicity of present lived realities.

Acknowledgment

This research was supported in part by a grant from the Social Science Research Council with funds from the Ford Foundation. The author would like to thank Bertram J. Cohler and Phillip L. Hammack.

NOTES

1. When referring to the sample and data as a whole, I use the plural possessive form to acknowledge the contributions of the broader research team, which included Bertram J. Cohler, Gilbert Herdt, the late Andrew Boxer, David deBoer, Michael Axelrod, Todd W. Rawls, Jeff Beeler, Samantha Bergmann, and Christine Glover.

REFERENCES

AARP. (2002). *The grandparent study 2002 report.* Washington, DC: Author.

Bakan, D. (1966). *The duality of human existence: Isolation and communion in Western man.* Boston: Beacon Press.

Bellah, R. N., Madsen, R., Sullivan, W. M., Swidler, A., & Tipton, S. M. (1985). *Habits of the heart: Individualism and commitment in American life.* Berkeley: University of California Press.

Benjamin, W. (1986). Theses on the philosophy of history. In H. Adams & L. Searle (Eds.), *Critical theory since 1965* (pp. 680–685). Tallahassee: Florida State University Press.

Bennett, K., & Thompson, N. (1991). Accelerated aging and male homosexuality: Australian evidence in a continuing debate. In J. A. Lee (Ed.), *Gay midlife and maturity* (pp. 65–75). New York: Haworth Press.

Bertaux, D. (1981). From the life-history approach to the transformation of sociological practice. In D. Bertaux (Ed.), *Biography and society: The life history approach in the social sciences* (pp. 28–46). Newbury Park, CA: Sage.

Blackwood, E., & Wieringa, S. E. (Eds.). (1999). *Female desires: Same-sex relations and transgender practices across cultures*. New York: Columbia University Press.

Borden, W. (1989). Life review as a therapeutic frame in the treatment of young adults with AIDS. *Health and Social Work, 14*, 253–259.

Boxer, A., & Cohler, B. (1989). The life course of gay and lesbian youth: An immodest proposal for the study of lives. *Journal of Homosexuality, 17*, 315–355.

Bronfenbrenner, U. (1979). *The ecology of human development: Experiments by nature and design*. Cambridge, MA: Harvard University Press.

Bronfenbrenner, U. (1986). Ecology of the family as a context for human development: Research perspectives. *Developmental Psychology, 22*, 723–742.

Brown, P. L. (2007, October 30). Gay enclaves face prospect of being passé. *New York Times*. Retrieved January 7, 2008, from www.nytimes.com

Bruner, J. (1987). Life as narrative. *Social Research, 54*(1), 11–32.

Bruner, J. (1990). *Acts of meaning*. Cambridge, MA: Harvard University Press.

Butler, J. (1990). *Gender trouble*. New York: Routledge.

Butler, J. (2004). *Undoing gender*. New York: Routledge.

Chauncey, G. (1994). *Gay New York: Gender, urban culture, and the making of the gay male world, 1890–1940*. New York: Basic Books.

Chauncey, G. (2004). *Why marriage? The history shaping today's debate over gay equality*. New York: Basic Books.

Clausen, J. A. (1991). Adolescent competence and the shaping of the life course. *American Journal of Sociology, 96*, 805–842.

Clausen, J. A. (1993). *American lives: Looking back at the children of the Great Depression*. New York: Free Press.

Cohler, B. J. (1982). Personal narrative and life course. In P. Baltes & O. G. Brim, Jr. (Eds.), *Life-span development and behavior* (Vol. 4, pp. 205–241). New York: Academic Press.

Cohler, B. J., & Boxer, A. (1984). Middle adulthood: Settling into the world-person, time, and context. In D. Offer & M. Sabshin (Eds.), *Normality and the life course* (pp. 145–203). New York: Basic Books.

Cohler, B. J., & Galatzer-Levy, R. M. (2000). *The course of gay and lesbian lives: Social and psychoanalytic perspectives*. Chicago: University of Chicago Press.

Cohler, B. J., Galatzer-Levy, R. M., & Hostetler, A. J. (2000). Gay and lesbian lives across the adult years. In B. J. Cohler & R. Galatzer-Levy (Eds.), *The course of gay and lesbian lives: Social and psychoanalytic perspectives* (pp. 193–251). Chicago: University of Chicago Press.

Cohler, B. J., Hostetler, A. J., & Boxer, A. (1998). Generativity, social context and lived experience: Narratives of gay men in middle adulthood. In D. McAdams & E. de St. Aubin (Eds.), *Generativity and adult development: How and why we care for the next generation* (pp. 265–309). Washington, DC: American Psychological Association Press.

Cornett, C. W., & Hudson, R. A. (1987). Middle adulthood and the theories of Erikson, Gould, and Vaillant: Where does the gay man fit? *Journal of Gerontological Social Work, 10*(3/4), 61–73.

Corporation for National and Community Service. (2006). *Volunteering in America: State trends and rankings 2002–2005.* Washington, DC: Author.

Csikszentmihalyi, M. (1996). *Creativity: Flow and the psychology of discovery and invention.* New York: Harper Perennial.

de Vries, B., & Blando, J. A. (2004). The study of gay and lesbian aging: Lessons for social gerontology. In G. Herdt & B. de Vries (Eds), *Gay and lesbian aging: A research agenda for the 21st century* (pp. 3–28). New York: Springer.

Denzin, N. (1989). *Interpretive biography.* Newbury Park, CA: Sage.

Edwards, D., & Potter, J. (1992). *Discursive psychology.* Newbury Park, CA: Sage.

Elder, G. H., Jr. (1974). *Children of the Great Depression.* Chicago: University of Chicago Press.

Elder, G. H., Jr. (1992). Life course. In E. Borgatta & M. Borgatta (Eds.), *Encyclopedia of sociology* (Vol. 3, pp. 1120–1130). New York: Macmillan.

Elder, G. H., Jr. (1998). The life course as developmental theory. *Child Development, 69*(1), 1–12.

Elder, G. H., Jr., & Caspi, A. (1988). Human development and social change: An emerging perspective on the life course. In N. Bolger, A. Caspi, G. Downey, & M. Moorehouse (Eds.), *Persons in context: Developmental processes* (pp. 77–113). New York: Cambridge University Press.

Elder, G. H., Jr., & Caspi, A. (1990). Studying lives in a changing society: Sociological and personological explorations. In A. I. Rabin, R. A. Zucker, R. A. Emmons, & S. Frank (Eds.), *Studying persons and lives* (pp. 201–247). New York: Springer.

Erikson, E. H. (1963). *Childhood and Society* (2nd ed.). New York: Norton.

Fontana, A., & Frey, J. H. (2000). The interview: From structured questions to negotiated text. In N. K. Denzin & Y. S. Lincoln (Eds.), *Handbook of qualitative research* (2nd ed., pp. 645–672). Thousand Oaks, CA: Sage.

Gagnon, J (1992). The self, its voices, and their discord. In C. Ellis & M. G. Flaherty (Eds.), *Investigating subjectivity: Research on lived experience* (pp. 221–243). Newbury Park, CA: Sage.

Gergen, K. J. (1991). *The saturated self: Dilemmas of identity in contemporary life.* New York: Basic Books.

Gergen, K. J. (1994). *Realities and relationships: Soundings in social construction.* Cambridge, MA: Harvard University Press.

Gergen, K. J., & Davis, K. E. (Eds.). (1985). *The social construction of the person.* New York: Springer-Verlag.

Giddens, A. (1991). *Modernity and self-identity: Self and society in the late modern age.* Stanford, CA: Stanford University Press.

Gould, D. B. (2000). *Sex, death, and the politics of anger: Emotions and reason in ACT UP's fight against AIDS.* Unpublished doctoral dissertation, University of Chicago.

Hagestad, G. (1996). On-time, off-time, out of time? Reflections on continuity and discontinuity from an illness process. In V. Bengtson (Ed.), *Adulthood and aging: Research on continuities and discontinuities* (pp. 204–222). New York: Springer.

Hebdige, D. (1981). *Subculture: The meaning of style*. London: Methuen.

Herdt, G. (1997). *Same sex, different cultures: Exploring gay and lesbian lives*. Boulder, CO: Westview Press.

Herdt, G., & Boxer, A. (1996). *Children of horizons: How gay and lesbian teens are leading a new way out of the closet* (Rev. ed.). Boston: Beacon Press.

Hostetler, A. J. (2004). Old, gay and alone? The ecology of well-being among middle-aged and older single gay men. In G. Herdt & B. de Vries (Eds.), *Gay and lesbian aging: A research agenda for the 21st century* (pp. 143–176). New York: Springer.

Hostetler, A. J. (In press-a). Homosexuality and bisexuality: Cultural and historical perspectives. In R. A., Shweder, Bidell, T. R., Dailey, A. C., Dixon, S. D., Miller, P. J., & Modell, J. (Eds.), *The Chicago companion to the child*. Chicago: University of Chicago Press, forthcoming 2009.

Hostetler, A. J. (In press-b). Single by choice? Assessing and understanding voluntary singlehood among mature gay men. *Journal of Homosexuality*.

Hostetler, A. J., & Herdt, G. (1998). Culture, sexual lifeways and developmental subjectivities: Rethinking sexual taxonomies. *Social Research, 65*, 249–290.

Kertzner, R. M., & Sved, M. (1996). Midlife gay men and lesbians: Adult development and mental health. In R. P. Cabaj & T. S. Stein (Eds.), *Textbook of homosexuality and mental health* (pp. 289–303). Washington, DC: American Psychiatric Press.

Kotre, J. (1984). *Outliving the self: Generativity and the interpretation of lives*. Baltimore: Johns Hopkins University Press.

Kotre, J. (2004). Generativity and culture: What meaning can do. In E. de St. Aubin, D. P. McAdams, & T. Kim (Eds.), *The generative society: Caring for future generations* (pp. 35–49). Washington, DC: American Psychological Association Press.

Laslett, P. (1991). *A fresh map of life: The emergence of the Third Age*. Cambridge, MA: Harvard University Press.

Lyotard, J. F. (1984). *The postmodern condition: A report on knowledge* (G. Bennington & B. Massumi, Trans.). Minneapolis: University of Minnesota Press.

Mannheim, K. (1928). The problem of generations. In K. Mannheim (Ed.), *Essays on the sociology of knowledge* (pp. 276–322). London: Routledge & Kegan Paul.

Markus, H. R. (2003). Culture and personality: Brief for an arranged marriage. *Journal of Research in Personality, 38*, 75–83.

Markus, H. R., & Kitayama, S. (1991). Culture and the self: Implications for cognition, emotion, and motivation. *Psychological Review, 98*, 224–253.

Markus, H. R., & Kitayama, S. (1998). The cultural psychology of personality. *Journal of Cross-Cultural Psychology, 29*, 63–87.

McAdams, D. (1993). *The stories we live by: Personal myths and the making of the self*. New York: William Morrow.

McAdams, D. P. (1996). Personality, modernity, and the storied self: A contemporary framework for studying persons. *Psychological Inquiry, 7*, 295–321.

McAdams, D. P., & de St. Aubin, E. (1992). A theory of generativity and its assessment through self-report, behavioral acts, and narrative themes in autobiography. *Journal of Personality and Social Psychology, 62,* 1003–1015.

McAdams, D. P., Hart, H. M., & Maruna, S. (1998). The anatomy of generativity. In D. P. McAdams (Ed.), *Generativity and adult development: How and why we care for the next generation* (pp. 7–43). Washington, DC: American Psychological Association Press.

McAdams, D. P., Hoffman, B. J., Mansfield, E. D., & Day, R. (1996). Themes of agency and communion in significant autobiographical scenes. *Journal of Personality, 64,* 339–377.

McPherson, M., Smith-Lovin, L., & Brashears, M. (2006). Social isolation in America: Changes in core discussion networks over two decades. *American Sociological Review, 71*(3), 353–375.

Meyer, I. H., & Colten, M. E. (1999). Sampling gay men: Random digit dialing versus sources in the gay community. *Journal of Homosexuality, 37*(4), 99–110.

Mishler, E. (1990). Validation in inquiry-guided research: The role of exemplars in narrative studies. *Harvard Educational Review, 60,* 415–442.

Nardi, P. M. (1999). *Gay men's friendships: Invincible communities.* Chicago: University of Chicago Press.

National Gay and Lesbian Task Force. (2006). Adoption laws in the United States. Retrieved January 12, 2007, from www.thetaskforce.org

Neugarten, B. L. (1964). Summary and implications. In B. L. Neugarten, *Personality in middle and later life: Empirical studies* (pp. 188–200). New York: Atherton.

Patterson, C. (2006). Children of lesbian and gay parents. *Current Directions in Psychological Science, 15*(5), 241–244.

Plummer, K. (1995a). Life story research. In J. A. Smith, R. Harré, and L. Van Langenhove (Eds.), *Rethinking methods in psychology* (pp. 50–63). Thousand Oaks, CA: Sage.

Plummer, K. (1995b). *Telling sexual stories: Power, change and social worlds.* New York: Routledge.

Rieff, P. (1966). *The triumph of the therapeutic: Uses of faith after Freud.* New York: Harper & Row.

Rubinstein, R. L. (2002). The third age. In R. S. Weiss & S. A. Bass (Eds.), *Challenges of the third age: Meaning and purpose in later life* (pp. 29–40). New York: Oxford University Press.

Sarbin, T. R. (Ed.). (1986). *Narrative psychology: The storied nature of human conduct.* New York: Praeger.

Sarbin, T. R., & Kitsuse, J. I. (Eds.). (1994). *Constructing the social.* Thousand Oaks, CA: Sage.

Savin-Williams, R. C. (2005). *The new gay teenager.* Cambridge, MA: Harvard University Press.

Siegel, S., & Lowe, E. (1994). *Uncharted lives: Understanding the life passages of gay men.* New York: Dutton.

Stacey, J. (2006). Gay parenthood and the decline of paternity as we knew it. *Sexualities, 9*(1), 27–55.

Stewart, A. J., & Vandewater, E. A. (1998). The course of generativity. In D. P. McAdams (Ed.), *Generativity and adult development: How and why we care for the next generation* (pp. 75–100). Washington, DC: American Psychological Association Press.

Strauss, A., & Corbin, J. (1990). *Basics of qualitative research.* Newbury Park, CA: Sage.

Sullivan, R. D. (2007, December 2). Last call: Why the gay bars of Boston are disappearing, and what it says about the future of city life. *Boston Globe.* Retrieved December 6, 2007, from www.boston.com

Vaid, U. (1995). *Virtual equality: The mainstreaming of gay and lesbian liberation.* New York: Anchor.

Vaillant, G. E. (1977). *Adaptation to life.* Cambridge, MA: Harvard University Press.

Vaillant, G. E. (2002). *Aging well.* New York: Little, Brown.

Warner, M. (1999). *The trouble with normal: Sex, politics, and the ethics of queer life.* Cambridge, MA: Harvard University Press.

Weeks, J., Heaphy, B., & Donovan, C. (2001). *Same sex intimacies: Families of choice and other life experiments.* New York: Routledge.

Weiss, R. S., & Bass, S. A. (Eds.). (2002). *Challenges of the third age: Meaning and purpose in later life.* New York: Oxford University Press.

Weston, K. (1991). *Families we choose: Lesbians, gays, kinship.* New York: Columbia University Press.

White, H. V. (1973). *Metahistory: The historical imagination in nineteenth-century Europe.* Baltimore: Johns Hopkins University Press.

18

From Same-Sex Desire to Homosexual Identity

History, Biography, and the Production of the Sexual Self in Lesbian and Gay Elders' Narratives

Dana Rosenfeld

That identity is a complex process of interpretation, negotiation, and declaration that unfolds in interaction is the basis on which most interactionist sociology is built, dating from symbolic interactionism's earliest work (Blumer, 1969; Goffman 1959, 1963; Mead, 1934). This work has shaped subsequent qualitative approaches, from social psychology (e.g., Burke & Reitzes, 1991; Howard, 2000) to ethnomethodology (Garfinkel, 1967/1984; Moerman, 1974) and conversation analysis (e.g., Sacks, 1984; Widdicombe, 1998; Zimmerman, 1998).

The role of historically grounded discourses of identity in the formation and enactment of identity has become an increasingly important focus as well, as the Foucauldian opus (Foucault, 1973, 1978, 1979; see Armstrong, 2002) points to the historical production of new categories of person and of related subjectivities, and Beck (2002), Giddens (1991), and Bauman (1996, 2000) theorize the emergence of more fluid postmodern identities (see also Holstein & Gubrium, 2000). Moreover, these historical contexts are shaped by powerful institutions and groups that variously provide, suppress, and shape the discourses (and opportunities to locate and use them) through which personhoods are built. As Cerulo (1997) writes, postmodernists critique constructionists for implying that "identity categories [are] built through interactive effort" alone and for failing

to appreciate "the role of power in the classification process" (p. 391). In contrast to ahistorical, developmental approaches to homosexual identity development inspired first by Dank's (1971) six-stage model of *coming out* and then by
Cass' (1979) *homosexual identity formation* (Floyd & Stein, 2002; Horowitz &
Newcomb, 2001; Minton & McDonald, 1983–1984; Troiden, 1989; Weinberg,
1978), the historically and interactionally sensitive approach I adopt here con-
ceives of identity construction as an ongoing process of interpreting desires
and experiences using existing cultural resources, and then situating the self
within existing categories of personhood that are both historically and politically contingent. *When* sexual identifications are made, then, can be conse-
quential for the *type and consequences* of sexual identity a person adopts, as
historical periods, and dominant groups within them, provide distinct cultural
resources that guide the actor's interpretations of desire and self.

This approach offers the cultural and historical variation in the way same-
sex desire is defined and experienced as evidence of the role of taxonomies
in shaping, rather than neutrally "representing" human feelings and actions,
including sexual ones. But while here, as with ethnicity (e.g., Waters, 1990),
identity is the product of choices made rather than essential attributes recognized, cataloged, and embraced (see Whisman, 1996), these choices are
made by reference to a symbolic field that is the product of a cultural legacy
consisting of typifications (Schutz, 1967) and representations of, inter alia,
self, other, men, women, morality, truth, and science, and of categories of and
cultural scripts for action and evaluation. As Gubrium and Holstein (2001)
write, "Taken together, cultural and institutional images set the 'conditions
of possibility' (Foucault, 1979) for who and what we might be—or are likely
not to become, as the case might be" (p. 9). These "conditions of possibility"
are, again, historically contingent, as categories of person (e.g., "the homosexual"; see Plummer, 1981; Weeks, 1977) emerge, change, and even disappear
(e.g., Boyarin, 1997; Foucault, 1978; Hacking, 1986; Jewson, 1976; McLaren,
1999; Nagel, 1995), and actors may encounter different languages with which
to interpret particular feelings and actions at different points in the life course.
(Someone born in 1852, for example, would have encountered the emergent
Freudian opus in late middle age and the identity politics of the late 1960s
not at all.) Actors' movement through history, then, and the intersection of
their biographies with historical events and contexts, affect not only concrete
life chances, as demonstrated by life course theory (Elder, 1974, 1995; Hardy
& Waite, 1997; Settersten, 1999), but also the range of subjectivities and identities we can fashion, as the interpretive resources we encounter are filtered
through circumstances in which we find ourselves at particular points in time,
and through the decisions and investments we have already made that were

themselves based upon interpretive resources that were available at the time. This brings the intersection of personal biography with historically specific discourses of subjectivity and social action to the forefront of homosexual (and any) identity formation and sensitizes us to the need to recognize identity as the product of interpretive work conducted in the context of shifting, and often complex and unclear, discursive fields (Anderson, 1991; Pollner & Rosenfeld, 2000; Rosenfeld, 1999, 2003a, 2003b; Stein, 1997).

Until the late 1960s, twentieth-century homosexuality, in its discursive formulation, cultural representation, formal regulation, social enactment, and lived experience, was driven by stigma—in Goffman's (1963) terms, a discreditable aspect of self best kept hidden and thus potentially, rather than actively, discrediting. This formulation was embedded in, but not reducible to, homosexuality's construction by medical, scientific, and psychological discourses as a pathology of mental, developmental, or physical etiology. While these discourses are too complex to investigate fully here (for a more complete investigation, see Irvine, 1990; Marshall, 1981; Weeks, 1991), their dominant and most popularly accessible versions centered on a nineteenth-century sexological literature (based on the pioneering work of Krafft-Ebbing and Havelock Ellis) that posited homosexuality as the product of *gender inversion* (Minton, 1986; Mort, 2000) and, later, by a Freudian discourse that conjured up an invisible sexual *pervert* born of a failure to graduate from one developmental stage to the next. This discourse offered the possibility of effectively containing one's homosexuality within gender-conforming surface appearances and behaviors, and of achieving public respectability in stark contrast to the evident discrediting of gender inversion.[1]

The political movements that emerged in the wake of the 1969 Stonewall uprising and that are glossed into the term *gay liberation* condemned this stigmatization as oppressive and misguided and those who embraced it as colluding in their own oppression. The discourse of these movements offered instead a construction of homosexuality as an accrediting, global, political identity that demanded open expression and celebration (Bernstein, 1997; D'Emilio, 1983; Valocchi, 1999a, 1999b). Rather than an *aspect of self*, homosexuality was conceived as *the authentic self*, which passing as heterosexual denied. In this frame, psychological damage and pathology were effects of an inadequate response to one's homosexuality rather than its cause—a stand that, according to Cain (1991), has become an accepted maxim in professional literature and various gay communities alike.

By the early 1970s, then, homosexuality as *stigma* and homosexuality as *status* had become two competing interpretive frames and guidelines for action through whose properties social actors experiencing same-sex desires could, and did, identify and pursue them. This rapid shift in how homosexuality was conceptualized makes the process of identifying as gay or lesbian during the first 70 years of the twentieth century a particularly clear instance of the intersection of historical period, power, interpretation, and agency in the formation of sexual identity. My informants—gay men and women born before 1930—came of age in a period when the only available discourse of same-sex desire was both stigmatizing and, given the strict censorship of sexual images in the post–World War II era (Chauncey, 1994; Johnson, 2003), elusive. The gay liberationist discourse became available when they were aged 39–63, and most had already identified, and begun to live, as homosexual through the properties of the stigmatizing discourse decades earlier. Others, however, had not identified as such, or had done so and then abandoned that stigmatized identity as too damaging to their self and life chances. How the interpretations and actions surrounding same-sex desire over the course of a lifetime unfolded in particular eras with distinctive discourses of homosexuality can tell us much about the nature of homosexual identity as a historically grounded yet creative process of interrogating the cultural context; of assessing, negotiating and, often, refashioning the implications of a particular category of person for self; and of either situating the self within that category or declining to do so.

The research discussed in this chapter is based on open-ended, in-depth interviews, each lasting for 2–3 hours, that I conducted in 1995 with 35 self-identified gay men and women aged 65 and over living in the greater Los Angeles area. Interviews were tape-recorded and transcribed verbatim, then analyzed using grounded theory (Charmaz, 2006; Glaser & Strauss, 1967). Interviews elicited demographic information, sexual and life histories, social relations, everyday life and problems of daily living, and feelings about and involvement with the lesbian and gay communities but were generally open-ended. With my encouragement, informants often raised issues of relevance to emergent as well as explicitly raised themes, as did I. Moreover, while the interviews were designed to capture past and present experiences and understandings, they were also occasions for the "situated construction and display" of identity (Rosenfeld, 2003a, p. 193; see also Holstein & Gubrium, 1995). Because the interviews were explicitly concerned with age and sexual identity, informants undoubtedly treated these qualities of self as more relevant to their daily lives than they would have outside the interview setting or in an interview concerned with other topics. I asked informants to assess the relevance of their homosexuality to their own lives, which often inspired lengthy narratives about the nature and consequences of same-sex desire, both in their own eyes and as depicted by various discourses of homosexuality.

I initially located informants through support groups for lesbian and gay elders and "snowballed" from the initial contacts I made through, and interviews I conducted with, these groups' members. With the exception of ethnicity (I interviewed one African American and four Latino/a informants), the final sample was heterogeneous.[2] But it is impossible to state whether the sample was representative of the elder lesbian and gay population, since, as Weston (1991) and others have argued, criteria for membership in the category homosexual is unclear at best. (As the narratives discussed in this chapter reveal, whether one is or is not homosexual is the result of interpretive work and social practice rather than of innate attributes.) However, my goal was to capture the *range* of self-identified lesbian and gay elders' identity practices, both in the past and in the interview itself, rather than their *incidence*. My analysis did uncover patterns in these identity practices, grounded in the discourses of homosexuality that prevailed in the twentieth century and in the specific discourse of homosexuality through which informants had crafted their sexual identities.

Encountering and Resisting Discourses of Homosexuality

Awareness of Difference: Sense-Making in a Conceptual Void

Most informants had been drawn to members of their own sex during childhood, although they did not always experience sexual desire for them. Several informants described their *fascination* with members of their own sex, and the pleasure that looking at them provided, as signifying a palpable but unidentifiable difference from others, of which they often became aware during key moments.

When Rodney was a teenager, he attended a state fair and realized "all day long, literally, that I was just ogling every attractive male that I saw, every guy that I saw. And it stood out in my mind how interested I am in them." He remembers "that one day in particular" because "it seemed to be a *demarcation* for me." These "demarcations" were also provided by the reactions of others to their own gender nonconformity, real or ascribed (for example, Rodney was taunted for being effeminate and a poor athlete), or to their suspicious same-sex interactions (at age 16, Jeannine "was walking around school with my girlfriend holding hands and people made remarks. I think somebody called us fairies"), to which they had not yet ascribed any significance.

Sexual encounters also constituted key moments in which previously inchoate desires were given shape, although not yet a name. George's growing awareness of his interest in males, for example, was sharpened by a sexual experience with another teen-age boy during which they "masturbated together. We didn't *touch* each other, but I knew at that time that there was something different about me." With no available sexual taxonomy, "the only thing I could think of was I enjoyed it. It was different than boys and girls touching each other." As he explained, "All the boys around 10, 11, 12 years old, at puberty time, they know, I don't want the girl. I am different. They might not know the word for it, but they know they are different."

Being *unable to interpret or name* their same-sex interests and/or desires was a central theme in these narratives. As a teen, Constance "liked [girls] a lot, but I didn't know, well you don't, you know, you don't know what's what." Similarly, when he "was a little kid," Dan "used to look at men relatives," sometimes seeing "a relative nude," but "didn't know why." Operating without an explicit language through which to describe their same-sex desires and interests was, of course, a product of both the postwar censorship of homosexuality and the state and medical enterprises' effective monopolization of any legitimate discussion of homosexuality. In retrospect, informants linked the elusive nature of their same-sex feelings to this conceptual and linguistic void.

George, who "did homosexual things before" he identified as homosexual, "never put it into words" because "you don't know it exists." Phoebe explained that, because "we didn't know gay in those days," she "didn't know what to think about it," adding that she "didn't really know what gay was 'til I got to [college]." This lack of nonpathological language to describe same-sex desire discouraged individuals from identifying as homosexual. When I asked Barbie, who recognized her same-sex desires in high school but did not pursue them until she was in her 20s, how she thought of herself at the time, she described having thought, "Oh, I'm having fun anyway, without doing." Similarly, Dan, who, while becoming aware of the existence of homosexual men when he was in the army in 1945, and while having "the awareness and the desire," understood himself as "active neuter. Nothing, no sex, nothing"—a status also informed by his having "never dated a woman." Dan was explicit about the connection between his own ignorance and the lack of a discourse to explain same-sex desire, linking his private lack of awareness to a public lack of the same:

> I wasn't aware but what I'm saying is, there was no public *awareness*, there was nothing for me to latch on to.... Well, there was no gay identity in those days, I mean you couldn't have an identity when you have nothing to—there was no...not hero, but what's the word I'm looking for? There was nothing to *represent* anything gay, you know.

With no way to articulate their desires, several informants described simply "*not thinking about it.*"

When I asked Rodney what he had thought the significance of the demar-cation he had experienced at the state fair had been, he answered that he hadn't known and didn't think that he had "thought in those terms." When they did begin to interpret their desires, though, some saw them as *personally idiosyn-cratic*, themselves as "the only one in the world," and their desires as different, fleeting, strange, and even, in Sharon's case, symptoms of mental illness (see below). Barbie, for example, "would wonder if there's other people who feel the same way as I do." While she "accepted that feeling," it made her feel lonely at times because "I didn't feel complete when I was out there."

Others saw their desires as *relationally idiosyncratic*, neither rooted in nor of any significance for their "true," essentially heterosexual, selves. Bracketing their desires and relationship allowed them to see these as natural. Jan, for example, had considered her relationship with her female high school teacher "the most natural thing in the world," a self-concept bolstered by her igno-rance of "what a homosexual was." During the relationship, she dated men and "always assumed that I would marry . . . because that was what people did where I grew up." Similarly, when I asked Kate, who became Jan's lover after Jan grad-uated from high school, if she had identified herself as "I am in love with Jan," she replied, "Yes. That was it. . . . I simply loved Jan! Both of us had expectations of getting married to a man." Finally, Susan, who had been "aware of certain girls" in high school, "*always* thought of myself as a typical young woman" who "always wanted to have a family [and] children." When her relationship with a fellow nurse, who was herself engaged to be married, ended, Susan simply "went on with my life," marrying and having three children.

Textual and Interactional Encounters with Stigma

Experiencing same-sex desires, interests, and even encounters and relation-ships in the absence of a discourse through which to interpret them, then, precluded identification as homosexual but allowed informants to sustain self-concepts as heterosexual. Their discovery of such a discourse—before 1969, an exclusively stigmatizing one—offered the opportunity to reevaluate these desires and their enactment as evidence of a new type of sexual identity. One place informants discovered this stigmatizing discourse of homosexuality was *written texts*, which depicted same-sex desires as (1) evidence of homosexuality and (2) a pathological but possibly curable condition.

Kate, for example, read sexologists Krafft-Ebbing and Havelock Ellis only to learn that "I was abnormal, a menace to children, that there was no hope for me, or that there was hope for me but that it would mean turning myself inside out on the therapist's couch or 20 years of psychoanalysis or God knows what.

But basically what I learned was that I was a mess." During her early teens, fearing that her interest in other girls was symptomatic of a "brain disorder," Sharon searched the same texts for a possible "cure," to find that they "told about all the horrible things that the insane people did, so I thought that's what gay people did."

It is important to note, though, that these texts, like all messages and representations, are resources whose relevance to self readers can negotiate rather than rigid claims that they must unreflexively accept and embrace. Thus, some informants report having engaged in a *creative reading* of these stigmatizing texts to produce a homosexual self while rejecting or ignoring their pathologizing stance. While reading Havelock Ellis taught Tony that "to find myself, to really go out and *be* myself and perform what I wanted to," he would "have to be secretive about" his tendencies and activities, he "didn't find it wrong" and "never thought about being sick. I thought it was being different."

Similarly, when Abby read Radclyffe Hall's obituary in the *New York Times* while in high school, she sent away for *The Well of Loneliness*, Hall's notorious book that was advertised beside the obituary, and found that the book's tragic, pathologizing ending was, while distasteful, balanced by its provision of an identity category, albeit a devaluing one. Emphasizing that this had been the first time she had read of the existence of women with same-sex desires, Abby noted that

> even though the book itself was ... basically an unhappy book, I
> didn't feel like that. I picked out only the parts that weren't negative.
> And I felt like, well, everybody, I think, feels the same thing: "I'm
> not the only one. There are other people."

A less scientific but equally severe stigmatizing discourse was visible in *everyday interactions and encounters* that equated homosexuality with gender inversion and publicly condemned both as shameful. Several informants spoke of having overheard people discussing gender inverts, usually described as *pansies*. Rhoda, for example, "heard about boys first, because their being feminine was so obvious," and remembers people using the word *sissy* to describe them. Informants also observed gender inverts in public, although they didn't necessarily connect them to their own desires. Indeed, the dominant equation of homosexuality with gender inversion (and, thus, of gender conformity with heterosexuality) allowed informants to maintain their heterosexual identities despite these desires, which remained ambiguous.

Dan "knew [that] in Greenwich Village there were like drag queens and things," but, ignorant of the homosexual subculture, he "didn't connect that with men loving men or anything." Julius had had sexual encounters with men, but "when I saw gay people"—specifically, "flaming types [who] acted real gay and swishy"—he thought, "Well, if that is gay people, then I am not gay." Those such as Rodney who did not themselves display the requisite level of gender conformity were vulnerable to taunting, but these taunts did not clarify their same-sex desires because they centered on gender rather than sexuality. "When I was called a sissy," he explained, "I wasn't called a faggot. They didn't use that much in those days, they called you a sissy or pansy or maybe a fruit." When I asked him if *sissy* meant the same thing as *faggot,* he answered, "Not to me, no. Although I didn't understand, there must be some relationship. It was all very, very vague, it was very, very unclear."

The public harassment and ridicule of *gender inverts*—and their public identification as homosexual—were both more clarifying and more painful, as they provided an identity category into which the individual might fall yet might induce humiliating treatment. Because these were immediate, embodied, and targeted *at* specific people, rather than global and scientized statements *about* them, these encounters were not as open to creative interpretation as were encounters with textual representations, which allowed readers to, in Abby's words, "pick out the good parts." Marge, for example, described having connected her desires to a stigmatized homosexuality as a child "because there was a female that everybody called 'old dyke' because she was out and she had a girlfriend"; the woman was, she said, "almost like an outcast." To Marge, "that she was called 'dyke'" by people who claimed that "she liked women [and] did not get along with men" was "a terrible thing."

Marge's discovery of a discourse provided an "identity peg" that made her desires intelligible and accountable but, at the same time, stigmatized her and invited ridicule and condemnation. This experience constituted a dilemma: how to construct the sexual self through a formulation that devalued it. Not all informants had found this so onerous as to discourage them from identifying as homosexual through this discourse; indeed, several identified as homosexual as soon as (or soon after) they encountered a stigmatizing discourse of difference, despite its implications. Patricia, for instance, "always knew I was gay," not only because she was always aware of her desire for women, but also because she encountered the discourse of difference, in the form of talk about homosexuals, at an early age and identified with its terms. As she explained, "There are things that you don't ever need to ask anybody. You just pick them up. You know it, you know what they're talking about." As a result, by the time she had sex with a woman for the first time, she "knew what it was, what gay meant. I knew that I was a lesbian, I knew that I was gay."

After Jeannine and her girlfriend were called "fairies" in high school, they "talked about it, and we thought we'd heard the term homosexual at some point, so we looked it up in the dictionary," where they found a relatively neutral construction defining "a homosexual [as] a person who has a sexual relationship with a person of the same sex." While the definition "made a lot of sense," Jeannine was "annoyed, because it appeared that I would never be able to follow the major mode of what women were expected to do: get married and have kids. It put me out of the norm.... I was annoyed because it put me beyond the pale, basically." Despite this insight, however, Jeannine "never had a negative reaction to it at all." Like those who creatively mined texts for identity categories while disattending to the negative messages they contained, these informants took advantage of the information the stigmatizing discourse provided—about what their own desires meant, and how those desires and their meanings connected them to others—to link themselves to a larger, newly identified group.

Others, however, felt caught between a need to understand and pursue their desires and the negative implications of a stigmatized homosexuality—specifically, a devalued self and associations that, while fulfilling sexual desires, may serve to discredit them and thus make them subject to ridicule. Many interviewees found the implications of a stigmatized identity so overwhelming that they worked to interpret their desires outside its parameters, managing the tension between their desires and the consequences of enacting them by distancing themselves from one, the other, or both. The stigmatized discourses as represented by the gender inversion and Freudian (sexual pervert) models, then, were not just oppressive constructions, but also fluid resources that agentic actors could negotiate to produce valued (heterosexual or asexual) selves.

Distancing

As we have seen, informants engaged in creative interpretive work to produce themselves as valued persons: for example, by disattending to devaluing aspects of the stigmatizing discourse and focusing instead on its identifying category. The same creativity can be seen in the distancing practices in which several informants engaged, some for many years. The term *distancing* refers to a range of practices to minimize, reject, or change the degree to which the term *homosexual* applies to self, desires, practices, and even relationships. The practices may appear similar to those we have already seen, such as viewing same-sex interactions and/or relationships as relationally idiosyncratic. But those instances were the result of an ignorance of the existence of others "such as themselves" and of the absence of a vocabulary through which to articulate their desires and interactions. By contrast, distancing was characterized by a decision to reject or negotiate the applicability of a known category to the self, often involving the pursuit of heterosexual relations or a heterosexual identity.

Informants practiced distancing by putting the issue *on the back burner*. This phrase refers to privileging and pursuing other, nonsexual needs and desires over same-sex ones. After witnessing the harassment and ridicule of the "old dyke," for example, Marge "knew I was connected with it, but I wanted to stay away from it because I did not want to be ridiculed." When I asked how she was defining herself at the time, she answered, "You mean as a person who had feelings towards females? I rejected it. I just put this out of my mind."

In response to the tense atmosphere that developed after other members of his Air Force squadron learned of his sexual encounter with another squadron member, Leonard began "avoiding it and being aware that, sure, I'd like to do something with this one or that one, [but] just avoiding it" because of the negative implications of homosexual associations and reputation. Putting it on the back burner often involved *pursuing heterosexual relations* as, in Ryan's words, "the lesser of two evils." Marge, for example, dated men instead of pursuing her same-sex desires, as did Leonard, who dated women and had a "heavy romance" throughout his 20s. These informants described having sought to prevent or compensate for the frustration of avoiding same-sex encounters and pursuits by tending to needs that could be met without the negative implications of homosexuality. After a failed course of psychoanalysis designed to "cure" her lesbianism, Kate became "deeply involved in my school and my teaching which was very satisfactory, very all-consuming. And the other stuff I put on the back burner."

While effective, suppressing certain needs and desires or redirecting them to other pursuits (a classic case of sublimation; see Freud, 1910) failed to produce a clear identity: Dan defined himself as "active neuter," Deborah explained that she "wasn't defining myself at all," and Kate considered herself "a mess, sexually, practically without identity." Thus, some informants committed to *conventional heterosexual marriages* to protect themselves from the negative reactions of others and to achieve a heterosexual identity that was fulfilling in itself. As Luke explained, "When I met her I was trying to get away from gay life. I don't know. I just wanted a family." Similarly, Mark left his lover, Jack, for a woman after he discovered that Jack did not love him and decided that there was "no future" in "being gay." After he got a woman pregnant, "I says, 'Well, better get married.' We got married and I gave up Jack."

Others constructed a *liminal heterosexuality*, treating the parameters of the scientific stigmatizing discourse as negotiable through a judicious foregrounding of certain features of these discourses to produce an actual or

potential heterosexuality. Because the gender-inversion model would depict
him as homosexual, for example, Rodney applied Freudian logic (again, an
understanding of homosexuality as caused by the individual's failure to proceed from one normal stage of sexual development to the next) to interpret his
interest in heterosexual men as evidence of a latent heterosexuality:

> Freud said that the male cannot get at the female without a torturous
> detour through another male. The fact that they would cohabit with
> women, that made him totally much more exciting, but I didn't want
> to touch the women, I was totally interested in him. 'Cause the way
> I defined it is that makes him heterosexual, and yet was I really after
> women? [For] some period of my life I thought I was a latent straight,
> and instead of being latent gay and having problems, I may have
> been latent straight.

In contrast to Rodney, Tony creatively invoked the gender inversion model to
produce himself as "different" but essentially heterosexual. While his desires
and his private "feminine attitudes" made him different, his outward gender
conformity placed him outside the homosexual category as constructed by the
gender inversion model; in his words, "I didn't think I was a fag.... A faggot was a sissy, a person [who] acted feminine. *Acted* feminine." Thus, while
his "feminine attitudes" and the "warm feeling" he had regarding feminine
men and behaviors, which grounded the "physical attraction and the physical
desire," were necessary to place him in the "faggot" category, that he did not
exhibit these behaviors allowed him to escape membership in it.

The liminal heterosexuality that Tony and Rodney fashioned for themselves was also available in the medical model's constructions of homosexuality as a curable sexual perversion and of the homosexual committed to a "cure"
as potentially heterosexual. Thus, some informants became *compliant patients*,
fashioning the positive identity of a homosexual in transition to a valued heterosexuality, therefore adequately oriented to medical goals and standards of
normality. For 9 years, for example, Kate consulted an array of medical experts
for a cure for her lesbianism, including an endocrinologist who was "bewil-
dered" to find that she had "too many female hormones, which I was supposed
to have at all." Kate was "relieved" to find that she was

> not a *male* in disguise kind of thing. You know, the doctrine was that
> female homosexuals were somehow or other *men* in disguise, there
> was something the matter with you in terms of your *basic* sexual-
> ity in the sense that you really were supposed to be a male but you
> turned out to be a female.

Each of these distancing techniques (putting it on the back burner, pursuing heterosexual relations, and developing a liminal heterosexual identity) involved reconceptualizing the meaning of same-sex desire and interactions from signifying membership in the homosexual *category* to being incidental to, or the basis for pursuing, a heterosexual *identity*. As it did for those who had adopted a homosexual identity upon encountering the stigmatizing discourse, identifying as homosexual required viewing their same-sex desire as both enduring and constituting the same basis for inclusion in the category homosexual as it did for those already thus identified, even though it might not carry with it the entire range of attributes that the stigmatizing discourse associated with homosexuality (e.g., gender inversion). These informants could have continued to experience, and even enact, their same-sex desires without making this symbolic shift indefinitely, as they were strongly committed to these distancing techniques and to the heterosexual identity they provided. All of my informants did, however, eventually identify as homosexual, and those who had engaged in distancing practices did so in response to the emergence of new emotions or to new contacts and contexts that led them to view their desires and activities in a new light.

Fashioning Gay Identities

As we have seen, informants described a number of divisions that permitted them to sustain heterosexual identities despite having experienced or pursued same-sex desires: between the gender invert and the sexual pervert (and between gender and sexuality more generally), internally experienced and externally displayed gender nonconformity, present and future selves, and the idiosyncratic and the generalizable. That sexual interactions may neither occasion nor proceed from emotions signifies another division (between the physical and the emotional) that also potentiated the production of a heterosexual self in the context of same-sex desire and pursuits. In several accounts, informants described having interpreted their "purely sexual" encounters as, if not isolated incidents, practices of little relevance to their heterosexual identities. The emergence of *emotional needs* that could only be met via romantic same-sex interactions, however, indicated a need for same-sex relations lasting beyond the immediate encounter, and thus invoked a future same-sex relational, as opposed to a purely sexual, self.

For example, while George "did homosexual things before," he did not "realize" he was gay until he experienced "this wave of emotion" while holding hands with James, whom he had just driven home: "I turned and looked out the window and I said, 'I want to tell you something.' And he said, 'Don't worry about it, so am I.'...I knew that I wanted him, he knew that he wanted me." George explained that falling in love with James made him "realize the urging towards [men]" and identify as homosexual.

Julius fell in love with a young man while engaged to a woman and recognized that he "had loved people before, but not this same way"; this experience led him "to raise more and more I'm gay." Gabrielle had had sexual encounters with men and women before and, during her two heterosexual marriages, found sex with men sexually fulfilling but emotionally unfulfilling. She found the obverse during sexual encounters with women. "Emotionally," she explained, "I have *never* been able to really love a man." After years of therapy, Gabrielle committed herself to Betty, whom she met when she was in her 40s. While she still finds sex unfulfilling with Betty (she considers giving up heterosexual sex a "compromise"), she declared their sex life to be "unimportant" both in itself and in relation to their emotional commitment and life together.

Just as these accounts describe a moment of clarification inspired by new emotions, other accounts describe similar moments inspired by same-sex *erotic feelings and/or encounters*. Dan, for example, was aware of his attraction to men throughout his childhood and had met homosexual men and women whom he had failed to recognize as such because he was "completely oblivious" to any discourse that would have allowed him to identify his feelings, or these persons, as homosexual. Thus, when he was in his 20s, he could not explain the "vibration" he felt when another man complimented him on his tie. While being massaged by a gay male physical therapist, however, Dan felt attracted to him, and when the man "finally kissed me," he understood that his desires related to sexual and romantic interactions with men—an understanding confirmed by a book on homosexuality that the therapist recommended.

When her female roommate propositioned her at age 28, Deborah "thought, 'well, I'm not getting anywhere, my whole life has just been so out of it,' so I did." The sexual encounter "probably convinced me of what I already knew, because emotionally I was always more attracted to women than men." As in other accounts, Deborah described having then retrospectively reevaluated her previous actions as signifying a previously unrecognized homosexual identity: "I guess that was one reason I didn't have any problem with dating men in the army, because I knew it was temporary."

By *encountering other homosexuals*, informants learned of the existence of others who shared these desires and had means of pursuing them within social settings, and perhaps networks, and that they could do so themselves. While observing the public harassment of gender inverts could inspire informants to distance themselves from the perceived implications of pursuing same-sex desire and even from that desire itself, these inverts also provided an opportunity to connect with members of the gay world. Connection with these individuals led them to lovers, social networks, even communities that cemented their identification as homosexual in concrete practices and cultural codes. For those not yet "in the life," however, these connections could be extraordinarily difficult to make, because places where homosexuals could present themselves as such were, although not always few and far between, necessarily secret and secretive.

As with all underground subcultures, gaining access depended upon the help of insiders, who were themselves difficult to find. Having entered gay bars under the guise of "heterosexual tourists," both Abby and Leonard quickly identified with the lesbian and gay patrons. As Abby put it, "As soon as I walked in there, I don't think it took me very long to realize that this is *exactly* where I belong." A coworker took Leonard to "a very nice bar that I'd been going to for a long time in Greenwich Village," which he had assumed was a heterosexual establishment because it was devoid of the stereotypical "fairies" he had seen elsewhere in the area. His equation of homosexual men with "dishing queens" made him suspicious of his coworker's claim that this was, in fact, a gay bar. But when he realized that he had been comfortably associating with gay men in a safe place, he recognized and embraced the new identity that these gender-conforming gay men embodied. Indeed, although he had been engaging in same-sex erotic encounters and had seen clear instances of "queers and things…running around," Leonard described his experience at the bar as "more like my first introduction to anything that was gay.… It was shortly thereafter that I picked somebody up or somebody picked me up. And so I came out at that point. That was coming out. [Because I] had sex with somebody and I committed myself basically that I was gay."

Fashioning Accredited Selves

The steps informants took to adopt a homosexual identity included becoming aware of same-sex desire as different; searching for, encountering, and adopting or negotiating a discourse of homosexuality; adopting a stigmatized identity or distancing the self from it; interpreting previously inchoate desires as homosexual in nature in the context of new encounters and contacts; and interpreting new emotional needs as signifying an emergent relational, rather than purely sexual, homosexual self. This process was undertaken within a historically distinct context in which the stigmatized discourse of homosexuality was not only dominant but exclusive. The raw symbolic matter out of which informants could fashion homosexual identities before the advent of gay liberation was therefore classically stigmatizing: homosexuality was a discred-itable aspect of self, whose public discovery would lead to negative treatment and was therefore best handled by passing as heterosexual and/or by seeking medical treatment for what the medical discourse claimed was a pathological condition.

While informants were artful in their negotiation of this discourse, they could not escape its basic parameters, as there was simply no other discourse through which to make sense of and pursue (or avoid) the same-sex desires and practices of which they had become increasingly aware. To identify as homosexual, then, these informants were condemned to stigmatization.

In 1969, however, the gay liberationist discourse offered a new formula-tion of homosexuality and a new homosexual identity, grounded not in *stigma* but in *status*. An explicit rejection of stigma, this accrediting discourse con-structed homosexuality as an essential global self rather than a discrete aspect of self, which could not be managed by passing as heterosexual, since this management denied the consequences of same-sex desires for the self. Rather, the adoption of a "true" homosexual identity demanded a commitment to its open declaration and enactment across a range of contexts, public and private. This stance would, gay liberation claimed, both reflect and encourage *(1)* the rejection of the stigmatized construction of homosexuality as pathological and shameful and *(2)* the celebration of homosexuality as a source of pride and as meriting social inclusion and respect.

For informants who were still engaged in distancing themselves from homosexuality when this new discourse emerged, gay liberation constituted a new context and provided a new set of contacts (e.g., feminist organizations), that offered an alternative to a stigmatized homosexual identity and expe-rience, on the one hand, and to the liminal heterosexuality that many were pursuing as an alternative to this stigmatized life, on the other. Again, given the age of these informants at the time gay liberation emerged (between 39 and 63), the likelihood of their encountering this discourse before they had identified as homosexual through the stigmatizing discourse was relatively small. While all eventually encountered the discourse of liberation, most did so after having invested themselves in the stigmatized homosexual world on which this new discourse had declared war. They thus experienced the new discourse as a threat to their practices and beliefs, as indeed it was. Not sur-prisingly, these informants did not abandon the homosexual lives and iden-tities that they had lived for years—even decades—to embrace the new ones demanded by gay liberation. Indeed, as Grube (1990) has demonstrated, gay liberation created a generational and political rift rather than a united ideolog-ical front. But a small minority encountered this new discourse—and the new homosexual identity it offered—at a time when they were not thus invested, and these informants did embrace it and identify themselves by reference to its core discursive properties.

Before we consider how this latter group accomplished this task of identification, however, it must be noted that their biographies cannot be simplistically divided into pre- and postdistancing periods. On the contrary, having come of age in an exclusively stigmatizing era, some of these actors had indeed adopted a stigmatized homosexual identity, only to reject it subsequently and distance themselves from it and its host discourse. Abby, for instance, had adopted a stigmatized homosexual identity in the 1950s. After she moved to California years later, however, she underwent treatment for her alcoholism, which she associated with her homosexuality. As a result, she distanced herself from her homosexuality in the quest for continued sobriety, putting it on the back burner and immersing herself in her professional life.

Kate, as already noted, had declined to define her relationship with Jan as anything other than relationally idiosyncratic. Eighteen months into the relationship, however, she "hit the panic button and threw Jan out" after having encountered lesbians at a summer camp where she was working and connected her relationship with Jan to the homosexual world. Having briefly adopted a stigmatized homosexual identity, she quickly entered therapy, questioning her lesbianism and pursuing a liminal heterosexuality. Indeed, of the seven informants who eventually adopted an accrediting homosexual identity, only two had avoided identifying as a stigmatized homosexual; the others had identified through the stigmatizing discourse, then distanced themselves from their (now stigmatized) same-sex desires, and then adopted an accrediting identity once they encountered its host discourse. Thus, while all accredited informants adopted an accrediting identity after encountering and embracing the gay liberationist discourse, and while all did so during a period of distancing, some had a personal history that included a previous identification as a stigmatized homosexual, whereas others had not.

The social and symbolic contexts provided by the accrediting discourse often overlapped in venues such as feminist meetings and consciousness-raising groups. Both Kate and Marilyn had almost identical experiences when they attended meetings hosted by the National Organization for Women (NOW, an organization that, until its notorious ousting of avowed lesbian-feminists, was an arena for an emergent lesbian-feminist movement). While Kate attended this meeting on the advice of her therapist, Marilyn did so on the advice of a woman whom she met at a workshop for career women. Both noted their surprise and delight at finding self-identified lesbians in an open political setting—in Kate's words, "interesting-looking, bright-looking, normal-looking women" and in Marilyn's words, "identifiable lesbians." In an instance reminiscent of Leonard's experience at a gay bar (see above), Kate asked a friend who was attending a NOW meeting with her if there were any lesbians among the "normal-looking women" there. When her friend told her that "almost all of them" were, in fact, lesbians, Kate felt that she was "home, I was home free."

Through her involvement with NOW, Kate was offered, and embraced, a homosexual identity shaped by membership in lesbian-feminist and feminist social movements, which stood in stark and explicit contrast to the stigmatized homosexual subculture from which she had distanced herself. Kate termed this a "rebirth":

> I have a certain amount of sympathy for a born-again Christian. It was like I was a born-again lesbian. Not only I wasn't a freak but I was a part of what was a really big important group *and* my lesbianism *fit in*, there was no problem with it.... I was not an outsider anymore. I belonged. I had full validation.... It was acceptance, it was validation, it was belonging. It was really remarkable. It was a wonderful feeling.

Marilyn described adopting an accrediting lesbian identity in almost identical terms: after attending her first NOW meeting, she read an article written by a NOW member and thought, "'Hey, that's me.' And it was just a revelation.... What she was describing was what I felt and thought and had experienced."

But the accrediting discourse of homosexuality was, while most clearly visible within the activities of lesbian-feminist and feminist organizations, available elsewhere as well. For example, Tex, who had been leading a double life (having sex with men while married to a woman), found an early gay liberationist book at an underground bookstore and embraced its construction of this life as inauthentic, of his homosexuality as comprising his entire "true" self, and of his agreement with these "true readings" as essential to personal integrity. As Tex explained, the book

> showed me not what I was, but what I wasn't. I wasn't what I was pretending to be. And that the only way I would get myself in order is to be myself. I don't think I was feeling anything until after I got through it and digested it. And it's really a great book! That's all I felt. You know, this is the answer to what my questions are.

Moreover, embedded in the identity politics of the late 1960s and early 1970s, gay liberation was part of a larger project of accrediting previously stigmatized identities, most notably those surrounding gender and race. Gay liberation and lesbian-feminism were also informing such institutions as the church, and Sharon encountered these movements through her immersion in the hippie counterculture and, later, the Metropolitan Community Church (the first and largest explicitly lesbian and gay church, founded in Los Angeles in 1968), which she found during a period of spiritual exploration.

Leonard, who had identified as gay through the stigmatizing discourse and then distanced himself from it, encountered a nascent identity politics, and its politicized condemnation of passing, when he became involved in the civil rights movement, whereupon he came to see homosexuality as an essential, inescapable self that demanded acceptance and proclamation. Abby, who had distanced herself from her lesbianism throughout the 1970s and 1980s, encountered the liberationist discourse, having seen an advertisement for the West Hollywood annual Gay Pride Festival, in the early 1990s, when it had become firmly enshrined in public gay life.

For those who had declined to identify as homosexual and/or had identified as such through the stigmatized discourse, adopting an accrediting homosexual identity forced a reevaluation—and accounting—of their previous actions and inactions. Because it constructed the stigmatized discourse as an oppressive distortion of the true nature of homosexuality, and those who embraced it as ignorant and/or colluding in their own oppression, the gay liberationist discourse through whose properties members of this smaller group eventually fashioned their sexual identities tacitly demanded that they explain how and why they came to align themselves with an ideology that they now recognized as not only personally destructive, but politically and morally deficient. Thus, Tex described having realized that he had to "get himself in order," demonstrating his recognition (1) that his previous "double life" was essentially "disorderly," a product of his having failed to place himself in his rightful category (see Douglas, 1966/1991), and (2) that placing himself in the right category—that of accredited homosexual—would both launch him on the path to personal authenticity and effectively end his previously inauthentic actions. Here, in a single account, the past is condemned through the properties of the very discourse whose adoption promises a morally valid future.

Similar to Tex, Kate depicted her early understanding of her relationship with Jan as irrelevant to her essential identity as heterosexual as "insanity"—a denial of its true character. Kate recast her pursuit of a liminal heterosexuality in the name of mental health as itself a form of insanity and embraced her "essential" lesbian identity as a sign of true mental health:

> We were together for a year and a half at that stage, and neither of us admitted that we were lesbian or even or homosexual, or—inverts, perverts, Uranians, any of the terms that were being used then, we

didn't admit anything, we just loved each other. Total, total, *total* denial of what was really happening.... It was total insanity, if you really want to look at it that way, I mean we were totally out of touch with reality.

Conclusion

The narrative accounts of gay and lesbian elders reported in this chapter demonstrate the active, reflexive negotiation of the meanings and implications of same-sex desire in the context of the shifting and often contradictory discourse of homosexuality. Indeed, while the core narrative of contemporary gay politics depicts the pre-Stonewall era as having been dominated by a relatively straightforward stigmatized and medicalized discourse of homosexuality, the symbolic terrain in which actors interpreted and managed their sexual desires in the first 70 years of the twentieth century was surprisingly complex, both in itself (the stigmatization of homosexuality, for example, took several forms) and in its creative refashioning by actors working to develop a valid and valued sexual identity through its parameters.

The complexity of the cultural and discursive terrain in which actors interpret and negotiate their identities is thus both a property of that terrain and the product of interpretive work, as well as concrete decisions actors make. Actors do not merely *respond* to discursive formulations; they *elaborate* and *complicate* them to produce a fit between the identity categories they contain and their own lives. This process suggests that, rather than merely trace the developmental stages through which actors move on their way to identifying as members of a group (in the essentialist argot, to recognize and give shape to biologically based sexual drives), we must consider that these steps may be less innate than historical, less universal than culturally located, less driven by internal processes and needs than shaped, even provided, by historically specific and politically regulated cultural repertoires of self, desire, and commonality. But, as signaled in this chapter's introduction, attention to the historical context requires that we attend as well to the suppression by agencies of social control of discourses that actors need to fashion particular identities and communities. In short, just as we recognize the role of discursive context in the formation of (sexual) identities, we must also recognize that particular discourses, however readily available they now appear, may be conspicuous by their absence and that identities are doubly political—they are fashioned *(1)* by reference to discourses that are upheld by dominant groups and *(2)* in the politically designed absence of discourses that potentiate particular selves. Indeed, identity-based social movements can and do emerge in response to the absence of particular discourses or to their inaccessibility.

Consider, for example, the disability rights movement, feminism, and the like—movements centered on refashioning target identities through, inter alia, creating and distributing new discourses of self. These movements represent actors' own sense of the absence of, and their need for, new discourses of self whose properties better reflect human experiences, desires, and attributes. In these accounts, we can see the challenges of producing a morally accountable homosexual identity in the absence of a valuing discourse of homosexuality— or, indeed, of any perceivable discourse of homosexuality.

In the narratives of elders, feelings and experiences were recognizable *as* feelings and experiences but were inarticulable in the absence of a discourse of same-sex desire. Once informants encountered a discourse of homosexuality, they minimized its devaluing. This experience highlights the importance of available discourses of self and the desire for identity formation.

This phenomenon also highlights the fluidity not only of self, but of the discourses that make claims about it. My informants are not unique in the creative agency they applied to their cultural repertoires of the sexual self (discourses shape our identities but do not determine them, as we reshape their meanings and claims to fit our own biographies and needs). But they are unique in having exercised this agency in a historical period providing a distinctive (stigmatizing) discourse of homosexuality whose basic tenets demanded particularly delicate interpretive work to produce a valid, valued homosexual self. For some, this self was possible within the parameters of the stigmatizing discourse; for others, it became possible only when a new politicized and accrediting discourse of homosexuality emerged.

Discourses of homosexuality, like all discourses, are thus not infinitely flexible; they allow for a *range* of possible selves but not for *any* self. Moreover, emergent discourses that potentiate new "conditions of possibility" are themselves interpreted in the light of previous familiar discourses that the former seek to supplement or replace. This interpretation, in turn, shapes their perceived flexibility. Social changes that construct new discourses of personhood, then, are filtered through biography and commitment, as were preexisting cultural repertoires. This process is evident in the accounting work in which Tex and Kate engaged: having adopted both the gay liberationist discourse of homosexuality and the identity it provided, they recast their previous homosexual identity work as inadequate. They did so in gay liberationist terms, as gay liberation's very existence was predicated upon the rejection of previous stigmatized versions and enactments of same-sex desire—indeed, of any formulation of homosexuality as anything other than an essential global self whose authenticity depended upon its public proclamation.

Kate, Tex, and the other informants who adopted an accrediting homosexual identity did so in a more complex symbolic field than did those informants who had adopted stigmatized homosexual identities. While the latter became aware of the gay liberationist discourse of homosexuality (and its claims upon them) after they had identified as homosexual, and thus experienced their homosexual identities and lives in a new political context that critiqued their past decisions and current affiliations, they *initially* identified as homosexual in a relatively simple discursive field. Although, as I have argued, the stigmatized discourse was more complex than was previously thought, it was the only discourse of homosexuality to which they had access when they eventually defined their same-sex desires as homosexual. But those who fashioned accredited identities did so in the context of competing discourses, and thus have more in common with those who conduct this interpretive and identity work in the twenty-first century, as we find ourselves constructing and negotiating sexual and other identities in a cultural context offering more and more options for who we are and how we live.

As Giddens (1991), Beck (2002), and others have argued, postmodernity is characterized by, among other things, an explosion of identity and lifestyle choices, to which we are no longer expected to adhere indefinitely. We could, then, assume that new generations will construct their sexual identities in contested fields similar to those faced by Kate, Tex, Marilyn, and others, and find themselves having to account for past identifications and practices through the guidelines of the discourse of sexuality with which they currently affiliate. But scholars of postmodernity suggest that the array of identity and lifestyle choices that characterizes contemporary social life is framed as just that—equally valid lifestyle choices—rather than pitted against each other in a tense identity-political battle for authenticity. If this is true, then the emergence of new homosexual categories, many of which are gender-based (e.g., the *macho man* and the *lipstick lesbian*), will be adopted in a less contested field than was the case in the 1970s and 1980s (Stein, 1993). Given the interpenetration of history, biography, discourse, and identity, how future cohorts of actors experiencing same-sex (or, indeed, any) sexual desire construct sexual identities is a question requiring continued investigation.

NOTES

1. These formulations were challenged only in 1948, with Kinsey et al.'s "reformulation of sexuality as a continuum with both behavioral and cognitive characteristics" (Risman & Schwartz, 1988, p. 126).

2. The average age was 72.5, with 46% of informants aged 75 or older and 13.5% aged 80 and above. Annual income ranged from below $10,000 to over $100,000, with male informants averaging $29,500 and females averaging $24,700. Three out of four informants lived alone; approximately one out of three had been heterosexually married, of whom two men and two women had children.

REFERENCES

Anderson, B. (1991). *Imagined communities* (2nd ed.). London: Verso.

Armstrong, D. (2002). *A new history of identity: A sociology of medical knowledge.* London: Palgrave.

Bauman, Z. (1996). From pilgrim to tourist—or a short history of identity. In S. Hall & P. du Gay (Eds.), *Questions of cultural identity* (pp. 18–36). London: Sage.

Bauman, Z. (2000). *Liquid modernity.* Cambridge: Polity Press.

Beck, U. (2002). The cosmopolitan society and its enemies. *Theory, Culture & Society, 19*(1–2), 17–44.

Bernstein, M. (1997). Celebration and suppression: The strategic uses of identity by the lesbian and gay movement. *American Journal of Sociology, 103*(3), 531–565.

Blumer, H. (1969). *Symbolic interactionism.* Englewood Cliffs, NJ: Prentice-Hall.

Boyarin, D. (1997) *Unheroic conduct: The rise of heterosexuality and the invention of the Jewish man.* Berkeley: University of California Press.

Burke, P. J., & Reitzes, D. C. (1991). An identity theory approach to commitment. *Social Psychology Quarterly, 54*(3), 239–251.

Cain, R. (1991). Stigma management and gay identity development. *Social Work, 36,* 67–73.

Cass, V. C. (1979). Homosexual identity formation: A theoretical model. *Journal of Homosexuality, 4*(3), 219–235.

Cerulo, K. A. (1997). Identity construction: New issues, new directions. *Annual Review of Sociology, 23,* 385–409.

Charmaz, K. C. (2006). *Constructing grounded theory: A practical guide through qualitative analysis.* Thousand Oaks, CA: Sage.

Chauncey, G. (1994). *Gay New York: Gender, urban culture, and the making of the gay male world, 1890–1940.* New York: Basic Books.

Dank, B. M. (1971). Coming out in the gay world. *Psychiatry, 34*(2), 180–197.

D'Emilio, J. (1983). *Sexual politics, sexual communities: The making of a homosexual minority in the United States.* Chicago: University of Chicago Press.

Douglas, M. (1991). *Purity and danger: An analysis of the concepts of pollution and taboo.* London: Routledge. (Original work published 1966)

Elder, G. H., Jr. (1974). *Children of the Great Depression: Social change and life experience.* Chicago: University of Chicago Press.

Elder, G. H., Jr. (1995). The life course paradigm: Social change and individual development. In P. Moen, G. H. Elder, & K. Luscher (Eds.), *Examining lives in context: Perspectives on the ecology of human development* (pp. 101–139). Washington, DC: American Psychological Association Press.

Floyd, F. J., & Stein, T. S. (2002). Sexual orientation identity formation among gay, lesbian, and bisexual youths: Multiple patterns of milestone experiences. *Journal of Research on Adolescence, 12*(2), 167–191.

Foucault, M. (1973). *The birth of the clinic*. London: Tavistock.

Foucault, M. (1978). *The history of sexuality, Vol. 1: An introduction*. New York: Vintage.

Foucault, M. (1979). *Discipline and punish*. New York: Vintage.

Freud, S. (1999). *Leonardo da Vinci and a memory of his childhood*. London: Routledge. (Original work published 1910)

Garfinkel, H. (1984). *Studies in ethnomethodology*. Cambridge: Polity Press. (Original work published 1967)

Giddens, A. (1991). *Modernity and self-identity. Self and society in the late modern age*. Cambridge: Polity Press.

Glaser, B. G., & Strauss, A. L. (1967). *The discovery of grounded theory: Strategies for qualitative research*. Chicago: Aldine.

Goffman, E. (1959). *The presentation of self in everyday life*. Garden City, NY: Doubleday.

Goffman, E. (1963). *Stigma: Notes on the management of spoiled identity*. New York: Simon & Schuster.

Gubrium, J. F., & Holstein, J. A. (2001). *Institutional selves: Troubled identities in a postmodern world*. New York: Oxford University Press.

Grube, J. (1990). Natives and settlers: An ethnographic note on early interaction of older homosexual men with younger gay liberationists. *Journal of Homosexuality, 20*(3/4), 119–135.

Hacking, I. (1986). Making up people. In T. C. Heller, M. Sosna, & F. E. Wellerby (Eds.), *Reconstructing individuality: Autonomy, individuality and the self in western thought* (pp. 222–237) . Stanford, CA: Stanford University Press.

Hardy, M. A., & Waite, L. (1997). Doing time: Reconciling biography with history in the study of social change. In M. A. Hardy (Ed.), *Studying aging and social change: Conceptual and methodological issues* (pp. 1–21). Thousand Oaks, CA: Sage.

Holstein, J. A., & Gubrium, J. F. (1995). *The active interview*. Thousand Oaks, CA: Sage.

Holstein, J. A., & Gubrium, J. F. (2000). *The self we live by: Narrative identity in a postmodern world*. New York: Oxford University Press.

Horowitz, J. L., & Newcomb, M. D. (2001). A multidimensional approach to homosexual identity. *Journal of Homosexuality, 42*(2), 1–19.

Howard, J. A. (2000). Social psychology of identities. *Annual Review of Sociology, 26*, 367–393.

Irvine, J. M. (1990). *Disorders of desire: Sex and gender in modern American sexology*. Philadelphia: Temple University Press.

Jewson, N. D. (1976). The disappearance of the sick-man from medical cosmology. *Sociology, 10*, 225–244.

Johnson, D. K. (2003). *The lavender scare: The Cold War persecution of gays and lesbians in the federal government*. Chicago: University of Chicago Press.

Marshall, J. (1981). Pansies, perverts and macho men: Changing conceptions of male homosexuality. In K. Plummer (Ed.), *The making of the modern homosexual* (pp. 133–154). Totowa, NJ: Barnes & Noble.

McLaren, A. (1999). *Trials of masculinity: Policing sexual boundaries, 1870–1930.* Chicago: University of Chicago Press.

Mead, G. H. (1934). *Mind, self and society.* Chicago: University of Chicago Press.

Minton, H. L. (1986). Femininity in men and masculinity in women: American psychiatry and psychology portray homosexuality in the 1930s. *Journal of Homosexuality, 13*(1), 19–22.

Minton, H. L., & McDonald, G. J. (1983–1984). Homosexual identity formation as a developmental process. *Journal of Homosexuality, 9*(2–3), 91–104.

Moerman, M. (1974). Accomplishing ethnicity. In R. Turner (Ed.), *Ethnomethodology* (pp. 54–68). Harmondsworth, UK: Penguin.

Mort, F. (2000). *Dangerous sexualities: Medico-moral politics in England since 1830* (2nd ed.). London: Routledge.

Nagel, J. (1995). American Indian ethnic renewal: Politics and the resurgence of identity. *American Sociological Review, 60*(6), 947–965.

Plummer, K. (1981). Building a sociology of homosexuality. In K. Plummer (Ed.), *The making of the modern homosexual* (pp. 17–29). Totowa, NJ: Barnes & Noble.

Pollner, M., & Rosenfeld, D. (2000). The cross-culturing work of gay and lesbian elderly. *Advances in Life Course Research: Identity Through the Life Course in Cross-Cultural Perspective, 5,* 99–117.

Risman, B., & Schwartz, P. (1988). Sociological research on male and female homosexuality. *Annual Review of Sociology, 14,* 125–147.

Rosenfeld, D. (1999). Identity work among lesbian and gay elderly. *Journal of Aging Studies, 13*(2), 121–144.

Rosenfeld, D. (2003a). *The changing of the guard: Lesbian and gay elders, identity, and social change.* Philadelphia: Temple University Press.

Rosenfeld, D. (2003b). Homosexual bodies in time and space: The homosexual body as a sexual signifier in lesbian and gay elders' narratives. In C. Faircloth (Ed.), *Aging bodies: Meanings and perspectives* (pp. 171–203). Walnut Creek, CA: Alta Mira Press.

Sacks, H. (1984). On doing "being ordinary." In J. M. Atkinson & J. C. Heritage (Eds.), *Structures of social action: Studies in conversation analysis* (pp. 413–429). Cambridge, England: Cambridge University Press.

Schutz, A. (1967). *The phenomenology of the social world.* Evanston, IL: Northwestern University Press.

Settersten, R. A., Jr. (1999). *Lives in time and place: The problems and promises of developmental science.* New York: Baywood.

Stein, A. S. (Ed.). (1993). *Sisters, sexperts, queers: Beyond the lesbian nation.* New York: Plume.

Stein, A. S. (1997). *Sex and sensibility: Stories of a lesbian generation.* Berkeley: University of California Press.

Troiden, R. R. (1989). The formation of homosexual identities. *Journal of Homosexuality, 17*(1), 43–73.

Valocchi, S. (1999a). Riding the crest of a protest wave? Collective action frames in the gay liberation movement, 1969–1973. *Mobilization: An International Quarterly, 4*(1), 59–73.

Valocchi, S. (1999b). The class-inflected nature of gay identity. *Social Problems, 46*(2), 207–224.

Waters, M. C. (1990). *Ethnic options: Choosing identities in America*. Berkeley: University of California Press.

Weeks, J. (1977). *Coming out: Homosexual politics in Britain from the 19th century to the present*. London: Quartet.

Weeks, J. (1991). *Against nature: Essays on history, sexuality and identity*. London: Rivers Oram Press.

Weinberg, T. S. A. (1978). On doing and being gay. *Journal of Homosexuality, 4*(2), 143–156.

Weston, K. (1991). *Families we choose: Lesbians, gays, kinship*. New York: Columbia University Press.

Weston, K. (1997). *Families we choose: Lesbians, gays, kinship* (Rev. ed.). New York: Columbia University Press.

Whisman, V. (1996). *Queer by choice: Lesbians, gay men, and the politics of identity*. New York: Routledge.

Widdicombe, S. (1998). Identity as an analyst's and a participant's resource. In C. Antaki & S. Widdicombe (Eds.), *Identities in talk.* (pp. 191–206). London: Sage.

Zimmerman, D. H. (1998). Identity, context and interaction. In C. Antaki & S. Widdicombe (Eds.), *Identities in talk* (pp. 87–106). London: Sage.

PART V

Concluding Perspectives

19

Lives, Times, and Narrative Engagement

Multiplicity and Meaning in Sexual Lives

Bertram J. Cohler and Phillip L. Hammack

The development of sexual identity always occurs in a particular social and cultural location. This *contextualized* approach to the study of sexuality represents the foundational premise of all the chapters in this volume. This context for the development of personal meaning of same-sex desire is characterized by a particular discourse or lexicon that we use to understand our feelings and actions (Hammack, 2005; Hostetler & Herdt, 1998). Thus, *narrative* becomes a fundamental analytic tool for the study of sexual lives, for narratives provide access to the meaning-making process as it actively occurs (Bruner, 1990; Polkinghorne, 1988).

In this concluding chapter, we begin by reviewing our general theoretical perspective on narrative, sexual identity, and the life course. We highlight the way in which a particular *paradigm* for the study of sexual identity development emerges when we integrate some of these critical social science perspectives. We then address each of the major sections of the book and connect the work of the contributors to this paradigm.

Time, Place, Story: Toward an Integrative Paradigm

This book has two goals: to highlight the importance of stories about same-sex desire and sexual orientation in the course of individual lives and to demonstrate the contextual basis of narrative—that is, the connection of personal narratives to specific sites of telling or writing. Narrative engagement necessarily includes social and historical change as a determinant. We remember the past, experience the present, and anticipate the future in quite specific ways, and we collectively remember our past in different ways and at different times. As Benjamin Shephard argues in his chapter, the history of same-sex attraction in American society has changed the manner in which men and women regard their sexual orientation. The stories we tell of same-sex attraction in our own lives are guided by these larger social and historical changes. Personal narratives are remade across the course of life and in the context of this social and historical change and further shape this shared understanding of sexuality (Cohler, 2007; Holland, 2000).

In our introductory chapter, we reviewed a model for understanding human development that highlights the importance of generation-cohort as a context within which we make meanings of our experiences. As Elder (1998) and Shanahan and Elder (2002) have observed, our life is a "career" marked by shared understanding of the nature and timing of the social positions we are expected to occupy. Both expectations and timing vary across generation-cohorts as a consequence of historical and social change. Our understanding of same-sex attraction and of the means that we use in realizing this attraction follow shared and ever-changing understandings of what it means to be aware of this same-sex attraction, including the manner in which we both understand this attraction and talk about it with a variety of others. That is, the way in which particular tellers of a life story construct that story is entirely a product of the discourse on sexuality that is deployed in a given sociohistorical context (Foucault, 1978). The personal narrative thus becomes more than an individualized document of life; it is, rather, a reflection of the lexicon available to make meaning of desire (Hammack, 2005). The personal narrative that constructs identity is, therefore, best understood as a *product* of linguistic possibility; it always relates to some master narrative of identity accessible in a culture (Hammack, 2008; Plummer, 1995).

Our intellectual agenda in this book—indeed, in our independent and collaborative work more generally—has been to integrate narrative and life course perspectives on identity to construct a theoretical account sensitive to the context of human development. As social scientists embrace their roles as "historians of the self" (Mishler, 2004; see also Gergen, 1973), the utility of such an integrative paradigm becomes apparent. Identity is not just the product of individual cognition; it is not characterized simply by the mastery or management of past identifications. Rather, identity represents a story constructed and reconstructed across the course of life, always in relation to some discourse available in a given social ecology (Cohler, 2007; Hammack, 2008; McAdams, 1996, 2001).

As we stated in our introductory chapter, though, we endorse an account of identity that recognizes both structure *and* agency in the context of human development. In other words, we do not view identity *merely* as a product of social discourse. Rather, we view identity and culture as coconstitutive. It is for this reason that we speak of narrative *engagement* as a process of human development. The process of narrative engagement speaks to the ability of an individual or a group of individuals to contest the content of a master narrative from within and, in the process, potentially repudiate and reformulate its story line. Hence, narrative engagement represents a vitally *social* process and can, in fact, catalyze collective action for social change. It was precisely this kind of process that was at work in the events of the gay rights movement of the twentieth century. And this process is still at work among contemporary youth with same-sex desire, who possess new discursive resources with which to construct personal narratives of identity (Cohler & Hammack, 2007).

The advent of the Internet has made it possible for persons with same-sex desire to share their experiences and to remake meanings within an international community. As Harper and his colleagues illustrate in their chapter, youth make significant use of this new tool for human interconnection as they construct their identities. The Internet has facilitated collective remembrance of a sometimes painful and stigmatized past and has fostered sharing of sexual stories in blogs and chat rooms. In this way, as Plummer (1995) suggests, stories flourish and lead to ever-changing meanings of sexuality as successive generations come of age and enter into the community of persons seeking same-sex intimacy.

A major issue—or point of tension—in queer scholarship concerns the impact of a shifting master narrative of same-sex desire and orientation for a new generation. Some scholars have suggested that we may be entering a "postidentity" phase of the narrative of a sexual self (e.g., Savin-Williams, 2005). If narratives of same-sex attraction and identity have been constructed in the past as counternarratives in the context of stigma (e.g., D'Augelli, 2002; Flowers & Buston, 2001), then as sexual diversity becomes recognized, "virtually normal" (Sullivan, 1995), and no longer contested within the larger society, succeeding generations will make new meanings of their life stories (Savin-Williams, 2005). Construction of a coherent personal narrative depends ever less on particular sexual lifeways as contested social terrain (Hostetler & Herdt, 1998) and perhaps more on other strivings, such as recognition for creative accomplishments or contributions to the welfare of the larger society. Who we are might depend ever less on our sexual lives.

We have argued that the story of social change is not quite so linear. Contemporary youth engage with multiple narratives of what it means to experience same-sex desire (Cohler & Hammack, 2007). The story of the interaction between David and Paul that we discussed in our introductory chapter plainly reveals this dynamic process among youth. Our view is that the process of narrative engagement, if examined empirically among individuals with same-sex desire, reveals much about the relationship between culture and the self. The shifting master narratives of queer identity in the twenty-first century provide incredible opportunities for empirical inquiry, but such an inquiry necessitates adequate sensitivity to and appreciation for the contextual basis of human development. We believe that a fusion of narrative and life course approaches constructs a paradigm sufficiently sensitized to the historical and cultural grounding of identity.

Culture, Identity, Narrative: Context and Multiplicity in Sexual Lives

In our introduction, we outlined a theory of identity grounded in notions of social change across generation cohorts, accessible at least in part through narrative. Findings reported in this book suggest further that a model of identity presuming a coherent self may be less relevant to contemporary society than a model of multiple coexisting selves with all the contradictions, conflict, and curious coherence. Blackburn's analysis of four tellings of the personal narrative of a young Black lesbian revealed the process of negotiating multiplicity. And the narratives of Black gay men and lesbians examined by Meyer and Ouellette suggested that coherence can indeed prevail in the face of conflict between multiple identities and axes of potential marginalization.

To the extent that sexual identity remains a salient category for understanding social life, it is that all identities are multiple and remade in the context of social ties (Hermans, 2001; Rodríguez Rust, this volume; Schiff, 2003). Rosenfeld observes in her chapter that events of the 1960s and 1970s overtook even those men and women who had previously attempted to avoid the challenge of integrating a gay identity into a previously established identity based on other social characteristics. The explosion of identity possibilities afforded by these social movements demanded reconsideration of self, thus disrupting the personal narratives of many of Rosenfeld's interviewees. Hermans (2001) has been explicit in maintaining that a coherent self is realized in the context of society and not as an individual apart from society. The task is the management of these several aspects of experience, recognizing the variety of contexts within which we lead our lives.

The concept of the dialogical self maintains that we make sense of lived experience by recognizing the multiplicity of experiences and contexts in our life. Gergen (2001) and Schiff (2003) emphasize that social ties are particularly important in the realization of self. Michel and Wortham (2002) implicitly accept Bruner's (2002) and McAdams' (2001) perspective on story as the foundation for identity but note that this story is itself constituted through the interplay of persons and their social worlds. As we would argue, the story is constructed through a process of *narrative engagement.*

Findings from Hall's study of same-sex attracted men across three postwar generations in Czech society demonstrate how identities are both multiple and "on the move" over time. In Czech society, where heterosexuality is viewed as an element of citizenship, Czech men are able to blend elements of both same-sex and opposite-sex attraction together into their understanding of self within their culture. These men find strange the American concern with constructing a distinct gay identity, as they are able to express their same-sex desires in their cultural context without assuming an identity.

The chapters on culture, narrative, and multiplicity reveal the dialogical nature of the self and the process of narrative engagement as it is actively undertaken in diverse settings. The significance of time, place, and story in the construction of sexual selves is revealed in the dynamic processes individuals undergo as they reconcile desire and discourse. Yet, a foundational premise of our perspective is that this process never occurs in solitude. Rather, it is embedded in a context for the possibilities of relational action. As such, the construction of identity necessarily entails the navigation of risk and relationships for individuals with same-sex desire.

Identities in Process: Stories of Risk and Relationships

The construction of a coherent and meaningful personal narrative occurs in a relational context. We come to understand our stories in connection to a larger social network, and our stories contain characters whose presence facilitates the process of personal meaning-making. Kurtz's chapter on the navigation of sex, drugs, and relationships in the Miami circuit scene offers an ethnographic perspective on the struggles of gay men to create communities and forge relationships that provide a sense of belonging. Weinstock's fusion of her personal narrative of relationships with an assessment of the larger scholarly field on gay and lesbian friendship reveals the sociohistorical grounding of the life course. As the meaning of gay and lesbian identity has shifted in American society, so too has the nature of community and friendship.

As rates of human immunodeficiency virus (HIV) infection are back on the rise after an incredibly successful prevention campaign in the 1990s, it is useful to consider the relational context for risky sexual behavior using a narrative approach. The chapters by Adam and Ridge and Wright address precisely this issue and contextualize contemporary risk behavior in the larger history of the acquired immune deficiency syndrome (AIDS) epidemic, as well as the narratives of sexual behavior that have circulated over time. If we are to understand how and why sexual practices associated with HIV transmission have risen, we must consider the personal meanings of risk and relationships by listening to the voices of these men. We must hear the challenges they face as they negotiate the boundaries of safety and pleasure, desire and rationality. And we must make sense of risk by directly probing the motivations of men.

Perz and Ussher's important chapter on lesbian relationships uses narrative methods to reveal the incredible ways in which women find mutual support and functionality. Their chapter offers itself a counternarrative to other perspectives on lesbian relationships, thereby engaging with a master narrative constructed within the scholarly literature.

Narrative approaches to the study of same-sex relationships and sexual risk are vital because they offer important insights into the contextualized *meaning* individuals make of experience. The voices of gay men and lesbians reveal the centrality of relationships in the course of their development, even as the shifting historical context of same-sex desire might radically transform this process across generations (e.g., Weinstock, this volume). The contextualization of risk and relationships through access to the voices of men and women navigating the waters of social interaction as they construct a life story provides social scientists with vital and salient data on the nature of sexual identity development.

Making Gay and Lesbian Identities: Development, Generativity, and the Life Course

The final section of the book focused on issues central to scholars of human development. Our intent in this section was to highlight the ways in which different cohorts have made meaning of sexual identity by appropriating particular narratives. In Cohler's chapter on American boyhood, for example, the way in which men of a particular generation called upon the cultural construction of boyhood to make sense of their remembered past and conceived present was readily apparent in their personal narratives. Other chapters in this section focused on the shifting nature of gay and lesbian identity development through engagement with new media (Harper et al.) or through new rites of passage (deBoer). Still others appreciate human development as a complete life cycle (Erikson, 1959) by investigating the narratives of gay and lesbian individuals at midlife and beyond (Read, Hostetler, and Rosenfeld).

The theme of multiplicity continues throughout these chapters on the gay and lesbian life course. These chapters dramatically reveal the impact of social change on the manner in which we understand the interplay of same-sex desire and shared understanding. In their chapters, Cohler and Harper and his colleagues each show the importance of social context represented as identity cohort (Rosenfeld, 2003) in managing same-sex desire across childhood and adolescence. Harper and his colleagues argue for the significance of the Internet in realizing this management of an adolescent self, subject to multiple social influences and multiple selves crafted in terms of social position within school and community. Adolescents and emerging adults are uniquely subject to multiple influences that are magnified by proximity to social change, reflected in rapid adoption of new technologies (Arnett, 2002).

One of the most contested arenas of modern social life is that of continuing, dedicated relationships between two men or two women and the realization of both social recognition and the expectable transitions accompanying these unions, such as parenthood. Same-sex parenthood challenges many of our assumptions about identity and the life course. DeBoer well illustrates the complexity involved in being a partner in a same-sex marriage or partnership and the social activity of child care. He notes the impact of gender expectations on gay men assuming the parental role.

Reverse socialization is having a renewed impact on the lives of middle-aged and particularly older adults who are aware of same-sex attraction. The oldest generation had to some extent avoided coping with multiple identities while growing up by remaining socially invisible. The new discourse on sexual identity that emerged in the late twentieth century and continues to evolve in the twenty-first century has led at least some of these self-identified gay and lesbian elders to become socially active for the first time. An older gay couple, a retired teacher and a retired librarian, led a quiet life in their urban neighborhood, mixing with other older gay and lesbian couples at dinner parties and other functions. One member of the couple had served in the armed forces during the Second World War and was incensed by the impact of the Clinton administration's decree, "don't ask, don't tell." Inspired by the gay youth movement that they had read about in both mainstream and lesbian, gay, bisexual, and transgender (LGBT) magazines, the couple organized a group of other self-identified gay veterans to protest dishonorable discharge from the military on account of sexual identity. Their sense of agency led them to organize what has now become the powerful gay veterans organization with access to the Pentagon. This couple represents new activism among older gay men and lesbians aware of and able to integrate multiple identities in society.

The example of gay and lesbian elders reveals the coconstitutive nature of culture and identity, as there has been a *reciprocal* process of socialization through intergenerational engagement. Rosenfeld's chapter well portrays the social context in which these lesbian and gay men came to adulthood in the postwar world. She observes that the requirement of adopting multiple selves was forced on the men and women coming of age in the 1960s and 1970s by the reality of social and historical change taking place in their communities and more generally in society. The new discourse of the feminist and gay rights movements, gaining ground in the aftermath of the civil rights movement, challenged men and women to integrate this new discourse into their personal narratives. The men and women of this generation, however, grew up in a world in which same-sex desire was a source of personal pain and collective repression and in which there was no way of understanding same-sex attractions. Thus, the process of narrative reconciliation for this generation was quite challenging. Rosenfeld argues that sexual identity is an interpretive activity within a community that is itself socially and historically informed. Challenged by their repressive postwar world to make sense of self and sexual desire in the context of censorship, and lacking models for constructing a coherent self, the men and women of this generation engaged with multiple master narratives across the course of their lives.

While contemporary scholarship on sexual identity development gives much attention to the process of narrative engagement for *youth*, the chapters in this section of the volume highlight this process for a previous generation. The multigenerational contestation of master narratives reveals human development as, at its core, a process of narrative engagement. Hostetler cautions that while history and social change impose demands for remaking identities, there is considerable variability in the meaning that we each make following such change. It is important to understand the subjective experience for those encountering social change in order to understand the manner in which we manage such change.

Read notes that the generation of lesbian women whose narratives she examines had few models of what it meant to realize and act upon same-sex attractions. The social movements of the 1970s reoriented these women's lives and created a new discursive context for the understanding of same-sex desire. Hostetler's general discussion of gay and lesbian aging in contemporary society complements Read's perspective and Rosenfeld's discussion of narrative integration. Hostetler shows that gay men within these several generation-cohorts realized multiple selves in somewhat different ways in keeping with the time at which they arrived at midlife. Within the generation coming to adulthood in the postwar years, before the emergence of the gay rights movement, the construction of a narrative of generativity was compromised by the impact of stigma about same-sex attraction.

Some men coming to adulthood within the first postwar generation managed this task of making a multiple self by compartmentalizing and keeping separate these aspects of self. Still struggling with issues of accepting a gay identity, postwar generations were then forced to struggle with AIDS, which meant so many losses of significant relationships. While few men in the immediate postwar generation had ever considered the issue of parenting, men in subsequent generations expressed the desire to have children and in other ways to care for the next generation. DeBoer's chapter illustrates the emergence of concern with generativity among a current generation of gay adult men. Hostetler sees the possibility of reconsidering the concept of generativity for future generations of individuals with same-sex desire.

As we have argued both here and in our introductory chapter, human development occurs within a particular discursive context for the construction of a personal narrative. A paradigm that fuses the fundamental principles of a life course approach—the significance of generation-cohort, the social timing of lives, and the agency and resilience individuals possess to drive the course of their own development—with the theoretical and methodological idea of narrative offers much new knowledge about sexual identity development. Such a paradigm recognizes that, like identity more generally, sexual identity is *made* in social practice and in a dynamic engagement with the stories of a cultural surround (Cohler, 2007; Cohler & Hammack, 2006; Hammack, 2005; Holland, Lachicotte, Skinner, & Cain, 1998). And we do not know enough about a person unless we know his or her life story (McAdams, 1995), for it is in the construction of a coherent life story that individuals find a sense of meaning and purpose (McAdams, 1990, 1997). The chapters in this book that have dealt specifically with issues of development, generativity, and the life course reveal the vitality of such an epistemological approach to the study of sexual lives.

Meaning and Multiplicity in Sexual Lives

As we conclude this chapter, we want to highlight the advantages of the paradigmatic approach we have outlined—an approach that has been exemplified in numerous ways in the chapters of this volume. In our view, a narrative and life course approach to sexual identity development is vital in the context of postmodern social science because it supplants archaic notions of "ages and stages" with a dynamic view of human development. In contrast to some views in postmodern psychology, however, we do not view the self as entirely frag- mented (Gergen, 1991), nor do we see the postmodern era entirely as charac- terized by the absence of coherent narrative (Lyotard, 1984). Rather, we agree with Giddens (1991) that late modernity is characterized by the significance of biography and by the need to construct a life narrative that provides integrity, purpose, and meaning (see also Bruner, 1990; Cohler, 1982; McAdams, 1997; Smith, 1994).

As Lifton (1993) argues, individuals possess remarkable resilience to the multiplicity that characterizes postmodernity, constructing what he calls *pro- tean* selves. The process of narrative engagement documented by the numer- ous contributors in this volume, we believe, reveals precisely this ability to construct coherent personal narratives in the midst of profound social change. The study of sexual identity is perhaps particularly illustrative of this artful management of multiplicity.

From the perspective of both time and place, individuals with same-sex desire have negotiated a multiplicity of narratives with which to make sense of their experience. What anchors their development is, in our view, the search for a vocabulary of desire and identity—a discourse with which to make mean- ing of their lives. It is through narrative that meaning is constructed (Bruner, 1990), and thus it is to narrative that we as social scientists of sexuality need turn to produce knowledge about sexual lives.

Future study of the narratives of men and women with same-sex desire must account for the multiplicity of narratives located in the community that become salient across the course of life. Generation-cohort reflects an ever- shifting multivocality of identity for individuals with same-sex desire. Earlier study of same-sex attraction focused on the issue of identity as a fixed entity, with a course defined by an essentialist and ontogenetic view of human devel- opment. This approach failed to recognize the impact of social change on the manner in which we make sense of our experiences. The very success of the gay rights movement and the success of the effort to make a gay identity and to change culture through practice have reshaped the sexual life course. One of our central tasks as social scientists of human sexuality is to document this historical shift in the process of making meaning of desire.

Herdt and Boxer (1996) demonstrated how a Chicago youth group made its own identity as queer youth through the establishment of community through ritual. The success of youth movements across the past decade, together with other social and political transformations, has led the present generation of teenagers and young adults to question the very concept of *gay* (Savin-Williams, 2005). More distal events have also changed the manner in which men and women understand same-sex attraction. From Supreme Court decisions supporting the right to privacy of consenting intimate relationships to the passage of gay marriage and civil union legislation in the United States and throughout Canada and Europe, the previous narrative of struggle and success in realizing a gay identity has given way to a narrative of emancipation among the youth of the present generation (Cohler & Hammack, 2007). This desire for emancipation from the sexual taxonomy of a previous generation, whose lives could not be rendered meaningful or *safe* without such a discourse of identity, clearly reveals the process of narrative engagement. The contestation of a master narrative of gay and lesbian identity creates a competitive discursive space for the construction of identity, but it also creates intergenerational tensions.

It is not clear how emergent narratives of sexual identity will be influenced by the multiplicity of voices as this generation moves into adulthood. What is clear is that narratives of same-sex attraction respond to larger social changes and that this dialogue of an ever-shifting desire must become the major focus of study on the course of gay, lesbian, bisexual, and transgender lives. We must move beyond unidimensional models in the study of same-sex attraction to recognition of the multiplicity of voices shaping sexuality and self across the course of life and across successive generations in society. Such a reorientation of sexual science—from a static conception of the discovery of an "essential" gay or lesbian identity to a more fluid understanding of culture and the life course—can transform the social reality of individuals with same-sex desire by demonstrating their lived experience in an authentic light. The transformative knowledge produced by such inquiry, we believe, might inspire a more complex appreciation for the reciprocal relationship between culture and identity, between discourse and self-understanding, and between power and human agency.

REFERENCES

Arnett, J. J. (2002). The psychology of globalization. *American Psychologist, 57,* 774–783.

Bruner, J. (1990). *Acts of meaning.* Cambridge, MA: Harvard University Press.

Bruner, J. (2002). *Making stories: Law, literature, life.* Cambridge, MA: Harvard University Press.

Cohler, B. J. (1982). Personal narrative and the life course. In P. Baltes & O. G. Brim (Eds.), *Life span development and behavior* (Vol. 4, pp. 205–241). New York: Academic Press.

Cohler, B. J. (2007). *Writing desire: Sixty years of gay autobiography.* Madison: University of Wisconsin Press.

Cohler, B. J., & Hammack, P. L. (2006). Making a gay identity: Life story and the construction of a coherent self. In D. P. McAdams, R. Josselson, & A. Lieblich (Eds.), *Identity and story: Creating self in narrative* (pp. 151–172). Washington, DC: American Psychological Association Press.

Cohler, B. J., & Hammack, P. L. (2007). The psychological world of the gay teenager: Social change, narrative, and "normality." *Journal of Youth and Adolescence, 36,* 47–59.

D'Augelli, A. R. (2002). Mental health problems among lesbian, gay, and bisexual youths ages 14 to 21. *Clinical Child Psychology and Psychiatry, 7,* 433–456.

Elder, G. H. (1998). The life course as developmental theory. *Child Development, 69,* 1–12.

Erikson, E. H. (1959). *Identity and the life cycle.* New York: Norton.

Flowers, P., & Buston, K. (2001). "I was terrified of being different": Exploring gay men's accounts of growing up in a heterosexist society. *Journal of Adolescence, 24,* 51–65.

Foucault, M. (1978). *The history of sexuality, Vol. 1: An introduction.* New York: Vintage.

Gergen, K. J. (1973). Social psychology as history. *Journal of Personality and Social Psychology, 26*(2), 309–320.

Gergen, K. J. (1991). *The saturated self: Dilemmas of identity in contemporary life.* New York: Basic Books.

Gergen, K. J. (2001). Psychological science in a postmodern context. *American Psychologist, 56,* 803–813.

Giddens, A. (1991). *Modernity and self-identity: Self and society in the late modern age.* Stanford, CA: Stanford University Press.

Hammack, P. L. (2005). The life course development of human sexual orientation: An integrative paradigm. *Human Development, 48,* 267–290.

Hammack, P. L. (2008). Narrative and the cultural psychology of identity. *Personality and Social Psychology Review, 12*(3), 222–247.

Herdt, G., & Boxer, A. (1996). *Children of Horizons: How gay and lesbian teens are leading a new way out of the closet* (2nd ed.). Boston: Beacon.

Hermans, H. J. M. (2001). The dialogical self: Toward a theory of personal and cultural positioning. *Culture and Psychology, 7*(3), 243–281.

Holland, D., Lachicotte, W., Skinner, D., & Cain, C. (1998). *Identity and agency in cultural worlds.* Cambridge, MA: Harvard University Press.

Holland, W. (2000). In the body's ghetto. In S. L. Jones (Ed.), *A sea of stories: The shaping power of narrative in gay and lesbian cultures* (pp. 109–138). New York: Harrington Park Press.

Hostetler, A. J., & Herdt, G. H. (1998). Culture, sexual lifeways, and developmental subjectivities: Rethinking sexual taxonomies. *Social Research, 65,* 249–290.

Lifton, R. J. (1993). *The protean self: Human resilience in an age of fragmentation.* Chicago: University of Chicago Press.

Lyotard, J. (1984). *The postmodern condition: A report on knowledge* (G. Bennington & B. Massumi, Trans.). Minneapolis: University of Minnesota Press.

McAdams, D. P. (1990). Unity and purpose in human lives: The emergence of identity as a life story. In A. I. Rabin, R.A. Zucker, R.A. Emmons, & S. Frank (Eds.), *Studying persons and lives* (pp. 148–200). New York: Springer.

McAdams, D. P. (1995). What do we know when we know a person? *Journal of Personality, 63*(3), 365–396.

McAdams, D. P. (1996). Personality, modernity, and the storied self: A contemporary framework for studying persons. *Psychological Inquiry, 7*(4), 295–321.

McAdams, D. P. (1997). The case for unity in the (post)modern self: A modest proposal. In R. D. Ashmore & L. Jussim (Eds.), *Self and identity: Fundamental issues* (pp. 46–80). New York: Oxford University Press.

McAdams, D. P. (2001). The psychology of life stories. *Review of General Psychology, 5*, 100–122.

Michel, A. A., & Wortham, S. E. F. (2002). Clearing away the self. *Theory and Psychology, 12*, 625–650.

Mishler, E. G. (2004). Historians of the self: Restorying lives, revising identities. *Research in Human Development, 1*, 101–121.

Plummer, K. (1995). *Telling sexual stories: Power, change and social worlds.* New York: Routledge.

Polkinghorne, D. (1988). *Narrative knowing and the human sciences.* Albany: State University of New York Press.

Rosenfeld, D. (2003). *The changing of the guard: Lesbian and gay elders, identity, and social change.* Philadelphia: Temple University Press.

Savin-Williams, R. C. (2005). *The new gay teenager.* Cambridge, MA: Harvard University Press.

Schiff, B. (2003). Talking about identity: Arab students at the Hebrew University of Jerusalem. *Ethos, 30*, 273–304.

Shanahan, M., & Elder, G. (2002). History, agency, and the life course. In R. A. Dienstbier & L. J. Crockett (Eds.), *Agency, motivation and the life course* (pp. 145–186). Lincoln: University of Nebraska Press.

Smith, M. B. (1994). Selfhood at risk: Postmodern perils and the perils of postmodernism. *American Psychologist, 49*(5), 405–411.

Sullivan, A. (1995). *Virtually normal: An argument about homosexuality.* New York: Knopf.

Index

Note: Page numbers in *italics* refer to figures and tables.